GUSTAVUS ADOLPHUS

GVSTAVVS ADOLPHVS D.G. REX SVEC. GOTH:
ET VAND. MAGNVS PRINCEPS FINLANDIÆ DVX ETC.

Paul. Pontius sculp.   Ant. van Dyck pinxit   Cum privilegio
                                      G. H.

FROM PORTRAIT NOW IN MUNICH

GUSTAVUS ADOLPHUS

A History of the Art of War
from its Revival After the Middle Ages
to the End of the Spanish Succession War,
with a Detailed Account of the Campaigns of
the Great Swede, and of the Most Famous
Campaigns of Turenne, Condé,
Eugene and Marlborough

Theodore Ayrault Dodge

DA CAPO PRESS • NEW YORK

Library of Congress Cataloging-in-Publication Data
Dodge, Theodore Ayrault, 1842–1909
  Gustavus Adolphus: a history of the art of war from its revival
after the Middle Ages to the end of the Spanish Succession War,
with a detailed account of the campaigns of the Great Swede, and
of the most famous campaigns of Turenne, Condé, Eugene and
Marlborough / Theodore Ayrault Dodge.—1st Da Capo Press ed.
    p.   cm.
  Originally published: Boston: Houghton, Mifflin, 1895.
  Includes index.
  ISBN 0-306-80863-3 (alk. paper)
    1. Gustaf II Adolf, King of Sweden, 1594–1632—Military
leadership. 2. Thirty years' war, 1618–1648. 3. Military history,
Modern. I. Title.
DL706.D6 1998
948.5′ 02′ 092—dc21   98-7699
                                                                          CIP

First Da Capo Press edition 1998

This Da Capo Press paperback edition of *Gustavus Adolphus*
is an unabridged republication of the edition published by
Houghton Mifflin Company in 1895.

Published by Da Capo Press, Inc.
A Subsidiary of Plenum Publishing Corporation
233 Spring Street, New York, N.Y. 10013

Manufactured in the United States of America

To
THE AMERICAN SOLDIER
Who, not bred to arms, but nurtured by
independence, has achieved the proudest
rank among the veterans of history

This Volume Is Dedicated

"*Faites la guerre offensive comme Alexandre, Annibal, César,
Gustave Adolphe, Turenne, le prince Eugène et Frédéric; lisez, reli-
lizes l'historie de leur quatre-vingt-huit campagnes; modélez-vous
sur eux,—c'est le seul moyen de devenir grand capitaine et de sur-
prendre le sécret de l'art; votre génie ainsi éclairé, vous fera rejeter
des maximes opposées à celles de ces grands hommes.*"—NAPOLEON

"*La tactique, les évolutions, la science de l'officier de génie, de
l'officier d'artillerie peuvent s'apprendre dans les traités;—mais la
connaissance de la grande tactique ne s'acquiert que par l'expéri-
ence et par l'étude de l'histoire des campagnes de tous les grands
capitaines.*"—NAPOLEON

PREFACE.

THAT the immense gap of sixteen and a half centuries which intervenes between the last campaign of Julius Cæsar and the first campaign of Gustavus Adolphus is left almost untouched, must be justified by once more reminding the reader that the author has made no attempt to cover the history of war, but seeks only to indicate the origin and growth of what to-day we call the art of war. No preface, however long, can explain the purpose of the volumes of which the present is one, so well as the few words of Napoleon which have been chosen as a motto, and which follow the dedicatory page. " Read, reread the history of their eighty-eight campaigns," says this last of the Great Captains. A history of the origin and growth of the art of war is in reality only the story of the campaigns of those leaders whose deeds have created the art. The history of war is beyond limit; to treat it in equal detail would call for hundreds of volumes, and the author has contemplated no such work.

A distinguished professor of history [1] recently wrote the author : " You will have an embarrassing wealth of material in the military changes from Cæsar to Gustavus Adolphus. As I run over the time, I see how you can use your narrative skill on the slaughter of the legions of Varus in the Teuto-wald ; the hurried marches of Aurelian while his soldiers sung that wild song of slaughter given by Flavius Vopiscus ; the Goths of Alaric and the Huns of Attila, and the struggle

---

[1] Samuel Willard, LL. D.

of armed mobs at Chalons; the skillful work of Belisarius; the saving of Europe by Leo the Isaurian, to whose work the picturesque battle of Tours was but a supplement; the campaigns of Charlemagne, earliest in modern times to march converging columns upon an enemy; knights and crusaders, and that greatest of all cavalry battles, greatest that ever was or ever will be, Dorylæum; the Normans at Hastings; the Swiss piling up the rampart of ten thousand dead at St. Jacobs; the vain charge of Talbot, representative of the outgoing chivalry, against cannon and earthworks at Chatillon; these, and two score more of the illustrations of the change from the old to the new, — how can you leave them out — how can you put them in?" And just because none of these acts in the drama of history had any influence on the art of war, it is not within the scope of this work to narrate them. Many of the deeds of the Great Captains, indeed, had no such influence; but though these may none the less have found a place in their general military history, there is nothing to warrant the author in going outside of the Great Captains to dilate upon mere acts of heroism or mere scenes of carnage.

Hence, though the period between Munda in 45 B. C. and the Danish campaign of 1611 is dismissed with a mere summary, the author does not believe that he has left any gap unfilled in the actual history of the art of war; and as its revival began with Gustavus Adolphus and was carried forward more or less expertly by his successors, it will be found that from the beginning of the seventeenth century down to 1815, the narrative in this and future volumes will cover most of the important wars.

Every nation, in gazing at the glories which surround its victories and its heroes, is apt to lose sight of the comparative standing of the latter. To the Prussian, Frederick the Only stands out unequaled; to the Scandinavian, Gustavus; to the

Frenchman, Napoleon; to the Austrian, Prince Eugene or the Archduke Charles; to the Englishman, Marlborough or Wellington. It is only when each of these generals is grouped with the others on the theatre of war where he played his part, that one can properly gauge his place among the captains. To some of us Anglo-Saxons it may seem heresy to assume that Prince Eugene was equal as a general to the Duke of Marlborough. And yet, such was the case. Alone, he conducted more successful campaigns, he won more victories and he did more first-rate work than Marlborough; while at Blenheim, Oudenarde and Malplaquet, he bore half the burden and won half the renown. When the facts are looked at dispassionately, the place assigned to each of the great generals in these volumes will, it is believed, be borne out by the mature judgment of any military student not suffering from patriotic astigmatism.

It is comparatively easy to write up a campaign without a map. This tell-tale absent, errors can be more easily covered; a general allegation will suffice for a more specific one. But the author has striven to so illustrate his work with charts as that every statement may be readily checked off by reference to the terrain. The ancient maps of the country and of battle-fields, while full of information and suggestiveness, are apt to be topographically wrong and hence misleading; it is hoped the maps and charts in this volume will prove more acceptable. The same care has been expended on them by personal visits to the battle-fields as was given to former volumes; but they are intended rather to illustrate the text and to aid in comprehending the campaigns than as samples of the geographer's art. The amount of ground to be covered has resulted in their being made on a smaller scale than heretofore.

Little space could be spared for the exploits of individual

generals or divisions; the battle descriptions have been confined to what was strictly essential to a clear understanding of the manœuvres. Particular heroism has been rarely mentioned; except in the case of the leading generals, it does not fit into the scheme of the work.

Dates in the old records are inaccurate and puzzling; but the New Style (ten days later than the Old Style) has been followed, — it is hoped without many errors. The political history of the times has been only incidentally mentioned; the author can scarcely vouch for its being free from error, — he pretends to no knowledge of the intricate state imbroglios of the sixteenth century.

The authorities to which this volume is indebted are very numerous. Having no knowledge of Swedish, the author has been obliged to rely upon German, French or Italian translations of the home records; but such eminent men as Droysen have carefully covered this ground; and most of the better class of historical works, such as Geijer's Sveriges Historia, or Gustavus' Letters, exist in German. Moreover, the campaigns which made Gustavus forever great were rather a part of the history of Germany than of Sweden.

The following works, among others, have been laid under contribution, some of them very freely: Arkenholtz, Beaurain, Bülow, Chemnitz, Coxe, Desormeaux, Droysen, Duvivier, Dudik, Feuquières, Förster, Gallitzin, Gfrörer, Grimoard, Gualdo Priorato, Harte, Hurter, Julius, Kausler, Keym, Khevenhüller, Lediard, Lossau, Mauvillon, Oman, Puffendorf, Quincy, Ramsay, Ranke, Swedish Intelligencer, Soden, Le Soldat Suédois, Sporschill, Theatrum Europæum, Villermont, Voltaire, Zaber, Zanthier, a great number of memoirs, dispatches and letters of many of the generals, and old Netherland, Nürnberg and other German records. The author has drawn from too many eminent historians and critics to do less than acknowledge gratefully his indebtedness to each and all. But he has uniformly got his best suggestions from visits to the battle-fields, which, however changed in minor details, still remain substantially as they were.

The volume perhaps errs in being bulky; but the reader can readily understand that it would have been easier to write thrice the number of pages than to condense so vast a subject into what may be placed between two covers. It is a far more satisfactory task to go into the minute details of a single campaign than to deal superficially with the manœuvres of many; but though the scheme of this work necessitates in places severe condensation, the author trusts that no important matter distinctly contributory to the art of war has been slighted.

TABLE OF CONTENTS.

LIST OF ILLUSTRATIONS.

GUSTAVUS ADOLPHUS.

I.

THE ERA OF CAVALRY. 378–1315.

As the ranks became filled with mercenaries, the Roman legion fell from its high estate. Hand to hand tactics gave way to missile weapons, the bow came into fashion, and ballistic machines and portable stakes appeared in line of battle. The barbarians grew in efficiency beyond the legionaries, and to protect the vast frontier of the empire, cavalry came to be essential. Adrianople proved that horse could ride down foot, and mounted service became the more honorable. German cavalry, enlisted by the emperors, proved its preëminence, and the footman sank into insignificance. While the western nations relied on hard knocks, the Byzantines kept up a species of military art, — one of form and stratagem, rather than pure tactics or strategy, in which valor was prized, but discretion ranked higher. The Teutonic races depended on stout infantry : in their great raids there was little horse. Feudalism introduced the mailed knight, who for centuries reigned supreme. Useful in holding back the Moor, the Viking and the Magyar, he was not a soldier in the best sense ; his instability equaled his courage. He knew but one tactics, — to charge straight at the enemy, — and he was frequently routed by bad ground. Armies were set up in deep squares, and accident often decided the day. Armored mercenaries succeeded the knights, but were no better. Feudalism called for castles ; castles led to a war of sieges. Of strategy and tactics there was none. The Crusades were full of prowess ; they gave us no military lessons, except that of blind devotion.

THE feature characterizing the history of the art of war, from the fall of the Roman empire to the era of the Reformation, is the rise of cavalry as the main reliance of nations, and the corresponding decadence of infantry. This condition lasted for many centuries, until the English long-bow and the

Swiss pike and halberd, coupled to the growth of firearms, again reduced the horseman to his true level. Cavalry is an essential arm ; even the rapid-firing weapon of to-day cannot quite displace it ; but it is neither fitted to stand alone, nor to dominate infantry. Only when the footman is the main reliance of the commander can the art of war reach its highest development.

We have seen how the Roman legion, which was at its zenith when the burgess-soldier's stanch courage put a term to Hannibal's splendid bid for the conquest of Italy, degenerated by easy and natural gradations until it became a merely mercenary body, unable to cope with the barbarian invaders of the peninsula. In proportion as it forfeited character it became burdened with ballistic machines, it grew unwieldy, and lost so much of its marching speed that, to have at hand forces which could effectually be transferred from one threatened point on the enormous imperial frontier to another, the Emperor Constantine began to increase the cavalry by taking from each legion its auxiliary turmæ, and collecting these into large bodies destined to serve alone.

The enemies of Rome, moreover, were no longer the ill-armed savages of yore. Their weapons and accoutrements had been vastly improved by contact with the empire, and the legion could not slash its way through a body of mere human brawn, — still less so with its own diminished stanchness. That the old Roman quality had perished was abundantly proven by the numerous ballistic machines, and by the beams and stakes carried along on pack-mules, not for the ancient purpose of intrenching the nightly camp, but to save the legion from cavalry attacks on the field of battle. These supplementary engines and tools meant that the legion had been reduced to an un-Roman defensive.

In the battle of Adrianople (A. D. 378), the Gothic squadrons accomplished what cavalry had never compassed since Hannibal's Numidians waded in the gore of Cannæ, — they destroyed a Roman army. This battle was the capstone to the belief that it was more honorable to fight on horseback than on foot, for the Goth had found that, unassisted, he could ride down the vaunted Roman legionary. While this was due more to the deterioration of the foot than to the melioration of the horse, yet while the latter continued to gain, the former continued to lose. For a thousand years to come cavalry was uppermost. It naturally deemed itself the superior of foot, as indeed it became and remained, — until the long-bow of the hardy British yeoman mowed down the supercilious French chivalry at Crécy.

Adrianople made it evident that the legions alone could no longer uphold the Roman supremacy.

With this lesson in mind, Theodosius began to enlist bands of Teutonic chiefs, and from now on the Roman soldier quite lost caste, and the barbarian horseman became the pillar of the empire. Indeed, he proved his right to the title by riding down the veteran Gallic legions which had risen under Magnus Maximus, and by more than one other noteworthy deed of prowess.

Another change soon became apparent. The Roman footman, already used to the support of ballistic machines and portable stakes in the line of battle, began to rely more and more on missile weapons, and to discard the arms of close quarters. The bow for the first time became a Roman weapon. Not but what the bow is an admirable arm, especially against cavalry; it has asserted itself at intervals from remotest ages; but it was a new thing to see the Roman legionary take kindly to long-distance weapons, and a thing to excite one's pity.

Cavalry reigned supreme. At a later day the Gothic horseman rode to and fro throughout Italy, and still further proved that infantry, such as the Roman legion had then become, was no match for the best of mounted troops. All Europe soon vied in arming and training cavalry, and infantry sank to a still lower level. It was fit only for garrison duty, — to defend walls. The Roman cavalry ended by adopting the bow, and became the same body which had annihilated Crassus on the plains of Mesopotamia. Horse-archers and horse-lancers were the choice of the day. The latter, the heavy squadrons, were more unwieldy, but they were able at least to ride down the Oriental horse-archer.

It was thus arose all over Europe the idea that cavalry should be the chief and only arm ; the idea that mounted service alone was honorable ; the idea that the footman was a sloven and a coward.

The Byzantines were, in matters military, the legitimate successors of the old Roman empire. Their armies for centuries held back the barbarian inroads from the east ; they were, during their life, the best of their kind. They have been much disparaged by historians, and in a sense it is true that the Byzantines were not successful ; but for all that, they had an art in their wars, while in the west of Europe thews and sinews won the day. And while the doughty blows of the Frank appeal to our Saxon instinct of manliness rather than the ambush, stratagem and studied method of the Byzantine, yet the latter showed more intelligence in what he did and in the way he did it. Several books of tactics remain to us from this era, and the means of successfully combating the various races that might be met — Frank, Magyar or Saracen — were assiduously discussed. Moreover the eastern emperors did succeed in holding their territory against western assaults for generations.

The strength of the Byzantines lay in their heavy cavalry,

and this they set up in two lines and a reserve, whose three successive shocks told well. Courage was valued highly, but discretion and a knowledge of how to utilize varying conditions were deemed a better quality. Bull-headed pluck was not so highly considered as it was in the west; stratagem showed a higher kind of soldierly ability, — even treachery held its place in the Byzantine scheme. A similar tendency was shown in the seventeenth century in the preference of manœuvres over battles; and was not Hannibal called perfidious because he resorted to ruse in his unequal struggle against ponderous Rome? Despite these facts, which sound worse in the telling than they actually were, the Byzantines, so far as an art in war is concerned, were a half dozen centuries ahead of any nation in the west.

From the era of the Byzantine empire onward for many centuries it is impossible to speak with much accuracy about war or the art of war. History there is none; chronicles mislead. Of war there was much; of art in war there was little — as we understand it, none — until Gustavus Adolphus again infused method into what others had done with no method at all. Strategy had rarely shown itself since the days of Cæsar; tactics was whatever suited each nation or tribe, and never rose to the rank of grand-tactics. If a commander was able enough to pattern his battle-tactics to the ground on which he fought and to the work he had to do, he was deemed a marvel of originality and skill.

All nations did not go to war mounted. It was Gothic infantry, not horse, which marched down the Italian peninsula under Totila; but it was the cavalry of Belisarius and of Narses which proved fatal to them; and for three centuries the Franks kept increasing their proportion of mounted men. The bulk of the Teutonic forces remained foot; and while Charles Martel and Charles the Great had a goodly array of

cavalry, their armies were really infantry, supplemented to a
moderate extent by horse.

When the kingdom of Charles the Great was broken up
and the local counts began to acquire a semi-independence,
feudalism arose, and horsemen acquired still greater importance. They had their merits. It was they who kept back
the vast inroads of that era from north, east and south.
Without them Christendom might have been overrun; no
wonder the knight in armor won the regard of the whole earth.

In England the superiority of the horseman was not demonstrated until the battle of Hastings, when William's horse,

backed by his archers, did their
share in overthrowing Harold's
brave but reckless axemen; but
the superiority of the knight in
armor was as marked during the
feudal period in Britain as it was
on the continent.

From the establishment of feudalism until the Swiss at Morgarten and the English at Crécy
proved the ability of good foot to
withstand the best of cavalry, the
horseman was preëminent. He was
not a good soldier; he had no idea

Knight.   (15th Century.)

of discipline; courage, a certain ability to use his cumbrous
weapons, and the sort of faith in his own invincibility which
helped to render him invincible, were his only recommenda-
tions. There was no art in what he did. His only tactics
was to charge straight at the enemy on sight. When he
charged on good ground, no foe could resist his impact; but
he might end his gallop in a marsh, or against a palisade.
At Mansoura, St. Louis' knights were entangled in the streets

of a town and utterly worsted. The knight was ignorant of art. Each army was formed in three great columns or " battles ; " these galloped upon the enemy similarly marshaled, and, after a tussle of hours, one or the other would be forced back, often by an accident of *terrain* or on account of the loss of a leader. To set a successful ambush was a rarity which was applauded as a wonder. For many centuries armies moved into the enemy's territory, not to secure

Dismounted Knight.
(13th Century.)

a strategic point, but to ravage the land and secure plunder from the harassed people. Victualing by any method was not attempted, and so soon as one section was eaten out, another must be sought, irrespective of its military value.

Battles were rare. The rival armies did no reconnoitring, and thus at times scarcely knew each other's whereabouts. They met by accident more often than by design, and not infrequently sent word to each other to meet at a given spot and fight it out, — as the Cimbri had invited Marius to battle at Vercellæ. Even then it exceeded their ability to marshal their forces on fair terms, for it took all day to deploy a small marching column into line of battle. A modern army manœuvres thrice as rapidly.

Knight.   (15th Century.)

The feudal knight was so utterly without discipline or reliability that mercenaries gradually crept into favor. But the mercenary was cast in the same mould; he was a man in

Knight in Armor.
(13th Century.)

armor, if not a knight, and was equally bold and useless, though more loyal to his chief. So long as he was paid, he would stay with the colors, which was more than you could count on in the knight. The mercenary became the support of autocratic monarchs; but when, at the end of a war, bands of mercenaries began to move to and fro over the face of the country, seeking a new lord and fresh campaigns, they became of questionable utility and unquestionable danger.

The feudal system called for castles; castles led to a war of sieges rather than a war of manœuvring and fighting. Many of these castles were to the armies of that day more serious obstacles than Ehrenbreitstein or Gibraltar to a modern force. They began by being simple in construction; they ended by being elaborate and solid. There were but two ways of capturing them : starvation or undermining the walls, and to the latter the mediæval armies were ill adapted. These castles robbed war of all skill, and reduced operations to the scale of raids which disregarded their existence, or to a series of tiresome sieges. For generations after the invention of gunpowder, artillery had small effect on these solid feudal structures ; less than the ancient catapults and rams.

The Crusades were the typical work of the mailed knight; and as this warrior made practically no impress on the art of war, so the Crusades teach us no useful lessons. Both were equally unpractical ; each served its purpose, but neither war

nor warrior was worthy of imitation, unless it be in the guile-
less devotion of the latter. There were abundant and splendid feats of arms; there was nothing to repay study. To
record all the deeds of valor which war has evoked is but to
record the history of the human race; our task is to evolve
the history of the art of war from these deeds: in other
words, to separate from the mere acts of courage those instances of intelligent application of courage which have added
to our knowledge of what constitutes modern war. The thousand years during which cavalry was the sole dependence
of Europe have in this sense few lessons for the military
student.

Knight. (12th Century.)

II.

REAPPEARANCE OF INFANTRY. 1315–1500.

IT was the plucky peasant of Switzerland and Britain who reëstablished the value of foot. The Swiss carried an eighteen-foot pike, or a heavy halberd; and in their muscular grasp these weapons were irresistible. They fought in an echeloned line of three solid bodies, which cavalry could not break, nor the infantry of the day withstand, and they were hardy marchers. At Morgarten (1315) they destroyed an army of knights in a mountain pass, and at Laupen (1339) one in the open field. Only when broken could they be beaten, as they later were by the Spanish sword and buckler. Equally splendid was the record of the English long-bow, with its cloth-yard shaft. At Crécy (1346) this weapon utterly overthrew the French chivalry; Poitiers (1356) and Agincourt (1415) proved that the day of infantry had come back. The long-bowman behind his stakes could not be approached by cavalry; when broken or on the march he was like other foot. Swiss and Briton proved to the knight in armor that he was not invincible. Zisca's wagon-fort was another link in the same chain; the Hussites became a terror in Germany. The disappearance of feudalism, the growth of intelligence, and the invention of gunpowder all contributed to reëstablish warfare as a science. The cross-bow began to be replaced by the musket; and the unwieldy knight gave way to the more active footman. As kings gained power and raised their own armies, war became more regular; and toward 1600 conditions arose which might rehabilitate the art of war.

IT was the courage of the hardy peasantry of two western nations quite as much as the invention of gunpowder, which put a term to the ascendancy of the feudal knight, and reëstablished infantry as the arm which should bear the brunt of battle. The English long-bowman with his cloth-yard shaft found that he could annihilate the best of cavalry from a distance; the Swiss pikeman proved that armored knights could not ride down his steady array of protended spears. These facts were a revelation, and at once modified the posi-

Swiss Halberdier.
(16th Century.)

tion of the horseman in war. Each represented a new development of shock and missile tactics. The Swiss array was a modern revival of the old phalanx of Philip and Alexander; and, though the bow was one of the most ancient of weapons, it had never yet been what the English yeoman made it.

The Swiss pike was eighteen feet long, with a steel head of from twelve to thirty-six inches, was grasped in both hands, and held shoulder high, with a downward slant. The second, third and fourth rank pikes protruded beyond the front; the rest were held upright. This arm resembled in length and application the sarissa of Macedon, but it was differently held. Around the central pennon of the Swiss column stood the halberdiers, who

Swiss Sergeant
Halberdier.

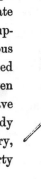

Swiss Pikeman.
(16th Century.)

wielded an eight-foot heavy-headed weapon which could cleave the best of armor, lop off arms or legs, or even, it is said, decapitate a horse. Without the upland brawn and tremendous national spirit which inspired the Swiss, however, even these weapons would have availed nothing. It was hardy strength, the love of country, and the instinct of liberty which lent them terror.

The Swiss were rapidly

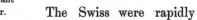

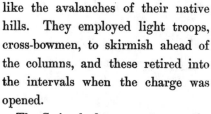

mobilized and swift on the march. Like the early Roman legions, they always attacked, and wearing no armor, could not only keep well ahead of the cumbrous armies of the day, but descend on the enemy's line with an impetus like the avalanches of their native hills. They employed light troops, cross-bowmen, to skirmish ahead of the columns, and these retired into the intervals when the charge was opened.

The Swiss had no great generals. It was the courage and steadfastness, the weapons and skill of the men which won. But they had an admirable battle-field tactics. They mar-

Swiss Captain.
(16th Century.)

shaled three columns, Vorhut (vanguard), Gewaltshaufen (power-mass) and Nachhut (rear-guard), and launched them on the foe in echelon, with the advantage of successive impact, independence of movement and the safety of each column from partaking of the repulse of another. At times the three columns were marshaled with the centre or the wings in advance, a partial checker-wise formation. The wedge and the hollow square, or "hedgehog," showed that the Swiss had studied the tactical forms of antiquity.

Lance and Halberd Heads.
(16th Century.)

The first victory of the Swiss foot, at Morgarten in 1315, was not due to its superior formation or tactics. The feudal horsemen were lured into

an icy mountain-pass, with a precipice above them on the
right, and a lake below them on the left: and here
they were destroyed by rolling
logs and bowlders down upon
their line, and thus hurling
them into the gulf beneath.
This, coupled to a furious
front attack with the
deadly halberd, gave the
knights no room to set
their lances in rest, or
to swing their swords.
Morgarten was not a
battle; it was a sur-
prise and butchery;
but it opened the eyes

Bernese Soldiers.
(15th Century.)

of the arrogant knight to the fact that, even
though he be afoot, a man's a man for a' that.

Swiss Pikeman. (16th Century.)

At Laupen (1339) the Swiss
infantry, quite unsustained
and in the open field, met,
with its serried ranks and
bristling pikes, an array of
heavy horse backed by the
best infantry of the day. The
foot was quickly dispersed,
and all the power of the
armored knights could not
drive the columns from their
ground. Infantry, after a
dozen centuries of decay, had again proved its worth.

Bannockburn accomplished the same end in another part
of the world and in a different way.

It was only by similar tactics to their own — by dismounted heavy cavalry, or by bodies of footmen formed on the same

method, such as the Landsknechte of Germany — that the Swiss met their match. Later on the Spaniards, with sword and buckler, found that they could annihilate the Swiss column, if, like the legionaries against the phalanx at Pydna, they could but once penetrate a gap. Foot could be matched by foot; but infantry had asserted its superiority over horse, and in a combat between the two arms, the pike was useful when sword and shield were of no account; the Swiss column

Genevese Mercenary.
(15th Century.)

had a distinct advantage over the Spanish line.

What placed a limit to the utility of the Swiss column was the revival of castrametation and the improve-

ment of artillery. A column with long spears was ill adapted to carrying works, nor could it live under well - plied salvos of cannon. These weak points, and yet more inter-cantonal jealousies and a consequent deterioration in discipline, eventually sealed the fate of the Swiss array.

English Long-
bowman.
(14th Century.)

English Long-
bowman.
(14th Century.)

Of even more interest than the Swiss footman's mastery of cavalry is the wonderful result obtained by the long-bow of the Englishman. Until the reign of John, the cross-bowman had been in the ascendant. Whatever its origin, it was Edward I. who brought the long-bow into favor. At Falkirk (1298) the long-bowmen did wonders, and while at Bannockburn (1314) want of support caused their overthrow, it was they who at Crécy (1346) proved to the haughty chivalry of France that a new era had arisen. With their flanks protected from the charges of horse and their stakes set up before them, the line of

Cross-bowman.
(12th Century.)

long - bowmen, vomiting its fire of three-foot shafts, could not be reached by the best of cavalry. Poitiers (1356) was cumulative testimony, and Agincourt (1415) made it plain beyond cavil that infantry was regaining its proper place in war.

That the French, later in this century, won victories against the Eng-

Cross-bowman.
(12th Century.)

lish is due to the fact that they had learned to attack the enemy only at a disadvantage, and not when the long-bowman could put in his best work; they fell upon them on the march in lieu of assaulting their chosen ground. Once broken up, the long-bowmen were no more invulnerable than any other foot; they were in fact at the mercy of cavalry charges, or of stout infantry armed with good hand to hand weapons and vigorously led.

Cross-bowman.
(15th Century.)

That the knights recognized the growing value of infantry is well shown in the fact that large bodies were now frequently dismounted to fight on foot, and that with their heavy armor and weapons they could more than once bear down the lighter line of unmailed infantry, — provided always that they had not to march far or fast.

The Germans learned another lesson as to the efficiency

Cross-bowmen.   (15th Century.)

of foot, in the Hussite wars of the fifteenth century. John Zisca was an extraordinary man. He well understood that his half-armed, undisciplined peasant rabble, with all their religious zeal, could not cope with trained troops, and least of all with feudal cavalry. But he stood at bay, and with his wagon-fortress scheme developed into a science of defensive tactics, he, too, helped teach the heavy-armed rider that the footman, well used, was more than his equal. This wagon-camp tactics grew to be so exact that Zisca's armies changed from the defensive to the offensive, and moved to and fro over the land with more swiftness than their opponents; and woe betide the heavy horse which dared to charge in on the wagon-burg. The Hussites, in open field, would march into the very teeth of a German army. They were marshaled in five columns, the artillery and cavalry in the centre; outside this two short wagon-columns, and then again two long ones. As by magic, the short wagon-columns would gallop up to form a front line and back to form a rear one; the whole structure was lashed together with chains or ropes ; on each wagon mounted its special squad of defenders, and lo, in the twinkling of an eye, almost a Roman camp in the midst of the enemy's battalions. And from out this camp would sally men with flails and pikes, whose fanatical fury was irresistible. So dreaded were they that a handful of Hussites would sometimes disperse an army. Nothing but artillery could successfully demolish these wagon-burgs, and Zisca had always a superior equipment of guns to silence the enemy's. German armies could finally not be got to face the Hussites. This tactics was not within the domain of regular warfare ; but it was an instance of able adaptation of means to end, and a further proof of the value of the foot-man properly put to use. Internal dissensions among Bohemians finally broke up this remarkable method of defensive tactics. But while it existed, it worked towards the same end of destroying the ascendancy of horse.

So long as the feudal power remained in force, there was small chance of a revival of the art of war. But princes, dissatisfied with the untrustworthiness of the forces raised under the feudal system, resorted to mercenaries, either in time of war, or to protect their real or pretended rights against their own vassals. Feudalism outgrew its usefulness. It accomplished its mission and gave way to something better, taking with it that warrior who from one point of view is the *preux chevalier* of all the ages, and from another the typical armed bully, — the mailed knight.

References to explosive substances like gunpowder, or to burning substances like Greek fire, are to be found in works literally as old as Moses. Among later references, some of the Brahmins of Alexander's time are said by Philostratus to have been able to " overthrow their enemies with tempests and thunderbolts shot from their walls ; " Archimedes, at Syracuse, is said by Plutarch to have " cast huge stones from

Hand Gun.

his machines with a great noise;" Ca-
ligula is stated by Dion Cassius to have
had machines which "imitated thunder
and lightning and emitted stones;"
and Marcus Graccus in the eighth cen-
tury gives a receipt of one pound of sulphur, two of willow
charcoal and six of saltpetre, for the discharge of what we
should call a rocket.

The use of Greek fire was understood as early as the sixth
century, but powder was earliest used in China, perhaps a
thousand years before Christ,
and was introduced to European notice by the Saracens.
Neither Schwartz nor Bacon
can be said to be its inventor.
Early in the fourteenth century cannon and gunpowder

Bombard of Rhodes. Calibre, 22 in.
Threw Stone Ball of 650 pounds.

appear to have been known in Florence; in 1338 mention is
made of them among the stores in the Tower of London and
the arsenal at Rouen; and in 1346 guns — perhaps hand
guns — are said to have been used at Crécy.

It is certain that the Spanish Moors, shortly after 1326,
had made the use
of gunpowder, fire-
arms and cannon
well known in west-
ern Europe, and by
the end of the cen-
tury they were the
common property of
all armies. At first
their high cost pre-
cluded their use ex-

Big Cannon.   (15th Century.)

cept in sieges and the defense of towns; it was much later,
at the battle of Rosabeck, in 1382, between the Dutch and
French, that field-ar-
tillery appeared.

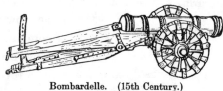

Bombardelle. (15th Century.)

At the end of the
fourteenth century
guns were cast of
bronze, copper and
iron, and called *bombardæ*.　Some of these were huge speci-
mens, which consumed large charges of powder, and hurled
stone balls of from one hundred to one thousand pounds
weight.　Mortars appeared in Italy about the middle of the
fifteenth century.

French Gun. (15th Century.)

The French first made
use of field-artillery,
which could be trans-
ported in the army train.
That which accompanied
Charles VIII. to Italy in 1494 was, comparatively speaking,
light, rapid of fire and well served.　Other nations gradually
fell into line, and Gustavus made artillery of really light calibre.

In the fifteenth and sixteenth centuries part of the
infantry bore fire-
arms. These were
at first extreme-
ly crude, being
merely a gun-bar-
rel lashed to a
stick and set off

Hand Bombardelle.
(15th Century.)

Mounted Culveri-
neer.

by a match; but by the end of the sixteenth century they
had all grown to have a lock, and the form of the weapon
began to approach the musket.

In the second half of the fifteenth century firearms and artillery had become a necessary part of the equipment of an army. The feudal organization was disappearing, and the power of kings received more recognition. Both these things combined to make possible a revival in the art of war. Standing armies had become the rule, and war was no longer the exclusive prerogative of the nobleman. As infantry resumed its sway and cavalry was

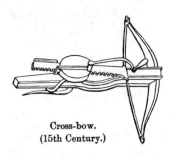

Cross-bow.
(15th Century.)

set back to its proper function ; as artillery improved and discipline was enforced, those conditions gradually obtained on which Gustavus Adolphus exercised so marked an influence. Since the Byzantine art disappeared, there had been no basis on which to build such a thing as a science of war ; but a proper basis was now formed.

By the middle of the sixteenth century the cross-bow disappeared, and infantry

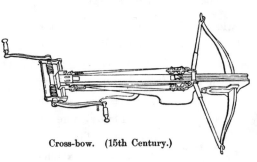

Cross-bow.   (15th Century.)

was armed with pikes, halberds and muskets. At first the musketeers were but ten or fifteen to a large company ; but the number increased until, early in the seventeenth century, two thirds of the men were armed with muskets. They all wore light helmets and breastplates.

The Dutch, in their wars against Spain, made marked tactical progress. Particularly, Maurice of Nassau improved

the musket and lock, made rules for the footmen, introduced
the cadenced step, and prescribed many evolutions, ployments
and deployments. Other able soldiers were working in the
same direction.

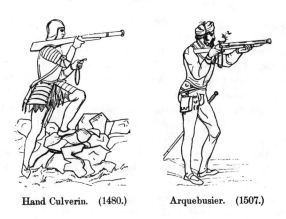

Hand Culverin. (1480.)   Arquebusier. (1507.)

III.

CHANGES IN TACTICS. — SIXTEENTH CENTURY.

HEAVY horse had fought in column; then in one long line; later the column was resumed. The foot was ployed into big battalia or "battles," huge squares of pikemen thirty or forty deep, with cross-bowmen or musketeers on the corners or sides. As artillery and firearms improved, the depth was reduced. These battles stood in line or checker-wise, and skirmishers operated in front of and between them. Up to the fifteenth century the horse stood in front of the line of battle; later it was mixed with it, and a reserve was kept. From the sixteenth century the cavalry was put on or behind the flanks. Artillery was too heavy to follow troops; it delayed their marches, and always fell to the victor. Parallel order was invariable; the lines were cumbrous, and battles were bloody because the troops once in could not be got out of action. Pursuit was unknown. Marches were in close column, with van and flankers, but at no great distance. The train was enormous. Food was got by plunder. The use of mercenary troops introduced rank and command; those who raised the men became the officers. There was no discipline. Punishments were Draconic; rewards brilliant. Up to about 1500 prisoners had been killed; the system of ransom then sprang up, to the sad increase of the train. Earthworks around camps grew into use. In besieging fortresses treachery was resorted to, and the ancient siege devices were used until the introduction of artillery. The art of besieging remained crude until the sixteenth century, when the Italians, and later the Dutch, improved it, and engineering began to take on a better form.

PRIOR to the sixteenth century it had been a habit to draw up heavy cavalry in one long line (*en haye*). The rule then grew up of marshaling all cavalry in solid columns, which opened in order to use their firearms. The foot was likewise marshaled in heavy squares, called battalia or "battles." The cross-bowmen, later the musketeers, formed the front and rear ranks of these battles, and a file on each flank. The rest of them were posted on the four corners in bodies, of which, when the front rank had fired, it retired behind the rest to load. The depth of these battles long remained thirty to forty men ; but as artillery became more dangerous, early in the seventeenth century, it was reduced to ten and eight men, and even to five. As a general rule, the pikemen and halberdiers fought in close, the cross-bowmen and musketeers in open, ranks ; in other words, the long-range and hand to hand fighters kept to their appropriate formations. The fight was opened by volunteers, or men chosen by lot (*enfants perdus*, forlorn hopes), who skirmished out in front, and though they rallied in groups in case they were attacked by cavalry, they were often ridden down.

In line of battle, the cavalry, up to the fifteenth century, was wont to be in front, the foot in the rear. Later, the columns of foot were for mutual support mixed with those of horse in the same line, as the fire of the cross-bowmen would, it was thought, make the work of the horse more easy ; and a reserve of heavy horse and foot was kept in the rear. From the sixteenth century on, the foot stood habitually in the centre, the cavalry on the flanks, or behind the flanks. There was no set battle-order. The battles were placed in one continuous line, or checker-wise, or at times in concave order. Open ground was sought and, if possible, with the sun and wind in the rear.

The artillery was placed in batteries at any commanding part of the line, and the horses or oxen which dragged it were sent to the rear. It could neither follow the troops in a victory nor sustain an advance, and in case of disaster was sure to fall into the enemy's hands. Despite these demerits, artillery grew in importance : its advantages outweighed its shortcomings.

The introduction of firearms brought about many changes. Open order became essential, and cavalry looked on its fire

as superior to the cold weapon. The horsemen awaited a
charge and received it with salvos of musketry, while during
a charge the men stopped to fire a volley, or often several;
though, if without firearms, they still charged as of old. The
dragoons dismounted and fought on foot. The infantry
fought in open or closed order, according as it bore missile or
close-quarter weapons.

The rival lines were slowly formed behind a cloud of skirmishers. Duels between champions or small bodies were frequent. Parallel order was almost invariable; flank attacks
or turning movements were rare or accidental. In the fourteenth and fifteenth centuries battles were often sanguinary,
and ended in the annihilation of one army. Firearms reduced
the casualties because battles were sooner decided. Pursuit
was almost never undertaken. It was in fact a traditional
habit to remain three days on the field of victory, to celebrate
the event and to divide the booty.

Marches were conducted in as heavy columns as the roads
allowed; the cavalry and foot were mixed; the artillery,
strongly escorted, was in a separate column. Van- and rear-
guard and flankers were put out, but at no great distance.
The baggage-train grew enormously in size; non-combatants
and women accompanied the army in almost incredible numbers, and the soldiers were followed by their prisoners and
booty, in whatever fashion they could be transported. Compared to the orderliness of an army of to-day, the army of
three hundred years ago was worse than a mob.

During the feudal era, rank and command, as we understand it, did not exist; but the employment of mercenary
troops gradually evolved a system. The monarch appointed
the army commanders and the colonels; the latter selected as
captains the men who raised the companies; the captains
chose their lieutenants; and the men were often permitted to

select the petty (or non-commissioned) officers. This ancient device was substantially the system which prevailed in raising volunteer regiments during our civil war.

On recruitment the men were expected to report with a given number of days' rations, after which the prince they served was supposed to keep them in victual; but this was so ill done that plunder was the universal means of subsistence. There were no magazines until much later; regular requisitions on the enemy's territory were unknown, food was usually brought from the army's base, and this was a long and tedious process, whose irregularity forbade rapid manœuvres, and gave rise to hunger and sickness, to desertions and plunder. Nor until long after regular armies had become the rule was there any method in feeding troops, and their payment was even more shiftlessly conducted than the rationing.

Even so late as the fourteenth and fifteenth centuries the feudal organizations showed no discipline whatever; but the growth of mercenary organizations made severer methods imperative. In the sixteenth, Ferdinand the Catholic in Spain, Francis I. and Henry II. in France, and Charles V. in Germany made codes of laws for their respective armies. Under these codes the punishments were Draconic, and rewards were allotted for courage and exemplary service; but unless a general was able and much beloved by his men, no laws could keep up a discipline such as to-day we take for granted.

Prisoners in feudal times had been habitually treated with such cruelty that few escaped with their lives. Only the nobles could buy release. But little by little a system of ransom sprang up under which even the common soldier could hope for freedom. This was a step in the right direction, but it increased the train to a dangerous degree, and hampered still further the movements of troops.

In the fourteenth and fifteenth centuries armies camped

without much artificial protection, though the wagons were used as defenses; but firearms soon made it essential for camps to be surrounded by earthworks, on which guns were mounted. The profiles of these works gradually became more marked, and bastions and outworks were erected. Especially the artillery parks were fortified lest the guns should be captured.

In attacking fortresses, the ancient means of rams, movable towers, catapults and ballistas, Greek fire and like devices remained in use until the introduction of gunpowder. Walls of circumvallation and contravallation were thrown up, and mining was commonly resorted to. In the sixteenth and seventeenth centuries great advance was made in the conduct of sieges, especially by the Italians. These new methods, improved on in the Netherlands, led up to the modern art of engineering. Treacherous dealings were first essayed with the commandant of a strong place, or with a friendly party within walls. Secret escalade might be attempted. If neither was available, a regular siege was undertaken. Trenches were dug, at first without system, later in zigzags. Batteries were erected to command the enemy's walls, and breaches were operated. Powder was too costly to use in mining; walls were undermined by heat, as in antiquity. The besieged kept up a heavy fire, threw burning substances at night to light up the siege-lines, built outworks from which to disturb the operations, made sorties, and defended themselves from assaults with stubbornness. To a storm-captured fortress no quarter was given, and the defenders fought with this knowledge.

The wars in the Netherlands in the last half of the sixteenth century gave a great impetus to engineering. Outworks grew in extent and importance, and inner works were built to enable the besieged to hold the fortress even after the loss of the walls. Regular sieges were long drawn out. Trenches were opened beyond cannon-shot; covered trenches or saps nearer to; and breastworks at given distances took the place of parallels. All but the breaching batteries were placed so as to command the tops of the walls. Many of our common devices, such as mantelets, fascines, sand-bags, had their modern origin in these days. Breaches were carried by storming parties made up of volunteers. The besieged gradually learned in a cruder way all the arts of defense which are now put into use.

The rôle played by the invention of gunpowder has been exaggerated; it was an effect, not a cause; gunpowder was but one manifestation of the growth of the world out of the darkness of the Middle Ages; the advance in military art was another. It was in reality the dawn of the new era of intelligence, the emergence from the ignorance which had engulfed Europe for a thousand years, which lay at the root of all these improvements. It was time mankind should redeem itself.

Officer. (14th Century.)

IV.

THE SWEDISH ARMY–CHANGES. 1523–1632.

FROM Alexander to Cæsar, the art of war rose to a great height; from Cæsar to Gustavus, it sank into oblivion; Gustavus re-created it. Gunpowder gave a new direction to war. Ancient arms were simple; armies needed no magazines, nor trains to carry munitions, and everything tended to battle. When firearms and cannon were introduced, the strong places where the munitions lay became so important as to be fortified, and armies sought rather to capture these than to fight battles. Hence a system of sieges. Armies could not go far from their munitions; artillery was heavy; marches were slow and tedious; victories could not be made decisive by pursuit; and all war was formal. Troops were raised by recruitment or press-gangs, and their quality was bad. Sweden first created a national militia, and its regular army, drawn therefrom, had no mercenaries. In France there were then but fifteen thousand men as a standing army. Marked tactical advance was soon made, and troops grew more mobile. Infantry was the bulk of the force; pikemen gradually gave way to musketeers, especially for light troops. The file was still deep; but Gustavus reduced it to six, which deployed to three deep to fire. The men wore light armor and a pot helmet. The pike was shortened. The musket, after many stages, grew light enough to dispense with the crutch-rest; paper cartridges were introduced; and finally the bayonet was added. The foot got organized into companies and regiments, and rank and command were settled. Fire grew more rapid, especially among the Swedes, but minor tactics was crude. Cavalry consisted of cuirassiers and dragoons; light horse existed in eastern Europe only; all was organized into cornets and regiments. Cavalry had grown to rely on its firearms; Gustavus taught it to charge at a gallop. The Swedish artillery was far ahead of any other. Gustavus made light and handy guns, which could keep up with the troops and fire with rapidity; and he invented fixed ammunition. At one time the king used leather guns. The artillery was reduced to a system of regular calibres, and the handling of guns became a science.

IT is desirable to review part of what has been said in former volumes, in order to lead up to the military status of Sweden, when Gustavus Adolphus was on the throne. History shows us three main periods in the art of war : the first from remote antiquity to the decadence of Rome; the second, during the Middle Ages, and down to Gustavus; the third, from the beginning of Gustavus' work to the present day. During the first period, the art of war under the Greeks and Romans, and notably under Alexander, Hannibal and Cæsar, attained a height such that, in view of the uncertainty in warfare and of the changeableness of tactics arising from the rapidity of modern invention, it may be said to dispute the palm with that of the nineteenth century. During the second period, the art of war sank to its lowest level, as letters and arts were forgotten, and began slowly to rise, as people again became intelligent; and to this rise the introduction of gunpowder contributed. From the genius of Gustavus in the third period, the art of war acquired a notable impetus and a life which, invigorated by the great deeds of Frederick and Napoleon, has brought it to the present high development.

It was the introduction of gunpowder into Europe which gave the key-note to the new science of war, so different from that which obtained among the ancients. The two periods in which war has really flourished, and which have been not over three hundred years in length, were separated by a gap of many centuries. The distinction between the two was a marked one.

The armies of the Greeks and Romans were, as a rule, not numerically large. Their method of victualing troops was such that food could be found almost everywhere, and it was not usually necessary to establish storehouses of provisions or to bring rations from a great distance. The weapons of the ancients were simple, and those which did not last long — spears, darts and arrows — could be readily manufactured in any place, and by the soldiers themselves. Great arsenals of military stores were unessential to an army in the field ; nor

had powder and ball, or other ammunition, to be brought up
from the rear to supply the waste of battle. For this reason
the ancients had no need of fortresses, or depots in their rear.
Communication with home was of less importance than after
the introduction of gunpowder with all its machinery, and the
reasons which make the security of a base so essential in
modern times were to the ancients of no moment whatever.

With the ancients battle was the one important feature.
The nature of their weapons brought them at once into close
quarters, and kept them there. To withdraw an army from
battle with a moderate loss if things went wrong was impossible, — to all but the very few great generals. There was
no artillery to keep the enemy at a distance and arrest his
pursuit while the beaten troops were retired out of action;
and the rival lines were too much intermingled to make this
possible if there had been. Battles commonly resulted in
victory for one side and fearful massacre for the other.

The average generals of antiquity needed no art except
the art of fighting battles, — in other words, tactics. To them
what we call strategy was an unessential art. They marched
their armies out to a convenient plain in which to fight, and
everything depended on the victory they there might win.
The great captains of antiquity were undeniably able strategists as well as fine tacticians; but strategy is the very essence
of intellectual common sense, and their clear vision enabled
them to see the advantage of doing that which we have now
reduced to rules and called a science, — which indeed is but
a collection of those things which the great captains have
taught us how to do.

In modern times, when the introduction of firearms, for
infantry and cavalry alike, became universal; when much
artillery accompanied armies; when their numerical force
became larger, and they had to be fed and supplied with

ammunition from magazines in their rear, the importance of these depots became so great that they were invariably turned into fortresses; and their value lent an equal importance to the lines of communication out to the army depending upon them. These lines had to be protected at all hazards, for their interruption for even a few days might bring disaster to the army thus cut off.

Again, the transportation of rations and material of war required long trains, and consumed much time. The loss of a convoy or of a fortress was as harmful as the loss of a battle. Thus in a certain sense battles forfeited their original importance, and people took instead to manœuvring on the enemy's communications or to capturing his fortresses.

Victories, to be decisive, must as a rule be followed by vigorous pursuit; and the armies of the early period of gunpowder, loaded down, depending on depots, and followed by a horde of non-combatants, often exceeding in number the arms-bearing men, were cumbrous and unsuited to pursuit. A further reason why battles were followed by so little gain was that they were delivered only to defeat, destroy or inflict loss on the enemy — from purely tactical reasons — without any ulterior purpose. The art of making battle subserve a larger purpose in the general campaign-scheme, so that a victory shall be of due effect, was not then understood. It is, in modern times, of recent origin. Thus, though there was an effort to make war a science, to reduce it to rules, the lack of broader knowledge and the cumbrous method of the day rendered the average campaigns, even up to the end of the seventeenth century, slow, long drawn-out and indecisive; full of wrong, ill-digested methods, of a curious sort of formality or subservience to certain hard and fast rules.

Sweden was the first country in Europe which built up for herself a regular and at the same time national military organization. In other countries what army there existed was small, — had originally served as a species of guard of honor to the king. In case of war, troops were raised by conscription, or under a rude militia system, by voluntary or press-gang enlistments, or by the purchase of mercenaries. In the sixteenth and seventeenth centuries the soldier of fortune

was a typical character, equally useful and unreliable in war, and dangerous in war and peace alike. These men earned their livelihood by arms as a trade, not as a profession; they expected to live on their pay and rations, and they hoped to grow rich by plunder. The free towns were garrisoned by their citizens, who were enrolled in a regular body for the defense and policing of their city; in case they needed additional forces they resorted to mercenaries.

Danzig Citizen Soldier (taking oath).
From an old print.

Sweden was a noteworthy exception. As early as the sixteenth century the Vasa kings laid the foundation of a national regular army, and Gustavus Adolphus perfected it. The Swedish army was a pattern organization, in which there were no mercenaries. It consisted of a given number of regular troops, raised, paid, fed and equipped by the state, and back of these stood a militia kept up by the people. The regulars were intended for wars outside the national territory, the militia for the defense of the fatherland; and the regulars were kept at full strength by drafts from the militia. The raising of the troops was based on a careful system of land-tenure, under which all able-bodied males from fifteen years up were called into service; and Gustavus introduced a novel method under which each soldier was supposed to own and to be supported and equipped by a certain parcel of land, rising in size and importance according to arm and grade.

The militia consisted of eight cavalry and twenty infantry regiments, each raised in whole or in part in a given district from its own inhabitants, and kept on foot at the expense of that district. The men there liable to duty assembled at a given time under its standard, and each district raised from three hundred to six hundred men. King Eric strove to make the conscripts from each set of twelve districts into a

Lansquenet.
(16th Century.)

regiment, but these proved too irregular in size. The early number of three thousand to a regiment was finally reduced to eleven hundred and seventy-six; and Gustavus equalized

Musketeer.
(1572.)

companies and regiments. The militia was carefully drilled, kept at its full complement by annual drafts, and relieved from taxes and some other burdens. As Sweden was poorly populated, and the militia contributed to the regular contingent no more than twelve or fifteen thousand men a year, Gustavus was eventually compelled to resort to mercenaries to fill his war-thinned ranks; and regiments came to his army from all parts of Germany, the Netherlands and England. But the Swedes were the leaven of the lump.

The other nations of Europe boasted no such settled organization. All middle Europe was split up into petty princi-

palities, of a size which precluded armies worthy
the name. Of the Catholic German troops, Wallenstein's were perhaps the best ; Tilly's ranked
next.   Of the Protestant German troops, the
Saxons were deemed to hold the palm, though
they did not prove it at Breitenfeld ; then the
Hessians, and the army of Brunswick-Lüneburg,
the latter being patterned on the Swedish. Denmark had practically no army system.   France,
at the time, had only fifteen thousand men as a
standing army, with cadres that could be increased to fifty thousand in case of need, of
which ten thousand would be mounted. This
was a mere fraction of what she called out
under the Grand Monarque.

Pikeman.
(1534.)

Though there had been little advance in general military organization, the tactical systems of the various countries had improved. William and
Maurice of Orange, Spinola,
Henry IV. and Coligny each contributed something to the discipline and structure of troops ;
and Gustavus put on the capstone in the Swedish army changes. The wars in the Netherlands and Germany in the sixteenth and seventeenth centuries had shown up the defects
which had come down from feudal times, and
the bright intellects among rulers and their
servants set themselves the task of supplying
the remedy.   But to create a system which
should permanently affect the art of war remained for Gustavus Adolphus.

Infantry, in the early part of the seventeenth

Pikeman.
(1572.)

century, consisted of pikemen and musketeers, and with the
efficiency of firearms the latter increased from one third to
two thirds of the force. In Swedish companies of one hundred and fifty men, there were sev-
enty-five musketeers and fifty-nine
pikemen, the rest being petty and
commissioned officers. The musketeers were reckoned as light
troops, best fitted for scouting and
outpost service ; they had a pot
helmet, a sabre and
a musket. The pike-
men were the heavy
armed, and were
deemed superior in
value, — what we
should call the troops
of the line. They

Grenadier. (1696.)

had full body-armor, and until the seventeenth
century thigh-pieces. Their eighteen-foot pikes
were finally replaced by partisans, with eleven-
foot shaft, and two-foot double-edged head,
four inches in width. Later, the length of the
partisan and shaft appears to have been cut
down to not over eight feet. Gustavus foresaw that musketry was the arm of the future,
and gradually decreased the number of pikemen as well as took from the weight of their
armor to add to their mobility. In 1631 he
introduced entire regiments of musketeers. The distinction
between riflemen who fired guns and grenadiers who threw
hand grenades dates back to him. The word "grenadier"
was coined at the defense of Ratisbon by the Swedes in 1632,

Officer of French
Foot. (1647.)

when those soldiers who took the risk of handling and casting hand grenades from the walls were given extra pay ; for the riflemen could fire from behind cover as they could not. The officers of infantry carried a partisan and a sword. Bowmen did not exist in Germany.

Arquebus and Rest.
(16th Century.)

In 1623 Gustavus organized the Swedish companies of one hundred and fifty men, set up in files six deep. Four companies made a " squadron " or battalion ; eight companies a regiment ; three regiments a " great regiment " or brigade. Some regiments enlisted in foreign parts had but one hundred and twenty men to the company. The companies and battalions stood in line with varying intervals between them.

The arming of the infantry underwent a considerable change. There appears to have been a number of " double-pay " men (veterans) as far back as Eric's time. They carried the pike and wore armor, and numbered at times nearly three fourths of the force. The old arquebus and cross-bow, heavy and clumsy, with their forked rest, were replaced by the musket ; but this still needed a rest. It was provided with a match-lock, a device originally more reliable than the flint-lock, which often missed fire ; but gradually the latter was improved, and drove out the match. About 1626

Musketeer. (1630.)

Gustavus lightened the musket sufficiently to dispense with the crutch, and introduced the wheel-lock; and in his wars against the Poles, not above taking a hint from any source, he resorted to the old Roman, or, one might say, the English long- bowman's habit of

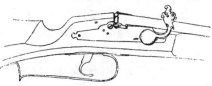

Matchlock. (Stockholm Museum.)

having the men carry sharpened palisades, not for camping, but to erect a defense against the Polish lancers from behind which they could fire upon them. This was a spe-

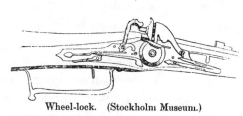

Wheel-lock. (Stockholm Museum.)

cies of survival of the musket - rest; it finally became only an iron-point- ed rod; and to it some have as- cribed the origin of the bayonet. It was carried after a while in the train, as it loaded down the men and militated against rapidity.

The next important improvement in firearms, and this was first made in the Swedish army, was the introduction of paper cartridges. Of these the men car- ried ten, together with spare powder and ball, in car-

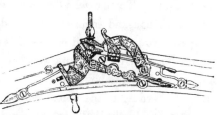

Pistol Flint-lock. (1613. Stockholm Museum.)

tridge-boxes or "bandoliers" slung across the chest from left shoulder to right side; while a sword hung in a belt from right shoulder to left side. The bayonet and flint-lock were introduced in France some time after Gustavus' death; and the troops armed with this handy musket (*facile — fusil ; though* the name probably came from *focus —* fire, Italian *focile*) were called fusiliers. The bayonet was mounted on a wooden plug to be inserted in the bore of the musket. It first made its appearance in the wars in the Netherlands.

Infantry, in all the European countries, finally got divided into regiments and companies; but these were of no especial numerical strength. The company occasionally ran up as high as three hundred men, and the regiment to over four thousand. Gustavus' regular regiments were more uniform. The companies had one hundred and fifty men, and eight to twelve companies made a regiment. In 1630 eight companies were deemed a battalion or regiment. It goes without saying that the exigencies of active service often changed all this. A note by Oxenstiern exists which speaks of foot regiments varying between fifteen hundred and nineteen hundred men; cavalry regiments with from four to eight companies; and they must have varied much more. To one who has served with regiments which from one thousand men would run down, in the course of a campaign, to two hundred or less, this seems a very small variation; but Swedish recruits were used to equalize old regiments, not to make new ones. The Swedish militia regiment varied according to the population of the district in which it was raised. In the bulk of the countries of Germany about two thousand men made up an infantry regiment, and its officers were a colonel, lieutenant-colonel, major, quartermaster and regimental clerk; a barber and one assistant, who were surgeon and apothecary; a provost-marshal and one as-

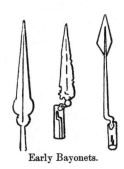

Early Bayonets.

sistant; a chaplain and one assistant; a judge advocate and his clerk. The infantry company had a captain, a lieutenant, an ensign, two sergeants, one muster-clerk, a quartermaster, an armorer, six corporals, two drummers and a fifer. In active service there were ninety to ninety-four common soldiers, fifteen upper and twenty-one lower file-leaders and four muster-boys.

Loading and firing, with the constant improvement in firearms, grew more rapid; and yet it took ninety-five to ninety-nine "motions" to complete the operation, though Gustavus had abolished a large number of useless ones. On the other hand, the minor tactics of the foot-soldier was very crude, and was confined to the

simple facings, wheelings, ployments and deployments. The solid masses or phalanxes of the Spanish style remained in use by all

English Soldier (unequipped).

German Officer. (1630.)

but the Swedes, while Gustavus set up his men six deep, the pikemen in the centre, the musketeers on the flanks or in small intermingled bodies, and later three deep.

The cavalry consisted of cuirassiers and dragoons, the latter being mounted infantry. There had been mounted arquebusiers, but Gustavus gave these weapons up in favor of lighter firearms in all cavalry regiments.

In the imperial armies were heavy cavalry, carbineers and Croats or Hungarian irregulars. These three species of horse were known by different names in different countries, and

Dragoon.   (1616.)

varied in them all. When Gustavus came to the throne, the cavalry was still considered the more honorable arm; but the nobility, which grew poorer as the commonalty gained in intelligence, were unable voluntarily to keep this arm up to its ancient standard, and Gustavus was finally compelled to recruit his cavalry in the same manner as his foot. It was not strong; in Sweden were only some thirty-five hundred mounted troops. As the firearm gained in efficiency, horse-armor was discarded; the lance gave way to the more useful carbine, and the dragoons, introduced into the Swedish army from Germany in 1611, were furnished with an infantry musket and dismounted to fight. They were really bodies of infantry, comprising both musketeers and pikemen,

and mounted to enable them to move fast. They lacked the cavalryman's distinctive boots and spurs. Yet they were not bad cavalry; their record as such was good. The cuirassier retained helmet, cuirass of front and back pieces, sword and two pistols; but from this time on light cavalry has constantly gained in relative efficiency over the heavy.

Hungarian Irregular.
(17th Century.)

Like foot, the horse was organized into regiments and companies, the latter also called "squadrons" or "cornets." The Swedish cavalry regiments had a colonel, a lieutenant-colonel and major, a quartermaster, regimental clerk and a barber-surgeon. The cavalry cornet, or company, had a captain with four horses, a lieutenant and an ensign with three horses each, two corporals with two horses each, a quartermaster with two horses, a muster-clerk, a chaplain, a provost, a barber, a farrier, each with one horse, two trumpeters and one hundred and two common soldiers; or, all told, one hundred and fifteen men with one hundred and twenty-five horses. The strength of the cavalry regiments of other countries was very various, and the difficulty of procuring horses often dismounted great numbers of men. The imperial companies averaged one hundred horses, the regiments eight hundred. The Swedish regiments of cavalry had eight cornets, aggregating one thousand horses.

Croat.

The main trouble with the horse prior to Gustavus' day was its slowness in charging. It would ride up to the enemy, when each rank would successively fire and then wheel off to reload. The light horsemen served as scouts; the heavy cavalry lacked *élan*, never undertaking the true rôle of horse. The Swedish cuirassiers, on the contrary, were taught to ride at a gallop, to fire their pistols at speed, and then take to the naked weapon. If they were superior to the German cavalry in any one point, it was in their better tactics, and this was Gustavus' doing. On the whole, the Swedish cavalry, barring discipline, was no better than the German; perhaps the heavy cavalry was not as good as the best German squadrons, on account of the smaller size of the Swedish horses, nor the light as good as the Croat irregulars.

But there was no question as to the superiority of Swedish artillery. Gustavus Adolphus introduced marked changes in this arm, mainly by making the guns and carriages lighter and handier, and by adapting their movements to those of the other arms and to the requirements of the battle-field. In this, as in all his military efforts, his motto was mobility and rapidity of fire.

There were, according to size, three kinds of guns: siege, ship, field. The twenty-four-pounder siege-gun weighed three tons; the twenty-four-pounder field-gun only twenty-seven hundred pounds. The twelve-pounder siege-gun weighed a ton and a half, the twelve-pounder field-gun only eighteen hundred pounds. The six-pounder siege-gun weighed three

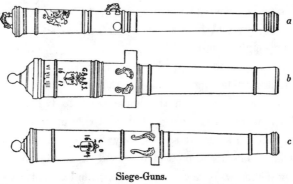

Siege-Guns.

a, Twenty-four pounder; calibre, 5 inches; weight, 6,000 pounds. (Stockholm Artillery Museum.) *b*, Twelve-pounder; calibre, 4 inches; weight, 2,600 pounds. (Stockholm Artillery Museum.) *c*, Six-pounder; calibre, 3.3 inches; weight, 1,700 pounds. (Stockholm Artillery Museum.)

fourths of a ton; the six-pounder field-gun twelve hundred pounds. There were also three-pounders and two-pounders for field use. The ship-guns were intermediate in heft. There was some variation in these measurements and weights. The heavy siege-guns took thirty-six horses to move, and could not go into the field. There were various patterns of guns, cannon-royal, culverins, falconets, single and double (*i. e.* heavy and light) and mortars; but the latter were not much used. All these pieces were extremely unhandy. The single cannon-royal was twelve feet long and called for twenty-four horses to transport it; culverins needed sixteen.

One of Gustavus' artillery officers, von Siegeroth, in doing practice work with guns, new and old, had found that shorter guns, properly con-structed, were equally ef-fective. In 1624 Gustavus commanded all old and

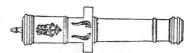

Three-pounder Regimental Gun.

Calibre, 2.6 inches; weight, 450 pounds.
(Stockholm Artillery Museum.)

unserviceable ordnance to be recast into newer patterns; and a year later he himself contrived a gun which one horse or three men could handle to good effect. This gun was in-tended as a regimental piece; and each regiment had one and later two of them. It was an iron three- and four-pounder, and the cartridge, which weighed less than a pound and a half, consisted of the charge held in a thin turned wooden case, wired to the ball. This was the first artillery cartridge,

Three-pounder Leather Gun.

Calibre, 2.6 inches; weight, 450 pounds.
(Stockholm Artillery Museum.)

the original fixed ammuni-tion. The gun was after-wards introduced into oth-er European armies as the *pièce Suédoise.* Not only had it the virtue of lesser weight, but its cartridge was always ready, and it could be fired eight times to six shots of a musketeer with the awkward arm of the day.

Gustavus' merit thus lay in making guns which could be handled more like our own than the cumbrous ordnance then in use. In the wars against the Poles he employed with profit the so-called leather cannon, a fact which shows how lacking in power the artillery of the day must have been. These guns were invented in the early twenties by Colonel Wurmbrandt, and consisted of a thin copper tube reinforced

Early Mortars.

by iron rings and bands, then bound with rope set in cement, the whole covered with sole leather. The tube was made to screw in and out, as it grew heated by from eight to twelve discharges and had to be cooled. The gun-carriage was shaped out of two oak planks. Three men could carry a gun, which without carriage weighed ninety pounds, and was fired with a light charge. Of fourteen of these cannon only is mention made ; and after being used in 1628–29 in Poland, they disappeared in favor of the king's four-pounder cast-iron guns. These last named regimental guns remained in common use in Europe until the artillery was reorganized and massed by Frederick. The capacity for evolutions and the rapidity of fire of Gustavus' batteries excited universal admiration. Grape

Early Mortar.

and canister were generally employed in the field-guns, round shot only in siege-guns. Gustavus used his cannon in masses as well as with regiments, and the excellence of his artillery largely contributed to his successes. This arm with the Swedes was immensely superior in effectiveness to that of any other European army; the king was the first to show of what artillery was really capable.

Mortars throwing bombs were first used at the siege of Lamotte in 1634. Hand grenades, shells, fire-balls, etc., came into more general use as the German chemists made their many new discoveries. Artillery-practice grew to be something of a science; experts took it up, and the troops were better instructed. The regimental guns were attended by grenadiers detailed for the work; and there were special companies for the reserve guns. Musketeers supported the guns among the Swedes; cavalry was wont to do so in the imperial army.

In this connection the following extract from Holingshed's Chronicles, showing what English ordnance at the end of the sixteenth century was, may not be uninteresting : —

The names of our greatest ordnance are commonly these : *Robinet*, whose weight is two hundred pounds, and it hath one inch and a quarter within the mouth. *Falconet* weigheth five hundred pounds, and his wideness is two inches within the mouth. *Falcon* hath eight hundred pounds, and two inches and a half within the mouth ; *Minion* poiseth eleven hundred pounds, and hath three inches and a quarter within the mouth ; *Sacre* hath sixteen hundred pounds, and is three inches and a half wide in the mouth ; *Demi-Culverin* weigheth three thousand pounds, and hath four inches and a half within the mouth ; *Culverin* hath four thousand pounds and five inches and a half within the mouth ; *Demi-Cannon*, six thousand pounds, and six inches and a half within the mouth ; *Cannon*, seven thousand pounds, and seven inches within the mouth ; *E-Cannon*, eight thousand pounds, and seven inches within the mouth ; *Basilisk*, nine thousand pounds, eight inches and three quarters within the mouth. By which proportions also it is easy to come by the weight of every shot, how many scores it doth flee at point blank, and how much powder is to be had to the same, and finally how many inches in height each bullet ought to carry.

The Names of the Greatest Ordnance.	Weight of the Shot.	Scores of Carriage.	Pounds of Powder.	Height of Bullet.
Robinet	1 pound.	0	$0\frac{1}{2}$	1 (inch)
Falconet	2 pounds.	14	2	$1\frac{1}{4}$
Falcon	$2\frac{1}{4}$ pounds.	16	$2\frac{1}{2}$	$2\frac{1}{4}$
Minion	$4\frac{1}{2}$ pounds.	17	$4\frac{1}{2}$	3
Sacre	5 pounds.	18	5	$3\frac{1}{4}$
Demi-Culverin	9 pounds.	20	9	4
Culverin	18 pounds.	25	18	$5\frac{1}{4}$
Demi-Cannon	30 pounds.	38	28	$6\frac{1}{4}$
Cannon	60 pounds.	20	44	$7\frac{3}{4}$
E-Cannon	42 pounds.	20	20	$6\frac{3}{4}$
Basilisk	60 pounds.	21	60	$8\frac{1}{4}$

Culverin. (1500.)

V.

THE SWEDISH ORGANIZATION AND TACTICS. 1611–1632.

GUSTAVUS was unable early to uniform his troops, but he gave each a special color of regimental flag. In arms and equipment there was uniformity, and the men were warmly clad in their peasant's dress, and had waterproof fur-lined boots for winter. His first improvement was to lessen the file to three deep in firing; but the pikemen stood in close serried order, six deep. The brigades had alternate bodies of musketeers and pikemen, and foot was mixed with horse in parts of the line. All changes tended towards rapid fire and mobility. The cavalry from ten was also cut down to three ranks, and was ployed into column to charge. From an inert body Gustavus made it an active one. Though the artillery was used in masses, each regiment kept its own pieces. In battle the skirmishers held the ground while the line formed; then the cavalry cleared the front, the artillery opened, and the line advanced, first to fire, then to push of pike. In marches Gustavus dispensed with a rear-guard when marching toward, with a van when marching from, the enemy. His men were rapid goers. In battle he paid keen heed to the *terrain*, and made his three arms work together. The discipline of the Swedes was wonderful; good conduct was universal; the usual military crimes were quite absent. The pay was small but regular; the food was ample, and was obtained, not by plunder, but from magazines carefully provided. The troops were quartered in towns or fortified camps. The train was much decreased. Religious duties were strictly observed. Promotion went by seniority and service. Rewards and punishments were just. There were regimental schools for the children of soldiers, many of whom, as well as their wives, went with the troops. Loose women were not tolerated. As an engineer, Gustavus was far ahead of his day; he had many experts; fortification was wonderfully well done; and field-works were constructed rapidly and efficiently. The Swedish navy as well as the army was largely increased and brought to a state of high efficiency.

GUSTAVUS ADOLPHUS is usually referred to as the originator of uniforms. This is not strictly correct. Some of the Swedish regiments were known by a color, not of the uniform

but of the standard. Ehrenreuter's regiment had red silk
for its ensign ; the Vizthum regiment, old blue ; Winkel's,
blue ; Teuffel's, yellow ; Hepburn's, green ; the Pomeranian
regiment, white ; the three Hanse regiments, black. The
ensign was of one solid color, on which figured an emblem.
Such was one of white damask, with the royal crown surmounted by a rose, and " Gustavus Adolphus " on one side,
and on the other, " Touch me not or you 'll get burnt ; "
or, again, a blood-red standard, with a flame and a figure
bearing sword and scales, and the motto " For King and
Justice."

For many years Gustavus had no uniforms for his troops.
At the beginning of his reign the men served, each in the
peasant's dress in which he reported. In arms and equipment alone was there uniformity, save in so far as the peasants dressed alike. In 1613 a uniformed royal body-guard
was organized, and in 1621 Gustavus ordered that the soldiers of the line be clad alike so far as possible, instead of
in the long jerkin and smock-frock of the peasant, " so that
they should not be despised among the nations of the out-
land." A year after he ordered that companies and regiments be uniformly clad ; but all this took time. The clothing
of the Swedish peasant was coarse, but being hand-made it
wore well, and a good garment might not be lightly discarded. So that even in 1626 people spoke of the Swedes
as ill-appearing louts in bad clothes. The uniformed troops
indeed donned their uniforms only on dress occasions, as at
the visit of princes, or at reviews in their honor. They sometimes had holiday insignia issued for special use ; at the
Altmarkt Conference the men on duty wore blue and gold
tabards. When the matter got settled, the men appear to
have worn a sleeveless tunic and loose knee-breeches, which,
indeed, was the national cut of dress ; and over this their

armor and equipments. An undergarment covered the arms; the legs were clad in coarse woolen stockings and the feet in shoes or bootees, according to season, for the foot and dragoons; in boots for the cavalry. The infantryman wore at times a species of gaiter from the knee down. Clothing depots were established at several of the Swedish cities; but although the work was all done in these depots, the patterns are said to have come from Paris, then already the centre of fashions, small and great. It is true that Gustavus eventually arrived at uniforming his troops; for years his efforts lay in that direction, but he aimed still more at providing warm and useful clothing. The men had fur garments and gloves, fur-lined boots and woolen stockings, and many had a sort of Russian bootee of waterproof leather.

Suit worn by Gustavus at the Dirschau Combat. (Stockholm Museum.)

These were in part issued to the troops, in part bought by the individual soldiers. It was the protection afforded by such clothing that enabled Gustavus to conduct his winter campaigns in Germany, — to the astonishment and confusion of his enemies.

The chief improvement in the tactical formation, and this was brought about by the introduction of gunpowder, lay in the lessening of the depth of the file; and yet it is curious how old-fashioned soldiers like Tilly stuck to their deep battles when artillery was becoming effective. Gustavus made many other changes in the formation and manœuvring of the troops. Infantry had already got set up in not exceeding ten ranks. The musketeers stood in closed files but with open ranks, which gave space for the rank which had fired to retire to reload, and they sometimes attacked in open order, almost in what we should call a skirmish line; the pikemen

stood in closed ranks and
files. Gustavus first reduced
the formation of musketeers
to six ranks, which for firing
closed into three; this remained the pattern for many
years, and at the close of the
Thirty Years' War was universal. The battle disap-
peared, and was succeeded
by a proper fire line.

Swedish Musketeer.

Swedish Pikeman.

In line the pike-
men were placed
in the centre, with the musketeers on the flanks
or grouped at the corners of the bodies; or else
the divisions of musketeers and pikemen alternated.
A mass of men ready for action was called a tertia,
or battalion (battle), or squadron. In Germany
and Spain these battles were several thousand
strong; among the French they consisted of not
over five or six hundred men. Gustavus
first brigaded his regiments, and gave to
many brigades a peculiar color of standard.
The exigencies of the service demanded frequent changes, and we hear of brigades of
two regiments formed in five lines, of which
the two rear ones were the reserve, and in
them the divisions of pikemen and musketeers alternated. Such a formation is shown
in Lord Reay's sketch, of which later; but
it was not universal. Or again, the brigade
was set up in three lines, so as to show more
front; this was the formation adopted by

Gustavus at Breitenfeld. At still another period the brigade was formed with a division of pikemen in advance, and four divisions of musketeers in two lines in the rear. At Lützen, a dozen Swedish companies were ployed into column, one behind the other, and had eight companies in one line as a reserve. Any one of these brigade-formations was handier in movement, and less endangered by artillery, than the usual deep masses; and it was particularly use-ful from having the reserve to call upon.

It seems odd that there should not be more certainty as to the organization and minor tactics of an army of modern days; but matters were in a transition period, due to the constant improvements in bal-listics, and there is no moment of time when any one method universally obtained, even in Sweden. It might be difficult, when arms of precision call forth so many changes, to say just what the organization of infantry is to-day, or may be within five years. Going back to include our civil war, in view of the changes in all civilized

Swedish Officer.

countries, it might indeed puzzle one to state without great prolixity just what a regiment or a brigade is; and records were not so carefully kept in the seventeenth century. Many of the foreign regiments in Gustavus' army had each its own formation and drill, which it was wise not to alter, lest the efficiency of the body should be affected.

Taught by his studies, Gustavus revived the ancient habit of mixing small detachments of infantry with cavalry. He made these composite bodies from two hundred to four hun-dred strong, and gave each one a field-gun. On important occasions he detailed men from different organizations to form a *corps d'élite* of musketeers.

The infantry commonly fired in salvos by ranks, succeeding ranks coming forward, while the one which had fired retired through the intervals to reload. Gustavus introduced the habit of having the front rank kneel so as to fire without shifting ranks, as this was apt to unsettle the line. On occasion he used what was virtually a fire by file.

The cavalry had hitherto been formed in from four to ten ranks. Gustavus cut it down to three ranks, which much increased its mobility. The fancy skirmishing (*caracoles*) was abolished, as well as the use of firearms as the sole resource in the attack. The king insisted that the squadrons should charge at a gallop with pistols or naked blade; a style quite in accordance with his own tremendous fire and energy.

Swedish Cuirassier.

The Swedish cavalry rode in two or more lines, company in rear of company, or checkerwise; occasionally in one line *en muraille*. Other horse still relied on its fire alone, which made it excessively slow. There were exceptions: no better cavalry stood in line than splendid Pappenheim's; but as a rule the cavalry of the day was inert. With Gustavus, on the contrary, even the dragoon partook more of the impulse of the cavalryman than of the stolidity of the infantry soldier; while in the other armies the dragoon remained a mere well-transported footman. In his intelligent management of both these arms Gustavus soon had imitators. His victories showed the superiority of his system so thoroughly that the whole world turned from the ancient methods to study what he had introduced.

It was the habit in all armies to place the horse in the wings; and a sort of precedence by seniority that decided the place in line made the constant shifting of regiments awkward and dangerous. Gustavus kept cavalry in the wings, but he also placed cavalry companies in rear of each line of infantry, where they served to aid in reestablishing any sudden check.

Swedish Ensign of Cuirassiers.

The artillery was posted along the front, or on advantageous ground. Under Gustavus the three arms supported each other much in the modern way. Herein consisted the value of the king's method. His army became a well-designed machine, with all parts operating smoothly, instead of a disjointed mass, whose several parts worked out of time, and failed at the critical moment to sustain one another.

The acts of a battle were these. The ground was first held by the small bodies of skirmishers, who, from their dangerous calling, were called forlorn hopes, or *enfants perdus;* and behind these the lines quietly formed in parallel order. Then, often not waiting to withdraw these skirmishers, the cavalry charged down the front to clear out the curtain they had formed, to the destruction of friend and foe alike; which done, the artillery opened fire along the entire line. Under its smoke the cavalry — usually on the flanks — would charge again; the foot would get into musket-range,

and if it could unsettle the enemy, would finally come to
" push of pike." There being rarely anything like grand-
tactics, or a battle plan, the lines got much intermixed.
Whichever side could retain the best semblance of formation,
or rather the side which showed the less confusion, would be
apt to win.

An army marched usually in van-guard, main force and
rear-guard; Gustavus dispensed with rear-guard when marching towards the enemy. Light troops formed the van and
flankers. There were two or three columns, each a line
when in order of battle, and so formed that the platoons or
companies could readily wheel into line. Occasionally the
columns marched checker-wise. Armies began to get over
more ground than formerly; especially the Swedes made
good marches ; but the rate was not equal to the best of this
century.

In battles more heed was now paid to topography, and
the operations were better suited to it. Artillery played a
more decided rôle. The utility of reserves came into recognition. While the order of battle remained parallel and there
was no grand-tactics, yet flanking marches, the advance of
a second line through a wearied first line, and other like
manœuvres, were not uncommon. Gustavus made none but
parallel front attacks. The value of his tactics lay in the
disposition of the troops : in so placing the pikemen as to
cover the musketeers ; the musketeers as to sustain the pikemen; while each brigade sustained the other and each was
all-sufficient to itself, with well-protected flanks, like a small
movable fortress. But it was rather the mobility of each
separate body than its solidity which lent it self-sustaining
power.

The parent of grand-tactics is ability to manœuvre ; without mobility bodies cannot do this ; and Gustavus, from the

new conditions imposed by gunpowder, first wrought out details which enabled men to move rapidly on the battle-field. Basing on his work, later commanders introduced what we now know as grand-tactics. Gustavus especially saw how to adapt his troops and position to the topography and the conditions; he seized the vital moment in a battle and made the most of it. To him belongs the credit of first, in modern times, forcing the passage of a rapid river in the face of a strong and able enemy. And even though he failed in his assault on the Alte Veste, Gustavus showed the world that there need be no hesitancy in storming intrenchments or strong positions. Both operations had imitators.

As the king's was better than any other European army in organization, so it was superior in discipline and *esprit de corps*. The Swedish primeval peasantry was excellent; big-fisted and stout-hearted, it in no wise feared danger or suffering. The Swedes "do not defend their men with walls, but their walls with men" was a contemporary saying. Since they had emerged from serfdom many peasants had acquired property, and each proprietor was held to furnish a man to the government or to the army. The crown had grown to rely greatly on the people, and the reason the Vasa family had so strong a hold on the masses was that they always sided with the peasantry against the nobles and clergy.

The pay of the Swedish troops was small; the narrow exchequer of the country allowed no greater. The budget in 1630 was twelve million rix dollars; but the troops were regularly paid during the life of Gustavus Adolphus. There is no table in the Swedish archives which details the entire pay-roll, and there is some question as to the amounts. The several records vary greatly. The following strikes us as high; but we do not know what each officer had to maintain, or what deductions may have been made for rations, clothing,

arms, etc. A lower scale is given in other records. The pay
of the generals and staff was : Field marshal, 1,000 rix dollars a month ; colonel-general of artillery, 600 ; colonel and
chief of scouts and colonel and chief quartermaster, 500
each ; colonel and quartermaster of cavalry, 300. The rate
of pay of the lesser staff-officers was presumably assimilated
to that of their regimental grade.

The scale of regimental pay in the foot was : —

Colonel	184 rix dollars a month.
Lieutenant-colonel	80 " " "
Major	61 " " "
Chief quartermaster	30 " " "
Chaplains (2) each	18 " " "
Judge advocates (2) each	30 " " "
Surgeons (4) each	12 " " "
Regimental clerk	30 " " "
Clerk of council of war	18 " " "
Provost-marshals (4) each	12 " " "
Assistant of marshal	10 " " "
Beadles (2) each	3 " " "
Hangman	7 " " "

The scale of company pay was : —

Captain	61 rix dollars a month.
Lieutenant	30 " " "
Ensign (ancient)	30 " " "
Sergeants (2) each	9 " " "
Assistant ensign	7 " " "
Assistant quartermaster	7 " " "
Armorer	7 " " "
Company clerk	7 " " "
Musicians	4 " " "
Corporals (6) each	6 " " "
File leaders (15) each	5 " " "
Under leaders (2) each	4 " " "
Privates	$3\frac{1}{2}$ " " "
Officers' servants	3 " " "

In the cavalry the rates were considerably higher, — especially for the field-officers.

The troops were fed from magazines, — one of the most important of the improvements of Gustavus, who established depots in suitable localities, and saw to it that they were kept full from Sweden, or by systematic contributions from the countries traversed. There was a regular staff of commissaries who distributed provisions to the regiments in bulk, and they were then issued to the men by the major, who seems also to have been charged with the fatigue and policing duties of the camp. Sutlers or traders were permitted at times to set up their booths near by. During Gustavus' life the troops were well cared for ; after his death things went on in a more hap-hazard way, and the army was apt to be fed and paid from the results of plunder.

Gustavus quartered his troops in towns or cities; if in fortified camps, in huts or tents. Wherever they were, camp and garrison duties were obligatory, and discipline was never relaxed.

The baggage-train was much decreased by Gustavus. A cavalry company was allowed ten wagons ; an infantry company three, the regimental staff eight. To us this seems a large allowance ; but the train and camp-followers of an army in the seventeenth century were far beyond any modern limit.

The one thing which made Gustavus' army a power was the infusion of the man himself into its very pith. The Swedish troops were instinct with strong religious feeling, and exhibited the qualities that spring from it, — good behavior, obedience, absence of crime, cheerful courage and good discipline. At the root of this lay Gustavus' own example, which was a never-varying pattern of soldierly bearing. Regular morning and evening prayers were introduced by the king ; he first

commissioned chaplains. Before battle there was a service
by the priests, and a dedication of the army to the service of
God. Regular days of prayer were appointed at intervals
in General Orders, and Gustavus caused to be printed and
distributed to the army a special Soldiers' Prayer-Book. In
Germany it was to most men a wonderful sight to see the
distinguished field-marshal kneeling upon the ground beside
the humblest private in earnest prayer.

Promotion went strictly by seniority and services; nepotism
was unknown. The highest in the land must begin at the
foot of the military ladder, as the king himself had done.

At the siege of Riga, in 1621, Gustavus issued a set of field
regulations which long remained in force. They established
a regimental court-martial, of which the commanding officer
was president and "assessors" elected by the regiment were
members; and a standing general court-martial, which had
the royal marshal of Sweden as president and higher officers
as members. To the monarch was the last appeal. Provost-
marshals might arrest on suspicion any offender, and imprison
and bring him before the court; but they might not hang for
any offense, except resistance to their orders. The regimental
court tried for thieving, insubordination, cowardice and all
minor crimes; the higher court had cognizance of civil causes
in the army, treason and the more serious crimes. Decimation, by beheading or hanging, was the lot of any regiment
which ran away in action, and the regiment was thenceforth
held to lie out of camp and do menial service till it retrieved
itself. "Riding the wooden horse" with a musket tied to
each foot, shackles, bread-and-water-arrest, were common.
There was no flogging. Even small breaches of discipline
were severely punished, and misdemeanors were visited impar-
tially with regard to persons. The higher crimes were punished with death, among others theft, plunder, violence to

women, cowardice, or the surrender of a fortress, except in extremity. The articles of war were excellent. The universal testimony is that there were few breaches of discipline. But they did occur : in 1631, Gustavus had to issue an *adhortatorium* to the troops on account of acts of plunder, and a number of men were executed. As a rule, however, the Swedish soldiers were exemplary, in word and deed, far beyond the soldier of that century. An officers' tribunal or court of honor existed for passing on their misdoings. Gustavus was especially severe on dueling, which was forbidden under pain of death. It is related that he permitted two officers, who especially requested leave, to meet ; that he himself attended the duel, and said to the principals : "Now, gentlemen, at it, and stop you not till one of you is killed ! Moreover, I have the provost-marshal at hand, who will at once execute the other ! " Cheerful prospect !

A soldier's wife was allowed to accompany the regiment ; but the bane of the German army, a troop of loose women among the camp-followers, was unknown. In each regiment were schools for the children of soldiers, many of whom, according to the curious custom of those days, accompanied their fathers, even on campaigns. As crimes were remorselessly punished, so were services adequately rewarded, by promotion, presents of money and pensions. But excellent as it was, it must be admitted that the perfect organization of the Swedish army did not outlive Gustavus himself.

All other European armies at this time were alike, and characterized by disorder and indiscipline. The troops were rarely paid, ill-fed and scantily clothed. The officers were over-luxurious ; the men barely provided for. The troops were carelessly quartered in the towns or wherever it came easiest, and their presence was the signal of grievous oppression ; while in the wake of a marching army stalked desolation. The baggage-train was enormous, as the men were permitted to carry along their plunder, and the number of non-combatants is hard to credit. In one army of forty thousand men, one hundred and forty thousand camp-followers are said to have been counted. The armies were full of cut-throats, outcasts and soldiers of fortune, and their conduct was that of highway robbers, even in the land of friends. Despite capital punishment for a number of crimes, and the penalty was often exacted, such a body could not be kept from gruesome atrocities, from which indeed neither man, woman nor child escaped. But prisoners had come to be well treated because they were expected to pay ransoms ; and acts of heroism were not uncommon. Rewards were as marked as punishments. Especially Wallenstein was distinguished for the severity of his punishments and the splendor of his rewards.

Gustavus was himself an expert, and he organized a superb corps of engineers. In Germany, folk were astonished to see scores of men of science accompany the army, and to note the way they were put to use in intrenching positions. Franz von Traytor was the "general of fortifications," or, as we should say, chief of engineers ; and an engineer-officer named Porticus was noted for excellent work. There was a special corps of miners ; but the entire army was drilled in throwing up fortifications and in pontoon-bridging. Even the cavalry were taught to throw a bridge. By spreading this knowledge so thoroughly throughout the army, Gustavus could intrench himself on unavailable ground, and quickly repair and make serviceable the walls of places he captured. He wrote a series of "Instructions" on this subject which are clear and sound. He had learned all that the Netherlands had to teach, and had bettered on some of it.

Field-fortification in this era was common. Outlying posts

were defended by redoubts and star-shaped forts with pali-sades, drawbridges and all manner of entanglements. Armies in the field, as well as those besieging strong places, covered themselves with works more or less complicated. A camp was not dissimilar to the Roman camp, with its wall and ditch, streets of tents, parade-ground and careful divisions, the difference being mainly one of arms and organization. Gustavus adopted the system of field-fortification which had been brought to perfection in the Netherlands; but he altered it in many ways. Instead of having a single line of unbroken works, he would build a series of mutually supporting isolated works, in two or more lines. In his camps he placed his troops with a much greater front than usual, and allowed each regiment to have its baggage in its own rear.

Rank and command were as follows : The king was supreme. Next came the royal marshal. Over a large army there was a general-field-colonel, and over smaller armies, commanders, general-commanders and field-marshals. In 1623 there were only two commanders, Jacob de la Gardie and Hermann Wrangel. There were field-majors, and general-field-majors. Bernard von Thürn, who came to Sweden from the Nether-lands with a regiment of foot, was made a general-field-major. Then came colonels, lieutenant-colonels and majors, and then the company officers. In 1626 there were fifteen colonels and nineteen lieutenant-colonels. In 1630 Gustavus Horn was made field-marshal, Åke Tott and John Banér generals. The nucleus of a general staff was begun ; Kniphausen was its chief, and he was succeeded by Baudissin. The chief of artillery in Germany was the twenty-seven-year-old, but exceptionally able, Colonel Torstenson.

Permanent fortification was rather blindly borrowed from the system of the Netherlands. Sieges were formally con-ducted with lines of circum- and contra-vallation carefully prepared. Regular trenches, as we understand them, did not appear till towards the end of the Thirty Years' War. The means of siege was laborious rather than scientific; nor can it be claimed that Gustavus was peculiarly able in his sieges.

The navy was much increased. Many ships were bought in Germany; more were built by Swedish private capital. In 1630 the Mercury of thirty-two guns was the flagship. The Westerwik had twenty-six guns, the Apollo and Pelican twenty each, the Andromeda eighteen, the Rainbow thirteen, the Stork twelve, the Parrot ten, the Black Dog eight, the Dolphin two. In 1632 there were five admirals and fifty-four ships of war, whose crews numbered from forty-eight to one hundred and sixty men.

Cannon suggested in the 15th Century.

VI.

THE YOUNG PRINCE AND KING. 1611–1617.

GUSTAVUS VASA, the grandfather of Gustavus Adolphus, was a prince of exceptional force. He introduced Protestantism into Sweden, raised and educated the peasantry, and took their part against the priests and nobles. He fostered commerce and created a merchant marine. All the Vasas were able, cultured and strong; but there was a touch of insanity in the family. Eric showed it and was deposed. John had a tendency to Romanism, and his son Sigismund turned Catholic on inheriting from his mother the throne of Poland. By this act he forfeited the Swedish crown; and Charles, the father of our hero, was made king. Gustavus was born in 1594, was carefully educated, and showed wonderful ability. He mastered several languages and was a keen student. His character as a lad was the promise of the man; he was a good writer and a fine speaker, and was physically strong, open hearted, brave and religious. At eleven he éntered the army, and was allowed to attend the meetings of the royal council. He watched the Russian campaign of 1610, and engaged in that of 1611 against Denmark. Though only successful in part, he showed intelligence, persistency and marked originality in what he did. Charles IX. died this year, and Gustavus, who, though only seventeen, was at once crowned, found himself at war with Russia, Poland and Denmark. The campaign of 1612 exhibited ability; but it was only successful in so far as it enabled Sweden to make a peace by purchasing from Denmark some territory in 1613. Next year there were no operations, but in 1615–16 the young king attacked Russia from Finland and won a large strip of territory. The eyes of Europe began to be attracted to him. In 1617 Russia ceded the conquered provinces, and the war closed.

THE grandfather of Gustavus Adolphus, the great Gustavus Vasa (1523–1560), was a man of sound and powerful character, and a truly noteworthy Protestant prince. It was he who laid the foundation of the growth of Sweden. When he came to the throne, the Swedes were all but a semi-barbarous people, who, said the king, were so shortsighted as to rob every merchant who ventured among them. The Reformation did so much for the country, however, that a hundred years later Gustavus Adolphus saw his people as advanced in intelligence and culture as any nation of northern Europe ; and the Swedish nobility held high rank among the aristocracies of the Continent. The growth of Lutheranism in Sweden was not merely a religious revival ; it was largely due to political facts. Gustavus Vasa, its founder, though a great man, was far from a profoundly religious man ; but he saw that by confiscating the estates of the church, he could help forward the national finances as well as bind the nobles to his cause ; and that by getting rid of the priests, who all desired a single and Catholic Scandinavia under the rule of Denmark, he would establish his own family more firmly on the throne. It was he, in fact, who made the throne hereditary in the Vasa family. In addition to introducing Protestantism, Gustavus I. established a commerce for Sweden by favoring the middle class as against the nobles ; and he added largely to the territory of the country by means of encroachments on his neighbors that were equally in fashion then as now. It was this head of the Vasas who created the Swedish fleet, and who improved the style of ship-building by bringing Venetian workmen to instruct his own thorough but less subtle designers. Under him the Swedish merchant marine grew to a reputable size. Gustavus Vasa left his crown to his eldest, and dukedoms to his other sons, and was succeeded in turn by his first son Eric, his second son John and the latter's son Sigismund ; and then by his fourth son Charles IX., the father of Gustavus Adolphus.[1]

The entire family were able men and broad. The Vasas stood so far above any of the other Swedes that they may be said to have reigned by a sort of Homeric right. Not only

[1] See Vasa Family-Tree, page 65.

possessed of force of character and brains, most of them were highly cultured, well read in literature, and versed in the arts and sciences. Many were truly noble men. The Vasa blood had a markedly good strain.

King Eric was able, but he showed evidences of the insanity which, coupled to its vigorous intellect, unquestionably resided in the Vasa family. He was deposed in 1567, and his brother John ascended the throne. John inclined to Catholicism, though he never avowed so much; but he married Catherine Jarghellon of Poland, and when the Jarghellon monarchs died out, his son Sigismund was made king of Poland, and, as was imperative, became a Catholic at the same time.

In order not to forfeit his claim to the throne of Sweden by his change of religion, Sigismund granted extravagant privileges to the nobles; but the country had a parliamentary government, the four Estates — nobles, clergy, citizens, peasants — having each a voice, and the three last named were stanch Protestants. Despite Sigismund's efforts, even by force of arms, to make Sweden a Catholic country, he failed in his end, was eventually deprived of the crown, and

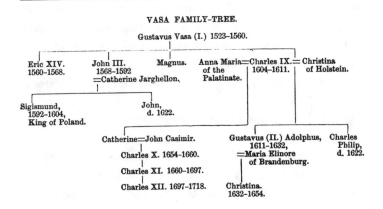

VASA FAMILY-TREE.

Gustavus Vasa (I.) 1523-1560.

Eric XIV. 1560-1568.

John III. 1568-1592 =Catherine Jarghellon,

Magnus.

Anna Maria=Charles IX.= Christina of the 1604-1611. of Holstein. Palatinate.

Sigismund, 1592-1604, King of Poland.

John, d. 1622.

Catherine=John Casimir.

Charles X. 1654-1660.

Charles XI. 1660-1697.

Charles XII. 1697-1718.

Gustavus (II.) Adolphus, 1611-1632, =Maria Elinore of Brandenburg.

Charles Philip, d. 1622.

Christina. 1632-1654.

retired to Poland, breathing vengeance. In 1604 Charles IX. became king, and the throne was entailed on his eldest son, Gustavus Adolphus, and his descendants, " being Protestants." With this patriarchal family back of him, the prince came honestly by his ability, his uprightness, his courage and his energy.

Gustavus II., or Gustavus Adolphus, was born in Stockholm, December 19 (N. S.), 1594, son by his second wife of the then Duke Charles, whose nephew Sigismund was on the throne. By his first wife Charles had had but one daughter, Catherine, who married Count John Casimir, and became the life-long friend and adviser of the future monarch, and the progenitress of the succeeding kings.

Charles was not as brilliant as most of the Vasas, but he was practical to the last degree, a quality at the time of more importance than high culture ; the mother of Gustavus had that which Charles lacked, and the young prince was surrounded by every advantage which strong intelligence and high mental and moral aims could bring him. If Charles IX. wanted some of the burly intellectual qualities of the family, he none the less exhibited in a high degree the common-sense ability of his father. He did much for the military organization of the kingdom ; he compiled the first code of Swedish laws ; he labored hard at the financial status and equalization of taxes, and gave a new impetus to mining ; he ordered topographical surveys of the kingdom to be made ; and he prepared the way for his son in a fashion which could scarcely have been bettered.

Charles was happily born to reign over an unspoiled people. The Swedish peasantry was rude and ignorant, but it was stout and loyal. Like the soil of New England, the Scandinavian land had trained its dwellers to work and to endure ; and religion had made them earnest and true. In fact, his faith represented to the Swedish peasant his fealty to both God and king, much as it does to the Russian of to-day, but with a broader intelligence.

Gustavus Adolphus was a lad of great personal beauty and strength, and his naturally alert mind was a pregnant soil for careful training. Even in his boyhood he showed that breadth of quality which later in life lent him such preëminence, — a deep and earnest religious nature, strongly imbued with the tenets of Protestantism, an unswerving moral character, warm affections, great amiability, frankness and a strict sense of rectitude. Coupled with these from earliest youth there were noted in him that species of courage which absolutely ignores danger, and those habits of mind and heart which are wont to call forth the manly virtues. And as this species of character usually possesses its purely human side, so we find in the king certain failings in temper and tricks of thought which all the more endear him to us. He was not a mere king of high heels and wig and ermine cloak ; he was a man enacting his rôle in the face and eyes of all the world.

Many a pretty story is told of his childhood. " Do not go into that wood," said his nurse to him one day ; " there are big snakes there ! " " But just give me a stout stick," replied the brave little fellow, " and I 'll soon kill them all ! " One day, when he was taken to see a naval review, an officer of rank asked him which ship he preferred. " Why, that one there," replied the five-year-old prince. " And why, Your Royal Highness ? " " Because she has got the most guns." It was natural that his tastes should run to war ; it was part of the Vasa education as well as inheritance.

The lad was a close student, and took a keen interest in languages, sciences and *belles-lettres*. His education was conducted under the oversight of his father and mother, and of

Axel Oxenstiern, who later became his prime minister as well as most intimate friend. His father drew up a memorandum of routine for him, which, by no means lacking the same religious impulse, stands out for its common sense in marked

Axel Oxenstiern.

contrast to that drawn up by the father of Frederick the Great. Charles had the utmost faith in the future of Gustavus. *Ille faciet*, said he on his death-bed, when an unusually knotty question arose which had puzzled him and his council, and which he was fain to put into other hands.

Gustavus' masters were selected after consultation with the Swedish Estates. His special tutor was John Skytte, clerk of the supreme court, assisted by a German, Helmer (or Otto) von Mörner, both traveled men and able; Count de la Gardie was his military instructor, and later one of his trusted generals. Sweden was noted for inviting distinguished foreigners to its court, and never failed to make the best use of their abilities.

Gustavus became an exceptionally clever linguist. He read and could fairly express himself in Greek, Latin, Dutch, Italian, Russian and Polish, beside his native tongue; he read history to good effect, — Xenophon in the original was his favorite book, — and was well rounded in his studies. During his campaigns, Grotius' Commentary, " De Jure Belli et Pacis," was his constant companion. He has left us a history of the Vasas which is distinguished by its clear grasp of his subject and 'dignified style; he spoke and wrote with equal pointedness and force, and was considered to be the best orator in Sweden. Many of his poems, particularly the religious ones, are still sung by rich and poor in Sweden, as Luther's are in Germany. In gymnastic sports, and in the use of weapons, he was unexcelled, and was a skillful horseman. Not only had he courage, but his bodily strength and health were exceptional. On one occasion, when he felt an attack of fever coming on from undue exposure, he sweated it off by a prolonged and violent fencing-bout with young Count Brahe. His temper was exceedingly quick, and in his youth a blow followed a word with scarce an interval; but he always made honest and ample amends for his hastiness, and later in life he learned the rare virtue of self-control. The eyes of all Sweden were early riveted on the promising heir to the throne, and great things were hoped of him.

When, in 1604, Gustavus reached ten years of age, his cousin Sigismund had already been deposed on account of his Catholic fanaticism, which had pushed him to acts intolerable to the Swedes, and Gustavus' father, as Charles IX., sat upon the throne. Sigismund retired to Poland, and both he and his powerful kingdom threatened and proved to be the most dangerous opponents Sweden could have.

In his eleventh year Gustavus entered the army at the lowest step, and worked his way patiently up. As a training in statecraft he was allowed to sit at the meetings of the ministry, and the council soon learned to appreciate his worth. Quite without pedantry, — a thing which speaks volumes for his instructors, — the lad exhibited a clean-cut idea of the strength and weakness of Sweden, of its proper rôle in the economy of northern Europe, and of his own duties as future ruler. The death of Philip II. had relieved hordes of soldiers of fortune from duty in the Netherlands, and many men trained in this famous school of war came to Stockholm to offer their services to the king, who was expected soon to measure swords with Poland. These veterans were dear to Gustavus, because from them he learned of the warlike deeds of Maurice of Nassau, his special hero. War was even then his pride and his dream; the old Viking blood throbbed lustily in his veins.

Much to his chagrin, Gustavus was not permitted to serve in the Russian campaign of 1610, but he went to Finland and watched it near by under the guidance of de la Gardie; and when he reached the age of seventeen, his father, with the consent of the Estates, declared him of age, — "worthy of wearing a sword," — and he was given a small command in the war with Denmark in 1611.

The Goth was strong in the young prince; it seethed indeed in the Vasa blood: Eric at times showed the tiger instinct; prosaic Charles once challenged the king of Denmark to personal combat. And in this his first taste of war, Gustavus showed the utmost coolness and disregard of danger, riding up into the immediate vicinity of the enemy when out reconnoitring, and scanning them through his glass, quite unconscious that fear was an instinct with most men.

The young general raised some forces in West Gothland and essayed to relieve Kalmar, then under siege; but fortune seemed to favor the Danes, who captured the fortress as well as Elfsborg on the west coast. Young Gustavus, however, shipped his detachment over to Öland, and took this island and the fortress of Borgholm. On his return there fell into his hands a letter from the Danish commander of the small fortress of Christianopel, begging the Danish king for five hundred horse. Gustavus at once made use of this lucky accident. He clad five hundred Swedes in Danish fashion, led them himself to Christianopel, reached the place at night, was admitted, and took possession of the fortress. These early exploits showed the stuff of which the prince was made, and exhibited that ability to utilize favorable opportunities which later became so marked a trait.

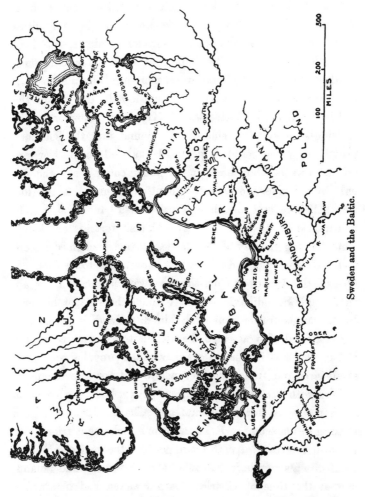

Sweden and the Baltic.

Genius for war is only genius given a warlike direction. The same mental tissue which makes the poet, the astronomer or the musician, if coupled to vigorous character, and given the opportunities of war, will make the captain. But the character must equal the intellect, and the opportunity be of the highest.

During the reign of Charles IX. Sweden was but a small and unconsidered country. Beside Stockholm, her only cities of importance were Westerås, Örebro and Kalmar. Gothenborg did not grow to be important until after Gustavus' death. Sweden's neighbors were, moreover, all in a position and mood to push her hard. Denmark held the key to the Baltic by her two fortresses of Kronborg (Elsinore) and Helsingborg on either side of The Sound, and the southern provinces of the Swedish peninsula, as well as all Norway, belonged to the Danish crown. Sweden could reach the sea only by the river Göte, at the mouth of which was the fortress Elfsborg, and this, though in Swedish hands, was largely neutralized by the not far distant Danish fortress of Bohus. Thus holding the key of the Baltic, Denmark claimed to control its commerce, and was a neighbor much to be dreaded. One of the dreams of Christian IV. was once more to organize a single Scandinavian dynasty under the rule of his own house; an aspiration that made him anti-Swedish to the core. Holland had also asserted herself in the commerce of the Baltic, but not in such a manner as to provoke war. All she desired was free trade everywhere and non-interference.

War with Russia, then a minor power, had been going on for some years, for Sigismund and Charles IX. were each seeking to place on the Russian throne a claimant friendly to his own interest. Apart from politics, the matter resolved itself into a struggle for Livonia between Sweden and Poland, and at the time of Charles' death, Sweden had obtained a sort of foothold in that province. Russia's ambition was to recover her Baltic possessions, and the king of Poland was intent on regaining the crown of Sweden.

The only other prince who had a hand in the game of northern European politics was George William, the elector of Brandenburg. This sleepy potentate had no broader idea of policy than to hold on to what he already had, and to keep out of war either for religion or any other cause. He was the distinct reverse of what a Hohenzollern is apt to be.

It was on October 30, 1611, that Charles IX. died. As a matter of precedent, Gustavus Adolphus could not ascend the throne until he was twenty-four years old. But so exceptional were the circumstances surrounding Sweden that within two months, on December 17, 1611, the ministry, to whom, as a species of regency, Charles had confided Gustavus and the welfare of Sweden, clad the seventeen-year-old prince in the fullest power as king; the people accepted him as such; and during his twenty-one years' reign, no Swedish subject ever regretted this action. Gustavus chose Axel Oxenstiern, himself only twenty-eight years old, as prime minister, and during life was devoted to him as one of the best of his statesmen and generals. Oxenstiern was as prudent and calm as Gustavus was impetuous and high-strung. The two, with a friendship so unusual between king and minister, could not have been better matched. The qualities of each were a complement of those of the other. It seems strange enough that these two men, whose united ages were but forty-five years, should have thus set forth on so gigantic an undertaking.

Few young monarchs have ever been so harassed on taking up the reins of government. Gustavus' situation recalls forcibly that of Alexander. Not only was there great distress in many parts of Sweden, not only were the finances of the country on a questionable basis, but Sweden was actually at war with Denmark, Russia and Poland; and these countries were apt to hold the young king cheap.

It was manifest that Gustavus could not cope with all

these powers at once ; that his only safety lay in finishing, if possible, the war with each one singly. The conflict with Denmark was the most pressing; the others were all but dormant, and could be staved off for a season.

Christian had begun the war in April, and within two months had appeared before and captured Kalmar, and greatly strengthened its works. The fortress of Elfsborg was also in the possession of the Danes, and the young king foresaw that to attempt their recapture would involve more time than he had at command. He determined on an incursion into Danish territory, as an easier means of accomplishing his object, and in 1612, leaving a force in the vicinity of Elfsborg to prevent further aggression by the Danes from that quarter, he marched with the bulk of his army into Schönen, where Christian had stationed a detachment.

According to the military art of the day, this was an unusual if not unwise proceeding. To undertake a sharp offensive on one point of the theatre of war as a defensive measure to another part, simple as the problem is, would never have occurred to the average general of the early seventeenth century. But Gustavus had not studied the lives of great captains in vain. Convinced that he was right in his theory, he followed up his movement by besieging Helsingborg. The plan should have succeeded, but the Danes, with a sudden onslaught on his army, placed him in grave danger, and forced him to raise the siege. This failure neither discouraged the young king nor drove him from his purpose. Its effect was the reverse; his mood was elasticity itself, and he determined on an irruption into Norway; but this too proved fruitless, and despite good calculation the whole campaign came to naught.

A severer test of Gustavus' character and ability could scarcely have been made. No doubt there were many innuendoes by the wiseacres of broken maxims of the science of war; such a failure would have drawn the temper of most men. But like Frederick after Mollwitz, the king only saw the clearer and felt the more reliant; and the operations, though unsuccessful, go to show that the bent of the future great warrior's mind had already grown beyond the formal limitations of the military art of his century.

One incident in the campaign came close to putting a term to the king's career. In a battle on the ice on the lake of Widsjö, he and his horse fell through, and he was with difficulty rescued. Military manœuvres on the ice, or the engulfing of many men, are no rarities in these northern latitudes. This was but one of a series of accidents and wounds, generally brought on by the king's inordinately reckless gallantry. He is the captain who most resembles Alexander in the Homeric quality of his courage. He could not keep out of the fray.

Meanwhile the Danes, under personal command of Christian, prepared an expedition against Elfsnabben and Jönköping. The latter was a border fortress, and both were important places from a military standpoint, to hold which would give the Danes a secondary base for the invasion of the interior of Sweden. Gustavus had taken up a position near by, to forestall any such movement, but was, both by land and sea, distinctly weaker than the enemy. Harboring small respect for his youthful opponent, Christian made bold to push for Stockholm, hoping to capture it out of hand during the absence of the king. He had already reached Waxholm, within a half dozen miles of the capital, when Gustavus, catching the alarm, returned at the head of a small force, roused and armed all the able-bodied population, and marching boldly out to meet Christian at Waxholm, compelled him to withdraw.

Disappointed in the results of this unimportant campaign, and under the influence of England, Christian, who utterly lacked the moral equipment of Gustavus, and who was moreover held much in check by his nobles, a turbulent, unreasonable set of men, now expressed his willingness to make peace. Gustavus, who was a soldier to his finger-tips, felt bitterly the necessity of ending by negotiation a first war which he would fain have ended by the sword ; but he was glad to be rid at any price of his nearest and most dangerous enemy, and Christian, at the peace of Knaröd, January 19, 1613, yielded up Kalmar, and later Elfsborg and his other conquests, on payment by Sweden of an indemnity of a million rix thaler, about eight hundred and fifty thousand dollars. This was a heavy tax for so small and poor a country, but the peace was made with honor, and was abundantly worth thrice the money. A special tax was imposed for the ransom of Elfsborg, and Swedish territory was left intact.

No sooner rid of Denmark than Gustavus turned to the Russian question. His father had already conquered Ingria and Carelia. His old tutor, de la Gardie, the general there in command, had won a reputation for energy and fair military skill. Gustavus' younger brother, Charles Philip, had some time before been selected as a candidate for the Russian throne, which at this time was a shuttlecock between several rival factions, but Charles IX. had not approved the act, and Gustavus now declined to assert the claim by arms. His sole purpose was to prevent the king of Poland from putting on the throne a tool of his own. Nor did he in 1613 consider himself quite ready to undertake so extensive an affair ; for the Danish war had delayed his preparations.

It was at this time that Gustavus' love affair with the beautiful young Countess von Brahe occurred, and it has been said that this too contributed to his delays. At all events, nothing was accomplished until the next year, 1614, by which time he had fully completed his equipment for a Russian campaign.

Michael Feodorovitch, the ancestor of the Romanoffs, had been elected czar; but de la Gardie, on behalf of Sweden, protested against the choice, for the general still favored the pretensions of his young prince. Though Gustavus' object was more an effort to strengthen the grasp of Sweden on the Baltic than to push his brother's claims, he was none the less keenly bent on war. After some effort, he managed to patch up a two years' truce with Poland, and sent Charles Philip with troops to Wiborg, in the Swedish province of Finland, to protect it from invasion. Some exchanges had already taken place between de la Gardie and the Russians, and the war was fairly inaugurated.

In 1615 the young monarch marched with an army from Finland into Ingria, past the present site of St. Petersburg, took Angdov by storm, conquered the whole province, besieged Pleskov, which was strongly fortified, and, finally successful in reducing it, made proposals of peace through the mediation of Great Britain. But these were rejected. In this campaign de la Gardie was the young king's second in command, and his teacher in the art, as he had been his tutor in the science, of war. He was to Gustavus what old Schwerin was to Frederick, or Parmenio to Alexander. But Gustavus himself made good use of his experience. Like these other great captains, from the start he overshadowed his pedagogue, and laid the first foundations of Swedish discipline. In lieu of the fearful acts of violence which accompanied the raising and the progress of any army of that day, all was order and quiet system. Even the Russians acknowledged that the behavior of the Swedes was vastly better than that of their own troops in their own land.

Every one who placed himself under Swedish protection was in fact protected; the army was fed by contributions regularly levied and paid for; plundering by individuals was punished by death. What the regulations prescribed from the cabinet was actually carried out on the field. The reputation of the young king began to spread all over Europe. The one man who gauged Gustavus accurately was Wallenstein, though he would allow him no ability as compared with himself. " By all means help Sigismund to crush him," said he at a later day. " He is a worse foe than ever was the Turk."

Gustavus was early approached to take part with the Protestants of Germany, where the wise foresaw the bitter struggle which promised to break out. An envoy from the University of Heidelberg came to beg him to act as mediator between the Lutherans and the Calvinists; and Landgrave Moritz of Hesse asked him to join a Protestant alliance for mutual protection. But while the young monarch watched events with a keen eye, he wisely refrained from any undertaking which might interfere with his activity against his hereditary enemies, and especially Sigismund. He kept on good terms with Christian, who, though he was often a cause of grave anxiety, never again overtly attacked Sweden, but with fair honesty held to the " brotherly compact " he had sworn with Gustavus over his wine; and a truce was made with Russia looking towards a peace. The year 1616 was spent in Finland, in building up this province, much exhausted with the burdens of war; and by the treaty of Stolbowa, February 27, 1617, Russia, hard pressed between Sweden and Poland, definitely ceded to Sweden the provinces of Ingria and Carelia, with the fortresses of Kexholm, Noteborg, Ivangorod, Janra and Koporie, and paid over a considerable sum of money.

VII.

THE POLISH WARS. 1617–1625.

HAVING vainly striven to make peace with Poland, and having secured only a truce, Gustavus set to work to carry out his projected army changes, and at intervals traveled in Germany. In 1620 he married the sister of the elector of Brandenburg. At the end of the Polish truce, in 1621, he sailed with a fleet to Livonia, and laid siege to Riga. Poland was harassed by the Turks, and though the siege was difficult, Riga fell in September, and the king occupied Courland. Thus hemmed in, Sigismund made a fresh truce, which, with one or two interruptions, lasted till 1625. The Polish king was under the control of the Jesuits and of the emperor, and would not agree to a permanent peace, looking on Gustavus as illegitimately king. The intervals made by the several truces gave Sweden leisure to establish herself on a sound financial and military basis, one which for her size was exceptional; and estates, people and king all worked in hearty harmony.

HAVING happily settled the differences with Denmark and Russia, Gustavus strove to transform into a permanent peace his two years' truce with Sigismund; but his best efforts produced no effect on this fanatic. Sigismund plotted in every conceivable manner against the country of his birth; and that war must eventuate was not doubtful. But circumstances delayed the crisis. The truce, already several times extended, was again in 1618, and very fortunately for Sweden, renewed by Sigismund, owing to the other complications of Poland, — mainly the invasion of the southern part of that kingdom by Bethlen Gabor, prince of Transylvania, — and through the mediation of King Christian. This aid was a first-fruit of the peace Gustavus had made with Denmark, and afforded the young monarch the leisure to carry out the changes in discipline and tactics which he had already so auspiciously begun.

During 1619 and 1620, at intervals in this work, Gustavus traveled, generally *incognito*, through a part of western Europe. Shortly after his accession — as already mentioned — he had had a passionate attachment for a beautiful young lady of the Swedish court, Countess Ebba von Brahe (who used, by the way, to accompany the king's playing of the flute, on which it is hoped that he was a better performer than that other great captain and petty musician of Sans Souci); and though his devotion was entirely honorable, the queen-mother contrived to break up his purpose of sharing his throne with the lady. In this connection it may be noted that there is but one record of immorality against Gustavus. He had by a Dutch lady a natural son, born in 1616, who, at Lützen, won his spurs on the field where his father fell. In an age of sexual laxity, this was a clean record. It was politically essential that Gustavus should wed; Sweden must have an heir, and after a trip to Berlin as Captain Gars (Gustavus Adolphus Rex Sueciae) he married the sister of the young elector of Brandenburg. From this alliance the Swedish Estates were warranted in hoping much; for Brandenburg was able to help in the complicated business with Poland. During this period of travel Gustavus' letters show that his thoughts were never away from home, nor his activity less in testing all the new things he saw which might contribute to the perfection of his army or the building up of Sweden. He journeyed as far as Heidelberg; the cultivated beauties of the Palatinate must have struck him as a singular contrast to his own rugged plains; and what he learned of places and people enabled him the better to understand the religious struggle which had already been inaugurated, and in which he was destined to bear the giant's part.

The Thirty Years' War was already two years old, and terror reigned in many parts of Germany. Gustavus foresaw that Sweden, though geographically removed from the scene of conflict, would sooner or later be drawn into the vortex; and in 1621 he sought once more to renew the truce with Poland, but in vain. Sigismund, under the political control of his relative the emperor, and under the religious control of the Jesuits, then the growing power of the Roman Church, could not be influenced, especially as a fourteen years' truce which he had just concluded with Russia saved him harmless from danger in that quarter. War supervened, but Sweden was in every sense more ready than ever before, and people and ministry alike sustained their young monarch with hearty good will.

If war it must be, no better time could perhaps have been chosen for Sweden. During the five years' respite Gustavus had organized both her finances and her troops. Taxes had been carefully laid, and the raising of men for the army had been systematically based on a tenure of land which equalized the burdens. The priests from the pulpit preached the war, the nobility was encouraged to yield its best efforts to the cause, and the soldier was given an honorable position in society. The officer who bore him well was considered the equal of the noble, and the aristocracy was thus merged into the military scheme. For the first time in modern days there arose a new form of government, — the military monarchy. East Gothland had fallen to the crown on the death of Gustavus' cousin John, diminishing the chances of internal strife; and his marriage, it was thought, had given him a political foothold in Germany despite the opposition of Poland.

As a first act in the opening of the campaign of 1621, Gustavus set out to conquer Livonia, to which the Swedish royal family ever since King Eric's time had some pretensions, though pretensions of this kind, in the sixteenth and seventeenth centuries, were wont to have a slender basis. With a fleet of one hundred and fifty-eight vessels, the king landed twenty-four thousand men, mostly infantry, at the mouth of the Dwina River, took the fort commanding it, and opened the siege of Riga on August 13. In this and his future Polish wars Gustavus had the assistance of his later so celebrated generals, Horn, Banér, Torstenson and Wrangel.

The siege of this important city proved difficult. It was strong, contained a goodly garrison, and, though on the score of religion Livonia was not warmly attached to Sigismund, the city had a public-spirited population. The Poles were noted for stout, if spasmodic, fighting. Luckily for Gustavus, Sigismund was unable to send reinforcements to Riga because of an inroad of three hundred thousand Turks, the result of his defeat at Jassy the year before; and no imperial aid was forthcoming. The siege was vigorously pushed; a line of contravallation was built, and the army divided into four unequal corps according to the lay of the land. The king was personally active in every step of the operation. While insisting on discipline unknown at that day, he encouraged the men by his presence and enthusiasm, and afforded them the example of what a commander-in-chief should be. He had the true soldier's way of winning their love. Gustavus thrice offered terms to the garrison before opening a bombardment, and a belated army of relief, ten thousand strong,

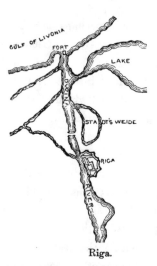

Riga.

under Prince Radziwill, was attacked and beaten. Two of the outer works, a redoubt and a half moon, were taken by storm; but two other assaults were driven back, and Horn and Banér both wounded. Mining was then resorted to in September; a gallery of the king's own invention was laid on to cross the wet ditch; this was partly filled up, and everything was prepared for an assault in force upon the breaches opened. Annoyed at the stubborn defense, the king had determined to explode all the mines at once, to storm the place, and give it up to plunder; but in the six hours' truce granted September 16, before the assault should begin, the garrison wisely concluded to surrender. The siege had lasted four weeks. Well satisfied at the victory, Gustavus treated the people of Riga with generosity, and after banishing the Jesuits, who had behaved in a peculiarly hostile manner, took an oath of fealty from the town. The campaign had opened felicitously.

From Riga Gustavus marched through Courland to Mittau, and as a matter of strategic safety, placed a friendly garrison of two thousand men in the town; for the duke of Courland was on terms of amity with Sweden.

Before moving into Poland, where he hoped to compel a peace, the king again approached Sigismund with offers of negotiation. Sigismund was only half tractable; he would not conclude peace; but owing to the trouble which the Turks and Tartars were giving him, he did agree to continue the truce another year, leaving to the Swedes, as a guaranty, the already conquered part of Livonia. Hereupon Gustavus evacuated Courland, and returned to Stockholm, late in 1621. The promise of the campaign had been fulfilled; but quiet was not restored without another warlike incident.

The king's brother, Charles Philip, died in 1622; he himself had as yet no heir; and these circumstances renewed the aspirations of Sigismund to the Swedish throne. Nothing could better fit into the plans of the Emperor Ferdinand, and under the advice of the latter, Sigismund began to think of carrying the war into Sweden. As Poland had no fleet, Sigismund betook himself to the free city of Danzig, hoping to build ships in its harbor, a work for which its vast commerce and connection with the Hanse towns afforded ample means. A less suspicious mind than Gustavus' would have seen no harm in this; but the Swedish king was alert; towards the middle of June, 1622, he appeared before Danzig with a strong fleet, and after some negotiation compelled the city to bind itself to neutrality. This prompt action led up to the proposal of an armistice by Sigismund himself, and to a further renewal of the old truce; whereupon Gustavus returned home. Signed in June, 1622, this truce left Sweden in possession of Livonia, and of some places in Courland; it was kept up by more or less irregular extensions for three years.

Sigismund's unwillingness to make peace was not unnatural. The Catholic princes of Germany looked on Protestant Gustavus, who came of the junior Vasas, as an usurper of the Swedish throne, and would gladly have seen Catholic Sigismund back in his place. They feared Gustavus' restless ability, and were ready for anything to humble him. The Jesuits ceased not to foster the oppression of the Protestants. Under their influence, Sigismund would not enter into a permanent peace, for that was treason to his religion, while a truce was a mere military incident. On the other hand, Gustavus showed himself at all times ready to make terms with Sigismund, on the basis of the good of Sweden. His constant offers of peace remind one of Cæsar's many proposals to Pompey. Both Cæsar and Gustavus were no doubt honestly desirous of peace on terms satisfactory to the cause of each;

each was careful to place himself on record as a peace-maker, though neither would have given up a substantial part of what he deemed his rights. Of the two, however, Gustavus was by far the more frank and upright in his protestations. If ever a man said what he meant and stuck to it, it was the king of Sweden; Cæsar veiled his meaning in diction which never committed him to any definite action.

At home Gustavus was sure of his ground. The unity of king, ministry and people was in marked contrast to the condition of any other country of Europe. Scarce a chapter in the world's history exhibits affection, confidence and mutual helpfulness between prince and people in equal measure. The king took no step without consulting the Estates, and they and the ministry never failed to sustain him. In the new organization of the Swedish army, which, in 1625, he more formally undertook, he had the hearty support of all classes. Under it, a regular army of eighty thousand men was raised, in addition to the equally large militia system already adverted to. He was now ready for any war which must come, though he felt that he was not yet prepared definitively to embrace the cause of his German brother Protestants.

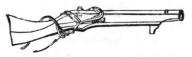

Arquebus. (16th Century.)

VIII.

THE THIRTY YEARS' WAR. RELIGIOUS PHASE. 1618-1625.

THE Thirty Years' War originated in the desire of the Catholic princes of Germany to prevent the growth of Protestantism, and in the desire of the emperor to make his rule a real instead of a nominal one. These two aims so lacked consistency that many princes would work for one and not the other. There were seven prince-electors who chose the emperor; there was a German Diet, but it did not represent the people. The several potentates were practical autocrats; the Diet was their meeting-place; only the free cities governed themselves. The emperor's power was small; though nominally the fountain head, he could enforce his will only by the ban of the empire. The two religions were more at odds in temporal than spiritual matters. Much of the property of the Catholic bishoprics had been secularized where people had adopted the new religion, and the Peace of Augsburg, in 1552, had settled questions thus arising. Fifty years later things could not revert to that status, and yet the Catholics were bent on recovering, the Protestants on holding, what they had since taken. Maximilian of Bavaria was the champion of the Catholics; Christian of Anhalt of the Protestants. The Lutherans and Calvinists did not act in common; the leading Protestant princes were not helpful. A Protestant Union was formed in 1608 to prevent the Catholics from retaking what the Protestants already had; a Catholic League followed. Though the struggle went on, war was not precipitated until 1618, when Bohemia drove out her new king, Ferdinand, and the emperor undertook to replace him. In 1619 Ferdinand himself was elected emperor, Frederick of the Palatinate was chosen king of Bohemia, and the war was prosecuted in earnest. There was no community of action among the Protestants, and neither party won success until, in 1620, Frederick was defeated near Prague by the imperial general Tilly, and driven from Bohemia, while Mansfeld and later Christian of Brunswick, who commanded Protestant armies, were driven up into the Weser country. The armies of the day, living by plunder, were barbarous beyond telling, and the land suffered much. Tilly kept on, until by 1623 all south Germany was reduced, and the emperor resolved on putting down Protestantism in north Germany as well. Mansfeld and Brunswick alone stood in the way.

THOUGH the operations of the Thirty Years' War, prior to the entrance on its stage of the great Swede, have little value as a military study, a few pages must be devoted to the subject to show the desperate situation of the war when Gustavus finally threw himself into the scale against the empire and the persecution of the Protestants. As little time as possible will be taken from the more important phases.

The remote causes of the war were twofold : the purpose of the Catholic powers to weld the chains of religion on protesting Europe ; and the purpose of the emperor to make his rule a real instead of a nominal one over entire Germany ; for the Hapsburgs had long dreamed of a universal European empire. These two purposes were inconsistent ; they could not live together. Potentates who would work faithfully to compass the religious end would sacrifice religion to prevent a reëstablishment of imperial rule. And it was this inconsistency which brought about the eccentricities of the war, and lay at the root of the never-ending changes among the contestants ; which led Catholic France to subsidize Protestant Sweden, and prevented Maximilian of Bavaria from working kindly under his brother in the faith, the Emperor Ferdinand.

Not but what the Protestants were to blame. The Lutherans and Calvinists were as incapable of continued joint effort, as they were intolerant of each other's dogmas ; and their quarrels, quite as much as the diverse purposes of the Catholics, operated to prolong the struggle. It was the knot of this imbroglio that Gustavus Adolphus essayed to cut ; and implacable as were the contestants, unreasonable as were their motives, he succeeded, before his early death, in permanently preventing the emperor from fettering Protestantism, and in giving the death-blow to imperialism. He thwarted the realization of both the causal aspirations. The sixteen

years of awful warfare which succeeded his death were due
to the shortsightedness and petty jealousies of those who continued the struggle in his name, and who during his life had
worked with reasonable unanimity with or against him. The
motif of the war was religious toleration; what Germany
began, France completed; but it was Gustavus who made the
success of France a possible thing.

There were four phases to the Thirty Years' War: the
Religious, the Danish, the Swedish, the French.

To us English peoples, the construction of the German
empire in the seventeenth century is an enigma. We hear
that there was an emperor, and we read of a diet, and it is
hard to comprehend why the people had no voice in the government. But they practically had none whatever. The
land was ruled by a few princes, each possessing within his
own borders almost absolute power.

There was a vast number of small principalities, among
which were seven princes called electors, who, on the death
of one, chose the succeeding emperor. Three of them were
religious : the archbishops of Cologne, Trier and Mainz;
four of them were temporal : the king of Bohemia, the electors of Brandenburg and Saxony and the elector-palatine.
The emperor was the acknowledged successor of the Roman
Cæsars and of Charles the Great; but he had no real power,
except in so far as he was also king of some particular country. As emperor he held a mere empty title. He was supposed to be the source of everything; from him all holdings
of kingdoms, principalities and powers were deemed to have
been derived, but the princes who so held under him resented
the slightest interference with their acts.

The Diet was in no sense a popular assembly. Far from
being a mouthpiece of the people, it did not even represent
the smaller princes. It was a mere congress of the larger

autocrats, to arrange their, so to speak, international rights. The only power the emperor could exert against a prince was to put him to the ban of the empire, a mild species of lay excommunication, which hurt him not the least, provided he had a good army and a full treasury, and was at peace with his neighbors. To be sure, Germany was divided into Circles, each of which had an imperial court to decide questions between the princes; but the decisions were far from being always fair, and yet farther from being generally respected.

The Estates of the empire, some of the princes to wit, met in the Diet in three Houses. The electors, excepting the king of Bohemia, who only voted in the election of an emperor, formed the first; the second contained a number of smaller princes, ecclesiastical and lay; the third, deemed an inferior body, was filled by representatives of the free cities. Except for the latter, the people was utterly without representation. Nothing better proves this than the fact that at the beginning of the seventeenth century the vast majority (stated at ninety per cent.) of the population of Germany was Protestant, while the Diet was opposed to Protestantism; and the further fact that most of the lay princes, members of the Diet, as individuals sustained the new religion, if they did not actually profess it. This condition of affairs was fraught with, and naturally resulted in, war.

Under Charles V., the Convention of Passau, in 1552, led to the Peace of Augsburg, which attempted to settle the many vexed questions arising from the very natural seizure of Catholic Church property in entirely Protestant countries; but the Augsburg .erms provided nothing for the future, and only Lutheranism, not Calvinism, was recognized. Meanwhile, the new religion was growing, and matters could not practically be measured by a standard fixed at any given time. There

were further seizures of ecclesiastical property and rifling of
monasteries; and eight of the great northern bishoprics
became Protestant. The bishop, as he was still called, was
in reality only a prince who sometimes spoke of himself as
Administrator. So things went on for a generation or more.
The Protestants did not grow in wisdom as they grew in
stature. Theological quarrels arose among them, which gave
the Jesuits, as being all of one mind, a fair claim to a hearing; and finally the Catholics began once more to gain
ground. The two main questions in dispute were the rights
of the Protestant administrators, and the status of the secularized lands. At the end of the century the Catholics insisted
on going back to the Augsburg basis of 1552; the Protestants
desired to modify matters to suit the conditions of the day.
The disputes waxed hotter, but there appears to have been
more hostility manifested by the princes than the people. As
a rule, the Catholic and Protestant populations tolerated each
other fairly well.

All this grew worse and worse. Maximilian of Bavaria
was the champion of the Catholics; Christian of Anhalt, a
Calvinist, was the leader of the Protestants; John George,
elector of Saxony, a Lutheran, played the part of peace-
maker.

Maximilian was an able man with an ample treasury and a
good army. He held to the Peace of Augsburg as the only
true measure of values, and to conform to this meant to uproot
all that had been done in more than fifty years. The Protestant princes found the ownership of the ancient Catholic
lands altogether too convenient to be given up; and their
faith agreed with their liking. The most unprotected part of
Protestantism was in the south German states, which lay
between Catholic Bavaria and the bishoprics of Bamberg and
Würzburg on the one side, and those of Worms and Speyer,

the electorates on the Rhine and the Spanish possessions on
the other. These south German Protestants were mainly Calvinists, as their brethren in the north were mostly Lutherans.
Christian of Anhalt was a stanch Calvinist, and an able
politician, in fact too much of a diplomat. Maximilian wisely
armed; Christian sought to accomplish results by finesse.
Every one foresaw an irrepressible conflict.

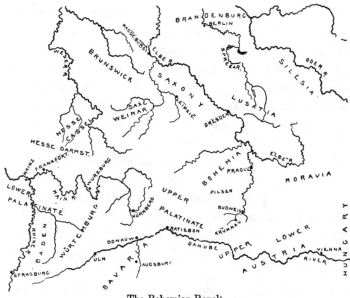

The Bohemian Revolt.

Finally, in 1607, a religious riot in Donauwörth induced
the emperor, with only a show of trial, to put it to the ban,
and Maximilian was appointed to execute the decree, which
he did with inexcusable rigor.   At this, the free cities of the
south — Nürnberg, Ulm and Strasburg — took alarm, and in
1608 a Protestant Union, under the leadership of Christian
(and incidentally of Frederick of the Palatinate), was formed
for mutual defense.   To it belonged Hesse-Cassel, Würtem-

berg, Baden-Durlach and many of the free towns; Saxony and Hesse-Darmstadt refused to join; Brandenburg, Mecklenburg, Pomerania and Brunswick-Lüneburg remained neutral. The Union in the same year was followed by the creation of a Catholic League under Maximilian, which was joined by nearly all the princes of south Germany, the Main and lower Rhine; but the emperor took no part in it. The two parties — Union and League — stood ready for war, and succeeding conventions and diets effected nothing toward peace. John George of Saxony, who was a good sportsman and a deep drinker rather than a wise ruler, despite his extensive power and his good intentions, had not the personality to enforce his moderate views, and the seething of the trouble went on. It is fruitless to follow all the phases of the singular struggle; but it never ceased until finally, in 1618, it broke out into open war.

In 1611 Rudolph, king of Bohemia, who was also archduke of Austria and German emperor, was driven from the throne of Bohemia by his brother Matthias, who next year, on Rudolph's death, was elected emperor. The Bohemians had extorted from Rudolph a sort of imperial charter for freedom of conscience. This charter Matthias sought to undermine, and in the Bohemian Diet of 1617, the Estates were persuaded into acknowledging Matthias' cousin, Catholic Ferdinand of Styria, as hereditary king of a throne which had always been elective. Thus the House of Austria fastened its talons upon Bohemia, and shortly, as was to be expected, the persecutions of the Protestants became more marked.

In 1618 the Bohemians rose under Count Henry of Thurn, the new king was deposed, his regents expelled in the famous defenestration of Prague, the Jesuits were driven from the land, and thirty directors were chosen who appealed for help to their brother Protestants. John George of Saxony refused any except such aid as would reconcile them to the empire, but Frederick of the Palatinate took up their cause in theory. The Protestants in Moravia, Silesia, Lusatia and Upper Austria began to arm. Every one was expecting a struggle and sought to be ready. The emperor was fairly driven into war; but his low treasury and internal troubles prepared for him a difficult task.

Bohemia raised thirty thousand men. Count Mansfeld, an able officer but distinctly a soldier of fortune, just at the end of his service under the duke of Savoy, joined the Bohemians with a small division; Silesia and Brunswick sent troops. Neutral Brandenburg and Saxe-Weimar promised secret aid, and other countries, notably Holland, money. Negative assistance in the way of an attack on Austria was hoped from Protestant Bethlen Gabor, and even from the Turks.

Three strong places in Bohemia had remained true to the emperor: Catholic Pilsen, Budweis and Krummau. Instead of advancing at once on the emperor, Counts Thurn and Mansfeld engaged in a siege of these fortresses, and Pilsen was actually taken. The emperor sent against them small armies under Dampierre and Bouquoi, the latter a general educated in the best school of that day, the Netherlands; but the operations of 1618 were trivial, and the Bohemian Diet, which had pulled down its king, showed no sign of replacing him by any effective government. The Protestant Union naturally promised its aid; but the disagreements between its members made the assistance of questionable utility to the Bohemians.

The succeeding winter was made noteworthy by the beginning of depredations on the part of the unfed, unpaid troops, of license which was the disgraceful characteristic of the Thirty Years' War, and which ended by transforming Germany into a desert and retarding her progress a hundred years.

In 1619 Matthias died, and in August Ferdinand II., the deposed king of Bohemia, was elected. Moravia and Silesia had openly revolted. Mansfeld remained during the year in Bohemia to watch Bouquoi. Thurn marched through Moravia on Vienna, and actually reached and cannonaded the city. Almost any man but Ferdinand would have succumbed; but the future emperor was made of iron, and luckily for him Dampierre turned to help Vienna and drove Thurn away, while Bouquoi faced Mansfeld and beat him in a battle near Prague. Thurn returned to Bohemia, and Bouquoi took to the defensive; Dampierre made an unsuccessful foray into Moravia. None of these operations had any result.

Never was a better chance for independence thrown away. Had the joint forces of Bohemia and its allies been used in one body, they could at this moment have secured anything at the gates of Vienna; but the Bohemians resorted to political means in lieu of pushing the war with military vigor. They chose as their king Frederick of the Palatinate, who was son-in-law of James of England, and who, they believed, possessed friends of the helpful sort. Their calculations proved false. Frederick — as king of Bohemia and elector-palatine — would become the strongest prince in Germany, possessing two out of the seven electoral votes, a fact which aroused the keenest jealousy of every other potentate, especially John George, and even stirred up the Union; while, on the other hand, King James did naught to aid his kinsman. The Bohemians made a treaty with Bethlen Gabor, though the latter was too busy in seeking to tear Hungary from the emperor's grasp to be more than an indirect ally; and they appealed to Gustavus for assistance. Bouquoi, with twelve thousand men, retired to the imperial capital, and established a camp on the left bank of the Danube, below Vienna, backing on the river, a position curiously considered by the mili-

tary men of that time the strongest a general could hold.
Thurn with ten thousand men joined Bethlen Gabor with
sixteen thousand; the two essayed in vain to drive out Bouquoi, and at last, wearied with winter campaigning, Bethlen
Gabor made a separate peace with the emperor, and Thurn
was compelled to retire. His several advances on Vienna,
too much in detail, had borne
no fruit. But they had been
brilliantly conceived.

These two years, neglected
by Bohemia, enabled the emperor to conduct a strong offensive in 1620. He had utilized
his time by inducing jealous
Saxony to side against Frederick; by inciting Bavaria and
Spain to activity; and by
frightening the Union into
withdrawing its aid from the

Tilly.

new king of Bohemia, so as to defend itself. The Lower
Palatinate was soon threatened by twenty thousand men under
the Spanish general Spinola, who marched up the Rhine from
the Netherlands to Mainz, and, despite the Union, reduced all
the Palatinate on the left bank of the Rhine; while Maximilian mobilized the Bavarian troops, and the Catholic
League collected an army at Donauwörth. The Bohemians
were inexpertly led by Christian of Anhalt, who was barely
able to hold them together. The duke of Bavaria, whose
general-in-chief was the celebrated Count Tilly, a Walloon,
Jan Tzerklas by name, reduced the Protestants of Upper
Austria in August, joined Bouquoi's forces, and with fifty
thousand men marched into Bohemia. Frederick, whose
friends at the first sign of danger all seemed to forsake him,

withdrew with his army towards Mansfeld at Pilsen. The
Bohemian armies were ill supplied, suffered from disease,
had no discipline, and plundered right and left. Frederick
and Mansfeld did not agree. The latter remained in Pilsen,
and Frederick retired towards Prague. Tilly, whose army
was equally ill behaved and ill supplied, followed Frederick
sharply, and on November 8, 1620, at the battle of the
White Hill, near Prague, utterly defeated him. Frederick
fled the country, and was put to the ban of the empire. The
operation on the part of Tilly deserves praise. He had
profited by his opponent's weakness.

Bohemia was soon subjugated. Mansfeld held Pilsen some
time, but eventually retired to the Upper Palatinate. The
land was punished in a frightful manner, according to the
fanatical method of the day. The elector of Saxony, meanwhile, reduced Silesia, and was allowed to annex Lusatia as
his reward. John George was a peace-maker, or at least he
was consistent in so proclaiming himself, but he was always
ready to earn a new strip of territory, and he kept his eye on
the main chance.

In 1621 the emperor set himself to reduce the Palatinate;
Frederick would not sue for amnesty. Spinola had already
put his foot on the Lower Palatinate, and was visiting the
land with the wonted atrocities. Hesse-Cassel, Strasburg,
Ulm and Nürnberg made terms. England, the Netherlands,
Denmark and Switzerland sought to encourage the Union to
better efforts, but this body lacked a capable leader whose
hands were free, and it broke up in April. Mansfeld endeavored to defend the Upper Palatinate for Frederick, but
his troops were if anything more lawless than the enemy's,
and it was well that he was eventually forced to retire.

It is impossible to describe the barbarity of these armies.
The soldier was a professional who hired himself to the gen-

eral promising the greatest chance of plunder, and there was
not a vice or a brutality from which he shrank, even among
friends, while in the enemy's country, murder, rapine and
incendiarism were the rule of every day. " Do you think my
men are nuns? " asked Tilly, in answer to complaints of ruf-
fianism ; and yet Tilly's army was comparatively well in hand.
Neither man, woman nor child escaped the ruthless savagery
of the soldier of the Thirty Years' War, — excepting always
those under the control of Gustavus Adolphus. And such soldiers were all the less efficient, for their habits clashed with
every military plan ; armies moved to seek plunder, not success. Yet such was the method of raising and maintaining
troops that it was deemed a matter of course that these things
should be. The effect on the country or on the army was not
considered.

From the Upper, Mansfeld marched to the Lower Palatinate, where he won some slight
successes against Spinola, and
then sat down in Hagenau,
watching Tilly on the Neckar,
and Spinola on the Main.
Meanwhile, Bethlen Gabor
again appeared on the scene.
Bouquoi had been killed, and
his army was in full retreat.
If Frederick was in desperate
straits, Ferdinand's position
was far from easy.

Now came an accession of
forces for the Protestants.

Tilly's Manœuvres.

Early in May, 1622, Christian of Brunswick, an adventurer
almost as desperate as Mansfeld, starting from the north, and
the margrave of Baden-Durlach from the south, each with

twenty thousand men, marched to join Mansfeld, who crossed the Rhine, and after meeting the margrave at Wiesloch, defeated Tilly in an ambush. But, wasting his time, he allowed Tilly to join the Spanish forces, and to march on the margrave, who had again separated from him. Falling on him at Wimpfen on May 6, before Mansfeld could come up, Tilly defeated him, meanwhile holding Brunswick in check by a detachment of Spinola's troops borrowed for the occasion. On these being later withdrawn, Brunswick marched down to the Main country to join Mansfeld. But Tilly caught him crossing the river at Höchst June 20, attacked him in the rear, and badly cut him up. Heidelberg, Mannheim and Frankenthal now easily fell to Tilly.

Space forbids us to detail this, as well as many other interesting operations. Tilly had manœuvred skillfully. By keeping in one body he had prevented the junction of three armies of twenty thousand men each, and beaten them in detail, by a set of manœuvres which abundantly deserve study. They are one of the early instances of clever strategic work following upon the blank page of the Middle Ages. And yet Tilly was not usually fertile in strategic manœuvres. Mansfeld and Brunswick were finally driven out of the Lower Palatinate, passed through and devastated Alsace and Lorraine, and retired to Metz; and from thence, after a brush with the Spanish troops, Mansfeld, with his army, entered the service of the Netherlands.

Claiming his reward for Tilly's accomplishment, Maximilian was made elector, and given the Upper Palatinate. Emboldened by success, the emperor resolved to carry the war to the north against the dukes of Mecklenburg, Brunswick and Pomerania. He had reason for congratulation.

The war was thus transferred to the Weser. Frederick had dismissed Mansfeld and Brunswick from his employ;

but far from disbanding their forces, these generals foresaw means of subsistence and renown in marching their armies to another section. There was nothing they so little desired as peace. Each was fighting, not for Protestantism, but for himself. North Germany was as much opposed to them as it was to Tilly. If Mansfeld and Brunswick had not moved north, it is improbable that the emperor would have sent Tilly beyond the Palatinate; some kind of a peace would have been patched up. But these free lances kept about their work, and the men who were supposed to be the champions of the new faith grew to be its most intolerable foes.

Mansfeld, in 1623, devastated the Catholic holdings on the left bank of the Rhine with his Netherlands troops, while Brunswick lay beyond the Werra with some twenty-five thousand Dutch and north·Germans, near Göttingen. Tilly moved upon him, crossed the river in his front, and sent a detachment around his left wing. This time, however, the veteran counted without his host. Brunswick fell successively on each part of Tilly's army, and beat it singly. But losing part of his forces by disbandment, he fell back to join Mansfeld. Tilly followed, and attacking him August 6 at Stadtlohn, west of Münster, on the Ems, defeated him with grievous loss. Only six thousand men out of twenty thousand succeeded in joining Mansfeld. No further operations were undertaken this year, but all the armies went into winter-quarters, accompanied by the usual course of atrocious devastation of the countries they occupied.

Halberd with Gun. (16th Century.)

IX.

THE DANISH PERIOD. 1625–1630.

GUSTAVUS had repeatedly been appealed to by the German Protestants for aid; but his Polish wars kept him too busy to respond. Recognizing that eventually Sweden would be involved, he expected to coöperate, but in his own fashion. France, England and Holland, all anti-Hapsburg, had been irregularly furnishing funds to the Protestant armies, but lacking a worthy leader, there was no consistent action. In 1625 Gustavus offered to undertake the war on certain distinct terms; but Christian of Denmark underbid him, and England made a treaty with Christian, under whom Brunswick and Mansfeld were to serve. Thus began the Danish phase. .To oppose Christian was Tilly, the Bavarian general; and the celebrated Wallenstein was commissioned by the emperor to raise an army. The two had seventy thousand men to Christian's sixty thousand. Living by plunder, all these armies weighed heavily on the land. While Tilly advanced against Christian, Wallenstein defeated Mansfeld at the Dessau bridge; but he then weakly followed when Mansfeld pushed south to join Bethlen Gabor in Transylvania, thus wasting the campaign. Mansfeld's army was eventually disbanded, and Wallenstein returned. Meanwhile Tilly defeated Christian at Lutter in 1626, and in 1627 drove him well back into Holstein. Wallenstein now arrived, took the reins, and pushed Christian into the Danish islands. All Germany was the emperor's, save the free cities and Stralsund; but from this latter place, in 1628, Wallenstein, after a long siege and heavy loss, was driven back. King Christian sued for peace, and in 1629 was let off on easy terms, so that Wallenstein might devote himself to Gustavus, who was shortly to come upon the scene. The war had been remorselessly conducted, and without broad method. Results had been obtained rather from weak opposition than by able measures.

To detail the complicated political and religious events of the Thirty Years' War is without the scope of the present work; nor can we dwell on its early military manœuvres. With the exception of a few of Tilly's and Wallenstein's, the marches and countermarches of the plundering hordes have no value; the military history of Gustavus, and of a few great captains who succeeded him, claims our attention.

During all this seething of the German imbroglio, Sweden was engaged on other business. As a strong Protestant, Gustavus was ambitious to help his downtrodden brethren of the faith; but he was a stronger Swede, and he looked primarily to the welfare of his fatherland. That this welfare was bound up in its religion, Gustavus had the intelligence to see, as his grandfather, the great Gustavus I., had seen; that the European conflict could be settled only by the sword and by means of strange political alliances; that, unless Sweden soon took an active part in the struggle she would eventually be passively crushed: all this was plain to him, and the young king was ready to act so soon as the time was ripe. But though hot-headed in the fray, though embracing with exceptional fervor a cause he had once joined, Gustavus was cool and dispassionate, prudent and calculating, in the cabinet. True Swedish polity would not permit him to undertake a work which might lay him open to the treachery of Sigismund, which might again bring Sweden under the dictation of Poland; nor could he put his hand to so great a business unless he was more amply equipped with the sinews of war than his own poor land could furnish. In the work to be done he was willing to join the man to whom public opinion was now pointing, King Christian of Denmark, or he was ready to see the latter undertake it single-handed. But of first importance to him was peace or a lasting truce with Poland; Gustavus would not needlessly sacrifice Sweden upon the altar even of Protestantism; she must be placed beyond danger from outside foes; and such a peace or truce Gustavus set himself resolutely to conquer. Not closing his eyes to the suffering in Germany, he limited his action to his manifest capacity.

There was, moreover, a feeling in Gustavus' mind, that, in a military sense, he could best aid the Protestant cause by an advance upon the emperor's dominions through Silesia, — by reaching out towards Bethlen Gabor, who had married the sister of his queen, and was one of his devout admirers. This plan likewise necessitated a previous conquest or neutralization of Poland, some place near which would then serve as a base of operations.

This idea was in fact worked out from the then standpoint in much detail. While Christian of Denmark should conduct a campaign in support of the Protestants in the west of Germany, Gustavus, with Danzig or Stettin as a base, would march up the Oder through Silesia, straight on the emperor's hereditary possessions. The Silesians, mainly Protestants, would, as he knew, rise in his support and contribute heavily in recruits; Bethlen Gabor would fall upon Poland and help to compel her neutrality; the countries to be marched through were fruitful and able to sustain large armies; the road was practicable, the Warta being the only considerable river to be passed. But all this demanded money; and England and Holland — who alone had elastic finances — would not produce it. With reference to this plan, it must be remarked that Gustavus recognized that it had weaknesses; for Bethlen Gabor was the most unreliable of men, and Poland was not beyond being a serious enemy in his rear. But it was much his habit to deal in the possibilities of any given situation. He had the true gift of imagination, without which the captain, alike with the musician, the poet, the astronomer, never grows to his greatest stature. We shall encounter many of his imaginings. They all had their practical value.

For twelve years before Gustavus had any part in the Thirty Years' War, hostilities and atrocities had been constantly going on; and France, England and Holland, unwilling to see the Hapsburgs gain the upper hand in Europe, but without consistent plans, had been alternately subsidizing and forsaking the Protestant princes of Germany. These three moneyed powers could not work in unison, having each a different motive and aim. In 1624 Gustavus made to England a proposal to undertake the German business on condition that a port on the south shore of the Baltic was assured him, and another in the North Sea; that he should have abundant subsidies; that England should pay for seventeen thousand of the fifty thousand men he deemed essential; that Denmark should be neutralized by an English fleet in The Sound; and that he himself should have sole command of all forces under arms. But Christian was negotiating towards the same end; he was willing to accept much lower terms;

Christian of Denmark.

he could not see as far as Gustavus did; and his offer the English government accepted in 1625. Until 1629 the Thirty Years' War was in what is known as the Danish period. The Danish king's object in undertaking the war cannot be said to have been as ingenuous as that of the Swede; he acted more from a desire to enrich himself out of the bishopric of Bremen and other neighboring ecclesiastical foundations, than from any strong championship of Protestantism. Nor was he fitted to the task of commanding the armies of several nationalities, officered by men of diverse training and ideas, which the Protestants would put under

Danish Period.

arms. But the Swedish monarch's war kept Sigismund away from Christian's field, which was a help *pro tanto*, and Christian never doubted his own ability. It was no doubt well that Gustavus was left to finish the Polish problem before he undertook a war so distant from the Vistula. He could afford to bide his time.

Christian thus assumed the lead of the German Protestants. To oppose him the emperor in 1625 commissioned Wallenstein to recruit an army. Tilly still commanded the forces of Maximilian. The Dane was promised a busy campaign.

England agreed to subsidize Mansfeld and Brunswick, who joined the new commander-in-chief, thus giving him some sixty thousand men. But these troops were not rendezvoused until November, 1625, while Tilly had crossed the Weser into lower Saxony in July. Lukewarm towards Mansfeld, the British subsidies were irregular ; but the latter's career as a bold and measurably successful adventurer was heightened in brilliancy by relying largely on his own resources.

Christian's opening was weak ; though he had in his service Count Thurn, and the margrave of Baden-Durlach (young Bernard of Saxe-Weimar, later so celebrated, was present too), he merely garrisoned sundry places and sat down in a fortified camp at Bremen, to conduct a small war with Tilly, who duly appeared in his front. He was apparently unmindful of the fact that Wallenstein was rapidly putting afield an army for the emperor, and that dangers were encompassing him on every side. Between them Tilly and Wallenstein may have had seventy thousand men.

Wallenstein.

Albrecht von Waldstein, or Wallenstein, was born a Bohemian Protestant, and educated as a Moravian ; but though he early threw himself into the arms of the Jesuits, his religion was limited to belief in himself and the tenets of astrology. He entered the service of the emperor as a young man, and earned his praise and gratitude by many able military and diplomatic schemes. He became wealthy by marriage, wealthier by his own speculations, and was already prince of Friedland, and one of the most powerful men in Bohemia, when Ferdinand needed to raise an army.

It is alleged that Wallenstein agreed with Ferdinand that he would sustain his army on the country; but it is probable that the emperor promised to support it. That his low treasury forbade his carrying out such an undertaking made the matter come to the same thing. On the other hand Wallenstein probably agreed that there should be no plundering; that he would raise victual by contributions from the regularly constituted authorities. It was all one; the countries through which Wallenstein passed were invariably left a desert. To create an army was what both emperor and general aimed at; the means by which it was raised or fed or paid was immaterial to either.

Wallenstein's method of supporting his army was no other than that of the adventurer Mansfeld, but he did it in a more systematic way, acting in every land he entered as if he were the supreme lord, whose only law was I will. He paid his men well; he took good care of them; he kept them out of danger until he disciplined them into the semblance of an army; he was himself magnificent, and deemed nothing too good for his followers. Tilly, on the other hand, was a rough, blunt soldier, whose men worked hard and had but an occasional reward in the sack of a town. Wallenstein's army was on a much more splendid, if no more efficient scale.

The Czech was unquestionably an able strategist; he preferred, to be sure, to avoid battle and resort to manœuvre; but according to the art of that day, he had few peers. An equally shrewd politician, he harbored schemes looking towards the unity of Germany under the Hapsburgs, with equality of the two religions, in which schemes he himself should figure

as leader ; but these material strivings not unfrequently interfered with his better military knowledge. Unlike a great
commander, he did not call the political situation to the aid
of his strategy ; he rather subordinated his strategy to his
political desires, forgetful that it is only after victory that one
may gainfully do this. While Wallenstein served a Catholic
master, he had the breadth to see that in religious toleration
lay the best chance to spread the imperial power ; and toward
this end he constantly strove.

Jealous of any competition in the field, Wallenstein resolved
to open a campaign on his own lines about the left flank of
Christian. He passed from Bohemia into Saxony, crossed to
the right bank of the Elbe at Dessau, where he fortified a
strong bridge-head, and prepared to advance on the Danish
king. To counteract this advance, Mansfeld, who had been
in the Lübeck country and in Brandenburg, crossed the
Havel, took Zerbst, and in late April, 1626, marched boldly
on towards the Dessau bridge. His attempt, April 25, to
capture it failed ; Wallenstein held his men behind their
defenses, and at the right moment debouched upon Mansfeld's exhausted troops, which had shown some gallantry in
the advance, and cut his army to pieces.

Mansfeld was elastic. With the help of John Ernest of
Saxe-Weimar, he again recruited forces in Brandenburg and
Silesia (the devastation of the war and the burning of home-
steads made half the population ready to enlist), and at the
end of May moved towards Hungary, via Crossen, Gross Glogau and the Jablunka Pass, to join Bethlen Gabor, who was
again at war with the emperor. Wallenstein, sending to Tilly
some six thousand men under Merode, followed Mansfeld, a
fact so singular, so eccentric in both a military and a collo-
quial sense, that only the fear of grave danger to Ferdinand
from the joint operations of Mansfeld and Bethlen Gabor, can

explain it. By some authorities he is stated to have received
especial instruction from Vienna to follow Mansfeld, and
that under these he unwillingly directed his march via Juter-
bogk towards the Oder. It was a creditable thing for Mansfeld to lure an old and able soldier like Wallenstein after
him, and away from his proper sphere; and it was equally
discreditable to Wallenstein to be so lured away by a man to
whom he would have referred with a sneer.

Mansfeld was not as fortunate as his manœuvre was bold.
In December, 1626, Bethlen Gabor made a new peace with
Ferdinand, and Mansfeld was driven to disband his army and
to make his own way to Venice, where he died. Brunswick
had died in the spring. Neither of these soldiers of fortune
lived to see the awful burning of the fire they had so largely
helped to kindle.

Wallenstein's retrograde march had been useless, and he
did not again get to work in north Germany until late in
1627. He had wasted two campaigns.

While Wallenstein was thus occupied, Tilly followed up
King Christian. In May, 1626, Christian marched towards
the Elbe to the aid of Mansfeld, or rather to lay his hand on
the Weser bishoprics, but found that both he and Wallenstein had moved towards Hungary. He attacked the Dessau
position, but, aided by a reinforcement from Tilly, the garrison left there by Wallenstein drove him back, and he
retired to Brunswick, and sat down to the siege of several
towns. Nothing but smaller operations took place between
the rival armies, and these mostly fell out in favor of Tilly.
After taking Göttingen, and learning that Christian had
advanced on him as far as Nordheim, Tilly moved toward
the reinforcements Wallenstein had sent him, drew them in,
and turned on his adversary. Christian withdrew, but Tilly
followed him up, reaching him at Lutter, August 27, 1626;

Christian's unpaid troops fought in a half-hearted manner, and Tilly defeated him badly. Christian retired to Holstein to recruit. This operation redounds to Tilly's credit, and caused the Protestant princes to shake their heads as to Christian's ability to carry out his programme. German Protestantism was not to be thus conserved.

In truth, Christian was in a bad way. The common folk had a song, of which the refrain ran, "Perhaps within a year he'll be, A king without a kingdom." He sent embassies everywhere, — to England, Holland, Venice. France and Holland gave only a part of the promised subsidies; yet by praiseworthy exertions he got together in the winter of 1626–27 an army of thirty thousand men. Cut off from the lower Saxon Circle, he had thrown that part of Germany into a defensive attitude; and now Brunswick turned to the emperor; Mecklenburg ordered the Danish troops out of its territory, and Brandenburg sent reinforcements to the Poles.

The wonderful imperial successes of the past five years in war and politics had left only Mecklenburg, Pomerania and Denmark to uphold the integrity of the Protestant faith. Ferdinand dreamed of extending his empire to the Baltic; and there were folk, even Protestants, who deemed such a consummation not wholly to be regretted; for as against the ill-doings of Mansfeld and Brunswick, Ferdinand and the empire stood for order. His armies opened the campaign of 1627 by reducing Silesia; Tilly crossed the Elbe at Arthenburg in August, and moved into Holstein. Christian stoutly defended himself against Tilly's advance; but Wallenstein, who had marched with nearly a hundred thousand men through Silesia and Brandenburg, burning and plundering, and extorting all manner of contributions, now appeared on the scene. Sending Arnim to Pomerania, and Schlick to Mecklenburg, each with a small army, Wallenstein crossed

the Elbe at Winsen towards the end of August, and moved
into Jutland. Tilly, meanwhile, had again beaten Christian
in September, and the king, leaving garrisons in Glückstadt
and other strong places, had gradually retired up the peninsula to avoid further battle. On the arrival of Wallenstein,
who, as the emperor's general, claimed to be the ranking officer, Tilly was sent back across the Elbe, ostensibly to protect the joint communications, but really to be got out of the
way, while Wallenstein cleared the peninsula of the Protestant forces, and drove the Danes to take refuge in the
islands, whither, having no fleet, he could not well pursue
them. Though one of his titles was that of " Imperial Admiral," he had no ships, and could not isolate towns with a
harbor.

There was widespread opposition to Wallenstein's military
sway, and especially to his soldiery. He had scarcely a
friend in north Germany. Every one protested against Ferdinand's army, while technically remaining loyal to the
emperor. The great Czech's work was, however, done with
zeal and military intelligence ; and he was shortly rewarded
by Ferdinand with the duchy of Mecklenburg, which, having
sustained Denmark, was declared to be forfeited ; and he had
already been created duke of Friedland. The end of 1627
saw the emperor in full control of the shore of the Baltic,
save only Stralsund, and in possession of all its abutting
countries. Pomerania was occupied; Wismar and Rostock were taken ; only the Hanse towns and Stettin still held
their own. Brunswick and Hesse-Cassel were the sole provinces which maintained any show of independence.

It must be said to Wallenstein's credit that, however intolerable his régime, he was not fighting the battles of the Jesuits, or of religious oppression. To him Protestant and
Catholic were one. His controlling idea was imperialism —

Hapsburgism — and to accomplish this he was willing to lay all religious disputes aside. But Ferdinand could not recognize his duties as emperor apart from his duties as a Catholic, and Wallenstein was compelled to follow his dictation. The Czech was at the height of his glory. He dreamed himself the conqueror of Germany, at the head of a powerful army, in the new rôle of deliverer of the empire, advancing

Stralsund.
Partly from an old plan.

on the Turks, and taking Constantinople. He forgot the Catholic League; he forgot Maximilian and Tilly. And he forgot in his dreams, but not in reality, the king of Sweden. So long as Gustavus held sway on the Baltic, as he now did, Wallenstein's power was an uncertain term, — and he knew it. He had been watching the career of the "Snow King," as he jeeringly called him, and while he did not hold him at a great value, as measured by his only standard, himself, he

yet saw in Gustavus' holding of the Baltic grave cause to
fear for his own schemes.

Stralsund was now the saving clause. This strongly fortified city was of equal importance to all Protestants. England, Holland, Sweden, Denmark, the Hanse towns, all joined
to help her. She could, like Danzig, be provisioned from the
sea. Gustavus had always recognized the value of Stralsund
as the best strategic base on the Baltic. He had at one
moment conceived the idea of conducting a defensive campaign in Germany, and of going to Stralsund in person to
organize it from there. It would be fatal if the Catholic
League should control so important a harbor. He had already sent Stralsund supplies, and dispatched six hundred
men under a good officer, Colonel Rosladin, with a naval
adviser, Admiral Flemming; and in 1625 he had made a
twenty years' treaty, offensive and defensive, with the town.

Stralsund was not one of the so-called free cities, but
was practically on the same basis, though she owed nominal
allegiance both to Pomerania and the emperor. But she
declined to admit the imperial army, whose ill fame had preceded it, whereupon Wallenstein ordered his lieutenant,
Count Arnim, to besiege the city. Arnim already held the
island of Rügen, and soon took Dänholm, which commanded
the mouth of the harbor; but in March, 1628, the Stralsund-
ers drove him out of this latter island.

The town held a number of old soldiers, six hundred
Danes, and six hundred Swedes, and the citizens were instinct
with courage. In May Gustavus had sent them a cargo of
powder, and Christian, who was now in earnest, joined in
putting Stralsund on a solid footing. Wallenstein, angered
at the unexpected resistance, was fain to come to the aid of
his lieutenant. " I will take Stralsund, were it hung to
heaven by chains," he is, somewhat doubtfully, quoted as

saying; and to a deputation of citizens he pointed to his table: " I will make your city as flat as this." The citizens sent their property and families aboard ship or to Sweden, but showed no signs of yielding. Wallenstein, surprised, nettled, disconcerted, kept on with the siege, but made no progress. Soon after his arrival at Stralsund, about the end of June, he ordered a storm, and kept it up three days. But it was met at all points, despite valor, ability and immense excess of force. No greater result followed a twenty-four hours' bombardment. Without a fleet, or means of creating one, the siege ran the same course as Gustavus' siege of Danzig. On July 9 and 10 more Danish troops and a Danish fleet arrived, and a week later two thousand Swedes under Leslie and Brahe. Wallenstein felt his weakness, and abated his demands, but with no result; and on July 24, 1628, he retired from the siege with a loss of twelve thousand men, baffled. Stralsund had taken the first step in saving Protestantism in Germany.

In 1628 matters in Germany were ripe for absolutism. The Jesuits anticipated full control of European affairs. The ideal of Ferdinand, to recover the lost dignities and power of the empire ; and either the ideal of Maximilian, to recover for the church its lost property, or the ideal of Wallenstein, to found unity on a military government, seemed about to be realized. Gustavus' ideal of a *Corpus Evangelicorum* — or union of all Protestant powers for self-defense — had not been formulated. No part of Germany now stood out except the Hanse towns ; and to reduce these seemed but a small work compared to what had already been accomplished. To a deputation of Hanse towns which pleaded for Stralsund, Wallenstein had replied : " I will have Stralsund first, and each of you in turn after ! " But when they had conquered all Germany, it was on this commercial rock that the efforts

of Ferdinand and Wallenstein were wrecked.   Truly, money
is the sinews of war.

Meanwhile Stade, at the mouth of the Elbe, had been taken
by Tilly, but Glückstadt held out, and in January, 1629,
Tilly retired from this place, though Wallenstein lent his
personal aid.   The towns, the merchant class in other words,
had demonstrated that they were greater than these vaunted
generals ; stronger in their rights than the successor of the
Cæsars.   They had put a limit to their conquests.

It was the siege of Stralsund which brought conviction to
the mind of Gustavus that Sweden must and now might throw
herself into the scale against the Hapsburgs.   He was far-
sighted, as Christian was not.   Denmark had been subdued
on land, but though at sea she still held her own, Christian
had lost courage.   Finally begging for mercy, Wallenstein,
who recognized, if he did not acknowledge, his own limitations,
was only too ready to show it.   At the Peace of Lübeck,
May 12, 1629, Christian was freed from the obligations he
had taken on himself at the inception of his luckless campaigns.   In this Danish period of the Thirty Years' War, the
emperor had been completely successful ; but Christian was
treated with uncommon leniency, for Wallenstein wanted
securely to shelve him before he undertook to master Gustavus ; and on the promise that he would thereafter stand aloof
from German affairs, Christian even received back the lands
which the emperor had taken.

Wallenstein had already received his reward.   Maximilian
was now given the Upper Palatinate and that part of the
Lower Palatinate which is on the right bank of the Rhine,
coupled to its electoral vote ; and within these lands Protestantism was soon interdicted.

The emperor had begun the war by seeking to discipline
some rebellious subjects ; he had ended by conquering all

Germany. The Edict of Restitution — issued May 19, 1629 — compelled the Protestants to restore to the Catholics all the religious property acquired by them since the Peace of Passau in 1552 ; and Wallenstein was charged to see this done. The archbishoprics of Magdeburg and Bremen, the bishoprics of Minden, Verden, Halberstadt, Lübeck, Ratzburg, Miznia, Merseburg, Naumburg, Brandenburg, Havelberg, Lebus and Camin, and one hundred and twenty smaller foundations, were torn from the Protestant clergy and their congregations, and restored to the Catholics. With Wallenstein at the head, this was not done leniently : all Germany, from the Alps to the Baltic, groaned under the awful manner of the doing. Protestantism was fairly proscribed. In some localities it was worse than in others. In Nördlingen there was not a single Catholic, but the imperial commissioners nevertheless marked all the churches and their property for surrender to Catholic priests.

To be truthful, the fault had lain with the Protestants. They had never stood by each other, nor acted for any time in concert ; their political jealousies had been stronger than their religious aspirations. On the other hand, the emperor, both in politics and war, had shown a persistency worthy of a better cause; while his generals, Wallenstein and Tilly, and his right-hand man, the elector of Bavaria, had well seconded his courage and intelligence.

Meanwhile two strong men had been watching the successes of Ferdinand : Richelieu from his jealousy of the Hapsburgs and dread of their ascendancy ; and Gustavus from his love of Sweden and fear that Protestantism would be trodden out of Germany.

There is little in the campaigns of the first twelve years of this war which savors of what to-day we call military method. Occasional smaller pieces of work were excellently done, but the whole was unsystematic, and the grand strategy of the field was forgotten in the political ideas of the leaders, and in the commissariat demands of the armies. In a country parceled out like Germany, this was not to be wondered at. The armies marched hither and yon without consistent purpose. Allies did not work into each other's hands. A town rich in booty was as much an objective of every commander as a fortress at a key-point or the army of the enemy; and the habit of living on the country was coupled with atrocities, the recital of the least of which makes one's blood curdle. Wallenstein, Tilly, Mansfeld and Brunswick were guilty of acts of savagery which would stamp them with eternal infamy, — except that such was the era. Marches were mere devastating raids, only then having an ulterior object when the conquest of a province lay in the way; and the fact that it was believed that no fortress should be left in the rear of a marching army made all operations slow and indecisive.

We shall see a different method while Gustavus Adolphus is in the field.

All this anticipates the Polish campaigns of Gustavus from 1625 to 1629, to which we must now return.

Genevese. (16th Century.)

X.

THE POLISH WARS CONTINUE. 1625–1627.

In 1625, unable to prolong the truce with Poland, Gustavus, with twenty thousand men, set sail for Livonia, and thence invaded Courland. Here he was met by a Polish army, which he defeated at Walhof in January. His idea still was that he might aid the Protestants by pushing a column through Silesia. In 1626, with reinforcements, he sailed for Pillau, which he took, though it belonged to Brandenburg; then advanced on Königsberg, and down towards Danzig, seizing all the towns on the way, and besieged this, to the Poles, essential harbor. Sigismund came up with an army and blockaded Mewe, which the Swedes had taken; but Gustavus relieved it by a brilliant *coup*. In 1627 the Poles under Koniezpolski tried, before the king's arrival, with partial success, to raise the siege of Danzig; and cut off some of the Swedish reinforcements; but when Gustavus reached Danzig, affairs changed. The king, too venturesome, was here wounded, and matters remained at a standstill. In August the Poles drew near; and in an ensuing engagement Gustavus was again and more severely wounded. While invalided, a naval engagement took place off Danzig, in which the Swedes were beaten, but the siege was not raised. When convalescent, the king captured some surrounding towns, and more effectually shut in the place. Owing to his late arrival and two wounds, this campaign was not of marked gain.

AFTER the completion of the new military organization of Sweden, and the failure of all attempts to negotiate a permanent peace with Sigismund to replace the existing truce, Gustavus, like a true soldier, made up his mind, if war it must be, to open hostilities by vigorous measures. With twenty thousand men, on a fleet of seventy-six vessels, he again set sail for the mouth of the Dwina, in June, 1625, captured Kockenhusen and other points held by the Poles in Livonia, and reduced the entire province. The attempt of a Polish colonel with two thousand men to retake Riga failed, the detachment being all but destroyed; and a second one by Marshal Stanislaus Sapieha, with three thousand men, was driven off with a loss of all the guns. From Riga Gustavus crossed the border into Courland and captured Mittau and Bauske. The cold weather had come, but the king was better equipped to conduct a winter campaign than the enemy; for his men, with their fur-lined boots of waterproof, oiled leather and thick stockings, and otherwise coarsely but serviceably, warmly and uniformly clad, could keep the field at any season.

Field - Marshals Leon Sapieha and Gosiecowski, with twenty-six hundred cavalry and thirteen hundred foot, advanced to the rescue of Bauske. Gustavus went out to meet them, relying mainly on his excellent infantry, for he had little horse. Early recognizing the value of foot, it was he who first in modern times put it in its proper place with relation to the other arms. He believed in it; and, moreover, the Swedish horses were too small for anything but light cavalry, so that, until bigger animals could be got in Germany, he fain must put up with what he had. Once Gustavus found how much reliance he could place upon his foot, he never ceased to devote his best energies to its development. On the other hand, the Polish generals' reliance was on their superior cavalry, which was their nation's favorite arm.

Polish Horseman.

Gustavus had as yet commanded in no pitched battle, and

he was eager to measure swords with the enemy. The armies met at Walhof, in Courland, January 16, 1626, and the king utterly worsted the Poles, with loss of sixteen hundred killed, many prisoners, much of the artillery, baggage and many standards, the Swedish loss being small. There are no details of this battle. Except the king's brief dispatches home, which dwelt on results rather than tactics, there is no record from which we can divine his method of attack. The fire in the Castle of Stockholm in 1697 destroyed many papers which might have given us more light. Sapieha fled to Lithuania, followed by Gustavus, who on the way took Birzen and another strong place; which success accomplished, the king again endeavored to make peace. But part of the embassy which he sent to Warsaw was seized, and with difficulty released. Peace was not upon the cards. The king demanded of Lithuania a heavy contribution in money, and, the season being advanced, left de la Gardie to secure his conquests in Livonia, and returned to Stockholm, with the intention of attacking from another quarter in the spring. Being still restricted in strategic operations by the Polish war, the king thought that by advancing up the Vistula, he might connect on his right with Christian of Denmark, or Mansfeld, and on his left with Bethlen Gabor. This project was the one already referred to for a joint effort to reach the heart of the empire. But it was never put into execution.

From Stockholm, on June 15, 1626, the king, with twenty-six thousand men on one hundred and fifty ships, sailed to the coast of East Prussia, landing near the fortress of Pillau, at the mouth of the Frische Haff. This place belonged to his brother-in-law, the elector of Brandenburg, as duke of Prussia, then a fief of Poland; and Gustavus asked permission to occupy it as a storehouse, and a strong place to protect his reëmbarkation. But the inert elector demanded

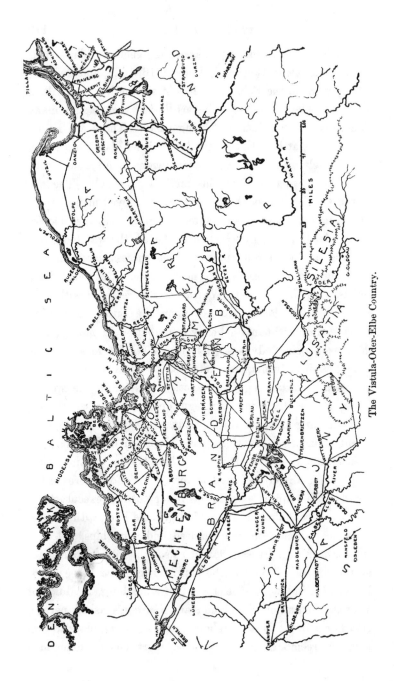

The Vistula-Oder-Elbe Country.

three weeks to consider the matter; Gustavus had no time to spare; he summarily took Pillau, and by equally unanswerable arguments compelled the elector to neutrality. With his characteristic bluntness he said to him : " I am aware that you prefer to keep a middle course, but such a course will break your neck. You must hold on to me or to Poland. I am your brother Protestant, and have married a Brandenburg princess ; I will fight for you and defend this city of yours. I have good engineers, and know a bit of the business myself. I doubt not I shall defend it against Poland or — the devil. My men, if you like, are poor Swedish peasant louts, dirty and ill-clad ; but they can deal you lusty blows, and shall soon be given finer clothing." His acts, moreover, argued better than his phrases.

In case he should make an advance through Brandenburg, Gustavus did not lose sight of the fact that his army would be moving into a position where it would become the strategic centre of a line, of which the king of Denmark, who stood between the Elbe and the Weser, was the right, and Mansfeld, on the Oder, was the left. All his lines of advance were duly weighed, and his active mind made potential plans far ahead. But his immediate task was simpler ; and superior to any plan for joining the German struggle was the intent to cut Poland off from access to the Baltic, as he already had Russia, by the occupation of the entire coast line. He never lost sight of his great aspiration, " *Dominium Maris Baltici.*" He gauged its value rightly.

Gustavus continued his advance. Königsberg was threatened until it promised neutrality. Braunsberg, Frauenburg and Tolkemit were surrendered July 1–3, and the Jesuits here and elsewhere were expelled from the cities, and their goods confiscated ; for these priests were mixed up in every political matter, and did infinite harm. Elbing, July 6, and Mari-

enburg, July 8, followed suit, as well as all the towns of West
Prussia.   But Dirschau and Danzig, which had broken neutrality, and were in dread accordingly, held out.   Gustavus
moved on Danzig, and camping in the Werder, near the
mouth of the Vistula, reconnoitred the town and the fortress
Weichselmünde.   He then began to recruit from the conquered districts, and crossing the Vistula on a bridge of boats

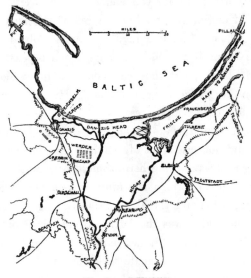

Danzig and Vicinity.

below Dirschau, July 12, he stormed that town and Mewe, to
hold which cut Danzig off from her trade with the interior.
The king's hope was not only to take Danzig as a base and
depot for himself — " *sedes belli* " was the phrase of the day
— but to hamper the Poles by cutting off from them access
to an essential harbor.   Everything looked promising, when
suddenly Sigismund appeared on the theatre of operations
with thirty thousand men, and camped at Graudenz, several
days' march up the Vistula.

Danzig was a strong place. It disputed with Novgorod the title of richest mart of eastern Europe. It was a free city, owing mere nominal allegiance to Poland, and was a prize for him who controlled it. But it could be provisioned from the sea, which Gustavus seemed unable to prevent. Danzig proved valuable to the Swedes as an object-lesson; and from his experience here the king was able to show Stralsund how to defy Wallenstein; but though it had this secondary value, its obstinacy in holding out largely neutralized the Swedish successes in the four years of the Polish war.

The presence of Sigismund quite altered Gustavus' plans. Though much weaker than the Poles, the king deemed it wise at once to march against them. The fortresses he had taken were no permanent defense; he must beat the Poles in the field. Led by Sigismund and his son, Vladislas, the enemy advanced to Marienburg; on meeting the Swedes, a few unimportant skirmishes occurred, when the Poles withdrew, crossed the Vistula near Neuenburg, and began a siege of Mewe from the south.

The Swedish commandant was prepared to resist to the uttermost, but Mewe needed victual, and, though such an operation was then unusual, Gustavus personally headed a reinforcement and succor-train for the garrison with three thousand foot and three hundred horse. Despite due attempts at secrecy, the plan was discovered; the Poles essayed to stop the convoy, and with light horse and some artillery occupied a position athwart its path. Rather than bring the whole Polish army down upon himself, the king resorted to a ruse, gave his movement the appearance of a reconnoissance, and proceeded to withdraw. His clever dispositions deceived the Poles, and throwing out Count Thurn with part of his force to divert the enemy's attention by active demonstrations, he himself made a detour with his convoy somewhat out of sight and covered by horse. Thurn performed his work so well that the Poles, under the impression that the Swedish garrison was about to be drawn from Mewe, and that the place would fall to them in any event, made no serious advance. Their manifest rôle was to attack sharply, and

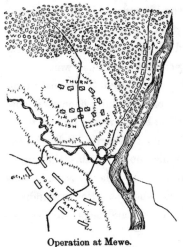

to closely observe the place to ascertain the real purpose of the Swedes. They did neither.

Thurn had a severe skirmish with the Polish light horse, which alone had been put in, and was obliged to withdraw a space for fear of being cut off from the king. But he held the force in check, and the Poles, though they had abundant time, neglected to reinforce it. Gustavus managed luckily to run

Operation at Mewe.

his convoy into Mewe from the north side, and then turned to protect the withdrawal of Thurn.

The Poles had used but a small part of their troops, though in actual numbers ten to one of the Swedes. They feared that Gustavus was in force, and feinting to draw them from their good position. A simple demonstration on either of the Swedish flanks would have disclosed the true situation, and been fatal to the king's project. Gustavus retired safely up river to Dirschau, and the Poles raised the blockade of Mewe. Their loss, stated at five hundred men, far exceeded that of the Swedes.

It is rare that a fortress has been re-victualed in this fashion in the teeth of so numerous besiegers. As an operation it was quite unusual then, and is not usual at any period. The management of the affair was perfect. In the fighting Gustavus had himself led his men, and, as was his wont, run grave danger, being, it is said, twice captured in the fray, and twice cut out by his immediate companions. He had tested the quality of the Poles, who, except for undoubted bravery, had little in the way of good soldiership to recommend them, and did not appear to be dangerous opponents. Sigismund's generals had a narrow appreciation of what a large army should do which blockades a town, and finds itself attacked by a handful of the enemy seeking to relieve the place. Bold as Gustavus' attempt had been, he was well seconded by Polish hebetude. On the succeeding day he marched in force into Mewe. Sigismund, less persistent in war than obstinate in politics, made signs of desiring peace, but coupled his proposals with impossible conditions. Placing his troops under Oxenstiern in winter-quarters, for the year was far spent, the king returned to Stockholm. The ministry and people supported his refusal to listen to the Polish conditions, and a more reasonable proposal was drawn up and sent to Warsaw; but as Sigismund did not answer before the next year, the war went on.

The command of the Poles, at the opening of 1627, was given to Crown-Marshal Koniezpolski, who was sent to raise the siege of Danzig. Gustavus was at home; but the Swedes held Putzig, Dirschau, Mewe, Elbing and Pillau, thus encircling the city. To break through this line, Koniezpolski saw that Putzig afforded the easiest means, and he was as successful in his venture as he was bold. The garrison of Putzig, unfortunately short of both munitions and food, was quickly reduced to straits; but though surrendering, it obtained the right to march out with colors flying. This again opened the communication of Danzig with Germany, and neutralized all

Gustavus' work so far done. Nor was this the end of ill-luck. Eight thousand recruits, coming to the Swedes from Germany, were met by Koniezpolski on the march from and driven back to Hammerstein, and the place forced, on April 15, to capitulate, in a manner not creditable to the Swedish garrison. The officers were made prisoners — among them Colonels Streif and Teufel — and the men released on a year's parole. This was a notable piece of partisan warfare.

During this period of Swedish reverses, Gustavus had been kept in Stockholm by contrary winds. By no means cast down by these backsets, he doubted not to overcome them when he should reach the ground. Sailing from Elfsnabben May 4, he landed on the 8th at Pillau. When he reached the army at Dirschau with the six thousand troops he had brought, he found it increased by recruitment up to thirty-five thousand men. But to his surprise he also found that the elector of Brandenburg had taken up arms against him, and had raised four thousand " blue coats " for his suzerain Sigismund. These were intrenched near Pillau, at Loch-städt. Gustavus made short work of the matter; he set out, speedily captured the little Prussian army, and forcibly enlisted the entire body under his own standard. George William learned his lesson, and thereafter remained neutral.

Gustavus began by a careful reconnoissance of the works surrounding Danzig. The citizens had occupied the " Danzig Head," or strip of land at the west mouths of the Vistula, and here was a redoubt which Gustavus especially desired to reconnoitre. While thus engaged, May 25, 1627, viewing the works from a boat, he was wounded by a bullet in the flesh of the hip, which laid him up, and further delayed operations. During this period the Poles concentrated their forces; Sigismund threatened de la Gardie in Livonia, and the king was compelled to send Horn to his assistance.

Gustavus Adolphus was personally much too venturesome for a commanding general. In this particular the family tendency to insanity perhaps manifested itself; but his was as admirable a form of the disease as that of "Macedonia's Madman." The same day on which he was wounded, he had been almost captured by two Polish horsemen, who suddenly sprang upon him while out reconnoitring and far from his attendants; and but a few weeks before, he had barely escaped being cut down in a cavalry skirmish. But no expostulations were of any avail. Gustavus would run risks fit only for officers of lower rank. For this venturesomeness Oxenstiern attempted to take him to task, saying that a monarch had no right to risk a life so needful to his subjects. But Gustavus cited Alexander, and the necessity of showing his men that they must despise danger. "What better fate could overtake me than to die doing my duty as king, in which place it has pleased heaven to set me?" he quietly replied. In this particular the monarch could not be controlled.

Meanwhile, Koniezpolski drew within six miles, and undertook, on August 18, a reconnoissance of the Swedish position. Gustavus headed a body of cavalry and drove back the Polish horse, which retired through the village of Rokitken. This place lay in a country much cut up by hills and ravines, and the village was held by Polish infantry and artillery. Gustavus had placed some batteries on a convenient hill, with orders to attack the village, and had galloped up an adjoining height to reconnoitre, when he was again wounded through the right shoulder, near the neck. The Swedes, somewhat disheartened, withdrew.

The bullet was deep and could not be cut out, and the wound proved dangerous. Gustavus at first feared that it was his mortal hurt; and, indeed, he was kept from duty for three months. Meanwhile the siege went slowly on. It is related that the king's body physician, while dressing the wound, was led to say that he had always feared this or worse, as His Majesty so constantly courted danger. " Ne sutor ultra crepidam," answered the royal patient.

On recovery Gustavus recaptured Putzig, and once more cut Danzig from its communication with Germany, while a Swedish fleet under Sternskjöld blockaded the port. The Danzigers had also patched up a fleet; and under command of Admiral Dickmann, a Dane, they made, November 28, an attack on the Swedish navy, and inflicted a severe defeat upon it, but not without heavy loss of their own. Dickmann and Sternskjöld both fell, and a Swedish captain — some say Sternskjöld — blew up his ship rather than surrender. This naval battle exhibits the strength and ability of Danzig. The misfortune seemed to cap the adverse occurrences of the year, though the Danzigers had won but an empty triumph, and at a loss of five hundred of their best sailors. A stronger fleet was brought up, and Gustavus began to draw his lines closer about the city. In order to do this effectually, it was essential to capture two towns south of the Frische Haff. The king, though not yet convalescent, headed the party against Wörmditt; General Tott that against Guttstädt. The former was taken by storm; the latter surrendered. No further operations, save another minor naval fight in the harbor of Danzig, occurred this year, and Gustavus returned to Stockholm in December, partly for the benefit of his health.

The campaign of this year was of small account, — indeed almost a failure, — owing to the adverse weather, which kept the king from the scene of action, and to the aggravating delays occasioned by his wounds. It was fortunate that the enemy took no better advantage of their opportunities.

Nothing can excuse their carelessness in not assuming the offensive during this period, in connection with the garrison of Danzig. The Poles never lacked courage, but they were rarely well led. A vigorous policy must have occasioned serious complications to Gustavus' lieutenants, and might have brought disaster; for Gustavus had not sufficient forces to blockade so strong a place as Danzig, and at the same time hold head to an army fully equaling his own, and vigorously directed. Koniezpolski opened against Gustavus' lieutenants with vigor; but he drew back to a strict defensive after the arrival of the king.

There were uncompleted fortifications on the Bischofsberg and Hagelberg, near Danzig, which it has been said should have been attacked by Gustavus, but even their capture would not necessarily have brought about the fall of the place; for the Swedish ordnance, though the best then known, was not capable of reaching every part of the town from those eminences; and the Danzigers would have fought hard. It seems that Gustavus might have been wiser to resort to a simple blockade, and in July, before the very dilatory enemy was ready, to fall on and cripple him for the campaign. Had he accomplished the latter, he could have turned on Danzig with a better chance; for without the moral support of the presence of Sigismund's army, the town would scarcely have resisted so stoutly; and easy terms might have secured it.

Moreover, in a military sense, the Swedes were not well placed. The time for the Polish army to attack Gustavus was while his attention was taken up by the siege. His desire to capture Danzig before moving on the enemy was perhaps a mistake. As Lossau has pointed out, had the Poles defeated Gustavus while he lay near the city, so as to punish his army badly and thrust it back towards the west, his line of retreat would have been through an extremely poor country, in which an army, especially one partly broken up, could scarcely subsist; whereas an advance on the Polish army up the Vistula, even if resulting in defeat, would have given Gustavus a better chance to retire and to save his army whole. But these were new problems of war, unknown to the soldiers of the day; and the Swedish monarch was slowly working them out. He cannot be held to look at war from our own point of view, illumined as it is by the work of a Frederick and a Napoleon, as well as by his own; for he was still hampered by the fear of fortresses, so strong a sentiment of his era. And happily Koniezpolski showed indolence to a degree which corrected the evils which might have flowed from Gustavus' position and wounds.

Danzig had so far resisted Gustavus' best efforts. It was a proud city, without religious prejudices, and while owing slender allegiance to Poland, it held its own rights at a high value. In this it was seconded by Holland, and morally sustained by all powers which preferred not to see the Baltic reduced to the position of a Swedish lake.

It must be said to the credit of Wallenstein's foresight that he was constant in his advice to the emperor to assist the Poles. If Gustavus was allowed to win success he would prove the worst enemy the empire could have, he wrote to Ferdinand. He would gladly have accepted Gustavus as an ally, if the monarch could at a cheap price be kept from entering into the German imbroglio, where he himself was now enacting the chief rôle. With his usual habit of sowing by all waters, Wallenstein even sought diplomatic means of establishing communication with Gustavus, meanwhile doing his best to cripple him, and instructing his lieutenant on the Baltic, Arnim, to prevent the Swedes at all hazards from landing in Pomerania or Mecklenburg.

XI.

THE POLISH WARS END. 1628–1629.

AGAIN joining his army near Danzig, in 1628, Gustavus pushed the siege; Koniezpolski indulged in making sundry diversions; but the king marched out against him, and in a sharp battle drove him up the Vistula. Danzig was about to fall, when unusual floods overflowed the country, and drove the Swedes out of their works. Gustavus had been studying the German situation, had made a treaty as to Baltic trade with Denmark, and had thrown a force and munitions into Stralsund. When the emperor overran all north Germany except the free towns, the king saw that he must shortly enter the contest, and he pushed the Poles hard for a peace. In 1629 the emperor sent a force to join them, and operations became active. The enemy moved sharply on Gustavus, and with initial success, but within a few days he turned the tables and defeated them with heavy loss. This, coupled to the exhaustion of Poland and the intervention of France, brought about a six years' truce, under which Gustavus held all his conquests. In these Polish wars Gustavus, like Cæsar in Gaul, had trained his army for its future work in Germany, and himself in war's broader problems. He had learned to know his men and they to lean on him; and he had gradually transformed the slow-moving army of the day into an active and mobile force. He was now ready to enter the lists for Protestantism.

DURING the winter, in relation to commerce in the Baltic, Gustavus had made a treaty with Denmark, which granted him a passage through The Sound, — a matter of prime importance. In the spring of 1628 he left Stockholm with thirty ships. Near Danzig he encountered seven of the city's vessels, of which he took five and sank one; and landed probably near Putzig. The Swedish fleet cruised opposite Danzig, but could not prevent the place from being victualed by Polish blockade-runners. The army was still concentrated near Dirschau, in its location of last year, but Gustavus desired to establish a foothold at some point nearer to Danzig ; he selected and personally headed a body of seven thousand męn, and, unexpectedly to the enemy, threw them across the Vistula, on a quickly constructed bridge, to the island called the Kleine Werder, which he took. This island gave him a better position from which to threaten and choke off the place. No serious fighting is spoken of ; very likely none occurred ; but in this respect there are many gaps in Swedish annals ; we have more data about Cæsar's battles than those of Gustavus. The Swede did not write commentaries ; and his dispatches are usually bare of military detail, though full of matter dwelt on at that day.

Without undertaking any serious operation, Koniezpolski endeavored to interrupt the siege by diversions against several of the towns held by the Swedes. He captured Mewe, again took Putzig, and, gradually approaching Danzig, hoped to effect something which might raise the siege. Gustavus detailed General Tott with a cavalry force to watch these operations. Tott fell into an ambush west of Grebin, but though surrounded by thrice his force, he cut himself out without harm ; he even captured some prisoners and flags, and brought in the news of the enemy's force. Unwilling to attack the Swedish army, Koniezpolski annoyed the besieging force materially, and Gustavus determined to rid himself of his interference. Immediately upon this affair of Tott, leaving a part of his forces before Danzig, he suddenly marched with the bulk of them on the Polish army, met and attacked it not far from his camp, — the exact locality, curiously, is not known, — and by his sharp initiative well kept up, the mobility of his foot and his vastly superior artillery, defeated it with a loss of three thousand men, four guns and fourteen flags, and drove it well up the Vistula. Koniezpolski himself fell, heavily wounded.

It is a grievous loss in the study of the life of Gustavus,

that so little is known of these Polish battles; so little of the siege of Danzig. Here was a general engagement with a high percentage of loss, and yet even the battle-field is neither named, nor can it be identified. This war was the monarch's schooling, as Gaul was Cæsar's, or Spain Hannibal's; but we know as much of Hannibal's Iberian, and much more of Cæsar's Gallic, battles than we do of these.

The king now tightened his grip on Danzig, by land and sea. It would soon have been reduced by hunger, had it not been for a serious flood in the Vistula, which drove the Swedes out of their trenches and camps, and forced Gustavus to raise the siege all but totally. And at the same time Sigismund came on the scene with heavy reinforcements for Koniezpolski, which complicated the situation still more.

Sigismund was more implacable than ever. Approaches from the Dutch states-general to bring about a peace were met with refusal. Leagued with the emperor, Spain and all the Catholic powers, and under the thumb of the Jesuits, he would listen to no argument. He looked forward to the probable arrival of a Spanish fleet in the Baltic as well as to an imperial auxiliary corps from Germany; he had received subsidies from both branches of the Hapsburgs, and the Polish parliament had voted him generous supplies. Moreover, as the emperor, in 1628, had succeeded in gaining the upper hand in Germany, Sigismund was emboldened by the failure of the Swedes at Danzig to hope, not only to drive them from Poland and Livonia, but eventually to carry the war into Sweden, and again lay claim to the throne of his ancestors.

After the failure of their own disjointed efforts, there had been but two sources from which the Protestants of Germany could expect assistance: from Gustavus, or from Christian of Denmark. They had enlisted the services of the latter to no great profit, and as it was inexpedient for Sweden to undertake two wars at the same time and the Polish king would not make peace, they could, for the moment, not count on Gustavus. But when Christian was driven back by Tilly and Wallenstein to the confines of Jutland, many of the Protestants again turned to the king with urgent appeals for help. Wallenstein had already selected Stralsund as the most available base for operations against Sweden or Denmark, and was blockading it. Such a threat to the Baltic had naturally brought Christian and Gustavus closer together, and the treaty they made included an agreement to defend the freedom of the Baltic. Christian went personally to Stralsund, provisioned it, and saw to its proper manning; and the Danish fleet destroyed several vessels sent by Sigismund to the help of Wallenstein. All this had occurred during the king's own blockade of Danzig; and finally Wallenstein was compelled by Stralsund's brave resistance, as well as by the command of the emperor, who disapproved of his generalissimo's obstinacy, to give up the blockade. This imperial reverse was in reality a Swedish victory; for it was due to the heroic defense of the town by the garrison which Gustavus had sent thither under Colonel Leslie.

The siege of Stralsund was so noteworthy a failure from every point of view that it alone, says Lossau, suffices to dispute the place of Wallenstein among remarkable generals. And yet Wallenstein was a great soldier. Did not Gustavus fail before Danzig?

The defense of Stralsund opened to Gustavus himself an important foothold for operations in Germany, as well as for the protection of the Baltic; and that he had well weighed this fact is shown in the treaty which he made with the city, one extremely favorable to it and of equal value to the projects of the king.

The imperial party paid small heed to Gustavus. Wallenstein by no means underrated the king, but he distinctly overrated himself. Had he stated the case as he saw it, he might have placed Gustavus next to himself among the coming captains of Europe, — *proximus, sed longo intervallo.* His structure of mind had not the self-confidence which accurately gauges the opposition while relying on its own powers; it rather possessed the self-esteem which arrogates all to its own capacity and allows nothing to the opponent. This was the secret of Wallenstein's great strength, and of his singular weakness as well. He won where self-assertion alone can win; when he met equal power, he lost.

The emperor did not keep Sigismund provided with money as had been agreed, and had Polish coffers not always been at a low ebb, the king might have found it more difficult to maintain his footing near Danzig. After the raising of the siege, Gustavus received considerable accessions of troops, including two thousand cavalry from Germany under Rhinegrave Otto Ludwig; but he was unable to bring the Polish army to a decisive battle on terms which he could accept. Koniezpolski confined himself to small operations and occupied strong positions; and Gustavus was fain to content himself with half measures. The Swedes took Neuenburg, Strasburg with much material, and Schwetz; and one detachment under Baudissin undertook a gallant raid to the gates of Warsaw, where it produced the utmost consternation, while Wrangel made a bold foraging expedition inland from Elbing. Later Baudissin was captured, but exchanged. The Poles made a few unimportant gains, and on one occasion actually surprised the Swedish army; but they failed to follow up their successes.

The singular political complications made the war in Germany drag slowly on. Having won his exceptional triumphs, the emperor, as we have seen, began tampering with Chris-

tian of Denmark, and finally (1628–29) a congress was held
at Lübeck, and May 22, 1629, peace ensued. From this
peace, Gustavus, king of Sweden, and Frederick, ex-elector
of the Palatinate, were expressly excluded. Gustavus had
sent his representatives to the congress, but Wallenstein had
arrogantly refused them admittance ; nor was any notice
taken of the king's protest by either the emperor or Wallenstein. Gustavus had at the time sent an embassy to Ferdinand ; but he recalled it when excluded from the Lübeck
Congress ; nor would he receive an imperial mission, because
in the accompanying documents the title of king had been
formally denied him. But he made a public demand for the
restoration of the *status quo ante bellum.* The refusal of
Wallenstein to recognize Sweden was one of the immediate
reasons of Gustavus undertaking the Protestant cause in Germany ; for it was the one thing wanting to convince him that
Sweden would shortly become involved.

The successes of the emperor and the many high-handed
acts of Wallenstein had the effect of bringing the Protestants
into warmer sympathy, and his brethren in Germany once
again turned to Gustavus for leadership. Distinct appeals
had been theretofore made in 1615, 1619, 1621 and 1622 ;
but never had the cause so sadly needed help, nor Sweden
been so nearly ready. The conditions seemed to drag the
king against his will into the contest which had been going
on for ten years. France had already flung herself in the
scale, out of antagonism to Spain and fear for the balance of
power in Europe, and had offered herself as intermediary
to procure a peace with Poland, so as to untie Gustavus'
hands. It was fully determined in Sweden, so early as February, 1629, that Gustavus should at no distant date move
to the assistance of Germany.

In the beginning of this year (1629), during the king's

absence at home, Wrangel fell upon the Polish army in its winter-quarters. The latter retired, but Wrangel followed, caught up with it at the village of Gurzno, near Strasburg, beat it, and drove it to Thorn, which place, however, he could not take. The Poles, severely oppressed by the burdens of the war, earnestly desired peace, but Sigismund was ready to consent to no more than a short truce even under the pressure of the Brandenburg and Dutch ministers ; and this truce even was so made as to be capable at any time of being broken.

Meanwhile an imperial army under Count Arnim, of seven thousand foot, two thousand horse and some artillery, was approaching to aid the Poles. Gustavus joined the Swedish army in June, about the time when Arnim made his junction with Koniezpolski at Graudenz. As Sweden was at peace with the empire, this was a gratuitous act of war by the emperor; it was really intended to retard the Swedish interference in Germany, and it accomplished its purpose. There was a considerable body of Swedish horse at Marienwerder, and this the king now reinforced with foot to meet the enemy's threat, sending at the same time a protest to Wallenstein for his breach of the comity of nations.

Gustavus had eight thousand foot and five thousand horse. Koniezpolski, with his much superior forces, determined to deliver battle. His plan was good, and might have been dangerous to any one not watchful. On June 27 he marched from Graudenz along the river flats towards Marienwerder, purposing to bear off to Stuhm and turn the left flank of the Swedes. But Gustavus had already concluded to retire to Marienburg, and his column was defiling along the Stuhm road. So soon as he was instructed as to Koniezpolski's march, he sent the rhinegrave with a body of eight hundred horse to protect the narrows between the lakes at Stuhm, so as to head off the enemy from the marching column and oblige them to make a long detour, and with strict orders not to bring on an engagement, but merely to occupy the enemy's

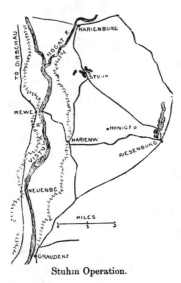

Stuhm Operation.

attention. The enemy's cavalry reached Honigfeld ; the king's orders were not obeyed, and when he shortly arrived with the rear-guard of his army, he found that the rhinegrave had attacked, fallen into an ambuscade, and been beaten with a loss of two hundred men. In his endeavor to sustain him, a hot combat of cavalry ensued. Gustavus again was in the thick of the fray, and narrowly escaped death or capture. A Polish cavalryman seized him by the shoulder-belt, but Gustavus slipped it over his head and escaped. His party was beaten back, but the defile at Stuhm was held, and the whole force regained Marienburg. He had lost a number of men, flags and guns.

The fault had lain with the landgrave ; but it appears from this engagement that Gustavus' light cavalry was not always as watchful as it should have been, or not always put to proper use. Perhaps the lack of enterprise on the part of Koniezpolski may have bred this carelessness. Nothing trains cavalry except an active enemy.

Gustavus' spirit was singularly elastic. Unable to sit still under defeat, he went again at the problem, and soon retrieved his disaster. The enemy advanced to the river Nogat, really a part of the delta of the Vistula. Gustavus moved upon them, and in a sharp and decisive encounter, defeated them with a loss of four thousand men. The details of the battle are not known. Some historians ignore it. But it is manifest that the campaign did not end with a defeat of the Swedes. The sole evidence of many of the operations of Gustavus lies in the dispatches from the army to the home government; and the king's singular modesty of statement robs the after-world of much it ought to know. His letter to Oxenstiern about the battle of Breitenfeld might be the description of a small cavalry combat. There were no war-correspondents in those days, and the Swedish officers were too busy with making history to write it. Fancy a battle in our day in which the enemy forfeits four thousand men being thus lost to fame! Triumphal columns are erected by some nations to perpetuate battles where the loss has been but a dozen! And yet this is not without parallel in modern days. Many of the actions about Petersburg in 1864 and 1865, where casualties ran up into the thousands, are barely recorded with a name; many outpost-combats where hundreds bit the dust are known only as "the picket-fight of such a date."

The ill-success of their late venture had a further tendency to make the Poles long for peace; and the barbarous conduct of the troops of Arnim, a pestilence which broke out in the camp of the allies and kept the country people from bringing in supplies, the growing fear of Gustavus, and the dwindling prospect of success combined to make Sigismund more tractable. Negotiations were opened in August, 1629, and, under the influence of the French ambassador, were ended in a six years' truce. This was signed, on October 5, at Stuhmsdorf; and by its terms Sweden retained all Livonia; Memel, Pillau and some other places in ducal Prussia; Braunsberg, Tolkemit and Elbing in Polish Prussia. Danzig remained neutral, but by a separate treaty agreed to pay two thirds of its customs into Gustavus' treasury. Sweden restored the rest of Poland and Courland to Sigismund. But in case no peace should result from the truce, Marienburg was to be again surrendered to Sweden, being meanwhile held by the elector of Brandenburg in trust. Gustavus was formally recognized as king, — a marked concession by Sigismund.

Richelieu no doubt had weight in bringing about this truce; he was the last ounce in the scale; but it is scarcely doubtful, even if France had not acted as intermediary, that Sigismund would have concluded peace. He and his subjects were exhausted by the war.

Thus, after eight years, ended the early wars of Gustavus Adolphus. The king had conducted six campaigns against Poland, and two against Denmark and Russia. These campaigns, not possessing the importance of his later ones, and lacking a record of their remarkable features, — for it is often the details which show up the military ability displayed in a campaign, — were yet what trained Gustavus in the habits of war, and permitted him to view the struggle in Germany from a broader basis of experience; they were a practical school in which he could teach his right hand the cunning it would so soon need on the European stage, and his army could be hardened into a body fit for its arduous task. He entered the Danish war a young and inexperienced leader of men; he emerged from the last Polish campaign ready equipped to prove himself in the coming two years one of the world's great captains.

In these campaigns Gustavus had observed the practical working of his new army organization, and learned *à fond* the then existing system of tactics and strategy. He was enabled to gauge the advantages of his own method, which, in the short remaining term of his life, he moulded into what was the origin of the modern art of war, — into what brought the world back to dispositions both intellectual and humane. These campaigns had been conducted against different peoples, — Danes, Russians, Poles, — and the king had gleaned varied experience. He learned the habits of different leaders and armies, and strove to adapt his own ways to theirs. His infantry underwent a good schooling against the large and excellent forces of Russian and Polish cavalry, and learned to protect itself against this arm. It was swift on the march, and steadier in defeat and victory than any imperial troops, even if no more stanch in battle than the Walloons of Father Tilly. His own cavalry the king had gradually improved by imitating the Poles, and by adding discipline and *ensemble* to it. There was superb horse on the other side, the Black Brigade, for instance, under its model cavalry leader, Pappenheim; but, headed by the king, the Swedish was as good. Had it earlier met the German cavalry, it could not have held head against it. Gustavus' artillery, much improved in organization, drill and technical knowledge, gave a wonderful account of itself. He had studied what the Turks had done, and had profited by their errors. They had got the biggest guns which could be cast; he made his handy, quickly served, and accurate of aim. Theirs were of all sizes and patterns; he reduced the matter to some sort of scale. There were heavy guns, needing thirty-six horses to transport; siege-guns, much smaller; and field-guns, six-, four- and two-pounders, the latter being handled by one horse. The regimental four-pounder could be fired faster than a musket; and the leather cannon, originally adopted for their small weight, were driven out by the monarch's light metal gun.

Swedish success was largely due to technical engineering and ordnance skill, which seconded the energy and ingenuity infused by Gustavus into the armies under his control. As

an engineer, he was far ahead of Wallenstein or Tilly. He
understood the value of field-works in their best sense; his
engineer companies were numerous; and by quickly building
works to protect his men, he would stand on ground the
enemy would abandon.

Under Gustavus' watchful eye, every branch of the service had grown in efficiency. Equipment, arms, rationing,
medical attendance, drill and discipline, field manœuvres,
camp and garrison duty, reached a high grade. Energy and
extra exertion were recognized; luxury was discountenanced;
the troops looked earnest, severe, but they were kindly. The
officers had all served from the bottom up, and had learned
to work and to obey. Promotion was by seniority and merit.
Justice was pronounced. Of the many Romanists in the
Swedish ranks, none complained of unfair treatment.

As in the little, so in the large. Gustavus treated each
country he entered with a strict eye to economics, instead of
sucking out its life-blood. The population made no complaints, and he could nourish and keep his men together in
camp, when the enemy must disperse in cantonments, and
run the risk of being destroyed before concentration.

In the seventeen years Gustavus had been king, each campaign had added to the skill and efficiency of the Swedish
army. There was no question of its distinct superiority over
any European army of its day. And chiefly was this shown
in substituting the idea of mobility for the old idea of weight.
Speed was the watchword of Gustavus' tactics; it was his
speed which won his victories. His motto was, " Action,
action, action ! "

In these campaigns, too, not only had Gustavus learned to
know his generals and men, but they had gauged their mon-
arch-leader; and there had arisen that mutual confidence,
esteem and affection which only the great captain effectually

commands. As there was no danger or labor which their general and king did not share, in which he did not bear an equal part, so the Swedish army saw in him a harbinger of victory, a sure protection in disaster; Gustavus' own character, bravery, religious ardor, honesty and humanity infused itself into every soldier in the army. Nothing can exaggerate the advantage which this good understanding between chief and army gives; no leader who lacks the divine spark ever reaches its full measure.

In listening to the last appeal of the Protestants to undertake their cause, Gustavus was actuated by faith in his religion, by an honest sense of the dangers and needs of Sweden, and by feelings in which personal or national ambition had no foothold. It is a difficult task to twist even isolated remarks or letters of the king into a semblance of personal ambition; it is impossible, from the whole of his utterances, to deduce any ambition but that of serving his country and his country's God. His address to the Estates in 1630 plainly shows his mood: "The Hapsburgs are threatening Sweden, and must be met instantly, stanchly. It is a question of defending the land of our sires. The times are bad, the danger is great. Let us not look at the unusual sacrifices and load we must all unite to bear. It is a fight for parents, for wife and child, for house and hearth, for country and religion." And the people's answer was as full of courage and of meaning as the king's address. It was like the upswelling of the old Roman burgess-blood when the unparalleled disaster of Cannæ threatened the state with annihilation; it was like the uprising of the North when the nation was threatened with disruption in 1861. Heavier taxes were willingly paid; individuals built and equipped vessels; every man laid aside his private broils and griefs, stood shoulder to shoulder and linked hands with his neighbor for God, King and Fatherland.

The openly expressed opinion of Wallenstein, — in a certain respect a measure of this great but arrogant man, — with regard to the undertaking of the king of Sweden to lead the Protestant cause in Germany, was well shown in his boast that he would "drive the Snow King from Germany with rods if he should dare to show his face there;" and Ferdinand, puffed up with his wonderful successes, echoed the opinion with: "So we have got a new little enemy, have we?" But Wallenstein knew better, if Ferdinand did not. His private correspondence and statements show a clear appreciation of the danger which the arrival of Gustavus threatened to his carefully erected structure. Alone, Wallenstein ruled Germany as its strongest warrior; with Gustavus there, he knew that he had a rival, he feared that he might find his master.

Albanese Horseman.

XII.

THE SWEDISH PERIOD BEGINS. JANUARY TO JUNE, 1630.

In twelve years (1618 to 1630) the emperor had overrun all Germany. No one had been found to hold head to Wallenstein and Tilly, and the Protestants turned in despair to Gustavus. It was a wrecked cause he was to champion, and none of the Powers lent active aid. Happily Wallenstein was put aside, and France was ready to pay money to check the dangerous rise of the Hapsburgs. Gustavus entered the lists. Whether Sweden should conduct a defensive or an offensive war was promptly settled by the king, sustained by his Estates and people. Though he placed too much reliance on the Protestant princes, his general calculations were just. The motives of the king were honorable; he had no personal ambition; he proposed to protect the interests of Sweden and of Protestantism, — and what Sweden needed was a " bastion " on the south shore of the Baltic, to enable her to control that sea. The winter of 1629–30 was a busy one. Munitions were collected, taxes equalized, troops raised and equipped under the new system, and seventy-six thousand men were placed under arms, of whom thirteen thousand were destined for Germany. This number the king expected to double by recruitment there, for the emperor had at least one hundred thousand men. What Gustavus took with him was a mere nucleus for accessions from the German princes.

BEFORE the beginning of the Thirty Years' War, Germany was about equally divided between the Protestant and Catholic princes; and when the former took up arms, the emperor's authority extended over not more than half of the territory which is comprised between the Rhine and the Oder, the Alps and the Baltic. At the expiration of twelve years of war (1618–1630) the entire territory named had been overrun by the imperial forces, save only the free towns of the north, Stettin and the fortress of Stralsund. The

Protestants had begun the war with encouraging prospects; they were now disunited and cowed. It was under these conditions that from many sources entreaties reached Gustavus to come to the rescue of his brothers in the faith; it was these conditions which the monarch faced in becoming the champion of Protestantism.

Gustavus had for at least two years foreseen that he must take a hand in the German imbroglio; early in 1629 such action was fully determined; but when, in 1630, he finally appeared upon the scene, he was called on to contemplate so wrecked a cause, that the boldest soldier with inexhaustible resources would scarce have cared to face it; while he stood almost alone, with the sole good-will of poverty-stricken Sweden at his back, and the very men who most ardently besought his aid were the ones who afforded him the least assistance. He had no earnest allies. Denmark was neutral if not an enemy, though Christian proffered friendship in public. France was uncertain, for though Richelieu was bound on the destruction of Austria and tendered subsidies, his method and his ultimate aim were not those of Gustavus. England could not be relied on. Holland, though the states-general approved its attitude, was jealous of Sweden's prestige in the Baltic, and was ready to take a hand in the matter from purely commercial motives, — ready to gain by Gustavus' defeat as much as by his victories. Lübeck and Hamburg limited their helpfulness to trading silver for the army-chest against Swedish copper. The dukes of Pomerania and Mecklenburg tendered assistance indeed, as well as the margrave of Baden, the administrator of Magdeburg and Landgrave William of Hesse; but we shall see how much this meant. And meanwhile Poland was bitter as gall, and Bethlen Gabor was dead. Not a power was ready to throw itself heartily into the scale; the German princes were at odds among themselves and cowed by overwhelming misfortune; and while the Hanse towns had armed to protect themselves, they cared not to aid Protestantism for any but selfish motives. Money was their god.

The one thing in Gustavus' favor was that the grasping measures of Ferdinand had for some time excited the gravest discontent among even the Catholic princes ; that the savage cruelties and ruthless devastation of the war had exasperated the Protestants and roused the horror of Europe. All potentates looked with distrust upon the growing manifestations of imperial ambition; for Austria now had at her feet the very liberties of Germany. Whither might not Ferdinand's greed of power lead him ? On the other hand, most of the Protestant princes, to save themselves, had accepted the emperor's sway ; some of them, led by personal motives, were in accord with him ; others again sought protection in a neutral bearing. A mere handful, notably the dukes of Hesse-Cassel and Brunswick-Lüneburg, as well as the free towns of the Hanseatic League, still maintained a bold front of opposition, while Stralsund had held her own with the aid of a Swedish garrison, and Magdeburg had stood a siege by Wallenstein. But with these few brave exceptions, Germany had bowed her head to the stroke, showing neither power nor will to withstand the imperial dictation, or to fight for her religion or independence. Ferdinand was master. The German princes would probably have gone over to him in a body, had they not feared his future policy. He had the entire matter in his grasp. But no man is all-wise ; Ferdinand foolishly quarreled with his electors on a side issue, and lost their loyal support, while the Edict of Restitution, issued in March, 1629, completed the break-up of confidence.

Not only were none of the other European powers anxious to come to Germany's assistance, but none of them were prepared to do so. England was busy with intestine disquiet, and in the end of the year made peace with Spain, which for once drew her closer to the Hapsburgs. The Netherlands were still at war with Spain, and the last thing they wanted was an inroad by the victorious armies of Wallenstein, Tilly or Pappenheim. Spain herself was Hapsburg, and were she not so, she had, in addition to the war in the Netherlands, the Mantuan imbroglio in Italy. Denmark had been beaten into peace, and then bought into neutrality for a price, and Christian was morbidly jealous of Gustavus, and ready to do anything underhand to thwart his plans. The Turks were an uncertain element. Brandenburg had sent troops to Poland, and had scarcely forgiven Gustavus' foray on her territory. Saxony felt bound by her oath to the emperor to resist armed aggression, while John George, the elector, was intent on peace at any price. The other Protestant princes were either frightened or reduced in means beyond power to help.

Only France and Sweden remained. Though France had at first inclined towards the emperor, or at least towards the League and Bavaria, when matters took too decided a turn in Ferdinand's favor, Cardinal Richelieu clearly saw that political gain lay in aiding the Protestants, so as to weaken the power of Austria ; but as Catholic France could not openly enter the lists on behalf of Protestantism, Richelieu preferred to use his influence with Sweden to take up the cause, relying for eventual results upon the location and healthy condition of the Swedish nation and the proven talents of its king.

The two marked features of European politics of the day were thus Austria's aggressiveness, and the change of the foreign policy of France.

It was not difficult to induce Gustavus to enter into this

plan. The Swedes, in his opinion, needed a " bastion " on the southern shore of the Baltic in order to maintain their supremacy on this sea; and Stralsund was just that. But Gustavus' demands were at first deemed too high by France. He asked a considerable lump sum down and six hundred thousand rix dollars a year as subsidy. This Richelieu declined, though his general course remained helpful, and he eventually came to Gustavus' terms.

Sweden was neither a populous nor a rich country. She numbered but a million and a half of souls, and her annual budget ran up to not exceeding twelve million rix dollars. But she made up in a great degree for this weakness in material resources by the simplicity and strength of her people, her well-regulated government and particularly her remarkable military organization. The army had been tried in its eight years' war against Denmark, Russia and Poland; and the genius of its king, sustained by the love and devotion of his people, and coupled to the strong Protestant sentiment of the nation, made Gustavus a noteworthy champion. Many reasons weighed with Sweden and the king. That the emperor had sent an army to help the king of Poland against him while he was at peace with the empire; that the Swedish embassy had been thrust from the congress at Lübeck and heaped with contumely, rankled deeply in Gustavus' nature. Sensible, frank and generous, he was yet sensitive in matters relating to his dignity, and prompt to resent any affront to Sweden. The oppressions of the Protestants appealed strongly to both king and nation. Danger unquestionably threatened Sweden now that Germany had succumbed, and Gustavus was ambitious to show that his country was not a cipher in the religious and political complications of Europe.

When the question came up as to whether Sweden should wage a defensive war within her own borders, or an offensive

war in Germany, many of the more conservative statesmen
inclined to the former view, notably the prime minister,
Oxenstiern. The emperor, said he, had one hundred and
sixty thousand veteran troops, while Protestant Germany was
exhausted. How could Sweden with her small army enter the
lists against such a host, and without aid? Better spend
money on a strong fleet and hold the south shore of the Baltic.
Oxenstiern's idea was perhaps not a mere inert defensive, for
he was willing to argue the other plan; but he proposed
to conduct any offensive which might be undertaken to the
east of the Oder, and to remain strictly on the defensive in
Pomerania. The king gave many reasons against this. His
idea was merely to observe the country to the east of the Oder,
and to resort to a stout offensive in north Germany. Sweden,
he argued, could count more than Oxenstiern would allow on
the aid of the Protestant princes and free towns of Germany,
if once upon its soil. The Hanse towns, which had held a
convention at Lübeck in November, 1629, where they had
agreed to arm for mutual defense, now sought alliance with
the several Protestant powers, and had made efforts to secure
the aid of Sweden. Stralsund must not be forsaken. Wallenstein had made a bid for the Hanse towns by flattery,
which failing, he had attacked Stralsund by force. This city
had shown the ability of the free towns to defend themselves,
and no time must be given for the idea of defense to grow
cold. Magdeburg had proven her stanchness. All were now
ready to aid. It was imperative for Sweden to hold the
German coast of the Baltic, and prevent the emperor from
building a fleet. An offensive war in Germany would cost
Sweden less than the defense of her own soil; and the saving
for her people of the atrocities of such a war as was being
waged on the mainland was a manifest duty. The defense of
Sweden could well be left to its militia and fleet, if a Swedish

army opposed the emperor in Germany. Delay was the most dangerous thing of all. Should he once become absolute master in Germany, the emperor could no longer be controlled, and Sweden would be in greater danger than ever.

In order to feel the pulse of the nation, the king convened in Upsala eleven of the leading Swedish senators; and on mature discussion of the case presented by the king, these men unanimously agreed that an offensive in Germany was the wiser course.

In the event, Gustavus was mistaken in his reliance on the willingness or ability of the Protestant princes of Germany to lend their aid; he had gauged them at too high a value, for they proved to be controlled by their fears or their selfish interests rather than by the good of their religion or their country. But he was not mistaken in his financial estimates; for in 1632 the war consumed only one sixth of the Swedish revenue.

The king's plan was comprehensive; and he never lost sight of the value of the sea. Unless he controlled the Baltic, he had no base whatsoever, and what he proposed was quite as much to equip a big Swedish fleet and a fair-sized Swedish army, as it was merely to land Swedish forces in Germany and there conduct a land campaign. That a base on the Baltic had no value without a powerful Swedish fleet no man saw more plainly than the king; for years he had striven for *dominium maris Baltici.*

Gustavus' motives in undertaking this war have been the subject of grave discussion and much disagreement. It cannot be alleged that they were purely religious, that it was solely as the champion of Protestantism that he risked so much. But it may be honestly claimed that he had no personal ambition to subserve. He was by birth and nature a Viking, a species of colonizing fighter; but he neither sought

foreign conquest nor foreign gold. Sweden later became over
lustful for both; but Gustavus strove first for the defense of
his fatherland, and next for the defense of his religion. He
has been accused of seeking to create a Protestant German
empire with himself as its ruler; but there is no tangible
evidence to sustain this view, while there is a multitude of
testimony to controvert it. No monarch ever had a more
intimate friend and confidant than Gustavus possessed in Axel
Oxenstiern, his chancellor, trusted adviser and one of his
able generals; nor was there ever a man in whom truth was
more ingrained. Many years after Gustavus' death, when the
subject first grew into a controversy, Oxenstiern wrote in a
private communication : " King Gustavus Adolphus wanted
the Baltic coast; he harbored the idea of some day becoming
emperor of Scandinavia, and this land was to contain Sweden,
Norway, Denmark to the Great Belt and the lands abutting
on the Baltic. With this in view it was that he first concluded a peace with Denmark, as favorable as it was then
possible to endure, and later one with Russia with regard to
the Baltic. He took the coast and river mouths from Poland
by seizing the lucrative customs. Then he attacked the Roman
emperor, and demanded as war-indemnity from the German
princes, to whom imperial lands should be given in exchange,
Pomerania and Mecklenburg. Denmark was also to be
clipped of all territory down to the Great Belt, and Norway
was to become ours. It was on these lines that this great
king intended to construct an independent kingdom. But
that, as the saying goes, he desired to be German emperor is
not true."

So unbounded was the confidence of his subjects that the
king had little difficulty in impressing his opinion on the
people, the Estates and ministry, and shortly the work began.
He opened negotiations with the anti-Hapsburg peoples. He

appointed his brother-in-law, Count John Casimir, his representative in Sweden, commissioned to act with the advice of the council and of Field-Marshals de la Gardie and Wrangel. He made arrangements for internal government for a long absence, leaving explicit instruction as to land administration, recruiting and taxes, loans, victual and war material for the future. He accumulated present moneys and supplies to accompany the army. He ordered new fortresses to be built on the coast opposite Denmark. He strengthened his fleet and built a number of transports.

There were great preparations in Sweden during the winter of 1629–30. The nitre and sulphur works were kept busy shipping to the powder-mills at Naka and Wätinge. Calculations were made for furnishing a ton and a half of powder per regiment per month, and about fifty cartridges per man, plus twenty-four hundred pounds of lead and thirty-six hundred pounds of match punk, of which the consumption was necessarily large. The armories in all parts of Sweden were driven; and armor, helmets, partisans, pikes, spades and picks were turned out by government and by private firms. Each regiment was to have issued to it five hundred and seventy-six muskets and bandoliers, four hundred and thirty-two sets of armor, four hundred and thirty-two pikes and one thousand and eight helmets and swords. In addition, forty-eight partisans were issued to the three officers and three non-commissioned officers of each of the eight companies, and sixteen drums to the regiment.

In order to equalize taxes so that the aristocracy should not escape, a mill-tax, or tax on corn, had been laid in 1625; in 1627 it was changed to a poll-tax; and now, in 1630, a war-tax was added. The income in 1630 was about twelve million rix dollars, of which three fourths was spent on the war; but in 1631 and 1632 the cost ran down to five and a half and two and a fourth million rix dollars ; for German and foreign subsidies began to help out.

The clergy preached the cause as heartily as the recruiting officers enforced it. All males from sixteen to sixty must report at the local rendezvous, and those who were not house-holders or who worked for wages were first enrolled. Of the rest, each tenth man was drawn by lot from those between eighteen and thirty, excepting miners, especially in the nitre and sulphur mines, and manufacturers of arms and ammuni-tion. Only one son was taken from a family ; a man having no sons was excused. On enlistment, papers in triplicate were made out, much as with us, and the men were subse-quently mustered in companies. The troops assembled at Kalmar, Elfsnabben and other places for shipment to general rendezvous, in May, 1630.

Arrangements had been made for raising men abroad as well as at home. Kniphausen and Spens were recruiting to good effect in England ; Falkenberg, in the Netherlands, had no luck. Many recruits were got from the mustered-out sol-diers of the late Danish war, and in Brandenburg, Poland and Danzig. In June, 1629, Colonel Morton arrived with two regiments of Scotchmen.

In the conquered towns of Livonia and Prussia there were still twelve thousand men. These were left as a reserve under Oxenstiern, who recruited them up to twenty-one thou-sand. Six thousand more, under Leslie, were in Stralsund and on the island of Rügen. Leslie was active in recruiting, and the Hanse towns furnished a few men. By the early months of 1630 there had been organized an army of seventy-six thousand men, of which forty-three thousand were Swedes ; and in the fleet were three thousand more. Of this total, thirteen thousand were destined for Germany, to which were added, by reinforcements during 1630, twenty-three hundred men from Sweden, twenty-eight hundred from Finland, two thousand from Livonia, thirteen thousand six hundred from Prussia, and the six thousand garrison of Stralsund, an aggregate of about forty thousand men. There were left in Sweden sixteen thousand men, in Finland six thousand five hundred, in the Baltic provinces five thousand, in Prussia seven thousand six hundred, — thirty-five thousand men in all.

The cost of the forty thousand men in Germany was estimated at eighteen hundred thousand rix dollars a year, or forty-five rix dollars per man. This amount varied during Gustavus' reign from forty-one and one third to fifty-two rix dollars per man per year. Cheap enough service for any class of men, and the Swedes were of the best.

Gustavus had no doubt that he would receive considerable accessions from the friendly princes of Germany; and men from the disbanded armies of Mansfeld and Brunswick, it was believed, only waited his arrival to join his standard in large squads. The armies of Denmark and Poland, lately mustered out, would furnish abundant recruits. His thirteen thousand men would, he calculated, be increased to a substantial body so soon as he placed foot on German soil. But as against the seventy-five thousand aggregate on Gustavus' muster-rolls, of which he led but thirteen thousand to Germany, Wallenstein and Tilly were yet afoot, with armies which easily reached a hundred thousand men.

Gustavus issued no formal declaration of war. The attack on his ally, Stralsund, made the war appear to him a defensive one. But certain negotiations between the king and the emperor, which Gustavus well knew would come to nothing, were carried on for a while through the intermediation of Christian of Denmark. Stettin, the capital of Pomerania, was being threatened by the imperial army, and Gustavus felt that he must save the town. He was ready to sail from

Elfsnabben, whither all the troops were forwarded, by the end of May, but adverse winds kept him in port three weeks. His forces were embarked on two hundred transports, protected by thirty men-of-war.

The mouths of the Oder were to be the point of debarkation, and Gustavus had made himself familiar with every rood of the country. From this point he proposed to seize, or treat with, the cities along the coast on either side of Stralsund, and especially Stettin, and make his base strong by a depot at the latter place, from whence he could advance up the Oder. The general plan was fully worked out; the details had to wait upon the conditions of the moment.

Pomerania had never been friendly, and had given aid and comfort to the imperialists; but when the news came that Gustavus would probably land on her shores, Duke Bogislav, a very old man, sent an embassy to Gustavus to pray him not to make a *sedes belli* on his territory. Gustavus answered, without mincing words, that on their own attitude depended his conduct to the Germans when he should have reached their shores. He should sail for Pomerania, establish himself within her borders, and use her as by her future acts she deserved to be used.

Before embarking, the king issued a proclamation appointing three days of public fasting and prayer for the success of the cause.

After making all arrangements for the government of his kingdom, Gustavus' three-year-old daughter Christina was accepted as his heir; to her all Swedes swore fealty, and the king left the fatherland in May, 1630, on what was to him and to all the world a holy mission, — to accomplish it, indeed, but never to return.

XIII.

GUSTAVUS LANDS IN GERMANY. JUNE TO AUGUST, 1630.

GUSTAVUS sailed May 30, and landed at the mouth of the Oder without opposition, the imperial generals retiring to Garz and Anklam. Occupying Usedom and Wollin, he set his fleet to cruise along the coast, advanced on Stettin, and though Duke Bogislav sought to preserve his neutrality, took and garrisoned it; upon which a favorable treaty was made, and the Swedes camped in Oderburg, near by. Every place taken was strongly fortified. As the enemy held the rest of the coast, the communication between Stralsund, Stettin and East Prussia was not secure, and Gustavus set to work to extend his holding, and to blockade the places along the coast which he could not take, while the enemy strengthened Garz, and there encamped the bulk of their force. The king first intended to secure his foothold and the line of the Tollense in his front; but while so operating, the enemy took Clempenow and Pasewalk, massacred the garrisons, and seized the Tollense. Oxenstiern, from East Prussia, was pushing out towards the king, who kept steadily at work making firm his standing on the coast; Magdeburg declared in favor of the Swedes, and Colonel Falkenberg was sent thither to take command.

THE troops were embarked June 9, 1630 ; and after a delay of three weeks, waiting for a favorable wind, the fleet set sail with its burden so precious to Protestant Germany. Heavy weather still further retarded its progress in the open off Stockholm ; a stormy passage ensued, during which the shipping beat about several days, and was with difficulty kept together; but it finally made land, and anchored July 4 in the lee of the island of Rügen, close to Usedom, near the mouth of the Peene River. The two hundred transports and men-of-war had aboard six thousand sailors, ninety-two companies of foot, one hundred and sixteen companies (half-squadrons) of horse, and eight hundred guns of all calibres. Denmark had recently made efforts to purchase the island

of Rügen, an acquisition which would have made a base at
the mouth of the Oder quite insecure for Sweden. For some
time the imperialists had held the bulk of the island, of which
a large part belonged to the city of Stralsund; and as it was
essential to clear the coast, it was determined by Gustavus
that Rügen should be recaptured. On March 13 Leslie
took the island of Hiddensee, and garrisoned it with three
hundred men; on the 29th he put over troops to Rügen, and
captured the works at the several landing-places out of hand.
The imperialists tried in vain to eject the Swedes, and at the
end of April retired wholly from Rügen, except a garrison
of three hundred men in one of the forts, which on June 7

The Landing-
place.

likewise fell. Rügen was thus secured to
the Swedes.

The imperial general, Torquato Conti, a
cruel man even among the wolves of that day,
and equally incompetent, was at Anklam,
twenty miles to the south. So soon as he
heard of the fleet being sighted, he sent detachments to light fires along the beach,
hoping Gustavus would believe that a large
hostile force was on hand. But the ruse
failed; Conti lost his best chance of dealing
the Swedes a hearty blow as they landed, and
his parties retired from the coast. Boats,
ordered some time before by Gustavus, were
on hand under control of his own officers;
the king headed the landing parties, and the troops were
disembarked on Usedom. As Cæsar is said to have fallen
when he reached Africa, so Gustavus, on landing here,
stumbled on the gang-plank, and slightly injured his knee;
but he is not recorded to have turned the matter into an
omen. The Swedish blood flowed too calmly to need such

adventitious aid. On putting foot on shore, he knelt and offered up unaffected prayer; then seized a spade, and began himself the work of intrenching a line to cover the landing. It took two days to disembark; the companies were successively set to work; an old line of defenses was occupied; new ones were drawn up, and soon the first intrenchments of Peenemünde, which place was included in the circuit, were completed. Victual issued to the men had been mostly consumed in the long delay and passage; provisions had been ordered to be collected in Stralsund, but the king found on hand only a small supply. It was not an encouraging beginning.

Gustavus was wont to speak his mind; and for this lack of provision he roundly held to task John Skytte, to whom he had committed the business; he moreover sent urgent dispatches to Oxenstiern, in Prussia, to hurry forward supplies; and feeling reasonably secure, on July 28 he sent six men-of-war and thirty-six other vessels to the chancellor for their transportation.

Further to protect from inroads the coast already occupied, Gustavus ordered a suitable naval force to cruise between Travemünde and Rügen. Two days after landing, he took twelve hundred musketeers and a small body of horse, and started out southerly towards the region opposite Wolgast to reconnoitre the country. Arrived there, he found that the imperialists had built a fort on the island to protect the crossing. Reconnoitring the rear of the fort from the water, and sending back for a force of four thousand men, and all the horse which had already got mounted, Gustavus prepared to take the place; but the imperial garrison retired to the mainland.

On July 11 Gustavus left a thousand musketeers in the fort, and with three thousand foot and twenty-five hundred

horse set out to sweep Usedom clear of the enemy. The
imperialists had built two forts to protect the passage from
Usedom to Wollin across the Swine inlet. On the Swedes'
approach the garrison fled over to Wollin, burned its boats

Oder-Elbe Country.

and the Wollin defenses, and retired to the back of the
island. Gustavus managed to get boats, put across to Wollin, garrisoned the fort, and made after the fugitives as far
as the Divenow inlet, but was too late to prevent their burning the bridge across it. Having thus secured the mouths
of the Oder, the king returned to headquarters in Usedom.

No sooner landed than Gustavus incorporated in his army five thousand of the garrison of Stralsund. He had made good progress; for not only did his possession of Stralsund, Usedom and Wollin secure the mouths of the Oder, but it gave him an almost certain claim to Stettin, the capital of Pomerania, still in the hands of Duke Bogislav. The entire coast of north Germany, save Stralsund, the island of Rügen, what Gustavus had taken and Stettin, was held, however, by the imperialists. Happily, Wallenstein was away, and no one made any sensible effort to arrest the Swedish advance.

Pomerania is divided into two parts by the Oder, and Stettin, from its position, was a natural capital of the duchy. It had been besieged by the imperialists, but without success. General Savelli was in the country southeast of Stralsund, while Conti was on the west bank of the Oder. When the imperial generals saw that the Swedes had actually landed, they retired, Savelli to Anklam and Conti up the Oder to Garz on the left and Greifenhagen on the right bank. This gave Gustavus a chance to thrust himself in between the two parts, and he made arrangements to advance on Stettin.

In April, before leaving Sweden, the king had sought to influence this well-fortified city in his behalf, and we have seen that Stettin had stoutly defended itself against the imperialists. While Conti was lax, Gustavus was active. He left Colonel Leslie in command of Wollin, General Kagg of Usedom, and both under Kniphausen, to whom was committed the general supervision of the territory so far taken; he detailed officers to patrol the coast to secure all possible landing-places; and went in person to the southern part of Usedom near the Swine, to collect boats on which to ship a suitable force for an advance on Stettin. On July 18 he had seventy-four companies, eight thousand seven hundred and twenty-three men, ready to be shipped. On July 19 they

were put aboard such vessels, fifty-one in number, as were
of suitable draught to sail up the river. Next day the fleet
made Stettin by noon, and Gustavus landed part of the

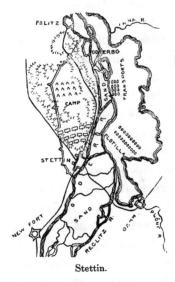

Stettin.

troops near the castle of Oderburg below, where he took up
a good position.

One would expect to see the
Evangelical powers of Germany
unite to receive Gustavus with
open arms. Nothing shows their
supineness more than the fact
that, save only Stralsund, —
and this was held by his own
garrison, — not a city, not a
prince, not a circle, did aught
to welcome the champion they
had called. Every one waited
to see how his perilous undertaking would result, before com-

mitting himself to the Swedish monarch's support. It was
an ill beginning; had not Gustavus been of a buoyant nature,
he might have faltered now; but worse was yet to come.

Pomerania would have liked to remain neutral, and
Bogislav tried his old tactics to influence the Swedes to leave
him so; but Gustavus would none of it. Colonel Damitz,
the commander of Stettin, under orders of the duke, declined
to admit the Swedes; in fact, threatened to fire on the flotilla
if it should approach closer. He sent a drummer as bearer
of a message, who was speedily turned back with answer that
Damitz should come himself, as the king of Sweden was not
in the habit of recognizing messages from men of regimental
rank. The colonel came with some ambassadors from the
duke, but they had no authority to allow the occupation of

the city; nor was any headway made until the king told Bogislav in so many words, at an interview which was shortly held, that he would countenance no neutrality on the part of the Germans, and that he had made suitable arrangements to take Stettin by force if not willingly yielded. Neither would he tolerate delay. "Every procrastinator is not a Fabius," said he. Gustavus already divined that the anticipated German support would not be forthcoming, and he proposed to handle this lethargic temperament without gloves. Stettin was given up.

The Swedish troops, owing perhaps to the lateness of the hour on that day, did not march into Stettin through the city gates, but through some incomplete defenses, and took formal possession on July 20. As the imperial forces were gathering near by at Garz, Gustavus would not prejudice his position by a minute's loss of time.

A treaty was concluded by which Swedish influence was made predominant in all matters, commercial and political, and three thousand men of the Pomeranian garrison of Stettin, under Damitz, were taken into the Swedish service as the "White Brigade." They proved to be excellent troops. The city of Stettin was garrisoned by three regiments and three companies of the Swedish guard. Having paid a goodly sum of money, Bogislav was permitted to resume nominal sway in Pomerania. The real control remained with the Swedes.

This acquisition of Stettin was a vast gain for Gustavus, and an equal detriment to Ferdinand. So far the foothold had been got without the loss of a man. Gustavus had secured his base of operations, and there shortly came an accession of troops from Prussia, from disbanded men who had served with Mansfeld or under the Danish flag, and from other sources. The conditions were such that a man could earn his bread as a soldier with greater safety from the perils of war than as a farmer, and many sought refuge in the ranks. These new enrollments ran the effective of Gustavus' army up to twenty-five thousand men.

After having thus yielded to Gustavus, Bogislav could scarcely make his peace with the emperor, though he with good right claimed that the imperial troops had abandoned him. Pomerania was pronounced rebellious, and the cruelties of the imperial forces were redoubled, a fact which added to Gustavus' welcome as a possible deliverer.

About this time there are said to have been several attempts to assassinate the Swedish king, prompted by fanatical Roman Catholics; but such matters have no special interest for us here.

Gustavus' habit was to secure his every step. A notable engineer, he put his knowledge into daily practice. Stettin, in lamentable condition, was at once taken in hand, and its fortifications strengthened according to the best art. Leslie had been ordered to do the like by Stralsund, as well as to fortify Bergen, the chief city of Rügen, to restore the works at the ferry, to erect forts at several important places, to make strong the camp at Peenemünde, and to fortify all the villages on Usedom. Wollin and Cammin opposite were to be placed in a state of good defense; the Divenow to be held by redoubts; and the bridge to the mainland to be rebuilt, and strengthened with a bridge-head.

The works of Stettin were extended to beyond Oderburg, with trenches, redoubts and well-devised lines, and near Oderburg was erected a large camp. In four days, by using the entire laboring population, the work was substantially done, and the army quartered there, except the three garrison regiments in the town.

Gustavus had brought only foot to Stettin. The cavalry —

thirteen companies under Colonel Teuffel — had been ordered
to follow with one thousand musketeers, by way of the bridge
at Wollin. The march of Teuffel was somewhat delayed;
and Gustavus, growing anxious, sent out a scouting party to
see what had become of the column. In this party was an
officer who had formerly been an imperialist. He now
deserted, and gave the enemy all the news he had been able
to gather; but though the imperialists broke up on July 23,
to intercept Teuffel, this officer headed them off and reached
camp in safety.

To celebrate worthily his successful landing Gustavus
appointed July 23 as a day of prayer, and it was duly
observed throughout the army.

While it is true that Gustavus had strongly established
himself on the Oder, there was still a deal left to be desired.
The imperialists held the whole country into which he had
thus driven a wedge; they extended in a huge semicircle
around his position at Stettin, from Colberg on the east, which
was held by a big detachment, to Wolgast on the west, where
troops were assembling; while the camp which they had established above Stettin, at Garz and Greifenhagen, allowed them
to make a diversion on any point along the Oder — say Pölitz,
or the mouth of the Ihna — from which they might cut off
the Swedes from Stralsund and the Peenemünde camp.

The town of Damm, opposite Stettin, was an important
point commanding the east branch of the Oder. On July 22
Gustavus sent Count Brahe with his squadron to seize the
place; and this drew within the Swedish lines the entire Oder
stream and the mouth of the Plöne River. As an outpost a
fort was begun between Stettin and Garz, and large stores
were accumulated in Stettin. Damitz was told off to take
Stargard, which capitulated after a short struggle. Treptow
and Greifenberg were shortly after taken; Damitz seized

Sazig in the beginning of August; and Naugart and Plate were captured. This series of operations gave the Swedes the possession of the territory inclosed by the Oder, Plöne and Rega rivers, and cut Colberg off from Garz and Greifenhagen. Each place taken was strengthened and garrisoned.

In reconnoitring towards Garz on one occasion, Gustavus again subjected himself to undue risk. He rode ahead with an escort of twenty horsemen, followed by a second detachment of seventy, and entering a defile not previously explored, he fell into an ambush, his escort was overpowered, and he himself was captured. His captors did not know him, and as good luck would have it the rear squadron rode up in season to rescue him. It was by mere chance that he had not been cut down.

Gradually the king extended his grasp towards Oxenstiern in Prussia, whom he ordered to send an able officer to occupy the Stolpe country, while he himself proposed to invest Colberg. Rügenwalde, by a lucky accident, was seized by a force of three small Scotch regiments from Pillau, under Colonel Munroe. This body, sent out on another errand, had been shipwrecked; but by a combination of daring and good sense, Munroe contrived to turn ill into good fortune, and seized the town. He won warm commendation from the king.

On the other hand it is related that an enterprising Swedish colonel conceived the project of a sudden attack on an outlying post of the enemy's at Garz; but, not possessing the virtue of silence, his plan leaked out, the enemy heard of it, and the attack was beaten back with loss. Though the officer brought in two stands of colors, the king gave him a sharp reprimand on the score of allowing his plan to become known. No courage or good conduct could excuse an idle tongue, said he.

Quite as important as the closing in on Colberg was to

reach out overland towards Leslie in Stralsund. Gustavus was theoretically well placed, with Oxenstiern on his left and Leslie on his right; but practically he was not certain in his communications with either. Only by water could he surely reach them. The imperialists still held Uckermünde and the Peene country, Anklam, Wolgast and Greifswalde. Especially Anklam was important, as it threatened Usedom, and here, on Gustavus' landing, Savelli had taken up his stand. But the imperialists were lacking in wisdom. Lest Gustavus should advance south from Stettin, the bulk of the forces in the Peene country were drawn into the Garz-Greifenhagen position, and Gustavus ordered Kagg from Usedom to occupy Anklam. So little could he understand the fatuity of the imperialists, that in the same breath he cautioned Kagg against a possible *ruse de guerre.* Anklam was taken and at once fortified; though as the population was not favorable to the Swedes, the work was slow.

Uckermünde was also occupied; and Barth, near Stralsund, fell to Gustavus without effort. Wolgast, one of the very important places, as it held the key to the road from the Swedish camp at Peenemünde to the continent, capitulated to Kniphausen, July 28; but the garrison retired to the castle, and held out with stubborn courage till August 16. Greifswalde seemed no longer tenable for the imperialists; and yet it held out.

The result of these manœuvres was practically to control the coast from Stralsund to Wollin on one side of the Oder mouth, and the shutting in of Colberg on the other.

Still Gustavus' occupation was far from being a perfect one. His main army lay in three detachments: his own at Oderburg and Stettin; Kagg's basing on Usedom, as a link in the chain; Kniphausen's on Peenemünde or Stralsund. Until all three were so placed as to be able to act as one body, Gustavus would not rest content. Nor would the possession of Anklam suffice. Unless the Swedes held the line of the Tollense, they could scarce present such a front to Savelli as to prevent his puncturing their defense. And though Stolpe alone would not control Farther (eastern) Pomerania, this section might wait. Hither (western) Pomerania was of greater importance, and this the king set out to occupy.

Such, then, was the first problem before Gustavus could venture on a march to Mecklenburg, which was one of his early projects. Kagg had already got a footing on the Peene, but as the imperialists might at any moment move on him, or on Kniphausen from the Mecklenburg garrisons, because they held the fords over the Tollense at Treptow and Demmin, Gustavus gave Kniphausen instructions to move forward on all places in his front; while Kagg was so to operate as to seize the line of the Tollense and prevent Kniphausen from being taken in flank while he pushed out from Stralsund. The joint operation would forestall reinforcements to the places they might attack.

A small Swedish outpost had already been pushed as far as Clempenow, and on August 12 Savelli, from Greifswalde, where he still was, sent a detachment to watch it. So soon as he heard of the fall of the Wolgast fort, he himself broke up from Greifswalde, and at the head of nearly all his force marched, by way of Demmin, on Clempenow, receiving on the way a reinforcement from Garz. On August 28 he stormed Clempenow. The garrison of barely a hundred men — far too small a force to put where it was — defended itself with true Swedish heroism; nearly the whole number fell; one officer and six men surrendered. This gave Savelli control of the Tollense region, and he at once strengthened Demmin, Loitz and Clempenow, while he garrisoned Trep-

tow, Neu-Brandenburg and Friedland. By this salient, basing
on the Tollense and with apex at Greifswalde, the Swedes
were thus held back to the coast, and Kniphausen feared that
Savelli would push on Anklam.

But Savelli had another idea. It was not so much a strategic success as a momentary triumph he desired. The small
and unprotected town of Pasewalk was held by a hundred and
fifty Swedes as an outpost to Stettin. It should have been
occupied in greater force, but Gustavus felt that he needed
all his troops in Oderburg, especially as he was organizing a
movement to Mecklenburg, and was reluctant to eat up his
aggregate in garrisons. For the moment, indeed, he was in
Stralsund ; and it is possible that he did not know how small
a force there was. Savelli sent to Pasewalk a body of a
thousand men, and on a foggy morning in early September
the imperialists surprised the place, of whose condition they
had learned by the treachery of some townsmen. The citizens who were on duty fled at the first assault ; and the
Swedes were left to defend themselves in scattered detachments against the overwhelming force. Nothing could be
done to save the place. They fell, arms in hand, to the last
man, and the town was burned to the ground.

The Swedes and imperialists could boast of about even
luck, but the Swedes had illustrated the noble qualities
infused into them by their monarch.

On the other side of the Oder, Oxenstiern was at the head
of the reserves in Pillau and Elbing. To open proper land
communications with him, and to afford safe transportation
for reinforcements and victual from there, Cammin and Colberg had still to be taken. The duty of clearing the country
between the Oder and the Elbing region was now intrusted
to Kniphausen, with whom Oxenstiern coöperated. According to the then military idea, that every strong place should

be either taken or observed before any advance could be made beyond it, this was no easy business.

It had been originally agreed between Bogislav and the imperialists that the two most important fords of the lower Oder, Garz and Greifenhagen, should remain in the hands of the Pomeranian troops. On Gustavus' landing, Conti had forcibly demanded admittance to these places ; the commandants yielded, and moving in, Conti strengthened the works, and imagined that he was after a fashion blockading Stettin. Astride the river, he lay strongly intrenched in the Garz camp on the left bank of the Oder, connected with the right bank by a bridge and a bridge-head, whose approaches were covered by the little town of Greifenhagen. Though his strength did not warrant Conti in interfering with the king's operations on the coast line and lower Oder, yet Garz and Greifenhagen were really the gates of Brandenburg, and merely to hold them was a benefit. All Conti pretended to do was to ravage the neighboring country, and to attempt to throw succor into Colberg. At the same time a small imperial force was assembling in western Mecklenburg.

It is no part of our province to detail the fiendish devastation, burning, rapine and murders of the imperial troops. Scarce a valuable within reach escaped these licensed thieves, scarce a woman escaped their lust ; not a home but was broken up, not a family but was ruined. The elector of Brandenburg issued an edict calling on all persons to arrest marauders, or, failing ability to do this, to shoot them down. But the peasantry was helpless. What could an unarmed countryman do against prowling ruffians armed to the teeth ?

In early August, under Christian William, the dispossessed administrator, who had secretly returned, Magdeburg rose in revolt against the imperial rule and declared in favor of a

Swedish alliance. The uprising was not cleverly managed, nor had Gustavus, unprepared for distant business, desired such early action; and no sooner had Christian William taken the first step than he called on the Swedes to help him take the second. Gustavus sent him Colonel Falkenberg, with instructions to do all that was possible to put Magdeburg in a state of perfect defense, and hold it for the Protestant cause. The king was preparing to march to Mecklenburg; but Magdeburg was another thing; it was but one factor in his larger calculations, not the main objective of a movement. Nor was the road thither open to him. Just now the question of good winter-quarters was occupying his thoughts. To extend his possession of the coast, so as to gain a foothold on the Elbe and parley with Hamburg and Lübeck, was on his programme, but not yet reached. Magdeburg was important, but it was not the one important thing, and it was far removed. Christian William looked at the Swedish plan of campaign from the narrow standpoint of his own interest; Gustavus kept the whole theatre of war in his eye.

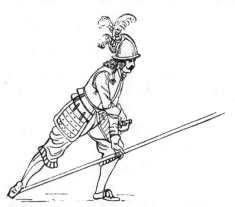

Pikeman of Thirty Years' War.

XIV.

GUSTAVUS ATTACKS THE ENEMY. SEPTEMBER TO DECEMBER, 1630.

MECKLENBURG had been given to Wallenstein, and Gustavus proposed to reinstate the dukes, as well as reach out towards Lübeck and Hamburg, Magdeburg, Hesse-Cassel and Lauenburg. He left Horn on the Oder, returned to Stralsund, and headed a column on Rostock and Wismar. He captured Ribnitz, but as the enemy threatened his holdings south of Stralsund, he advanced no further, and returned to his "bastion." Tilly now replaced Wallenstein, whose arrogance had given general dissatisfaction, and hosts of the latter's disbanded men enlisted with the Swedes. The king returned to Stettin, whence he dispersed a large imperial force near Demmin, and shortly after visited the siege of Colberg, from which he had beaten back several relief parties. Though contemplating an advance to the Elbe, he deemed it wise to complete his bastion first, and not to close the year without some handsome stroke; he made careful preparations to attack Greifenhagen and Garz, fell suddenly on them, carried them by storm, and drove the imperialists headlong up the Oder towards Cüstrin. This was a marked success. The king now practically held the entire coast line of Pomerania, and out to East Prussia, and had a wedge firmly driven into Germany along the Oder. His standing for the coming year was good, if only some of the German princes would join him.

So soon as Gustavus had made his base secure, he contemplated a movement into Mecklenburg to restore his cousins, the dukes, whose territory had been given to Wallenstein for his services against northern Germany; to open up connection with the duke of Hesse-Cassel, who, so far, was the only German prince who had volunteered active aid, with the administrator of Magdeburg, who asked for assistance, and with the duke of Saxe-Lauenburg, who promised it. Lübeck and Hamburg were also on his programme; and while the route proposed was not direct, it was the only one he could

pursue without the permission of the electors to cross Brandenburg and Saxony. The king had been up to Wolgast and
Stralsund, but had returned early in September.

The imperialists held Wismar and Rostock, towns which
Gustavus was anxious to secure, as this route would enable
him to provision himself for the winter and to keep the imperial forces from the coast near the lower Oder. Before moving towards Mecklenburg, Gustavus made a reconnoissance to
ascertain whether he could push the enemy from Garz. But
he found their camp so strong that for the moment he declined
the attack. It looks as if it would have been wiser to dispose
of the imperial general in his front before undertaking an
advance apparently so eccentric as one towards Mecklenburg.
But Gustavus saw that as Conti was bound to remain, like a
mole, buried within his fortifications, it was safe to disregard
him ; he recognized the danger in the enemy's holding Rostock and Wismar, which ports were necessary to his scheme
for controlling the shore of the Baltic so as to exclude an
inimical or even neutral fleet ; he believed that a handsome
diversion elsewhere would aid eventual operations on the
Oder ; and he must carefully consider the matter of winter-
quarters, for which purpose Mecklenburg was well adapted.

General Gustavus Horn had, in August, brought reinforcements from Finland and Livonia, and him the king left with
a large part of the army in Stettin, giving him orders to act
on the defensive, forward what reinforcements he could collect, and in case of being attacked by overwhelming odds to
retire towards his chief. He might use his time in making a
diversion on Greifswalde, which ought to be had before spring,
so as to keep communications open between Stettin and Stralsund. Should the Garz army attempt an operation in force
towards the king, Horn was to let the Greifswalde project go,
and march to his assistance.

The king left Stettin by boat, September 4, with three thousand men, and reached Wolgast the next day. He expected to take over some troops from Teuffel and the Finlanders, and calculated that the " Hamburg" and "Lübeck" regiments, with some forces from Prussia, would give his column not far from nine thousand foot and four thousand horse. But he had pitched his expectations too high. Purposing to move by sea on Rostock, it not only turned out that there were not ships enough, but the reinforcements from Prussia were not at hand; there was a deal of sickness in camp, and supplies and money came in slowly. The enemy was growing stronger in Garz, and Teuffel was needed in Stettin. Worse still, apathy reigned in a population which should have risen *en masse* to welcome Gustavus; the Germans had seen their hope so constantly fail, they had been so woefully ground under the imperial heel, that they dared not afford aid and comfort to their new champion.

Ribnitz.

It was September 9 when Gustavus reached Stralsund. The troops followed six days later, and were embarked; but rough weather holding them aboard for nearly three weeks, about every sixth man was ill, and the cavalry well-nigh exhausted. Under stress of these adverse circumstances, Gustavus substituted a land invasion for the one by sea, and put his men and material ashore.

From Stralsund the column headed for Mecklenburg, the frontiers of which were stoutly held by Savelli. Passing Barth, the Recknitz was reached, where in the morass made by the river near its mouth lay the village of Dammgarten, while on the further side of the river, in Mecklenburg, approachable by a ford from Dammgarten, was Ribnitz. The country had been wasted by the imperial forces; so much so that the king was not only called on in many places to distribute corn to the famishing peasantry, but to refrain from victualing in others. He paid in coin for all that the soldiers needed and could collect.

Dammgarten, though possessing a tower of some strength, was held but by ten men, who at once gave it up, and on September 25 General Banér marched in. In Ribnitz were one hundred and fifty foot and two hundred horse, and the ford was protected by a redoubt in the marsh, with a ditch twenty-five feet wide and fifteen feet deep, a palisaded wall, eighty men, and a number of guns. Two smaller redoubts flanked the main one. Expecting the fleet to cooperate in taking Rostock and Wismar, Gustavus had no siege-guns with him; bad weather still kept the ships at Stralsund, and only the light fieldpieces were on hand. To avoid this redoubt, Gustavus threw two pontoon bridges across the river near the mouth, and though the imperial garrison sought to disturb the work, on the 26th it was ready, and next day Gustavus appeared before Ribnitz.

The enemy's horse came out for a skirmish, but meeting a bold front they retired towards Rostock. The foot resisted for a short hour, when the gates were blown open by petards, the place entered, and the imperialists taken prisoners. The heavy guns having arrived, the garrison in the redoubt which had refused to surrender was battered out. A foothold in Mecklenburg was thus obtained, and the troops were given a short rest in Ribnitz.

Here the king learned that the imperial forces were assembling in the Demmin country, where Montecuculi — later so distinguished — had arrived with a body of horse; and believing that they were about to follow him into Mecklenburg to head off his further advance, he ordered Horn to send him all the troops he could spare, keeping in Stettin and Anklam only what was needed for defense.

Meanwhile on October 2, with one thousand men, Gustavus set out to capture a small but strong fort near Wüstrow, on the inlet known as the Binnensee; next day the garrison surrendered, and the ground so far occupied was duly strengthened.

The imperialists had formerly got possession of Rostock by a ruse. It was guarded only by its citizens, and the imperial troops asked permission to march through the place to save an inconvenient circuit. Once in, they remained, and held the town for Wallenstein. It was a place of importance; this port and Wismar once secured by the Swedes, they would control the entire coast from Stralsund to Lübeck, on the friendship of which city Gustavus placed considerable reliance. Ribnitz was a sort of outwork to Rostock; but the capture of the latter place would consume time; the situation in the Demmin region in the centre of his line appeared to require the king's personal attention more than a siege on an extreme flank; and he renounced his present design upon Rostock and turned to other business.

While Gustavus was threatening Mecklenburg, the imperialists had not been idle. Conti had tried the strength of the Stettin works, but was driven back with a loss of three hundred men; and some slight exchanges occurred between foragers, with attempts on Damm and Gollnow, and on Buchholtz near Damm. To watch Gustavus' operations so as to join him if necessary, and to conduct the small war thus forced upon him, kept Horn busy enough.

Gustavus had a singularly fertile brain, and his correspondence details a variety of plans which from time to time he considered, generally rejecting all but that which was at the moment most available. Though the matter has no bearing on the manœuvres which now ensued, it is interesting to follow out the king's ideas. His general scheme before pushing the imperial army to battle — always his ultimate object — was to stimulate the activity of the friends of the cause, and to encourage the arming of the Protestant population all over the theatre of war. He hoped from available resources, the Netherlands, Prussia, Poland, Livonia, as well as Germany, to increase his aggregate force to seventy or eighty thousand men, not counting allies. With this strength he had considered a specific scheme of moving in five different armies forward from along the whole coast line, Colberg, Stralsund, Lübeck, the Weser and Bremen, in more or less concentric lines, upon the heart of Germany. This was an apparently dangerous division of forces, warrantable only on the assumption that some of these columns would be those of allies whose active aid he could not otherwise hope to obtain, and who would for the time being assist in a negative if not a positive way. In effect it was to be an operation on two lines: one through central Germany and one up the Oder, straight on Vienna.

This five-column plan is spread out in a letter to Oxenstiern from Ribnitz, dated October 8, 1630. Horn and Teuffel, says the king, should have forty-six thousand men, march up the Oder, holding Brandenburg and Silesia; the king with forty-two thousand, the " Royal Army," would base on Pomerania and Mecklenburg; the fourth should be a Magdeburg army of ten thousand men, whose task should be the Elbe country; the Hanse towns, led by the archbishop of Bremen, should coöperate with Hamilton and Leslie, both of whom were expected to raise considerable forces. These columns, a hundred thousand and over strong, would, thought the king, be sure to compel a peace. This was a sanguine view of the case, and though it was based on a strength which Gustavus was fairly warranted in believing that he could raise during the coming winter, it was perhaps too rose-colored a scheme ; and to do Oxenstiern justice, he saw this aspect of the plan, and told the king that he would find his means unequal to it. The chancellor was, unquestionably, an able man, much more conservative than the king, and his best adviser. His weakness lay in his sometimes leaning towards a defensive policy, and with all his strong sense, he lacked the divine afflatus. His own plan, which in this same month he worked out with a great deal of care, was to garrison Pomerania with twelve thousand men ; to project a column of fourteen or fifteen thousand men along the Oder through Silesia, under Horn ; while the Royal Army should consist of over thirty thousand, and be manœuvred to meet the imperial forces on the Elbe.

The king in this instance gave heed to Oxenstiern's ideas, especially as the late harvest in Sweden had not been up to the usual mark, and taxes lay heavily on the people. His own plan had been but tentatively drawn up; for, long before it could be inaugurated, there came about a marked change in the existing conditions, very much in his favor, and still he did not attempt to carry it out.

A congress in Ratisbon to devise means to put an end to the war in Germany had been sitting nearly six months, and it ended, in November, 1630, in the emperor's investing Count Tilly with supreme command in the place of Wallenstein, against whom the Catholic potentates had conceived a great prejudice, for his unmeasured assumption and the utter license of his troops. The result of this change was that a large part of the army, enlisted for service under Wallenstein's personal command, was disbanded, and the total imperial forces were reduced to some seventy thousand men, of which the bulk were in southwestern Germany, or engaged in the war in Italy. Thus in the early part of the German campaign, the emperor was unable to meet Gustavus' invasion with sufficient forces. Considerable numbers of these disbanded men enlisted under Gustavus' banner ; and it is as wonderful a thing to say of the king that he made good soldiers of men spoiled by Wallenstein's fearful indiscipline, as to tell of Hannibal that he made out of the riff-raff of southern Italy soldiers who could stand up against the legions of Marcellus and Nero. Thus reinforcements came from an unexpected quarter; and Falkenberg's men began to come forward from Holland. Had Gustavus intended a definite adherence to the five-column plan, he would have been in better shape to carry it out than in October he could have hoped to be.

It appears singular to us that upon the displacement of Wallenstein the disbanding of substantially all the imperial army should follow. But the method of raising troops at that day was peculiar. Wallenstein no doubt had, with each regimental commander, a personal contract under which the latter served and received pay for himself and his men; and this contract fell when Wallenstein ceased from command. Many who had been in the imperial service before may have remained as a nucleus of a fresh army ; many may have been sent in small bodies to other armies ; but most of the men were mustered out with their general, and were at liberty to enlist where they would. It was all one to them.

The chief complaint made by every member of the Congress of Ratisbon was the ill behavior of Wallenstein's forces, from whose depredations friends and foes alike had suffered ; and after his dismissal, orders were issued to keep the men under severe restraint; but troops which have once enjoyed a loose rein cannot be fully brought in hand; and Germany was never freed from the worst horrors of war until her territory was occupied by Gustavus; nor indeed after the king's death was humanity in war an element recognized by his successors, or if recognized, enforced.

At the time of Wallenstein's dismissal, it is said that Gustavus approached him through Count Thurn to negotiate for his services; but this will be referred to later.

Gustavus definitively gave up his five-column scheme. He was not ready to launch out on so broad a manœuvre. Taught by the apathy of the Protestant princes, his caution came to the surface, as in his German campaigns it so often and so felicitously did; he choked down the Vasa recklessness,— as Charles XII. was never able to do, — and concluded to narrow his operations to the completion of his bastion, to concentrate instead of parceling out his forces, and for the nonce to operate on some point in the Tollense line. This looks like a marked descent from his larger scheme; but it was just this caution, method, exactness, which Gustavus was to teach the world. His base was not yet perfectly secure, and he delayed bolder operations until he should have made it so. We shall see him in rapid action before many months. He selected Demmin as his objective, and left Banér with some three or four thousand troops to blockade the place, and to hold the territory between it and the Recknitz River, while he returned to Stettin with four thousand men. Shortly after, learning that six thousand troops under Savelli had marched to the relief of Demmin, he broke up thither with a force of four thousand men, met the imperialists in the vicinity of the place, engaged them, and, by the greater mobility of the Swedish infantry and its dashing courage, defeated and drove them back to Rostock with loss of their entire artillery and train and many standards.

Here again was a brilliant feat of arms, the details and the exact locality even of which are unknown. Records were ill kept in this era. Were it not that the bare facts are sufficiently vouched for by the Swedish dispatches and the imperial records, we should be tempted to set down some of these successes as mere paper-victories. But Gustavus was quite free from that particular weakness which induces a man to claim a victory or hide a defeat. His mind was too comprehensive to seek for such adventitious aid. It is we who lose by not knowing the details; the victor himself loses nothing.

Gustavus returned to Stettin. During his absence Schaumberg, the successor of Conti, had made a further useless attempt to take Stettin, and had then sent a force to release Colberg from the Swedish blockade. At the moment, this was one of the most important places along the coast. The king's initial plan was to extend his base so as to include the whole Baltic shore, much as Alexander deemed the whole east coast of the Mediterranean essential as a base from which to advance into Persia. The Swedes already held a goodly part of the shore line, and Colberg, a strong fortress, was indispensable to complete it. The operations so far had isolated the town, and cut it off from Garz; but so long as it was held by an imperial garrison, it threatened the left flank of the Swedish line, as well as communications with Oxenstiern in Prussia; and even Gustavus was not yet free from the prejudice of the day with regard to fortresses.

Colberg was held by Colonel Mörs, and blockaded by Colonel Sperreuter. On September 23 the imperialists at Garz sent five companies of cavalry to make their way into the place; but Horn heard of their presence, headed them off, and compelled them to return by a long circuit. The garrison feared its ability to hold out.

Kniphausen, who was now in charge of the Colberg region, expected to operate mainly with troops to come from Oxenstiern. Towards the end of October Horn ascertained from deserters and scouts that a marked stir in Garz indicated a movement in force towards Colberg. He strengthened Gollnow, and sent word to Kniphausen to hurry forward the oncoming Prussian troops to Belgard or Cörlin, and occupy the line of the Persante. Kniphausen was active. He made Schievelbein the rallying-point of all arriving troops, and threw several companies into it; but the Prussian troops were much delayed.

On November 7 Horn got news of the actual march of a heavy column from Garz in the direction of Colberg. Delaying a day lest the manœuvre should be a mere feint to lure him from Stettin, Horn marched by Gollnow and Greifenberg to Treptow. Instructed of his purpose, Kniphausen, still on the Persante, left a suitable force under Colonel Hepburn to hold this position, cautioned Sperreuter to stand firm, and contain the garrison of Colberg, and himself marched to Treptow, which he reached November 10. From here the two Swedish generals moved to Rossentin near Colberg to await the enemy.

The imperialists had made a big circuit to avoid detection, and on the night of November 10 their column reached Schievelbein. Here Colonel Munroe held head against their attack, and they swerved off towards Colberg. Keeping out his patrols, Horn was well advised of their movements, and they advanced until they found that Horn stood athwart their path. Discouraged, they turned to retire, but Horn followed and gave them battle. A heavy fog prevented the possibilities of good management, and after desultory fighting, Horn, who had accomplished his aim, fell back to the Persante, and the imperialists towards their base, their attempt to relieve Colberg having proven a dismal failure. Lest in his absence his camp should be attacked, Horn then returned to Stettin by the direct road.

The movements of the Swedes in Mecklenburg and Pomerania had so far been parts of one great whole. From Ribnitz Gustavus was reaching out towards Lübeck and projecting an operation towards the Elbe. The duke of Saxe-Lauenburg, a small principality on the lower Elbe, was preparing to join him, while Magdeburg, further up the river, stood as an allied outpost in front of this right flank. As Gustavus progressed with his movement on Ribnitz, Magdeburg loomed up in his mind as a suitable point on the Elbe for him to occupy in force. But it was not to be. Christian William, the administrator, was unfortunately not the man to second Gustavus' broad plan, even in so far as his one city fitted into it; and Lauenburg proved too weak to accomplish his aim. After a short period of success the latter succumbed to Pappenheim in a battle at Ratzburg, — a failure that drew the fire of Lübeck, which had been recruiting for the king. These new factors in the problem made it doubtful whether Gustavus could accomplish any strategic good by pushing forward to the Elbe at the present moment. To entertain an army might be difficult, as the season was getting late, and the financial question was not an easy one. Troops and material arrived slowly from Prussia, and an advance meant to consume large forces for garrisons. The enemy had reinforced the troops in Mecklenburg, and to advance would open to attack the newly conquered bastion. Already somewhat reduced by labor and sickness, the army ought soon to be given its winter rest.

As he could place no reliance on German aid, Gustavus was convinced that he must concentrate his efforts. Yet his instinct as a soldier called on him to end the campaign by some stroke worthy of his reputation. It was as much a matter of moral effect as of material gain that he was aiming to compass, to show that the Snow King had come to Germany on no child's errand. But how? By advancing towards the Elbe he could make no sensible gain, and not to win was of itself failure. On studying the entire situation, he determined to return to Stettin, to draw the enemy from Garz and beat him in the field, or to attack him where he stood. Kniphausen still held for the advance to the Elbe. Horn and Teuffel were of Gustavus' opinion, but they counseled speed, lest the enemy should retire to Frankfort and intrench his winter-quarters.

Gustavus had returned to Stralsund. Oxenstiern was ordered to forward cavalry as soon as possible; Kniphausen was drawn on for troops for Stettin; Banér was to complete the works near Ribnitz, garrison it, and then join Gustavus; the infantry to be sent via Wolgast to Horn; Gustavus himself, with the cavalry, would march to Stargard, be joined by Sperreuter and the Prussian cavalry, making a total of thirteen thousand five hundred foot and six thousand horse, and with these the king purposed to move on Garz.

All this was admirably planned. But Oxenstiern wrote that he could only send the Prussian troops by detachments, and Kniphausen reported that he could scarce spare a hundred men. For a moment Gustavus was uncertain what to do; then his courage rose to the occasion, and he determined to go on with the plan, be his force more or less.

It was at this time that he heard of the enemy's failure to relieve Colberg. On November 16 he reached Greifenberg, and here Horn, Kniphausen and Baudissin were ordered for consultation. As a result, Horn was instructed to remain near Colberg; Banér and Ake Tott were drawn in from Mecklenburg to reinforce him; Gustavus returned to Stettin.

On November 21 he reached the city, and heard sundry rumors of a renewed attempt on Colberg. He scarcely believed this probable, for the enemy, after the late experience, would be unapt to break up with a small force, and a large one would at this season have difficulty in victualing ; but he notified Horn to instruct the population along the probable route to drive their cattle to a place of safety. The imperialists, however, were contemplating a movement, in the belief that the Swedes would not expect one. So soon as Gustavus satisfied himself of the fact, he ordered Horn from Greifenberg down to the line of the Ihna, to take up a position between Stargard and Gollnow and hold the fords, and to draw, if essential, from Banér's and Dargess' troops. On December 1, while Horn was carrying out his instructions, he received new ones from Gustavus, who had ascertained that the proposed movement was delayed or postponed, that only five or six thousand foot remained in Garz, and that, owing to scant forage, the cavalry had been cantoned in various villages on the east side. Here was an opportunity for a stroke. Gustavus could either collect his cavalry and fall smartly on the enemy's scattered horse ; or he could call in from Horn all available forces, join them to his own, and with this column attack the depleted Garz intrenchments. He summoned Horn, Kniphausen and Baudissin to Gollnow for a conference.

Gustavus was one of the men who belies the old military saw that a council of war never fights. Having sought the opinion of his marshals and thus become familiar with all the facts, he himself decided, and always for a vigorous policy.

It is not usual to detail the to and fro manœuvres of troops under the orders and counter-orders given by the commanding general as the kaleidoscopic game changes under his eye ; only the marches or attacks finally decided on are wont to be

mentioned, while the intermediate period, during which the
commander is fencing to discover his enemy's weak guard, is
ignored ; but it is interesting now and then to enter into even
petty details ; for all operations, however large, are made up
of these, and it is the general who gauges accurately the meaning of the information brought in by his scouts, and who
then orders skillfully, that succeeds on the chessboard of war.

Gustavus was by no means certain of the outcome of the
attack he proposed to deliver ; but to make provision for an
unsuccessful result and then to put his whole soul into the
work was natural to his character. He had determined that
the campaign should not end until he had forced a battle on
the enemy, but he recognized the dangers which might follow
failure. Like all his utterances, his letter dated December 5,
to John Casimir, commending Sweden and his own wife and
daughter. to his care in case of disaster, is affecting. And
his instructions to the Swedish people were to the last degree
explicit. When Tott and Banér were ordered away from
Stralsund, Generals Sten Bjelke, Rynnig and Soop were left
in joint command, — a curious division of authority which
largely obtained all through the era of which we are treating.
Eighteen hundred and fifty men were left in Stralsund, and
Anklam, Wollin, Cammin, Uckermünde, Barth and Ribnitz
each had a garrison, — the total of garrisons in places already
captured running up to ten thousand six hundred men. To
these joint commanders Gustavus gave orders, in case of disaster, to look well to Stralsund, — so that it might be at all
hazards kept safe for Sweden. Should they need it, they were
at liberty to draw in some or all of the garrisons of adjoining
towns ; but they were in no case to lose courage or to give up
Stralsund. The command in Stettin, where forty-four hundred men were left in garrison, was given to Colonels Carl
Banér and Leslie. Early in December the available troops

were got together; Tott's and Banér's regiments were ordered
in from west Pomerania, Horn's corps and other troops from
east Pomerania. Some twenty-five hundred horse came from
Prussia and, added to the force from Stettin, the king collected eight thousand foot and six thousand horse, ten siege-
guns, each drawn by twenty-four horses, and a number of
field-pieces. Part of the force was to go by land from Damm,
where they rendezvoused, part by water on the fleet, which
had been all along lying in the Oder at Stettin; and after
careful inspection, on December 24 the start was made, and
Gustavus set out to drive the enemy from his intrenchments.

That the imperial forces in Garz were in a wretched plight
from cold and hunger, and in a worse state of discipline, —
actually in no condition at this season to withstand the
Swedish army, — justified the selection by the king of this
moment for moving upon them, though he had no entirely
reliable evidence to go upon, but rather judged from his
military experience and instincts. It was in truth so. Count
Schaumberg, the new commander of the imperial forces on
the Oder, gave to his chief, Tilly, the most distressing reports
of the condition of the army, in which, said he, there were
not over four thousand footmen fit for service. The cavalry
was better, but half was dismounted and all inefficient. He
begged for an inspector who should report the state of the
forces turned over to him by Conti, and with which he was
held to show results. It was the lack of victual which had
driven him to send away the horse to the outlying districts,
even so far as the Neumark. In the Swedish camp matters
were on a better footing. The home troops were in good
shape; the newer recruits were getting into order; all were
warmly clad, fairly well fed, full of an excellent spirit, and
in condition for any work. The difference between the old
system and that introduced by Gustavus was pronounced.

Colonel di Capua held Greifenhagen with some thousand men ; the rest lay in the camp at Garz. Schaumberg began already to think of retreat to Landsberg to defend the line

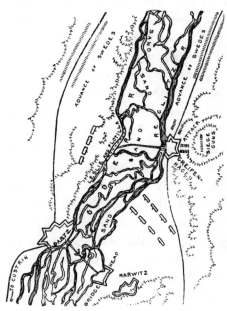

The Attack on Garz.

of the Warta. He harbored fears that both it and Frankfort might fall, and his retreat to Silesia be cut off, but he did not feel warranted in leaving his post without instructions from Tilly. He did not anticipate an immediate attack ; and his position was good though his troops were not.

Greifenhagen lay on low ground between the Reglitz and a line of hills which slope down towards it. These hills command the town, which had only a wall of no great strength, with a few towers but no flanking bastions, and a dry ditch protected by another light wall.

The route of the Swedes lay along both sides of the Oder, and the army was accompanied by the flotilla and a flying bridge, to keep up connection between the separated wings. Marching on the right bank, the Swedish van reached Greifenhagen late in the evening, and after a smart skirmish, drove the imperialists within walls. Don Capua had no idea that Gustavus with his entire army was upon him ; he looked on

the body as a mere reconnoissance. The Swedes camped overnight in a wood near by. Next morning all joined in a solemn
Christmas-day service, and the attack was begun. Some of
the siege-guns were hauled up to the highest hill, not a musket-
shot distant from the town, and, protected by an infantry
detachment, opened fire. In a short while a breach was made,
and the king in person headed the assaulting party. Twice
the Swedes were driven back, but on the third attempt the
imperialists gave ground, and Don Capua, who had behaved
with gallantry, was forced to turn from the fierce onslaught.
But Leslie lay in wait in the rear of the imperialists, on the
Oder, aboard the boats, and by a heavy fire drove them back
on the Swedish line of musketry. Thus hemmed in, the
entire force surrendered. Gustavus' loss was small; that of
the enemy was reported between one and two hundred.
Startled from his fancied security, Schaumberg made up his
mind to summary retreat, if possible towards west Pomerania
to join the imperial forces on the Tollense, where, by a vigorous push, he might make the Swedes nervous as to their
communications, and thus draw the fire of their advance up
the Oder.

Next day Gustavus broke up early and marched along the
right bank towards Marwitz, near by which a fort protected
the bridge to Garz. This bridge-head had a deep wet ditch
and was strongly held. The king anticipated resistance, and
the army marched on the place in order of battle. But the
garrison did not even wait their coming. So soon as the van
of horse put in its appearance, they withdrew over the bridge,
burned it, and took up a position in a work on the further
side. Out of this they were driven by the Swedish artillery,
and thence retired to Garz.

Schaumberg no longer delayed; he could not reach west
Pomerania, for the Swedes on the left bank were upon him.

He burned the Oder bridge at Garz, threw his guns into the
marsh, destroyed so far as he was able the public buildings,
gates and defenses, as well as the victual he could not carry
off, and marched hastily away to the south, putting the torch
to every village on the route, and leaving scarce a spear of
grass behind.

Cavalry under Baudissin was sent in pursuit, which captured much material, said to have included three hundred
wagons full of plunder; and detachments were hurried on
towards Cüstrin and Landsberg to cut the enemy off from the
fords and bridges there. Following to Pyritz, Gustavus drove
out the garrison, which fled headlong; and Schaumberg
retired rapidly up the left bank to Frankfort, and marched
part of his forces to Landsberg on the Warta, to hold the line
of that important river. The Swedes followed them up, and
in several rear-guard combats inflicted considerable loss upon
them, badly cutting up four of the best imperial regiments.
The king headed direct for Landsberg, and it was lucky for
the town that he did not know that it was in bad case, with
few troops, empty magazines, twelve guns, and only eight or
nine hundred-weight of powder. Ignorant of the facts, Gustavus did not attack; moreover his men were weary, it was
bitter cold, his own victual was getting short, and he feared
imperial concentration on the line of the Warta, which would
prevent his holding Landsberg, if taken. He retired to
Königsberg in the Neumark, where he rested his troops, calling on Horn with the foot and Tott with the cavalry to follow
up and complete the rout; while Leslie on the left bank
should advance inland and seize Löcknitz, Prenzlow and the
Uckermark. Patrols were set along the river as far up as
Schwedt. To be ready for further operations, if these should
be forced upon him, Gustavus called for all available troops
from Oxenstiern and Horn.

Though the king's army had been much the better and the opposition had been weak, it cannot be denied that he had won a brilliant advantage. He had driven the enemy out of good intrenchments, at that day considered a distinguished feat of arms, and although the operations were neither bloody nor on a vast scale, they redounded greatly to his credit. All Germany rang with his praises ; in Vienna "they shook with fear."

" Advance Pikes ! "

XV.

WINTER–QUARTERS AT BÄRWALDE. JANUARY, 1631.

GUSTAVUS had as yet no idea of the petty jealousies of the German princes. He had every right to expect the elector of Brandenburg to stand by him. But George William felt more bound to the emperor than to his religion; he aimed at neutrality, but allowed the imperial troops what he denied the Swedes. Gustavus built a fortified camp at Bärwalde, and housed his troops. Here Richelieu made a treaty to pay him for keeping thirty-six thousand troops in Germany, all mutual friendly states to have due protection, and no violent upheavals to be made. Tilly was on the Weser. On hearing of the capture of Garz, he started towards the Oder, but shortly returned and undertook, with Pappenheim, the siege of Magdeburg. The Protestants held a convention in Leipsic, and though Gustavus was in Germany at the request of many of them, there was no mention of the king in their deliberations. Anxious to complete his base on the Oder before he moved to the Elbe, Gustavus sought to aid Magdeburg by threatening Frankfort, so as to draw Tilly away from there, and in February Tilly marched to the Oder. Some slight manœuvring took place, but no serious operations, except that Tilly compelled the Swedes to raise the siege of Landsberg. Gustavus determined to draw him from the Oder into the open country.

GUSTAVUS' trials were about to begin. The military problem was difficult enough; but as yet the king had no idea of the complex network of paltry prides and jealousies, of private grudges and selfish interests, in which he would now be caught, and which would seriously hamper his best efforts. It is wonderful that he had the courage to enter upon any campaign in Germany, after tasting the difficulties which from the start beset him; it is doubly wonderful that within two years he should have reduced to possession the whole land.

George William, the drowsy elector of Brandenburg, had repeatedly exchanged embassies with Gustavus, but not to offer assistance; his one aspiration was to save his dominions from invasion. Neutrality was his only thought; despite which he allowed the passage of Schaumberg's fleeing forces through his fortress of Cüstrin, — of itself the baldest breach of neutrality. Gustavus demanded equal passage. The elector was between the devil and the deep sea. He must offend either Gustavus or the emperor; and either was able to visit him with condign punishment. He began early in January with a declination to allow Gustavus to pass Cüstrin, on a number of trivial pretexts, mainly his duty to the empire; the king answered by demanding actual possession of the fortress, instead of free passage; the elector must not, said Gustavus, shield the imperialists and prate of neutrality. Though Gustavus was long-suffering, when he acted it was without fear, favor or affection; but it was difficult to say how far he might trench on the rights of Brandenburg, lest he should force George William into open enmity. He needed him as a friend; he must keep him at least neutral.

The imperialists had reassembled twelve thousand men in Frankfort, and as the elector persisted in denying the Swedes a passage through Cüstrin, Gustavus, unwilling to advance with this fortress and Landsberg in his rear, for the moment pocketed his wrath, and took up quarters at Schwedt, and at Bärwalde, on the right bank of the Oder, at which latter place he constructed an intrenched camp, and housed his main force. He repaired the Garz works in order to keep open his Oder line; blockaded Landsberg with four thousand men under Tott; and sent out detachments to clean Brandenburg of the isolated plundering bands of imperialists which were overrunning the country and harassing a friendly population. He would have been glad to push on and relieve Magdeburg from Pappenheim's blockade; but his Swedes needed rest; it was winter; his new recruits had to be got into shape; and, above all, his base was not yet free from danger. Should he march to the Elbe, his line of operation would be open to interruption by the imperialists from Frankfort; and indeed, in the present tone of the electors of Brandenburg and Saxony, he could not venture to cross their territory.

Gustavus had good reason for self-gratulation. In six months the Swedes had advanced from the seacoast to the line of the Warta, leaving in the emperor's possession, within the line covered by the Trebel-Tollense-Ucker, only Demmin and Greifswalde, and east of the Oder only Colberg; these places were blockaded by his forces, and Banér lay on the frontier of Mecklenburg with four thousand men.

It is true that Gustavus had secured so easy a triumph against no well-organized resistance. Conti had been distinctly unskillful; and what with Wallenstein dismissed and his forces disbanding, with Tilly far off in the Weser country, seeking to gather Wallenstein's men into the fold of the League, though the aggregate of the enemy had been large, only isolated garrisons and weak divisions had been on hand to oppose him. He had encountered more political than military opposition. With the true soldier's ardor, he had hoped for a battle; but not only had he met no real army in the field to outmanœuvre and beat; it took many weary months to force Tilly to the point of risking his master's cause in a general engagement.

In the camp at Bärwalde Gustavus lay in the early weeks of 1631, busying himself with recruitment and discipline, to prepare his men for more vigorous measures in the spring, and with urging the Protestant princes to concerted action. He issued a proclamation to all who had fled from imperial cruelties to return, and many did so. Contributions on the country were regularly levied and paid for. Billeted soldiers were forbidden to ask more than bed, the right to cook at the general fire, salt, and vinegar to correct the bad quality of the water of the plains.

To win the elector of Brandenburg's active help, Gustavus used his best endeavors, but this Protestant sovereign, and brother-in-law of the king, preferred an ignominious neutrality ; and — more discreditable still — the head of the Lutherans in Germany, John George of Saxony, simply ignored Gustavus' advances. Such was the attitude of the men the king had come to aid. In George William's case it was hebetude ; in John George's it was jealousy.

To counterbalance this, there was one real cause of congratulation. Richelieu plainly desired to coöperate with Gustavus. Former negotiations had failed, owing to certain formalities on which both parties could not agree. But on January 23, 1631, Gustavus and Louis XIII. concluded a five years' treaty, by which the king of Sweden agreed to maintain thirty thousand infantry and six thousand horse in Germany, against a payment of three hundred thousand livres (five livres equaled two rix dollars) for the past year's expenses, and a future annual subvention of a million livres, payable May 15 and November 15, in Paris or Amsterdam, at Gustavus' option.

The other terms of the treaty contemplated protection of mutual friends and of the Baltic, the freedom of commerce, and generally the restitution of the *status quo ante bellum.* In conquered territory Gustavus agreed to respect certain laws of the empire, and not to disturb the Catholic religion where he found it duly established. The treaty was to be open for any princes to join who desired to coöperate in the common cause. With Bavaria and the League neutrality or friendship should be maintained, if they would do their part.

Count Tilly, now in supreme command of the imperial forces, lay on the Weser awaiting reinforcements from Italy and recruits from the League. Though he knew how worthless were his lieutenants and troops on the Oder and the coast, he took no action to direct or relieve them. A slow, old-fashioned soldier, not able, if measured by the high standard, yet not without marked capacity in his way, Tilly was noted for never having lost a great battle. He had always waited for the advantage to be on his side before engaging; but he was far behind the times in dealing with such an antagonist as Gustavus. Count Pappenheim had repeatedly urged his chief to head off the Swedes in overrunning the land, but to no avail. Tilly would not move till he got ready.

Out of this inert mood he was rudely startled by the disaster to Schaumberg, who wrote that he had saved a bare four thousand foot and an equal number of horse; and that it would be lucky if he could hold Frankfort and Landsberg, for the king was aiming at the roads to Silesia, and his own men were down-hearted to the last degree. On receiving Schaumberg's first intelligence, Tilly had broken camp; on January 9 he was in Halberstadt; January 13, in Calbe. His lax habit had lost him Garz and Greifenhagen.

The Protestant princes, in the beginning of February, 1631, assembled in Leipsic at the invitation of the elector of Saxony. There were represented the houses of Saxony, Brandenburg and Hesse, and some smaller principalities, as well as all the free towns. This body was convened to devise measures for withstanding the imperial tyranny, but it actually accomplished nothing, and it is a marvelous fact that in their deliberations, which lasted two months, Gustavus was not even mentioned. The tone of the convention was given by the elector of Saxony, who still deemed it possible, by simple appeals to Ferdinand and without war, to bring back matters to their original basis and to reconcile the Protestant and Catholic claims. The convention acted as if Germany was in a state of profound peace, instead of almost on the eve of political and social disruption. Except for what was said by William of Hesse, not a voice was raised which fairly represented the disturbance which prevailed. In answer to all the advances of Gustavus, only a timid outside intimation was conveyed to him that, under favorable conditions and on his own pledges to do and to refrain from doing all manner of uncertain things, the friendship and good-will of the Evangelical principalities might perhaps be extended to him. John George still believed Gustavus to be an unessential factor in the problem, and still hoped that he could sway obstinate, high-handed Ferdinand by meekly worded correspondence. For all the Protestant body paid any heed to him or his doings, Gustavus might as well have remained quietly in Sweden. Such were his German friends.

Meanwhile, the imperial forces had been winning some successes in the Elbe country. Christian William, in the late summer of 1630, had armed Magdeburg, Halberstadt and other neighboring towns, had driven the imperial forces from the region, and carried on an assiduous small war. But his success was short-lived. Pappenheim, with seventeen thousand men, having, as already narrated, surrounded the duke of Lauenburg and captured his army on the lower Elbe, returned and blockaded Magdeburg in September.

This was not the first attack on this proud Hanse city. In the summer of 1629 Wallenstein, engaged in enforcing the Edict of Restitution, had laid siege to it, but mindful of the failure at Stralsund and of his own reputation, had accepted a ransom of one hundred thousand dollars, and left in September. Magdeburg then patched up a treaty, offensive and defensive, with the other League towns, — Ham-

burg, Lübeck, Bremen, Brunswick and Hildesheim. In
June, 1630, the ex-administrator got possession of the place,
and made the treaty already mentioned with Gustavus in
August, by which the king agreed to have a heed to the city
in all its dangers, to defend it without cost, never to forsake
it, or to conclude any peace in which it was not protected.
No sooner was this treaty made than Pappenheim appeared
before it, and opened his lines.

The fact that such a treaty was made, and the additional
fact that Magdeburg was captured and sacked before Gustavus could reach it, have been made the text of many accusa-
tions against the Swedish king. It is a common allegation
that before this disaster could occur, Gustavus was bound to
march to the relief of the city. This is a charge easily made ;
but there were many considerations for the king to weigh.
He had but half won his base on the sea or the Oder, and he
might not lightly prejudice it. Until he could, beyond a peradventure, command the Oder from the line of the Warta
north, and the entire territory back of the Trebel-Tollense
line, he was scarcely justified in advancing inland. According to all reports from Magdeburg, and to all military
probabilities, the city could hold out against Pappenheim
indefinitely, and, if Tilly joined him, against both for two or
three months. The king had small doubt that he could keep
Tilly in the Oder country by threatening Frankfort, the loss
of which would open the road through Silesia directly to the
hereditary possessions of the emperor. He was in constant
communication with Magdeburg, and thought he knew
whereof he spoke, and his letters to Falkenberg show his
feelings in the matter with perfect clearness. Despite all
that may be said, it remains true that Gustavus did what was
humanly possible to succor Magdeburg. He may not have
foreseen all the difficulties in his path when he made the

treaty, but he was fairly justified in assuming that Magdeburg could resist a longer siege, and that it would not be (as it was) treacherously surrendered by the imperial party within its walls; he sent one of his best officers to take command, and money to raise troops; and he received credible information that Tilly was on the point of abandoning the siege, as he actually was on the eve of the storm. Still more to the point, Gustavus could hardly anticipate the unreasoning opposition of Brandenburg and Saxony; he had the best of reasons for believing that he would have forced the enemy to battle long before Magdeburg should weaken; and he was actually within a short march of the city when it was taken. It is not worth while, in view of Gustavus' life-work, to combat the statement that he deliberately abandoned Magdeburg to her fate. If any accusation be brought against him, it should be for miscalculation of what he could accomplish while Magdeburg held out. All this anticipates the narration of the facts, but it is well to bear the matter in mind, in order to appreciate the king's operations between the date of the treaty and the fall of Magdeburg.

In February, 1631, the main imperial army under Tilly finally made its appearance in Gustavus' front. The aged and rather inert generalissimo had been at fault in not sooner sustaining his forces on the Oder, but he was unused to the winter operations to which the Snow King's activity had forced him. After his ineffectual start for the Oder, he had been tempted to move to the assistance of Pappenheim at Magdeburg; but when he heard how hard pressed Schaumberg was, Tilly began to fear for Silesia, should the line of the Warta be lost; so he abandoned the Magdeburg scheme and crossed the Elbe at Dessau. Then via Treuenbrietzen and Saarmund, some twenty thousand strong, he marched on Frankfort, which he reached January 18, 1631. This gave the imperialists thirty-four thousand men. Gustavus had succeeded in helping Magdeburg by drawing Tilly from its gates.

From Frankfort, leaving a garrison of five hundred of his best troops in the place, Tilly marched to Landsberg, and compelled the Swedes to raise the siege and fall back to the main camp at Bärwalde. The sturdy old warrior gave certain indications of a readiness to draw the king, who had but twenty-five thousand men and many of these detached, from his intrenched camp to a battle in the open; but he did not choose to assault the Bärwalde works, nor was a special offer of battle made. Gustavus was engrossed with the Mecklenburg problem. Until he should quite clear the imperialists out of the territory near the coast, he could not be satisfied of its security; and to sustain Magdeburg in her courageous defense, he must advance from a base which could not be threatened. The antagonism of Brandenburg and Saxony made this all the more true. There was another idea lurking in Gustavus' mind: that a threat towards the towns still held by the enemy in Mecklenburg would draw Tilly thither from the Frankfort region, and afford him an opportunity to return and capture this city and Landsberg out of hand. These strong places were essential to the operations he contemplated between the Elbe and the Oder, but he could scarcely hope to get hold of them so long as Tilly was within their walls. And by luring Tilly to follow him, he might so manœuvre as to get a chance of battle in the open, or of catching the imperial army at a disadvantage, while not affording the enemy an occasion to return to Magdeburg.

Swiss Pikehead. (15th Century.)

XVI.

GUSTAVUS AND TILLY MANŒUVRE. FEBRUARY TO
APRIL, 1630.

WITH twelve thousand men Gustavus moved into the Demmin region. Tilly slowly followed on a southerly route. The king captured Demmin and several minor towns. Colberg shortly fell, and only Greifswalde held out within his bastion. He contemplated a movement on the Elbe, but Tilly showed signs of attacking his lines, and the king feared he might break through. Instead of so large a scheme, Tilly took Neu-Brandenburg, and, massacring the garrison, retired towards Magdeburg. Gustavus believed that a sharp threat on Frankfort would again draw Tilly away from this ally, and in March, with fourteen thousand men and a large force of guns, he advanced up the Oder. Cüstrin fell, and Frankfort was taken by storm, with a number of general officers. This was a brilliant exploit, and for his lesson in audacity modern war is indebted to the Swedish king. Advancing on Landsberg, the place surrendered. The bastion was thus pushed forward to the Warta, and the road to Vienna was open. Such a situation should have called Tilly away from Magdeburg. Had not Gustavus felt it his duty to relieve the city, he might have advanced directly on the emperor. Tilly did indeed start to the relief of Frankfort, but being too late, headed back to Magdeburg. The Swedish holding was now a semicircle from Mecklenburg to Prussia, with a chain of strong places all the way, Frankfort in the centre.

IN pursuance of his design to entice Tilly away from the Oder, Gustavus left Horn in a camp at Soldin, with six cavalry and six infantry regiments fronting towards the Warta, and under orders to hold the enemy to the Landsberg-Cüstrin line; not to risk an engagement, but to act defensively against superior forces; and to seize Frankfort and Landsberg if the opportunity offered. Horn's reserves would lie in Pyritz, Stargard and Gollnow, so as to protect the Oder, the Neumark and eastern Pomerania. Should the enemy go into winter-quarters, Horn might attack Landsberg and Driesen, the two most important points on the line of the Warta-Netze.

On January 26 Gustavus himself set out with six cavalry and four infantry regiments, plus some Stettin battalions, in all twelve thousand men. Kniphausen, who commanded in the Stralsund region and was now besieging Greifswalde, was sent orders to be ready to join the king. Marching by way of Stettin, where he crossed the Oder, past Löcknitz, which he took, Pasewalk and Waldeck, Gustavus left a small garrison in Prenzlow. At Neu-Brandenburg the imperialists capitulated February 2, and were paroled. The small garrison of Treptow retired lest it should be taken prisoner, and

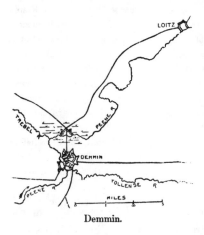

Demmin.

Clempenow was captured a day or two later. To hold these towns protected the proposed siege of Demmin. It was cold winter weather, but the possession of western Pomerania was too important to delay till spring.

Demmin, anciently a strong place, had been repaired by the imperialists. It was the apex of the Peene-Trebel-Tollense region. Savelli held it with seventeen hundred men, while in Loitz, near by, lay six hundred more, and fifteen hundred in Greifswalde. Demmin was easy to fortify, and art had been called to the aid of nature. It was surrounded by a bastioned earthwork with a wide wet ditch and glacis; and the vicinity was commanded by a field-work inclosing a strong tower, north of the town, on the left bank of the Peene and surrounded by the morass made by the river. Tilly had told Savelli that he must hold the place at least fourteen days, as he had supplies and ammunition in abundance. That the marsh was frozen helped the besiegers somewhat. In addition to ordering Kniphausen to join him at Demmin with all his available foot and some siege-guns, the king had instructed Baudissin to march to Treptow with his cavalry; and with eight hundred musketeers he went forward to reconnoitre Demmin. Torstenson with the artillery was to follow to Clempenow.

The king saw that Loitz had first to be taken, for it stood like a detached work on the left bank of the Peene, and possessed a castle of some strength. This was accomplished, Savelli was cut off from Greifswalde, and the road from Stralsund was opened for Kniphausen, whom the king again admonished to bring his batteries.

Tilly met this march of Gustavus by leaving Schaumberg in the vicinity of Frankfort with eight thousand men, and starting himself with twenty thousand for Mecklenburg. Perturbed at the situation, he had delayed some time. If he left Frankfort, he feared that Horn would seize on Landsberg; if he stayed, that Gustavus would advance across the Havel on Magdeburg. Finally he chose the least dangerous course and set out early in February. He could break through Gustavus' lines at Prenzlow, Neu-Brandenburg, or some point on the Trebel-Recknitz, if he wanted to go to the relief of Greifswalde; or he could march straight to the Havel, if he proposed to attack Magdeburg. His course was plain. During the ensuing manœuvres Tilly was seeking to draw Gustavus away from Frankfort and the open road to Silesia, as well as to prevent his marching to the relief of Magdeburg; and Gustavus' aim was to keep Tilly from adding his army to the besieging forces at Magdeburg, and to take Frankfort and

Landsberg from him by a stratagem. On the direct road up the Oder the king had got possession of all the towns, so that Tilly was obliged to move his columns by a detour south of Berlin: via Beskow, Fürstenwalde, Mittenwalde, Saarmund, Brandenburg and Neu-Ruppin. This, to be sure, enabled him to cover the line of the Havel, which would head Gustavus off from Magdeburg; but he was seriously delayed on his march by the opposition of several towns.

The king learned of Tilly's march, from Horn, on February 10. Selecting Malchin as a good outpost to prevent interference with his operations against Demmin, he ordered Kniphausen and Baudissin thither; and meanwhile dispatched Captain Moltke with thirty-six horse to reconnoitre the place. This officer managed to make the enemy believe that the king was close by with the Demmin army, and seized the town, though the garrison was thrice the size of his own force. For a mere scouting party, this was a pretty operation, and opened the way for the approaching troops. On February 12 Gustavus marched from Loitz on Demmin, sending cavalry ahead to cut off Savelli from retreat. On the 13th he reached the work on the left bank, whose garrison of Landsknechte retired to the tower. Out of this they were driven by mining, and rather than be blown into the air they surrendered, the men enlisting under the Swedish colors. At the same time approaches were opened and pushed on the right bank against Demmin. In two days Savelli concluded he had better make terms. He was allowed to retire with the honors of war, conditioned on his army and himself not serving in Pomerania and Mecklenburg for three ensuing months. Having yielded up a place which could have offered a long resistance, Savelli withdrew to Neu-Ruppin. Much artillery and a large supply of corn and forage fell to the Swedes. Tilly found grievous fault with his lieutenant; he would accept, and indeed there was, no excuse. He desired to make an example of Savelli; but this officer, who had friends at court, got off with a few months' arrest, and was later given higher employment. The capitulation of Demmin allowed free exit for all personal effects. Among these was the baggage of Quinti del Ponte, a deserter and traitor, who had made an attempt on the king's life, and in it the money he had received from his treachery. On being asked whether he would confiscate the stuff, Gustavus replied that it was included in the terms, and that he had no mind to take petty revenge on the man.

In view of the Swedish successes all along the line, the Pomeranian Estates were now persuaded to raise ten thousand foot and three thousand horse to garrison the land, a help which released an equal number of Swedes for the field. Gustavus had surely deserved this first assistance.

For the moment, and not anticipating much manœuvring on Tilly's part, the king appears to have deferred his designs on Frankfort in favor of putting his men for needed rest in winter-quarters. Behind his curtain of strong places, he designed to clean up his work by the capture of Colberg and Greifswalde, and perhaps of Rostock and Wismar, and with nothing in his rear, the more safely advance to the relief of Magdeburg, and approach Hamburg and Lübeck. The projected line of winter-quarters was to extend from the Oder to Stralsund: Banér in command of the right along the Trebel and Tollense; Kniphausen at Neu-Brandenburg in the centre; Teuffel and Baudissin on the left, along the upper Ucker; beyond the Oder, Horn. The strong places on the line were Ribnitz, Dammgarten, Tribsies, Demmin, Malchin, Clempenow, Treptow, Neu-Brandenburg, Prenzlow, Garz and Schwedt. East of the Oder the line would run parallel to the Warta-Netze. Near Wolgast were Kagg and Tott with the reserve cavalry. The king personally went to Stettin to oversee the whole or to plan new operations. Opposite this Swedish line lay the imperialists, with an irregular front from Frankfort to Magdeburg, and outlying forces in the Rostock-Wismar country.

Not meaning to lie idle because he contemplated winter-quarters, Banér was instructed by the king to press the siege of Greifswalde from the south, but to have a heed lest the enemy should break through the line to relieve it. Tott was to help with his cavalry, and to lend a hand to Banér or Kniphausen, as needed. Now that he was quite cut off from the imperial army, Banér called on the commandant of Greifswalde to surrender, but Colonel Perusi refused terms and prepared for defense.

Gustavus had seriously considered a march up the Oder through Silesia ; but the attitude of Brandenburg and Saxony held him back. Tilly's dread in this quarter was ill-founded ; but the old-fashioned soldier justly feared some operation which he could not fathom, and chose the Ruppin country as a good place from which to attack any novel problem. In going to Stettin the king left his lieutenants with some distrust ; but he had a right to believe that they could hold their own. Kniphausen was active in procuring information in his front, and late in February had come to the conclusion that Tilly was about to attack Prenzlow, so as to break through the line to relieve Greifswalde. Gustavus had the same notion, and cautioned the officers in command to be ready to concentrate to oppose any such attempt. Later indications were that Tilly was aiming at Neu-Brandenburg, and Kniphausen sent notice to Banér and Baudissin. Like information was received by the king, who sent word to Banér to sustain Kniphausen, as he could do without weakening his siege lines. On March 6 Banér reached Friedland, where he was to await the king's further orders; Baudissin had broken up towards the same place; and the king likewise prepared to move to Kniphausen's assistance.

The siege of Colberg had been going on continuously for months under Boëtius, and finally, on March 2, from lack of victual, Colonel Mörs surrendered, marched out with the honors of war, and was given free passage to Landsberg. The fall of Colberg made available the bulk of the garrisons of the surrounding places in the Neumark; Leslie was left in command of what remained; the surplus force was ordered to Stettin, and on March 7 Gustavus, thus reinforced, reached Pasewalk.

Meanwhile Tilly slowly advanced to Neu-Ruppin, found Savelli there with the Demmin garrison, and learned of the loss of Colberg. Thence he headed for Neu-Brandenburg.

Gustavus had sent word to Kniphausen to hold Neu-Brandenburg manfully (or, if he had to surrender, to make good terms), and he would within a few days either relieve him or undertake an operation to draw Tilly away. The fact was that Gustavus had begun to revert to his old plan of an attack on Frankfort. He did not believe that Tilly was merely aiming at Neu-Brandenburg. It scarcely seemed worth his while; he concluded that the imperial general was concentrating for a dash on either Stettin or Greifswalde. The apex of the Stralsund-Greifswalde position is Demmin, and even should Neu-Brandenburg fall, it was no fatal loss, for the place could be got back later. It looks a little as if Tilly, angered at the loss of Colberg, was at this moment willing to come to battle with the king; but Gustavus thought best to draw him away from his Mecklenburg lines by a diversion on Frankfort and Landsberg, convinced that he would follow. There was a greater gain here, and less danger in case of defeat. In pursuance of this plan, the king ordered some of the troops east of the Oder to Krähnig, opposite Schwedt, and Torstenson and Carl Banér, with some artillery, bridge materials and victual, to a camp he had intrenched on the Oder between Schwedt and Vierraden. Purposing to call Banér to his own side, he left Horn in command of the forces behind the Peene, Trebel and Recknitz, with orders to cover Wolgast, Loitz and Demmin ; to retire, if necessary, on Anklam and Stralsund ; and in case Tilly should advance on Gustavus, to follow him up, leaving only a small force behind him.

The king miscalculated. Tilly paid no heed to his movements. He had indeed no deep design, but was looking for some small success. He was not active enough to be seduced away by able manœuvring. From Neu-Ruppin, on March 12, he reached Stargard, just south of Neu-Brandenburg. This latter was not a place which could be easily defended. Gustavus called it a " naked spot," and Kniphausen had not a single gun. Nor had he got the king's final orders ; the messengers had been captured ; and instead of capitulating honorably, the brave old man determined to hold on, and thrice refused Tilly's demand, replying that he would defend the town to the last man.

Tilly began a furious cannonade, and kept it up two days, breached the mean walls with his artillery, and stormed the town March 23. The resistance was heroic ; the fighting of the Swedes surprised Tilly beyond measure. Quarter was neither asked nor given ; four hundred imperialists fell ; Tilly gave the town up to plunder, and annihilated the garrison. Every male was ruthlessly slaughtered, except Kniphausen and three other officers. Outrage of every kind ran riot. Nothing was spared, — as a species of revenge for the capture of Demmin and Colberg ; but it was a sad contrast to the recent conduct of the Swedes under parallel conditions.

It did the imperialists no strategic good, for Tilly saw no advantage in advancing farther. He was not a man to be encouraged by success, nor had he any surplus enterprise to boast of.

Friedland is a bare twenty miles from Neu-Brandenburg. Why neither Banér nor Baudissin came to Kniphausen's aid is not explained. The error may have lain in the king's failure to guess Tilly's rather blind design, and in orders a record of which is not on hand.

When Horn ascertained the fall of Neu-Brandenburg, he withdrew the troops from Friedland, leaving only a garrison, broke down the bridge at Treptow, and retired to Demmin, to protect the approaches to Stralsund and Greifswalde by holding the fords of the Peene and Trebel. Tilly, on weighing the difficulty of marching on either Stralsund, Greifswalde or Anklam, and fearing that, by a sudden dash, Gustavus might seize the passage of the Havel, concluded to retire to Neu-Ruppin. When he did so, Horn returned to Friedland.

A small compensation for the Neu-Brandenburg disaster shortly occurred when the rhinegrave met a detachment of a thousand horse on its way from Rostock to the imperial army, and completely destroyed it.

Count Pappenheim had made to the elector of Bavaria many complaints of Tilly's dilatoriness, and about this time there came orders to Tilly to let everything lapse which interfered with the capture of Magdeburg. No doubt Tilly would have retired as it was, for without reason he became nervous about the Dessau bridge. He wanted to be near Leipsic, where the convention was being held; and as his position as representative of both the empire and the League subjected him to contradictory instructions, he chose an operation which should suit every one's ideas, — the siege of Magdeburg.

On Tilly's retiring from the Neu-Brandenburg holocaust, Gustavus imagined that he was aiming at Prenzlow, to march up the Ucker to the sea, interpose between Horn and himself, and deliver battle to one or other ; he ordered Horn to march via Pasewalk to Löcknitz, so as to be able at any moment to join him, while Carl Banér was instructed to make secure the works of Schwedt. Gustavus thus prepared to fight in one body and with a good camp in his rear. But when he ascertained that Tilly had retired to Neu-Ruppin, he gave up his defensive attitude, and struck so as to draw Tilly away from his now manifest intention to return to Magdeburg. He believed that a direct threat on Frankfort would do this, and sent Horn back to the command of the Stralsund-Stettin country, with orders to push the siege of Greifswalde, and to send a body of horse to watch the east side of the Oder. If he captured Greifswalde, he could make a move on Rostock, or threaten Mecklenburg in some other quarter. Banér accompanied the king.

Just as the king was about to start, he heard that the imperialists from Landsberg had sent out a detachment and had captured Arnswalde. This moved him to speed. With fourteen thousand men and two hundred guns, on March 27, 1631, he broke up from Schwedt, headed his column along both Oder banks for Frankfort, the main force on the left bank, and the flotilla and flying-bridge in company. The right flank and rear of the army was protected by the camp at Schwedt, as well as by flanking detachments. Baudissin led the column with the cavalry ; the king followed with foot and artillery. The horse scoured the country well to the west, and a detachment captured Oranienburg, to forestall a possible threat to the flank. On March 30 the column reached Wrietzen.

Cüstrin was of the first importance. Gustavus had an

intelligent observer here, received frequent information, and knew all about the place. The commandant, Colonel Kracht, was speedily convinced of the uselessness of resistance, and gave up the place on demand. Continuing the advance on April 1, the outlying posts and scouting parties of the imperialists were encountered. On the 2d the army was in front of Frankfort.

No sooner arrived than the king set about a siege. Some six thousand imperial troops were in the town, and a number of distinguished officers, Marshal Tiefenbach, Count Schaumberg, General Montecuculi and Colonel Sparre. They had determined on defense, and burned the suburbs.

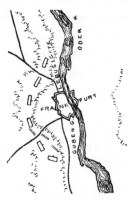

Frankfort.

The Swedish army lay on the hills to await the fleet, and prepare material for the siege. Gustavus reconnoitred. On the first night trenches were opened, not without opposition. On April 3 three batteries were planted opposite the Guben gate, and three regiments posted opposite the Lebus gate. The fire from the batteries was effective, and a small breach was made. In the late afternoon a body of men was sent forward to capture the outworks, so as to drive the enemy within walls, or, as some authorities rather improbably state, an attack was begun by a junior Swedish officer on his own motion, and then followed up. However started, the Swedes advanced with exceptional gallantry, got through the ditch, clambered up the wall, tore down the palisades, and drove the imperialists helter-skelter from the town gates. But they did not stop here. Some musketeers planted ladders, reached the wall, and blew the gates down with petards. Nothing

could resist the fury of the soldiery. Every man met in arms
was cut down; seventeen hundred were killed, Count Schaumberg among them, and one thousand were captured, including
many officers; a large amount of stores was taken. The
town was given up for three hours to plunder, in retaliation
for the massacre at Neu-Brandenburg; but no citizen's life
was taken. A part of the garrison made efforts to escape;
many were drowned in the Oder. A small part, including
two general officers, escaped towards Silesia; individuals
reached refuge even as far as Glogau.

This capture of a walled city with strong defenses and
heavily garrisoned, containing a number of capable military
men, without waiting for a perfect breach, was an exceptional
venture, and earned the Swedes great credit. The news
spread fast, and the king hoped that the victory would influence the German princes to join him.

The modern art of war is indebted to Gustavus Adolphus
for more than one lesson in audacity. It was well that the
world should learn that bold assaults are justifiable; and in
this the Swedish hero led the way. This capture of Frankfort,
and especially the later crossing of the Lech and the assault
on the Alte Veste, were object lessons of exceptional value. Not
but what breaches had been stormed before Gustavus' time. It
is not for ordinary boldness that he deserves credit; but he
should be awarded the highest encomium for doing those
acts which in his era were condemned as foolhardy, and for
showing the world that intelligent audacity is not of necessity
rashness.

From Frankfort, on April 5, Gustavus with all the horse
and three thousand foot advanced on Landsberg. The van of
dragoons drove before it the Croats, of whom many still
infested the country, and inflicted heavy loss on these savage
marauders. Out of twelve hundred, not two hundred got

away. On April 7 the Swedes reached the vicinity of the town. Horn had been ordered to cross the river from Schwedt, and head for Landsberg, with all the force he could collect, to help shut in the town. He arrived the same day as the king.

Gustavus had supposed that Tilly would take some vigorous action to relieve Landsberg, and ordered Banér to break down the Cüstrin bridge, to finish a redoubt already commenced there and make it as strong as possible, and to hold Frankfort stoutly. This would head the imperial army off, as Tilly could not cross at Schwedt. Should he try Crossen, up river, Gustavus purposed to check him with his cavalry; should he go as far south as Glogau, Gustavus would pay no heed to him, as he hoped in that case to be through with Landsberg before the enemy could reach it.

Banér, with five regiments from Frankfort, joined the king April 15. On the same day operations were opened against Landsberg. The town lay in the valley, and possessed a castle, and an outlying fort, on whose possession depended the security of the castle. Gustavus directed his artillery against the fort, and placed guns so as to take it in reverse. After no great interchange of fire, and the repulse of a sortie, a demand was made ; and, April 16, in pursuance of a short negotiation, the garrison of four thousand men surrendered, and received free exit on agreement not to serve for eight months. Crossen speedily followed. The Swedish left flank was thus abundantly secured, and the king drew in the bulk of his forces to Frankfort. The road to Silesia was open.

Now, had Gustavus, as is sometimes alleged, really been indifferent as to Magdeburg, would he not have chosen the plan long urged by Oxenstiern, and have himself advanced through Silesia on Vienna, instead as he did of intrusting

this section to Count Horn? Such an advance would have
suited his paymaster, Richelieu; it would have struck at the
heart of his enemy; he was justified by the neglect of the
men he had come to help in looking solely to his own and
Swedish interests; he would have had a walk-over to Vienna,
and have possibly made a brilliant *coup*. That, instead of
the alluring route, he chose to turn back towards the men
who needed help, but who said no thanks for what he tendered, is sufficient proof that he was faithful to the cause he
had undertaken beyond what can be said of most great
captains.

Tilly had remained a long time inactive at Neu-Ruppin,
and then started in the direction of Magdeburg. When he
learned that Gustavus had moved against Frankfort, he also
turned that way, sending word to the place that he was on
the road to relieve it; but hearing at Brandenburg that he
was too late, he sat down not far from Berlin to wait. He
believed that Gustavus would either march on Silesia or back
to Magdeburg, and he was unwilling to follow him to Silesia.
His desire was to draw the king from the Oder towards the
Elbe, so that he might engage battle with him on favorable
terms; failing which, to capture Magdeburg, and make such
an example of it as would frighten the Protestants into submission. But for some time he embraced no action. Not
until Landsberg fell did he start for the Elbe.

The king sent word of his wonderful success to Magdeburg, promised succor within two months, and said that he
based his calculations on the belief that the town could hold
out easily at least so long.

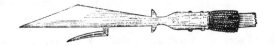

XVII.

MAGDEBURG. SEPTEMBER, 1630, TO MAY, 1631.

MAGDEBURG had been well fortified by Falkenberg, whom Gustavus had
sent thither. The Elbe bridge was protected by several forts, the walls made
strong, and the city became a fortress. After taking Frankfort, as Tilly
returned to Magdeburg to help Pappenheim, who had been there many months,
Gustavus decided to march to its relief. But he was opposed by the electors of
Brandenburg and Saxony. The former forbade the Swedes to cross his territory, or to occupy the fortresses essential to the Swedish advance, until the
king threatened force, when he reluctantly yielded; even the danger to Magdeburg would not induce the latter to permit a Swedish march across his land to its
relief, though the imperialists had gone to and fro at will. As John George with
forty thousand men held the balance of power, Gustavus might not provoke
his enmity; and believing with reason that Magdeburg could hold out several
weeks longer, he urged his negotiations for passage. Meanwhile, the siege was
sharply pushed. Falkenberg had twenty-five hundred men, Tilly and Pappenheim thirty thousand, but the resistance was stubborn. Finally, Tilly, fearing
the advent of the king, contemplated withdrawal; but during previous negotiations, when the garrison was off its guard because an imperial herald was within
walls awaiting answer to Tilly's ultimatum, an assault, aided by the treachery of
citizens, was made on May 20, the place was taken, given up to plunder, burned,
and forty thousand souls perished. This holocaust was properly charged by
Gustavus to John George.

IN the light of his recent success, Gustavus might contemplate an advance on the Elbe. His base was secure. There
was no danger of interruption from Poland, and Silesia was
open to him. Tilly gave up hope of regaining the Oder, but
for a while he lay near Brandenburg, and sent parties out as
far as Crossen. He threatened Berlin, but the citizens put
the city in a state of defense, burned the suburbs, and flatly
denied him victual; and on the fall of Landsberg he marched

towards Magdeburg, and crossed at Dessau. The Oder gone, he felt that he must hold the Elbe, and he was impelled to wreak on Magdeburg a vengeance for the loss of Frankfort. Tilly was still a slave to the old method, in which the deterrent virtue of cruelty was an article of faith. It is proven by modern investigation that the wanton slaughter and burning at Magdeburg were not by his command, but the fact remains that Tilly was a representative of the old school, one of whose tenets was that the sack of a city was a species of right to which the soldier had a claim. In this light he cannot be absolved from the barbarism exhibited in that unfortunate city.

Now was surely Gustavus' time to relieve Magdeburg, and he resolutely set about it. The military danger of such an advance was past, and the king's assurances of speedy succor were founded on this fact. But Gustavus had as yet no conception of the political difficulties which lay athwart his path, and the military and logistic difficulties were by no means all surmounted. Victual was hard to get; Pomerania was slow in filling her quota; remittances from home and abroad came in after tedious delays; the cavalry had run down by excess of the winter's hard work and deprivation so as to be appreciably below that of the enemy in effectiveness. So much was this the fact that the king was called on for the first time to punish depredations, and yet the troops — horse and foot alike — suffered at times almost to the verge of mutiny. " Many excuses, little support," complained the king.

But all this was of small account compared to the difficulty of bringing the electors of Brandenburg and Saxony to a helpful attitude. Gustavus could not begin an unauthorized march through the territory of either, lest the prince concerned should fall upon his rear; and he was able to make no impression upon them. They were not small potentates like Bogislav; should Brandenburg and Saxony join hands to resist the king, his helpfulness to the cause of Protestantism was at an end. The business called for diplomacy, not force; and George William had already been antagonized by the Cüstrin matter.

On April 21 the king himself was in Cüstrin, where he worked out his plans for the Magdeburg expedition. His next step must be to the fortress of Spandau, as a secondary base to secure his advance. Horn was left in command on the Oder, with headquarters in Cüstrin, and was to make up a new army from the recruits collected in Pomerania and arriving from Sweden. A garrison was placed in Landsberg, and a rendezvous was given for May 1, at Köpenick, to all troops destined for the army of the Elbe.

It was hard to argue George William out of his neutrality; commissioners effected nothing; a personal interview in Berlin proved of no avail. Until Gustavus, in a fit of righteous indignation, declared almost at the cannon's mouth that unless Cüstrin and Spandau were voluntarily yielded, he would occupy them by force, he made no headway. It was manifest that he must rely on possession, not promises. George William could expect no imperial aid; he placed no reliance on Saxony; he believed himself in Gustavus' military power; he weakened, and finally came to terms. Control of both Cüstrin and Spandau was given to Gustavus until the Magdeburg incident should be closed; but the vacillation of the man is no better shown than in the fact that George William wrote an apologetic letter to the emperor, excusing his action, and stating that he had caused as great a delay as possible. A pretty champion of his faith indeed!

No sooner in Spandau than, on May 8, Gustavus started for the Dessau bridge, in the hope that he would have less

trouble with the elector of Saxony. His back was scarcely
turned when George William alleged fresh difficulties —
mostly his duty to the empire — in delivering up full control
of Spandau, where Gustavus had left but a small body of
men. The opposition amounted to nothing, but was an additional source of worry. Compulsion alone was an argument
with this shortsighted potentate, who, from a species of moral
cowardice difficult to understand, still clung to his pretended neutrality. It was hard to rupture the old imperial
tie, even for religion.

When Tilly finally retired from the Oder country, Gustavus intended promptly to follow him up; but the road open
to the imperialists had been completely barred to him. Brandenburg once opened, he must reckon with Saxony; and
John George would not allow him to cross his fords at Wittenberg or Dessau. The only other road was via Brandenburg and Möckern, through a country which had been so
completely devastated that it gave an ill promise to the Swedish commissariat, which was at ebb-tide; and moreover
the bridge at Magdeburg was already in the hands of the
besiegers. He could not well advance to the aid of Magdeburg from any point lower down the Elbe; for the bridges
were scarce, or had been destroyed; the boats had all been
seized by the enemy; the river was wide; he had no pon-
toon-train, and to secure means of crossing would consume
much time; the vicinity he must occupy had been devastated,
so as to be unfit to sustain operations; and wherever he
should attempt to cross, it must be in the face of a superior
enemy.

Every avenue to his objective seemed closed; and while
anxious to relieve his faithful ally, Gustavus could scarcely
be held — as a matter of good faith or a matter of common
sense — to compromise his whole military scheme, built up

with endless care and caution, by so moving as to endanger his communications, magazines and *points d'appui*, to risk an uprising of Brandenburg and Saxony in his rear.

His difficulties can scarcely be overestimated. Most Protestant princes still looked at him as a second Christian of Denmark, who, at the proper time, might sell their cause to save himself ; they not only refused his advances, but declined to raise troops for the common cause. The electors of Brandenburg and Saxony could not have done less for him had they been open enemies. In truth they would have proven a simpler factor in the problem had they met him sword in hand.

Gustavus represented to John George with the utmost frankness the condition of Magdeburg, as also his own and Tilly's relative strength, and by correspondence and embassies, begged this head of the German Protestants for aid in his perilous venture. The elector would scarcely deign to answer ; and answers, when they came, were argumentative solely. The diplomatic interchanges are interesting, but they do not come within our province. That John George forbade a march through his territory suffices to explain Gustavus' long delay in carrying out his promise to stand by the city of Magdeburg in its distress. Tilly outnumbered him ; the elector of Saxony, with an army of forty thousand men, held the balance of power ; the elector of Brandenburg in his rear was not to be relied upon, — and to be brief, Gustavus was not a Charles XII. Had he been so, he might have relieved Magdeburg — perhaps — while the dull-witted electors were gaping at his boldness ; but he would not have been of the stuff to save Protestantism in Germany. Happily for us, he was better balanced, and would not risk Sweden and the future of the faith on a hair-brained advance, however brilliant. He felt constrained to remain on the Havel, along which he advanced as far as he might, until he could overcome the inertia of the Saxon elector.

Putting aside politics — in this case John George with his forty thousand men — the military problem could be readily solved. Three or four stout marches by way of Dessau, the destruction there of Tilly's force, the building of a bridgehead to preserve his line, and the summary attack of the enemy besieging Magdeburg were among the possibilities. But if we assume that Gustavus' duty was merely a military one, and that he was bound to disregard all political complications, we can scarcely imagine his pushing far into the tangled network before him. All great soldiers have succeeded because they made politics subserve their military scheme; and so did the Swedish monarch. We may imagine the bold and rapid advance which some historians have told us it was his duty to make, to redeem his pledge to Magdeburg; we may picture its success; but we shall have created a paper campaign, and a paper hero, we shall not have depicted the Gustavus who saved the Reformation in Germany, and who was the father of modern war. Gustavus was not great because he was either cautious or bold; he was great because he knew when to be cautious and when to be bold. We shall see him bold enough by and by.

To return to Magdeburg. Colonel Falkenberg had been sent by Gustavus to take charge of its defense in the fall of 1630, and had entered the city October 19. He found the situation far from bad. The enemy had less than six thousand men, was merely observing the city, and Falkenberg felt confident that he could hold the place for many months. He was warmly welcomed, and his influence was at once felt. He took full command, — the administrator retaining only his body-guard and a sort of advisory control, — and began recruiting outside and repairing the works within.

The Elbe at Magdeburg has a number of islands close together. The bridge over the river utilized these, and a bridge-head stood on the right bank. Perceiving that the enemy, by attacking the islands from up river, could cut off the bridge, Falkenberg built a big work at the south end of the most important one, and for the several sections of the bridge redoubts. To strengthen the bridge-head on the right bank, a work called " Trutzkaiser " was erected on the Mühlberg, a hill near by which commanded it. Two heavy works

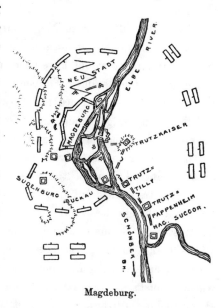

Magdeburg.

were built on the south of the town, one on the water's edge, and one in the outer corner; a number of bastions were constructed to strengthen the city wall, and the Sudenberg suburb was protected by a strong redoubt. On the west the two gates were strengthened by two horn-works and a crown-work. The north side, where the Neustadt lay, possessed a round bastion on a point surrounded by a dry arm of the Elbe. The gate here was fortified with two towers, and the suburb was itself intrenched. Work was vigorously pushed, and by the end of the year the citizens could truly claim that Magdeburg was a fortress. Falkenberg had shown energy and intelligence. But Magdeburg had a weak spot within walls. Christian William, the town council, the military under Falkenberg, the common folk, and a strong party of disaffected Catholics — each group of a different mind — furnished abundant means for disagreement and promise of treachery.

Tilly paid small heed to Magdeburg. Between Gustavus and that scornful city, he scarcely knew which way to turn ; and yet its capture would have been almost the hardest blow he could deal the Swedes. Pappenheim understood this well. For months correspondence ran between the imperial army and the Magdeburg council, and efforts were made to bring the city back to the empire. But Falkenberg never permitted it to waver in its fealty to Gustavus, though the imperialists numbered some of the most influential citizens. He was not infrequently put to it to reconcile conflicting interests ; but though he could not accomplish the moral task, he mastered the material one, and during the winter of 1630–31, he labored to make the surrounding defenses stronger, and at designing new ones. On the right bank, whence Gustavus was expected, were erected the "Trutz-Pappenheim" furthest to the east, and the "Trutz-Tilly" nearer the town ; and upstream a large work, the "Magdeburg Succor." A line of heavy intrenchments arose along the right bank, and Falkenberg had twenty-five hundred men, plus citizen-militia, to man them.

In November Tilly had proposed to besiege the city, but contented himself with leaving Pappenheim to blockade it while he turned towards Gustavus. He left his lieutenant with ten thousand men, but at times drew on this number for other service. Pappenheim was a hot-headed officer, ill adapted to so slow a process as this blockade ; to storm the city was more in his style ; and he fretted under the task. Count Wolf von Mansfeld had a small army near by, but lent no assistance, a fact which irritated Pappenheim still more.

Finally, toward the beginning of April, Tilly was moved by Pappenheim's entreaties to permit him to take active measures ; and the gallant lieutenant needed no second order. Falkenberg could not pretend to hold his long *enceinte* with his limited number of men. He might have been wise sooner to withdraw into the city. The defiant " Trutz-Pappenheim " was selected as a beginning, and after equally gallant assault and resistance, this redoubt, with the " Magdeburg Succor " and the " Trutz-Tilly," fell on April 9. On the morrow two more works on the right bank succumbed to Pappenheim's impetuous energy and heavy excess of forces ; while Mansfeld did a more moderate share in taking the three Buckau redoubts. The Magdeburgers lost all their outlying works and fully five hundred men. Some ten days later Tilly arrived. The joint forces before the town amounted to twenty-five thousand men, plus a detachment of nearly five thousand more at the Dessau bridge. This was fearful odds for Falkenberg's small garrison, now reduced to little more than two thousand soldiers. He had felt able to hold his works against Pappenheim, but now he had twelve times his force to face.

Shortly after the fall of Frankfort, Tilly had received orders to march to the protection of the emperor's hereditary lands, which would be threatened by the capture of that city. To do this was impossible. To divide forces would be to insure the failure of both detachments ; and the emperor had troops in Silesia, as it was. Tilly served both the League and the empire ; and a council of war decided to capture Magdeburg as a first step.

The imperialists were now able to attack the works at the bridge-head and on the islands. The garrisons defended themselves nobly, even according to Pappenheim's high estimate, but eventually, about April 30, Falkenberg deemed it best to draw them in, and the bridge and islands were lost. The citizens began to despair, and Gustavus seemed as far off as months ago.

News came from time to time from the Swedish army, and its successes faintly cheered the weary waiters ; but the negotiations with Brandenburg and Saxony were to the last degree disheartening. Falkenberg and the council wrote repeatedly to the king, representing the growing scarcity of victual and powder, the intention of the enemy to control the Elbe by a bridge at Schönebeck, eight miles up river, the almost mutinous condition of the people, the unhelpfulness of the administrator ; and prayed for speedy succor — " or we are lost." But Gustavus was powerless ; the two electors barred his way.

There may have been men in the world's history who would have braved even these conditions, who would have frayed a path across Brandenburg and Saxony in the teeth of any opposition, and have marched to the relief of Magdeburg without regard to what lay behind them. But there have also been gigantic failures in the world's history from just such impetuousness. No one can accuse Gustavus of lack of personal boldness. Of all great captains he is most like Alexander in his reckless disregard of danger, and even the Macedonian could show no more wounds. His moral force — his capacity to face responsibility — was as marked. But what Gustavus did for the art of war sprang less from the exuberance of his courage, less from that species of moral bravery which impels a man to take abnormal risks, than it did from his exceptional power of calculating correctly by the existing conditions what course would most certainly tend to the eventual success of the whole scheme. He had not the gambler's instinct so strongly as Napoleon. Had he let loose the reins of his gallantry, he would never have grown to be the champion of Protestantism ; no one can tell what might have become of the cause of Reform in Germany. Such a Gustavus certainly could not have saved it.

Falkenberg now leveled the suburbs to protect the town. On May 4 the inhabitants of the Sudenberg retired within the walls, and this suburb was burned ; and when Pappenheim moved to the Neustadt, this too was fired. When all outlying garrisons were drawn in, there were not quite twenty-two hundred and fifty men, horse and foot. Pappenheim began regular approaches in the ruins of the Neustadt.

Fearing that Gustavus would come to its relief before he had reduced it, Tilly opened negotiations with the town early in May. He wrote to the mayor and council, to the administrator, to Falkenberg. But the advances were refused and messages again sent to Gustavus, praying hard for immediate succor. The council, however, offered to leave the whole matter to the joint decision of the electors of Brandenburg and Saxony, and the Hanse towns ; they held their messengers ready to depart upon this errand, so soon as Tilly should send a safe-conduct ; and of all this he received clear notice.

Tilly was puzzled what to do. He heard of Gustavus' successive advances to Köpenick, Berlin, Spandau, Potsdam. He learned that negotiations were going on with John George, as well as George William, and he feared their early success. He was apprehensive lest the Saxon army should appear at Dessau. He must get possession of Magdeburg speedily, or else retire, baffled, as Wallenstein had done at Stralsund. He deemed himself in bad case, when he really had no cause to fear, for he had a larger force than Gustavus, unless Saxony should join the king. On the first appearance of Swedish cavalry near Zerbst, Tilly destroyed the Dessau bridge.

While using his most persuasive measures against the town, the work in the trenches went on. The bombardment was opened on May 17, and was kept up three days. Under cover of it, the approaches in the Neustadt, in the Sudenberg and on the island progressed. Pappenheim, in the Neustadt, got to the very margin of the ditch, and fairly seamed the Neustadt with trenches. He sapped the counterscarp and pushed a covered gallery over the ditch, while the defenders were kept off the walls by a heavy fire. Breaches were operated; the biggest of the towers fell; indefatigable Pappenheim pushed five approaches to the *fausse-braye* of the new bastion, tore out the palisades, and laid several hundred ladders. He worked on the other side of this bastion as well, making it a key-point for his proposed assault. The defenses of the town were also weakened on the west and on the river fronts.

The defenders opposed this work with equal energy. Fires from the enemy's hot balls were kept down by systematic measures. The besieged countermined, and patched up the works as fast as these were disturbed; but from want of powder they could not maintain a steady fire.

On May 18 Tilly again dispatched a herald into the town. During the two weeks since the proposal to arbitrate, he had neither refused it nor sent a safe-conduct; and now, on the score of time, he declined to allow the submission of the case. He practically demanded unconditioned surrender, or threatened to storm the town. The approach of the Swedes, of which Tilly now hourly expected to hear, spurred his determination to adopt any course, right or wrong, to get possession of the city.

The council was convened, and the citizens were called together on May 19 to frame an answer. It was determined to treat with Tilly. Falkenberg protested, and asked for a meeting with the council, to be held at 4 A. M. on the 20th.

On the afternoon of the 19th the fire of the imperialists ceased, and they could be seen, from the town, moving the

siege-guns to the rear. The townspeople began to hope that
Gustavus was nearing, and Tilly was in fact on the point of
giving up the siege, lest he should be interrupted by the
" Snow King." He still hoped that at the last moment the
town would accept his ultimatum, and he called a council of
war to determine what to do. At this council it was suggested that an assault, delivered at an early morning hour,
had succeeded elsewhere and might succeed here, and this
suggestion Tilly eagerly grasped at. He determined to storm
the breaches at daylight next day.

Through the disaffected Catholics Tilly knew all that was
going on in the town. They kept him posted as to the
strength of the guard at various points, the hours of relief,
the means of defense, the want of powder ; and there is not
wanting evidence that messages were thrown from the walls
on the morning of the 20th, before sunrise, to the effect that
now was the very time.

Whatever the other facts, it is beyond dispute that while
the council was sitting in debate on Tilly's ultimatum, while
the imperial herald was still within the walls of Magdeburg
awaiting the council's answer, the army of Tilly was ordered
forward to the walls. It is beyond dispute that the generalissimo had given every indication to the town that he was
still negotiating and would await a final answer, and yet he
sent Pappenheim to storm the works. This treachery is on
a par with that of Cæsar against the Usipetes and Tench-
theri.

At daylight some of the guard had left the walls, prompted
thereto by the knowledge that the ultimatum was being discussed, and the belief that there was nothing for the moment
to fear. The officers of rank were all at the council. Matters were more lax than usual. At 7 A. M., after quiet preparation, Pappenheim assaulted at two points : the round bas-

tion near the Elbe, where a party of Croats was sent forward, and the bastion which he had so vigorously approached, where he in person led the party. The Croats easily forced their way in. Pappenheim found only a few sentries on hand and the watch surrounding the chaplain at morning prayers; and he pushed his party over the walls with scarce a semblance of opposition. He was having things all his own way, when Falkenberg appeared, hastily summoned from the council chamber, and met him with what men he could instantly collect. For a brief moment Falkenberg was able to check both the Croats and Pappenheim; but he soon fell. Pappenheim was receiving constant accessions to his force, and in less than an hour there remained nothing to resist him. Mansfeld was slow in storming; but when Pappenheim had effected his entrance, he too forced his way into the town.

The city was given over to plunder. The horrors of the scene have been all too often dwelt on. There perished forty thousand souls. Treachery was followed by its fellow, massacre.

It will always remain doubtful how Magdeburg was burned. It is charged to Tilly unjustly; Pappenheim, Falkenberg, the citizens, the imperial troops, have each in turn been accused of deliberately destroying the beautiful city. The event left Magdeburg a pile of ashes surrounding the cathedral, which alone escaped.

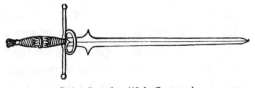

Swiss Sword. (15th Century.)

XVIII.

GUSTAVUS ADVANCES TO THE ELBE. JUNE AND JULY, 1631.

THE capture of Magdeburg meant retreat for Gustavus, lest Brandenburg and Saxony should side with the emperor and endanger his bastion. He fell back to the Havel, and here awaited Tilly. But the Walloon had won fame enough; he essayed no forward movement; reinforcements were coming up from Italy, which he desired to draw in before attacking Gustavus; and he was shortly ordered to move on Hesse-Cassel and Saxony, to compel their submission to the imperial dictates. Pappenheim remained in the Magdeburg country. Hesse-Cassel prepared for resistance; the landgrave and the duke of Saxe-Weimar were stanch allies of Gustavus. Seeing that Tilly did not advance on him, Gustavus strengthened the Havel line, and compelled George William to yield up Spandau for the war. Shortly Greifswalde, the last town within the bastion, fell; Mecklenburg was overrun, and the dukes reinstated. Gustavus, now secure at all points, extended his right flank to the Elbe, to draw Tilly from Hesse-Cassel; crossed the river, and intrenched a camp at Werben. Tilly did in fact come up, joined Pappenheim and moved towards the king. The latter fell on his advanced cavalry-parties and cut them up. Incensed, Tilly marched on Werben and attacked the camp; but, severely punished, he retired.

AT the downfall of the proud Lutheran city, the Catholics rejoiced with cruel taunts; many Protestants were disheartened, many cowed by her awful fate. Who knew where next the imperial lightning might strike? No one was seer enough to foretell a deliverer in the Swedish monarch. The only man in Germany who gauged his value was Wallenstein.

The capture of Magdeburg meant retreat for Gustavus. Had he reached the place in time to drive off Tilly, Brandenburg and Saxony might have joined his cause; now they

were more likely to be enemies who might cut him off from
the sea. He must force Brandenburg to his will without
delay; Saxony must wait. As some were inclined to blame
the king for forsaking Magdeburg, he issued a manifesto,
couched in no equivocal terms, putting the blame on John
George, where it properly belonged, for his obstructive measures; and, quite out of patience with the time-serving of the
Protestants, prepared to retire.

He was fortunate in one thing. Had Tilly followed him
up, sustained by Saxony, the Swedes might have been crowded
back to the coast. But Tilly sat down to enjoy his success,
and never dreamed of an advance. He deemed Gustavus'
entire venture at an end, as a less well-poised leader's might
have been, as Christian's had been. Pappenheim chafed
under this restraint; but he was young and ardent, and he
was not the commander-in-chief.

Having for the moment no inducement to advance to the
Elbe, and uncertain as to Tilly's manœuvres, Gustavus again
assumed the line of the Oder as a *point d'appui*. He dispatched orders to Horn to rebuild the Oder bridge at
Schaumberg, so that the Swedish army might retire on it if
driven back; and Frankfort was to be fortified to the highest
degree by chief engineer Porticus. These precautions were
wise, but, as matters eventuated, they were not needed.

There was no doubt in Gustavus' mind that the enemy
would now seize the opportunity which victory had given
him, and be prepared to meet him. The Swedish line was
open to attack from Silesia, and this was to be guarded
against on the line of the Oder-Warta. It was open to
attack from Dessau, and this could be met by holding the
line of the Spree-Havel. An imperial attack from Mecklenburg was improbable on account of the promised restoration
of its dukes; and if Greifswalde were once secured, Pome-

rania was tolerably safe. This left a long but good defensive
line, and from it Gustavus could debouch towards the Elbe,
if the enemy did not break down his defense. By pivoting
on Frankfort he could swing forward his right, and by securing a strong place on the Elbe, his new base would be more
firmly held than ever. Its front would cover much territory,
but it would be protected by such places as Stettin and
Frankfort on the left, and Hamburg and Lübeck on the
right; while in the centre Gustavus would fortify a strong
line on the Havel. Hamilton was shortly expected in the
Weser with a goodly force, and this would add Bremen to
the cause and extend the line to the North Sea.

The command of the important centre was given to Banér
early in July. He had three brigades: Teuffel's at Brandenburg and Rathenow; Hepburn's at Potsdam; a third
was divided between Bernau and the Bützow country, which
latter place was a defile in the network of lakes in this part
of Mecklenburg. Headquarters were at Fehrbellin.

The left was intrusted to Horn. He had a bare fifteen
hundred men, and news came that the imperialists in Silesia,
encouraged by the Magdeburg success, would soon move
down the Oder. The outpost at Crossen occasionally had
touch with the enemy, and in May, as suggested by Pappenheim, a number of regiments assembled in the Glogau country, and threatened Crossen and Züllichau. To meet this
threat, Gustavus ordered Horn to strengthen Crossen, to
recruit up his garrisons in the Neumark, and particularly
to hold the bridges at Frankfort, Cüstrin and Schaumberg.
He was to turn Arenswalde, Bärwalde and Königsberg into
strong places to retire on. If Crossen was attacked, Gustavus assured Horn that he would hurry to his relief with
troops from the Havel and Spree.

Happily for the cause, the imperialists lacked earnestness.

They had stomach for their plundering; they had none for serious war. Horn had time to carry out his orders; the imperialists played with the business. They took Kotbus; Horn captured Grüneberg; and soon after Gustavus advanced him to Crossen, where he erected a strongly intrenched camp.

On the whole, the horror of Magdeburg enraged rather than discouraged the Protestants; and despite the threats of the emperor they continued to equip troops, though without joint action. Hesse-Cassel and Saxe-Weimar were among the most active; while the elector of Saxony used his large army to preserve his neutrality.

It was at Stettin that Gustavus received an embassy from Russia, tendering good-will and an auxiliary corps. The king declined the troops, but received the minister with pleasure, and sent back friendly thanks to the czar.

Tilly's conduct after his victory at Magdeburg was not that of a great soldier. He lamely explained, in a letter of May 26 to the elector of Bavaria, that until he knew which way Gustavus had retired, he was unable to pursue him, and must remain *in situ ;* that it would take some time to raze the walls, fill up the ditch, and see to victualing Magdeburg; that the enemy had seized all the defiles in Brandenburg; that this electorate was so destitute of provision that no army could move through it; and, as victual was growing scarce, he suggested a march against Hesse-Cassel and Thuringia, where was abundance. This he wrote, while Gustavus stood on the Havel, anxious as to the enemy's advance from a military standpoint; actually dreading its political effect on George William; fearing that he might lose his initiative, mistrusting some combination that might drive him back to the sea. How Tilly could imagine that he might absent himself from the theatre of active operations without opening the way to farther Swedish advance, it is hard to see. Curiously,

Pappenheim, who usually had the happy trick of seeking the enemy, rather favored the plan of Tilly; but he was not the man to dally in its execution, if adopted.

In view of the generalissimo's representations and the continued arming of the Protestants, the emperor did order Tilly to take measures to compel the minor powers to cease warlike preparations, as being inconsistent with their fealty; but the old general was hard to get started. He remained in Magdeburg till the beginning of June; and wrote to Maximilian that with the Swedes and Saxons joining hands, which he expected daily, and with Hesse-Cassel arming in his rear, he feared to be surrounded and his army compromised.

Tilly was a queer compound of courage and the want of it. No man possessed more personal gallantry, as he had demonstrated on a hundred fields; but he lacked that larger intellectual and moral force which enables one to gauge danger and to accept responsibility. He was a noble battle-field fighter; but he suffered from strategic myopia. Finally the old man took courage, left five thousand foot and seven hundred horse in Magdeburg, under Mansfeld, and Pappenheim near by with a small army, and at the head of seventeen thousand five hundred foot, seven thousand horse and twenty-eight guns, broke up towards Hesse-Cassel. On the way the imperial troops devastated the country with fire and sword, and committed untold atrocities. To swell their numbers the League furnished nine thousand foot and two thousand horse; the Netherlands, four Spanish regiments; in Silesia were ten thousand men; from Italy twenty-five thousand were started north under Aldringer and Fürstenberg. The latter came up very slowly; some of the columns took a year to reach the Elbe from Mantua, being delayed in Swabia and Franconia by their orders to compel the Leipsic Convention states to submit to the emperor and disarm. Matters looked serious for Hesse-Cassel; but for all the dangers menacing him, the gallant landgrave ceased not from his work.

William of Hesse-Cassel was young, but a man of action. So early as August, 1630, he had offered his assistance to Gustavus, averring that he could not bring much, but that his two fortresses, Cassel and Ziegenhain, should be shut to the imperialists and open to him. Gustavus concluded a treaty with him ; and urged him to combine with the states of Weimar, Culmbach and Würtemberg, and the free towns of Frankfort-on-the-Main, Merseburg and Strasburg, which between them could readily arm ten thousand men. The landgrave did his best, but the interference of the imperialists prevented him, and Duke Bernard of Weimar, who worked with him, from accomplishing much. At the Leipsic Convention, these two were almost the only ones who spoke for the Swedes. Under the Leipsic agreement, they armed, as it was understood, for defense, but really proposing to aid Gustavus and to seek his aid. As Tilly approached, the landgrave mobilized his men, beset the defiles and roads, strengthened his fortresses, and peremptorily refused Tilly's demands for contribution. Fortunately for the cause, the elector of Saxony, though still claiming neutrality, was angered by the menaces of Tilly, and determined to resist to the uttermost any inroads on his territory by either party.

Gustavus kept strictly to his agreement with Brandenburg, and after some tedious negotiations succeeding the fall of Magdeburg, on June 9 surrendered Spandau, which had been turned over to him only until the fate of that city should be decided.

If we look at the mere military question, Gustavus was not justified in his anxiety ; but a study of the entire situation, political and military, shows us that the antagonism of

Saxony and the unreliability of Brandenburg placed the king
in a questionable case. To surrender Spandau meant to give
up the line of the Havel, as well as touch with the Elbe;
and if the elector should demand back Cüstrin, Stettin itself
would not be safe. Gustavus felt that he was justified in
any course to prevent such a catastrophe. He told George
William that if he so chose he would leave him to fight the
imperial army single-handed. This was in reality the last
thing the time-serving elector dared face. He would have
been happy to leave Spandau and Cüstrin in Swedish hands
as the price of support, but, as was his habit, he delayed and
talked, while Gustavus, along the Havel, awaited Tilly's
advance. Had it not been for abandoning Hesse-Cassel and
Weimar, he would have gladly returned to the Oder.

Gustavus had complied with his obligation; but, sick of
the fast and loose conduct of George William, he made up
his mind to cut the knot of the difficulty; and some days
after the surrender of Spandau, he marched on Berlin, and
at the mouth of his cannon, supported by his army in line of
battle, forced the elector to a fresh treaty, by which the
Swedes should retain Spandau for good; have constant passage through Cüstrin, or indeed occupy it with their troops;
and the elector should pay the Swedes thirty thousand thalers
a month. The trifling of George William was thus brought
to an end; he concluded to come to an amicable understanding, and the treaty was subscribed amid festivities.

The king concentrated near Brandenburg some twelve
thousand men, and while awaiting events, secured his position
by taking and strengthening neighboring towns on the Elbe
and Havel. Greifswalde in his rear was the last outstanding
fortress in Pomerania. Early in June a stray party of imperialists, perhaps on a reconnoissance, appeared before Malchin,
and led Gustavus to believe that an attack on Stralsund or

the relief of Greifswalde was in contemplation. He ordered General Åke Tott, one of his best officers, to collect all available troops in Loitz on June 20, where he intended to meet him; but unable to leave Brandenburg, he intrusted the entire conduct of the affair to Tott, who, with twenty-two hundred men, marched on Greifswalde, and on the night of June 22–23 opened his trenches. On the 23d a sortie was repelled and a bombardment begun. This was followed by the appearance of a herald, and on June 25 the imperialists marched out. The commandant, Perusi, had been killed, or the matter would have been less easy. For this brilliant success Tott was made field-marshal, and ordered to advance against Rostock and Wismar, to open the road to Lübeck. To have an eye to the situation, Gustavus shortly after went on to Greifswalde; but finding that Tott was abreast of the business, he returned to Spandau July 2.

With a suitable van of cavalry, the new field-marshal moved into Mecklenburg, spread all over the country, took Bützow and Schwan, drove the imperialists before him, and blockaded Rostock. A detachment marched south from Malchin, and seized Mirow and Plau. The dukes were in Lübeck, waiting with a small army, and in connection with them, though Güstrow and Schwerin held out till midsummer, Tott reduced all Mecklenburg except Rostock, Wismar and Dömitz. Many men from the garrisons thus taken preferred to enlist in the Swedish service to being paroled or held as prisoners. On July 5 the dukes were formally reinstated in their rights; but they showed small gratitude; they acted in a selfish and shortsighted manner, and every pound of bread for the troops which had reinstated them had to be wrung from their unwilling grasp.

Banér, whom Gustavus had left on the Havel, with instructions to occupy all the strong places on that river, to strengthen the works of Spandau and Brandenburg, and to build a redoubt at Potsdam, took Havelberg by storm on June 22, and strongly garrisoned it. Gustavus could now see his way clear to a campaign on the Elbe; with Pomerania, Mecklenburg and Brandenburg under his control, he practically commanded all the country to the north of that river; and Tilly was otherwise occupied. The scene had changed.

After what seemed to many his decisive victory at Magdeburg, Tilly, under his instructions to enforce the Edict of Restitution, to compel the disarmament of the German princes, or to incorporate their troops in his own army, moved via Aschersleben June 9, Oldisleben and Mühlhausen June 16–26, and captured Gotha, Eisenach and Weimar, while Erfurt bought itself off by a payment of money. He sent out detachments right and left, demanding that the imperialists be admitted into the fortresses; that the landgrave should disband his army, furnish the empire five regiments, give over Cassel and Ziegenhain to imperial garrisons, and pay the contributions which he should assess. Assembling his forces at Cassel, William firmly refused. Tilly wavered. The landgrave had six thousand or more men, recruits to be sure, but still soldiers, in his fortresses, and the victor of Magdeburg was loth to attack them. Age was encroaching on his energy; but his presence none the less put Hesse-Cassel in a perilous case.

About this time some eight thousand men from Sweden were arriving in Stettin. Of these, four thousand were brought to the main force on the Havel, and four thousand were sent to Tott, who was to join the king with old troops to an equal number. At the same time seven thousand English troops, under Marquis Hamilton, landed in the mouth of the Peene, instead of in the Weser, as expected. These regiments were sent to Horn on the Oder, and he was ordered to

leave a total of four thousand new men on that line, and prepare to join the king with the balance. Gustavus aimed at
having service-hardened men at the front. Hamilton's troops
are said not to have been of the best quality ; before the end
of the campaign they ran down to fifteen hundred men by
disease and desertion, and were in a sad state of discipline.
Heartily tired of the timidity and unhelpfulness of the
Protestant princes, the king now saw himself by his own
efforts in possession of the bastion on the south of the Baltic
which he had originally aimed to possess for the safety of
Sweden ; and the idea began to impress itself upon him that
if his brothers in the faith cared so little for his help, he
might hold this bastion, whose walls would be the lines of
the Oder-Warta, Spree-Havel and Elbe, and stand in a
purely defensive attitude against the emperor. Both the lack
of funds and the questionable tendencies of Denmark made
this course seem not unadvisable ; but to complete the work,
Gustavus must plant his foot firmly on the Elbe, and to this
he now addressed himself. The question of the defensive
might wait.

Arrived in Spandau, he determined to push at once for the
Elbe, not only to complete his bastion, but to draw Tilly away
from Hesse-Cassel. Heading seven thousand foot and three
thousand horse, he moved from Brandenburg out towards
Burg. He imagined that he might tempt Pappenheim from
Magdeburg across the river, and engage him ; but failing
this, he headed downstream, to Jerichow, which he reached
July 8. Pappenheim had an outpost at Tangermünde, opposite, and was at the moment there. On July 9 the king again
moved upstream, to lead him to believe that he was aiming
for Magdeburg, and Pappenheim marched up to anticipate
him. Like Cæsar on the Elaver, Gustavus immediately
marched back to Jerichow, put a few hundred men across

on boats, captured Tangermünde and its castle July 10, as well as Stendal and Arneburg, collected all the boats up and down river and built a bridge, on which he crossed his army, and took up a strongly fortified camp near the town of Werben, opposite the confluence of the Havel and the Elbe. Utilizing the embankments as works, he built a fort on the right bank to protect his bridge, which he moved up from Tangermünde, and threw up another fort at the mouth of the Havel. Havelberg had already been taken, and Gusta-

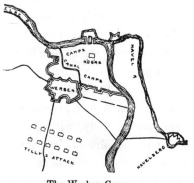

The Werben Camp.

vus' position on the Elbe was made reasonably secure. Pappenheim retired to Halberstadt.

The garrisons of these places were captured, and the men sent in a body to headquarters. As the king came out to inspect them, they fell on their knees to beg for mercy. " Get up," said the king, " I am no god for you to fall down before." Then he added, " You have all acted like brigands and deserve the gallows ; but I will make you a present of your lives."

Though he would have liked to march on Magdeburg, Gustavus contented himself with what he had got. His feeling for the offensive was damped by the conduct of the men he had expected to find frank and faithful allies. He held Brandenburg in the leash, but Saxony was not to be moved, and he was at a loss to explain Tilly's queer lack of enterprise. Gustavus could get no money ; victualing was so difficult that on one or two occasions the population had cause to complain of excesses by the troops ; there was a vast deal of sickness. The weeks in Werben during July and August, 1631, were perhaps the monarch's most disheartening period. One of his objects — to draw the enemy away from his allies — had been accomplished by the march to Werben. Pappenheim, single-handed, felt unequal to the task of facing Gustavus, and called Tilly to his aid. His chief threw up his half-hearted attack on Hesse-Cassel, left a portion of his troops on its borders, and hurried back to the Elbe. Despite his victory he had lost two months and accomplished nothing, while Gustavus had greatly bettered his position. Joining Pappenheim, Tilly, with twenty-seven thousand men, took position at Wolmirstädt below Magdeburg, and on July 27 threw out three regiments of cavalry towards Werben to reconnoitre. Gustavus was ready to meet him in earnest. To help protect the Havel line, he ordered Horn to leave suitable garrisons in Frankfort, Landsberg and Crossen, and some cavalry to scout the Oder-Warta, and to march with all his available force to Fürstenwalde, detaching meanwhile a thousand musketeers to Brandenburg. Tott was to send an equal number.

The king had not exceeding sixteen thousand men, but he took advantage of the isolation of Tilly's cavalry party. From Arneburg, twelve miles up the river, where he had concentrated his own cavalry, he marched, August 1, to Bellingen, and sent out patrols, and later an intelligent staff-officer to reconnoitre. The latter brought in some prisoners and information as to the enemy's whereabouts, acting on which the king advanced at nightfall halfway to Burgstall. Here he divided his force, which was about four thousand strong, into three columns. The first, under the rhinegrave, was to attack Burgstall ; the second, under Baudissin, was to fall on Angern ; the king with the third would advance between the two others on Rheindorf. The columns were set in motion.

The rhinegrave captured Burgstall, cut down or dispersed the imperial regiment there stationed, and took its baggage. At Angern the attack was equally successful, the enemy losing three hundred killed and many prisoners. When the king reached Rheindorf, he found Tilly's men, who had caught the alarm, drawn up in line. Though he had with him but three hundred horse, he fell with fury upon the imperial regiment, which offered no worthy resistance, and cut it to pieces; part escaped in the darkness, but all the baggage was taken. In the fray Gustavus, with his usual recklessness, rode into the midst of the enemy, was surrounded, and but for the fidelity and courage of Captain Harold Stake, would have lost his life. After this brilliant foray the party retired to Bellingen, and to Werben the next day, stationing the cavalry at Stendal. This capital stroke decidedly

Burgstall Operation.

raised the morale of the men, while the imperialists felt the blow to a greater degree than the loss warranted.

To make up for this defeat, which he appeared to resent keenly, Tilly, leaving Wolmirstädt with fifteen thousand foot and seven thousand horse, moved on August 6 to the camp at Werben, drew up in battle order, and cannonaded the works with sixteen heavy guns, sharply but ineffectively. He was doubtful about assault, as no practicable breach had

been made, until he was given to understand by what he supposed were disaffected soldiers in Gustavus' service, that at
a given time next day the Swedish guns would be spiked at
a particular part of the line. Relying upon this information, which he had no means of verifying, he sent his men to
the assault August 7. But the Swedish guns — as always —
were in good hands; Tilly's onslaught, though delivered with
the old soldier's wonted *élan* and in massed columns, was met
by so murderous a fire that its onset was checked; while the
cavalry under Baudissin at the opportune moment debouched
from a side gate, and galloping in on the Walloon's flank,
completed his discomfiture with extremely heavy losses.

In this cavalry charge young Duke Bernard of Saxe-
Weimar distinguished himself and attracted the monarch's
eye. While Gustavus' reckless exposure of his person in
battle was often without justification, his example none the
less produced a wonderful effect on the officers of the army.
Where the king exhibited such a spirit, how should any
man lack bravery? The result of Gustavus' gallantry was
markedly for good, — indefensible as it was, and sad as its
results proved in the succeeding year.

Seeing no gain from remaining in Gustavus' front, Tilly
retired to Tangermünde August 9. He had incurred a loss
of six thousand killed and wounded within a few days, plus
a great number of desertions. Thence, hearing that on
August 7 Horn had arrived at Rathenow with nine thousand
men, he hastily retired to Wolmirstädt, lest he should be taken
in flank. The imperial general thus left under a cloud the
vicinity where so long he had triumphed. The two captains
had measured swords, and unconquered Tilly had given up
the field without a victory.

As Tilly might be about to cross the Elbe, to pierce the
Havel line, Gustavus prepared a bridge over the Dosse, so as

readily to retire to its defense, and ordered Banér to dam
and flood the river. But Tilly did not venture any forward
movement.

The king had consumed a year in securing his bastion on
the southern shore of the Baltic. At times his conduct had
seemed to savor of over-caution; but when we consider that
he landed in Germany with but thirteen thousand men; that
he had received no assistance from the folk he had come to
aid; that he was opposed by superior numbers, the sum total
of the year shows up splendidly, and his caution had been
worth any amount of recklessness. His base was now
assured, and the time for action had come. We shall see
how nobly he improved it.

Horse and Equipments used by Gustavus at Lützen. (Stockholm Museum.)

XIX.

TILLY INVADES HESSE–CASSEL AND SAXONY. AUGUST, 1631.

THE south German Protestants had all submitted to the imperial decrees; it remained to force the north German principalities into line. Gustavus left the Werben camp well garrisoned, and assumed position on the Havel. Tilly marched on Hesse-Cassel, where the landgrave and Bernard held head to him, and then against Saxony, with orders to disarm it. Marking his progress with fire and sword, he reached Leipsic and gave his ultimatum. The elector was in sad case, but he had brought his troubles on his own head. After a few days' resistance, Tilly captured Leipsic, and sat down to await reinforcements. Meanwhile Gustavus advanced to the Elbe, anticipating what must follow. Driven to desperation, John George made a treaty, offensive and defensive, with the king, and Gustavus crossed the Elbe and marched to join the Saxon army, which was put at his entire disposal. A council of war determined on attack, and the two armies advanced towards Leipsic. Gustavus, with his line of small brigades and shallow formation, armed with handy muskets, and aided by quick-firing cannon, was to measure himself against the heavy battles of renowned Tilly. It was activity against bulk. Tilly lay with his back to Leipsic, facing north; Gustavus was advancing southerly.

FOR many months the imperial troops under Fürstenberg, Aldringer and Fugger had been marching up from Italy, had moved into Swabia and Franconia, and by untold outrage compelled the Protestant princes who were acting under the Leipsic Convention, to submit to the emperor, to enlist under the imperial banners the troops raised for their own defense, and to pay heavy penalties. These officers had orders to reinforce Tilly, and their head of column had already crossed the Main. Tilly remained at Wolmirstädt, which was a central point between Brandenburg, Saxony and Hesse-

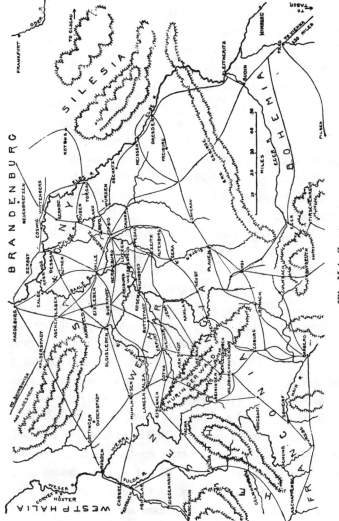

Elbe-Main Country.

Cassel, and enabled him to watch them all. His troops were
badly off as to health and victual, and quite wanting in camp
discipline, though in battle, be it said to their credit, Tilly's
men always behaved well, as their chief commanded nobly.

While the king was awaiting events, Landgrave William
of Hesse-Cassel came to Werben, definitely to cast in his fortunes with the Swedes; and a treaty offensive and defensive
was made, in which Weimar was included. Ten thousand
men could be raised by these states; and it was agreed that
the Swedes should protect the new allies, who would open
their fortresses to Gustavus and close them to the emperor.
The landgrave did not feel that Gustavus had failed in his
obligations to Magdeburg, and shortly went back to watch
his territory.

For his gallantry displayed in Tilly's attack on Werben,
Duke Bernard of Saxe-Weimar had been made colonel of
Gustavus' body-guard cavalry regiment. With the landgrave
the king sent back two of his best battalions as a nucleus for
drill and discipline, and it was arranged that Bernard should
take command of the Hessian contingent, as the landgrave had
much confidence in his military skill. Then, in mid-August,
leaving in the Werben camp, under Baudissin and Teuffel, a
force sufficient to defend it, with eighteen thousand troops the
king moved by his left, back of the Havel, and took post at
Havelberg, Brandenburg and Rathenow, in a position to concentrate and move on any point. He considered the Havel,
under the circumstances, a better rendezvous than Werben.
Each detachment had orders to act on the defensive if
attacked, utilizing the near-by strong places, until the king
came up to its assistance. Gustavus had materially gained
since the disaster at Magdeburg, but he was still compelled
to wait on Saxony, whose action he believed the enemy under
the positive orders of the emperor would shortly force; or

should Tilly advance, by confining him to the devastated strip between the Havel and the Elbe, the king hoped to drive him back on Saxony, and thus oblige the elector the quicker to decide whose cause he would embrace. Meanwhile, as Tilly moved on his new errand, Gustavus advanced nearer the Saxon border, to be ready to help John George whenever the elector should be ready to help himself. The imperialists played into his hands.

Tilly had definite orders to bring the north German princes back to their fealty, as those of south Germany had been, — by the sword. From Tangermünde he had notified the Hessians that they must choose between landgrave and emperor, and the loyal Hessians gave a noble reply. With but five thousand men under his command, Bernard threw down the gauntlet. He captured Fritzlar at the end of August, while the duke of Hersfeld laid Fulda under contribution. This was bold conduct in face of the approach of the Italian troops, eager to do by Hesse-Cassel as they had done by the south German states. But the danger to Hesse and Weimar settled itself. Tilly reached Eisleben August 28; and from here, under his new instructions, he ordered Aldringer with his seven thousand men, and Fürstenberg with his twenty thousand, to join him for an attack on Saxony. Tiefenbach from Silesia was to demonstrate on the Saxon rear, while Fugger was sent against Hesse-Cassel.

The reason of this change of plan was that the emperor felt that it was time to compel Saxony to disarm and submit to his authority. He had already made some demands in May and July, after a long correspondence dating back to 1630, and he now proposed to show that his demands must be met. It was for this purpose that Ferdinand ordered Tilly to move on John George and enforce the Edict of Restitution.

Between them the imperial generals had thirty-four thou-

sand men, and Aldringer had got as far as Jena. Tilly's
troops moved towards Leipsic with the usual barbarous devastation, — two hundred burning villages lay in his wake, —
and reached Halle September 4, and Merseburg next day.
They finally went into camp between the two places, and
roving about, plundered the entire neighborhood of Merseburg, Naumburg and Zeitz. Here Tilly declared himself.
He demanded that John George should quarter and feed the
imperial army, disband his new levies, serve under his (Tilly's)
orders with a suitable contingent, formally recognize the
emperor, and disavow any and all connection with the Swedish business.

John George was in pitiable case; but sympathy for him
would be wasted. Saxony was torn by three parties, the
Swedish, the imperial and the neutral. Between his ties to
the emperor, his Lutheranism, and his desire to erect in Germany a Third Party which should grow to be strong enough
to control both the emperor and the emperor's enemies, he
knew not which way to turn. And yet fire and sword were
at his gates. He was at this moment under the control of
Count Arnim, who was a Brandenburger and a Lutheran, had
been Wallenstein's lieutenant at Stralsund, had served with
Koniezpolski against Gustavus in Poland, and had now
become Saxon generalissimo. The Third Party notion was
as much Arnim's pet idea as the *Corpus Evangelicorum*, or
union of the Protestant powers, was Gustavus'.

In all his negotiations with John George, the king had
shown himself frank and aboveboard in his desire to subserve the cause of religion in Germany. He was even now
ready to leave the cause with John George and retire to
Sweden, providing his rights and those of his fatherland were
fitly recognized. He had done everything to persuade the
elector to joint efforts, but John George could not bring him-

self to an alliance with Sweden until the last ray of hope was gone of reconciling the two religions under the empire.

Nearing Leipsic, Tilly, on September 8, demanded a supply of victual from this city; but the citizens were bold in their reply. Unless their master, the elector, consented, they would have no dealings with Tilly. The imperial general appeared before the gates, devastated the entire region, and again demanded quarters and rations. Again refused, he moved on the town, camped near Möckern, and threatened Leipsic with utter destruction unless it surrendered. More

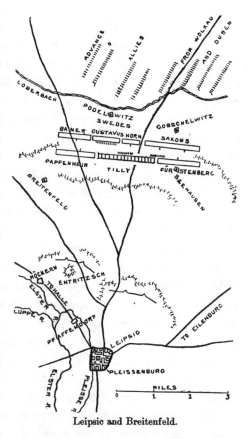

Leipsic and Breitenfeld.

bold than discreet, the citizens replied as before. Tilly opened trenches, planted a heavy battery of siege-guns and mortars at Pfaffendorf, and intrenched the heights at Entritsch to bar the road from Düben, by which the Swedes might come. The citizens burned the suburbs, manned the walls, and replied with some effect to Tilly's fire, which began

September 14. After nearly a day's bombardment Tilly again demanded surrender, and threatened the city with the fate of Magdeburg in case the gates were not forthwith opened.

The three messengers sent by the elector had been captured; Leipsic did not know how near relief was; and further resistance being mere madness, Tilly's ultimatum was accepted September 16. Four hundred thousand florins were paid, the small garrison marched out with the honors of war, and Tilly occupied the town. Scarcely within walls, Tilly received news of the approach of the allies. He at once marched to the north of the city, and drew up in battle order on the hills opposite Podelwitz and Göbschelwitz, and with Leipsic in his rear. He would have been glad to wait for Aldringer and Fugger, but reinforcements were to be denied him.

The plundering and devastation of the imperial army had embittered the elector, whose obstinate clinging to his impossible neutrality was now reaping its reward, and finally prevailed on him to declare against the empire. Not counting garrisons, he had some eighteen thousand men assembled in Torgau to prevent Tilly's reaching Dresden.

Gustavus had advanced to Wittenberg on September 2, with five thousand cavalry. Banér and Teuffel followed, while to Tott was committed the duty of holding the bastion, should matters turn out badly. Horn was to form a new army, on the nucleus of the Havel troops, from a promised Brandenburg contingent, some Swedish cavalry to arrive, the Scotch battalions, and the men of Hamilton and Leslie; and to be ready, if ordered, to move on Silesia.

The Swedish army, on September 3, had reached Coswig and Wittenberg. John George having succumbed, Brandenburg and Saxony, from whatever motives, were arrayed on the

Swedish side, and Gustavus saw daylight before him. An alliance offensive and defensive was made at Coswig, September 10, by which the elector agreed to give the Swedish army a month's pay, furnish it with rations, and admit it to his most important cities. All defiles were to be open to Gustavus and closed to the imperialists ; the conduct of military affairs was to be left to Gustavus, and no peace was to be concluded without him. The king agreed to drive the imperialists from Saxony, and stand by John George to the last. Had Brandenburg and Saxony joined him a year before, what might not have been accomplished ! Hereupon, instant orders were given to break up, all available forces were called in to the colors, Horn was instructed to join the king, and the army crossed the Elbe at Wittenberg and headed for Düben on the Mulde, the rendezvous with the Saxons.

The " order of battle " in which they passed the bridge is interesting. On September 9 a cavalry detachment of five hundred men had crossed and been spread out as a curtain to cover the bridge ; and on September 12 Quartermaster-General Bouillon, with three hundred cavalry and a small wagon-train, joined them. The army itself began to cross September 13. First marched a vanguard of two thousand foot, a detachment of cavalry, and twelve guns drawn by teams of eleven to thirty-one horses ; ordnance and munition wagons came next, carts loaded with cannon-balls, nine regimental pieces with their munition wagons, all followed by four blue and white cornets. His majesty of Sweden in person followed, under special escort of two cavalry cornets, with black and gold pennants, his battle-charger led behind him ; and then several other cornets, blue and red, white, orange, yellow, red, blue, green. Behind these filed four royal six-horse canopy coaches and two royal baggage wagons, and again cavalry cornets, green, blue and red. Then followed the infantry regiments with their pieces and powder and ball carts, the baggage wagons and pack-horses; and then the bulk of the cavalry with all its baggage. Last filed the general wagon-column under escort of horse and foot.

The army halted at Kernberg towards evening, and next day, September 14, it reached Düben.

From Torgau the elector reached the vicinity of Düben September 15. Gustavus rode over to the Saxon army, warmly greeted the elector, and narrowly inspected the troops, which were drawn up in parade order. He estimated the six regiments each of horse and foot at twenty thousand men, though they are elsewhere given at sixteen thousand. A joint inspection of the Swedish army followed. There were twenty thousand foot and seventy-five hundred horse in line.

At a council of war immediately succeeding these ceremonials, Gustavus advised a series of manœuvres to tire out the imperial army and seek to place it at a disadvantage before a general battle. He spoke of his ability to do this as superior to Tilly's, and suggested the distress Brandenburg and Saxony would be in in case of a defeat. For himself, he said, he could retire beyond seas, for which purpose he had a good base to embark from and a fleet. Curiously, John George the procrastinator now urged immediate battle. He was anxious to save Saxony from the plundering to which it was being subjected, was unwilling to subsist two armies during the suggested manœuvres, and had great confidence in the Swedish capacity for fighting. Gustavus was not loth to deliver battle, and it was determined to march without delay to the relief of Leipsic. On the 16th the allied army marched from Düben to Wolkau.

" In the early twilight of the 6th (16th N. S.) we passed through Düben and reached the hamlet of Wolkau, one and a half (German) miles from Leipsic, near evening," writes the king, from whose letters or dispatches comes a good bit of information; "and here we rested over night. On the 7th (17th), in the gray of the morning, I ordered the bugles to sound the march, and as between us and Leipsic there were no woods, but a vast plain, I deployed the army into battle order and marched towards that city. After an hour and a half's march, we saw the enemy's vanguard with artillery on a hill in our front, and behind it the bulk of his army."

It is not possible accurately to gauge the numbers of the two armies. Apparently good authorities differ, and even the Swedish records are at variance with regard to the Saxons. On the day of the battle the Swedes, according to the official list, had twenty-six thousand eight hundred men in line, viz.: nineteen thousand one hundred foot, and seven thousand seven hundred horse. The joint forces may have been forty-five thousand men. Neither can the strength of Tilly's army be justly given, but it no doubt fell a good deal short of forty thousand men.

Until Frederick the Great astonished Europe with his grand-tactics, there are but few battles of modern times which exhibit novelty in manœuvre. Armies met in a formal way, drew up in parallel order, advanced on each other, and there ensued a hand to hand conflict much wanting in the element of calculation or the utilization of favorable conditions; whoever stood the hammering or staved off demoralization the longer won.

The battle of Breitenfeld was a good sample of retrieving, by quick decision and action, an impending disaster, of utilizing an opportunity offered, of true battle-captain's work. It was not noteworthy for any special exhibition of what we now call grand-tactics, for it was not fought as it was intended it should be; but it was essentially noteworthy as being the first great engagement in which the modern tactics of mobility, of which Gustavus Adolphus was the originator and exponent, were opposed to the Middle Ages tactics of weight; in which the new Swedish was opposed to the old Spanish method. In this sense the contest was as interesting as the matching of phalanx against legion.

The Spanish tactics, as already explained, consisted in marshaling heavy bodies — battalia or battles — of troops in such masses that their mere advance should be irresistible, and that they should break a charge of cavalry upon them as the cliff breaks up the waves. The line was set up with foot in heavy squares in the centre, and horse in heavy columns on the wings, and after the fire of the artillery and the charge of the squares had shaken the enemy, the duty of the horse was to ride him down. The infantry battalia were wont to consist of fifty files ten deep, of which mass the bulk was mere pushing, not fighting force; and on the four corners stood groups of musketeers, two or three deep; while other musketeers were put out as skirmishers to protect the flanks of the battalia. Such was the Spanish battalion; it was an oblong fortress with bastions at the corners, and surrounded by outworks.

In these huge masses of human brawn the weapons were equally cumbersome. The pike was long and heavy, of use only to keep an opponent at a distance, not to demolish him by stroke of arm; and the old musket, requiring ninety-nine "times and motions" to handle, and a crutch to lean it on to fire, was as slow and ineffective as the artillery. Nor was the cavalry much less lumbering. Like a child with a new toy, it had fallen in love with its firearms, had come to discard its shock-tactics, and had learned to rely on repeated salvos of its carbines or pistols. These salvos were delivered from near at hand, and the squadrons lost the momentum of the full gallop charge from a distance. It was really mounted infantry, one regiment differing from another only in weight of armor or weapons. No doubt all this had a defensive value; but set it going at any pace, and it would fall apart by its own weight.

What Gustavus had been introducing and practicing his troops to use, ever since he ascended the throne, was a gun which could be rapidly fired, and a formation in which men could readily manœuvre. The Swedes had now next to no armor to hamper their movements; their musket was so light as to need no crutch, and its wheel-lock was vastly better than the match-lock of the imperialists. In addition to this, Gustavus' artillery was immeasurably superior, and the regimental pieces could actually follow the regiments.

Moreover, instead of these large bodies, which were intended to act together and be mutually dependent, the Swedes had a line made up of smaller battle groups, each of which was independent and self-sustaining. Gustavus had the habit not of collecting all his horse in a mass on each flank, but of alternating bodies of horse and foot in parts of the line itself. To soldiers brought up under the modern system, this formation seems odd enough, but it well suited the fire of that day, as it had suited at times the ancient tactics; bodies of cavalry need no longer dash uselessly against the battles, but the horse and foot were able to support each other in an advance. When the musketeers had broken the enemy by their fire, the horse pushed out and charged him. In retreat they worked equally well; the musketeers protected the horse, and the horse prevented the broken foot from being ridden down. In the centre of the line the foot was not always mixed with horse; but the units were smaller. The full Swedish brigade is stated at one thousand two hundred and twenty-four men, and was made up of either one strong or two or three weak regiments. It was a sort of wedge of one body of pikemen backed by two others, and in the intervals and on the flanks bodies of musketeers who might break out, deploy to fire, and again retire into the brigade. At Breitenfeld the brigades stood in three lines. The sketch of Lord Reay was not the common order of the Swedish brigade formation, though it

HALF BRIGADE

HALF BRIGADE

M=MUSKETEERS   P.= PIKEMEN

Brigade and Half-brigade.
Lord Reay's sketch.

may have applied to foreign bodies in Swedish service. Perhaps the difference exists in the use of the words " half-brigade " for what others called " brigade." The leading half-brigade of Lord Reay's diagram corresponds to what is usually referred to as a brigade ; the rear half-brigade does not.

As already explained, the line had been reduced to files three deep for firing in battle, though supposed to be six deep in fact; the first rank knelt and the other two stood. This gave much more effective fire and reduced casualties. Fire was delivered by platoon or by rank, and each rank having fired had but two others to pass to go to the rear and load. In the imperial army it might have nine ranks to pass.

What Gustavus gained in men by his shallow formation, he utilized by carefully marshaling his second line ; and what his first line lost in weight was made up by a second line or by reserves. It must not be supposed that the Swedish line lacked strength. It had nearly as many men, over six to the lineal metre of front, as the imperialists. Its organization gave it both power and elasticity. The two armies differed as a rigid cast-iron bar differs from an elastic steel sword-blade. The latter has life which the other lacks.

We shall see how these two systems worked in the first general engagement where they fairly and squarely met.

XX.

BREITENFELD. SEPTEMBER 17, 1631.

THE Leipsic plain is wide and flat, with here and there a rolling hillock good for artillery. Tilly had an admirable line, and a splendid array of veterans. He had never lost a great battle, and his men were eager to fight. The Swedes were not handsome, but the stuff was there. The Saxons were a bespangled lot, but they did not know what fighting meant. Tilly stood in a line of seventeen great battles, with Pappenheim and Fürstenberg on the flanks, and with his guns admirably posted. Early astir, the Swedes marched towards the enemy with cheer. Brushing away Tilly's outposts, they came into line with the Saxons on their left. In the Swedish wings horse was mixed with the foot in alternate small detachments; the right wing under Banér was principally horse; the king led the centre, mostly of foot; Horn on the left, with horse and foot. Each regiment had its guns, and the reserve artillery under Torstenson was on the left centre. The Saxon formation is not known. The battle opened with artillery, and restless Pappenheim rode out, unordered, to break the Swedish right; but Banér met him manfully, and drove him off in flight. Next, Fürstenberg charged in on the Saxons, and sent them flying to the rear. Tilly had viewed these unauthorized advances in dismay; but the flight of the Saxons uncovered Gustavus' flank; he prepared to strike him there, and wheeled in upon him. Gustavus was ready. Forming a crotchet of his left, he reinforced Horn, and then, heading the cavalry of the right, he rode down the late line of battle, captured Tilly's guns, and turned them on the enemy. The centre swung round so as to prolong Horn's new line, and Torstenson's guns took Tilly's squares in flank. The battle was won; but brave Tilly with his Walloons held firm until fairly torn to shreds. Then, thrice wounded, the old hero was borne off the field by his beaten troops *d'élite*. The victory was complete. Activity had proved superior to weight.

THE original intention of Tilly had been to operate defensively behind the Elster and Saale until his belated lieutenants should arrive, but Pappenheim had been hotly urging on his chief the necessity of at once quelling the spirit of the

Protestants by beating them in battle, as he had no doubt
unconquered Tilly could do. Few of the generals sustained
the chief in waiting for reinforcements, and Tilly listened to
the plea of his young and ardent officers. The events around
Leipsic brought the armies together, and after the capture
of the city, Tilly sat down with his back to it to await the
onmarch of the new allies.

The plain north of Leipsic is admirably adapted for the
evolutions of an army. It stretches for miles in either direction with but slight accentuation, and what slopes do exist
are as if created for the play of artillery. Tilly had previously sent out and intrenched some heights at Entritsch so
as to hold the road from Düben, and had selected for his line
the elevation facing Podelwitz and Göbschelwitz athwart the
allied advance; his batteries, protected in a slight way by
earthworks, lay near the turnpike.

While the Swedes and Saxons, in the gray of the morning
of September 17, 1631, were preparing to cross the Loberbach in their advance on Leipsic, Tilly led his brilliant
column to these same heights and out beyond; and some
time before the arrival of the allies, had drawn up his long
array, with Breitenfeld to the rear of his left, a mile or so
away, and Seehausen behind his right. The sun and wind
were both at his back, a feature much in his favor.

In contrast to the rough and rusty Swedes, Tilly commanded a splendid-looking set of veterans. His army numbered men who had followed him for years, and knew that
he had never yet been conquered in a battle. Prominent
among these were his Walloons, at the head of whom he
took his stand on his white battle-charger, which was known
to every man in line. As the rugged old veteran of seventy-
two passed along, shouts of "Father Tilly!" rang from
battalion to battalion. There was no feeling of uncertainty

in the imperial army. That full-throated cheer presaged success.

As variously computed, Tilly had from thirty-two to forty thousand men, of which a quarter was cavalry. He drew up the infantry in seventeen great battalia, of fifteen hundred to two thousand men each, in the centre, and ranged the horse in similar masses of about one thousand men, ten deep, on the flanks. Pappenheim with his famous black cuirassiers was on the left, Fürstenberg, who had personally come up, was on the right, with the cavalry just back from Italy, under Isolani, in first line. Tilly is credited with but twenty-six guns. This was the number reported as captured by the Swedes, but it seems as if there must have been more. His guns were difficult to handle, but he would scarcely meet his new antagonist without an effort to place in line batteries more nearly equal to the Swedish, whose effectiveness he must well know. His heavy guns were placed between the right wing and the centre; his light guns in front of the centre.

It has been asserted on the generally plausible ground of the custom of the day, that Tilly's army was drawn up in two lines. But all old pictures of the battle show but one line, and Tilly covered so great a stretch of front that, with his deep battalia, he had scarce enough men to form a regular second line. Only the Italian author Gualdo speaks of two lines; other accounts mention no second one. However disposed, the imperial line was longer than the allied, considerably overlapping the Swedish. Tilly had many times won success by wheeling in on the enemy's flank, and he may have hoped to do so here. Not prolific of novelties in tactics, he based his faith on the time-tried manœuvre. His men bound white kerchiefs in their hats, and the watchword was "Jesu-Maria!"

With a small column of cavalry, Pappenheim had been sent forward to arrest the allied advance at the little stream Loberbach, if perchance some advantage might be had of them.

At early daylight the Swedes had fallen into line, and advanced in battle order across the even plain from Wolkau, towards Leipsic. After an hour and a half's march they ran across the enemy's van, and then caught sight of the imperial array on the slopes where it had taken up its stand. To cross the Loberbach, the armies were compelled to ploy into column, and here they encountered the skirmishers of Pappenheim; but they threw them back, and crossed at the several fords.

The Swedes held the right and centre; the Saxons the left; but the two armies fought as separate organizations. There is no record of the Saxon formation; the Swedish may be of interest. The Saxons lay on the east of the Düben road; the Swedes on the west.

The Swedish centre had in first line four brigades of foot under Generals Winkel, Carl Hall, Teuffel and Åke Oxenstiern; in reserve to the first line the cavalry regiment of Ortenburg, and the Scottish infantry under Monroe and Ramsey. In second line the centre had three brigades, of which one Scotch under General Hepburn, and two German under Generals Vitzthum and Thurn. Behind this stood the reserve cavalry under Schafmann and Kochtitzky.

At the head of the right wing, which was mostly cavalry, stood Field-Marshal Banér, second in command. In first line were the East Gothland, Småland, West Gothland, and two Finland regiments under Tott; and the Wünsch and Stålhandske regiments, the best of their kind. Between each two of the small cavalry divisions there was stationed a body of two hundred musketeers. In reserve was the Rhinegrave regiment. In second line stood the cavalry regiments of Sperreuter, Damitz, and the Courland and Livonia regiments.

Field-Marshal Horn commanded the left wing. In first line stood the cavalry regiments of Baudissin, Calenbach and Horn, interspersed with the bodies of two hundred musketeers already mentioned. There was no reserve to this first line. In second line came Courville's and Hall's cavalry regiments. Between each two cavalry divisions was the same body of two hundred musketeers.

The regimental pieces were in front of the regiments; what we might call the reserve artillery was massed in front of the left centre under Torstenson.

On the left of Horn came the Saxons, destined by their utter lack of discipline, not to say cowardice, to aid in winning the battle.

The whole Swedish army wore hopeful green branches in their headgear, and the pass-word was "God with us!" Gustavus, who, despite his growing bulkiness, was always a noble figure, addressed the troops amid great enthusiasm. He wore but his common buff coat, and a gray hat with a green feather. Armor he had long ago discarded as uncomfortable; for the Danzig bullet still lay in his shoulder, and he was irritated by the weight of the cuirass. He sought but the protection of the Almighty.

The Saxon army was freshly equipped, and looked well. The imperialists wore gold and silver ornamented clothes, — the plunder of an hundred towns, — and from their headgear nodded fine plumes. Their horses were big showy Germans; the Swedish horses were small and gaunt. Compared to the other soldiers on this field, the Swedish peasant made a slender show; but the stuff was in him, as his fine friends and foes alike found out and long remembered.

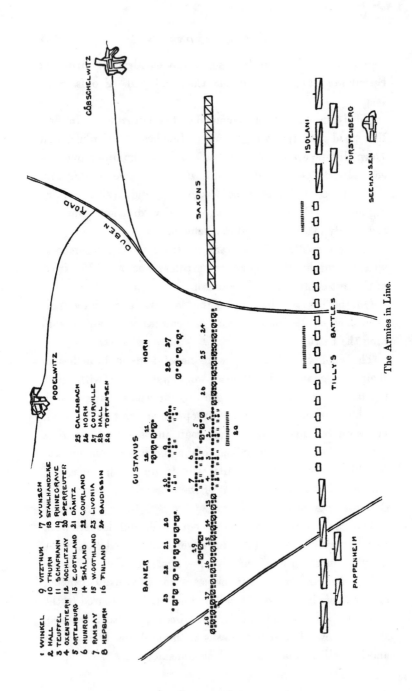

The Armies in Line.

So soon as they came within range, the imperial artillery began playing on the allies, and their marshaling took place under constant fire; but when the Swedish guns could be got up, they were put in battery, and replied three shots for one. The advance and deployment of the allied line had taken till nearly noon, and for two hours and a half after that time, there was no exchange except a cannonade, which indeed went on during the whole day.

Pappenheim's splendid cuirassiers had returned from the Loberbach and had taken place in line. All were now awaiting some incident to call for an opening attack; the imperialists expected the allies to advance, and Gustavus was making sure that all was ready, to give the signal call.

Pappenheim was growing restless. He was bold and impatient. Having stood the Swedish artillery fire for a number of hours, he could contain himself no longer. Gathering his five thousand horse in hand, and without awaiting orders from his chief, he thundered down upon Banér, who held the Swedish right, galloping in on him at the head of the best cavalry division then in arms. Tilly recognized his lieutenant's mistake before he had ridden a hundred yards. "They have robbed me of my honor and my glory!" he cried, throwing up his arms in despair.

In order to place his line where the disadvantage of dust would not be so great — the wind was southwest and the plain parched from a long drouth — Gustavus had, after crossing the Loberbach, moved well to his right, to establish his position.

The idea of Pappenheim was that he could edge to the left enough to outflank the Swedes, and then, by a half right wheel, push in and destroy their flank. He did not know Banér. He forgot, too, that his advance would separate him from the main body of the army at a time when he

might be sadly needed. His action was in every sense to
blame.

Not only was Pappenheim's advance an error, what was
worse, it failed.

The Swedish formation and excellent behavior easily withstood the shock. The "commanded musketeers" — as the
small bodies interspersed with the cavalry were called —
received the cuirassiers with withering salvos, and between
shots the Finns and Goths charged out on the horsemen
with a gallantry which cheered the whole right flank. Banér
at once understood the purpose of the brave but over-impetu-
ous Pappenheim; and when the imperial commander turned
from the Swedish front, and rode around its flank, he was
met before he was ready by a stiff counter-charge from one
of the cavalry regiments in reserve behind the first line.
Not discouraged, though checked, Pappenheim renewed and
renewed his charges. Seven times did he rally his men, and
dash down upon the Swedish front and flank; but the musketeers — fit prototype of Fritz's Prussian foot — stood their
ground as steadily in the hand to hand conflict as if they had
been on parade, and the Swedish cavalry, though lighter by
far, wavered not from their doughty resistance. The Holstein infantry regiment, which was sent by Tilly to Pappenheim's support, was cut to pieces, and the duke fell at the
head of his men. No impression whatever had been created
by Pappenheim's advance; and even this *preux chevalier* was
eventually thrown back, decimated and unnerved, was followed sharply by Banér and driven off the field. The wreck
fled towards Halle, and Gustavus discreetly recalled the pur-
suers to the line.

It must be remembered that the cavalry charge of that
day was not delivered at a gallop. The troops rather rode
at a trot, and at a convenient distance halted to use their

firearms. So long as there was a volley left, they did not draw their swords. It was not a question of solid impact; cavalry was not then the "arm of the moment;" it fought like infantry on horseback, and the footman's "push of pike" was much more common than the horseman's cold steel, so long as the enemy showed a front. When he lost steadiness, came the cavalryman's chance; he could slash up broken infantry if he could not break it.

On the allied left the result was different indeed. The charge of the imperial cavalry, under Fürstenberg and Isolani, could not long be held back after Pappenheim had started on his gallant but mistaken ride; the squadrons drove forward, straight upon the Saxon array. Nor did they meet a line of Swedish veterans; except for some efforts by the horse and artillery, they crushed in the Saxon formation the moment they reached it; and the loss of a few gunners, the unseating of a few officers, was enough to send the bespangled battalions of John George to the right-about. The elector was seized with an equal terror; he and his body-guard turned and spurred away to Eilenburg. In a short half hour the imperial cavalry of the right had driven the whole Saxon contingent — nearly half the army — from the field; having done which, it prepared to turn in upon the now naked left flank of the king of Sweden.

The Swedish train behind the army caught the infection from the flying Saxons, and made its way to the rear, in much disorder. As non-combatants they were mostly hired Germans, on whose stanchness no reliance could be placed.

The battle had begun without the orders of Father Tilly; it was running its course without any interference by him; it was going quite against his wishes. But at this juncture, from his position in the centre, he was quick to see that the Saxon flight had opened a chance by which he might repair

the errors already made, and win the day. The Swedish
left was open; and Tilly's centre of irresistible Spanish
battalia not only overlapped it, but he now outnumbered the
king at least three to two. Moreover Tilly was compelled
to act, for the fire from Torstenson's quick-served guns was
growing deadlier every minute. He gave the order to
advance in the wake of Fürstenberg, and, in the belief that
the king would not separate his left from his centre, obliqued
to the right, so as to get well beyond Gustavus' left. The
direction of his movement was to the east of the Düben
road; and be it said for the credit of Tilly's manœuvring
capacity, that a part of his heavy line of battalia was able
to march obliquely to the right, make a partial wheel to the
left, and still advance in serried ranks against the position
where, when it started out over two hours before, had stood
the Swedish naked flank; while Fürstenberg rode further to
the north, to come down upon its rear.

But Gustavus was alive to the danger, and Horn could
manœuvre twice as fast as the best of Tilly's battles. Under
Gustavus' instructions Horn smartly wheeled his wing to
the left, threw out detachments to hold the ditches of the
Düben road, and was ready to meet the imperial general
long before he reached the spot; while the king, hastily
drawing Vitzthum's and Hepburn's brigades from the second
line of the centre, threw them in to sustain the new line on
the left. The fight here was thus established on a safe basis,
and despite their heroic charges the Swedes drove the imperial cavalry back, and were ready to attack the battalia when
they should put in their appearance.

Now came the moment for Gustavus and his mobile line,
and the king grasped it in a twinkling. Riding back to the
right, he gave hurried orders to Banér, and heading the
West Gothland horse down along the front of the Swedish

line, he sent them charging at a furious gallop in on the
flank of Tilly's battles. Here it was cold steel; not a volley
was fired, but the squadrons dashed straight at the enemy
with the momentum of a
pas de charge. Gustavus
himself waited but to seize
the Smålanders, East
Gothlanders and Finns, —
four regiments, — and followed hard along, bearing
to the right up the slope
where still stood the im-
perial guns. These were
heavy and hard to move,
and the king and his

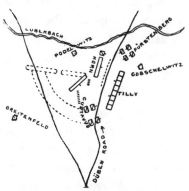

Battle of Breitenfeld. (2d Phase.)

horsemen swept over them wholesale, captured them in a
trice, sabred the gunners where they stood, and in a few
minutes turned the battery against the flank of Tilly's line,
now standing at bay where the brave old soldier had hoped
to turn the tide. Never, in modern days, had the chances
of battle been improved by so rapid, so masterly, so bold a
manœuvre.

The temporary promise of success of the imperial right,
and the failure of its left, had thus given a new and curious
direction to the line of battle. The Swedish left stood
almost at right angles to where it had first been marshaled,
with Tilly, in more or less irregular order from his unwonted
manœuvre, facing it. The king had captured Tilly's original position, and was not only pounding the imperialists
with their own cannon-balls, but Torstenson had swung round
his reserve artillery, which had stood in front of the Swedish
centre, and was pouring the contents of his munition wagons,
on a line parallel to the late Swedish front, into the huge,

defiant squares. Gustavus now made a general wheel to the left by his centre and right, so as to prolong the new front of Horn. He had already, by capturing the imperial batteries, cut the enemy off from Leipsic, but the battle was still to be won, and there was a fierce and prolonged hand to hand fight along the Düben road. With all the artillery in his hands and all the cavalry now left upon the field, it could, however, end but one way. It was solely a question of how complete the victory should be; of what losses the imperialists would stand before their resistance was turned into flight; of how tough Father Tilly was.

Tilly's veterans fought in a way to preserve their own fame and their general's reputation. Standing at bay with the Swedish array on two sides of them, torn by the fire of their own and the enemy's guns; with their cavalry in distant flight, no reserves to aid, no hope of anything but destruction, the battles of Tilly stuck manfully to their task. Gaps were torn in their ranks to no purpose. There they stood, partly from gallant love of their rough old chief, partly from the sheer inertia of their massed formation, — as the ranks of Porus had stood at the Hydaspes, as the Russian hollow square would stand at Kunersdorf. Finally, towards nightfall, the stampede began. Once begun, it spread fast, and shortly, save a small body of braves who surrounded Tilly, the infantry battalia melted into a mass of fugitives. There was no organization left. Pappenheim's famous horsemen had hours ago been broken, and with Fürstenberg's had fled; and Tilly's battles crumbled before the activity of the Swedish onslaught.

The Saxon guns were recaptured by the Swedes. The imperial army lost seven thousand killed, six thousand wounded and captured, all its artillery, ninety flags and the whole train. The rest of the army fled in every direction, mostly towards Halle, whither, thrice wounded and scarcely escaping capture, Tilly also made his way, and from thence to Halberstadt. Here he joined Pappenheim, collected what he could of his forces, and retired to the line of the Weser.

It is related that, so soon as the battle was fairly won, Gustavus dismounted, kneeled on the blood-stained field, and offered up thanks to the Giver of Victory, while all near by him joined earnestly in his pious act. With Gustavus such sincerity was inbred, — like the unspoken battle prayers of Stonewall Jackson.

The king, whose loss had not exceeded twenty-one hundred killed and wounded, left the Saxon contingent to capture Leipsic, and followed up the retreating imperialists. With his usual push he himself headed a body of fifteen hundred horse, and at Merseburg, on September 19, overtook a considerable detachment, beat it, and captured three thousand prisoners. He occupied Halle, September 21, but did not pursue beyond the Saale, for he wished to be secure in his foothold in Saxony before he moved decisively into western or southern Germany. The imperial garrison in Leipsic surrendered September 23, and the Saxons returned to Torgau.

After lying some time in the Halberstadt region, Tilly moved to the Weser, where he recovered his strength rapidly. "Whose house doth burn, Must soldier turn" was true, and he found plenty of recruits.

Breitenfeld, the first great battle of the modern era, is peculiar in more than one way. Counting out the Saxons, who were but a source of weakness, the king was heavily outnumbered, and was attacked successively and in force on both flanks, in a manner which on more than one occasion has proved fatal to an army. Attempted flank attacks sometimes open gaps in the line which delivers them, and result in more harm to it than gain made against the enemy. In this case, the flank attacks, while not lacking in direction and vigor, were met with great constancy; and Pappenheim's being delivered without orders, took the control of the battle out of the hands of the general in command. The situation which led up to Tilly's overthrow was none of his making, though Pappenheim afterwards complained of not being supported in his first charge, and it was Tilly's putting all his strength into the manœuvre on the naked Swedish left flank which practically broke up his line. This would not have happened had Tilly been faced by a line of slow-moving battles; and few generals, in any era, would have neglected so apparently good an opening. It was the Swedish mobility, led by Gustavus' splendid vigor, and his true *coup d'œil* to seize the moment and order the manœuvre needed, which won the battle, rather than Tilly's errors which lost it. Against a heavy line like his own the imperial general would doubtless have been victorious, despite the error of Pappenheim.

Gustavus was at once recognized as the Protestant Hero. Those who had looked askance at him, who had likened him to Christian of Denmark, were now vociferous in his praise; those who had feared to join his standard by word or deed, lest heavy retribution should await them in case of failure, now openly declared for him. All Germany was overrun with pamphlets to laud him, with pictures and medals of Gustavus the Great. For once the Catholic press and pamphleteers were silenced. Their defeat had been too overwhelming. Nothing could be said to excuse it.

The spirit of the Swedes was as much heightened by this victory as the king had gained in glory. The enlistment of prisoners and the gathering up of garrisons swelled the ranks

of the Protestant allies. A new army assembled on the
lower Elbe; Tott besieged Rostock, while Landgrave William and Duke Bernard held Fugger in check, cleaned
Hesse-Cassel of imperial troops, and made enterprising raids
into adjoining Catholic territory.

GUSTAVE ADOLPHE, ROI DE SUEDE
(Peint par Michiel van Mierevelt et gravé par W. J. Delff, 1633.)

XXI.

TOWARDS THE MAIN. SEPTEMBER AND OCTOBER, 1631.

In fourteen months Gustavus had not only securely established his bastion, but at Breitenfeld had quite changed the aspect of the cause; all laggards now crowded around him with offers of help. Tilly retired behind the Weser; the Catholics saw in the Snow King a dangerous opponent; and the Protestant prospects were flattering. Even Wallenstein aspired to serve the king, but Gustavus mistrusted him. With Saxony and Brandenburg as allies, Gustavus moved confidently to the Erfurt country, through Thuringia to the Main, and to the bishoprics dubbed the Priest's Alley, leaving John George to command an operation towards Silesia. Many thought the king should march direct on Vienna; but it was method, not temerity, which distinguished Gustavus, and he preferred not to prejudice what was already won. Tilly was watched by a minor column, and the king pushed on to the Main. He used his interior lines; every strip gained was carefully guarded; treaties were made with the lands he crossed, and with the free cities, such as Nürnberg. The Main was reached early in October, Würzburg and its castle taken, contributions levied, and the Jesuits banished. Tilly meanwhile raised a new army, marched to Aschaffenburg, joined the duke of Lorraine, and began to operate timorously in the region south of the Main, with near forty thousand men.

ONLY fourteen months had elapsed since Gustavus had landed in Germany, but by his far-seeing, cautious and well-digested plans, crowned by the decisive victory of Breitenfeld, he had completely changed the prospects of the Protestants. He had secured a firm footing in northern Germany, where he held all but a few of the strong places down to Saxony, and had isolated these. His communications with Sweden were secured by the control of the sea, and he had practically established his long-coveted *Dominium Maris Baltici*. After many and vexatious delays he had concluded treaties with Brandenburg, Saxony, Hesse-Cassel and Weimar, and was strengthened by accessions of troops, tendered and promised from many other quarters. On landing, the horizon was dark and unpromising; the sky had now cleared, and the sun of success blazed forth to cheer the hearts of all.

As Gustavus had gained in moral weight, so his army had gained in aplomb and confidence. His operations had at times appeared slow and cautious, but they had been sure, and, what is better, were justified by the results. He had met with but one serious failure, — Magdeburg, — and this was chargeable to the elector of Saxony. Breitenfeld had placed him on the most prominent pedestal in Europe. The Catholics no longer looked *de haut en bas* on the "Snow King." He was a redoubtable opponent as well as the Protestant Hero, — the "Lion of the North and Bulwark of the Faith." The imperialists had lost in spirit and organization all that the Swedes had gained. Their retreat to the Weser opened the heart of the emperor's possessions to the king's thrust, with but a trivial force in the way. The emperor's authority had received from his "new little enemy" an almost fatal blow, and the Protestants of north and west Germany, who, cowed into submission, had feared to welcome the uncertainty of Swedish aid, now rose, and with hearty good-will enlisted under Gustavus' standards. These fourteen months had distinctly shifted the moral superiority from the Catholic to the Protestant party. Gustavus had risen beyond being king of Sweden. He was now the leader of the attack in a great German war, in which the task he had undertaken was to establish beyond future question the equality of religions all over the land. But the work was not yet in a condition to leave to others. Gustavus had put his hand to the plow, and might not look back. It required the same wise and vigorous action in the future, to complete the structure which had been so well builded in the past.

Tilly's lamentable failure to withstand the Swedish advance began again to draw attention to Wallenstein, who had been nursing his wrath in a species of court in his Bohemian castles, or nursing his gout in Karlsbad. The terror which had been engendered by Gustavus' successes on the Oder now sank into insignificance before the terror inspired by the battle of Breitenfeld. The walls of cities hundreds of miles distant from the scene of action were kept manned; Bohemian forests were laid low to block the roads upon which it was feared that the king might advance; in Prague they equipped a new army; in the Ingolstadt churches they prayed to be "delivered from the devil and the Swedes, the Finns and the Lapps." Vienna was said to be "dumb with fright;" the emperor was so nearly at the end of his wits, say some questionable chroniclers, that he sought means of bringing about peace, and even contemplated flight to Gratz. Universal terror pointed the world to Wallenstein. Only he could inspire confidence; the popular sentiment was in his favor, in the army and outside.

It is a curious fact that of the noted soldiers of the Thirty Years' War, only Pappenheim was a German, and while Pappenheim was a bold and able lieutenant, he was killed before he rose to higher command. Gustavus was a Swede; Wallenstein was a Czech; Tilly a Walloon; Turenne a Frenchman; of the minor generals, the only German who won repute was Bernard of Weimar, and he forfeited his all at Nördlingen.

Oddly, Wallenstein had been looking in another direction, — towards his old antagonist, Gustavus. Approaches are said to have been made to him about these days by England; they certainly were by the Swedish monarch, and these

Wallenstein had not thrust aside, though he openly denied them. Tilly heard the rumor of such negotiations and taxed the Czech with it; but Wallenstein reassured him. In the same way Gustavus sought to influence Arnim, so as to reach Saxony. He was not above any honorable means to accomplish his end, and Wallenstein was in no man's employ. Nor would it have made any odds if he had been. Like the rest he was a mercenary, even if a great one. Still more important to the fortunes of Germany, Wallenstein stood in correspondence with Arnim. It was in keeping with the spirit of the times that these secret negotiations should go on. Save Gustavus, scarce a potentate in Europe had a disinterested servant. The great Bohemian, unlike most of his contemporaries, was not hide-bound by religion. He had broader aims, and would have welcomed an era of tolerance, in which he could strive for a German empire, under the Hapsburgs, to be upheld by himself as military chief. In another sense Gustavus had equal aspirations, but not for the German crown.

His dismissal from command had hit Wallenstein hard. In the summer of 1631 he undoubtedly stood ready to enter into an alliance with Gustavus, and to serve the Protestant cause, to revenge his wrongs on Ferdinand. Gustavus was almost on the point of intrusting him with an army, but it is doubtful if, in the Swedish service, Wallenstein would have proved a success. Then came the battle of Breitenfeld; and the emperor began once more to look towards his ancient general. But Wallenstein was disinclined to listen, and for a while it appeared as if the three strongest men in Europe — Gustavus, Richelieu, and Wallenstein — were to form an anti-Hapsburg triumvirate.

Now that Gustavus had shown his strength, the Anhalt princes joined the cause. They made a treaty at Halle to

pay three thousand rix dollars a month, to build forts and
bridges as directed by the king and at their own cost, to
hold their strong places and defiles for the Swedes while
denying passage to the emperor, and generally to act under
Gustavus' direction, in exchange for the protection afforded
by the alliance.

As when Magdeburg was crying aloud for succor, there
was again more than one road open to Gustavus. He must
choose his plan. Should he move against west Germany and
the beaten army of Tilly, who was now basing himself on
the Catholic princes of the Rhine; should he march through
the Thuringian forest on Franconia and the "Priest's
Alley;" or should he move southeastward, on the emperor's
hereditary possessions? At a council of war held at Halle
shortly after the victory, the elector of Saxony and William
of Weimar were present. John George had recovered from
the disgrace of his own and his army's flight from the battle-
field, for Gustavus had treated him, as he could well afford
to do, with an easy touch. After the battle the king had
sent to congratulate him on the victory, and to thank him
for having suggested an immediate movement on the enemy,
— and dull John George was as far from appreciating the
touch of satire in the facts as Gustavus was from intending
any slur. At this council Oxenstiern and many others
advised a march on Vienna. Count Horn made a strong
military plea for it. A summary operation, they thought,
against the emperor in his capital would bring him to a
peace which would set all the questions of Europe at rest.
There were few forces — perhaps ten thousand men under
Tiefenbach in Silesia, and less in Bohemia under Maradas
— to oppose such a march, and the elector of Saxony promised to care for the southwest. That the sentiment was
strongly in favor of such a project is shown by the fact that,

twenty years afterwards, Oxenstiern reiterated his opinion before the senate in Stockholm that such a march would have been the wisest one to make. The chancellor could be venturesome on occasion.

But though not slow to see the advantages suggested, the plan did not meet with the king's idea of a systematic method of carrying on the campaign; nor, be it said to his honor, did it chime with the pledges he had given his Protestant friends. So far results had come, not from the boldness, but the caution of his operations. What he had won and held was by intelligently securing each step as he progressed, and by doing nothing which had not its place in the general plan. Still, as was his wont, the king weighed carefully all the *pros* and *cons*, and listened patiently to every suggestion.

Small confidence could be felt in the ability of the Saxon army, beaten so easily at Breitenfeld, to do satisfactory work against imperial forces in the Main country, if Ferdinand should order a concentration there. John George, and especially Arnim, would be glad to control the south German territory; for John George had political and financial schemes to push there, and Arnim his Third Party business; none of which appealed to Gustavus' common sense. The king preferred personally to undertake south Germany, while the Saxons should sustain a force of twelve thousand Swedes, and a Bohemian army to be placed under Wallenstein's command (should he be won over), and the latter with this force might push on to Vienna. Moreover, Gustavus never quite lost his anxiety as to his communications, for he reposed no faith in the constancy of John George or George William, and could still conceive the possibility, even if remote, of Saxony and Brandenburg rising behind him, should he be too far distant. A single check in a movement on Vienna by his main force would be surely fatal. He knew the iron will of Ferdinand, and did not believe that even the sack of his capital would bring him to terms. The emperor had already been tried in this matter, — and Vienna at that day was not the capital which it now is. Like the Madrid of the eighteenth century, it might be taken by an enemy a dozen times without affecting the war. Ferdinand might retire to the south and involve Gustavus in an extremely dangerous stern chase. Nor was a march on Vienna the best way to compel the withdrawal of the Edict of Restitution. Nothing but Gustavus' presence could stay Tilly from visiting on any of the Protestant cities the fate of Magdeburg. The king must consider the work to be done before winter, and decide where he might best dispose his troops. Along the Main lay the rich Catholic bishoprics, — and here he could not only victual his men, but repair the wrongs of his brother Protestants. How much more negotiation was needful to induce the Protestant princes to work together was uncertain. Breitenfeld had changed people's faces, but the king had not forgotten his long struggle with Brandenburg and Saxony, and he believed that a single failure would renew the doubtful attitude of most of his present supporters.

The king's immediate idea was that he would personally move to the Erfurt country for winter-quarters, and govern his further operations from there. Not that he would disperse his men, but he would accumulate magazines, and make his own headquarters here, while the troops lay in Thuringia, with Hesse, Weimar and Saxony near by; and from here he would move on the Franconian bishoprics, compel contributions, recruit up an army for a brilliant campaign in 1632, and utilize the winter to consolidate his conquests, and to bring his allies to work in unison and furnish men and money as well as smiles and promises. Tilly must be considered; but the king deemed it sufficient to secure his own right by defensive means against him and the Rhineland princes, and his proposal to occupy, free and arm south-western Germany would cut Tilly off from Bavaria and the emperor; while, if successful, it would win as firm a footing in western Germany as he already had in northern. All parties agreed that it was not worth while to follow Tilly to the Weser. Such an advance with his main force would be taking the king away from his general direction, which should lead to southern Germany and towards the emperor. Though he must not be overlooked, operations against Tilly need not be conducted by the main force; a part of the allied armies, while protecting the king's flank, could prevent the imperialists gaining dangerous headway.

The march on Vienna was given over. Gustavus preferred to operate from his interior lines against all his enemies at the same time. With his main force he would move through Thuringia and Franconia to Swabia, to rouse southern Germany into activity, and gain a vantage-ground from which to attack Bavaria. When he should have secured the whole region from the lower Oder to the middle and upper Rhine, he could operate against Bavaria and Austria from the west. Meanwhile the Saxon, and perhaps Wallenstein's, campaign against Silesia, Bohemia and Moravia would secure the king's left in his advance, and keep up the semblance of an operation against Vienna; and the army of Hesse-Cassel and Weimar would operate against Tilly, prevent his venturing into western Germany, and secure the king's right. No doubt this plan was the wisest, though it did not suit all the Swedish generals, as it certainly did not satisfy the king's paymaster, Richelieu. But this far-seeing statesman did not withdraw his financial support.

The plan thus finally adopted by Gustavus has been much criticised by soldiers. Folard likens his declination to march on Vienna to that of Hannibal, who failed to march on Rome after the overwhelming victory of Cannæ. The comparison — though not so intended — is an apt one. Both Gustavus and Hannibal were right in their action.

Lossau gives a better set of reasons. Tilly, he argues, was beaten, but he should, with Fugger and Aldringer, have been followed up and annihilated. For this purpose, eight to ten thousand men under Horn or Banér sufficed; and when the work was accomplished, the corps could rejoin the main army. The elector of Saxony could easily manage the problem of the south German states with a small force, — there being no great opposition there, and could lend Gustavus a large part of his forces for a march on Vienna, which there was at the moment no organized army to oppose. Through Bohemia and Moravia the Swedish army could be easily victualed, and such a march might have made the subsequent raising of Wallenstein's army impossible. In the event, he says, Gustavus was compelled to operate on the Danube under much less favorable conditions. On the Baltic, in Saxony, in Bohemia, in Westphalia, in Hesse, in Thuringia, in Franconia, everything went well for Gustavus; ill for the emperor. Ferdinand had but fifty thousand men; he had lost more than half Germany; Hungary was threatened; Bavaria was unreliable; the Protestants of Upper and Lower Austria were in revolt. What better time for Gustavus to push home than the present?

All this is fair and proper criticism. But, prior to Gustavus' advent in Germany, there had been, in the history of the Christian era, many bold operations, and there had been no methodical ones. It was method that Gustavus was to teach in war, not alone boldness. This last quality is common, when taken by itself; combined with discretion it is rare. As Alexander would not advance into the heart of Persia until he had acquired as a base the entire eastern Mediterranean coast; as Hannibal declined after both Trasimene and Cannæ to march on Rome; as Cæsar, after crossing the Rubicon, took all the towns on the Adriatic before he would march to the capital, so Gustavus now decided to make sure of what he had, and to risk nothing for a questionable gain. In the purely military aspect, he was right; taking the political factors into account, doubly so.

In pursuance of this general scheme — which was far-sighted, reckoned on all the political and military factors, paid due heed to the demands of his Protestant allies, and had a basis of broad but to the world novel military judgment — the Swedish monarch set to work. Banér was ordered to leave a garrison in Landsberg, to deliver up possession of Frankfort and Crossen to the elector of Brandenburg, to take command of the Saxon army when it should be in condition for the field, to draw in the Havel and Werben garrisons, and to assume a strong position near Calbe on the Elbe, building forts at Rosenburg and Dessau, the mouths of the Saale and the Mulde. He was to send a cavalry force to take Halberstadt, and to aim at capturing Magdeburg; in fact, Banér was to clear the western skirts of the bastion of all imperialists and then to watch it.

Tott, who lay on the lower Elbe, with the same end in view was instructed to seek helpful alliances in the Brunswick-Lüneburg-Lauenburg territory, and with the free cities of Bremen, Lübeck and Hamburg. He was to besiege Rostock, and capture the outstanding towns in the Bremen region. All recruits to arrive from England, Scotland and the Netherlands — and they were a large body — were to land in the Weser and join Tott.

Oxenstiern was instructed to order sundry Prussian garrisons to Pomerania, from which most of the seasoned troops
had been drawn. He had already reported in person to the
king, who was glad to have him near at hand as an adviser.

Starting on September 27 from Halle, the king, with
twenty-six thousand men, headed for Thuringia, by way of
Querfurt. He was not sure that he could push beyond this
section before winter.

On October 2 Erfurt, one of the chief cities of the elector
of Mainz, primate of Catholic Germany, was seized by a
clever stratagem of Duke William, and after much discussion agreed to serve the cause, and was strongly garrisoned.
Here a final treaty was made with the four brothers of the
house of Saxe-Weimar.

The operations of the year had brought about a change in
the strategic position. In securing his bastion on the Baltic,
Gustavus had a base which called for a front of operations
running east and west, from say Landsberg to Werben.
He now found himself backing on the Elbe and Saale. His
rear was protected by the Frankfort-Crossen line, and no
enemy was near it except Tiefenbach in Silesia. Along the
Elbe-Saale he lay practically facing west, with the centre
point of operations at Erfurt, and groups of forces on his
right extending down the Elbe. These groups, under Tott
and Banér, on completing their work would join Landgrave
William in the Saale region; while the Royal Army would
push through the Thuringian Forest to the Werra, and on
through Franconia to the Main. This advance would help
the forces on the Oder by driving back the enemy, as well
as aid the Saxons in their advance through Silesia and
Bohemia. But until the imperial allies along the Rhine,
with the Spanish Netherlands at their back, could be neutralized, Gustavus could not safely extend his base so as to
project a line of advance on the heart of the empire.

At Erfurt the forces controlled by Gustavus and expected to be raised were substantially as follows: The Royal Army numbered eighteen thousand foot, six hundred dragoons and seventy-five hundred cavalry, which it was purposed to increase by eleven thousand foot and seventy-five hundred horse. Banér had four thousand men in the field and thirty-five hundred in garrison, which were to be increased by six thousand and twenty-six hundred respectively. Tott had five thousand five hundred Swedes and eight thousand Mecklenburgers, plus ten thousand eight hundred in garrison; all to be increased by six thousand Dutch troops, five thousand recruits, eight thousand in new regiments and thirty - five hundred Swedish cavalry. Hesse - Cassel had ten thousand men, to be increased by seven thousand; and Weimar was to raise eleven thousand five hundred. Thus the seventy thousand men already under the colors, it was hoped, would be nearly doubled. These calculations were well borne out by the promise.

As Bernard preferred to serve immediately under the king, Gustavus left the reigning duke, William of Weimar, in command of the Thuringian territory, to recruit for the above contingents, and gave him as a nucleus twenty-six hundred foot and four hundred horse.

How far Gustavus planned his advance from Erfurt cannot be said; but he sent embassies to Bayreuth and to Nürnberg to pave the way. He took no step in the dark. The army advanced through the Thüringerwald range in two columns: one via Gotha and Meiningen, one under the king in person via Arnstadt (October 7), Ilmenau and Schleusingen (October 8), where headquarters were established. The two columns reunited at the fortress of Königshofen, the key to the bishopric of Würzburg, which succumbed only to Torstenson's heavy guns, and was left with a strong garrison.

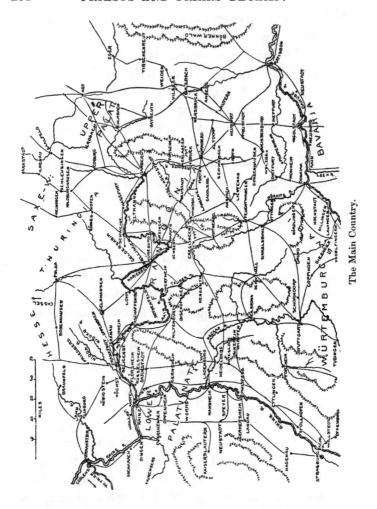

The next place essential to clear the country between the Saale and the Main was Schweinfurt, which surrendered, and received a sure commandant with a suitable garrison. Gustavus was greeted by the laity as the harbinger of freedom, but there was a great flight of priests and friars. He issued a proclamation covering all kinds and conditions of men. He had come, he said, to protect the Protestants from further injustice; but all, whatever their faith, who obeyed the law, would be protected from injury. Arrived October 13 at Würzburg, the capital of Franconia, whose prince-bishop had fled, the town capitulated October 15; but the garrison and chief inhabitants retired with their valuables to the castle of Marienburg, on the further bank, where they deemed themselves quite beyond reach.

This castle lies on a high rock, perpendicular on the water side, but approachable from the land. The gate was protected by a deep ditch, with a half-moon outwork; there were no other defenses. The bridge over the Main had been broken down, but this was repaired; Colonel Ramsay was sent over it, and Colonel Leslie put across in boats, each with a detachment, under a heavy fire, by which they suffered considerably. The place refused terms, and the Swedes opened lines and erected batteries. After the destruction of one of the towers, on October 18, about 5 A. M., the castle was stormed by several regiments, led by Colonels Lillie and Burt. Though stoutly defended, the party gained the half-moon with ladders, and drove out the garrison, pursuing which through the drawbridge, let down for the fugitives, the Swedes pushed on, blew down the gate, and captured the place. Immense booty was taken, as Marienburg was the strongest place on the Main, and had been made a storehouse for valuables; a vast amount of ordnance-stores was got; and the bishop's valuable library was sent to Upsala University. Würzburg was mulcted eighty thousand rix dollars, and town and castle were strengthened and suitably held. All Jesuit property was confiscated, but no person was injured. The Jesuit was, according to Gustavus, *hostis humani generis*, and was treated accordingly. Protestant worship was restored.

At Würzburg was made a treaty between the king and the Franconian Circle; the duke of Lüneburg came with offers to raise some regiments; and an embassy from Würtemberg arrived. With Nürnberg, after long negotiations and delays, a treaty offensive and defensive was concluded October 21, and the city raised a garrison of three thousand foot and two hundred and fifty horse, and strengthened its defenses. Similar treaties were made with Anspach and Bayreuth. At the same time a demand was made on the bishop-electors of Cologne, Mainz and Trier to acknowledge Gustavus' authority; to pay forty thousand rix dollars a month; to furnish provisions; to open forts and defiles to the Swedes, and to deny these to the emperor; and to give Protestants full religious equality with Catholics. Recruiting had good results. Franconia was rich; it had suffered little from the war; and its joining the cause was a marked gain. Business kept Gustavus in Würzburg a month.

The progress of the Swedes began to excite terror all through Catholic Germany; some of the princes were content to accept the situation, some fled, some showed a bold front. The bishop of Bamberg, to gain time, entered into feigned negotiations with Gustavus, who decided to press on to the Rhine, and wished to avoid a present expedition up the Main; by which ruse the bishop managed to hold his possessions until Tilly later came to the rescue. He cleverly baffled the king, — as a rule a difficult matter.

After his defeat at Breitenfeld, as already narrated, Tilly had made his way north, with the relics of his army, a mere disorganized mob, of which barely half were armed. On September 20 he reached Halberstadt, where Pappenheim joined him; thence he marched to Hildesheim, crossed the Weser at Corvey near Höxter, and drew in the Cologne troops on September 23. Hearing that Gustavus had headed south to Thuringia, after a while he himself turned towards Hesse. Early in October, at Fritzlar, Aldringer, who from Jena had retired via Erfurt, and Fugger joined him, giving Tilly eighteen thousand foot, and half as much cavalry.

Seeing that Gustavus still continued onward to the Main, Tilly moved in the same direction by way of Fulda and Aschaffenburg, so as to move around the head of the Swedish advance, cross the Main, and work south of the king, to regain possession of Würzburg. He had in view to join to his own forces the thirteen thousand men of the shifty duke of Lorraine, who had made a treaty with the emperor, had crossed the Rhine in September at Worms, and was moving on Aschaffenburg. But the duke did not escape disaster. As it happened, Gustavus had gone down the Main, reconnoitring. On November 2, not many miles from Würzburg, he ran across the enemy's van of four thousand men. Sending back for Baudissin's body of four thousand horse and two thousand musketeers, he fell on the enemy's camp not far from Bischofsheim and dispersed the entire body. The duke retired, with the relics, on his main body, managed to join Tilly in Miltenburg, and the joint forces amounted to some thirty-eight thousand men. Gustavus learned of Tilly's movements at Würzburg. He understood that he was aiming on either Würzburg, Schweinfurt, or Bamberg; but though he cared little for him so long as Nürnberg could take care of herself, he was careful to protect his allied cities and to close all available defiles.

When Tilly marched away from the Weser and towards Franconia, Landgrave William and Duke Bernard put in some good work. The latter gave a hearty blow to Fugger; and the landgrave fell on Vacha, took a big convoy intended for Tilly at Corbach, and captured Münden and Höxter. These outside operations cannot be detailed.

XXII.

MAINZ. NOVEMBER, 1631.

LEAVING Tilly, Pappenheim returned to the Weser; Tilly was ordered by
Maximilian to protect Bavaria, and sat down at Windsheim. Gustavus moved
down river to secure his hold on the Main and the Rhine before turning toward
the Danube. Taking all the cities on the way, he reached Frankfort November
16. He had thirty-two thousand men. Mainz, which had a Spanish garrison,
resisted; and Gustavus marched up the Rhine, crossed, and attacked the city
from the left bank. While so engaged, he heard that Tilly was besieging
Nürnberg, and at once started with a column of twenty-six thousand men
towards his ally; but at Frankfort he learned that Tilly had failed before the
place, which had resisted all his threats. Returning to Mainz, Gustavus took
the place December 22, and quartered his army there. During this period
Pappenheim was operating against Gustavus' lieutenants on the Weser, showing
ability, but accomplishing no substantial result. On retiring from Nürnberg,
Tilly took up quarters in the Nördlingen country. The official list of Gustavus' troops and allies at this time shows eighty thousand men under the colors,
with an equal number to be raised during the winter, — a marked contrast to
the thirteen thousand men who landed near Stralsund a year and a half before.

WITH Fugger and Aldringer Tilly had marched from
Miltenburg and taken Rothemburg and Windsheim, had
devastated Franconia where he crossed it, and reached
Anspach November 20. Gustavus had not succeeded in
cutting him off from Bavaria. He had separated from Pappenheim, who, unable to agree with his chief, preferred to
march back to Westphalia, a territory some one must defend
for the emperor. It is asserted that Tilly intended to bring
on another general engagement at an early date. This is
perhaps doubtful; for though Tilly never lacked courage, he
lacked enterprise of a certain stamp, and had scarcely yet

forgotten Breitenfeld. When he reached the Tauber, he had recovered his base and could choose a safe defensive, or a march to the Main to seek his adversary. He did not do the latter; for, whatever his intentions, his master, Maximilian, nervously fearing for his borders, ordered him to stop at covering Bavaria, and not to undertake operations which might lead to battle. Tilly took up positions with twelve thousand men at Donauwörth and Guntzenhausen, sent an equal number to the Upper Palatinate, and began to recruit. From annoyance at his orders, he was tempted to lay down the command, but was dissuaded by his immediate officers and Maximilian's personal request. He sent a detachment to seize on Wertheim, but without success, for the king, who was watching his operations, laid an ambuscade for the detachment and severely handled it; and immediately after made a descent on four imperial regiments at Creglingen, and all but destroyed them. Shortly receiving fourteen thousand men of reinforcement from Alsatia, the Lower Palatinate and Würtemberg, and emboldened by his numbers, Tilly advanced columns to Rothemburg, Windsheim and Ochsenfurt, and took up a position at Windsheim, the king being for the moment sick in Würzburg.

Considering the total defeat of Tilly not many weeks back, he had shown commendable energy in coming to the protection of his master's territory, and in making even partial attacks on the new allies of Sweden. But the timidity of the elector had prevented the veteran from utilizing his numerical, if not actual, superiority at the points attacked; and it had enabled the Swedes, without opposition, to plant themselves firmly on the Main. That Tilly could have prevented the seizure of the Main is improbable, but he might have made it difficult.

Holding Thuringia and Franconia, the king did not for the

moment care to move on Tilly; the possession of the Main down to the Rhine seemed more important; and Tilly, by moving to the upper Main, had yielded up all power to defend the lower. Leaving Horn with five thousand foot and two thousand horse to hold the Würzburg bishopric, and to complete the subjection of Franconia, the king started down the Main November 9, with eighteen thousand men, intending to gain control of or neutralize the bishoprics of Mainz, Trier and Cologne, the other Catholic Rhine princes and the Spanish troops, to relieve the Palatinate, and to take advantage of the richness of the country to add to his material strength before moving against southern Germany, Bavaria and Austria. His general scheme, as we have seen, was built on procuring large accessions of troops.

Whatever historians may say of Gustavus' declination to march on Vienna after the victory of Breitenfeld, they cannot complain that he was not thorough in what he undertook to do in lieu thereof; and the event proves his own plan the wiser. While one cannot prove that a march on Vienna would not have brought Ferdinand to his knees, it remains certain that, had Gustavus undertaken this course, the world would have remained the poorer by many lessons in methodical war.

The task he was now undertaking was not difficult, for the Catholic princes were unable to offer much opposition, and the garrisons along the Main were weak. Before leaving Würzburg, he sent out Colonel Hubald, with twenty-two hundred dragoons and cuirassiers, to capture Hanau, which this officer did by storm on November 10; Gelnhausen, Friedburg and Höchst surrendered, and on November 17 Rothenfels did the like. As the enemy was at Rothemburg, the king personally headed a detachment and fully garrisoned Schweinfurt; and a strong body was left in Würzburg.

The bulk of the Royal Army marched down on the left bank of the Main, a smaller body on the right bank. The baggage, artillery and supplies were floated down on boats between the troops. A large number of the towns were found ready to join the Swedish cause, Wertheim on the 20th, Miltenburg on the 21st, Aschaffenburg on the 22d, Steinheim on the 25th, and Offenbach on the 26th. Frankfort, after some delay, concluded to swell this number on the 28th. The garrisons, as a rule, entered the Swedish service.

At Frankfort a mild treaty was made with Hesse Darmstadt, which until now had held aloof; that principality reserved all its powers, but gave up, until the war should be ended, the fortress of Rüsselsheim, which, standing between Mainz and Frankfort, was of marked importance.

On November 28, through Frankfort, Gustavus marched to Höchst, Königstein, Flörsheim and Kostheim; and at Höchst there joined him fourteen thousand men from Hesse-Cassel, under Landgrave William, which, as Tilly had moved away from the Weser, were no longer needed there. This gave Gustavus thirty-two thousand men, with which he sat down on the right bank of the Rhine, astride the Main, the bulk of the force threatening Mainz.

This great city possessed a powerful bridge-head in the fortified town of Kastel on the right bank of the Rhine; two thousand Spanish troops under Count Silva which formed the garrison of Mainz vowed they would die to the last man sooner than give up the place; and on being asked by the elector if he had enough troops, Silva replied that he had enough to whip three kings of Sweden. The citizens made some advances, but Gustavus recalled to their mind their hitherto stubborn refusals to treat, and declined any but surrender without terms. The elector prepared for defense; he drove piles in the Main at its mouth, sank ships, and clogged up the river with stones; having done which he lost heart, left Silva to protect his capital, and fled with the bishop of Worms to Cologne. The garrison ill-treated the citizens and prepared for a stout resistance.

The king did not deem it possible to take Mainz from the right bank, and it was difficult to cross the river below the city in order to besiege it, though Bernard had taken the Mouse Tower and Ehrenfels near Bingen. There was a

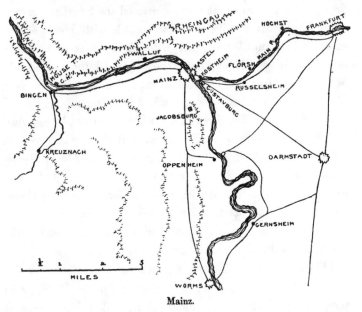

Mainz.

bridge of boats at Höchst; numerous boats fitted with guns and breastworks lay in the river, and Gustavus began to isolate Mainz. He seized the custom-house buildings oppo-site Bingen, and Walluf, and levied on the country contri-butions of forty-five thousand rix dollars a month. He sent out detachments to the Lahn, and took Limburg and other places, with much booty. Having meanwhile reduced the right bank as far up as the Neckar, he was preparing to cross above, when news reached him that Tilly was besieging Nürnberg.

This was a surprise. Gustavus postponed his designs against Mainz, left things as they were, and started December 9, determined to relieve Nürnberg by a battle. He had with him seventeen thousand foot and nine thousand horse of the Swedish, Hesse-Cassel and Weimar troops. While his columns were defiling through Frankfort, he made a definitive treaty with that city; and learning at the same time that Tilly had given up the siege of Nürnberg and retired to the Danube, he again returned to the Rhine.

This raid persuaded the king that Tilly might push in on his communications, and he made dispositions accordingly. Horn's corps was strengthened by drafts on Teuffel and on Nürnberg, with headquarters at Windsheim, so as to sustain at need either the king or Saxony; Duke William was ordered to push his army from Thuringia forward towards Schweinfurt, lest Horn should be suddenly detached. Thus Horn and the Weimar armies were made a link between, or a reserve to the king or the elector of Saxony.

While strictly maintaining his kingly dignity, Gustavus was easily approached by all. One day, in Frankfort, a priest was discovered in the anteroom with a concealed dagger; it was currently reported that a band of Jesuits had bound themselves with an oath to take his life; and bets were laid in Augsburg that Gustavus would not live six months. Much of this may have been idle talk, but when Gustavus was urged to keep a body-guard about him, he is said to have replied: "Then you would have me disregard the protection of God?" His very contempt of death was in some respects a safeguard. About this time are recorded some utterances of the king concerning his mission in Germany and his duty to Protestantism. One day at table with

the king of Bohemia, the landgrave of Darmstadt and many
other princes, the king said: "Believe me, I love a comfort-
able life as well as any man, and I have no desire to die an
early death. The emperor would readily make a separate
peace with me to get me to return to Sweden. But I dare
not leave so many innocent people subject to his revenge.
Were it not for this, I would soon get me gone."

On his return Gustavus went seriously at the Mainz problem. He left the landgrave to blockade the city from the
right bank, — the Rhinegau, — and to occupy the country up
and down on either side the Main; he himself passed over
to the south side, and on December 10 made a demonstration
towards Heidelberg. On December 13, from Gernsheim,
he turned quickly down river to a point opposite Oppenheim
where was a redoubt held by Spanish troops. These refused
to surrender; but having undertaken a piece of work, Gustavus was not easily arrested. Despite the opposition of the
Spanish cavalry on both banks, on the night of December
16–17 he put three hundred men in boats across the Rhine,
built a bridge near Gernsheim, probably at one of the bends
where his guns could protect the operation, crossed in the
succeeding two days, December 17 and 18, with all his
troops, took Oppenheim, stormed the castle, advanced
towards and blockaded Mainz, and cut the city off from the
Rhine up and down, as well as from the Main. The isolated
redoubt on the right bank surrendered. In a reconnoissance
here, the king by his reckless pushing out to the front, not
properly accompanied, was again all but captured. His
disregard of danger was a growing evil. No wonder he
eventually fell a victim to it.

On December 22, after two days' siege, Count Silva,
despite his heroic protests to do or die, surrendered Mainz,
and the troops were allowed the honors of war. Most of

them entered the king's service. It was a question whether this capture of Mainz was not an act of war against Spain, which Gustavus would have preferred to avoid, as his quarrel was one against the Austrian Hapsburgs. But Silva had received orders to be helpful to Mainz against Sweden, and Spain was already in the Baltic at Wismar. No war had been declared or was considered to exist, and yet acts of war had been committed by both parties. Gustavus was ready for what must come, and the ministry and estates sustained him. A contribution of eighty thousand rix dollars was levied on Mainz; one of forty-one thousand rix dollars on the Jesuits, and another of forty thousand on the Catholic priests. These were hard terms, for the Spaniards had already plundered the town; but the money was paid.

The king quartered his foot in Mainz, the horse in the surrounding country. He put the city in a state of excellent defense, surrounded it with works, built a strong redoubt on the Jacobsberg, replaced the bridge of boats across the Rhine to Kastel and made a new one to Kostheim, fortified the confluence of the Main and Rhine by a strong fortress, "Gustavburg," on the left Main bank, gave the left bank of the Rhine in charge of Duke Bernard, established his winter-quarters and his court in the city, and moved for the moment to Frankfort, where he was made happy by the queen joining him. The elector of Mainz soon after broke off his connection with the emperor. About this time, also, the duke of Lorraine withdrew his forces, much weakened by sickness and desertion, from Tilly's army, and hurried home to defend his territory, threatened by France on one side and the Swedes on the other. His army was soon disbanded by active contact with the French, who took Trier, Coblentz and Hermannstein (now Ehrenbreitstein), and he too forswore his fealty to the emperor.

The Spanish troops were lying on the Moselle, and from Mainz Gustavus organized an army to operate against them. Rhinegrave Otto Ludwig, in command of its vanguard, defeated at Creuznach a body of Spaniards with a loss of seven hundred killed, and later captured a number of places near by. It is asserted that Gustavus contemplated a march to the Netherlands to give the Spaniards the *coup de grace;* but Tilly was too threatening a factor, and the Dutch promised to keep the Spanish army busy. Whatever his project, he did not in fact move far from the Mainz country; nor did it prove essential, for in the course of January and February, 1632, under the instances of Duke Bernard, all the Catholic princes of the Rhine, as far as the Netherlands, pledged themselves to neutrality; Worms, Speyer and Mannheim did the like; the Spanish troops were forced to withdraw to the Netherlands, and the Protestant allies securely occupied both banks of the middle Rhine, Alsatia, the Lower Palatinate, Cologne, and other principalities.

When Tilly marched from the Weser to Swabia, he left in the region between the Elbe, the sea and the Weser but a small body of troops to sustain the Catholic garrisons. The most important imperial towns were Magdeburg, Rostock, Wismar, and Dömitz. Pappenheim, who, it will be remembered, had parted with Tilly in the Anspach region, and returned to Westphalia, had collected some eight thousand men, and, in November, 1631, raised the siege of Madgeburg, which an equal force of Swedes under Banér had just brought to the point of surrender. Banér retired into his strong position at Calbe, and Pappenheim shortly evacuated Magdeburg, burned the Elbe bridge and moved against Lüneburg. He soon found himself surrounded by the superior forces of Tott, Hamilton, Banér, and the bishop of Bremen, and a considerable accession of men raised for

Banér in Thuringia; he was compelled to retire behind the Weser, into the lower Rhenish Provinces, against which the duke of Hesse-Cassel continued to operate from the south, in such a manner as distinctly to aid Lüneburg, the lower Saxon Circle and Bremen by his diversions. Then Magdeburg, Dömitz, Rostock, Wismar and other towns were successively captured by Tott and the Protestant allies.

All this was not, however, accomplished without some difficulty; for Pappenheim operated with boldness and skill, prevented the allies from joining forces, compelled Tott to give up the siege of Stade, and when, in consequence of Banér and Duke William joining in his front, he was constrained to retire to Westphalia, he sat down near Cassel and held himself until he was ordered to join Wallenstein in Saxony. After he left, Baudissin and Lüneburg had freer play; the lower Elbe and the Weser region were quite cleared of the emperor's troops, and Banér, after taking Magdeburg, was able to move with a considerable part of his force by way of Thuringia and Franconia to join Gustavus, as Duke William, after taking Göttingen and Duderstadt, also did. But this is anticipating events; and there is no space to devote to the details of these minor operations. Their object and result were to conserve the bastion which the king had erected with so much time and skill.

When Gustavus marched down the Main, Tilly, though much superior in force, still undertook no operations against Horn, whom the king had left with eight to ten thousand men to hold the upper river, — a fact largely due to the contrary orders and pusillanimity of the elector of Bavaria. He contented himself with devastating the region between Windsheim and Anspach; and on November 28 he marched from Anspach, via Schwabach, on Nürnberg, demanded money and rations, and threatened to lay siege to the place. The citizens manned the walls, and even sent out the newly levied troops to skirmish with the enemy. Tilly threatened the city with the fate of Magdeburg, unless it complied with his demands; but the threat was idle and the siege short-lived. Tilly's army suffered from a want of provisions; the elector feared that he would get cut off from Bavaria, and ordered him back; a portion of his forces was already detached to Bohemia; a Protestant officer in the emperor's service proved traitor, and brought about an explosion in the ammunition depot of Tilly's artillery park; everything seemed to conspire against him, and, on December 4, he withdrew to Nördlingen, and quartered his troops on the left bank of the Danube, from the borders of Bohemia to the upper Neckar and Würtemberg. It was to meet this threat of Tilly's on Nürnberg that Gustavus had so suddenly left Mainz.

Instead of making his winter-quarters in Erfurt, Gustavus had advanced to the Rhine and Main, had conquered a large territory, and could choose his winter-quarters where he would. A year before, he had wintered at Bärwalde in the midst of privation and danger, with disappointment and uncertainty staring him in the face; now, he could winter in the golden city of the Rhine, in the enjoyment of plenty, and with the approbation of all Germany. Booty was immense; the arsenals of Würzburg supplied quantities of munition and clothing; victual was abundant; and the poor Swedish peasant reveled in Franconian wheat and wine. He had never dreamed of such luxury; he ate and drank to his heart's content. A Capua was more to be feared than a Valley Forge.

There is in the Swedish archives an official list, giving the troops at this time under Gustavus' command, and indicating what was needed to bring the companies and regiments up to full strength.

In the Army of the Rhine, under the king's command, there were with the colors 113 companies of foot, viz. : the Royal regiment of 12 companies ; Hogendorf, 12 ; Winkel, 12 ; Banér, 8 ; Wallenstein, 8 ; Vitzthum, 8 ; Hepburn, 12 ; Lunsdel, 8 ; Munroe, 8 ; Ruthven, 8 ; Ramsay, 8 ; Hamilton, 8. Total, 10,521 men, plus 3,000 of Hamilton's recruits. To bring these up to normal strength of 150 men per company, there were to be raised 6,521 men. And a further increase of 18,000 men was contemplated, viz. : 40 companies of 3,000 men of Hamilton's recruits ; 80 companies of 150 men each, to be recruited by von Solms, Isemburg and Nassau, and by Hubald and Hörnig. The cavalry had in line 83 companies, viz. : Smålanders, 8 companies ; West Goths, 8 ; Finns, 8 ; Duke Bernard, 8 ; the rhinegrave, 12 ; Tott, 12 ; Ussler, 10 ; Callenbach, 8 ; Livonians, 5 ; Courlanders, 4. Total, 5,300 men, to be recruited up to normal of 9,175 men. To these were to be added 20 companies, with 2,500 men ; to be raised by von Solms, John of Hesse, and Taupadel. The present total was 18,821 men. The grand total would thus be 46,717 men.

In the Franconian Army, under Horn, were 63 companies of foot, viz.: Axel Lillie, 8 companies ; Oxenstiern, 8 ; Erich Hand, 8 ; Härd, 8 ; von Thurn, 8 ; von Reike, 12 ; Wallenstein, 8 ; Dragoons, 3. Total, 5,161 men, to be increased by 12,844 men, by recruits from von Solms, Margrave Hans George, Truchsetz, Mussfeld, Canoski and Hastfehr. The cavalry had 36 companies, viz. : Baudissin, 12 ; Kochtitzki, 8 ; Witzleben, 8 ; Sperreuter, 4 ; East Goths, 4 ; and 600 recruits under Hastfehr. Total, 3,119 men, to be increased by 8,531 men, by recruits from Duke Ernest, von Solms, the margrave of Brandenburg, the duke of Weimar, von Dundorp, von Hoffenhült and Truchsetz. The present for duty were 8,280 men. The grand total was to be 29,655 men.

The landgrave of Hesse had 6 regiments of foot, with 6,000 men, to be raised to 7,200 ; 32 companies of cavalry, with 2,000 men, to be raised to 4,000. He proposed to raise 6 new regiments of 7,200 men. Present total, 8,000 men. Proposed total, 18,400 men.

The Mecklenburg corps had 56 companies of 3,900 men, to be raised to 11,100 men.

The Lower Saxon Army, under Tott, had 136 companies of 12,000 foot ; 8 companies of 1,000 horse. To be raised, 7,850 men. Present total, 13,000 men. Proposed total, 20,850 men.

The Magdeburg Army, under Banér, had 194 companies, with 10,437 men, to be raised to 30,821 men ; 69 companies cavalry, with

1,800 men, to be raised to 8,375 men.   Total present, 12,237 men.   Proposed total, 39,196 men.

The Weimar Corps, under Duke William, had 5 regiments of 3,000 men, to be raised to 6,000 ; and 20 companies of 1,000 horse, to be raised to 2,500.   Present total, 4,000 ; proposed total, 8,500.

Garrison troops were 10,416 men, to be increased to 13,150.   In Erfurt were 2,545 men, to be increased to 4,825.

In addition to these new German troops, Gustavus expected in the spring of 1632 from Sweden, 48 companies of foot, of 7,200 men, and 12 companies of cavalry, of 1,500 men.

The grand total, then, which Gustavus had under the colors at the end of 1631 was 63,700 foot and 16,000 cavalry ; and this he had good reason to hope, for the campaign of 1632, to increase up to 153,000 foot and 43,500 horse. Such an army had never yet been seen in Germany.

Landsknecht.   (16th Century.)

XXIII.

TO THE DANUBE. DECEMBER, 1631, TO APRIL, 1632.

At Mainz Gustavus held his winter's court, — the most prominent monarch in Europe. At this time he could have claimed the crown of Germany; that he did not shows the purity of his ambition. Everything looked smiling; and yet everything hinged on the king's life. All Europe was agog at his wonderful accomplishments, but the graybeards shook their heads, and wondered whether Germany was to be made subservient to Sweden. Still, on the surface, all went well; the Protestants were in the ascendant both in a political and military sense, while the emperor was crowded to the wall. In 1632, however, the theatre was too extended. There were too many places to hold, too many new regions to reduce; the king rarely had under his personal command as large an army as he should. At Mainz he had over one hundred thousand men, but these were in eight several parcels, all apparently essential: Mainz, Würzburg, Hesse, Saxony, Magdeburg, Mecklenburg, lower Saxony and garrisons. During the late winter Horn and Tilly did some manœuvring on the upper Main. Gustavus came to Horn's assistance, and Tilly moved back to the Danube. The king followed, crossed the Danube at Donauwörth, and Tilly intrenched himself behind the Lech at Rain, to protect Bavaria.

It was a splendid court rather than the rude winter-quarters of a campaigning army which was seen at Mainz in the winter of 1631–32; and ambassadors from every European power paid their respects to the victorious monarch. Negotiations consumed the days and weeks. Treaties were made with the duke of Brunswick and the city; a new one with Mecklenburg and formal ones with Lübeck, Lüneburg and Bremen. Negotiations were pursued with Würtemberg, Ulm and Strasburg. Gustavus was the centre-point, the observed of all observers, the most powerful of the kings of the earth, the most brilliant individual of the times. And

yet the Swedish standing was uncertain; everything hinged
on Gustavus and his purposes; and what he could accomplish hinged on his own life, for there was no one to succeed
him in his peculiar work. Gustavus recognized this fact
without arrogance. He might have claimed, and without
contest have been allowed, the crown of a new kingdom of
Germany; all he asked was a German Protestant Confeder-
ation — a *Corpus Evangelicorum* — under himself as chief.
This desire might have taken formal shape, had the electors
of Brandenburg and Saxony been like the other allies; but
they remained intractable, the one from hebetude, the other
from envy.

The whole of Europe was still at odds and evens. The
dictates of religion were buried under the selfish personal or
political motives which governed every monarch. England
was shifty; Charles I. promised nothing, and his promises,
if made, would be worthless. He was, in fact, plotting with
the emperor, and would do anything to secure the restoration of Frederick to the Palatinate. Maximilian was for
a while in league with Richelieu, who was eager to secure
neutrality for the Catholic League while humiliating the
House of Hapsburg. He sought to compass some agreement
between the League and Gustavus; but this was difficult;
and finally, when he accepted Gustavus' conditions to allow
the League a neutrality which should reduce its army to
twelve thousand men and tie it hand and foot, Maximilian
in anger threw over Richelieu, and thereafter clave to the
emperor. Denmark was jealous of Swedish successes; but
her recent punishment forbade her to act. The Netherlands
followed their loadstone, gold. Spain was or was not at
war with Gustavus, as either saw fit to construe the situation. Poland was bitter as gall, but impotent. Russia was
friendly. Brandenburg was inert. Ferdinand kept on his

way with his usual directness. Richelieu and Gustavus were equally anti-Hapsburg, but from different standpoints. And finally John George of Saxony, ruled by Arnim, leaned first to Gustavus, then to Ferdinand. His great foible was jealousy of the king; his worst defect was an ancient and unreasoning sense of fealty to the empire; his main aim was a Third Party in Germany, which, under his lead, should dominate both the emperor and the king; and he alternately corresponded with Gustavus and with Wallenstein. Faithful to neither because faithless to himself, he was destined to be the means of wrecking his own cause, and of visiting the horrors of war on his own dominions. And yet John George believed that he was honesty personified, and in a certain sense he was so; but he had dropped so far behind the times that he could neither gauge the German situation, nor appreciate what kind of honesty the times demanded.

Our attention is constantly drawn to the transformation which had taken place since the king had come upon the scene. The situation forces itself upon us. When Gustavus landed with his thirteen thousand men, the Protestant cause was on the wane, the party utterly discouraged, and the emperor everywhere successful. Now Gustavus had nearly one hundred and fifty thousand men in garrison and in the field. Recruiting was active. All the Protestant princes were in league with the Swedes. France was sustaining the cause by means which neutralized the Catholic princes on the Rhine, and the rest were dominated by the conditions surrounding them. The Swedes were on the borders of Bavaria, cutting the emperor from the Rhine bishoprics, — Cologne and Trier, — and were about to invade his dominions, while his "buffer-state," Bavaria, was made unreliable by the abject fear of the elector for his possessions. Ferdinand had sent to Poland for troops, but these were refused

on the plea of a threat from Russia, — perhaps fostered by
Gustavus. Pope Urban refused Ferdinand countenance,
alleging the war to be not for Catholicism, but for Hapsburg
aggrandizement. From Spain he could hope nothing, for she
was busy in the Netherlands. Upper Austria was in readiness for revolt. Turkey was threatening to invade Lower
Austria. Switzerland favored the Protestants. And still
worse, the emperor had but eighty thousand men, of which
sixty thousand, ill-cared for and in bad heart, lay on the
left bank of the Danube, from Swabia to Moravia, striving
to protect the inheritance of the emperor from further
inroads, and the rest in garrisons or detachments in Silesia,
lower Saxony, Westphalia, on the Elbe, Weser and Rhine,
where they scarcely held their own. He was recruiting in
all directions, but to small effect. And more than all, the
moral superiority had gone over to the side of the Protestants. This astonishing change was entirely due to Gustavus'
methodical handiwork.

There had been a suggestion, hard to be traced to its
source, that peace could be had on terms indefinitely
stated, but these were not such that Ferdinand could accept
them. It was sheer inability to help himself that induced
him again to turn to Wallenstein, the idea of employing
whom Gustavus had given up for fear that he could not be
trusted.

The casual observer might be led to say that all these
results sprang directly from the victory of Breitenfeld; that
had Gustavus beaten the enemy in a great battle at an earlier day, his standing would have been as good and much
time saved. But a careful survey of the king's problem,
and of the results as he worked them out, will convince the
student that the solid gain Gustavus had made came more
from his careful method than from his splendid victory. A

Breitenfeld in 1630 would not have taught him the true inwardness of the German situation. He would have leaned more heavily on German support; he would have taken too favorable a view of the helpfulness of his allies, and he might have undertaken operations which would have resulted in his overthrow. Had he pushed for an early victory, won it, and utilized it for an advance into Germany without his carefully established base, not only would he not have been the great exponent of methodical war, but he would scarcely have redeemed the Protestant cause. Gustavus belongs to the six Great Captains because of his careful method and his boldness combined; if either quality won him more than the other, it was his scrupulous care in doing well whatever he undertook to do.

But brilliant as Gustavus' standing was, splendid as had been his achievements, the conditions existing in the German political structure promised no certainty of continuing welfare; and these conditions reacted on the military problem vastly more than they would in a war of conquest. In 1632 there was altogether too extended a theatre of operations; such, in fact, as to forbid one leadership. Gustavus' operations in Franconia and Bavaria had small influence on those of his lieutenants; but the outside operations were of no great moment, except in so far as they weakened the Royal Army. What interest there is centres in the work of the king and of his great opponent, Wallenstein.

There is nowhere a crisp statement of Gustavus' plan for the campaign of 1632; nor anything to show that he formulated a definite one, beyond the general scheme of moving down the Danube and occupying the lands on its either bank. In no other war was the influence of petty states on the general military scheme so prominent; no other great captain waging an offensive war was ever compelled to weigh so

many and inconsiderable questions. Had Gustavus come as
a conqueror, — the rôle of all other great captains, save
Frederick, — he might have brushed aside these smaller
requirements, and have dealt solely with the larger factors;
but he came as a liberator, to restore and not take away,
to build up and not tear down; and every one of the petty
principalities had to be considered as a sovereign nation.
The contrast between his patience with the German princes
and Napoleon's brusque method of dealing with them is
marked. It is all the more astonishing that, in the short
twenty-eight months Gustavus enacted his part on the
European stage, he accomplished so vast a result.

From a military point of view, his forces were in detachments altogether too small. While Gustavus was at Mainz,
his active roll of over one hundred thousand men was in eight
armies: eighteen thousand under his own command; twenty
thousand under Horn on the Main; thirteen thousand under
Banér in Magdeburg; Tott moving from Mecklenburg to
lower Saxony had thirteen thousand; the Saxons had twenty
thousand; William of Hesse, eight thousand; the duke of
Mecklenburg, four thousand; and in various garrisons fifteen
to twenty thousand more. Every one of these armies was
essential where it stood; and yet it seemed as if none of them
could stand alone, and the year 1632 shows us Gustavus
striding from place to place to help first this detachment and
then that, arresting a necessary manœuvre here to save an
irretrievable loss yonder; a condition due to the lamentable
division of Germany into petty sovereignties. Still, despite
his difficulties, the king accomplished a year's work perhaps
unequaled in all military history; and, as no other great
captain was happy enough to do, he sealed the deed of
conserved Protestantism which, unrequited, he gave to his
German brethren, with his life's blood.

When, towards the close of 1631, Tilly had withdrawn from before Nürnberg, Horn gathered what forces he could readily spare from other work and marched from Rothemburg along the Tauber to Mergentheim, and thence to the Neckar, took Heilbronn and Wimpfen, and drove Tilly's troops in that region back to the Danube. Having cleaned Swabia of Catholic troops, he was ordered by Gustavus to Windsheim, to recruit, for part of his army had been detached to Magdeburg, where Pappenheim was confronting Banér. Horn's quota was fourteen thousand men; but he did not reach it, being hindered by a two weeks' truce between Gustavus and the League pending certain negotiations. At its expiration Horn turned towards Franconia, where he threw back a force of a thousand foot and horse coming from Forscheim, and after occupying Hochstädt by surrender, captured Bamberg and sat down there.

This was an open town without defenses. At the end of February Tilly advanced against it from his winter-quarters in Nördlingen. Horn made preparations to hold out, as he expected reinforcements from lower Saxony, and built long lines of works around the town. But his new troops were not yet in hand. Tilly had at least twenty thousand men, thrice his force, and coming from Nördlingen, had assembled at Neumarkt and thence advanced. Horn had not got Bamberg in order for defense, when the enemy's van put in its appearance. One of his cavalry regiments was, against orders, drawn into action, was beaten, and in falling back, demoralized a newly recruited infantry battalion. The panic spread, the troops abandoned the works and fled over the bridge on the Regnitz into the town, with the enemy at their heels. Horn headed a regiment of foot and one of horse, drove the enemy back over the river, and held him until the bridge could be broken down; and he saved his

artillery and baggage. But he deemed it prudent to retire
to Eltman, down the Main, and then collecting his army at
Hassfurt (where in a cavalry combat he won a handsome
success), he marched to Schweinfurt, and later took up a
position at Würzburg. Gustavus blamed Horn for this
affair, which he said unduly encouraged the enemy. Tilly
retook Bamberg, and went on to Hassfurt to attack Horn,
but the Swede had already retired with all his impedimenta,
and had marched on to join Gustavus at Geldersheim. Tilly
ceased his pursuit to besiege Schweinfurt, where, after
intrenching the town, Horn had left a garrison of three regiments.

Early in 1632 Gustavus seems to have made a plan to
base on Mainz, march up the Rhine into the Palatinate,
take Heidelberg, move thence into Würtemberg, and follow
down the Danube from its headwaters into Bavaria. His
lieutenants had captured Braunfels on the Lahn, Boben-
hausen, Kirchberg and Bacharach, and had just taken
Creuznach by storm, all of which tended to keep the Spaniards from too great activity in Alsatia, and he was about
ready to start, when he heard of Tilly's advance on Horn.
He at once changed his plan to a march up the Main, to join
Horn, hoping between them to drive Tilly beyond the Danube and to follow him into Bavaria.

Duke Bernard was left under Oxenstiern in Alsatia, to
hold head against the Spaniards. But the two did not
agree; and Gustavus soon called Bernard to his own side.
He committed to the landgrave the duty of keeping watch
of the elector of Cologne and other Rhenish princes; he left
Tott to act against Pappenheim on the Weser with the
troops of the lower Saxon Circle, and Banér on the Elbe;
and now, secure in every step he had so far taken, he started
from Höchst, March 15, with twenty thousand men, through

Frankfort and Steinheim to Aschaffenburg, and across to
Lohr, where he rested March 18. He had written to Nürnberg and Schweinfurt not to lose heart at the fall of Bamberg, but to persevere in the good cause. He joined Horn
near Schweinfurt, and concentrated the bulk of his troops
at Kitzingen, March 21–24. His avowed purpose was to
bring Tilly's army to battle, for Wallenstein was again
afoot, and the king would like to disable Tilly before the
imperial forces could concentrate. He was working to this
end when he heard what turned out to be the false news that
Tilly had marched towards the Upper Palatinate.

On this the king resolved to leave three thousand men to
act as an outpost to Franconia, and head for the Danube,
instead of following Tilly away from the more essential work
in Swabia. He ordered in Banér and William of Weimar,
and with forty-five thousand men set out via Windsheim
(March 26–28) and Fürth (March 30) towards Nürnberg, on
the way to the Danube. The fact that Tilly had not moved
did not now affect his plan.

Up to the 24th Tilly had lain in the Bamberg country,
but on the king's approach he declined to again tempt his
fortune in a battle, gathered all the forces under his command, and withdrew up the Regnitz by way of Forscheim
and Erlangen. The king's smart advance had prevented
Tilly from detaching any forces against Oxenstiern on the
Rhine. Both armies were apparently aiming for Nürnberg,
but Tilly concluded to pass by the city, and marched through
Neumarkt to Ingolstadt. Here he crossed the Danube,
proceeded upstream, and sat down near the fortress of Rain,
behind the Lech.

Maximilian had conceived the notion that Gustavus would
prefer battle with Tilly to an invasion of Bavaria, and had
ordered his generalissimo to withdraw towards Bohemia or

Austria, and manœuvre to join Wallenstein's new imperial
army. He hoped thus to draw Gustavus from Bavaria.
But his war council strongly opposed leaving the entrance to
Bavaria open; and Tilly was withdrawn to the Danube, and
his army so placed as to prevent Gustavus' inroad. As the
Swedish king would probably aim for Swabia, the Lech
would be a strong line on which to defend the land. It was
this lack of purpose in the elector which had given rise to
the rumor Gustavus had heard, and it was the later decision which had shaped Tilly's march. Under such contradictory orders, no wonder that Tilly was unequal to a situation with which at his best he was scarcely abreast.

At this time Gustavus would have been glad to enter into
a bond of neutrality with Maximilian, and rather expected
an embassy to treat of peace; but the elector was yet too
sure of his ground to make advances. He placed great
reliance on what Wallenstein would accomplish when once
he took the field, and felt reasonably confident of the future.

Gustavus, accompanied by Frederick of the Palatinate
and other notables, entered Nürnberg in state, March 31,
and was received by the population with enthusiasm. But
he could not delay; his movements were decided by the
retreat of the enemy. Having inspected the defenses, he
turned to follow Tilly, moved via Schwabach and Monheim,
and reached Donauwörth April 5. Here he bombarded and
captured the works on the Schellenberg in front of the town,
forced the two thousand infantry there to a precipitate flight
across the Danube with a loss of five hundred men, took
Donauwörth, restored its works, and rebuilt the bridge
which the enemy had tried to destroy. Horn was sent along
the left bank with a suitable force, to occupy Ulm, which
had already agreed to an alliance, and take other fords and
places on the way. This duty Horn accomplished in good

style, collecting much provision and material. Hochstädt was garrisoned by two thousand foot and eight hundred horse; Dillingen, Lauingen, Grundelfingen, Guntzburg were all friendly; Lichtenau, Pappenheim and Wülzburg were taken by Sperreuter. The duke of Würtemberg declared against the emperor, and raised eight thousand men for the cause.

Tilly made no pretense to oppose all this. He had, since Breitenfeld, lost much of his desire to cross swords with the Swedes, and his present orders were limited to the defense of Bavaria.

Statue of Gustavus Adolphus in Stockholm.

XXIV.

THE CROSSING OF THE LECH. APRIL 15, 1632.

HAVING crossed the Danube, Gustavus was on the left bank of the Lech. Tilly held an apparently inexpugnable position on the other side; but a reconnoissance satisfied the king that the position could be forced. Such a thing was unheard of; but Gustavus did unheard-of things. Establishing a heavy battery on the river bank, under cover of its fire and of the smoke of burning straw, he sent over a party to build a bridge-head, threw a pontoon bridge, and crossed his men. The imperialists met the crossing in force, but the king pushed on and drove them out of Rain. Tilly was mortally wounded. From Rain the king moved up the Lech to take Augsburg, and then marched on Ingolstadt. Maximilian retired to Ratisbon; the king crossed the Danube and laid siege to Ingolstadt. Wallenstein, again in command of the imperial armies, was threatening Saxony; Gustavus marched on Munich, to draw him from thence. In Swabia he seized the principal towns, and was fast reducing the country, when Wallenstein's inroad into Saxony constrained him to move north. Worse than the military threat was that, through Arnim, Wallenstein was tampering with the elector, and thus sapping Gustavus' communications.

CROSSING the Danube at Donauwörth, the king found himself on the left bank of the Lech, behind which, intrenched north of Rain, lay Tilly and the elector, who here came up to direct his generalissimo's operations. At a council of war, it had been decided that Tilly's army was too much lacking in morale to face Gustavus offensively, and that it should act strictly on the defensive until Wallenstein, who was again afoot, could come up, or at least send reinforcements. In their front was the Lech, and in their rear the small river Ach; the right flank leaned on the Danube; the left was protected by Rain. Redoubts had been built along the low-lying river front and joined by intrenchments; and

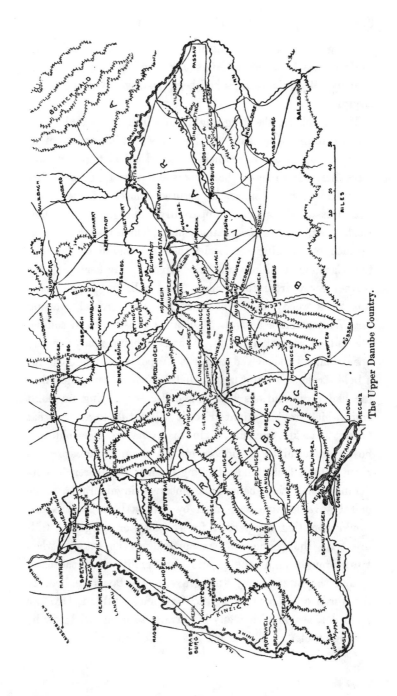

The Upper Danube Country.

heavy guns in suitable batteries stood at intervals. The fords of the Lech, up to Augsburg, and this city also, were held by Tilly; the bridges had been destroyed and the towns occupied.

If he so chose, the king might turn Tilly out of his position at Rain by crossing the Lech above him, or he might coop him up in a corner where he could not victual and thus force him out to fight; but this would take time, and after a careful reconnoissance, he assured himself of the actual weakness of the enemy's apparently impregnable position. Both banks were a low, marshy plain, which to-day has been drained by canaling the Lech; then the marsh lay between the Catholic position and the river. Higher land lay further away from the banks. The bulk of Tilly's army was in a woody defile back of the low ground, waiting for Wallenstein's arrival. Gustavus chose a third course. He had concentrated his forces at Nordheim, ready for any operation. He believed that the proper time had come for a bold stroke. From the fact that his whole campaign thus far had been cautious and systematic, neglecting no point from which trouble might arise, it will not do to assume that Gustavus lacked audacity. He was by nature overbold, and he now determined to impose on the enemy by crossing the river in their teeth, and attacking them in the intrenchments behind which they believed themselves invulnerable. The moral advantage to be gained by such a blow he esteemed would more than compensate for the loss, or danger of failure. At the council of war preceding the attack, when Horn brought up all the questionable conditions of the case, — and they were many and grave, — Gustavus replied, in the words of Alexander at the Granicus: "What, have we crossed a sea and so many big rivers, to be stopped now by a mere brook?" The attack was decided on.

On April 13, at early dawn, Gustavus made a reconnoissance close to the enemy's works. Coming near an imperial outpost on the other side, the king shouted across to the sentry: "Good morning, mein Herr! Where is old Tilly?" "Thank you, Herr, Tilly is in quarters in Rain," replied the man, and then asked: "Comrade, where is the king?" "Oh, he's in his quarters too!" replied Gustavus. "Why, you don't say the king gives you quarters?" "Oh, yes, indeed ; come over to us and you shall have fine quarters!" laughed Gustavus as he rode away, merry over the adventure.

Preparations had been speedily begun, a battery of seventy - two guns was erected on the left bank where it was higher than the right, and where was a bend in the stream with convex-

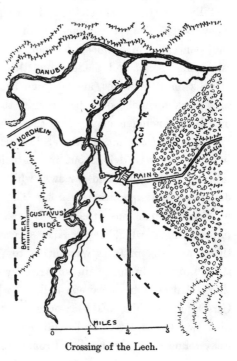

Crossing of the Lech.

ity toward the Swedes; and under cover of a constant fire, directed by the king in person, a bridge was thrown in the bend in such a way that the artillery and musketeers on the banks could protect it; and when it was nearly done, there was set over a party of three hundred Finns, who were concealed by burning damp straw to produce thick smoke, and to each of whom was promised ten rix dollars in case of success. In the night of April 14–15 the boat-bridge was completed and a bridge-head of earthworks thrown up. The king led the infantry across, and sent some of the cavalry upstream to ford the river just above the enemy's position, while the rest with the artillery filed across the bridge April 16.

Tilly and the elector strove to interrupt these proceedings. They issued from their camp with selected troops, which they concealed in a wood on their left, opposite the Swedish bridge-head, and made from this cover a number of attacks on the Swedes, at the same time opening fire from all the guns which could be brought to bear on the bridge or the advancing enemy. But the cross fire of the Swedish batteries inflicted much greater loss on them. The troops in the wood were driven out in confusion, and the Swedish infantry more than held its own, while the cavalry made a demonstration upon their flank. The engagement was of no mean proportions; the Swedish cavalry threw back the imperial horse which was sent in successive columns against them, and the infantry was put in to quite an extent; but the affair was in the main an artillery duel. Tilly had his thigh shattered by a cannon-ball, of which wound, though Gustavus sent him his body-surgeon, the grim old soldier died two weeks later, and Aldringer, who succeeded him, was wounded in the head. From twelve hundred to two thousand men were killed or wounded on the Swedish side; the imperial casualties are stated at four thousand men.

At the loss of their leaders — the elector being held of small account as a soldier — the imperial troops lost heart, and took refuge in their intrenched camp. The king made no assault, owing to oncoming darkness, ignorance of the work, and the exhaustion of his men, but remained on the battle-field. He had gained his object. The imperial army had lost morale and organization, and his own had gained in equal measure. Though the enemy should have been able to hold the works, which were strong, against the attack which would have been made next day, the elector retired during the night to Neuburg and thence to Ingolstadt, where he took up a position surrounding the fortress and intrenched.

Gustavus has been criticised for not following the enemy sharply and seeking to beat him in at least a rear-guard fight; for their retreat was made in much disorder; but so to take advantage of a victory had not yet been recognized as a maxim of war. Practically, until Napoleon's day, there was no pursuit. Indeed, vigorously to pursue is almost the rarest feat of any victorious general. It has not been over frequently seen since Napoleon's day. Nor may a captain be fairly criticised from the standpoint of the art of a later day. He must be tried by the standard of the art as he found it and left it. But it would seem that even if Gustavus did not tactically pursue the enemy after the victory on the Lech, he might have been wise to follow him up as a strategic operation. He could have sent part of his forces to Augsburg under Banér or Horn, and have himself sought to inflict a fresh defeat on Maximilian before he could recover from his late demoralization, or be joined by Wallenstein. But the king had his own way of doing things; he now repeated the procedure which had succeeded so well in Pomerania and the Franconian country, and began to occupy the newly taken territory in a systematic manner.

He crossed the Lech, April 17, with the remainder of his cavalry and the infantry, took Rain, seized all the towns along the right bank of the river to Augsburg, and ordered Torstenson and the heavy guns up the left bank to Oberhausen; and, to collect victual and contributions from all the tributary towns, he sent out a detachment into the Neuburg country. Augsburg, though a free city, was held in subjection by the imperial garrison. There was a bridge across the Lech, but this had been smeared with pitch, preparatory to setting it on fire. Gustavus moved up the right bank, camped at Lechhausen, and threw his pontoon bridges across the stream.

The triangle Ulm-Augsburg-Donauwörth was exceptionally strong. Had Gustavus desired it as a defensive "*sedem belli*," as he calls it, he could have held it against large odds. But defense was the last thing to think of. Swabia occupied, he proposed to move down the Danube, and on April 20 he entered Augsburg, which made some opposition to his demands, took its oath of fealty and promise of contribution, left Lechhausen April 26, and headed down the river Paar towards Ingolstadt, the strongest fortress in Bavaria.

Horn was in advance with the cavalry. The main column got to Aichach on the 26th, to Schrobenhausen the 27th, and to within eight miles of the river opposite Ingolstadt on the 28th. In reconnoitring, Gustavus found the enemy on the north bank, with a strong bridge-head on the south to protect the stone bridge leading across the Danube from Ingolstadt. Alongside of this stone bridge the enemy had thrown a pontoon bridge, and built a redoubt as its bridge-head. At daylight on the 29th an attack was made on this redoubt, but the Swedes were driven back with a loss of twenty killed. The troops were put into camp opposite Ingolstadt.

Early on April 30 Gustavus made a second reconnoissance, and riding too near the works, had his horse shot under him. A cannon-ball passed just behind the calf of his leg and went through the horse, which fell. Without any expression of astonishment Gustavus extricated himself, mounted another horse and went on with his work. Shortly after, one of the princes of Baden was killed near him by a cannon-ball, and when Gustavus returned to camp, these events were made the subject of discussion between him and his generals at dinner. Among other things Gustavus said: "I take God and my conscience to witness, as well as all the tribulation I am undergoing and shall undergo, that I have left my kingdom and all I deem of value, solely for the security of my fatherland, to put an end to the fearful religious tyranny which exists, to replace in their rights and freedom the Evangelical princes and estates of Germany, and to win for us all a permanent peace." He concluded his conversation by referring lightly to his danger: "Whoso lives for honor must know how to die for the universal good," he said.

More curious than the military situation was the political status. The elector of Bavaria had formerly refused Gustavus' offers of neutrality; now he was flying from the king and appealing for aid to Wallenstein, whose fall he had been chiefly instrumental in causing not many months ago; and it was he who now desired an accommodation. He made propositions for a truce and subsequent peace, but the king refused these as the elector had refused his own. He had no confidence in Maximilian, and believed, as was the fact, that he desired a truce merely to wait for Wallenstein.

It is thought by some critics that Gustavus should have embraced his present opportunity of cutting the elector off from Bohemia and Austria; but it was no easy task. After Tilly's death Maximilian lost his head, and on May 2 forsook Ingolstadt, which, from the nature of the case, had not been yet blockaded. He had lost confidence in his

army, as his army had in him, and was eager for Wallenstein, to have some strong soul to lean on.   He withdrew
unhindered by Neustadt, where he crossed the river, to Ratisbon, which, though a free city, he occupied by stratagem,
and thus secured his communications with Bohemia.

So soon as Gustavus saw that the garrison was being withdrawn from the bridge-head redoubt, he stormed it, crossed
the Danube, sat down to besiege Ingolstadt, and sent Horn
on to ascertain the enemy's movements.   Horn followed to
Neustadt, found that the Bavarian army had headed to
Ratisbon, scoured the country thoroughly, and sent detachments as far as its gates.

While opening the siege of Ingolstadt, the king heard that
Wallenstein had left part of his army to worry the elector
of Saxony, and was advancing on Bavaria with twenty thousand men.   It was important to save Saxony from imperial
badgering or influence, for comparatively little of either
might induce John George to make his peace with the
emperor; and Arnim, who practically controlled him, was
really in league with Wallenstein.   Gustavus deemed it
wise to make matters so threatening in Bavaria as not only
to rouse Maximilian to follow and fight him, but to entice
Wallenstein away from Saxony.   He raised the siege of
Ingolstadt May 4, — he had but just begun the work, —
left a corps of observation at its gates, and marched into
the interior of Bavaria.   Horn was recalled, and reached
Wollenzach May 5, took Landshut two days later, and levied
ten thousand rix dollars contribution.   Mosburg fell May
6, and Freising surrendered and paid its tribute.

As Gustavus advanced on Munich, he heard that Wallenstein showed no sign of following him.   He had miscalculated: the Czech was the more intent on Saxony.   For a
moment the king thought he would move to the aid of this,

his most important ally. He prepared to leave Banér in Bavaria, to send Horn to help Oxenstiern against the Spaniards in the Rhine-Main country, and himself to march to succor John George. While so engaged, he heard fresh news, — that Wallenstein proposed to join the elector of Bavaria with his whole force. This made it imperative that Gustavus should not parcel out his own army, but keep well concentrated. He reverted to his first view and moved on Munich. The capital was taken without difficulty, a contribution of forty thousand rix dollars was levied, and there was found great store of material and guns, of which latter one hundred and nineteen buried ones were dug up. Gustavus remained here three weeks.

The cities received the Swedes without great difficulty, but the population of the country districts of Bavaria and Swabia remained hostile, and kept up a constant small war. Soldiers who were caught singly or away from their companies were visited with mayhem, or death by torture, and many hundred soldiers thus perished. Prayers in the Bavarian churches were said to run: "God save us from our country's enemy, the Swedish devil." Gustavus took no revenge for this conduct, but levied contributions only. To Munich he said: "I could inflict on you the penalties of Magdeburg, — but fear not, my word is worth more than your capitulation papers."

Gustavus' troops in Swabia had captured Nördlingen, Landsberg, Füssen, Memmingen, Kempten, Leutkirch and other places. But the holding was insecure. The peasantry rose and killed the Swedish garrisons in some of these towns, and a few imperial officers headed the rising, which finally reached ten thousand men. Colonel Taupadel was unable to handle the business, and Colonel Ruthven from Ulm tried his hand with equal unsuccess. Towards the end of May,

Ulm was threatened by Ossa with detachments of troops
raised for Wallenstein. Gustavus left Banér in Munich,
and started for Ulm, via Memmingen. Here he heard to
his great distress that the Saxons were treating with Wallenstein, and that the latter had taken Prague. He had paid
too little heed to the growth in strength of the great Czech
and to his operations in Bohemia; and yet he could not have
arrested Wallenstein's movements without the coöperation
of the Saxon army, whose theatre was to have been Bohemia,
but which had as miserably failed in its action as the elector
had in his promises.

To go back some months: two imperial generals, Tiefenbach and Götz, with ten thousand men, had pushed their
way, in October, 1631, from Silesia into Lusatia and Brandenburg, had, as usual, devastated their route, and had sent
parties out as far as Berlin and Dresden. Their career was
happily of no long duration. Ferdinand had made up his
mind that a policy of excoriation towards Saxony was not a
paying one, and to try a milder experiment, recalled these
raiders. After they had left, there moved, in accordance
with Gustavus' general scheme, from Torgau and Frankfort
on the Oder into Bohemia and Silesia, a force of Saxons
under Arnim, of Swedes from the Elbe under Banér, and
of English under Hamilton, numbering from twenty to
twenty-five thousand men. In Bohemia they received help
from the population, and no great imperial force offered
resistance. On November 10 they took Budin and Prague,
where they beat the enemy in a smart combat, thrust the
imperialists back from Nimburg on Tabor, and in December captured Eger and Pilsen. The emperor was con-
strainèd to call to the business Marshal Gallas, who had
just come up from Italy; but this officer was slow. Everything was redolent of success. Bohemia was friendly; impe-

rial opposition scarcely existed; the Protestants of Austria
were gaining heart for action; the Transylvanian prince
Rakoczi fell upon Hungary and penetrated as far as Austria,
— an admirable diversion. But the Saxon elector, apparently on the eve of success, began to listen to the wily councils of Arnim, who was in correspondence with Wallenstein,
and instead of pushing on towards Moravia and into Austria,
to second Gustavus' manœuvres, returned to Dresden, sat
him down, and considered whether he could not make satisfactory terms with the emperor and save himself from so
big a military budget. It was at this time that Wallenstein
reappeared on the scene in person. This trickery separated
the English and Swedish brigades from the Saxons; they
retired from the undertaking, while the Saxons under Arnim
remained in Bohemia to conduct a petty war and to plunder
the land.

The new set of conditions centring about Wallenstein
induced Gustavus to return to Ingolstadt with his main force.
William of Weimar was left with a corps in Bavaria, on the
right bank of the Danube, and Horn with a corps was to
occupy the upper Rhine and Swabia. Recruiting for the
Swedes went on even as far as Switzerland.

Meanwhile the Rhine was a scene of conflict in which
Swedes, French, Spanish and Germans all bore a hand. A
French army had app'ared in Lorraine to chastise its duke
for joining Tilly a year before, and, isolated, he was glad to
return to his fealty on any terms. When Gustavus left the
Main, he gave the control of the left bank of the Rhine into
French hands; for it was better that Richelieu should have
control here than to let the section lapse into the hands of
the Spaniards or Austrians.

Oxenstiern had orders to respect the French holdings,
little as Gustavus liked the attitude of Richelieu; and the

operations of the prince of Orange came to the chancellor's aid. But meanwhile the imperialists and Spaniards were not idle. Generals Ossa, Fürstenburg and Montecuculi gave trouble; and Count Embden moved up the Rhine capturing sundry places. At Speyer a Swedish colonel capitulated, but the place was later evacuated by the imperialists. Pappenheim moved from the Weser on the Rhine country. On the other hand Horn, who had been ordered to the Rhine from the confines of Bavaria, took Lahneck, Stolzenfels and Coblenz in July.

These Hapsburg successes again induced the French, despite their strained relations with Sweden, to work against the common enemy; and what they did west of the Rhine had the effect of making the work on the east bank the lighter for Oxenstiern and Horn.

Then came the king's orders, of which more anon, to march to his support in Nürnberg. Oxenstiern left Horn to conduct the Moselle campaign, and prepared to send all available troops to the main army.

To the forces of the duke of Würtemberg, who had declared against the emperor and raised eight thousand men, Gustavus added some Alsatian regiments and some of Oxenstiern's old troops, and this army, under Horn, reduced Baden-Durlach, and made a handsome campaign in Alsatia.

The details of these operations cannot be given. They were merely the policing of the outside of the arena, within whose bounds the giants struggled for the mastery.

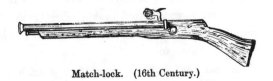

Match-lock. (16th Century.)

XXV.

THE REAPPEARANCE OF WALLENSTEIN. JANUARY TO JUNE, 1632.

DESPITE Gustavus' open-handed dealing, many princes of Europe did not trust him. Unselfish devotion to any cause was too rare to make the king's honorable conduct seem real. Too great success had the same effect as too great disaster; suspicion was as bad as abject fear. When Ferdinand found himself so hard beset he returned to Wallenstein, the only soldier who might stem the engulfing tide. The great Czech, still smarting from his deposition in 1630, would make none but his own terms; and these were practically the emperor's transfer of all his powers on the theatre of war. Thus equipped, Wallenstein soon raised an army, and assembling it in Bohemia, attacked the Swedes in their weakest point by tampering with Saxony. John George, jealous of Gustavus' playing first rôle in Germany, clung to his Third Party to offset Gustavus' *Corpus Evangelicorum;* Brandenburg was uncertain; France was fearful of too much Swedish influence; other powers held aloof. When Wallenstein entered Saxony, John George called for aid, and leaving Banér to continue his work in Bavaria, the king started north with eighteen thousand men. He was anxious to interpose between Wallenstein and Maximilian, who was marching to join the new commander-in-chief, but was two days late. Wallenstein lay at Eger. Gustavus was unable to fathom his design so as to determine his own action; but, having ordered reinforcements from all his lieutenants, he finally moved to Nürnberg, and put the place in a state of defense. Works were erected all round it, and here Gustavus awaited his opponent. Instead of smartly attacking the king near Eger with his threefold larger force, Wallenstein slowly followed, reaching Nürnberg the end of June.

THE success won by Gustavus Adolphus had not been without its disadvantages. As his brothers in the faith had looked on him with distrust when he first landed in Germany, so now both the Protestant and Catholic extremists began to fear that the astonishing victories he had won might lead the king to extend his empire over Germany.

Self-control and honest purpose were not the common attributes of the rulers of that day; and however frank and consistent Gustavus had been, few people but fancied that there was something back of his generous, outspoken conduct which they could not fathom, but none the less dreaded. In addition to this the Catholics harbored an especial fear for their religion. They knew that the Lutherans had been hardly dealt with. When would their own turn come? France, too, had begun to see a danger in Swedish victories; Richelieu wanted an agent, if not a tool; he had no use for a master, and he was already half inclined to enter the lists to put a limit to Gustavus' career of triumph. He would surely do so, should it reach a stage dangerous to Europe or to France. Richelieu was able to understand Gustavus if any one could, but he acted on the theory of distrusting every one until he proved himself honest; of not trusting too far either honest man or rogue.

It was true from the other standpoint that Gustavus had reached the highest pinnacle of fame and material success, and that the emperor had correspondingly lost. Ferdinand's case at the end of 1631 was desperate. He had not only been beaten in the game of war, but he seemed to have forfeited all his friends. He had turned to England, France, the Italian princes, the pope, and could get help from none. Even the pope was an out and out Gustavus man. Ferdinand had tried to make peace with the elector of Saxony, but Wallenstein, who was smarting from his dismissal, had Arnim under his thumb, and Arnim swayed John George. His position had grown worse and worse. From the Baltic to the boundary of France and to the foothills of Switzerland, the Swedish king had carved his victorious path, and now stood in absolute control. France was threatening Trier, whose elector had been forced into neutrality.

The elector of Mainz, the bishops of Bamberg and Würzburg had fled. The elector of Saxony had overrun Bohemia. The duke of Lorraine had been disarmed. The Protestants were everywhere under arms, and there was revolution in the Ems country. Bavaria was unreliable. The Spaniards had been beaten out of the Lower Palatinate. The Turks threatened. The Swiss had all but joined Gustavus. Ferdinand was not himself capable of commanding his armies. What could he do? Wallenstein against him was too dangerous. He must win him back or succumb. Under these circumstances, towards the close of 1631 the emperor turned to the Bohemian, who alone seemed able to save him from a further downward course.

We have seen how Wallenstein had been sowing by all waters; how near he had come to entering into the service of Gustavus; how he had sought means, by negotiations with his enemies, of paying back Ferdinand in his own coin. Now that he was needed, Wallenstein was not to be had on any but the most humiliating terms. He took rather than was given the command. The imperial treasury was empty; Ferdinand was at the very end of his resources, material and moral; and he stood out against no conditions to buy back the only soldier in Germany capable of matching the Swedish hero. Before Wallenstein would consent to enter the lists again, the emperor formally agreed to leave to him the exclusive military power over all imperial possessions; the civil power over all imperial territory in the possession of the enemy, including the right to confiscate lands; the absolute right to dictate operations; and in all cases of reward and punishment the emperor's action was to require Wallenstein's consent. Ferdinand agreed to stay personally away from the army, and to keep it furnished with provision, money and material. In addition to this Wallenstein was to have free entry into all imperial lands, to be reinstated in the duchy of Mecklenburg, and at the expiration of the war, of whose event he had no manner of doubt, to be rewarded by one of the imperial hereditary dukedoms. He received, in January, 1632, a provisional appointment to supreme command for three months; in April it was made permanent.

Such a contract with a subject was as degrading as it was unusual; and it of necessity meant that, when his usefulness should have past, Wallenstein would be put out of harm's way by fair means or foul. There could be no other outcome to it. Wallenstein, in assuming command, practically put a term to his own career, however brilliant it might meanwhile be.

The promise to victual the new army was a mere farce. Ferdinand had no money, and both he and Wallenstein knew that the forces must live by plunder. Even the Magdeburg wolves were tame compared to the wild beasts of Wallenstein's new divisions. Never, perhaps, have so many brutes under one standard disgraced the name of soldier, in every act except the mere common virtue of courage. On appointment, Wallenstein at once began to recruit, in the Netherlands, Poland, Austria, Silesia, Moravia, Croatia, the Tyrol, — everywhere. It was not long before his reputation, his riches, his generosity, brought about him forty thousand men. These he assembled near Znaim in Moravia, twenty-five miles north of Vienna.

This activity soon changed the political conditions in favor of Ferdinand. Wallenstein was a real power as well as an able soldier, and his apparent reconciliation with the emperor brightened the Catholic horizon beyond anything since the horror of Magdeburg. The situation, already colored by jealousy of Gustavus, seemed to shift as by the turning of a kaleidoscope. France was an uncertain ally. Brandenburg and Saxony could not be counted on: John George had already invited George William to join in an anti-Swedish alliance. Gustavus' friends in Germany feared the result of the reconciliation. These circumstances tended to put an end to the king's bold offensive, inclined him to greater caution than he had exhibited since Breitenfeld, warned him to hold fast to the position he had conquered in Bavaria and Swabia, on the upper Danube, on the Main, and the Rhenish country, rather than press farther on into the bowels of the land.

The most uncertain element was Saxony. John George was born to keep his friends and his enemies in equal perplexity. On the very eve of destruction, he had thrown himself into the arms of Gustavus, and the king had treated him with exceptional generosity, — a fact of which he now seemed oblivious. Under the suasion of Arnim, his every effort was to rid himself of Swedish influence. He could not bear to have Gustavus enact the first rôle in Protestant Germany. John George had long imagined that Gustavus could be bought off by money; he now believed that an accession of territory would do it. He forgot his own solemn compact of the days of sore distress; he could not appreciate the danger Sweden was running in this war on German soil. He claimed support from Gustavus; he forswore in the same breath the fealty he had pledged to the man who had saved Saxony from fire and sword. Gustavus foresaw the vacillation of John George; and he did his best to prevent it. He ceased not in his negotiations; he kept a diplomatic agent at the elector's elbow; he wearied not in urging John George to hold fast to the right, and he promised rescue from Wallenstein, even as he had delivered him from Tilly. But an evil star reigned over the court of Dresden.

Maximilian, fearful of Wallenstein's revenge for his share in the latter's dismissal, begged the emperor to forbid his entering Bavaria; but Ferdinand's voice had no weight with the new generalissimo. Wallenstein's desire to rescue Bohemia from the Saxons, to break their treaty with Gustavus, to weaken the king's communications with his base, and to draw him out of south Germany, was more potent; it constrained the Czech to march to Bohemia rather than Bavaria. This he did in February, 1632, and without a pretense of opposition, the Saxons fled from Wallenstein's army on its first appearance.

For many months Wallenstein had been tampering with Arnim, who practically controlled John George. The Czech now represented that he was anxious to keep peace with Saxony; he showed the emperor's formal authority, and assured the elector that the Edict of Restitution should be annulled in his dominions. He pretended that his warlike advance was but a matter of form, lest the Jesuits should suspect his design; but that he was ready at any time to conclude an alliance with John George, who might also persuade Brandenburg to join the compact. The elector was disposed to an accord, if it would save his land; but he was slow in making up his mind. Meanwhile Wallenstein took Prague on May 18, and drove the Saxons back to their own borders.

By this time the king had moved into Bavaria, and Maximilian again appealed to the emperor, now praying for Wallenstein's aid, and agreeing to serve under his command. Placated by this concession, Wallenstein left ten thousand men under Maradas to protect Bohemia, and marched with his army to Eger. From here he made an inroad into Saxony, plundering and burning as he advanced. He wished to show John George the sort of thing he might expect in case he delayed too long. Then, hearing that Maximilian was seeking a junction with him, Wallenstein returned to Eger, and thence advanced to Tirschenreut, to receive the elector, and to gain the advantage which the Bavarian army would lend him.

John George had eighteen thousand foot and eight thousand horse. This was a large body to throw from one to the other side. He lay at Leitmeritz, and a march for Gustavus from Munich thither was far from easy. Properly employed, there was enough of an army to defend Saxony, while to leave the Danube at this moment looked like a sacrifice of what had been so far accomplished. Gustavus ceased not his negotiations, and urged, in lieu of every other matter, his *Corpus Evangelicorum.* But no appeal to John George weighed against what this shortsighted potentate deemed for the present advantage of Saxony.

When Gustavus at Memmingen learned of the fall of Prague, he also heard of a raid on Munich by Colonel Craatz, who had been sent by the elector to spy out the disaster to the land, and who, finding his way barred, sat down to besiege Weissemburg. The king had at once determined to march north. He returned to Munich at the head of a small body of horse, and gathering all the news he could, marched to Donauwörth, which he reached June 12. Here he called in Banér with troops from Munich, and some regiments from Memmingen. He was too late to save Weissemburg, which had capitulated June 7; but as the articles of capitulation were broken, he wrote to Maximilian demanding Craatz's punishment, or he would visit the breach of faith on Munich.

Of the first importance was to sustain John George, as a political and military necessity. The king sent William of Weimar to Magdeburg to collect all the available troops and march to Saxony, where he would himself join him, and wrote the elector that he should rely on him for victual to the daily amount of sixteen thousand pounds of bread, eight thousand pounds of beef and sixteen thousand "measures" of beer, at the places mentioned on the itinerary, viz.: the 15th of June, Aschersleben; 16th, Eisleben and Friedsburg; 17th, Halle; 18th, Skeuditz; 19th, Leipsic; 20th, Würzen; 21st, Oschatz; 22d, Meissen; 23, Dresden. As matters eventuated, these supplies were never sent.

His mind once made up to march north and interpose between Wallenstein and the Bavarians, Gustavus left ten thousand men under Banér in Bavaria, and Bernard at Memmingen, with orders to keep the enemy out of Swabia and Bavaria by every practicable means, paying especial heed to Augsburg; and started June 14 from Donauwörth, with ten thousand foot and eight thousand horse, in pursuit of Maximilian. On June 16 he was at Schwabach; on the 18th at Fürth.

During the spring of 1632 Gustavus had not kept sufficiently concentrated. He cannot well be held to have foreseen the turn affairs were to take, but it is scarcely to his credit to be forced to move against two armies numbering at least sixty thousand men, with only eighteen thousand of all arms, and no reinforcements within many days' march. If the monarch is subject to criticism at any time during his German campaigns, it is at this moment, and for this lapse. Where were the one hundred and fifty thousand men with which he was to open the campaign of 1632? The rôle of pacificator, protector, had induced him to spread them all over the theatre of war. His desire to rescue his Protestant friends led him to prejudice his military standing.

The immediate task was to interpose between Maximilian and Wallenstein: nothing more helpful could be done for

John George. It was June 20 that Gustavus learned that
Maximilian had left garrisons in Ingolstadt and Ratisbon
and was marching by way of Amberg, and that Wallenstein
had started from the Eger country to meet him. There was
just one chance. If he could reach Weiden first, he might still
head off and beat Maximilian before Wallenstein came up.
He could reckon on both of these generals being slow. On
June 21 he left Fürth via Lauf, and on the 22d was at
Hersbruck, with van at Sulzbach, which the Bavarians had
reached June 17. On June 25 the army was at Vilseck,
where it could threaten the road leading from Amberg to
Weiden, over which the Bavarians must pass to join Wallenstein. But despite good calculation and good marching,
Gustavus was just too late. He learned at Vilseck that, the
day before, the Bavarian van had met Wallenstein's van at
Weiden.

Now comes what some historians have characterized as
a curious phase in Gustavus' character. Throughout his
campaigns he had shown caution as remarkable as Cæsar's;
but he had exhibited a boldness and a power of taking and
holding the initiative which were as wonderful as Alexander's. All Europe looked with open eyes at this Lion of
the North, who in two short years had marched from the
seacoast well up the Oder, to the Elbe, to the Main, to the
Rhine, to far beyond the Danube, — even to the confines of
the Alps; who so covered his ground as to hold against all
opposition the territory he traversed; who had not only
beaten the best armies of the empire and the League, but
had reduced Ferdinand to the very verge of ruin. Here he
stood, still with the initiative in his hand, and though with
small numbers, yet with troops flushed with success, and
able to compass the almost impossible. What would he do?
For some days Gustavus hesitated; he shifted plans contin-

ually, and for the first time appeared to forfeit his initiative.
He had never done this before, except when Saxony stood
between him and Magdeburg; and there had then been a
more than valid excuse. To be sure, he was hampered by
want of troops; he must wait for reinforcements, and was
necessarily reduced to a rôle of extreme caution; but he was
slower to decide than we have been wont to see him. His
first idea was that Wallenstein and Maximilian purposed to
overrun Saxony; and in lieu of marching the Royal Army
to the aid of the elector, he bethought him to return to the
Danube, lay siege to Ingolstadt, and seek to draw the enemy
away from Saxony by a smart diversion on the hereditary
possessions of Ferdinand. Again, he thought that should
the enemy actually enter Saxony, he would march to Dresden
with his own column, sustained by the Rhine and Thuringian armies. Again, he planned to march via Coburg, draw
in the Lüneburg and Hesse forces, and head for Meissen.
Again, after a couple of days, as the enemy still remained at
Eger, Gustavus imagined they might be aiming for Franconia, or perhaps for Bavaria, and he would stand where he
was and wait developments. He called in Duke William
and the duke of Lüneburg by rapid marches, via Coburg to
the Bamberg country, while Landgrave William should
remain as a check to Pappenheim. But Hersbruck, where
he now lay, lacked victual, and was a bad point for a rendezvous, and if Gustavus was to give up offensive action, it
was evident that he must retire.

Should he move to the Main — the natural rendezvous?
That would be to give up Bavaria, and especially Nürnberg,
which was not to be thought of. Finally, Gustavus settled
on Nürnberg for concentration, as the place where he was
nearest to all the points demanding his attention.

This apparent indecision has been much discussed, and by

some critics has been held up against the king. It does not appear to need much notice, except because it has already provoked it. Gustavus with his small force had merely been mentally alert, while his bulky opponents, Wallenstein and Maximilian, had inertly lain in quarters, waiting for the king to decamp. The fact is that Gustavus had a hyperactive mind; we have seen evidences of it before. He was continually conjuring up some new idea as to what the enemy might do, and framing schemes to counteract it. He was, so to speak, constantly casting an anchor to windward. He wrote much to Sweden, or to Oxenstiern, or to some intimate; he was free in stating his plans to his correspondents; and this amplitude of resources looks like indecision, when it was a mere discussion of hypothetical cases. Gustavus did not, like Cæsar, write commentaries at the close of his campaign, in which he could state motives which accorded with the event; he wrote as and when he thought, in the midst of the utter uncertainty of events, and he voiced his every idea. The apparent indecision was a mere habit of thinking aloud. What great captain who always voiced his thoughts would escape the charge of indecision? We judge the captain Alexander from the records of his friends; Hannibal from the story of his enemies; Cæsar from what he himself penned after the achievement; Frederick from his silent deeds alone; and we are but even now finding what the real Napoleon was, from the memoirs of his contemporaries. What we know of Gustavus is largely drawn from his own letters written at the moment. Let us be slow to criticise.

Consistency is a jewel, no doubt; but a man who is honest with himself, and who keeps up with the events of stirring times, cannot always be consistent. What seems true to-day may prove false to-morrow; the wise step of the morning may be a fatal one at sundown. As events chase each other onward, no one can long remain of the same mind. In a certain sense consistency is narrowness, and in this sense the great Swede was broad; he took no pains to conceal a change of purpose when he made it.

The forces Gustavus reckoned on concentrating by mid-June at Hersbruck, or in the Nürnberg region, were: —

	Foot.	Horse.
Royal Army, now numbering	9,000	6,500
Duke of Weimar, from the Saale	4,000	1,500
Oxenstiern, from the Rhine	4,000	1,500
Duke of Lüneburg, from the Weser . . .	2,000	1,500
Landgrave of Hesse, from Cologne . . .	2,000	1,500
Baudissin, from lower Saxony	3,000	2,000
Total	24,000	14,500

In addition to which Saxony was to furnish 6,000 foot, 4,000 horse. Grand total, 30,000 foot, 18,500 horse. Later, Bernard from Swabia and Banér from Bavaria were ordered to Nürnberg.

When Gustavus definitely ascertained that his operation to hinder the enemy's junction had failed, and comprehended that Wallenstein might now operate on his communications with north Germany, he all the more stood firmly for Nürnberg. He had visited the place June 19, when the army was at Fürth, had inspected the walls and works, and discussed peace and the *Corpus Evangelicorum* with the council. To protect this city, to lure Wallenstein from Saxony, and to act on the defensive until he could recruit his forces, was now his manifest rôle.

A strong sense of fidelity was mixed with the king's decision to march to Nürnberg: he could not desert the city he had agreed to stand or fall by. There was no *force majeure* as there was at Magdeburg. He had no choice. Nürnberg was at that time the cross-roads of the great routes between

Saxony and the Main, the upper Rhine and the Danube countries. The city was Gustavus' choicest ally, and held not only a Swedish and friendly garrison, but a large supply of victual and material of war.

Despite these advantages, Nürnberg was not his best place. From a military standpoint, Mainz or Würzburg was preferable. At Mainz the king was more strongly posted; at Würzburg, with Oxenstiern in the Palatinate, and Bernard in Swabia, he would have been at the apex of a strong triangle; and the only outside enemy was Pappenheim on the Weser, and he was neutralized by Tott. Maximilian would not have moved far from Bavaria, and of Wallenstein Gustavus had no fear, so soon as he backed up against his reserves. Once defeat Wallenstein, and Ferdinand would be hopeless. This was the purely military aspect, but the moral fact remained that he might not desert Nürnberg. Moreover the king was unwilling to leave south Germany, lest he should create an unfortunate impression, lose the fruits of his hard-won successes, and prejudice his new-made allies. The alternative of battle remained; but he could not now advance on Wallenstein, having no more than a third his force. For Wallenstein numbered more than sixty thousand men, and rumor ran that Pappenheim was on the march to join him.

Quite apart from the military situation, Gustavus was ready to make a universal peace, if it included the *Corpus Evangelicorum*. This project he had submitted to John George some time since; he now again did so to Nürnberg, and it was made a subject of careful consideration as to means and terms. Gustavus could certainly have made peace with Ferdinand, and have kept for himself Mecklenburg and Pomerania. But what then became of the *Corpus Evangelicorum*, for which he had sacrificed so much?

Gustavus had sent ahead his engineer, Hans Olaf, to examine the defenses of Nürnberg. Arrived there June 29, he inspected the works in person, and gave directions where to build new intrenchments. He made requisition on Nürnberg for fourteen thousand pounds of bread a day; the balance he expected to get from Franconia. Returning to Hersbruck, he started with the army on July 1. The foot

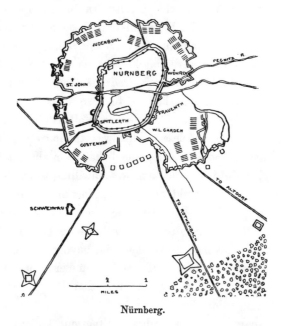

Nürnberg.

marched direct; the horse via Altdorf; on July 3 the army arrived at Nürnberg, and with the aid of the citizens, Gustavus began to surround the town with a cordon of redoubts.

Nürnberg is irregularly oval in shape from northeast to southwest, and the Pegnitz runs through it from east to west. The walls were good, and the citizens had already done much to strengthen them. Gustavus planned a new set of outer works, according to the most approved Swedish theory; soldiers and citizens were alike told off in fatigue parties; all worked with a will, and in fourteen days the task was done. These works, destined to contain the Swedish army, were strongest on south and west, for Gustavus rightly conjectured that Wallenstein, if he followed him, as was hardly to be questioned, would camp on the hills at the foot of which the Rednitz ran, and which lay on the southwest of, and four miles from, the town across the plain. The moat was twelve feet wide and eight feet deep, and the line was strengthened by a great number of minor works. A new redoubt was built at the entrance of the river Pegnitz into the city, and one at its outlet, and a ravelin and a hornwork were constructed between the Spittler and the Lady Gates on the south of the town. A line of earthworks extended around the entire place, from the market village of Wöhrd on the east to the Judenbuhl on the north, and round to the Pegnitz at St. John's. On the other side of the Pegnitz were two extensive redoubts, at the "White Lead Garden" and the Gostenhof, connected by suitable works and ditches, and in front of the Gostenhof redoubt were several outworks and half-moons. South of the city gates was meadow land, which was protected by extra strong works, one between Steinbühl and Schweinau, another between Steinbühl and the city; and on the Rötenbach road, on the edge of the wood, there was a strong redoubt, and still another on the Altdorf road. The works, broadly speaking, formed a big bow on the north of the city from the outlet of the Pegnitz to its inlet. On the south there were two bows, one from the Pegnitz inlet and one from its outlet, both ending at the main gates. On these works Gustavus mounted some three hundred guns of all sizes, the captured Bavarian and Swabian guns among them.

The good spirits and the determination of the Nürnber-

gers to stand by Gustavus were marked. All citizens from
eighteen to fifty years old were put under arms. The elderly
men undertook guard duty in the town and on the town
walls. For the outworks, there were made up of the enrolled
young men twenty-four bodies of from eighty-one to one
hundred and fourteen men, each known by a red and white
flag, and on a blue square in the upper corner a golden
letter of the alphabet. The militia was about three thousand
strong, plus two regiments of recruits, one being of three
thousand, one of eighteen hundred men. Thus from the
Nürnbergers Gustavus had eight thousand foot and three
hundred horse.

The Swedish troops outside the city were at first well
supplied with rations; but these soon rose in price, and some
excesses were complained of. These breaches of discipline
were treated summarily, by hanging the common soldiers,
and making the officers pay heavy damages. There was, no
doubt, cause of complaint; but the Swedes were angels compared to the fiends in Wallenstein's army. The king ordered the population to bring into the town all the provisions
of the adjoining country. The several armies or reinforcements had already been ordered to head towards Nürnberg.
The king pushed out a part of the cavalry to Neumarkt to
reconnoitre. This party was, however, driven in, and Wallenstein moved with more than sixty thousand men to Nürnberg, reaching the place early in July.

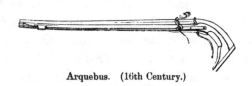

Arquebus. (16th Century.)

XXVI.

NÜRNBERG. JULY AND AUGUST, 1632.

IF Gustavus is taxable with ill management for being in Wallenstein's front with but a third his force, his activity made up for lack of numbers. Wallenstein erected a vast camp four miles from Nürnberg, and strengthened it by every means known to the military art; but he showed no symptom of attack. He was more than cautious. Gustavus waited for his reinforcements. There were sixty thousand men in the imperial camp, one hundred and twenty thousand souls in Nürnberg, and supplies soon ran short. Nothing but small war was waged. Gustavus captured a convoy, and Wallenstein took some adjoining towns. In the crowded city sickness supervened. In this starving-match neither side could claim an advantage. Gustavus was not certain that Wallenstein might not decamp and march toward Franconia or the north, and so ordered his arriving reinforcements as to head off either movement. Finally, in mid-August, Oxenstiern arrived. By every rule of warfare Wallenstein should have attacked Oxenstiern or Gustavus before the junction; but he did neither. Gustavus marched out, ready for battle, but there was no stir in the imperial camp, and he met his lieutenant at Bruck.

IF caution as a general may be said to have been one of the solid merits of Gustavus, so may it be called one of the glaring defects of Wallenstein. Though outnumbering his opponent three to one, the imperial general remained at Eger until Gustavus withdrew from his front. Having argued out his course for this campaign, he had concluded to play a waiting game. Wallenstein had not the instinct of battle which inspired Gustavus: against an enemy whom he had contemptuously threatened to drive from before him with a rod, and whom he ought to have crushed in the first engagement, he deliberately declined to undertake the offensive. So soon as the Swedish army left his front, he followed on sev-

eral roads via Tirschenreut, Weiden, Amberg and Sulzbach,
which place he left July 5 for Lauterhofen.   In this town
Gustavus had left a detachment under Taupadel, who, out
with a regiment of dragoons and some squadrons of cuirassiers on a reconnoissance, learned that the enemy's artillery,
covered by four thousand men, was in Neumarkt.   More
brave than discreet, Taupadel sallied forth to attack Neumarkt, ran across the enemy, was lured into an ambush, and
on July 6 was all but annihilated.   The king heard of his

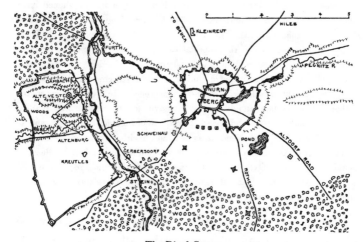

The Rival Camps.

dilemma and sought to cut him out, but the harm was done
before he could come up.

On July 10, at Neumarkt, the Bavarian and imperial
armies were completely merged.   As to their strength, authorities vary between sixty and eighty thousand men.   Next day
Roth and Schwabach were seized, and the upper Rednitz was
occupied.   Marching out with his cavalry by way of Fürth,
Gustavus carefully observed his opponent, and drew up in
line at Cadolzburg, in a position whose flanks were secure.

Far too weak for battle, he yet invited attack, which Wallenstein declined. "There has been enough fighting; I will
show them another method," said the Czech.

Gustavus' road to Donauwörth was now cut off. After a
two days' rest, the enemy advanced to Stein, and here and at
Zirndorf they intrenched a camp some four miles from Nürnberg, which in three days, by employing large details, was
completed. It stretched from Stein to Fürth along the left
bank of the Rednitz; it had a circumference of a dozen
miles, and was cut in halves by the little stream Bibert,
which empties into the Rednitz. Over the Bibert, within the
lines, were a wagon bridge and a foot bridge. The east and
north sides of the camp were the more strongly intrenched.
The south and larger half contained the villages of Kreutles
and Altenburg, and was well fortified at its southeast extremity. Opposite Gerbersdorf the trees were cut down, and
redoubts built along the Rednitz. A strong square redoubt
lay on the southwest corner. The smaller north half, around
Zirndorf, was the strongest part of the camp; it leaned on
wooded hills, and was especially well defended on the east
side, where it had three redoubts, with a fourth one in front
and opposite Dambach. Three strong batteries were established at the most northerly point of the *enceinte*, and the
heights were made as safe as art could do it. In the wood at
the northern extremity, on the Burgstall, a hill two hundred
and fifty feet above the Rednitz, lay a ruined castle, called
the Alte Veste, with a lodge near by; and these were peculiarly strengthened, being surrounded by palisades and
ditches; heavy guns were mounted, and through the woods
slashings were cut for their fire. Further to the west lay one
more strong, square fort. The rest of the camp had only a
single wall and ditch.

The Swedes had sought to interfere with these operations,

but had, whenever a small party ventured out and crossed
the Rednitz, been thrust back ; and when Gustavus, at the
head of a big division of horse, filed out one day, in the hope
of luring the enemy from his defenses, he was unable to
induce a single regiment to come forth. Wallenstein's new
method manifestly excluded fighting, unless he was forced
into it.

Despite his vast superiority of numbers, and though the
elector urged an attack, lest his land should be entirely eaten
out, the imperial commander refrained from a vigorous policy
against the king, fancying that he could blockade him in
Nürnberg and compel him by hunger to submit to a peace.
He had already cut him off from Swabia and Bavaria, and
he harbored great faith in this Fabian policy. The conception
of the plan cannot be said to do credit to Wallenstein's intelligence or energy ; but the execution was consistent and
thorough. The method was weak, but Wallenstein was well
adapted to the task. He was brought to it, moreover, by the
fact that the king's fortified camp was exceptionally strong,
and that, according to the ideas of the times, it was unwise
to attack intrenchments even with overwhelming forces. It
was Wallenstein's habit not to fight unless all the conditions
were beyond question in his favor, — or he had to. He had
conceived a different opinion of the ability of the Snow King
from what he originally held, and was unwilling to operate
against him by any but the very safest system. No really
great man ever more markedly lacked the fighting instinct ;
and that Wallenstein was a great man — a great soldier — is
not to be questioned. Again, Wallenstein estimated the provision of the allies to be much more limited than it really
was ; and it is alleged that, being a devout believer in astrology, he had had it foretold him that Gustavus' fortune would
last only till toward the close of the current year. For some

months the king had shown a willingness to conclude peace, on terms which should protect both Sweden and the German Protestants, a fact which Wallenstein misconstrued. He was far from understanding the firm character of the monarch, and the impossibility of compelling him to a peace which he would feel to be harmful to his allies or to Sweden, or in the slightest degree derogatory to his own dignity. Gustavus better understood Wallenstein. He knew him to be an ambitious man and an able soldier ; but he did not credit him with being a great general. As Wallenstein had originally erred in underrating Gustavus, so Gustavus now erred — but in a lesser degree — in underrating Wallenstein, for the Bohemian had a marvelous power of biding his time, and a conception of strategy leagued to politics beyond that of any man of his day, — save only the king. That the quality of Wallenstein's troops was not high Gustavus knew, while his own, though few, were of the very best. He believed that, despite his small force, he could hold his own until his reinforcements arrived, and, as he was habituated to do, he put his trust in Providence, and relied upon his army and his own genius.

Wallenstein was surrounded by his old officers, Gallas and Aldringer, Holcke, Sparre and Piccolomini among them ; but it cannot be said that his men were of the best. There was not the leaven in the imperial army which the rugged, honest Swede made in the body commanded by Gustavus, although this, too, had its questionable elements. But Wallenstein's position was strategically and tactically a strong one. It commanded the road from Nürnberg to the Main and the middle Rhine country, as well as those to Bavaria and Swabia ; it was, in the light of those days, in the light of almost any day, inexpugnable ; and the Czech was strong on the defensive, and believed that he was so placed as to await events longer than his enemy. Detachments of restless Croats were sent out to the north, south and even east of Nürnberg, to seize and keep the roads the more effectually, and with orders to hold the Swedes to their defenses and prevent their foraging.

In this situation the rival armies lay for weeks, waging only a small war, in which the Swedes were generally successful. The most important of these operations was an attack of Wallenstein's, July 15, on a part of the Swedish defenses erroneously pointed out to him as a vulnerable spot, which, not driven home, failed with a loss of three hundred men ; but on August 6 the imperialists captured the fortress of Lichtenau, by which they could threaten the king's communications with Würtemberg. To offset this, Gustavus sent out Taupadel, with three regiments of dragoons and cuirassiers, to capture a train of a thousand wagons of victual which was on the way to Wallenstein's camp from Bavaria, and on August 9 Taupadel escaladed Freistadt and captured the convoy. On his way back he met Gustavus, who had gone out to sustain him with three thousand men. Wallenstein had dispatched a force to intercept Taupadel, but its commander, Sparre, was not fortunate. He had four squadrons of cavalry, twenty companies of Croats and five hundred foot. The king attacked him with his customary fury, riding into the midst of the combat, in which he lost a number of his escort, but after a short, sharp fight he corraled the whole force. Sparre was himself taken prisoner. The officers engaged were rewarded with gold medals, and each man was given a rix dollar.

The opposing forces remained inactive. Gustavus waited far beyond his calculation for his reinforcements ; and it was fortunate that Wallenstein was unwilling to attack, and preferred the slower process of starvation. So far-seeing had the king's preparations been that for some weeks there was no scarcity of food in the city and camp beyond what is common in any beleaguered place. There was, however, lack of forage for the beasts, and many died. Wallenstein's Croats were the more able foragers, and soon had better mounts to keep up the work. Foreseeing want of bread, should the imperial general persist in his policy, Gustavus offered to make peace if Nürnberg so elected, but the city bravely stood to its guns. Actual hunger first appeared in Nürnberg; then in the Swedish camp; last in Wallenstein's. This general's severity and natural lack of feeling stood him in good stead in holding down his men.

It did not take long to reduce both armies to a pitiable condition. There were one hundred and thirty-eight bakers in Nürnberg, but they could not bake bread fast enough to fill the hungry mouths of citizens, soldiers and numerous refugees. All told, there were one hundred and twenty-five thousand souls; the companion of hunger, disease, by and by set in, and ere long deaths grew beyond the capacity to bury. Corpses lay in the streets; the graveyard and the pauper's ditch were filled; lack of forage had killed half the horses, and the stench of decaying carcases and unburied bodies bred a pestilence. Under circumstances like these, order could not always be preserved; it was a wonder that it was preserved so well. In the imperial camp matters were not much better; hunger and disease claimed an almost equal number of victims.

This sitting down to starve each other out seems an unwarranted method of conducting war, as well as a costly one; but it was with good reason that Gustavus remained quiet, for he could neither desert Nürnberg nor strike until he could gather his forces. Whatever the king's excuse, there was no good reason for Wallenstein's failure to bring about active work before Gustavus could be reinforced. Those who claim for the Bohemian an ability beyond his contemporaries are called on to explain this singular want of enterprise, as well as other lapses in the Nürnberg campaign.

Gustavus had not been, and still was not, certain as to what Wallenstein's movements would be. When at Nürnberg he heard of his march on Schwabach, he imagined that his purpose might be to march to the Rhine or to Würzburg, or to interpose between Oxenstiern and himself. This would be a serious matter, and Gustavus altered his former orders to his lieutenants. He instructed Oxenstiern to march to Würzburg, and to keep in touch with the enemy, hold the Main, and prevent Wallenstein from getting victual from that region. Banér he ordered to leave Ulm and Augsburg strongly garrisoned, and to join Oxenstiern at Würzburg. Loth to give up his hold on either the Main or the Danube, the king's idea was to keep a line of strong places between these rivers, along the Tauber and the Wörmitz, — Mergentheim, Rothemburg, Dinkelsbühl, Nördlingen, — to head off Wallenstein from marching to the Rhine. The position at Nürnberg would cut him off from the Bamberg and Culmbach country, and compel him to victual from Bavaria or the eaten-out Upper Palatinate, and perhaps to retire from want of food, as Wallenstein was seeking to make him do.

Swabia proved a weak link. Banér and Bernard had at first done well, and had extended their holdings, but General Craatz, sustained by the Catholic population, had then forced them back to Augsburg; had taken Friedberg, Landsberg and Füssen, and had even entered into secret dealings with Augsburg. Banér found that neither he nor Bernard could leave the country until Craatz was definitely beaten.

On July 30 Bernard was at Füssen, Banér in Dietfurt. Oxenstiern had reached Würzburg July 23 with seven thou-

sand men, — none too soon, as Wallenstein's light cavalry
was overrunning the region; and the landgrave joined the
chancellor with four thousand more on the 28th. Duke William, who was marching on Saxony, on receiving his new
orders, headed for the Main, and on the 27th was at Hildburghausen, where he received a reinforcement of four foot
and two horse regiments from Saxony. From the news
received from Banér and Bernard, Oxenstiern made up his
mind that it was not possible to carry out the king's orders.
He could not hold the line from Würzburg to Donauwörth
with his own troops alone. In view of the approach of the
landgrave, of Duke William and the Saxons, he adopted a
plan of his own, viz.: to hold the strong places on the Main,
leave a free corps to manœuvre in the region, and to march
with the rest up river to the Bamberg territory. Duke William from Schweinfurt, which he had reached, was to meet
him near Hassfurt, and between them they would use up
Holcke, who was assembling in the vicinity. Should Holcke
retire from Bamberg, they would follow him up, beat him,
and be ready to join Gustavus at Nürnberg when desired.
The chancellor began to execute this scheme July 31, and
did actually drive back the enemy towards Bamberg, and
recapture Hassfurt.

This change Gustavus did not approve. He still desired
to keep Wallenstein from marching to the Rhine, or from
victualing on the Main country, as he imagined he might.
He preferred a concentration near Rothemburg, with an advance on Anspach or Lichtenau, from whence Oxenstiern
could either join Gustavus or push the enemy. The advantage of this plan was the control of a rich country for victualing. Holcke could be disregarded; for with the strong places
in the Bamberg country held by the Swedes, he could accomplish no permanent harm. Gustavus' plan would keep Wal-

lenstein away from Swabia, which Oxenstiern's plan would
not ; and if the game was to be famine, the king was anxious
to confine him to a limited area. Still Gustavus, who reposed
the greatest confidence in his chancellor, wrote him to act as
appeared most advantageous; but urged him to keep the
main intention in view, to get together the troops, keep up
communications with Nürnberg, and not to be drawn into
battle before joining the king. This Oxenstiern did. Duke
William joined him August 16 at Kitzingen; and all Swabian forces which could possibly be spared marched towards
him, Ruthven being left to hold the land.

Banér had lately been successful in that region. He had
recaptured Friedburg and Landsberg, and pushed Craatz out
of the country. On August 7 he reached Nördlingen in obedience to Oxenstiern's call, awaited Bernard from Öttingen,
and August 15 both stood at Kitzingen.

To reach Gustavus, three roads were open to the new army:
to move direct towards the enemy and intrench in his front;
or via Anspach to the south of him; or to Windsheim or
Neustadt on the Aisch, then down to the Aurach at Ems-
kirchen, and the Rednitz at Bruck, and thus pass to the north
of him. Gustavus preferred the last because, once at Bruck,
the enemy could not hinder the junction; but he wisely left
the decision to Oxenstiern, bidding him not to call the enemy
down upon himself. In case of attack he must hold himself
at least a day, the king would come to his relief, and between
them they would give the enemy a beating. These preliminary instructions were rendered nugatory by Wallenstein's
remaining inert, but they were much in the king's style;
and so soon as he concluded that Wallenstein would venture
nothing, he bade Oxenstiern hurry forward his troops.

The chancellor broke up from Kitzingen August 17; on
the 19th he was at Windsheim, and rested two days. Receiv-

ing Gustavus' orders to march direct to Bruck, after a day of prayer on the 22d, — rather an odd delay under existing orders, — he moved to Neustadt the 23d, and on to Bruck, where he found that Gustavus had built a bridge across the Rednitz. Wallenstein could now no longer prevent the junction, if he wished to do so. The king's small army of twenty thousand men had been reinforced by Oxenstiern's thirteen thousand, the landgrave's four thousand, the duke's six thousand, and five thousand Saxons, to more than double its strength.

By every rule of the art, even in that day, Wallenstein should have taken steps to prevent these reinforcements from reaching the king. That he would do so was anticipated and provided for in Gustavus' movements; that he did not was made a matter of sneering criticism in the Swedish camp. Gustavus now welcomed a general engagement as an outlet to a situation which every day and every additional mouth rendered more critical. But Wallenstein kept close to his lines, and it is distinctly to his discredit to have done so. His conduct has been called Fabian, but the phrase is not a happy one. Fabius had no troops which could encounter Hannibal's. He refused to fight, because there was no gain in fighting. Hannibal had shown the Romans all too often that he could beat them under any conditions in the field ; Fabius chose a policy of small war, of cutting Hannibal's communications, of fighting detached forces ; and, having chosen it, he carried it out, and so worked as seriously to hamper the Carthaginians. But Wallenstein had a huge overweight of men, not, to be sure, the equals of the Swedish veterans, but troops which had been under his command for six to eight months, largely composed of mercenaries who were old soldiers, and men who shortly at Lützen showed that they could fight ; he had always boasted that he was in every mili-

tary respect Gustavus' superior; his one chance of annihilat-
ing the Snow King, at whom he had jeered for years, was in
delivering battle while Gustavus had but a fraction of his
force, and in then turning on his lieutenants; and to do this
he had had abundant opportunity, gallantly offered him by the
battle-eager Swede. But Wallenstein did nothing. Fabius
in his own way was active; Wallenstein was lethargy itself.

The utmost that can be said for him was that he lacked
confidence in his troops; but he was not occupying a position
where he could better them. If he desired opportunity for
organization and discipline, he had ill chosen time and place.
Deliberately to starve any army is a poor way of preparing
it for battle. After this criticism, however, it is but justice
to say that to the plan which Wallenstein had with premedi-
tation adopted, he clung with perfect consistency. The plan
itself ranks him low as a general; the execution of the plan
was masterly.

Having heard that Oxenstiern had reached Bruck, the
king, with part of his forces, moved out to meet him, fully
prepared for attack in case Wallenstein should interfere with
his manœuvre. But there was not even a show of it, and the
king and his lieutenant safely joined hands.

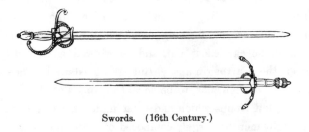

Swords.   (16th Century.)

XXVII.

THE ASSAULT ON THE ALTE VESTE. SEPTEMBER, 1632.

ADDITIONAL forces consumed more food. Starvation was depleting both armies. Gustavus sought battle. On August 31 he drew up in order along the Rednitz to invite Wallenstein out, but the Czech would not stir. Next day Gustavus bombarded his camp, but with no better result. The king was bound to have the matter out. He could fight, but not bear his men's distress. On September 2 he captured Fürth. To effect a lodgment here, the strongest point, would command the enemy's entire camp; to force an entrance elsewhere would not do so. On September 3 the king assaulted the Alte Veste. He had calculated to get artillery up the hill to force his way in, but no guns could be hauled up; the Swedes had but their muskets, pikes and brave hearts to break down defenses manned by cannon and equal numbers. For a whole day and night, and next morning, they stood to their work like heroes, at a loss of perhaps four thousand men; but in vain; Gustavus retired baffled. Still he nearly succeeded, and he deserves credit for showing the world that good infantry may attack stout works heavily manned, with the hope of carrying them. The Swedes were beaten, but not demoralized. Wallenstein took no advantage of his victory. The armies remained two more weeks on the spot. On September 17 the king sent Wallenstein a formal challenge to come out to battle, and drew up on the 18th to meet him. But the Czech did not budge. Disheartened, Gustavus moved towards Würzburg. Three days later Wallenstein decamped and marched to Forscheim.

THE concentration of his forces gave Gustavus nearly fifty thousand men; but it ran up the number to be fed, including Nürnberg, to thrice as many. The situation grew critical. There was little food left, and no forage within twenty miles; the whole vicinity had been eaten up. Disease and hunger made big gaps in the Swedish ranks, and yet more among the citizens. Matters were not better in Wallenstein's camp. Fugger had arrived from Bavaria with eight thousand men, and though Wallenstein sent Holcke with six thousand to Saxony, he still had over forty-five thousand men in camp. Here were two hundred thousand mouths crying for bread. The exhaustion of the country, the small war waged by the Swedes, and the capture of his great convoy brought grave distress to the imperialists. At Eger, Wallenstein had had sixty thousand men. Sundry detachments and depletion from want of victual had run down this force by a good quarter. The number is given in the Swedish archives as thirty-six thousand men; but there is some error in the estimate. Both Swedish camps — Bruck and Nürnberg — had, say letters of that day, to be rationed from Nürnberg. This is hard to understand: convoys might have come from the Main country. However this may be, the king's present equality of forces, and the bald fact that he could not long hold starvation aloof, induced him to move on the enemy. To beat or force him back from Nürnberg was the only outlet, and he sought to entice Wallenstein from his intrenchments.

It was on Tuesday, August 31, that out of both the camps the Swedish army debouched for battle. The lines about Nürnberg were occupied by the militia, and a camp guard was left at Bruck. The forces united in Kleinreut, and went into battle order opposite the imperial camp along the Rednitz, with three heavy batteries suitably posted.

Here was a challenge to tempt any soldier. But Wallenstein raised not a finger. A mere artillery fire, not even a severe one, was all he condescended to. A couple of small bodies issued from the gates, and advanced to skirmishing contact, but on being pressed by the Swedes, retired quickly within walls. In one of these skirmishes Banér was unfortunately wounded. Remaining in position, the Swedes threw up intrenchments for the batteries during the night; and the next day bombarded the enemy's camp. But on account of its vast area the fire was ineffective, and the reply was weak.

As Wallenstein's camp lay close to the edge of the Rednitz, an attack upon it by fording the river was hardly advisable, lest the men, disarranged by crossing in the teeth of the enemy, should be unable to resist a stout sally. But the matter must be brought to a head. The king lacked the patience of Wallenstein. Whatever we may say of the want of audacity of the imperial general (and he was the very opposite of Napoleon's "De l'audace, encore de l'audace, toujours de l'audace!"), we cannot deny him the ability to hold in hand a large body of the most insubordinate elements during a period of the utmost distress; or the persistency to carry through his plan without swerving, however tempted by his enemy to the arbitrament of battle. This is no small honor.

During the night of September 1–2, Gustavus, intent on battle, broke up from camp, captured Fürth, crossed the Rednitz, and, opposite Wallenstein's fortifications, encamped close to the enemy, so disposed that the cavalry should attack on his right, where was the weakest part of the wall, while the foot, under his own command, should assault on the left.

Why Gustavus chose this, the strongest place in Wallenstein's line, is not certain; but he accurately gauged it as the key of the position, from which, once taken, he would dominate the camp. If he ruptured the wall at any other point, he would not succeed in the same measure as if he forced an entrance on the north, where on the Burgstall lay the Alte Veste. From no other point could he use his artillery to such advantage; from no other point could he be so sure of his victory. The front along the Rednitz had been condemned; the side furthest from the city was too distant as a tactical point; to gain a foothold on the south end gave but promise of a half success. Be his reasons as they may, he chose this place, not doubting that his guns could be got up to aid in the attack.

All day long on the 2d Gustavus was busy fortifying the new camp and making approaches to the formidable lines. While so engaged he received word from scouts and some prisoners that Wallenstein was on the point of retiring, and would leave a strong rear-guard behind in the trenches. The work was hurried on, and the Swedish approaches were got close to the camp-ditch. The news proved to be false; Wallenstein was in truth moving, but it was only a change of quarters, from the north end further down the camp, to clear the ground for the coming attack; but Gustavus stood to his decision for an assault next day.

On Friday, September 3, 1632, somewhat before 10 A. M., the Swedish foot, who had stuck green boughs in their hats as a token of good cheer, were launched against the heights crowned by the Alte Veste. The hill was steep and rugged; with great effort only could a few light guns be hauled up by hand and got into position; most of them remained behind. It was, on the Swedish side, entirely an infantry battle. Practically the artillery accomplished nothing, and while the horse aided what it could, it had to fight dismounted and not as cavalry. The Swedes advanced with the utmost enthusiasm and confidence. Had they not defeated better troops than these at Breitenfeld? What were intrenchments to them, every man of whom had stormed breaches time and again? The fire grew deadly. Aldringer, who commanded at this point, was sharply reinforced by Wallenstein with six infantry regiments, on whose heels came speeding almost all the rest of the army. Gustavus was omnipresent, leading on his men, putting in regiments here and companies there, and laboring hard to get guns up the slope. This was all-important. The enemy afterwards confessed that a good battery at the Alte Veste would have driven them out of camp. The Swedes acted the part of men. Despite the grape and canister from the imperial cannon, of which there were over a hundred in line, and the volleys of musketry from the walls, so constant as to make one continuous roar, they held their own with utter contempt of death. Many imperial officers fell, Fugger among the number. The Swedes fared no better : scores of superior officers were killed ; every one was in the thick of it. Torstenson was captured ; Bernard's horse was shot under him ; the king's boot-sole was shot away. The general officers were doing their full duty. The troops were freely put in, and from time to time seemed to have success just within their grasp. To meet one desperate advance, Wallenstein launched one of his best cavalry regiments, the Kronberg, at the Swedish line, but Stålhandske's Finns thrust it back decimated.

Thrice the gallant Swedish foot captured the Burgstall ; thrice were they hustled out with grievous loss. A new line followed each one that lost ground. No troops ever showed better heart, but the Alte Veste could not be held if taken. They took, however, under gallant Bernard, a height facing the castle, and had they been able to get guns up there, they could have pounded the castle to pieces, and raked Wallenstein's camp. Scandinavian grit well seconded a Viking's courage. For twelve mortal hours the bloody work went on, — as Wallenstein expressed it in a letter to the emperor, " *caldissimamente,*" — but the Swedes had made no real gain. All agree that the fighting was hot, — the Swedes said hotter than Breitenfeld ; the imperialists, hotter than the battle of the White Hill.

At dusk a slow rain began to fall, which made the roads and slopes too slippery to leave any hope of success. Had

the fight been continued two hours more, said prisoners, the
imperialists would have run out of ammunition and been compelled to retire. But Gustavus called a halt. The Swedes
held their ground through the night, and the firing between
the lines never ceased. Early next morning the king tried
the chances of one more sally from the woods which he held,
but to no effect. Wallenstein saw his advantage, and redoubled the force of his counter attack. By 10 A. M. he
pushed the Swedes out of the wood they had all along held,
down the slope and back to Fürth. The battle had lasted
twenty-four hours. Many dead and wounded were left upon
the field. The Swedish loss is variously given at from two
thousand to four thousand killed and wounded. There is no
official list. Wallenstein lost half as many as the Swedes.

In this first battle between Wallenstein and Gustavus, to
the Swede belonged the honor, to the Czech the victory. But
not to win here was to lose; and the king had not won.

Though it had been the only means left to the king to
break the deadlock, it was none the less true that the assault
had failed, and with a heavy loss. Like all similar unsuccessful assaults, like Fredericksburg, Kenesaw, Cold Harbor,
in our civil war, Gustavus' attack on the Alte Veste has been
denounced as reckless and out of place. But for all that, it
was a distinct gain to the modern art of war; and as a first
attempt to compass what was then deemed impossible, should
be exempt from the blame which may sometimes be visited
on other failures. It had at that day been usual to operate a breach in the wall of a fortress, and then to launch
a column perhaps many times greater in numbers than
the entire garrison of the place to storm it, but no such
assault was attempted unless the breach was practicable.
It had been considered impossible to storm a fortified camp,
not because the walls could not be breached, but because the

defenders were presumably as numerous as the attacking force. And yet it was essential that attacks on such positions should find their place in war. Without them, the modern art could not be developed. Some brave soul was called on to prove that such an attack was feasible, and therefore justifiable; Gustavus' very failure demonstrated this; that his men were not disheartened by the failure, they shortly proved by their gallantry at Lützen; and since the introduction of firearms, the king deserves credit for first showing the world the ability of good infantry to attack and hold themselves in front of strong intrenchments manned by equal numbers and mounted by plenty of artillery. His great successor, Frederick, made it plain that what Gustavus attempted was achievable; and the heroic effort of the king and his gallant Swedes to force their way into the Alte Veste was as distinct a step forward in the art of war as it was a splendid exploit. Defeat is not always a disgrace or loss; nor is victory always a gain or glory. Had the attack on the Alte Veste succeeded, it would have won unstinted praise.

Gustavus understood his failure; with a vigorous commander in his front, he would be running a grave risk; with Wallenstein he was, barring loss of men, no whit worse off. In a letter to the Nürnberg council he explained the reason of his assault, acknowledged his failure, and asked care for the wounded and continued issues of bread, as well as six or seven thousand workmen to finish his intrenchments near Fürth. He was determined not to leave Nürnberg so long as there was any hope of success.

Gustavus had, since his negotiations with Wallenstein in the fall of 1631, made several further attempts to influence the imperial general. In the spring of 1632 he is said to have approached him, and he did so again when first in Nürnberg. But at this time Wallenstein was in negotiation with John George, and would listen to no advances, though Gustavus is said to have offered to help him to the Bohemian crown. In July there were renewed evidences of Wallenstein's willingness to work toward a peace ; and now Gustavus sent Colonel Sparre, recently captured, to Wallenstein, with overtures for the exchange of prisoners and incidentally to treat of peace. Exchanges were effected, but Wallenstein referred the other question to Vienna, where it was so long delayed that it was practically dropped.

Gustavus worked uninterruptedly on the Fürth intrenchments, which he prolonged from the Rednitz above the village with a northerly sweep to the rear, a distance of over two miles. So long as there was any chance, he still hoped for success. Rations had grown so short that the men got bread but once in three or four days ; no forage could be had within a day's march. Yet the Swedes had open communications to Kitzingen and Würzburg, while Wallenstein had not even the road to Neumarkt. It was reported September 9 that he could not hold himself over three days more. For all that, Wallenstein did not budge. He sat sullenly in place. It was a game of patience.

The rival armies — starving though they were — remained on the spot two weeks after the battle, the Swedes alone carrying on a small war, while Wallenstein forbade replies to their attacks. Hunger was now at its height, and was perhaps the worse in the imperial camp. Contemporary writers state the loss of each army to have been twenty thousand men in the two and a half months they lay near Nürnberg. This number, in the Swedish army at least, is exaggerated. In the city ten thousand people are said to have died. The cattle all perished, and the vicinity was transformed into a desert.

It was evident to the king that no further advantage could

be gained by remaining at Nürnberg. He could neither entice nor force Wallenstein out to battle; he could not capture his camp. He determined to cut the knot; either to reëstablish himself upon his direct communications with north Germany, or else to go on with his operations in Swabia, basing on the Mainz-Würzburg country. He was too highstrung to play longer at this game. He had tried assault; he had offered battle; he had sought negotiation. All had failed. Wallenstein was the colder-blooded, and, in such a contest, the stronger. Nürnberg was left well supplied with men, — eight regiments of foot, numbering forty-four hundred men, and three hundred horse, under brave old Kniphausen; while Oxenstiern was to remain in the city to represent the king.

Having done this, Gustavus sent Wallenstein, on September 17, a formal challenge to come out to battle on the next day; at the appointed hour he drew up the entire army and marched past the imperial camp, stopping on the way to cannonade it. But Wallenstein would not be tempted; he did not even answer the defiance.

There is a touch of pathetic gallantry in Gustavus' act, which appeals to the heart of every man who has ever felt the intoxication of battle; there is a touch of sullen grandeur in the refusal of the challenge by the proud Czech, who would not be moved by any taunt. The veteran salutes with a thrill of enthusiasm the *manes* of the noble Swede; he cannot reverence the memory of his foeman.

Failing in every effort to obtain an advantage over Wallenstein, Gustavus concluded to leave the field; he broke camp and marched unchallenged past Wallenstein's intrenchments towards Würzburg. His first camp was at Langenzenn; the next at Weinsheim; he then marched to Neustadt, whence he started September 23 for Windsheim. The army

with detachments had shrunk to about twenty-four thousand
men.

Here occurred a curious episode. An embassy from Tar-
tary reached the king, to see the Wonder of the North, and
to congratulate him on his splendid achievements. The time
was less appropriate than after Breitenfeld or Rain.

Wallenstein, who had watched this proceeding without
apparent interest, now waited until the 22d, when Gustavus
had reached Neustadt. As there was no further danger of
an ambush, after burning his camp and the inclosed hamlets,
and leaving a vast number of sick and wounded behind and a
quantity of baggage, he also broke up, and passing almost
under the walls of Nürnberg, moved, September 23, through
Fürth and Bruck to Forscheim, burning all the villages near
Nürnberg. The indignant garrison sallied out, and inflicted
considerable loss on Wallenstein's rear-guard.

The imperial general had won, — won by standing famine
three days longer than the Swedes, and by refusing every
offer of battle. What he had won it is difficult to say. He
had come to Nürnberg to capture the city; he had followed
Gustavus presumably to beat him in battle. But he had
conducted solely a campaign of depletion. Each army had
lost thrice the lives a battle would have consumed; no substantial advantage had been gained except by Gustavus in
the safety of Nürnberg. Each leader again took to manœuvring. Arrived in Forscheim, Wallenstein also could muster
a bare twenty-four thousand men.

The reasons Wallenstein gave the emperor for not following up Gustavus in what he was pleased to call his retreat
after a lost battle were that he could not quickly collect, nor
did he wish to tire out, his cavalry, which was dispersed about
the country to forage; that Gustavus held all the passes and
could head him off at every point; and that he preferred not

to risk the gain he had already made. Gustavus had no excuses to offer. " I attacked the enemy's intrenchments and was beaten back," said he; "but could I have had him in the open field, I would have shown another result." He proved his words good at Lützen.

Statesmen may differ as to who had shown himself the greater man ; but the fame of the captain may safely be left with the soldiers of all generations.

Gustavus Adolphus.
From bust modeled in 1632, at Augsburg (considered the best portrait of the king at the time of his death).

XXVIII.

SPARRING. SEPTEMBER, 1632.

AFTER the breaking of the Nürnberg deadlock, Gustavus imagined that Wallenstein would head for Saxony to resume operations; and he sought to so manœuvre as to tempt him away. The Saxon army under Arnim, with some Swedes, was in Silesia, where it had pushed the enemy well up the Oder. In September Wallenstein's lieutenants invaded Saxony from south and east, and devastated the region. But uncertain what Wallenstein would do, Gustavus marched back to Swabia and resumed his operations, hoping that a threat to move down the Danube would forestall the Saxon campaign. An insurrection in Upper Austria offered an opening, and Gustavus believed that John George could hold head for a while against Wallenstein. Oxenstiern strongly favored this plan; but Gustavus eventually chose to reduce Swabia. While proceeding with this work he ascertained that Wallenstein, paying no heed to the Danube, was steadily marching on Saxony, the one weak spot in the Swedish armor. This he must meet. Meanwhile the operations on the Weser and near Gustavus' bastion were progressing, on the whole in favor of the Swedes, though Pappenheim had been active and intelligent; but finally the bulk of all these forces was ordered to Saxony, where the great struggle promised to occur. The instability of John George had again resulted in bringing war within his own borders.

WALLENSTEIN advanced to Bamberg, took it, sent detachments to the most important neighboring towns, and detailed Gallas with a small corps towards Saxony. His intention was clear. He would now compel John George to bend to the imperial will, as he was on the point of doing when interrupted by the presence of Gustavus at Weiden and by his march to Nürnberg.

When Wallenstein followed Gustavus to Nürnberg the king had utilized some of the Saxon troops, thus become available, while the bulk under Arnim, with the Pomeranian and Brandenburg armies, held Lusatia and Silesia.

Shortly after Saxony had sent some regiments to Gustavus — thus convincing him of John George's loyalty — Holcke had marched from the Nürnberg country on that state, and by the beginning of September, devastating unmercifully, he reached the vicinity of Dresden. In the beginning of October Gallas joined him near Freiburg, which they took as well as Meissen. Here the Saxons defended the river, and the imperialists marched on Oschatz, keeping up their devastations in a manner as systematic as it was fiendish. The result of John George's vacillation was to make his country again the battle-field. Had he heartily joined with his brother Protestants, Saxony would have been spared most of the ills she suffered at the hands of the emperor's armies.

On September 26, at Windsheim, the king ascertained Wallenstein's retirement from Nürnberg, but he learned none of the details, nor whether the elector had separated from him. If, by his hesitation opposite Wallenstein at Eger, the king had prejudiced his initiative, here was a chance to regain it; but he had barely sufficient information on which to act. He might leave a part of his forces in Thuringia, to be ready to march to the aid of Saxony if threatened; with the rest, resume the conquest of Swabia, and from there push down the Danube on the emperor's hereditary possessions. Or he might send a slender column to Swabia, and march with the bulk of his force against Wallenstein, who, he already guessed, was bound for Saxony. Frederick or Napoleon would have done the latter; but Gustavus reasoned otherwise; he could not desert his friends along the Danube. Battle-eager as he was, his feeling for method in what he did was the stronger instinct.

Gustavus had learned that Wallenstein would not necessa-

rily follow his lead, — the Czech cared not for the devastation
of Bavaria or Austria, provided he personally suffered not,
— and by marching down the Danube, it was not certain that
the imperial commander would be induced to give up his own
designs.   It might mean to leave Saxony to her fate, should
he go far from the Main.   Still, he believed that John George
would. have force enough, with his own army and a small
Swedish contingent, to hold head against Wallenstein, who
during the approaching winter season would not be exceptionally active, and he began work on a broader scheme.   A
rebellion of the peasantry had long been brewing in the
Austrian provinces, where Protestantism had been put down
with much cruelty ; and it was still a question whether a
march down the Danube to their aid might not give the
imperialists enough to think about at home to prevent Wallenstein from pushing his offensive.   These provinces were
already on the verge of an uprising, and had sent messages
begging for aid, which Gustavus had indeed promised.   He
proposed to leave, out of his royal army, five thousand foot
and two thousand horse on the Main, and to head seven
thousand foot and forty-three hundred horse on the foray
named.

Oxenstiern, though far more cautious than the king, was
warmly in favor of the plan, as he had been, after Breitenfeld, of a march on Vienna.   He believed that Wallenstein
and Maximilian could not refrain from flying to the succor of
these threatened lands, from which they drew their supply
of recruits, and which should be protected at any sacrifice.

Gustavus finally declined the plan, and curiously chose
instead an operation towards the Lake of Constance, in order
to reduce the country at the headwaters of the Rhine and
Danube.   This does not strike the modern soldier as a wise
manœuvre, though it was much in Gustavus' style, whose

general scheme always included the possession of all lands from the point of entrance to some natural boundary. Postponing the Danube matter, he left Bernard in command of eight thousand men in the Schweinfurt country to watch the imperial army, prevent a raid into Franconia, and in case it started towards Saxony, to move north and protect John George. Ruthven, with ten thousand men, was left on the Danube and Lech to control Bavaria. Baudissin, with the Rhine and Hesse troops, continued to watch Pappenheim along the Weser. Duke George of Lüneburg was to guard Brunswick and the lower Saxon Circle. Oxenstiern was sent from Nürnberg to lower Saxony to administer that territory, which had fallen into bad repair.

On the way back to Windsheim from Nürnberg, whither he had gone to discuss plans with Oxenstiern, Gustavus inspected the wrecked imperial camp, where so many of his men had bravely sacrificed themselves; and on October 1 he broke up from Windsheim and marched south by way of Dinkelsbühl, Nördlingen and Donauwörth (October 3, 4 and 5), where he crossed the Danube to the relief of Rain, which the Bavarians were besieging. On arrival, he found that the Swedish commander, Colonel Mitschefal, had surrendered the place the day before, with the Swedish army right at hand. Of this act of cowardice Gustavus made an example: Mitschefal was tried and executed. The king made preparations to recapture Rain, for its possession by the enemy cut him off from Augsburg. He marched up the Lech, across at Biberbach, and down to Rain. The capitulation of the town brushed away what the king would have felt was a threat to the communications between Bavaria, Swabia and the Main.

Ready to continue his march towards the Lake of Constance, Gustavus heard from Oxenstiern that Wallenstein

had marched to Bamberg, and from Baudissin that Pappenheim was threatening Hesse. He delayed action for further
news. Should Wallenstein move on Bernard and join Pappenheim, he instructed Bernard to hold the fords of the
Main and withdraw to Rothemburg or Nördlingen, where
Gustavus would meet him and move promptly on the enemy.
Should Pappenheim march on Franconia, Bernard was to
stay on the Main and throw him back. Should Wallenstein
move on Saxony, there was at this season not much danger
to anticipate, providing John George remained true to his
compact. Should Wallenstein seek to winter in Franconia,
Gustavus would continue on to the uplands. He was again
pushing his initiative; Wallenstein's campaign so far had
only checked the Swedish programme; in reality nothing
had been lost. The summer's operations had interrupted, not
discontinued, Gustavus' general plan. He still hoped to
draw Wallenstein south and get at him in the open; or at
least to sever Maximilian from him, and reduce to the lowest
point his capacity to harm Saxony.

Meanwhile Horn, on the Rhine, had captured Coblenz,
Strasburg and other places, and had driven the Spanish and
Lorraine forces out of Germany. The king instructed him
to clean the Lower Palatinate, while the rhinegrave drove the
imperialists out of Alsatia. Benfeld, Schlettstadt, Türkheim,
Colmar were occupied, Frankenthal captured, and Heidelberg
blockaded. In the bastion country, Pappenheim and Tott
were equally matched, but the Swedes had got possession of
the Bremen archbishopric.

Wallenstein paid no heed to Gustavus' operations. He
remained for a while near Bamberg, quartered his troops for
their needed rest over a large area, collected food, and levied
contributions to pay his troops. Bernard prevented his taking
Schweinfurt, and beset the passes of the Thüringerwald to

keep him from Erfurt. Wallenstein finally broke up, marched on and took Coburg, — Taupadel held out in the fort, — purposing to move through the Forest to attack Saxony from the west. But hearing that Bernard from Schweinfurt, by a march on Hildburghausen and Schleusingen, was threatening his flank, and unwilling to encounter even his small force, he changed his plan, marched by way of Cronach and Hof, on October 20 reached Plauen, and at Altenburg joined Gallas and Holcke. At Coburg Maximilian withdrew his eight thousand men, leaving Wallenstein sixteen thousand, and, glad to quit the haughty duke of Friedland, returned to save his possessions. At Ratisbon he was joined by six thousand troops raised by the Spaniards in Italy.

Ordering Pappenheim to join him in Franconia or Saxony, Wallenstein from Altenburg advanced on Leipsic. While Gustavus was hoping to draw him away from John George, the Czech had remorselessly marched on this ally. In strategic manœuvring and persistency of purpose, Gustavus had met his match.

A page may well be devoted to the operations on the Weser. Since his separation from Tilly, Pappenheim had been conducting an active campaign in Westphalia and the lower Saxon Circle. Early in 1632 Mansfeld had been besieged in Magdeburg by Banér, and was on the point of capitulation when Pappenheim suddenly appeared, and by a *coup de main* relieved him. Gustavus, then in the Main region, debated a march to the assistance of Banér, but it was quite too late. Banér joined Duke William in January, and Pappenheim retired across the Weser. When the king called these forces to the south, Pappenheim recrossed the Weser and fell on the corps of Kagg, who alone was left behind, and pushed him back to Hildesheim. Landgrave William was compelled to retire to Cassel.

In January Tott had finally captured Wismar, had crossed the Elbe at Dömitz, and had sat down to besiege Stade at its mouth. Tott had formerly done efficient work, but he now appeared to lose his energy. He needed the immediate control of the king. Repeatedly instructed to join Kagg and the landgrave, on one pretense or other he neglected to do so, and remained in the Bremen territory, the government of which drifted into the worst condition. Kagg's command sank into an equally low state, and frequent serious complaints reached the king's ears. Ready to utilize the situation, Pappenheim marched against Tott, who continued lazily to blockade Stade.

To replace Tott Gustavus sent Baudissin, who, less strong than Pappenheim, at all events went to work; and his first attempt was to hem his enemy in the Bremen peninsula, and cut him off from the Weser. Pappenheim was skillful enough to disconcert this plan, and while Baudissin joined Duke George in June at Hildesheim, Pappenheim prevented the landgrave from meeting his allies by a threat to his territory. From Hesse Pappenheim moved towards Hildesheim, and July 8 captured the Moritzburg, but withdrew without battle and across the Weser and Rhine to Maestricht, heedless of the orders of Maximilian to march on Nürnberg, where he was much needed.

Gustavus equally needed Duke George at Nürnberg, but for fear of Pappenheim he only drew some troops from him, and left him to sustain Baudissin. The latter, in August, marched across the Weser with eight thousand men into Westphalia, to hold head against Pappenheim's forces left there under Gronfeld, and Duke George undertook the siege of Wolfenbüttel. Both were succeeding well when Pappenheim reappeared on the scene, forced Baudissin back, slightly defeated him at Brakel, and crossed the Weser at Höxter, in

the teeth of the Swede, who retired to Hesse. He then captured Hildesheim, October 9, and thus had open to him the
whole country as far as the Elbe.

This was the moment when Maradas was threatening and
Holcke and Gallas were invading Saxony, and Wallenstein
was at Coburg. John George called on Lüneburg to come
to his aid; and already in retreat before Pappenheim, he
made haste to do so, marching towards Wittenburg and
Torgau.

The situation in Germany had undergone a remarkable
change during the past year. The Swedish bastion, from
Danzig to Hamburg, remained substantially the same. The
line of the Warta was still held, with Frankfort as an
advanced work, and outposts in Silesia. The entire country
between the Elbe and the Weser was practically in the hands
of the Protestants ; for though Pappenheim, while manœuvring
on the Weser, had kept that region in constant turmoil, now
that he had moved to Saxony, Baudissin, utilizing his absence,
overran Berg and Cologne, and, capturing almost all the
cities, again compelled the bishop elector of Cologne to neutrality. Thuringia and the entire Main country were firmly
held by the Swedes. Horn, as we have seen, had conquered
Alsatia, and driven the Spaniards from the Lower Palatinate.
Würtemberg and Swabia were occupied by the Swedes, and
there was only Maximilian — a weak opponent — in the way
of the march of a strong and well-led column down the
Danube to Vienna.

But there was a weak spot in the king of Sweden's harness,
and Wallenstein had thrust straight at it. Saxony was the
one uncertain element, and though formally in alliance with
Gustavus, and bound to him by every tie of gratitude and honor,
now, at the critical moment, — when to keep faith meant
certain Protestant success, to break faith meant almost as cer-

tain failure, — the elector violated all his pledges.   The
emperor had failed in the policy of conciliation, which Wallenstein had so dubiously carried out with fair words coupled
to fire and sword, and it had been concluded between them
to resume the old system of coercion.   Moving in June from
Silesia into Lusatia, Maradas had as usual destroyed in the
most cold-blooded manner every hamlet along the route.
Arnim marched to meet this threat, a corps of Swedes
from the Oder joined him, and the imperial army retired to
the upper Oder, and from there back to the borders of Hungary, leaving the Saxons to reconquer and hold all Silesia.
But while Arnim was thus winning an apparent success, he
was at a distance, and the two other columns of imperialists
sent by Wallenstein under Gallas and Holcke moved into
Saxony and took possession of the whole electorate west of
the Elbe.   This should have drawn the Saxon army back
from Silesia, but it did not.   Saxon indecision was again,
as at Breitenfeld, the cause of a vast change in the Swedish
plan of campaign, and her soil became, as it was but just it
should, the theatre of conflict.

A Burgundian.
(15th Century.)

XXIX.

BACK TO SAXONY. OCTOBER AND NOVEMBER, 1632.

THE struggle for initiative between Gustavus and Wallenstein had been about even. The king had drawn Wallenstein from Saxony to Nürnberg, but Wallenstein had now resumed his work there, ordering Pappenheim to join him. Nearing Leipsic with threats to level it unless surrendered, he took it, and sat down to await events and ravage the land. The uncertain attitude of Saxony and Brandenburg, and the questionable bearing of the greater powers with regard to further Swedish conquests, warned the king to look well to his bastion. Anxiety as to what John George might do, despite his treaty, determined him to march to Saxony. Leaving a sufficient force in Swabia and on the Main, he headed for Erfurt, joined Bernard November 2, thence pushed on, and November 9 crossed the Saale, whose fords he had been wise enough to seize. Writing to the elector to send him what troops he could, he reconnoitred in his front at Naumburg. Arnim would not return from Silesia, and the elector sent Gustavus no assistance. Wallenstein was uncertain what to do. Not believing that Gustavus would attack him, he dispersed his forces, sending Pappenheim to Halle ; but when he saw that the king meant to fight, he quickly ordered him back. Gustavus would have liked to join the Saxons before engaging, but aware that Pappenheim was away, he decided on battle as he was.

FOR some months there had been a measuring of moral strength between Gustavus and Wallenstein, and so far there had been no great advantage on the side of either, though from a military aspect distinctly greater ability and character had been exhibited by the king. Wallenstein's threat to Saxony had drawn Gustavus away from work he had undertaken in Bavaria ; Gustavus' threat on Eger and his taking position at Nürnberg had drawn Wallenstein from work he had begun in Saxony. In the operations around Nürnberg, the initiative had all come from Gustavus, as it

had prior to his leaving Munich; Wallenstein had constantly declined the gage of battle. It was Gustavus' movement which broke up the deadlock, though he had failed in his
assault on the Alte Veste. Then Gustavus resumed the lead;
but Wallenstein, with a persistency which does him vast
credit, paid no heed to the king's threat against the Austrian
possessions, leisurely marched on Saxony, and resumed his
efforts to drive John George back into the imperial fold.
His movement was designed to draw the king away from the
Danube by seriously threatening his communications. It was
a question as to who should yield to the other; and in this
case Wallenstein's utter disregard of misfortune which did
not personally affect himself stood him in good stead; while
Gustavus' loyalty to Saxony weakened his strategic purpose.
There is no denying Wallenstein the title of a great man;
nor can large military ability be gainsaid him, despite his
utter lack of the true soldier's audacity. He is the only general Gustavus ever met who was a foeman worthy of his steel,
who on more than one occasion compelled the Swede to
change his own manœuvres to follow those of his opponent.
This was largely due to the complex political conditions
enlacing the Swedish problem, while the Czech was practically untrammeled; but it was in part due to Wallenstein's
strong character and indisputable if unadventurous military
skill. A touch of the divine spark would have made Wallenstein truly great; and were not so many vices and so much
human suffering to be laid at his door, he would almost stand
unsurpassed in the history of his times.

Wallenstein's general plan was not to surround Saxony,
but to concentrate his forces so as to meet Gustavus, who,
about the end of October, he learned was already on the
march towards him. From Coburg he ordered Pappenheim
to march on Leipsic or Merseburg, and to seize Torgau or

some other Elbe crossing; and, impatient at his slowness, reprimanded him for conducting war on his own score instead of obeying orders. But Wallenstein was in error. Pappenheim had grasped the necessity of joining his chief, and was already aiming for Erfurt via Mühlhausen and Langensalza; and when he heard that Gustavus had reached Erfurt, he turned aside past Buttstädt towards Merseburg, there crossed the Saale and reported. The imperial armies went into camp at Weissenfels.

With threats like those of Tilly a year before, Wallenstein marched against Leipsic, and was met by a similar refusal. The commandant of the Pleissenburg, or inner fortress, was on two successive days called on to surrender, but he gallantly refused. Early on October 31 Holcke advanced on the city, captured the suburbs despite a heavy fire, and began to bombard it. A third demand was refused, as was a fourth, which threatened not to leave man or dog alive in the place. Then Wallenstein opened his batteries. The town, well aware that it could not make a prolonged resistance, finally gave in, and received favorable conditions; and two days later the Pleissenburg did the like.

Wallenstein's light troops now raided the entire country between the Saale and the Elbe, and even beyond. Neustadt, Kahla and Saalfeld were taken; the peasantry sought refuge wherever they could, — in Erfurt, Wittenberg and Magdeburg. Torgau, Weissenfels, Merseburg, Naumburg, surrendered; Halle was occupied, but the fortress held out.

Gustavus had learned that Wallenstein had left Bamberg, and was marching north towards Coburg. Oxenstiern was anxious to have him disregard this manœuvre, and continue his own scheme. The king and the chancellor both believed that the forces in and about Saxony sufficed for her to hold her own; that Wallenstein would not quietly permit the devastation of the emperor's hereditary possessions; that, having once drawn Wallenstein away from Saxony, it could be done again by vigorous measures on the Danube. If the Main and Saxon armies held the fortresses, — such as Magdeburg, Wittenberg and Dresden, Frankfort, Würzburg and Schweinfurt, — and stood on a strict defensive, Wallenstein would be able to do no permanent damage to the cause; he would probably not conduct larger operations; while Gustavus could all but destroy Bavaria and the entire Danube country. If Saxony suffered, it would be her own fault.

This was sound military reasoning; it had been Gustavus' own idea; but he had promised John George to come to his assistance at just such a juncture as this. He had striven to save Magdeburg; he had saved Nürnberg; should he do less for Saxony? Moreover, he feared for his bastion; he knew that Wallenstein was his equal in persistent manœuvring, if not in battle; and, what was worse, the European powers were beginning to look on Gustavus' cause as the losing one. His star was, they feared, declining.

The latter was an element of the utmost gravity. The Netherlanders had never been warmly interested in the Swedes, — commercial relations forbade it; should a peace be made by the king with Spain, their position would be still less friendly. France stood in a questionable attitude, despite Gustavus' help in securing for Louis the control of the left bank of the Rhine, and the payment of the subsidies agreed on at Bärwalde stood in danger. Denmark had never been frank in her peaceful declarations, and, now that she had lost control of the Baltic, was ripe for any anti-Swedish plot; indeed, rumors came that such negotiations were on foot. England ought surely to be Gustavus' ally; but relations with her were strained, and all attempts to patch up a reasonable treaty had failed. Frederick had not yet been restored to the Palatinate, though Gustavus certainly intended that he should be, and this was a further cause for English grumbling. The brilliant successes of Gustavus where all others had failed had begun by provoking universal jealousy, and had been followed by apprehension of his downfall and of what might prove to be its result. These puzzling political conditions weighed sorely on Gustavus, and it was they rather than the military situation which led him to his action. With the aid of his old allies, or at least their ingenuous neutrality, he felt himself quite abreast of the situation. But with less than this, he was too good a soldier to risk what he had won at so vast a cost. His letters at this time show what he considered his problem to be.

His first duty was to put Saxony beyond question on such a basis as once more to be the outwork of his Baltic bastion. He had not quite lost hope of personally controlling Wallenstein; failing which, he had faith that he could beat him in battle. Alive with this feeling, he left Pfalzgraf Christian with four brigades and three thousand cavalry, to contain Maximilian, so that he might not again join Wallenstein; put necessary garrisons along the Danube, — Donauwörth, Rain, Augsburg and other places, — and on October 18 started for Erfurt. He ordered Duke William and Baudissin thither with all their troops and at all hazards. Bernard was to join him on the march; should Maximilian have passed Nürnberg on his way south, he purposed to take along Kniphausen too.

Passing Donauwörth, the column reached Nördlingen October 20, and Rothemburg (via Dinkelsbühl) October 27. On the 22d, with an escort of seven hundred cavalry, Gustavus went ahead to Nürnberg, to consult with Oxenstiern. The chancellor was to remain in south Germany, with headquarters in Ulm, and, as a general scheme, was to convene all the

Circles having the good of Protestantism at heart, and join their fighting and victualing powers, to sustain the king and oppose the emperor. In this interview Gustavus, as if in anticipation of his early death, gave Oxenstiern all necessary instructions as to the government of Sweden during the minority of his daughter Christina.

From Rothemburg the army marched via Kitzingen to Schweinfurt and Schleusingen. Decamping from here No-

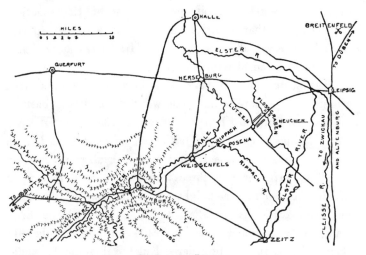

Region near Lützen.

vember 1, the Thuringian Forest was passed at night; and at Arnstadt, November 2, Gustavus joined Bernard, who had wisely crossed the mountains to head off Pappenheim from Erfurt and Weimar. The troops needed rest, and two days were given them at Arnstadt, whence, November 5, they marched to Erfurt, and remained in camp several days.

Breaking up from Erfurt, the king, eager for battle, headed the army for Buttstädt, which Pappenheim had recently passed; and Colonel Brandenstein was wisely sent forward through Kösen defile to Naumburg, which he took. In the presence of the enemy the army was ployed into battle columns and the country suitably patrolled. The enemy's light troops fell back along the Saale, and on November 8 Kösen was occupied in force, which, unless held, might compel the army to make a long detour to cross the Saale. In that day, the defile was of great importance. To-day, the country has many roads.

At early morning on November 9 Gustavus crossed the Saale at the Altenburg ford with the Swedish cavalry; the foot crossed at Kösen. At noon the whole army passed Naumburg, and occupying a camp in front of the Jacob's gate, proceeded to throw up works. The king's intention was to do here what he had done at Nürnberg: intrench a camp, wait for the Saxon army, and then force battle on Wallenstein.

Constantly in touch with John George, Gustavus had uninterruptedly advised him of the situation; he had too much at stake in the loyalty of Saxony to neglect these negotiations; and he had kept the elector well posted as to what troops would be in his vicinity and ready to lend a hand in case of attack. On starting north, he begged John George to draw his troops together so as to join the Swedish army; to occupy all defiles and strong places with large detachments; to cut off victual from Wallenstein; and not to be frightened by the reputed strength of the enemy, whose actual strength had been depleted numerically and morally. From Arnstadt he wrote again, asking for at least three thousand horse to be sent to Naumburg. From Naumburg he conjured the elector to send all available forces to the Saale, first of all those of Duke George; to hurry forward the cavalry, and let the foot, artillery and baggage come by the safest road, — perhaps via Mansfeld. There was no time to bring troops from afar ; the immediate work must be done with those at hand ; though, indeed, Arnim should be ordered in from Silesia. A small cavalry force, said the king, should be sent to Wittenberg and scout out towards Halle to clear the country. He urged John George to rouse the entire population, and order the peasantry to carry on a small war against the invaders. He had come to save Saxony; but Saxony must put her own shoulder to the wheel. He himself was waiting only to learn the enemy's whereabouts and intentions. Above all he urged an immediate junction of the Saxon with the Swedish army.

Duke George was sent orders to break up from Torgau and Wittenberg, and to join the king as quickly as possible with the cavalry.

Arnim, despite orders to return, was prolonging his stay in Silesia, while the imperialists had concentrated in the Leipsic region. He finally in person visited Dresden, November 5, but still foolishly urged that the place for the Saxon army was Silesia; and after making a flimsy inspection of the Lüneburg troops, he again left, insisting that he could at best spare a couple of regiments for Saxony. And he managed to convince the elector that he was right.

John George was conducting a political, not a military campaign. He again took to petty discussions of trivial points, while the enemy was within his dominions, and was prevented from desolating them by the sole presence of Gustavus. With every desire, he said, of sending troops, the bulk of the army was in Silesia, and that on hand was essential to protect the fortresses and the crossings of the Elbe. To exhibit his good-will, however, he would send two regiments, a force of about fifteen hundred cavalry, which should join Duke George and with him march to the Swedish army. John George had by solemn treaty agreed to give Gustavus the control of his

entire army; the king had forsaken his own plans on the
Danube to fly to the aid of his ally, and now John George
offered him a paltry fifteen hundred men! Even this force
came too late.

By November 14 Gustavus had substantially ascertained
the situation of the imperialists. There were but two of his
trusted generals with him, Bernard and old Kniphausen, in
which latter officer, brave though not always lucky, Gustavus
reposed much confidence. As was natural, Bernard advised
fighting, — and this was the mood of the king. Kniphausen
advised waiting for the Saxon and Lüneburg reinforcements,
the weight of which advice Gustavus recognized. But to
delay for these meant to permit Wallenstein to collect his own
forces, which Gustavus learned were much scattered. Before
the Saxons, Hessians and Lüneburgers could arrive, Pappenheim would be back, said the king, and his desire was to fight
before this took place. The enemy was never so weak as
when unexpectedly attacked, and Wallenstein seemed to be
undecided what to do. " I, your king and leader, will go
ahead and show every one the path of honor." Gustavus
decided to advance on the morrow and fight.

Wallenstein had taken measures to have his outlying armies
join him. Aldringer had been ordered away from Maximilian; Gallas had been called in, but the imperial commander did not anticipate an immediate challenge. It was
suggested by Pappenheim to make a raid on Erfurt, but as
Bernard had already joined the king, this was a useless operation. The generalissimo sent detachments to Naumburg,
hoping to be able to occupy the defile at Kösen, and the passages of the Saale, but these detachments came too late;
Gustavus had anticipated him.

While Gustavus was straining every nerve for battle, Wallenstein acted with indecision. He called a council of

war. This light-headed body advised against an attack on the Swedish camp as dangerous; counseled going into winter-quarters, which they alleged would oblige the king to do the same; to send a corps to Westphalia and the Rhine against Baudissin, to prevent the inroads and growth in importance of the Protestants in that section; and to quarter over a limited area so as easily to concentrate. This lamentable counsel Wallenstein was weak enough to accept. There is perhaps no better measure of the two men than the manner in which Gustavus dominated his council of war and decided for attack, and the manner in which Wallenstein listened to the trivial decision of his. Yet both commanders were equal autocrats, and, in a certain sense, of equal strength.

In pursuance of the advice of the imperial council, Pappenheim was kept till some other troops came to hand, and was then sent to Halle, with orders to hold this town, or if advisable, to send a couple of regiments to Cologne, and free it from the threat of Count Berg, whom Baudissin had dispatched thither. Leaving a garrison under Colloredo in the castle of Weissenfels, and sending detachments southerly towards Altenburg and Zwickau to observe the Swedes and keep the Saxons from joining them, Wallenstein retired, November 14, with his entire force towards Merseburg, to take up quarters between the Saale and the Flossgraben, so as to be near both Halle and Leipsic. He smelled not the battle afar off.

Wallenstein's strategic situation was remarkably good; he had blundered into it unawares; if he recognized he did not utilize it. His army lay in the midst of the three allied bodies: the Swedes at Naumburg; the Saxons at Torgau; and the force from the lower Saxon Circle with the Brunswick-Lüneburgers, who were marching from Wittenberg up the Elbe. Taken together, these forces exceeded Wallenstein's, but singly he was largely superior to any one of them. Here was his chance to fall on and destroy either of the three, before they should concentrate. He might take the Swedish army first, as the most dangerous, or he might lop off the Wittenberg column and by so much reduce his enemy's strength. No doubt the Saxons intrenched at Torgau and Gustavus in camp at Naumburg were better able to hold their own, even against odds. But Wallenstein's laxness now appeared as marked as his former persistency. He was at best not inclined to do battle, when he could accomplish his end by any other means. He harbored a dread of the king, despite his success at the Alte Veste; and he again adopted the strictly defensive rôle.

On the other hand, the decisiveness and energy of Gustavus grew as he advanced. The speed with which he had marched from Bavaria — Donauwörth to Naumburg in eighteen days — had enabled him to anticipate Wallenstein at the crossing of the Saale, as well as to prevent him from imposing on the fears of the elector. Determined to come at once to battle, the king was about to march on Grimma, via Pegau, to unite with the Saxons; but when he heard, November 15, of Wallenstein's retrograde movement on Merseburg, he followed him instead, giving up his original intention of intrenching a camp at Naumburg. He would wait, he thought, until he had concentrated his forces and advanced somewhat farther.

Divining the king's intention, when Colloredo, from the castle of Weissenfels, saw the heads of the Swedish columns and fired the three guns agreed on as a signal, Wallenstein called a new council of war, and under its advice again undertook to bar the road to Leipsic to the Swedes, and thus prevent the junction with the Saxons which he believed Gustavus was aiming to make. He ordered Pappenheim, who was besieging the Moritzburg at Halle, to return, to drop everything else, and hurry back by forced marches, — a thing he should have done without waiting for the council. " Let nothing prevent your being with me early to-morrow (November 16) with all your forces," wrote the general, anxious not to fight without his fiery lieutenant to uphold his hands. In consequence of this manœuvre, Wallenstein found the bulk of his army at Lützen on the 15th, and from here he sent out parties to scour the country. In his front were the fords of the Rippach, held by Isolani's Croat cavalry outposts. As Gustavus advanced to Rippach and Poserna, he met these detachments, which disputed the passage ; but they were brushed aside, and late on November 15 the Swedes crossed the stream. Gustavus spent some hours in reconnoitring the ground in his front.

It is a question whether the line of the Rippach itself would not have been a stronger defensive line for the imperialists. But Wallenstein had given his cavalry no clear instructions to hold the passage, nor had he arranged to sustain the outposts with any vigor, and the latter withdrew on the approach of the Swedes. Darkness prevented pursuit. Between the Rippach, the Saale and Lützen — the exact spot is not known — the Swedes lay on their arms in line of battle.

It is impossible to do more than guess at the force of the two armies which were to wrestle for the mastery on the morrow. For the Swedes the data vary between fifteen and thirty thousand men. It is only certain that Gustavus' army was much weaker than Wallenstein's. It may have numbered eighteen thousand men ; while the imperialists can scarcely have had less than twenty-five thousand ; and this number was to be reinforced by fully eight thousand more, whenever Pappenheim should come up.

Once set on battle, Gustavus took no account of the disparity of numbers. He knew that it was Wallenstein's strong intrenchments, and not lack of Swedish stomach, which had lost him the fight at the Alte Veste; and he advanced with entire confidence in himself and in them. Late at night on the 15th the general officers assembled round the traveling-coach in which the king spent the night, to receive instructions for the morrow. Some spoke of the enemy's superior strength, but Gustavus plainly gave his own views, and ended by saying that he could no longer endure to be within reach of Wallenstein and not move on him sword in hand. He burned to show him what he and his Swedes could do in the open field. This answered every objection; and all present crowded around to assure the king of their fidelity even unto death. This interview is a prototype of the famous speech of grim old Frederick to his generals on the eve of Leuthen.

Gustavus Praying before Lützen.
(From Braun's Historical Painting.)

XXX.

LÜTZEN. NOVEMBER 16, 1632.

WALLENSTEIN must hold Leipsic to prevent the junction of Swedes and Saxons; and the Merseburg turnpike for Pappenheim. He advanced to Lützen and established himself, facing southerly along the causeway, whose ditches made a line of works in which Wallenstein hoped to duplicate the battle of the Alte Veste. On reconnoitring, Gustavus planned to turn the enemy's left by a sharp attack and cut him off from Leipsic; not to be driven from his ground was victory enough for Wallenstein. The imperial left leaned on the Flossgraben, the right on Lützen, and in its front and in front of the right centre were two big batteries. The foot stood in four great battles in the centre, the cavalry on the wings; the ditches were lined with musketeers. Solidity was the theory of the imperial line. Gustavus drew up parallel to the enemy in his lighter order. In the wings was horse, mixed with foot, and cavalry was in reserve. The centre was of foot, with a heavy battery in front; and regimental pieces stood all along the line. Bernard was on the left; Kniphausen in the centre; the king led the right, where was to be the bulk of the fighting. After a cannonade, the Swedes attacked. The resistance was hearty, but the Swedish right forced its way across the causeway and pushed in the imperial left. The left was equally happy; and the centre crossed the causeway and began to swing in on Wallenstein's battles. But taken in flank by a column of horse, the Swedish centre fell back in some confusion. The king heard of the disaster to his centre; and heading some cavalry regiments, he galloped towards the place from whence they had fallen back. It was foggy, and, far ahead of his men, he ran into a stray party of imperial cavalry and was killed. About this time Pappenheim came on the field, and drove back the advanced Swedish right by a superb charge in which he also lost his life. The king's death maddened the Swedes. Bernard and Kniphausen reëstablished the Swedish line; and the Northlanders swept everything before them, and revenged their dead hero in a holocaust of blood. Wallenstein retreated to Bohemia; part of his army fled to Leipsic, part to Merseburg. He is said to have lost ten thousand men.

No engagement of modern times has a greater mass of conflicting records than the battle of Lützen. From the various statements you may sketch out a dozen different theories of the manner in which it was lost and won. It was, however, in the main a simple battle in parallel order, fought out with extraordinary obstinacy, and one whose phases were only those which may always occur in such an action, as the several parts of each line roll forward and back, in response to rein-

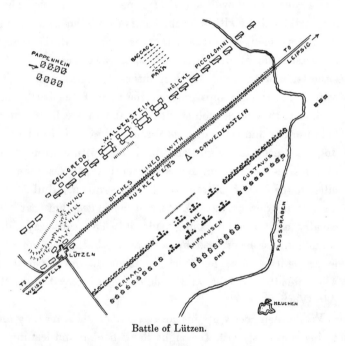

Battle of Lützen.

forcements brought up, or to gallant attacks made or repulsed. The principal facts are clear; but such interesting ones as the hour at which Pappenheim came upon the field, or the periods in the battle at which Gustavus and Pappenheim were killed, or indeed which was killed first, are wrapped in contradictory statement. There are indeed many different stories of the manner of Gustavus' death.

The plain of Lützen is low and flat. Cutting it substan-

tially from southwest to northeast runs the turnpike which
leads through Lützen village from Weissenfels to Leipsic.
This was Wallenstein's proper line of retreat, for he could
not well give up Leipsic, if he was to stand between John
George at Dresden and Gustavus at Naumburg; and he
needed it for winter-quarters as well. The road here lies
like a causeway above the plain ; some of the old maps show
it straight, others with a marked curve between Lützen and
the Flossgraben, — as it may then have had ; but the matter
is unessential : all details cannot possibly be reconciled. On
either side of the road are deep ditches, generally containing
water ; but though apparently at the time of the battle they
were dry, they were such still as to make an excellent line of
field-works ; and these ditches Wallenstein ordered to be well
dug out during the night, and lined them with a strong force
of musketeers. Running north and south a trifle less than two
miles to the east of Lützen was the Flossgraben, a dull stream
meandering down towards Zeitz, and not so deep but that both
cavalry and infantry could wade it. The causeway ditch
could likewise be crossed by both arms ; but it was none the
less a serious obstacle, much in favor of the imperialists,
who intended to fight on the defensive, as they had at the
Alte Veste.

Wallenstein drew up his army back of the causeway and
facing southeast, with the right flank behind and leaning on
the village of Lützen, which he had set afire to prevent the
Swedes from attempting to drive his forces out ; and with
the left flank leaning on the Flossgraben` and somewhat
refused, say some authorities. If the road was not straight,
the imperial line may have conformed to its direction and
thus have had a wing thrown back. It is probable that he
had a small flying wing out beyond the Flossgraben ; certainly the ubiquitous Croats must have pushed to the other

side, to put their harassing tactics to better use than they could do in the line of battle.

Along Wallenstein's front, then, ran the causeway, which stood up noticeably above the surrounding plain; and to the eye of the imperial general it seemed to yield a good chance of duplicating the victory of last August, if he could hold his men equally well to their task. To retain it and throw back the Swedish attack meant to keep Leipsic and to hold his route towards Merseburg and Halle, where lay part of his troops, and from which he was anxiously expecting the return of Pappenheim, — his stanchest lieutenant. Not to be driven from the causeway was victory enough for Wallenstein, just as the defense of the Alte Veste was in his eyes a notable feat of arms. He did not gauge victory from the standpoint of the great captain.

Not far back of the causeway, in front of the imperial right wing, was posted a battery of heavy guns, and another was in front of the right centre. The former stood on a slight rise just north of Lützen, in the midst of windmills. The number of guns has been, like that of the forces engaged, very variously stated. The greater part of the infantry was in the centre in four great battalia, set up in the Spanish style, and arrayed substantially as they had been at Breitenfeld. Much discussion has been indulged in to show that the imperial general had his army set up in three lines, and there exists a plan in Wallenstein's own hand for such a disposition. Be this as it may, the battle does not appear to have depended on there being any given number of lines. The imperial forces were drawn up in an order in which solidity played the main part, and it was Wallenstein's purpose to fight a strictly defensive battle, holding the causeway from Lützen to the Flossgraben as his line of works.

A portion of the infantry was posted in the windmills and

in the gardens which surround the village of Lützen. The imperial cavalry composed the wings of the army, the left under Holcke and Piccolomini, though it was hoped that Pappenheim would arrive in season to command the left wing. It is said that, in imitation of Gustavus' tactics, foot was interspersed with horse in the imperial right, under Colloredo; and they could well have been put to use behind the many garden walls.

Wallenstein himself remained with the centre, and was carried in a litter, as his gout prevented his mounting a horse.

The advance of the Swedes from Naumburg was such that they were marching directly upon the flank of the imperial army. It would seem as if Wallenstein's better line would have been across the turnpike, not along it, — perhaps, as suggested, behind the Rippach, — so as to enable Pappenheim to fall in on his right when he should arrive. Frederick would have sharply punished the great Czech for such a tactical blunder; but, like Alexander at Arbela, Gustavus declined to "steal a victory," and drew up for a parallel battle. Unless the king's idea of marching on Pegau and Grimma to join the Saxons, coupled to the knowledge that Wallenstein lay in and about Lützen, had led him to camp the day before somewhat to the south of the village, it is hard to see why he should not have used his opportunity for a flank attack. But battle-tactics was as yet a simple affair; Gustavus had done enough for the art of war in teaching armies mobility; he cannot be held to complete the science to which he contributed so much. Perhaps the best explanation is that the king desired to drive the enemy away from Leipsic and not towards it; or, in case of defeat, to retire towards the Saxons on the Elbe.

In two columns corresponding to the two lines of battle he proposed to fight in, Gustavus advanced, and drew up in line

at a distance of less than a mile from, and parallel to, the
enemy. We know his formation better than Wallenstein's.
Four half brigades were posted in the centre of each line.
Count Brahe was in command of those in the first line;
Kniphausen of those in the second line. The right and left
wings of the second line of the centre, under Kniphausen,
were composed of horse. In reserve was cavalry under
Colonel Ohm, in rear of Kniphausen. In front of the infantry centre there was one battery (some authorities say
two) of twenty-six heavy guns; and near forty light regimental pieces stood in front of the musketeers who sustained the horse. On both wings of the first line were
squadrons of horse, each two separated by detachments of
foot. In the wings of the second line there was only cavalry. Lützen lay in front of the Swedish left wing, and the
right lay on the Flossgraben. No doubt a Swedish flying
wing was placed or later got beyond this waterway. Bernard commanded the left wing, and the king, with Stäl-
handske and his Finns as a body guard, the right. The
baggage was near Meuchen, behind the Flossgraben.

Gustavus rarely slept much in the presence of the enemy,
but he passed the night in his traveling-coach with Bernard
and Kniphausen. The drums were beaten long before daylight, and the Swedish army bestirred itself. Prayers were
said by the chaplains, and " Eine Feste Burg " and one of
Gustavus' own hymns were sung as the men fell in.

Gustavus rode his brown charger and wore no armor.
Bernard and Kniphausen begged him to wear cuirass and
helmet. But a cuirass irritated his old shoulder-wound, and
he refused. His battle-speech to his men was short and to
the point, and he rode ahead with " Forward in God's name!
Jesu! Jesu! " on his lips.

The object Gustavus aimed at was to cut Wallenstein off

from Leipsic, so as to recapture the place and unite with John George. His tactics then was to pivot on his own left, which faced Lützen, and to drive the imperial left and centre away from the causeway. To this he addressed himself.

Though the troops had stood to arms at daylight, it was ten o'clock before they reached contact with the enemy. This delay was largely due to the fog which blanketed the plain, but it is an interesting thing for those of us who have seen an army on the march deploy from marching column into line, and win a pitched battle with high percentage of casualties in three or four hours, to note the length of time the formal marshaling of an army took prior to the day of that restless tactician, Frederick. Once aligned, the Swedes opened a heavy artillery duel, which lasted a full hour, and under its cover they advanced near the turnpike and stood ready for hand to hand work.

When he deemed that his artillery had made a sufficient impression, the king personally led forward his right wing of horse and foot, and gallantly charged on the causeway. He was received by a heavy fire; but after a sharp and prolonged tussle, the king drove the imperial musketeers from the ditches on both sides of the causeway, crossed this obstacle, and made a successful attack on the enemy's left wing beyond, driving the Croats off in the wildest flight. So stanch had their advance been that the imperial baggage park was threatened, and was summarily transferred from the left to the rear of the right, where lay the heavy batteries.

The king gave orders to pay small heed to the Croats, but at all hazards to break the ranks of the cuirassiers. These fine troops under Piccolomini fought like the black devils they were, and their intrepid commander was repeatedly wounded; but despite their bravery, they were forced back by the tremendous successive impacts of the squadrons headed by the king. Meanwhile the cavalry of the Swedish left wing was all but equally fortunate against the horse on the imperial right. And not to be behindhand, the infantry in the centre had advanced, driven the musketeers pell-mell out of their ditches, crossed the causeway, and taken the imperial battery opposite the centre. The initial gain had been sharp and marked all along the line.

But the success was short-lived. After crossing the causeway, the foot brigades wheeled somewhat to the left to take the imperial centre in flank, a manœuvre which exposed their own ; and before they could make an impression which was effectual on the battles of Wallenstein, several of the imperial cavalry regiments of the left centre and left, which had somewhat retired, were again massed, and bore down on the victorious Swedes like a torrent. Thus taken crisply in flank and in the face of a superior force, the gallant brigades failed to hold their own, and after a stout struggle were driven back and lost the battery they had taken. They had fought stanchly. In one regiment every captain was shot down. The Yellow cavalry and the Blues had successively advanced to the rescue, but only to be thrown back in disorder. The line was wavering. A disaster might result. The loss was as sudden as the gain had been, and the infantry was retiring across the causeway. Word of this state of affairs was sent to Gustavus, who was still driving the enemy on the right, and who believed that the whole line had kept its initial advance. As at the Alte Veste, Wallenstein had no ambition to fight a battle offensive. If he could hold the turnpike, the victory, so far as he needed it, would be won. And now that the Swedish central attack had failed, and his men had reoccupied the causeway ditches, he did not push them out to accentuate his gain, but held them in their place. A few squadrons alone galloped out beyond the imperial front.

While the king was reëstablishing order in his right wing, somewhat unsettled by its hard-earned advance, and was preparing for a second blow, he learned of the retreat of his centre. His fears were aroused for the success of the day, and he at once headed the Småland cavalry regiment, and with his usual impetuosity galloped over to the aid of his hard-pressed infantry. The king was heavy, but he rode good stock and fast. In his over-eagerness, and followed only by three companions, he galloped far ahead of his column, and in the fog which was again coming down upon the field, aimed for the place, slightly back of the causeway, where he expected to find his infantry, but from which the brigades had just now fallen back; here, between the lines, a stray party of imperial cuirassiers rode down upon him by simple accident, unaware of who it was. The king was shot in the bridle-arm; and, his horse swerving towards his own line, he received a bullet through the body. He fell from his horse with his last and mortal wound.

There was at the time a species of lull in the battle, caused by the falling back of the Swedish centre and the momentary pause of the right. As the imperialists had no idea of advancing beyond the causeway, there was a wide open space in their front, and it was during this lull and between the causeway and his own front that Gustavus fell. His death was announced to the army by his charger galloping riderless back to the Swedish lines, covered with blood, and his appearance excited the men to a frenzy of revenge.

Some time after midday Count Pappenheim appeared on the field from Halle, leading his van of cavalry. He had come with his best troops at a double-quick. Eagerly inquiring where Gustavus fought, — his death was not yet known to the enemy, — with a column composed of eight cavalry regiments, which he quickly assembled, he fell sharply on the

Swedish right wing and forced it back, practically regaining the ground their initial advance had won. Centre and right were weakening before the imperial attack ; but the Swedish left held its own in and about Lützen, and Wallenstein's lack of push saved the Swedes harmless from disaster. At this juncture, or somewhat later, gallant Pappenheim was killed, and his regiments, lacking his fiery leadership, hesitated and fell back; the Swedish right could once more gather for a blow.

On learning of the king's death, Bernard, who was on the Swedish left, immediately took command, and replaced the king on the right. Kniphausen led the centre. Count Brahe replaced Bernard on the left, where the cavalry had already sharply and successfully attacked the causeway, Lützen and the enemy's right wing. Re-forming the ranks in the intervals of quiet, which only Torstenson's guns now interrupted, Bernard ordered an advance all along the line, though the day was fast wearing away. The Swedes again pressed forward, this time screwed up to the highest pitch. Between the darkness and the fog, manœuvring had become impossible. It was a mere brute push for mastery. Piccolomini took Pappenheim's place, and led several regiments up to resist the renewed attack of the Swedish horse on the imperial left. The rival lines clashed, mixed, and rolled to and fro in a frantic death-struggle. In their first charge the Swedes carried everything before them. They recovered the body of the king, and again drove the imperialists far beyond the causeway. But some time after 4 P. M. the rest of Pappenheim's cavalry came up, and, maddened by the news of their splendid leader's death, they drove home a charge on the Swedish line which gained the lost ground, and once more pushed the assailants back across the causeway. No man could presage victory.

But gallant Bernard of Weimar would hear of no retreat, though even brave old Kniphausen is said to have suggested it. Torstenson's guns were still able ; the line could be again patched up, and every Swedish heart was nerved to avenge the king. One more effort was made for the *manes* of the dead hero, and the charge was given with the vigor of loving despair. The decimated ranks of the Northlanders closed up shoulder to shoulder, the first and second lines were merged into one, and forward they went in the foggy dusk, with a will which even they had never shown before. Nothing could resist their tremendous onset. On right, centre, left, everywhere and without a gap, the Swedes carried all before them. The imperial army was torn into shreds and swept far back of the causeway, where so many brave men had that day bitten the dust. At this moment some ammunition chests in rear of the imperial line exploded, which multiplied the confusion in the enemy's ranks. Darkness had descended on the field ; but the Swedes remained there to mourn their beloved king, while the imperial forces sought refuge from the fearful slaughter and retired out of range.

Lützen has been called a drawn battle. It was unequivocally a Swedish victory. The imperialists lost all their artillery, a number of standards, and, it is said, ten or twelve thousand men in killed, wounded and prisoners. Part of the force fled to Merseburg, part to Leipsic. That Wallenstein could reach Leipsic is cited as proof that the battle was drawn. But this was rather the usual want of pursuit. The Swedes slept on the field, and next day returned leisurely to Weissenfels, to weep for their dead lord.

Quite unaware that any future historian would find ground to state that the battle was drawn, Wallenstein retreated with the relics of his army to Bohemia. The loss of the Swedes has been called numerically equal to that of the enemy. Especially was it greater in the loss of its king and captain.

The dispositions of the Swedes and the vigor of their repeated attacks had been eminently praiseworthy. Wallenstein showed indecision in fighting a defensive battle; but no criticism can be passed on the manner of his fighting. It was a battle-royal in every sense, nobly fought out by each side.

The Swedes had destroyed the last army of the emperor. At the opening of the year Ferdinand had been at the end of his resources, when Wallenstein came to his aid; and the great Czech had now been utterly defeated. We know what Gustavus had already accomplished; he stood on the threshold of the imperial hereditary possessions, with every land from the Rhine and the Alps to the Baltic and the Vistula subject to his control, and firmly held. Had he outlived the battle of Lützen, can we doubt that he would have dictated peace on his own terms in Vienna? And would it not have been a peace promising more durable results than if he had reached Vienna after his initial victory at Breitenfeld? His wisdom was fully proven; but a higher power had disposed of his life.

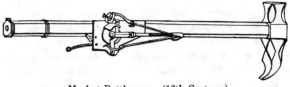

Musket Battle-axe. (16th Century.)

XXXI.

THE MAN AND SOLDIER.

GUSTAVUS was tall, strong and handsome, royal in bearing, condescending in manner, with noble features, golden hair and a clear blue eye. In intellect and scholarship he had no superiors; he was an eloquent speaker, and wrote hymns which are sung to-day all over Sweden. His dignity never left him; but though intimate with few, he was approachable by all. Of a sensitive nature, he was in youth quick of word, but he learned self-control and patience. Earnest piety was a constant guide, impelling him to justice and good deeds. His ambition was pure. In strength of will he was unchanging; he consulted all, but himself decided. No captain ever bore him with more splendid courage; Alexander had no more wounds; he went to danger as to a feast. Splendid in reward, he was just but summary in punishment. A hard worker, he was doubly busy in the field, trusting no man's eyes but his own, nor leaving work to others which he might do himself. He can scarcely be said to have been aided by Fortune. In dealing with his half-hearted allies, Gustavus exhibited the patience of Hannibal, the persuasiveness of Cæsar. He taught the modern soldier many lessons: method according to one well-considered plan; careful accumulation of supplies; activity in marches and manœuvres; rapidity of fire; the value of taking and holding key-points; the necessity of a sure base and communications; the security which resides in discipline; the fact that well-timed audacity is not foolhardiness. In winning his bastion, Gustavus showed caution backed by vigor; in defeating Tilly and overrunning the Main country, boldness, rapidity and rare skill; on the Lech and at the Alte Veste, magnificent contempt of danger and difficulty; at Nürnberg, admirable constancy; and at Lützen he sealed his honorable purpose with his blood. More than all this, he taught the world that war may be conducted on civilized lines. Had he lived, he would have dictated religious peace in Germany; as it was, he won it. He is properly called the Father of the Modern Art of War.

IT is a curious fact, and much to be regretted, that we know so little about the Hero of the Thirty Years' War. We are told endless facts about Frederick and Napoleon; we know much less about Gustavus.

Gustavus Adolphus was of tall and powerful frame; he had a royal bearing, great dignity, coupled to suavity, and a noble carriage ; but he was inclined, in the last few years of his life, to corpulence. This condition, however, so little interfered with his virility that his fondness for physical exertion led him into danger as to a feast. His hair and beard were golden yellow ; he had large light blue eyes, very expressive, eager and luminous, with a soft and kindly, yet proud look. His forehead was lofty and his nose strongly Roman. His daughter, Queen Christina, wrote of him as a very handsome man ; he was certainly kingly in his demeanor, as is testified by all his contemporaries. Earnest and liberal in all he did, no one who came near him but felt the influence of his character.

To an uncommon breadth of intellect Gustavus joined the well-poised knowledge of the apt scholar and the iron will of the true soldier. Once convinced that he was right, nothing could bar the execution of his project. He was of a quick, sensitive — one might say touchy — habit, coupled, as is rare, to a deep feeling for right, truth and religion. His quick temper was but superficial; at heart he was kindly, charitable and patient. His piety was honest, outwardly and inwardly, and impelled him to fair dealing and uprightness. Religion was never a cloak. He read daily and at length in his Bible, and prayed as openly and unreservedly as he spoke. He was fond of reading, well acquainted with the classics, and studied keenly the works of Hugo Grotius. He once, however, said that had Grotius himself been a commanding general, he would have seen that many of his precepts could not be carried out.

Gustavus spoke eloquently, and wrote easily and with a certain directness which in itself is the best style for a clear thinker. His hymns are still sung among the country folk of Sweden with the fervor in which the people shrines his memory.

Condescending, kind and generous, Gustavus was often splendid in his rewards for bravery and merit. When, in his youth, the later Field-Marshal Åke Tott performed some act of signal gallantry, the king thanked him before the whole forces paraded under arms, ennobled him on the spot, and with his own hands hung his sword upon him. But Gustavus was equally summary and severe. Once, on complaint being made of marauding by Swedish soldiers, the king assembled all his officers and severely held them to task; then, going into the camp and seeing a stolen cow in front of the tent of a petty officer, he seized the man by the hair and handed him over to the executioner. "Come here, my son," said he; "better that I punish thee, than that God, for thy sin, visit vengeance on me and the whole army."

While singularly quick tempered, Gustavus was eager to undo a wrong he might commit. "I bear my subjects' errors with patience," he said, "but they too must put up with my quick speech." He condescended often, at times too much, but no one was ever known to take advantage of his affability. Every one in his presence felt the subtle influence of greatness; his meed was the hearty respect of all who approached him.

Intimate with few men, and these only his leading generals or the princes he happened to be cast with, Gustavus was much attached to his chancellor, Axel Oxenstiern, and relied markedly on his judgment. Only Oxenstiern was privileged to speak plainly to the king. "You are too cold in all things, and hamper me too much," once said the monarch. "True," replied the chancellor, "but did I not now and then throw cold water on the fire, your Majesty had long since burned up." It was chiefly at dinner, which at that day was eaten before noon, that the king talked, and discussion then was ample.

This always busy monarch was especially busy in the field. Like Napoleon in his early years, he saw throughout life everything with his own eye; he would not rely on others, and always rode with the van of the army. His eagerness to know what was in his front many times put him in peril of his life; but he never overlooked an advantage of ground, nor was late in giving an order to meet the requirements of the occasion. In the cabinet he was strong and suggestive, the prime mover in every scheme; and though he constantly held councils of war, they never failed to fight.

He studied to know his opponents. He gauged Pappenheim high; Tilly was "brave, but nothing but an old corporal;" Wallenstein he underrated, partly because he disliked his pomp and egotism, and feared his loyalty. And yet he did him ample justice. Gustavus himself was too great to harbor petty jealousy of greatness in others. What he admired in Pappenheim was that which he himself so notably possessed, — a quick decision and fiery execution.

Sensitive to a degree with regard to his royal name and dignity, Gustavus hated adulation. Just prior to Lützen, when, in passing through Naumburg, the people prostrated themselves, he remarked with a protest: "Our cause stands well, but I fear God will punish me for the folly of this people."

Except Alexander, no great captain showed the true love of battle as it burned in the breast of Gustavus Adolphus. Such was his own contempt of death, that his army could not but fight. When the king was ready at any moment to lay down his life for victory, how should not the rank and file sustain him? With such a leader, a defeat like Tilly's at Breitenfeld, or Wallenstein's at Lützen, was not possible.

Nor was his courage a mere physical quality; his moral and intellectual courage equaled it. Hannibal's march into Italy was but one grade bolder than Gustavus' into Germany; Cæsar's attack at Zela was no more reckless, if less matured, than Gustavus' at the Lech.

The military student may read the records of war for seventeen centuries succeeding the death of Cæsar, without finding in its conduct any mark of that art and purpose which the great Roman, as well as Alexander and Hannibal, so constantly exhibited. Abundant courage, abundant intelligence, abundant opportunity will be found, but no broad, clean-cut method. When, however, the student turns to the page which narrates the operations of the Swedish king, he once again recognizes the hand of the master. The same method which has delighted him in the annals of the Macedonian, the Carthaginian and the Roman is apparent; the broad, firm ideal and never swerving moral force of which those captains were such brilliant examples may be seen; and from now on, thanks to the impress made on the art, he will find generals of the second rank who intelligently carry forward what Gustavus Adolphus rescued from the oblivion of so many centuries.

The operations of Gustavus in the Thirty Years' War are divisible into three epochs. From his appearance in Germany to his passing of the Elbe, his conduct of affairs was marked by great caution. It must be borne in mind that Gustavus had, barring the technical skill of the day, no military teaching except that which came from his study of the deeds of the ancients, and no guide except his own genius. War, up to his day and in his day, had been unmethodical and purposeless. This first epoch was of fourteen months' duration, and was consumed in securing a foothold in Pomerania, Mecklenburg and Brandenburg, in so careful and methodical a

manner as to stand out in contrast to any other campaign of
this era. Every circumstance was against him. He had but
slender means to oppose the emperor's apparently unlimited
resources. He came upon the scene at a time when the cause
he had embraced was a wreck. The Protestant princes whom
he sought to help, at whose request he had undertaken the
gigantic task, in lieu of flocking to his standard, looked on
him with suspicion, and afforded him small countenance.
Yet he lost not courage. With a clear aim in view, he pressed
steadily on, and reached his end gradually, step by step. He
bent every effort to secure the coöperation of the men who so
coldly scanned his work. He exhibited patience akin to Hannibal's, persuasiveness like to Cæsar's, boldness equal to Alexander's. He captured fortresses at the key-points and held
them : rarely was a strong place wrested from the Swedish
grasp. He accumulated supplies where he could be sure of
keeping them : but once during his German campaign — at
Nürnberg — was he out of victual. He firmly secured his
communications with the base he thus carefully established
and with Sweden, and never manœuvred so as to lose them.
He gradually overcame the shortsighted policy of his brother
Protestants, and strengthened himself with allies and fresh
accessions of recruits. He acted, not as the leaders of armies
for many centuries had acted, as if the population of the
countries they traversed were mere brute beasts, mere pro-
ducers of food for the great and their hirelings, but with a
spirit of kindliness and Christian charity which won over all
the populations to his side. He kept troops under a discipline
which was the marvel of its day, supplied their wants by legitimate means, paid them regularly, and allowed no marauding
or plunder. The few instances in which the Swedes were
convicted of crimes which were then the daily accompaniment
of the profession of arms were summarily punished. Gusta-

vus understood how to avoid battle with an enemy who was
too strong to beat ; how to lead him away from the key-points
of the theatre of operations, so as to secure them himself ;
how to operate energetically against an enemy who was his
equal or his inferior in strength ; how to employ the tactical
ability of his troops ; how to infuse into his men his own
enthusiasm on the battle-field ; how to utilize a victory to a
greater extent than any of his predecessors of the Middle
Ages or of his own era, and how to heighten and maintain
the morale of his troops in victory and defeat alike.   The
only failure of Gustavus' first epoch was his inability to save
Magdeburg from the hands of Tilly.   This was due not to his
failure to advance to her rescue, but to a natural miscalculation of her powers of resistance, of Tilly's perseverance, and
to the perverse refusal of the Saxon elector to allow the
Swedes a passage over his territory.

Then came the second epoch.   So soon as, by his cautious
and intelligent conduct, the king had set himself firmly in
place between the sea, the Oder and the Elbe, had protected
his flanks and rear from all probability of danger, and had
persuaded the electors of Brandenburg and Saxony to join
his standard, in other words had established his bastion, he
at once altered his method of operation.   When the enemy
would stand he assumed the offensive, crossed the Elbe,
attacked him at Breitenfeld, added immensely to his strength
and morale by beating him, and, leaving a portion of his
troops to operate with the allies and to protect his flanks and
communications, he advanced rapidly into the very heart of
Germany.   In three weeks, he had established himself firmly
on the Main, in Franconia and Thuringia ; in ten days after,
he had advanced down the Main to the Rhine, taking all the
strong places on the way ; in three months more, he had laid
his hands on the whole middle Rhine country ; and in two

and a half months from this last period, he had crossed the
Danube, beaten the enemy at the Lech by one of the boldest
operations undertaken since the Christian era, and had occupied almost all Bavaria. Thus in eight months, from September, 1631, to June, 1632, he had traversed and held a
much larger territory than he had previously gained in fourteen, and had become the most powerful of the monarchs of
Europe. He put to use the boldest and most decisive operations, and yet never failed in the method and caution which
were his guide; by his skill, courage and intelligence he
established himself as firmly in southern Germany as he had
previously done in northern. A glance at the territory he
covered, — from the north shores of the Baltic to the foothills
of the Alps, — and a comparison of it with that conquered by
any other captain of modern times, and the measure of the
few months during which he was actively a combatant in the
Thirty Years' War, will satisfy the most exacting admirer of
the past masters in the military art; and this especially so, if
we remember the political entanglements in which the king
was caught, the fact that he came to save and not to conquer,
and that statesmanship often dictated his manœuvres rather
than his clear grasp of the strategic situation.

Gustavus was now at the height of his reputation and success; the eyes of all Europe were upon him, and he was
ready to attack Austria from the west. Here begins the third
epoch of his operations. At this juncture the policy of France
changed; she feared that Gustavus would aspire to a political
prominence which would unsettle the balance of power in
Europe; his allies began to suspect him of aspiring to the
crown of Germany; and Wallenstein, the only soldier in
Germany who was in any sense worthy to be matched against
the king, raised a large army, and by marching on Saxony
threatened the Swedish communications with the Baltic, estab-

lished with so much care and skill. The whole situation changed. Gustavus was no longer so secure as he had been when his allies were whole-hearted, and his policy suddenly changed back to the cautious one he had early shown. Of the first importance in all his operations, whether offensive or defensive, particularly so as he was now apt to be thrown on his own resources, were his communications with the Main and the Rhine, and with his bastion in north Germany. Second to this was the protection of allied Nürnberg, to which city he had promised succor, should she be attacked. By taking position at Nürnberg, he accomplished all these ends, for he drew Wallenstein away from Saxony, and kept him away from the Main and Rhine. At Nürnberg, so long as his forces remained largely inferior to Wallenstein's, Gustavus acted on the defensive, indulging only in small war; but when, by his lieutenants coming up, the Swedish army grew to equal Wallenstein's, Gustavus again went over to an offensive startling in its boldness.

It cannot be denied that, while Wallenstein was in the field, Gustavus gave over part of his initiative to the Bohemian as he had never done before. But this was in a great measure owing to the political difficulties by which he was beset. Had the elector of Saxony been the firm and loyal ally to Gustavus that Gustavus was to him; had the king not been compelled to look sharply for treason in his rear, it is doubtful whether he would have yielded any part of his initiative, even to his great opponent.

When his offensive at Nürnberg failed and his provision quite gave out, Gustavus retired, not at once to Bavaria, but to the Main, to make sure of his communications there; and so soon as it appeared that Wallenstein had no immediate thought of disturbing these, leaving a lieutenant to observe him, Gustavus again took up his old thread and returned to

Bavaria to complete his conquest of Swabia and Würtemberg. Then, for the second time, Wallenstein, by moving on Saxony, coupled to the weak attitude of the elector, threatened, and now more seriously, the king's communications with the Baltic, and compelled him again to resort to quick and decisive operations. His march to Saxony and his attack on the enemy at Lützen were rapid, bold and skillful.

His life's striving here closed in a glorious death ; but the work the great king accomplished in little over two years in Germany was so vast, so solid and so intelligently planned, that it remains scarcely doubtful that, had he lived, he would have dictated to entire Germany the terms upon which the religious faith of all men should be held and practiced.

The student of Gustavus' life will notice in these several epochs a peculiarly intelligent adaptation of his work to the existing conditions. From his landing at Rügen to his passage of the Elbe, there was a cautious but by no means indecisive policy, to be largely ascribed to the unexpected coldness of the German Protestants ; to the ungrateful laxness of his cousins, the dukes of Mecklenburg; to the brainless hebetude of the elector of Brandenburg ; to the unintelligent yearning for neutrality of the elector of Saxony. The problem was one of politics, not war. From the crossing of the Elbe to the starving-match at Nürnberg, the student will see exceptional activity and courage, in no wise lacking intelligent, methodical caution. From the break-up at Nürnberg to Gustavus' death upon the field at Lützen, he will recognize an alternation as the circumstances dictated, from the cautious manœuvring of the first epoch to the intrepid energy of the second.

From Cæsar's time on, Gustavus was the first who firmly and intellectually carried through a campaign on one well-considered, fully digested, broad, and far-seeing plan, and who swerved therefrom only for the time being to meet conditions which could not be foreseen from the beginning; whose grasp was such that, whatever the conduct of the enemy, he was never compelled to abandon, but at most to vary, his plan; and whose work was done against an enemy at most times much his superior, and among friends whose half-hearted loyalty made them more dangerous than the foe.

Gustavus was in the habit of assembling his generals in council. The advice of his most trusted lieutenants was often opposed to what he did; but they could not see as far as he did. Not even Oxenstiern's crisp judgment was equal to the king's. And a council of war under Gustavus never deterred the king from pushing home. He listened patiently to all his generals; but he decided the action himself. It was he who maintained the consistency of his course through good and evil fortune alike. Each variation had its definite object, which attained, the general plan was at once resumed. In all Gustavus did there was a certain intelligent sequence and interdependence of movements that produced a perfectly systematic whole, in which the unity of plan was never disturbed. And with this broad plan there always went hand in hand a careful execution of detail upon which depended the success of the whole. His occupation remained firm; his victualing was sufficient to his needs; his movements accomplished what he sought to attain. Even when, as before Nürnberg, or before Lützen, he was driven to change his operation lest his allies in north Germany should play him false, it was only to defer, not to abandon, his own project.

In pursuance of his cautious policy Gustavus neglected no step of his advance. He left behind him no important fortress or city without observing, blockading or besieging it; he held the passages of all important rivers in his path by erecting suitable bridge-heads, or by occupying necessary

towns which controlled them; he kept upon his line of operations suitable detachments, often armies, or met threats in
force upon them by a prompt movement of his main force
upon the enemy. He so managed the division of his armies
as not to decrease his own strength, nor to lose the ability to
concentrate at least as rapidly as the enemy; he used his
allies for the work they could best perform; he kept the
main offensive in his own hands, generally so ordering that
his lieutenants should act on the defensive, unless they outnumbered the enemy, and then he urged them to all due
vigor; while he himself always undertook the part which
entailed the greatest labor, and called for the most courage
and intelligence.

Noteworthy as was Gustavus' caution, his vigor of execution when he undertook a fighting offensive was as remarkable. His caution was not the caution of Wallenstein, who
fought shy of battle, and fed his men by devastating the land
of foe and friend; it was the caution which watched his base
and line of communications, his victual, his munition and his
allies; while his decisiveness lay in his intelligent choice
between sharp movement upon the enemy with his whole
force when the conditions were favorable to a battle, or when
the moral superiority of the troops would allow, and the
policy of seizing important provinces and cities, and of utilizing the resources of the country and of allies so as to increase
the circle of his operations. His caution was such that, by
every step he advanced into the heart of Germany, he weakened the enemy by just so much. Wallenstein left the land
he crossed useless to the enemy because he had pillaged it as
he went; Gustavus spared the country he traversed, but he
held it by enlisting the population in his favor, and by careful military occupation. The simple recital of his marches
and manœuvres shows their value.

The secret of Gustavus' successes lay, not in the element of luck, for luck may be said on the whole to have run against him rather than in his favor, — not against him as it ran against the Carthaginian, but certainly not in his favor as it ran in Cæsar's, — the secret lay in his broad and intelligent general plan, in his adherence to the work as he had originally cut it out, and in his suiting his bold operations or cautious manœuvres to the circumstances as they existed or arose. As with Alexander, Hannibal and Cæsar, it was the man himself whose very brain and soul were put into his work; and this man possessed all those qualities of head and heart which produce results in war whenever they coexist with that other factor, opportunity. Equally great as monarch and as soldier, he united in his one person the art of both. His nation and his army were devoted to him as history has rarely shown devotion. His motives were perhaps the highest and purest which have ever inspired any of the great captains; his pursuit of them was steadfast and noble, open-handed and above-board, courageous and discreet. In weighing his intelligence, sound judgment, strong will, perseverance, hardihood and carefulness, he is properly put in the rank of the six great captains, — three of ancient, three of modern days. If we look further and gauge the results of what he did, if we view the purposeless and barbarous nature of war as it was conducted up to his day; if we weigh the influence which his short two years' campaign had upon all modern war, we may indeed in a moral sense, and in a sense making toward civilization, place Gustavus Adolphus yet higher. His pointing out the importance of key-points — at that time generally fortresses — in holding a country; the value of feeding an army by careful accumulation of supplies, instead of by ravaging every territory traversed; the use of a carefully drawn plan of operations, extending over the whole ground to be covered;

and the propriety of waging war in a more Christian and civilized spirit, marks the first step towards the modern system. Gustavus Adolphus has fairly earned the title of Father of the Modern Art of War, and must be acknowledged as the captain of all others who re-created methodical, systematic, intellectual war, and who taught the world that there could exist such a thing as civilized warfare.

After his death his lieutenants endeavored to carry out his system; but there was no one, not even Oxenstiern, who was equal to the task. They retained something of what he gave them; in many things they slid back into the old ruts; and war again assumed the aspect of gigantic raids.

Among his enemies, during the remainder of the Thirty Years' War, history shows nothing but inhumanity, over which it is well to draw a veil.

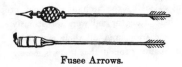

Fusee Arrows.

XXXII.

NÖRDLINGEN. 1633–1634.

THE death of Gustavus altered the entire aspect of German affairs. There was no longer a centre point, for Oxenstiern was not a monarch; but he and Richelieu kept on with the work which Gustavus had so well builded. Many of the powers stepped out of the Swedish programme, but the war went on. Bernard next year was to operate down the Danube; a Saxon-Swedish force was to manœuvre in Silesia; a third army in Westphalia. The Weser army succeeded well; Bernard and Banér, along the Danube, advanced as far as Upper Austria; Horn kept the imperialists out of Swabia. The Silesian force advanced against Wallenstein, who prudently retired to a fortified camp, while his lieutenants invaded Saxony. He then moved on the Oder; but his conduct was weak; and later returning to Bohemia, he was assassinated in February, 1634. Archduke Ferdinand took command of the imperial force, captured Ratisbon and Donauwörth, and sat down before Nördlingen. Bernard and Horn went to its relief, but attacking the archduke without proper concentration, they frittered away their strength, and were disastrously defeated, with the loss of the bulk of their army, and all their material. Men who made a mark as lieutenants of Gustavus found that there is more to war than they had understood.

THE death of Gustavus Adolphus completely changed the current of affairs in Germany. Its first effect was a practical rupture of all the treaties which bound the Protestant princes to the Swedish cause. The majority of them shortly began to make approaches leading to reconciliation to the empire. Richelieu was the only man who saw that now more than ever was it essential to uphold the balance of power against the Hapsburgs. It was he who stepped in and induced the Swedes to continue the war. Oxenstiern was the natural successor of Gustavus in the control of both the military and political issues; he agreed with the French minister, and despite her exhaustion, Sweden went on, hoping to gain, in the end, the object for which Gustavus had fought, as far at least as Swedish security was concerned. The treaty with Russia was renewed; Poland agreed to a continuance of the existing truce; and the entire resources and confidence of the Swedish nation were given to the great chancellor. But even Oxenstiern was not a Gustavus. The German princes, who had been ready to follow the lead of the splendid king, were unwilling to subordinate themselves to a mere prime minister; and Richelieu had much ado in prevailing on them to so act as not to forfeit the gain already made. In one way or other, however, they were fairly well committed to the cause; and for two years the work and method of Gustavus went on under Oxenstiern, — so far at least as was possible without the presence of the man and king himself.

The strategic plan contemplated three lines of operation. Bernard, with the bulk of the Swedish army, was to move into south Germany, pick up the troops left there by Gustavus, and then, basing on the Main, work down the valley of the Danube. Part of the Swedish army, with the Saxon and Brandenburg contingents, was to operate in Bohemia and Silesia. Another part, with the troops of the Hessian and lower Saxon Circle, was to hold Westphalia and protect north Germany. The winter succeeding Lützen was consumed in preparing for the execution of the comprehensive plan.

But Ferdinand was not idle. The fortune of war had rid him of his arch-enemy, and he foresaw greater advantages from a continuance of the struggle than from any peace which could be made with Richelieu at the council-board. To be sure, the army of Wallenstein was almost broken up, and had to be recruited anew; but the Bavarian forces were intact, and had been considerably increased by accessions from Lorraine and from Spanish troops. Few things go further to disprove the standing which has been claimed for Wallenstein as the best captain of his era than the secondary rôle he now played, after the only man who was called his equal had been removed by the accident of battle.

In the spring of 1633 the allies began operations more vigorously than the imperialists. In the Weser country they beat the forces of Merode and Gronfeld, and captured many fortresses. On the Danube, Bernard joined Banér, who had been forced out of Bavaria; and while Horn drove the imperialists out of Swabia into Switzerland and besieged Constance, Bernard pushed the emperor's army down the river, took Ratisbon before Gallas, whom Wallenstein at once dispatched from Bohemia to its succor, could arrive on the spot, and then crossed the Isar and moved on Upper Austria.

Meanwhile Aldringer, whose duty it was to contain Horn, marched into the Tyrol, where he joined a heavy body of Spanish troops and pushed his way through Swabia on Alsatia, hoping both to neutralize Horn and to entice Bernard away from his Danube conquests. Horn followed, after drawing in what reinforcements he could; and Aldringer found his scheme so unpromising of success that he retired.

To offset these gains, the Catholic armies had the upper hand in Silesia and Saxony. The allies, early in the year, marched through Lusatia into Silesia and overran that province. Wallenstein met this operation by moving from Bohemia into Silesia, where he took up a fortified camp at Münsterberg, from which, despite very great superiority in force, he retired on the approach of the allies. This defensive policy on Wallenstein's part is difficult to understand, and redounds little to his credit. Meanwhile Holcke and Pic-

colomini invaded Saxony; the former took Leipsic, the latter
threatened Dresden. Arnim hurried back to defend the
electorate, leaving Thurn with but twenty-five hundred men
in Silesia. This was Wallenstein's opportunity, for he had
forty thousand men. He moved on Thurn, beat him, and
marched down the Oder, captured Frankfort and Landsberg,
and even raided beyond the Warta. But the imperial general's operations essentially lacked vigor, even with nothing to
oppose him; and he finally yielded to the entreaties of the
emperor and returned to Bohemia, from whence he marched
on Bavaria to hold head against Bernard. His approach of
the Upper Palatinate did indeed force Bernard to retire;
but Wallenstein went into winter-quarters, owing to the late
season, ready to march on Saxony or back to Bavaria in the
spring. The great Czech's career was, however, summarily
cut short. His peculiar character and faithlessness had made
him too many enemies among the rich and powerful, from
Ferdinand down. He was assassinated in February, 1634,
in the fortress of Eger.

At the beginning of the spring of 1634 Bernard again
advanced on Upper Austria. The imperial army was now
wholly at the disposition of the emperor; and his son, the
Archduke Ferdinand, was placed in command, with Gallas
as his second. This force marched on Ratisbon, joined the
duke of Lorraine, who with the Bavarian army was besieging
the place, captured it on the 26th of July, and marched up
the left bank of the river. Bernard retired to Augsburg,
gathered in Horn's troops, and took post at Lauingen. The
archduke moved to Donauwörth, and taking it August 16,
marched on and laid siege to Nördlingen.

Meanwhile Banér and Arnim had advanced into Bohemia,
but had been beaten at Prague on the 28th of June, and had
returned to Saxony.

Nördlingen called on Bernard for assistance. The duke, with Horn, had sixteen thousand foot and ten thousand horse, but the archduke and Gallas had thirty-five thousand men or over. Bernard desired to await the rhinegrave, but the situation of the town had become desperate ; it had withstood one assault, but could not much longer hold out. He decided on attacking the imperial army.

The archduke was carrying on the siege from the south only ; but a reinforcement that Bernard managed to send the garrison did not hinder the operations, which were pressed vigorously. Horn advised taking up a strong position and trying to cut off the besiegers from victual ; but Bernard was for a battle, and he was sustained by a majority of the higher officers. He still felt the enthusiasm of Lützen. It was, however, with great surprise that, on the 5th of September, the imperial commander saw the army of the allies, which had lain back in the hills on the road to Ulm, appear and offer battle.

The plain of Nördlingen is bounded on the southwest and south, at a distance of three or four miles from the city, by a chain of hills, which rise from three hundred to six hundred feet. Nearer the town, across the road to Ulm, are other hills, perhaps one hundred feet high, and between the two runs a small brook, the Goldbach or Forellenbach. It was here that the archduke undertook to defend his siege operations from interruption by the allies. On the approach of the latter, he left only five thousand men in the lines, and advanced to meet Bernard with the rest. He was able to anticipate them, and as the vanguard filed out from the higher hills, the imperial cavalry fell upon it and drove it back. It was essential for Bernard to gain full possession of the debouches from these hills, and this he accomplished. He was anxious, before the enemy could do so, to seize the lower chain of hills, as these were practically the key to the battle-field; and he sent out a brigade of infantry with a battery to get a foothold there, while he himself deployed his army in the valley along the Goldbach. But the day was far gone, and as the allied artillery was not able to get a satisfactory position, the duke deferred the attack till the morrow.

The archduke spent the night fortifying the hills he had secured, and in placing batteries to advantage. He occupied

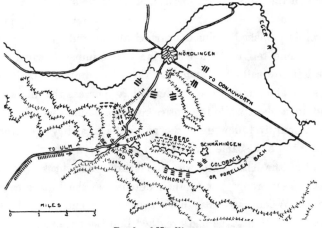

Battle of Nördlingen.

a line from Schmähingen to Hohlheim. On the heights of Aalburg on his left he expended special care, and placed there his best troops, the Spanish foot. The cavalry of the left wing lay behind works in two lines; the German foot held the right with a good part of the cavalry. There were, all told, seventeen thousand foot and thirteen thousand horse.

At daybreak of September 6 the allies broke out from their position in two columns, the right under Horn, the left under Bernard. Horn was to attack near Schmähingen, Bernard near Ederheim and along the Ulm road. The duke had no difficulty in seizing the rest of the higher hills, which only the imperial van had occupied. The imperialists contented themselves with bombarding the hills so occupied from their batteries opposite. Horn's cavalry, meanwhile, by a circuit, had got around the Aalburg position and attacked it in flank, while the foot had deployed in front of the imperial works and had advanced to the assault. But the cavalry was driven back on the infantry line, and though the Swedes, with their ancient gallantry, captured the first line of intrenchments and some of the guns, they paused, and after holding themselves some time, were thrust out with loss; a few of the most severely punished regiments turned to flee, and gradually the whole line fell back in confusion. The imperial cavalry of the left now sallied out against them; an unlucky explosion in some ammunition wagons tended to increase the difficulty, and in a short while the entire Swedish column was drifting back, sharply followed by the archduke's cavalry squadrons. Were these the same Swedes who stood twenty-four hours in front of the Alte Veste, who time and again thrust Wallenstein's best troops out of their defenses at the Lützen causeway? Where was that bold spirit, that endurance under trial, which Gustavus had breathed into their ranks ?

This failure of the allied right made a bad impression upon the centre and left. Their work ceased to show that energy which commands success. Bernard sent some regiments to the aid of Horn, and committed the grave error of detailing a considerable part of his troops towards Nördlingen to seek communication with the garrison, at a moment when he should have concentrated all his forces for a decisive blow on some one spot to stave off the impending disaster. There was but one outcome to such conduct. The division sent on this absurd errand was attacked and cut up by the imperialists, and the archduke at once assumed the offensive.

Horn, during this time, had reassembled his scattered regiments, and was ready to advance anew; but the Spaniards had taken all the positions he had vacated, and he was unable to recapture one of them. The reinforcement which Bernard had sent to him lost its way, and began operations on its own account. There was a lack of common purpose in the allied army. The imperial artillery was so effectively served that Horn, after a six hours' battle, was fain to withdraw. On the allied left matters were no better; and after much creditable fighting, so ill-directed as to be useless, this wing too gave way in confusion, and fled down the Ulm turnpike. Horn's cavalry had decamped; his foot, under his own courageous example, stood its ground where he had last rallied them; but the entire column was cut up or captured, Horn and three general officers among the latter.

The defeat of the allies was total, and it was due to Bernard's lack of definite plan. It is said that twelve thousand men were killed or wounded, eight thousand men captured; one hundred and seventy flags and eighty guns, and the entire train, fell into the hands of the archduke, whose losses are set down as a bare twelve hundred men.

Nördlingen surrendered next day. Bernard retired to Alsatia with his broken forces. The allied cause had been fatally checked. This battle ended what we have called the Swedish period of the Thirty Years' War.

In May, 1635, peace was made at Prague between the empire and Saxony. The elector received Lusatia, and the archbishopric of Magdeburg was given for life to his son Augustus. It was agreed that the ecclesiastical estates which were not held immediately from the emperor, and which had been confiscated before the convention of Passau (1552), should remain to the present possessors forever; all others should remain until 1667 in the hands of the present possessors, and then forever, unless some new arrangement should meanwhile be made. A general amnesty was given to all except the Bohemian and Palatinate rebels. Common cause was to be made against Sweden, and only Lutheran worship was to be tolerated. This peace was accepted by the elector of Brandenburg and most of the Protestant potentates.

French Sergeant.
(1630.)

XXXIII.

CROMWELL. 1642–1651.

CROMWELL was one of the greatest of men. His rank among generals is less high. He was the originator of the New Model soldier of the Commonwealth, — the regular who defeated successively all the militia of the royalists. He was an accomplished cavalry leader, who never failed to win whenever he charged. But Cromwell was not a great strategist, however good a tactician; and the opposition to him was never serious. His record of victories is interesting rather than brilliant; Marston Moor, Naseby, Dunbar, Worcester, make grand chapters in English history, but they do not teach us what Breitenfeld and Blenheim do. No one can underrate the services of Cromwell to England; he was a man capable of doing splendidly anything to which he put his hand; as statesman he has had few equals, but as a mere soldier he can scarcely aspire to the second rank. That he copied Gustavus was but natural; the whole of Europe, ever since 1630, had been copying him; and it is a slur on Cromwell's memory to assert that he was so lacking in intelligence as not to know what Gustavus had been doing. As a soldier he is strictly a product of the Swedish school. As a man he was essentially English — and his own prototype.

TEN years after the death of Gustavus on the field of Lützen, the civil war in England broke out. Charles stood at Nottingham with a patchwork army of ten thousand men. Prince Rupert ("Rupert of the Rhine," son of Frederick of the Palatinate and Elizabeth of England) was in command of the horse. The parliament army of double its numbers, but equally scrappy, lay in its front, under Devereux. Many officers in both armies had been trained in the Thirty Years' War; but there were as many tramps under both colors as there were soldiers. Roughly, the middle classes and the southern and eastern counties were with the parliament; the upper classes, the peasantry and the northern and western

counties were with the king; but there was no such line
of demarcation as in our civil war. Except unmethodical
operations, and the fact that Cromwell began to discipline
his "Ironsides" in the winter of 1642, little occurred for
two years. The parliament lost rather than gained ground,
and England felt in a lesser degree what had been the horrors of the war in Germany.

Cromwell began his "New Model" discipline with a troop,
of which he was captain. There was nothing new in it; it
was but the imitation by a strong, resolute, intelligent man of
what another great man and greater captain had done within
the generation. Cromwell was broad enough to understand
what he and all other Englishmen had watched, the wonderful campaigns of 1630, 1631 and 1632 in Germany; and
wise enough, when the occasion came, to apply the lessons
they taught. To assert that his military skill was but a
reflection of Gustavus' is no slight to Cromwell, who as
a man and a ruler was the equal of the Swede.

Cromwell's men were honest, pious yeomen. He asked, he
could have, no better material on which to work; and he
trained himself as he trained them, rising from captain of a
troop to colonel of a regiment, general of a brigade of horse,
commander of an army, captain-general. On the parliament
muster-rolls were twenty thousand foot and five thousand
horse, or twenty regiments and seventy-five troops of sixty
sabres each. In the cavalry, as it first stood, Cromwell
served as captain, and among the officers of regiments and
troops were numbers of his relations and friends. The cavalry corps was home to him.

At Edgehill, on October 23, 1642, the royalists had twelve
thousand men, the parliament fifteen thousand. Volcanic
Rupert, on the royal right, charged and routed Essex's left,
and then characteristically turned to plunder in Kineton.

The royal left had equal success, and the battle seemed lost, when there came up thirteen troops of the cavalry of the parliament, among them Cromwell's. They had other ideas in their heads than plunder. Riding in on the victorious royal foot, they at once turned the tide. The infantry was helpless; it was mowed down like grass. Rupert only returned in season to save the king from capture and to cover the retreat. Of the four (some say six) thousand loss the royal army bore the most. Edgehill proved that Rupert was gallant but unsteady; that the royal foot was wretched; and that the army of the parliament lacked cohesion. But it also showed in England what Gustavus had shown in Germany, that a man may carry the Bible into camp, and yet use his sabre-arm like the best of the fire-eaters, — as no fire-eater ever can.

Cromwell recognized what *noblesse oblige* meant. He knew that the parliamentary army was made up (as he said) of "old decayed serving-men, and tapsters and such kind of fellows;" he saw that "the spirits of such base, mean fellows" could not encounter "gentlemen's sons, younger sons and persons of quality;" he must have "men of a spirit, of a spirit that is likely to go as far as gentlemen will go," men imbued with a motive; and he "raised such men as had the fear of God before them, and made some conscience of what they did." And "from that day forward, they were never beaten." Their *noblesse* was the fear of God.

We English peoples are wont to ascribe all this to Cromwell's own invention. He himself would not have done so. It is an ill compliment to Oliver Cromwell's intelligence to say that with the Thirty Years' War drawing to a close, with confessedly numerous Englishmen and Scotchmen under his standard who had served with the Swedes, he should not have known what Gustavus Adolphus had begun to do twenty, had completed ten, years before; how he had transformed his poor Swedish peasant louts into invincible soldiers, who could beat the emperor's chivalry with no other talisman than the Bible. Cromwell, says Baxter, "had especial care to get religious men into his troop; these men were of greater understanding than common soldiers, and made not money but that which they took for the public felicity to be their end."

The minutiæ of drill Cromwell early learned from Captain (or Colonel) John Dalbier, a Dutch veteran, who had seen

Cromwell.

service on the continent; but he made his own rules of discipline, and so well conducted were his men that "the countries where they came leaped for joy of them." It was he who, following Gustavus, created in England the nucleus of what was really a body of regular troops.

In May, 1643, he won his first independent fight near Grantham; and though twice outnumbered, his horse rode through the enemy without a check. It was a notable lesson to see plain countrymen ride down cavaliers who were two to one of them; it rings in one's ears like the story of the Swiss pike or the English long-bow. In July Cromwell again met the enemy near Gainsborough, where, in hand to hand work with the pistol and naked blade, he drove them off and sharply pursued them; but unable to meet the larger body of royal infantry, he cleverly covered the retreat. Attention was attracted to him. In August Cromwell became second to the earl of Manchester, who commanded ten thousand

foot; and in October — in a combat in which he was un-
horsed and narrowly escaped with his life — he again defeated
a large force of cavalry at Winceby. His career of victory
had begun, and his activity was unceasing. His men had
won a reputation. " As for Colonel Cromwell, he hath two
thousand brave men, well disciplined; and no man swears
but he pays his twelvepence; if he be drunk he is set in
the stocks or worse: if one calls the other Roundhead, he is
cashiered."

In 1644 the parliamentary forces began to gain ground,
especially as the
Scotch sustained
them with twenty
thousand men ;
and near York,
at Marston Moor,
on July 2, the
combined army
of over twenty-
five thousand
men met a roy-
alist force of
somewhat less
strength.

Marston Moor.

The Roundheads were retiring from York, with Rupert on
their trail. They drew up to meet the fiery royalist on a
slight slope behind the White Syke Ditch, between Long
Marston and Tockwith. Rupert marshaled his army facing
them, on the moor, with Wilstrup wood in his rear. It took
some hours to put the men in line. In the parliamentary
army Cromwell commanded the left wing, of horse, with
Leslie in reserve. He had some four thousand men ; and on
this field he was to earn the sobriquet of Ironsides for him-

self and his God-fearing yeomen. The Scotch, nine thousand strong, in two long lines, held the centre, under Lord Fairfax. The cavalry of the right was led by Sir Thomas Fairfax. The artillery was on either flank of the centre.

Facing this array, Rupert drew up the foot, under Newcastle and King. The left, of horse, he commanded in person. The right was equally of horse. The artillery was near the foot, and there were good reserves.

It was seven in the evening before an attack was made. Battle was thought to be deferred to the morrow. But an attack was precipitated by the parliamentary foot, a part of which pushed through the ditch, and got roughly handled by the royal artillery. The right under Fairfax followed on, but the bad ground somewhat unsettled the line, and, met half way by the hot charge of Rupert, it was broken, and Rupert could turn inward on the infantry centre. When Cromwell, on the left, saw the difficulty which the centre had in passing the ditch, he obliqued his wing to the left, so as to clear this treacherous obstacle, and, outflanking the royal right wing, went thundering down upon the moor. Though slightly wounded in the neck, he paused not in his advance. Striking terror into the royalist ranks as he rode on, " God made them as stubble to our swords," he said. Rupert's right was utterly routed, and the centre of foot began to feel that initial success was not a presage of victory. Only Newcastle's White Coats arrested his advance.

Cromwell's charge was not what we call a charge to-day; it was an advance, with an occasional pause to fire and load; but it had a concentrated energy in it which even Rupert's mad gallop could not equal.

The right of each army had been destroyed. The centre of each was in perilous case. On whose banners would victory perch ?

Rupert's success had unsettled his squadrons; Cromwell's were in perfect order. Returning from pursuit, the royalist found the commoner drawn up on the moor, astride his own late line of battle, ready to test one more struggle; while Fairfax had collected part of his men on the edge of Wilstrup wood to prolong his line. Before he could re-form, Cromwell was upon him. There was no resisting the Ironsides; Rupert and his men took to flight.

Four thousand men bit the dust on this field. Marston Moor won the north of England for the parliament.

Cromwell was becoming the leading soldier of England.

The successes in the north were offset by corresponding losses in the south of England, and there was need of the Self-Denying Ordinance, under which members of parliament who cumbered the army must resign their commands. The passage of this measure, which was Cromwell's work, removed much useless material from the army, and made room for the New Model reorganization, which was equally his. The three armies of about ten thousand men each were, during the winter of 1644-45, consolidated into a regular body of twenty-two thousand men, and placed under Sir Thomas Fairfax; but Cromwell was the moving spirit. His cavalry body, like our volunteers in 1864 and 1865, had long been a regular corps, and it now gave the leaven to the whole lump. The fact that this new army was also the nucleus of the Commonwealth towards which England was tending has here no especial interest for us; as an army it was a notable institution. The New Model was voted in February, 1645. There were to be fourteen thousand four hundred foot, six thousand six hundred horse, and one thousand dragoons; and the whole body underwent a thorough drill and discipline. The effect was apparent as soon as it met the enemy.

In June, 1645, Fairfax lay near Naseby awaiting Crom-

well, whom he had specially desired to come and command the
cavalry, and for whom the Self-Denying Ordinance had been
suspended. His arrival was the sign for battle. On June
14, at early dawn, Fairfax drew up opposite the king with
fourteen thousand men; the foot in the centre, the cavalry
under Cromwell, who chose to place Ireton with five regiments and the dragoons on the left, while he retained the
right with six regiments, — some thirty-six hundred men.

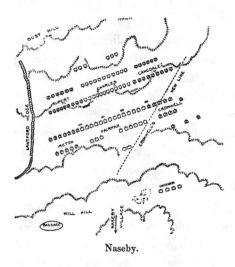

Naseby.

The royal army was
considerably less in
numbers, and on its
right stood Rupert,
opposite Ireton; on
its left Langdale;
and in the centre the
king. The composi-
tion of both forces
was better than at
Marston Moor; in
the royal army were
said to be fifteen hun-
dred officers who had
seen service, and the

parliamentary army was well drilled and disciplined. The
royalists had an admirable position on Dust Hill; the Roundheads one near Naseby. Lantford Hedge had been lined
with parliamentary dragoons.

The royalists opened the action by an advance. They
would have been wise not to leave their vantage-ground so
soon. On his side Cromwell, with "God our strength!" as
a watch-cry, met this onset by a counter charge with his
entire wing. The several columns of horse rode at the enemy
with perfect confidence in their cause and in their chief, and

" not one body of the enemy's horse which they charged but they routed." There was no question of the victory here.

Not so on the left. Rupert had ridden up Mill Hill at the head of the royal squadrons, had charged home, and Ireton, stanch as he was, could not stand the impact. The charge here was, as at Marston, probably at a trot. It was up an incline, and Ireton advanced to meet him, halting to fire. Rupert no doubt equally halted; and only after each rank had successively fired was the charge resumed. Real charges were not known in England at that day, — they were rare on the continent. Twice wounded, Ireton was captured, and the elated royalists pursued this routed wing almost to Naseby, and began to make for the parliamentary train. In the centre Fairfax's foot was at first driven in on the reserves by Charles' rapid charge; but they rallied, and once more made good countenance to the foe. At the same moment Cromwell, having dispersed the royal left wing of horse, wheeled inward on the royal centre, taking it in flank and rear, and, leaving but one *tertia* standing, drove the rest headlong from the field. This gallant *tertia*, like the White Coats at Marston Moor, held themselves until Fairfax's own regiment of foot went at them with clubbed muskets; then with Cromwell's sabres they were hewn in pieces. Charles had behaved with conspicuous gallantry.

Rupert and Cromwell had done equal work; but Cromwell had held his men in hand, as Rupert had not. A cavalry officer needs discretion as much as dash; and certainly it is harder to teach troopers to obey the "Recall" than it is to follow the "Charge." This virtue in Cromwell now bore fruit. Rupert's men, returning from the pursuit of Ireton, had they been in hand, and had Cromwell, in excess of ardor, met them in cavalry combat alone, were quite capable of retrieving the day. But Rupert was fiery; Cromwell was wary and fiery both. Like Gustavus he knew when to be prudent. Instead of trusting to his Ironsides alone, he and Fairfax drew up the foot, the guns and the horse in an irreproachable new line, and when Charles and Rupert, who still hoped for a chance of mending the day, saw the solid array in their front, they gave up the contest and retired in confusion, chased nearly all the way to Leicester.

The royal loss was heavy, but the killed were never known. There were five thousand prisoners, all the guns, standards and baggage, and best of all the king's private papers, — which sealed his political fate. His army was annihilated; he never collected another.

The likeness of Naseby to Marston Moor is marked; and it was Cromwell who won both battles.

For a year following Naseby, Cromwell and Fairfax were engaged in crushing the royalists in the south of England. In all there were some sixty small sieges, combats and storms, ending with the capture by assault of Bristol, September 10 and 11, where Rupert was extinguished; and of Basing House, October 14.

In August, 1647, the army asserted its right to dictate to the parliament. In April, 1648, the second civil war broke out, coupled with the invasion of the Scotch. Cromwell first subdued the rising in Wales, and then turned to Scotland. In August he fought the battle of Preston Pans, in Yorkshire, the first in which he was in chief command. The enemy, twenty-four thousand strong, was marching south in a long, straggling column, without any pretense to tactical skill, and without scouting the country. Cromwell fell on them with his nine thousand men, broke their column in two, and for three days (17th to 20th) pursued them some thirty miles, cutting them down right and left and fighting them when they would stand. It was not a battle, but rather a running pursuit; the loss of the Scotch and northern-country men was enormous; Cromwell's was trivial. This stroke ended the second civil war.

Ireland had embraced the cause of Charles II.; Scotland had proclaimed him king. To preserve the union, Scotland had to be conquered, Ireland subdued; and to Cromwell's lot fell Ireland. He landed in Dublin in May, 1649, with nine thousand men, which he shortly increased to fifteen thousand. With ten thousand men he first advanced on Drogheda, just north of Dublin. The enemy had a garrison three thousand strong in this well-walled town. On September 3 Cromwell reached the place, but not until the 10th did the batteries open. This was slow work, but when begun, the rest was sharply done. A formal demand of surrender was refused. On the 12th the place was stormed. The first assault was driven back; Cromwell headed the second, pushed in and annihilated the garrison, losing less than one hundred men. In a military sense the work was good; and in the history of the Thirty Years' War a soldier finds an answer to the charge of barbarity which will suffice for that era, if not for our days. "I forbade them to spare any that were in arms in the town," explains Cromwell's rule, and war is not a gentle art. From a religious standpoint, as the "rooting out of Papists," it is not our province to examine the act. The similar siege and destruction of Wexford (south of Dublin) followed, with the cutting down of two thousand men and a loss of twenty Cromwellians. No doubt many non-combatants, presumably some women, perished; but this was an unfortunate incident of the capture. During the winter Cromwell overran the land. At Clonmel he lost heavily in storming the town; elsewhere his losses were curiously small. These lessons sufficed. Though the revolution in Ireland lasted three years more, there was little of it.

No doubt both these so-called massacres are in a sense as inexcusable as that of Magdeburg, where forty thousand souls were cut off in one day; but there was in neither the same treachery. The rule was plain: " Refusing conditions seasonably offered, all were put to the sword." It was the way of the era, to free the world from which Gustavus had done so much. The fact that priests were not spared by Cromwell speaks less for the Briton than the leniency of Gustavus does for the Swede.

It was after this campaign that so many, it is said forty

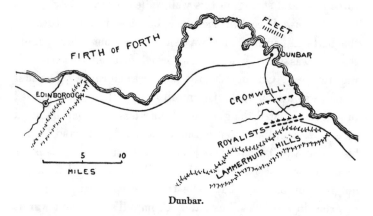

Dunbar.

thousand, Irishmen passed as professional soldiers to the continent.

As a mere soldier Cromwell had done well in Ireland, and with no great means; as man and soldier, he would have done better to heed the lessons of Gustavus. His conduct was the very essence of narrow Puritanism. But he had intentionally cut down none but men in arms.

Fairfax resigned; Cromwell retired to England, and was made captain-general; and in July he crossed the Scotch border with sixteen thousand men. Leslie was in command of the Scotch army, some twenty-two thousand strong, and sought to tire out Cromwell by a Fabian policy. This all but succeeded, and, worn by wet and hunger, the English army retired to Dunbar, to be near the fleet. The city was on a sort of peninsula, a mile and a half wide, and the only road to it ran over hills otherwise inaccessible. As they approached Dunbar, Leslie followed and held the road. He had trapped Cromwell; and drawing up along the Lammermuir hills, he cut him off from the only road to England. Cromwell's "poor, scattered, hungry, discouraged army" of eleven thousand men was in sad case, with twice their number of well-provisioned Scots in their front. Had Leslie kept to his Fabian strategy, it might have gone hard with Cromwell. But fearing that the English might embark and escape him, he pushed out his right wing to the coast, hoping to surround and cut them to pieces in the operation.

Leslie's left lay on the hills, with an impassable ravine in its front, but the brook which ran through the ravine to the sea broadened out lower down so as to be easily fordable. Cromwell was not slow to see the lapse, and to grasp its possibilities; he made his plans accordingly. On September 3, 1650, before daylight, he got his men under arms, put his guns in a position to keep up a heavy fire on, and thus prevent Leslie's left from deploying, and marshaled his army to attack his right in force. By 6 A. M. Cromwell advanced; the artillery fire sufficed to prevent the Scotch left from forming line and crossing the ravine in their front, and thus covered the disgarnishing of his own right; and meanwhile Cromwell fell lustily upon Leslie's right wing. Bar an initial check which was quickly repaired, the onset met with entire success. Cromwell sent a column around by the sea to take the Scotch line in flank, and within an hour the enemy was fully routed. The right flank was crushed, and when the left finally came to its support, it was but to be ridden down by its own flying squadrons, and to partake of their demoralization. The whole Scotch army fled in dismay. The victory was completed while singing "O praise the Lord, all ye nations."

There were three thousand Scotch slain, ten thousand taken, with all the baggage and material. Of the English only two officers and twenty men had fallen. It had been discipline which had won over numbers, and undoubted courage. The battle leads one to overlook the faults in strategy preceding it. Edinburgh and Glasgow surrendered.

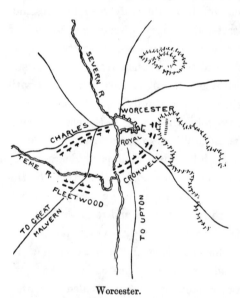

Worcester.

Next year, after some operations in Scotland, Charles II. made a bold dash for England. Nothing abashed, Cromwell followed him. Charles found little of the support he anticipated, and reached Worcester with not over fifteen thousand men, while at the end of August Cromwell arrived with thirty thousand.

Charles took up a position in the angle made by the Teme as it runs into the Severn. Just above, on the left bank of the Severn, lay Worcester, well fortified, with the Royal Fort on the southeast corner, and a bridge across the river; and Charles also held in force the bridge over the Teme and the road leading to the Malvern Hills. The Severn bridge lower

down, at Upton, he destroyed. His Worcester bridge enabled him to cross quickly to and fro, and here he prepared to
play his last card, expecting that Cromwell would assault
from the north.

With his excess of troops Cromwell could safely divide
his forces, having in this a manifest advantage. He closed
in the town, set up his batteries on the hill on the east of the
river, and cannonaded it for nearly a week, waiting for his
lucky day, the 3d of September, but meanwhile drawing his
lines in more and more. He had sent Fleetwood down the
Severn to cross and hold the enemy to the Teme.

On the day set Fleetwood attacked the Teme bridge, and
under cover of this attack two bridges were thrown, one
across the Severn and one across the Teme, close together,
thus taking Charles' triangle in reverse, and obliging him to
withdraw into Worcester, which he did in the afternoon.
From here he broke out on Cromwell's force on the left bank,
and for a moment gained success ; but the bridges enabled
Cromwell to reinforce this wing in season to prevent disaster ; and the royalists were forced within walls, after a hearty
struggle. The Royal Fort was taken by storm, and by eight
in the evening the city gates were captured. The rest was
mere massacre ; three thousand Scotch were killed, ten thousand taken. Cromwell lost two hundred men.

The tactics of this battle was admirable. It was a fit closing to Cromwell's military career, which had lasted from his
forty-third to his fifty-second year.

Judged by success, Cromwell was a greater soldier than
if gauged by the rules of the art. He was not a skillful
strategist ; in tactics, within a certain limit, he was admirable. Following immediately in the steps of the great continental captain, he organized and disciplined a wonderful
army, which none of the less well-drilled royalists could ever

resist. The forces he opposed never stood his blows long; and judged by opposition, he does not stand high. His losses in storming strong places, except at Clonmel, were always small, testifying to poor defense. At Preston Pans he lost fifty men; at Dunbar twenty-two; at Worcester two hundred. While mere losses do not necessarily measure the general, they must still be considered in the light of what he had to oppose him.

That Cromwell was one of the great men of history is undeniable; that for England he wrought as almost no other of its rulers ever did is but a truism; that, tried by the highest standard, he may be called a great general is less certain. He was what some other truly great men (Washington, for instance) have been, eminent in arms; but that he deserves to rank with the great captains no capable critic familiar with their history has ever pretended; that he may rank with the second class — with Turenne, Marlborough, Eugene and their fellows — can scarcely be allowed. That he did such splendid work for England came from his exceptional equipment of character and intelligence.

He was a worthy follower and, like all the rest of Europe, an imitator of Gustavus Adolphus.

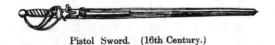

Pistol Sword. (16th Century.)

XXXIV.

TURENNE. 1634 TO AUGUST, 1644.

THREE sets of great soldiers exist in the seventeenth and eighteenth centuries: those grouped about Gustavus, about Condé and Turenne, and about
Eugene and Marlborough. It was they who created the modern art of war,
and by narrating their deeds we are writing its history. We have dealt with
the first set, and now come to the second. After the death of Gustavus, the
Swedish generals whom he had trained — Bernard, Banér, Torstenson — in
connection with France conducted brilliant campaigns over all Germany; but,
lacking the solid method of their great chief, their work had no result. In
1646 the last of these generals, Wrangel, operated successfully with Turenne.
Born in 1611, Turenne first saw service in Holland with his uncle, the prince
of Orange, proved himself gallant and intelligent, and rapidly rose in his profession, under successive commanders on the Rhine and in Italy. His first
independent campaign as field-marshal, in 1644, opened with a successful raid
across the Rhine and towards the upper Danube; this was followed by a march
on Freiburg, which was blockaded by the Bavarian Mercy. Turenne attempted to relieve it, but his army, which had been given over to him in the
worst order, proved weak, and his operation failed. Condé was sent to his aid.

IN the military era to which Gustavus Adolphus by right
of eminence and priority gives the title, there are three periods into which our subject-matter may conveniently be divided.
The first includes those generals who were grouped about
Gustavus, and the events in which they enacted their brilliant
parts. The second includes those generals who were on the
stage when Turenne conducted his campaigns in the Thirty
Years' War, the War with Spain, and the Wars in the Netherlands. The third period includes the generals who acted with
or against Prince Eugene and Marlborough in the War of
the Spanish Succession. By narrating the military life of Gus-

tavus, we have already covered the first period. We can best make clear the second and third periods not by an attempt to narrate all the war history of their times, but by keeping more or less closely to the masterly campaigns of Turenne, Prince Eugene and Marlborough themselves; to the skillful work of Condé, Vendome, Villars and Montecuculi; to the campaigns of Luxemburg and Catinat; for it was the novel and useful elements in what they did which so distinctly enriched the art of war, and which prepared the way for that greater teacher, Frederick, king of Prussia. If we depart from the course thus prescribed by this History of the Art of War, it will be but to notice such a splendid event as the defense of Vienna by John Sobieski, or such an erratic genius as Charles XII.

In this design, space limits us to the narration of a portion only of the campaigns of these able captains. Part must be omitted; another part can be sketched with but few strokes; to still other parts more time will be allotted; and from the ground thus covered we shall conceive a fairly good idea of what was done by them towards developing the art of which they were past masters.

From 1635 to the Peace of Westphalia in 1648, the Thirty Years' War was in what is called the French, or the Swedish-French phase. Because of Gustavus' death, or of the defection of Saxony, Brandenburg and other late Protestant allies, the Swedes were none the less intent on carrying out the purpose bequeathed to them by their great monarch, though indeed Sweden was compelled to fight if she would preserve her " bastion " on the Baltic. France would make no peace on terms acceptable to the empire, and so the war went on. The north German potentates were to an extent eliminated from the problem, and the theatre of war was somewhat changed even as the ideal of the war was modified, but Riche-

lieu and Oxenstiern never wavered. By the battle of Nördlingen Bernard had forfeited his duchy of Franconia, and he
was glad to serve under the ægis of France, with the hope of
carving for himself a new duchy out of Alsatia. On his death
in 1639 the French retained his army.

After the battle of Nördlingen, the operations of the Protestant allies had been mainly in two bodies. The Swedes
under Banér, based on Gustavus' bastion, had manœuvred
toward Saxony and Bohemia, while the army of Bernard,
properly a part of the Swedish forces, but entertained by
France, had operated on the Rhine, in Alsatia and Swabia,
sometimes in connection with the French armies, sometimes
alone.

In 1638 Bernard crossed the Rhine above Basle, captured
many towns in Swabia, besieged Breisach and beat off several
imperial armies of relief. His other campaigns were rather
weak.

The operations of Banér from 1636 to 1641 showed great
energy; but his boldness was misplaced, and despite many
fine forays into Saxony and Bohemia, and even as far as
Ratisbon, he was invariably forced back to Pomerania by the
larger imperial armies and their allies. No victories, and he
won some splendid ones, as at Wittstock, secured him a foothold beyond the bastion, which Wrangel meanwhile defended.
In 1641 Banér died and Torstenson assumed command.

Extending over the entire territory from Denmark to Vienna, the latter's manœuvres were in a high degree bold and
brilliant; but they were quite without result. In 1642 he
won a victory at Leipsic; again in 1644 at Juterbok, and in
1645 at Jankowitz, over the imperial troops; but though
much which is admirable characterized his work; though he
markedly aided the operations of the French, his campaigns
cannot be pronounced successful. Like that of the others,

his work lacked the solidity shown by his king and teacher. As a lieutenant, especially as an artillerist, he had been beyond criticism.

This want of permanent success by the generals he had brought up, and who had no superiors at the time, emphasizes the value of Gustavus' own careful method. His lieutenants covered the same ground which he had won; they marched as far; they won victories apparently as splendid; they had opponents less able than Tilly, or Wallenstein, or Pappenheim; and yet the result of all they did was naught, or at

best they merely kept the ball in play until exhaustion put an end to the long drawn out match of nations.

In 1646 Field - Marshal Wrangel, the last of Gustavus' lieutenants, commanded the Swedish army, and worked in connection with Turenne. Inspired by the great Frenchman, their joint campaigns were quite out of the ordinary.

Turenne.

Henri de la Tour d'Auvergne, Viscount of Turenne, was born in 1611 in Sedan, son of the Duke of Bouillon and Elizabeth, daughter of William of Orange. He was a sickly youth, and up to his twelfth year gave no promise of ability. But his father, who superintended his education, roused the lad's latent ambition, and he finally excelled in his studies. He was educated a Protestant. Like Gustavus Adolphus, he was fond of reading the heroic deeds of Alexander the Great in Quintus Curtius, and from these romantic pages he imbibed his early love of war, then as always the noblest of professions, but then more highly considered, as it was more essential, than it is to-day.

When twelve years old, his father died, his elder brother inherited the title, and Henri was sent to his uncle, Prince Maurice of Orange. But soon this guardian also died; and that Henri was thrown on his own resources contributed much to develop his extraordinary character. Entering the Dutch service as a private in 1625, he rose within a year to a captaincy, and, especially by distinguished conduct at Herzogenbusch in 1629, earned the respect and approbation of Prince Maurice, who then said of him that he would become a great leader. When nineteen, he entered the French service as colonel, and in command of his regiment, at the siege of La Motte, in 1634, he so approved himself for bravery that he was promoted on the spot to be maréchal de camp. The next year he served under Cardinal La Vallette, who went to the aid of the Swedes and, in connection with Duke Bernard, relieved Mainz. On the retreat of the army Turenne was noted for his untiring activity and his intelligence in procuring rations. In 1636 La Vallette made special request for Turenne's services, and at the siege of Zabern, while Bernard, after two failures, captured the upper town, Turenne stormed and took the lower town and citadel, doing wonders of courage and receiving a serious wound. Towards the end of the campaign he forced Gallas from Franche Comté in a rapid, dashing style, defeating his veteran opponent near Jussey, following him up and taking many prisoners. When later Gallas endeavored to raise the siege which Bernard was conducting against Joinville, Turenne intercepted and drove him back across the Rhine.

In 1637 Turenne took part in La Vallette's campaign in Picardy, and during the rainy season at Landrecies, when the trenches were constantly full of water, was again prominent in rationing the troops, working incessantly himself and enduring privation cheerfully. This solicitude for the welfare of his men was a trait which distinguished Turenne all through life. Demanding much of the soldiers, he devoted all his efforts to their good ; he was singularly careful of their health, — sometimes to his own strategic loss; and he never for a moment thought of self. His men were devoted to him.

At the age of twenty-six, for the capture of the castle of Solre in the Hennegau, and the heroic defense of the fortified camp at Maubeuge, Turenne was given his step as lieutenant-general, and as such in 1638 led reinforcements to Bernard at the siege of Breisach. During the eight months of this siege, he fought in three combats and three general engagements ; and a long attack of intermittent fever did not abate his energy. Finally, he stormed and captured an isolated fort which was a key-point of the investment, and the fortress of Breisach surrendered.

Sent to Lombardy in the spring of 1639, to serve in the army of Count Harcourt, Turenne covered the siege of Chieri, and fought successfully at La Route. Next year he pursued the enemy, after the siege of Casale, and captured many trophies and all his train. Hereupon he induced Harcourt to invest Turin, where Prince Thomas of Savoy was in command, while the citadel was held by a French garrison. Singularly, General Lleganes now came up and blockaded Harcourt. Thus the French force in the citadel was besieged by the prince of Savoy, he by Harcourt, and the latter by Lleganes, — a quite unparalleled situation. Lleganes was driven off; Turenne, though again wounded, victualed Harcourt by bringing a large convoy safely from Pignerol ; and shortly thereupon Turin surrendered. Harcourt was called to Paris, and during his absence, Turenne captured Moncalvo and besieged Ivrea, which surrendered to Harcourt on his return. Prince Thomas now entered the French service; Turenne was appointed to the command, under him, of the army in Italy; and recognizing the remarkable qualities of the young general, the prince intrusted him with the main direction. To induce the Spaniards to evacuate Piedmont, Turenne made apparent arrangements to transfer operations to the duchy of Milan, and laid siege to Alexandria, which he blockaded, so disposing his troops as purposely to leave a gap in his lines. Through this gap the Spanish general, at the head of almost the entire garrison of the fortress of Trino, essayed to relieve Alexandria. Allowing this to take place, Turenne sharply turned on Trino and captured it, for which skillful feat of arms he was made field-marshal, and here, after seventeen years' active apprenticeship, ended his services under other generals.

Turenne had learned his trade, was well equipped for a leader, and understood how to distinguish the true from the false in military situations. In his memoirs he has said that he owed certain qualities to those under whom he served. From the prince of Orange he had learned how to choose positions, the besieger's art, and especially how to draw up plans, to maturely consider them, and then to alter nothing so long as it was possible to carry them out. From Bernard he had learned not to be blinded by success nor cast down by failure; neither to blame himself nor to forgive his own errors, but to correct these and strive to change ill fortune. From La Vallette he had learned the importance of keeping in touch with his soldiers in the field. From Harcourt he had learned that mature consideration of the problem, followed by unceasing activity and rapid decision, were the surest elements of success in war.

We know more of the detail of Turenne's campaigns than we do of those of Gustavus, — indeed, we have the memoirs of the French marshal, — and there is a marked difference in the manner in which they wrought. In narrating the work of the king we are dealing with immense issues, — issues on which the whole civilized world depended for its future progress and welfare; in narrating that of Turenne we deal with the operations of bodies which occupied a position of less prominence on the theatre of war, and form a less important page in history. But Turenne, though deprived of the opportunity of working on so broad a field, was yet a soldier with few rivals; and many of his lesser operations deserve the closest study. War is wont to depend as much on smaller work well done as on the labors of the giants; and to few generals is it allotted to expend their efforts on the broadest fields. Like Stonewall Jackson or Sheridan in our own civil war, Turenne, in his early campaigns, was not in command of large-sized armies; nor indeed was he often allowed that complete independence of action which breeds the highest results; but whether in command of an army corps or in command of an army, he was always solid, original and brilliant. No better pattern exists in military annals; no captain has done more uniformly excellent work. If we were to select the material we possess of any one soldier's campaigns from which to study all the operations of war, from the minor to the grand, it is perhaps to those of Turenne we might best turn. It must be, moreover, borne in mind that he was the first great soldier to succeed Gustavus, and that as such he was called on to create much of what he did. Turenne is one of the most sagacious, profound of our teachers.

As an independent commander, Turenne began his campaigns towards the close of the Thirty Years' War, 1644 to 1648. His first army, as field-marshal, was given over to him in the worst possible condition. It was the army of the upper Rhine, which had been beaten at Tuttlingen, had lost the bulk of its officers, six or seven thousand prisoners, together with all its artillery and baggage; and had made its way, with difficulty and in utter disorder, back to Alsatia. This force, as a mark of confidence, was intrusted by Cardinal Mazarin to Turenne for the purpose of reorganization; but it was a sad compliment to pay him. Had he not already won a name for exceptional ability, he would scarce have been awarded so onerous a duty.

In December, 1643, though not long back from the siege of Trino, and still invalided, Turenne undertook his thankless task, and joined the army at Colmar; and because Alsatia had been devastated in January, he went into his winter-quarters in the mountains of Lorraine, and began his labor by salutary and sensible methods. The French government was illiberal in moneys, and Turenne was compelled to largely use his own capital and credit, which happily were excellent. His cavalry became good, but though his infantry could not be put on an equal footing, in four months he was able to take the field.

It will be noted, in all the wars of the period upon which we are now entering, that the cavalry was the principal arm, almost always equal, often superior, in numbers to the infantry, and thus, in the line of battle or in other operations, occupying a space and a position unduly prominent. It was a final flickering up again of the mediæval idea of the superior efficiency of mounted men, which Gustavus had proved to be erroneous, and to which Frederick, with the wonderful battalions drilled by his father, gave the death-blow at Mollwitz.

The enemy had lain quietly in winter-quarters, doing nothing except to besiege Ueberlingen, which fell in May. Early in the same month Turenne assembled his army in Alsatia, and, crossing the Rhine near Breisach with a part of

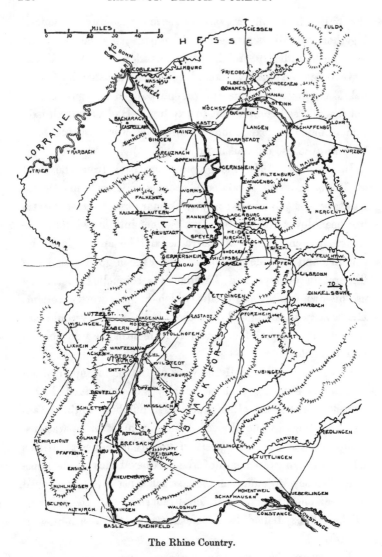

The Rhine Country.

his troops, marched toward the sources of the Danube. Hearing in the hills of the Black Forest of a body of two thousand raiding Bavarian horse, he hunted it up; and attacking

it smartly, beat it and captured many officers and four hundred men. The rest retired on the Bavarian army, which had captured Hohentwiel. This little foray instructed and heightened the spirits of the French army, which then returned to Lorraine, and enabled Turenne to gauge its quality.

The enemy had rested in good winter-quarters, and by enlisting a number of the French prisoners taken at Tuttlingen, had materially increased their strength. In the month of July Freiburg in the Breisgau was blockaded by the Bavarian field-marshal, Mercy, who had marched on the place through the Black Forest. The garrison had been increased to eight hundred men, which then was beyond the usual size. Artillery at that time was not powerful, and the belief in works was greater, — or rather the disinclination to attack them was so. In the siege of a place, the inhabitants were apt to serve on the walls as well as the garrison ; and many defenses of towns in which even big breaches had been made were long and gallant in the extreme. The smallness of the garrisons of important places, and the stanch resistance of which they were capable, strike us to-day with wonder.

Freiburg lies at the foot of the mountains of that rugged section of country known as the Black Forest, at a place where they inclose the alluvial plain of the Rhine in the form of a crescent. This inclosed level has high and inaccessible rocks on the right as you come from Breisach, and at that day had a wooded swamp on the left ; it was approachable from the Rhine by only a single road through a defile which ran several miles between the hills, and might be easily defended.

Turenne had a short five thousand foot and the same number of horse, with twenty guns. He again crossed the Rhine at Breisach, and moved on Freiburg, hoping to surprise

Mercy and to raise the blockade. The enemy had sent out a
large foraging party, and did not learn of the approach of
the French until the latter came within six miles of them,
when, recalling his foragers, Mercy prepared for action.
Turenne reconnoitred the enemy's position, and sought to
occupy a hill near Ufhaufen which commanded it; but the
infantry sent forward proved inefficient, and, owing to the
cowardice of two color-bearers, got panic-stricken and fell
back in disorder from the hill, which at the moment was held

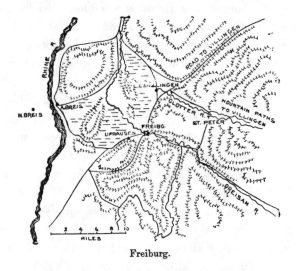

Freiburg.

by only a picket of twenty men. The enemy at once reinforced the picket, but did not follow the French. Turenne
remained on the field some time, during which a cavalry
combat fell out to his advantage; but his plan of a surprise
having failed, the dominant force of the enemy induced him
to retire after these slight engagements, and Freiburg surrendered to Mercy, being, however, allowed the honors of war.

  This failure was perhaps less the fault of Turenne than of
the miserable condition of his troops, especially the infantry.

And yet this same infantry, as we shall see, shortly after stood decimation under which even veterans might have quailed. Napoleon casts a slur at Turenne for this operation, which was, indeed, rather pitiable, and suggests that he should have taken up a strong position and gone into camp, so as to annoy the enemy. But Turenne probably saw after the panic that he could not count on his foot to serve him well at this juncture, and preferred to harden it by minor manœuvres before encountering larger forces. Merely to sit down opposite an enemy he could not attack was of no utility. The news of the backset having reached Versailles, he was, morever, ordered by the court to suspend operations until he could be reinforced by the duke of Enghien, — later the Great Condé, — who had leaped into fame by the victory of Rocroy, and despite his youth was deemed able to accomplish all things.

French Halberdiers.
(15th Century.)

XXXV.

CONDÉ AT ROCROY. MAY 19, 1643.

BORN in 1621, Condé distinguished himself in his nineteenth year at the
siege of Arras, and his royal connections rapidly advanced him. In 1643, in
command of the northern frontier of France, he advanced to Rocroy, besieged
by the Spaniards under Marshal Melos, and attacked the enemy despite marked
difficulties. With his right wing of cavalry he destroyed the Spanish left, and
turned in on the infantry centre under Fuentes. The Spanish right having
meanwhile broken up the French left, Condé rode with his cavalry column completely around the Spanish army, and took the successful enemy in the rear.
He thus dispersed both cavalry wings of the Spaniards. But the centre of foot
resisted so stanchly that the victory was dearly bought and at grave risk. As
the work of a young commander, this was a doubly famous victory ; and it at
once made Condé the national hero.

LOUIS of Bourbon, duke of Enghien, and, on his father's
death, prince of Condé, was born September 8, 1621. He
was early, and all through life,
noted for diligent application to
literature and arts, and ranked
as a man of fine culture and
broad ability. He distinguished
himself in war as early as his
nineteenth year, at the siege of
Arras ; and two years later, in
the campaign of Roussillon, won
commendation for skill and bravery. His royal connections yielded him exceptional opportunities,
and in 1643 he was given charge
of the defense of the northern frontier of France.

Condé at Rocroy.

The preceding campaign here had been disastrous; a French army had been destroyed at Honnecourt, and Field-Marshal Melos, governor-general of the Low Countries, who stood at the head of a splendid army of twenty-seven thousand men, already imagined Picardy and Champagne to lie at his feet. Condé, as we will continue to call him, though he remained duke of Enghien until 1646, was able to concentrate forces amounting to twenty-three thousand men, — of which seven thousand were horse, — and had under him Marshals de l'Hopital and Gassion. The former had been placed at his side to check any possible excess of youthful ardor, a thing which he was, however, unable to do.

Melos had opened his trenches before Rocroy. The town lay in a plain then covered with woods and marshes, — it is to-day full of forests, — and was approachable only through long and narrow paths, except from the Champagne side, where the woods were less extensive. In a military sense it was unapproachable. Melos had occupied all the avenues, and had bodies of scouts patrolling the country on every side. Condé had a strong instinct for battle. He felt that to destroy the enemy was the way to secure the safety of France; he determined to relieve Rocroy, even at the risk of fighting; and in order to reach the three or four miles wide plain near the city, where alone there was room to manœuvre, at the head of a body of cavalry, suitably sustained by foot, he forced his way through the woods early on May 18, took possession of a height at the outlet to cover his columns, and successfully debouched into the open. Melos did not oppose his passage because he himself desired battle, was not averse to winning a victory when the enemy had no chance of retreat, and believed the French army to be much smaller than it actually was. He was well seconded by Field-Marshal Fuentes, a veteran of experience and proven courage.

Condé had fully matured his plans the day before, had issued exact instructions, and the troops all filed into line in the prescribed order.   He himself commanded the right with Gassion as his second; de l'Hopital commanded the left; d'Espenant was at the head of the foot (*corps de bataille*) in

Battle of Rocroy.

the centre; and there was a reserve under Marshal Sirot. Between each two squadrons was a body of fifty "commanded musketeers," — Gustavus' old disposition, so successful at Breitenfeld and Lützen.   Dragoons and light cavalry were on either flank, and the baggage had been sent to Aubenton.

Melos, who harbored no doubt that with his veteran army

he could beat the unseasoned French troops of his young and inexperienced opponent, drew up his army, but with the sensible belief that on the day of battle you should have in line every available man, he sent word to General Beck, who lay a day's march to the rear, to come up rapidly with his six thousand men. Melos' line occupied a height facing that on which Condé had marshaled his army. The duke of Albuquerque commanded the left, and he himself the right. Count Fuentes, whom many years of war had crippled so that he could not ride, like Wallenstein at Lützen, led the famous Spanish infantry from a litter.

To marshal an army was, in the seventeenth century, an affair of time; and it was six o'clock in the evening before the rival generals were ready to join issue, though an artillery duel had been going on all day, rather to the disadvantage of the French, who lost three hundred men; for the Spanish batteries were the better. Even though late, Condé was about to attack, and, accompanied by de l'Hopital, was busy with his final dispositions, when La Ferté, inspired by the foolish idea of making a brilliant *coup* and of throwing a force into Rocroy, left his post in the line at the head of the left wing cavalry, and enabled Melos, who had a keen military eye, to sharply advance his own right. Had the Spaniard pushed boldly in, the day would have been beyond a peradventure his; but he did not do so; La Ferté was recalled, and the gap he had made was patched up. Daylight had gone, however, and Condé reluctantly put off his attack to the morrow.

Between the two armies lay lower land, and here, in the underbrush opposite the Spanish left, Melos had hidden a thousand musketeers, hoping to fall on Condé's flank when he should lead out his right wing of cavalry; but Condé had got wind of the ambush, and his first act in the morning twi-

light was to fall on these men and cut them to pieces; after
which he sent Gassion forward and well to the right with the
first line of his cavalry to attack Albuquerque in flank, while
he himself with the remainder should attack in front. His
line of retreat lay back of his right, and this he must protect
at all hazards. Surprised at the manœuvre, Albuquerque
nevertheless detached eight squadrons against Gassion, and
prepared to receive Condé with a firm foot. But the French
charge was too fiery; Condé drove in upon the enemy with
the fury of hot-headed youth; his horsemen followed the
impulse of the prince of the blood; Albuquerque's cavalry
was ridden down and fled; and Condé sent Gassion in pursuit, while he himself turned in on the flank of Melos' infantry,
in which he wrought fearful carnage among the Germans,
Walloons and Italians. On the French right the success
was beyond all expectation. Victory seemed near at hand.

Not so on the left. Marshal de l'Hopital had started his
cavalry out at too fast a gait, so that it reached the enemy
winded and in some disorder; Melos met it by a sharp
counter-charge and drove it back; de l'Hopital was wounded,
and Melos pursued his advantage just as Condé had done
his, fell on the flank of part of the French infantry, cut it to
pieces, captured La Ferté and all his guns, and actually
reached the reserve. The enemy had purchased a promise of
victory with equal ease as Condé. The case looked desperate.
The merest accident would turn the scale either way. Sirot,
who led the reserve, was urged by many of the runaways to
retire, for the battle was lost, said they. "Not lost, sirs; for
Sirot and his companions have not yet fought!" replied the
brave officer, and manfully held his ground. It was an even
chance on either side.

But Condé, learning of the disaster to his own left, now did
what only the true instinct of war, the clear soldier's eye and

heart, could dictate. If he did not win with the squadrons he
personally led, he saw that the battle was lost; and with the
energy of a Cœnus or a Hasdrubal he spurred on, and still on,
back of the Spanish foot, round to the enemy's right, out to
the front, took Melos' victorious cavalry in the rear, sent it
whirling back in the wake of the fugitives of the left, recaptured La Ferté and the guns, and took every one of the
Spanish batteries on that flank. Few such superb rides have
been made by any squadrons. Gassion ably seconded his
chief by completing the rout, and nothing remained on the
field except the splendid old Spanish infantry, which, like
Father Tilly's Walloons at Breitenfeld, refused to decamp.
It had been confronted by d'Espenant, who, however, with
his newer battalions, had not dared to come hand to hand
with the veterans. These, grouped with teeth set around
their guns, and in the midst of panic and disaster, resolved to
pluck victory from defeat, or to die where they stood. Who
knew what so brave a body might yet accomplish?

Beck was near at hand with six thousand fresh troops, — a
dreaded factor in the uncertain problem. Detaching gallant
Gassion with his handful of cavalry to hold him in check at
every hazard, Condé himself prepared to beat down the stern
resistance of the Spanish battalions. He had now again
taken his place in line after having made an entire circuit
of the Spanish centre and having destroyed both its wings.
Reassembling his squadrons, with the superb battle decision
which always characterized him, and inspiring them with his
own undaunted courage, he drove them home upon the Spanish foot. But he had not counted on what these men could
do, nor on the iron will of old Fuentes. Masking his guns
by a thin line of foot, and reserving his fire until the French
squadrons were within fifty paces, the veteran uncovered his
batteries, and opened upon the approaching horsemen his

eighteen pieces charged with grape, while the line gave so
withering a volley that even Condé's men, flushed with victory and their prince's ardor, could not face the hail, but fell
back in grave disorder. Had Fuentes possessed but a few
squadrons, he might still have wrested a victory from the
French. Not a Spanish sabre was on the field. Every man
had fled.

A second time the prince headed his horse, a second time
he was thrown back. A third charge was no more successful;
the crisis was doubtful. Fuentes, from his litter, could watch
with grim satisfaction his youthful antagonist breaking his
lines on the Spanish square as the waves break on the rock.
He had not lost yet.

But at this moment the reserve under Sirot came up.
Condé changed his tactics to a less reckless one, as he should
have sooner done: with the gendarmes he rode round the
flanks of the Spanish foot, and put his infantry in in front.
Fuentes saw himself surrounded by superior numbers on all
sides. This was decisive. The day was irretrievably gone.
To save a remnant of his men, the old Spaniard made an
attempt to surrender; but the French either understood not
or could not be restrained, and a frightful butchery ensued.
The battle of Rocroy ended in a bath of blood; and Beck,
learning that there was no more Spanish army left to rescue,
came to a right-about and precipitately retired, leaving behind some guns.

The Spanish losses were immense. Out of eighteen thousand foot, nine thousand are said to have been killed where
they stood, and seven thousand were taken, with all the guns,
three hundred flags and immense booty. Splendid Fuentes
died where he had fought. The French losses are stated at
only two thousand killed and wounded. If the figures are
correct, it was but a modern sample of the butchery usual in

ancient warfare. "How many are you?" asked a French of a Spanish officer after the battle. "Count the dead and the prisoners, — they are all!" was the answer.

After this magnificent victory, in which Condé exhibited singular courage and energy, and proved himself a born battle-captain, he took Diedenhofen (Thionville) on the Moselle and returned to Paris, where he was the hero of the hour. His princely blood, coupled to marked courage and ability, made too rare a combination to be overlooked.

French Musketeer. (1647.)

XXXVI.

FREIBURG. AUGUST, 1644.

AFTER Turenne's failure at Freiburg, Condé, who was believed equal to any emergency, was sent with ten thousand men to reinforce him and take command. On his arrival the two generals attacked Mercy in his works, Turenne by a long circuit around his left flank. The fighting was prolonged and bloody, and the French were divided; but Mercy withdrew to another position, and allowed them to reunite. Two days after, a second and rather miscalculated attack was made on the new works and was equally sanguinary; and again Mercy withdrew. After four days a turning manœuvre was attempted; but Mercy retired definitively. The French commander then marched to Philipsburg, and after a handsome siege captured it; upon which Turenne moved down the Rhine, taking Speyer, Worms, Mainz and other towns; and later Landau. Condé returned to France, and Turenne resumed his position at Philipsburg. The two French generals were warm friends throughout life; neither was jealous of the other; each was active in his colleague's interests.

To return to Turenne's operations. Shortly after his failure at Freiburg, Condé crossed the Rhine at Breisach with his army of ten thousand men and Marshal Grammont second in command. He had marched from the Moselle, one hundred and eighty miles in thirteen days, then a rapid progress. Condé joined Turenne, August 2, at the camp which the latter had taken up fifteen or twenty miles from Breisach, and, as superior taking command of the combined forces, he moved forward to Freiburg. Mercy had fortified the height which Turenne had tried to seize some weeks before, and now held it in force. He had eight thousand foot and seven thousand horse, excellent troops, and had added to the strength which discipline had given the regiments all that art could do for their position. The hill he occupied was strongly intrenched

with a redoubt on the right and a line of works and abatis ;
and with the swamp on one side and the mountains on the
other, he quite shut out approach to the city. The main
camp lay in the rear of the intrenched hill. A careful reconnoissance was at once undertaken by Condé and Turenne up
to the enemy's position, and it was determined that the chief
should advance against the height in front while, under cover
of his sharp demonstration, Turenne should make his way
through the woods and defiles round Mercy's left flank, push
in on the plain, and thus take him in reverse. The main

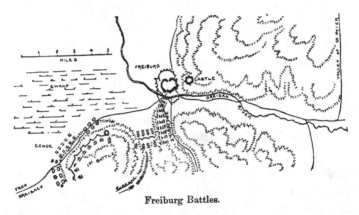

Freiburg Battles.

attack was set for five o'clock in the afternoon of August 3,
so as to give Turenne what was deemed ample time to make
his way by the long and difficult circuit mentioned. It was
not then known that the enemy had made the route almost
impassable by an intrenchment at the outlet of the defile, and
by trees felled across the path. The plan was made in the
dark. If Condé or Turenne could break through or turn
Mercy's line, they could reach the Freiburg plain; but by no
other means could this be done from the direction on which
they were operating. Their division was extra hazardous,
even on the assumption that Mercy would keep to his works.

Condé had six thousand foot and three to four thousand horse, and among his lieutenants were Marshal Grammont and Generals d'Espenant and Marsin. Turenne had ten thousand men, half horse, half foot.

At 5 P. M. Condé launched his men to the attack, there having been no special signal agreed on between him and Turenne. It was work for infantry only, and the cavalry was held in reserve on the flanks, to protect it so far as possible. The hill was one of those vine-terraced slopes, so common on the Rhine. Up it the troops went in gallant order, and took the line of abatis; but their loss was considerable, and they paused at the foot of the works, and began to spread in their uncertainty to right and left in search of shelter. This pause looked critical. Failure stared the young generalissimo in the face; and there was too much at stake to hesitate. Dismounting, with all his generals and staff, he and they dashed up the slope on foot, and personally headed the troops for a fresh assault. No nation responds to gallantry of this sort quicker than the French; the battalions again knit ranks, took fresh heart, and poured over the intrenchments like a flood. The hill was won, and out of the three thousand Bavarians who had so bravely defended it, a bare hundred escaped the ensuing massacre.

The situation was still desperate. Not knowing the ground, Condé feared a night attack by Mercy with fresh troops on his own men, who were unsettled by victory. He occupied the fort he had taken; with immense exertion got his cavalry up the slopes, and there waited anxiously for Turenne and the morning. Had he known the situation, he might have taken the enemy who lay in front of Turenne in reverse; but the uncertainty of darkness precluded any further action.

Turenne had started at daylight, had made his way with much exertion for sixteen or eighteen miles through the rugged ground to within a short distance of the mouth of the defile; but here a much larger force of the Bavarians than had faced Condé held head to him behind their stout line of works. Unable to get his cavalry out into open ground where it could deploy to support him, he was baffled. But as the best way out of a desperate position, he boldly attacked. Both lines stood in close fighting contact, — the reports say forty paces, — and the battle lasted fiercely through the late afternoon and evening, and scarcely ceased at night. The French troops behaved well, and stood a loss of fifteen hundred men without flinching. These were the same men who had decamped not long since before a picket of twenty men, — a phenomenon constantly occurring in war, and always curious. At this spot the Bavarians lost two thousand five hundred men. In fact, the casualties of both sides are by some authorities stated at an aggregate of six thousand. Each army was severely punished.

Haply, the action of Mercy cut the knot of the French leaders' difficulty. On account of his depletion he dreaded a fresh battle under the same conditions; and during the night, lest between the prince and the marshal he should not be able to hold himself on the lower ground and should suffer a more marked defeat, he withdrew to a new position back of the old one, leaning his right, which was of horse, on the outworks of Freiburg. Turenne and Condé were able to join hands and once more breathe freely. Their situation had been a bad one, but Mercy's retiring had saved them harmless.

Turenne advised an attack on the 4th, but Condé declined to make one on the score of the exhaustion of the troops. Mercy threw up fresh works. His position was if possible stronger than the first one, but cramped. His artillery, sustained by four thousand foot, was posted so as to sweep the approaches of the hill, and he was able to utilize the lines he had erected in the late siege. His front he covered with works constructed of rough logs, and with abatis.

The succeeding day, August 5, brought on another hotly contested battle. Turenne felt the enemy early, edging to the right to make room for Condé on his left, and the latter's troops were got into touch with the enemy. During a lull in the opening of the fighting, when the two French commanders were reconnoitring with a view to a combined assault on the Bavarian lines, and had ordered that no manœuvres should be undertaken in their absence, the restless commander of Condé's French infantry of the left, General d'Espenant, carried away by imprudent ardor, advanced on a work in his front that seemed weakly held; seeing which, General Taupadel, who understood that he was to follow the lead of the left, also threw forward his first line from the right. Both attacks were met in force, and brought on a series of partial engagements quite lacking *ensemble;* the French battalions lost heart and fell back from work which, well inaugurated, they would have cheerfully done; and the result was to disturb the tactical plans of the French commanders, and to bring about heavy losses on both sides, followed by an indecisive result. Turenne confesses in his memoirs that, had the enemy known the French situation, they could have destroyed the army, as the losses during the day had been between two and three thousand men in the wasteful fighting. But the Bavarians were in equally bad case, for Mercy had lost some twelve hundred killed, and his men were apparently more demoralized than the French, who had Condé and Turenne to sustain their flagging zeal.

The line of communications and supply, and now sole line of retreat, of Mercy was through the valley of St. Peter's Abbey in his rear to Villingen. Condé, being unable to see success in another front attack, on the 9th essayed to cut this line by a flank march via Langendenzlingen. This march was conducted expertly, but Mercy at once perceived its purpose, for the ground was open and revealed the direction of the French columns. He promptly withdrew, and marched on his base in Würtemberg.

If the joint attack of Condé and Turenne on the 5th had not been spoiled by the folly of d'Espenant, there was promise of a handsome victory. As it was, the Bavarian army had been reduced by nearly half, and the French joint forces by over five thousand men, in this three days' work. Desormeaux states the French loss in killed and wounded at six thousand men, and the Bavarian at nine thousand. But the French had captured all Mercy's guns.

The French followed Mercy, but their van under Rosen suffered a check in a gallantly sustained cavalry combat; and the extent of their present gain was the capture of a part of Mercy's train. The country was too mountainous to make a pursuit profitable, and lack of victual drove them back to Freiburg, as well as the fact that they were not equipped for lengthy operations and considered themselves too far from their base, the Rhine. They concluded, though it had but five hundred men in garrison, not to lay siege to Freiburg, whose possession Condé thought would bring no marked advantage, and would scarcely save the army from the necessity of retiring to Alsatia and Lorraine to winter.

Condé, whose ideas were always broad, deemed it wiser to turn downstream on Philipsburg, to capture which fortress would result in commanding a large section of country on the right bank of the Rhine, on which the army might more readily subsist till spring. The siege would be a difficult one, but the enemy could not now reach the place in season to head him off; Strasburg would furnish victual by boats

down the river; and in this city he could, on his own credit,
borrow money for the paymasters. Lack of sufficient infantry was the main objection to the plan.

Batteries were prepared in Breisach and floated down the
Rhine on pontoons, with as much material and food as
could be gathered. Cavalry parties were sent out to seize
places likely to offer opposition on the march; and the van

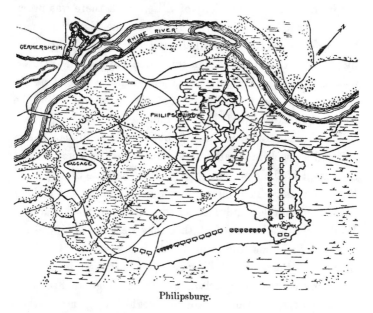

Philipsburg.

under Rosen followed. On August 16 the army broke up,
with Turenne in the lead, and advanced down the Rhine
valley to Philipsburg, where they arrived August 25, and
Turenne at once blockaded the place. The garrison was
probably under a thousand men.

Philipsburg was one of the most important places on the
Rhine, and lay in a plain surrounded by woods and marshes.
It had only earthwork defenses, but these were very strong,
mounted with one hundred guns, and the water from the river

flowed into wide and deep ditches. Approachable on but one side, — the south, — it had a fort which fairly well commanded the river. Philipsburg had been acquired by France from the Swedes, who had captured it, but the emperor had retaken it, and Condé saw the strategic advantage of its possession.

In order to control the river, the redoubt there situated was first captured by Turenne in a night attack. Contravallation and circumvallation lines were then opened. Two approaches were made, one by Grammont and one by Turenne, on the 7th of September; next day a sortie was driven back, and a few days later an attempt to relieve the place was successfully resisted. The approaches were vigorously pushed, and the commander, Colonel Bamberg, despairing of holding out, and anxious to save the large stores and treasury for the emperor, finally accepted terms, and Philipsburg surrendered September 12. During the siege, the French sent out a small detachment, which took Germersheim and occupied Speyer.

In his memoirs Turenne complains that the French infantry had lost heart in the Freiburg campaign. They had behaved well at times, and ill at times, proving a certain lack of discipline; and yet they had shown exceptional ability to stand hammering, — not the only, but the most essential requisite of the soldier. They had lost an exceptionally heavy percentage of men; and those who served through our 1864 campaign in Virginia will remember that the extreme depletion of a rapid succession of battles will sometimes react on even the best of troops.

The day after the surrender Turenne, under instructions from Condé, crossed the Rhine with his two thousand German cavalry and a chosen body of five hundred musketeers, and learning that a Spanish column was on the march to

Frankenthal, he sent a suitable detachment, which attacked this body, captured five hundred, and dispersed or killed the rest. The marshal then moved his infantry on boats down to Worms and Oppenheim, of which he took the former out of hand, while the latter fell to Rosen's cavalry; disembarked, and advanced by forced marches without baggage to Mainz, which was at the moment disgarnished of troops. This important city, whose possession secured the highway between France and her ally Hesse, though a Bavarian dragoon force under Colonel Wolf sought to relieve it, after some negotiations surrendered, on a threat to storm it if surrender was refused or Wolf admitted. Condé shortly put in an appearance with the army, and took possession. The elector of Mainz had gone to Frankfort; and the French occupied the whole vicinity, except only the castle of Creuznach, which held out. Small forces were left in Mainz, Oppenheim and Worms, and the French generals returned to Philipsburg. After reducing Creuznach, Turenne undertook the siege of Landau, where the French forces had just lost their commander, and on September 19, with a delay of only a few days, the place fell.

After the capture of a few more smaller fortresses (Neustadt, Mannheim, Bacharach and others) Condé withdrew to France by way of Kaiserslautern and Metz, and Turenne remained at Philipsburg, with a much reduced force. The campaign had eventuated in decided gain.

Condé and Turenne were worthy of each other. Except for a later temporary estrangement during the wars of the Fronde, they remained firm friends through life, neither jealous of the other's accomplishment or ability, and able when together to work in perfect accord. Condé, who in these early campaigns was his superior in rank, knew how to utilize Turenne's experience, energy and skill to his own advantage, but he never begrudged his lieutenant the appreciation which was his just due, nor denied him his share of the honor in the victories won by their joint efforts. And while opposed to each other in the wars of the Fronde, their friendship remained firm, as was the case with many of the generals in our own civil war. As general in command, Condé was of course entitled to the technical credit of success; yet no one can fail to see how largely Turenne contributed to this; and justice requires, as in the case of Marlborough and Eugene, — though these generals were equal in command, — that we should award to each his good half of the glory won. There are campaigns and battles of which the glory is universally yielded rather to the lieutenant than to the captain. Such was Chancellorsville. Though Lee was in supreme command, our thoughts instinctively award to Stonewall Jackson the credit of the flank march and attack which were the beginning of the end in that, from the Confederate aspect, superb campaign. It was so in some of the campaigns of Turenne and Condé.

French Infantry Soldier.
(1660.)

XXXVII.

MERGENTHEIM. MAY 5, 1645.

BEFORE going into winter-quarters, Turenne once more crossed the Rhine ; but as he found Mercy quiet on the Neckar, he undertook nothing. Next spring (1645) he again put over his army, and turning Mercy's position by the left, cut him off from Swabia. Mercy retired to Dinkelsbühl ; Turenne followed to Mergentheim. Here, for ease of victualing, he spread out his forces over too wide an area; Mercy and Werth moved sharply on him, and in the battle ensuing, by his troops behaving badly, Turenne was defeated with heavy loss. But he skillfully retired to Hesse, where he was joined by ten thousand Hessians and Swedes, and again immediately advanced on the enemy, who was besieging Kirchhain. Condé with eight thousand men now came up, and took command of the joint army. The Swedes retired, leaving him seventeen thousand men. Crossing the Neckar, the French at Heilbronn turned the Bavarians' position, who retired to Feuchtwangen, and after a few days' manœuvring to Dinkelsbühl. Following them up, the French generals forced them back to Allerheim, where they determined to attack them.

SHORTLY after Condé's departure, Turenne ascertained that, after repairing his losses, Mercy had left Würtemberg, and was marching on Heidelberg and Mannheim. He suspected that the Bavarian general designed to entice him away to cover Speyer, Worms and Mainz, in order meanwhile to seize Philipsburg by a *coup de main*. He accordingly left two thousand men near this fortress in an intrenched camp, threw a bridge, and crossed the Rhine near Speyer with his cavalry and a few musketeers, sent small detachments to Worms and Mainz, and took full precaution to protect all four places. It was a common habit of Turenne, as it was of Gustavus, to provide for remote contingencies. Mercy, however, had no such far-reaching intention ; he remained quiet between Heidelberg and Mannheim, and Turenne assumed that for want of provision he preferred not to cross the Rhine. He therefore sent the bulk of his troops to Lorraine into winter-quarters, keeping but a few cavalry regiments near the Rhine, and these he billeted in the towns. The two thousand foot remained at Philipsburg ; what remained of the foot Turenne marched to Alsatia.

Soon afterwards Turenne heard that the duke of Lorraine had passed the Moselle with six thousand men, had captured several places, Castellaun and Simmern among them, and was investing Bacharach. Hurriedly marching with five hundred horse on Mainz and Bingen, he spread the rumor that this was but the van of the entire army, which in truth he made arrangements to mobilize, and forced the duke back. Then taking the castle of Creuznach, which had held out in the last siege, he definitely retired, in December, 1644, into winter-quarters along the left bank of the Rhine, with head-quarters in Speyer. The year had been full of activity, and fairly successful.

In early April of 1645 Turenne again entered the field with six thousand foot, five thousand horse and fifteen guns, crossed the Rhine on a bridge of boats at Speyer, and moved on Pforzheim. He hoped in opening the campaign to anticipate Mercy, who lay beyond the Neckar with a force which had been diminished to six or seven thousand men by sending reinforcements to the imperial army in Bohemia, and whose troops were yet spread all over the country in cantonments. With his cavalry alone, and leaving his foot to follow on by rapid marches, Turenne crossed the Neckar near Marbach, April 16, through a ford which was not watched by the enemy, and marched along the right bank past Heilbronn to Schwäbisch-Hall, in order to throw Mercy, who had intended to move southward into Swabia, back in a

northerly direction. This was a neat and well-executed
manœuvre; and to follow out his plan, now that Turenne
had cut him off, and recover his communications with the
Danube country, Mercy was obliged at once to move easterly,
towards Dinkelsbühl and Feuchtwangen, by a considerable
circuit.

At one moment during his advance with his cavalry
Turenne feared that Mercy would fall on his infantry column, which was far in the rear and separated from the horse,
and turned back towards it. This afforded watchful Mercy
a chance to slip by him; he did not, however, venture to
attack the column of foot. But for thus retracing his steps,
Turenne would have earned the chance to follow Mercy with
his horse, and to give his rear-guard a hearty slap; but all
through his career he was noted for scrupulous care; and
while this in the long run served him admirably, at times it
looks like over-caution. In this case Mercy gained abundant
leisure to escape.

Turenne had accomplished his object, and had warded off
any danger of the enemy's invasion of Alsatia; but as Mercy
had got away from him without a blow, Turenne assembled
all his forces at Hall, and moved north on Mergentheim (or
Marienthal) on the Tauber, so as to have in his rear and
open to him the allied Hessian country. He had good reason
to hope that before summer he should receive reinforcements
from there; on the arrival of which he counted on pushing
into the heart of Germany, a thing which at the moment he
did not feel strong enough to attempt. Near this town he
put the foot and artillery into camp.

By his able turning manœuvre he had hustled the enemy
out of a position threatening to France, and then reëstablished
himself by a change of base where he could rely either upon
his holdings in Alsatia or on his Hessian allies. The entire

operation was skillful ; in it we see a gleam of the purposeful manœuvring of the future.

From Mergentheim Turenne sent General Rosen with four or five cavalry regiments as an outpost up the Tauber towards Rothemburg, and quartered the rest of his cavalry, for greater convenience of foraging, in towns two or three hours in the rear. This was a manifest error, for the enemy was not far distant, was in good heart and ably led, and Turenne knew

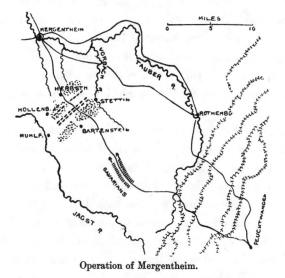

Operation of Mergentheim.

nothing of his intentions; he ought to have kept well concentrated. In effect, within a day or so, he learned that the Bavarians had broken up at Feuchtwangen, and were moving on him at Mergentheim. Rosen had not had enough scouting parties out, and the information preceded the enemy's van but a few hours.

Immediately ordering Rosen back to a position where he could be sustained, Turenne called in his outlying cavalry parties, and instructed Rosen to take position in rear of a wood which lay some distance in front of Mergentheim, at which obstacle he could conveniently assemble all his forces, and if desirable retire to a better point for battle. He should, observes Napoleon, have ordered his forces to assemble at Mergentheim, which was behind the Tauber and nearer for all the outlying regiments, certainly at a point further behind the outposts than the one he chose. But to make matters worse, by misunderstanding his orders, Rosen took position in front of the wood, where, as alleged by Turenne, he could neither hold himself, nor easily retreat, nor be readily supported, and where the enemy, if he attacked him, was sure to bring on an engagement on unfavorable ground. This was in fact what occurred. Mercy advanced on him, and Turenne found himself compelled to sustain his lieutenant under awkward conditions.

Our own habit of frequently fighting in the woods during the civil war breeds among American soldiers a belief that a forest is not so marked an obstacle as it is wont to be considered in Europe. But in Turenne's days, and in fact at all times, a wood even free from the underbrush of the American forest was considered a very serious post to attack, if held by foot ; and so difficult was it deemed to get troops through an open wood in good order, that a few squadrons posted beyond it were believed to be able to break up the organization of troops emerging from it. The nature of the wood had naturally much to do with the matter ; but on such a terrain as our " Wilderness," no European army would for a moment think of manœuvring. They are too much used to the open plain ; and it was under such conditions that Turenne proposed to fall upon his enemy after the latter had passed through the wood and was apt to be in broken order.

The three thousand infantry which had arrived Turenne placed on the right of the cavalry, equally in the wood, and

sustained by two other squadrons. He himself took up post
in the left wing. As the Bavarians advanced in two lines, the
foot in the centre and the horse on the wings, the right under
command of Mercy and the left of John de Werth, Turenne
led forward his own cavalry, fell upon the horse in first line
on the Bavarian right, and threw it back on the second line
in much disorder. But meanwhile Werth attacked the
French infantry in the wood, and the latter, which had been
hurried into action
and felt as if it had
been surprised, and
was moreover in
poor order from
having been pushed
through the wood,
after but a single
salvo seemed to lose
heart, and, attacked
in front and on both
flanks, fled, carry-
ing with it the two
squadrons of cav-
alry which sustained

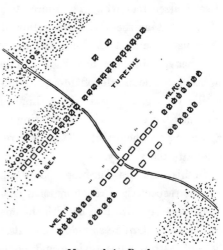

Mergentheim Battle.

it. This disgraceful conduct, which now enabled Werth
to threaten Turenne's flank, forced the French left wing of
horse to retire also, which it did in equal disorder. Rosen
was captured, and Turenne so nearly compromised that he
was forced to cut himself out sword in hand. The fault here
appears to have been not more due to the position than to
the lack of endurance of the troops; and yet this was the
same infantry which at Freiburg the year before had so
cheerfully stood decimation.

In Turenne's rear lay still another wood. Here he boldly

essayed a further defense with three fresh cavalry regiments
which had just come up, and some twenty-five hundred rallied
runaways. But as the enemy prudently took time to reform
and came on in fine shape, and he could make no headway in
retrieving his loss, Turenne accepted his defeat in good part,
and definitively retired. He personally covered the retreat
up the Tauber on the Main with two of the three cavalry regiments that were intact, detailing the third to accompany the
disorganized foot, which he ordered to retreat to the border of
Hesse; but as the Bavarians followed him up more sharply
than usual, and as he disputed every inch of the way, he
lost heavily in men and flags and guns in the rear-guard
fighting. The battle of Mergentheim had cost him all his
artillery, baggage and fifteen hundred men. The tactical
pursuit, however, did not continue far. The Bavarians,
according to the habit of the day, remained on the field to
celebrate the victory.

In his memoirs Turenne openly acknowledges his defeat.
In this respect the French marshal is a model. Whether the
advantage lay with him or with the enemy, he always frankly
confesses it. Unlike so many generals, whose retreat from the
field of battle belies their grandiloquent reports of victory,
Turenne lays bare the facts, shows us his errors, and thus
gives us lessons which can never be learned from prevaricat-
ing dispatches.

The Bavarians soon followed Turenne to Hesse and laid
siege to Kirchhain; Turenne retired to Cassel. Near this
place he joined the six thousand Hessians, and the Swedes
who, four thousand strong, had come up from Brunswick
under Königsmark; by which accessions, with his own four
thousand horse and one thousand five hundred foot, he made
up a force of fifteen thousand men; and with these he at
once advanced on Kirchhain. This was all done within twelve

days after his defeat, showing an elasticity and a quickness of movement which were admirable; for Cassel is about a hundred miles from Mergentheim, and there were negotiations which consumed some days and delayed Turenne's action as much as the reorganization of his troops. Raising the siege of Kirchhain, the Bavarians at once retired to Franconia. Turenne shortly led his forces to join the eight thousand men coming by way of Speyer under Condé, which he did at Ladenburg, near Mannheim, on July 5.

Condé again assumed command. He had been campaigning on the Meuse, where France desired a foothold strong enough to control Lorraine, a province essential to her communications with Germany; and having left Villeroi to continue his work, he had been ordered to the relief of Turenne, whose defeat had demoralized the French court. They had abundant confidence in Condé, but lacked belief in Turenne, — a rather curious want of discrimination, yet easily bred of Rocroy and the two last campaigns. They changed their mind ere long.

Though in command, Condé, unlike the court, had the good sense to recognize the worth of Turenne, and took counsel of his ample knowledge and courage; and the two generals at once moved up the left bank of the Neckar on Heilbronn. But Mercy anticipated them at this important place; and finding the Bavarians beyond the river and holding the passage there so as to make it difficult to force, they had to choose between a march up river towards Swabia or another crossing and a march towards the Danube country. The Swedish contingent refused to entertain the former plan, fearing by so distant an operation to be cut off from north Germany; and the French commanders finally decided on Wimpfen, which place they took, and crossed the Neckar on a bridge they built. Here Königsmark, in consequence of a disagreement with Condé, and restless at serving under so young a commander, left the French and led his Swedes back towards the Main. The Hessians stood by, and Condé and Turenne, taking a number of places on the way, moved on Rothemburg. So soon as the French had crossed the Neckar, the Bavarians retired on a substantially parallel line to Feuchtwangen, where they set up an intrenched camp. The French commanders offered Mercy battle, but without avail; for Mercy deemed it better to retire to another intrenched camp, behind Dinkelsbühl. The rival armies had got back to the same campaigning ground on which they had manœuvred a month or two before. From Dinkelsbühl, in a few days, leaving a small garrison in this place, the enemy retired, and camped behind a wood several miles further back, apparently as a stratagem to induce the French to besiege the camp just left, an operation which might afford them an occasion of making a favorable attack. Turenne and Condé followed up this retreat, and stopping at Dinkelsbühl to capture the intrenched camp, soon learned that the army under Mercy was advancing on them. Leaving a small body to observe the camp, the French set out to meet the enemy. Both Condé and Turenne accompanied the van, while Grammont brought up the main army.

At break of day the French, who had marched at night, struck the Bavarian van, and this retired on its main body, which was intrenched in a difficult position behind a marshy brook and some ponds. An all-day's cannonade resulted, with a loss of three hundred men on each side; but though the Bavarians could not be successfully attacked in their position, they feared for their line of retreat, and concluded to retire towards Nördlingen. Having so far failed by front operations to gain any advantage over the enemy, two hours before daylight next day the French generals, turning the

Bavarian position by the right, also marched on Nördlingen, which they reached by nine o'clock, and camped in the plain, leaving the baggage train in some of the villages in the rear. The Bavarian army, which had been reinforced by seven thousand imperial troops under General Glein, had divined the manœuvre, and lest they should be cut off, had already reached Nördlingen plain in light order, and seized an advantageous position.

French Dragoon. (17th Century.)

XXXVIII.

ALLERHEIM. AUGUST 5, 1645.

THE Bavarian right, under Glein, lay on the Wennenberg; their centre, under Mercy, back of and in Allerheim village; their left, under Werth, on the hill and in the castle of Allerheim. Condé, in the French centre, essayed with his infantry to capture Allerheim, but was driven back; Werth broke the French right under Grammont and drove it well to the rear: the day was very doubtful. But Turenne, on the French left, by splendid efforts broke Glein's formation and captured the Wennenberg. After defeating Grammont, Werth, by striking Turenne's right, might have completed the Bavarian victory; but he did not utilize his advantage in the best manner, and night came on. The Bavarians retired, and the French kept the field. The losses were very heavy. Nördlingen surrendered; the enemy moved back of the Danube. The French would have liked to winter in Swabia, but the Bavarians demonstrated towards them and they retired to the Rhine. After capturing Trier and Oberwesel, Turenne went into winter-quarters. On the whole, the campaign was favorable to the French; for its activity, it was highly creditable to Turenne.

THE rolling plain of Nördlingen, watered by the Wörmitz and Eger, is a dozen miles in diameter, and the town lies near its southwestern edge. Near the southeastern edge, backing up against the Wörmitz, lay the enemy, between two hills, a mile and a half apart. The Wennenberg is about one hundred and sixty feet above the plain, and steep; the other, about one hundred and twenty feet high and less steep, was at the time crowned by the castle of Allerheim. Between them, a quarter of a mile further forward, lay the village of Allerheim. From the castle hill to Allerheim ran a wide and deep gully; from Allerheim to the Wennenberg the ground is much cut up. In this admirable defensive position, proposing to fight for the possession of Nördlingen and the protection of Bavaria, Mercy took his stand early on August 3, and began to intrench; and shortly there arose a strong line of earthworks, hard to force, easy to hold. In prolongation of his left through the hills ran the short road to the Danube at Donauwörth, a good day's march away.

The Bavarian right leaned on the Wörmitz, and its left on the castle of Allerheim. This stronghold and the village opposite the centre were occupied by foot; the main force lay on the heights behind the village, and the cavalry was posted on both flanks. Glein was on the right; John de Werth, an able veteran officer, on the left; Mercy in the centre.

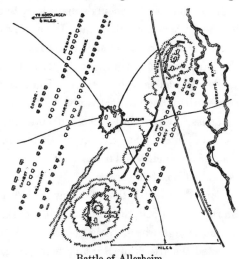

Battle of Allerheim.

Artillery was posted all along the lines, and the *élite* of the infantry held the village. Mercy had about sixteen thousand men.

Condé, with Turenne and Grammont, made a reconnoissance early in the day; and though the position of the enemy evoked some serious comments, he decided to fight, and was sustained by the council then usual. His force was slightly superior to Mercy's. He posted Count Grammont in two lines and a reserve on the right, opposite Werth; the foot, — the *corps de bataille,* — also in two lines, was in the centre, under Marsin; and Turenne, with his own forces and the

Hessians in reserve, held the left opposite Glein. The usual artillery duel opened the action.

Towards noon the French troops began to move forward, but they took till four o'clock marshaling for the attack; a period which, with an army of so small a size, suggests very mediocre capacity to manœuvre. They then advanced, artillery in front, and smartly attacked the village, which lay well in front of the enemy's main line, but lost more heavily by the Bavarian artillery than the enemy did by theirs. Batteries at that day were slow of movement, and on both sides the guns were, according to modern standard, clumsily managed. It was not the artillery of Gustavus, and the Swedes then still possessed the only well-managed, easily-handled batteries. Even the French, despite their imitative ability and the intelligent manner of their equipment, had as yet reached no such standard of excellence in field-guns as Gustavus had boasted.

Condé believed that no impression could be made on Mercy's line until the force which was thrust out as a salient in the village was disposed of; he took his stand here, and directed the attack of Marsin's foot. At that point the action began, and very heavy fighting was kept up, with especial severity in the churchyard. The French behaved with commendable gallantry, and were met with equal courage by the Bavarians; the village was captured and recaptured five times, the ground being fought over with admirable tenacity. Condé, whose peculiar style of fighting and experience was suited to cavalry rather than foot, was somewhat out of his element, but he clung to his work; his staff were nearly all disabled, he himself had several horses shot under him during the day, and received bullets on his breastplate and through his clothing. Mercy was killed, and both parties lost heavily. Success in the centre was disputed. Condé began to see that he could not compass a victory here by even his best efforts; the victor of Rocroy had met a more stubborn task than he had yet faced. This cold-blooded infantry fighting lacked the touch-and-go of cavalry work.

While this was going on, Condé had directed Grammont to attack Werth; but the count, on ascertaining the presence of the gully above referred to, maintained that he could not reach the Bavarian line; and Condé rode over to the left, leaving him to a defensive rôle. To show how mistaken he was, soon after Condé's departure the Bavarian cavalry of the left wing, led by Werth in person, rode out, crossed the gully without difficulty, and attacked the French cavalry under Grammont, striking it partly in flank, and driving it back after a mere attempt at resistance. In the confusion Marshal Grammont was shot and captured. Had it not been for the reserve of this wing, Werth would have won the victory right here; but General Chabot somewhat checked his progress, and so much time elapsed before Werth could complete the wreck of the French right, that the opportunity slipped out of his hands. Werth did, however, eventually crush Grammont, and this disaster threw the French infantry of the centre and the cavalry in its support completely out of Allerheim.

Matters looked dubious for the French. Happily, on their left there was a man of energy and resources, of caution when called for, of gallantry not second to Condé's; a man who could deal you lusty blows. During this time, while Condé had been unable to capture Allerheim, and Grammont had been driven from his foothold on the right, Turenne, with the cavalry of the French left, had gallantly and repeatedly charged in on the enemy's right, and, after a tough conflict and much loss, had, despite the bad ground, driven the first line back on the second. Here he was for a moment checked,

partly by the fresh troops brought up by Glein, and partly
by the view of the French disaster in the village and on the
right.   It was a critical moment, one of those which show up
the man.   The only French troops which had not been beaten
were under his command; but Turenne, who though wounded
still kept in the saddle, was not to be easily discouraged; he
saw that he held the fate of victory in his grasp; only he
could save the French from another defeat.   He ordered up
the Hessians, who were fresh and eager; Condé put in an
appearance to help encourage the troops, and, returning to
the charge, the two generals definitely drove back the Bavarian right wing of cavalry, which had advanced into the plain.
At the same time, under cover of this charge, the Bavarian
infantry of their right on the Wennenberg was sharply
attacked; Turenne's men caught the ardor of victory and
the heroism of their chief; and in the mêlée General Glein
and all the artillery were captured.

Having completed the discomfiture of the French right,
despite the success of the French left, Werth now had the
battle in his own hands.   He should have turned directly
against Turenne and have struck a blow at his naked flank,
while he was busy breaking up the Bavarian right.   Had he
done so, Turenne would have been destroyed, and there was
no obstacle in Werth's way.   The French right was broken,
and the centre had been driven out of Allerheim and well
back.   The Bavarians held the town, and the road was open.
But Werth, though instinct with gallantry of the first water,
and of unquestioned ability, did not here exhibit the *coup
d'œil* of a battle captain.   Instead of riding across the front
of Allerheim, directly at Turenne's open flank, he returned
by the way he had gone out, and came into action by the rear
of the village, arriving too late to be of any use.   When he
reached Turenne, in fact, he struck him, not in flank, as he

might have done, but in front, or at best at an oblique angle. His work was thus quite ineffective, and Turenne was able to turn against him and throw him back from the Wennenberg.

Night had come on. The left of each army was victorious, the French somewhat the more advanced, and well beyond Allerheim. The right wing of each had been utterly worsted. Supposing themselves cut off by Turenne's advance, the Bavarian troops in Allerheim surrendered. Neither side had won an undisputed victory, but after midnight the Bavarian army confessed defeat by quietly withdrawing from the field, unaware that the French were as badly demoralized as they themselves were; and their retreat compensated Turenne, to whom the credit of the victory was due, for his late defeat at Mergentheim. "Were I not Condé, I would wish to be Turenne!" exclaimed the young general-in-chief in his exultation over what his lieutenant had accomplished; and despite the fact that Napoleon awards the main praise of this victory to Condé, it was really Turenne's battle — as Condé in a letter to the queen of Sweden generously acknowledges.

Had the fighting continued next day, it is more than probable that the Bavarians would have been beaten, as they had lost their leaders, and with a woody defile in their rear on their route to the Danube, in case of defeat they were badly placed. The French had suffered heavily in casualties, — four thousand in killed and wounded, — but had captured all the Bavarian guns. The Bavarians lost an equal number and two thousand captured beside, with nearly all their battle flags. Of their generals, Mercy was killed, Glein captured, and Werth in full retreat; of the French generals, all three were wounded. The battle was contested in the handsomest manner. The French loss had been most severe in the infantry; a bare twelve hundred serviceable foot could be gathered under arms.

In this battle of Allerheim (or, as it is often called, of
Nördlingen) the French cavalry of the right had behaved
badly; that of the left with commendable steadiness. The
French infantry at that time has been taxed by contemporary
writers with being lamentably bad. The men, they said,
would attack once in good heart, but if beaten in an assault,
there was no more fight left in them. Once dispersed, they
could not be rallied. And yet they fought stanchly here, and
we shall see that they did noble work under the influence of
such men as Turenne, Condé, Vendome and Villars. Despite
their uncertain mood, they were at times capable of very gallant fighting, as their percentage of loss well shows.

Heavy casualties are not always a sure test of steadiness.
A division which marches straight at the foe may win at a
small loss; a division which hesitates may suffer decimation
under the enemy's fire, and if defeated — or even if it wins —
its loss will be no test of its push or its resistance. Butchery
apart, only long-protracted fighting between equally matched
divisions, with heavy losses on both sides, — the Bloody Angle
as an instance, — is a test of battle courage and discipline.
Heavy losses may be accidental.

Nördlingen did not await the French attack, but at once
surrendered, and the captured Bavarians were allowed to
leave for home without weapons. Turenne followed up the
enemy's retreat to Donauwörth with his cavalry, whence he
returned to the army; and Condé and he, after a few days'
rest, retired to Dinkelsbühl, which likewise surrendered.
This rearward movement Turenne explains by lack of money
and consequent inability to victual so far from the Rhine and
Neckar country.

Condé now left the army, seriously ill, and Count Grammont, who had been released, took his place; but Turenne
and he continued operations jointly. Turenne was so far his

superior, as even that of Condé, that it grates upon one's sense of justice to see him so often second in command. It was by an extension of the ancient belief that kings divinely inherit their rights into the superstition that princes are born generals, that the command of armies was often placed in hands unfit to hold it, and that Turenne did not always stand where he deserved to be. But his merit was so well recognized by his superiors that he was uniformly given entire latitude in his operations.

The French now marched back to Heilbronn, but having small siege material, could not take this strongly garrisoned place; and thence by a sudden change of plan they advanced on Schwäbisch-Hall, hoping to push the enemy back over the Danube, so as to enable them to winter in Swabia. But the Bavarian army, reinforced by seven thousand imperial cavalry and dragoons, took up its stand at Donauwörth on the left bank, and demonstrated towards the French; when the latter, not liking to go into winter-quarters too near an army superior to itself in numbers, deemed it best to retire on the Main and Neckar. This withdrawal appears to have been made on a slender pretext; but the reasons alleged by the old historians are often quoted in these pages, even when they do not appeal to us as sound. The French left a garrison of six hundred men in Wimpfen, and retired across the Neckar at this point. The water was so deep that the cavalry had to swim the river, each one taking a footman with him, and a number of men and wagons were lost.

From here the French army again withdrew to Philipsburg, hoping to camp permanently on the right bank, and the Bavarians followed it up. Turenne began an intrenched position between Philipsburg and the Rhine, and sent his cavalry and baggage over to the left bank on boats; while, finding that they could accomplish nothing further, the Bavarians returned to Wimpfen, captured it, as was to be expected, and went into winter-quarters.

The French army under Grammont marched back to France, but Turenne, learning that the enemy was kept too busy in Flanders to hinder him, moved on Trier, captured it by a two days' siege, gave it over for occupation to the allied elector of Trier, besieged and stormed the castle of Oberwesel on the Rhine, and then, placing his army in winter-quarters along the Rhine and Moselle, he personally repaired to Paris.

This campaign is distinguished from those of the period by its stirring activity, and by seeking battle rather than by besieging strong places. Against the defeat at Mergentheim may fairly be placed the victory at Allerheim, and the speed shown by Condé and Turenne is highly commendable, compared with that of other commanders. The Bavarian movements followed the French, who in every case retained the initiative. The advantage, if any, was on the French side, though they ended where they began; and it was rather technical than real. Many of the campaigns of this era appear to us to have no very manifest objective, as they had no very definite outcome; and armies were wont to return to their base for winter-quarters. Such campaigns were mere rounds in a boxing match; each opponent sought to tire out the other, if there was no particular object to gain. It is the peculiar indefiniteness of almost all campaigns of the day preceding and following him which throws the clear-cut purpose of Gustavus into such relief. What Gustavus once took, he held; other generals rarely did so.

The biographers of Condé are wont to ascribe to him all the credit of this and other campaigns in which Turenne and he worked jointly; but the after history of both these captains best indicates who was the more able man. Condé knew well how to put Turenne's ability to use, and the latter's modesty never permitted him to trench on his superior's prerogative; but it must be said to Condé's credit that he was always generous in the division of honors.

Norman Soldier.
(7th Century.)

XXXIX.

CONDÉ AT DUNKIRK. SEPTEMBER AND OCTOBER, 1646.

THE duke of Orleans commanded the French in the Netherlands in 1646. Under him Condé served until the duke had captured Mardyk, when he succeeded to the command and undertook the capture of Dunkirk, the most important fortress on the coast. First proceeding to Hondschoten, he thence took and fortified Furnes. From here he advanced along the coast on Dunkirk, whose commander, Leyden, inundated the vicinity to prevent Condé from getting supplies. The difficulties were grave: the garrison of ten thousand men could be victualed by sea; there was danger of an army of relief coming up; Condé was put to it to get victual or material. But he made a treaty with the Dutch, who not only helped shut the place in by sea, but began a diversion against the Spaniards. He worked incessantly, and was lucky in having no serious interference from the outside. His lines and approaches were duly completed, and several sorties repulsed. On October 1 and 2 assaults were made, a footing gained in the place, and ten days later, Dunkirk surrendered. Condé then relieved Cambray, and the campaign closed.

ON account of his royal birth the duke of Orleans had been put in command of the troops operating in the Low Countries, and in 1646 Condé, though conscious of his superior ability, appears to have willingly and conscientiously served under him. The army had cautiously advanced as far as Mardyk, below Dunkirk, when Condé proposed the siege of the latter place, the most important and strongest fortress on the coast; but his chief had not the courage to undertake it. Mardyk had been captured the previous year by the duke of Orleans after a costly twenty days' siege, and had been later seized by the Spaniards in a cleverly designed and sudden attack, with merely nominal loss; now, after opening lines and trenches, and after several bloody sorties and attempts to relieve the town from the outside, the French managed to cut the place off from Dunkirk, and took it; upon which the duke, despairing of further successes, and satisfied with his few laurels, prudently retired to Paris to celebrate his triumph, and Condé received command of an exhausted army of ten thousand men. With this handful he undertook the proposed operation against Dunkirk, to reduce which he had to contain the large Spanish army, beat the marquis of Caracena, — who lay in the way, intrenched

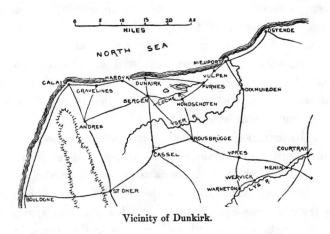

Vicinity of Dunkirk.

within a network of canals and rivers, — capture Furnes, and hold the sea against a Spanish fleet. The communication in this singular country is mostly by canal; the roads run along the dikes; the rivers are largely turned into artificial waterways; and campaigning is correspondingly difficult. The region between Mardyk and Nieuport is entirely cut up by small streams and canals; it is well adapted for defense, difficult for the offensive.

In pursuance of his bold plan, Condé marched September 4 to Hondschoten, where he deposited his heavy train. His first objective was Furnes. To cross the several canals fed by the Colme and held by troops as numerous as his own, he organized three columns which he himself was to sustain with the reserve, as might be needed. The first column, under Marshal Gassion, headed for Furnes and threw back the Spanish force towards Caracena at Nieuport. The second, under General Laval, marched on Gassion's left to force the line of the Colme canals, and accomplished its object with equal celerity. The third, under Villequier, was headed on Gassion's right towards Vulpen. This column met unexpected resistance, but, being properly supported by Condé, drove in the enemy, and then pushed for Furnes, which town was taken by assault, the Spanish general having declined to sustain it, though it was essential to whoever should undertake a siege of Dunkirk. It is not probable that the Spaniards anticipated so apparently foolhardy an act as an investment of that fortress.

At the council of war which Condé called, there was some desire manifested to besiege Menin in lieu of Dunkirk; but Condé convinced his lieutenants that the latter was vastly the more important place, while the difficulty of besieging the other was equally great; and his plan was approved by the court, to whom all such matters had customarily to be referred.

Dunkirk is built on the dunes which extend up the coast all the way from Calais. The sea bounds it on the north; Furnes and Nieuport lie on the east; Bergen on the south, and on the west Mardyk. The old town was fortified; the new town lay outside. The walls were thick and flanked by huge towers; while a brick-lined ditch one hundred and twenty feet wide was fed by canals from the river Colme. The sea, breaking in towards the town, opened a fine port, which art had made capable of holding eight hundred vessels, and its entrance was defended by an extension of the fortifications on the dunes, and by two breakwaters on which artillery was mounted. Three great canals led out of Dunkirk, and boats could sail thither to every city of the Low Countries. The dried-herring trade had originally given importance to this city; and since its growth to wealth and power it had been captured by several of the nations in succession. Charles V. had granted it many privileges, and it was the bulwark of the Hapsburg dominion in the Nether-

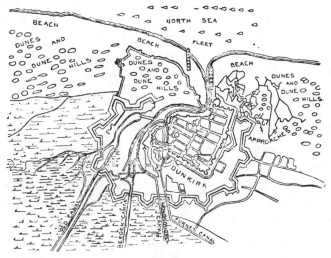

Dunkirk.

lands. Its trade with the interior and by sea was immense; it maintained a number of privateers which did much damage to the French ports and commerce, and it had successfully engaged the Dutch fleet. Its garrison consisted of three thousand soldiers, four thousand sailors and three thousand trained burghers, and was under command of the marquis of Leyden, who had won great repute by defending Maestricht for three months against a large Dutch army.

The difficulties were indeed great. Condé's army of ten

thousand men was tired out, and had little left but good-will
with which to undertake further work ; the vicinity of Dunkirk is a waste of sand, with none but swamp water, affording
no subsistence for troops, nor indeed means of constructing
works deserving the name. Furnes, the base for the siege,
was not strong and might fall into the hands of the Spaniards, who, moreover, were able at any time to relieve Dunkirk from the sea or along the beach at low tide. The Dutch
were uncertain and somewhat jealous allies, liable at any
moment to be bought off by the enemy. Victual had to come
from Calais, and the Dunkirkers had inundated the land by
opening the canal-sluices, so that provision could not be
hauled overland, while a tempestuous sea or the enemy's fleet
might at any moment interrupt the supply coming by water.
Worse than all, the season was getting late, and success must
be won soon or not at all.

The duke of Lorraine was in camp on the border of Holland ; Marshals Piccolomini and Beck, with the main Spanish
army, lay under the cannon of Dendermonde ; Caracena
under those of Nieuport. On the other hand, the French
troops believed in Condé, while the enemy was supine. The
Dutch question was the most pressing, and Condé settled that
by sending an able ambassador to the Hague, who so far won
the assistance of the States-General that Van Tromp soon
patroled the sea near Dunkirk, and the prince of Orange
undertook a diversion against the Spaniards.

Condé ordered La Ferté, who had four thousand men on
the Lys, to be ready at any moment to join him ; he sent for
part of the garrisons in Picardy ; the Boulognese militia was
armed ; six thousand men came to him by sea and were put
for rest and drill into Mardyk ; two thousand Poles recruited
by Baron Sirot and one thousand English recruits were
placed in Calais. All these were so posted that they could

be concentrated in twenty-four hours, and fifteen small frigates were ordered to patrol the mouth of the port of Dunkirk. Furnes was stoutly fortified under Condé's own eye, a garrison of one thousand five hundred men was put in the town, and a large supply of provision was collected there. Two weeks after the army reached Furnes, so active had been his measures that Condé advanced on Dunkirk with ten thousand foot and five thousand horse.

The leader himself with the first column took the road nearest to the enemy, along the coast; Gassion with the second marched on his left, along the canal running from Furnes to Dunkirk; Rantzau with the third marched across country towards the Colme. All the columns reached their objectives in good season.

Once quartered in front of Dunkirk, the French were in no danger of attack save from the direction of Nieuport. Gassion held the line from the sea to the middle of the dunes; next him Condé to the Furnes canal; then Rantzau astride the canal of Bergen. Villequier, with the Boulognese, held the west of the town to the sea to head off succor from St. Omer. Marshes or places controlled by the French closed the circuit. Ten Dutch men-of-war and the fifteen frigates effectually shut the mouth of the port. The canals were bridged, and a line of circumvallation begun, which consisted of a palisaded and sodded wall and a ditch, the latter twelve feet wide and six feet deep, and another similar one forty paces from the first. The highest of the dune-hills were crowned by forts mounted with suitable guns, while on the wide beach, where the low tide afforded an approach, the defenses were held in place by a multitude of piles, left open to admit the waves. Rations were brought by the canals, and as this means was insufficient and the country roads had to be utilized, the inundation was arrested by driving piles at the mouths of the sluices, backing these up with huge stones, and then stopping the whole with a prodigious mass of earth. All useless horses and men were sent to the rear, and troops were moved from place to place as most needed. The distribution of rations, in which it was essential to economize, was made under Condé's own eye, for enough victual could not be got up, on account of the bad weather at sea and the deep roads on land. The men soon felt the lack of good food; and the bad weather and absence of material made it impossible suitably to house them.

In five days from arrival of the army the lines were done; and trenches were at once opened. Seeing that the health of the men could not long be kept up under the existing conditions, Condé pressed the siege with vigor, determining wisely to sacrifice men in assaults rather than lose an equal number by disease. He made a careful reconnoissance of the place, and concluded to open two approaches: one, which he was to conduct in person, covered the last bastion towards the sea on the east side; the other was directed at the horn-work north of it under the two marshals. This was executed on the night of September 24–25, and sixty guns in all were mounted.

Next day, the marshals delivered a fierce attack on a dune-hill near the horn-work, and captured it; but Leyden made gallant efforts to retake it, and sharp fighting, lasting twenty-four hours, with heavy loss, resulted. At the approaches of Condé fighting was carried on daily with great determination; Leyden was active, and as fast as the French gained one point, they found fresh works to encounter; behind every breach they uncovered a demi-lune.

Meanwhile the Spaniards had concentrated their several armies, but they delayed action in the belief that the difficulties of the siege and the unfavorable elements would drive

Condé from his task without their interference. After a careful reconnoissance of the French position, moreover, the Spanish commanders found the works too strong to make it wise to attack them; and the fact that the prince of Orange was learned to be preparing a diversion to assist the French compelled them to carefully consider their plans. An attack on Furnes was proposed; but the works at this place proved, on reconnoissance, to be likewise too strong to promise success. The unenterprising Spanish commanders eventually deemed it best to resort to relieving Dunkirk by sea; but this project being attempted, also failed; for no sooner had the pilots caught sight of the Dutch and French squadrons cruising in the offing than they sought refuge in flight.

On the night of October 1–2 a serious assault was made both on the bastion and the horn-work, and a lodgment was effectuated. Three days later the Spaniards made an attempt to break through the French lines near the beach, but failed. Leyden now saw that the end was approaching; he listened to proposals, and on October 11 he capitulated with the honors of war. He had made a noble defense, but his friends on the outside had acted with a pitiful lack of vigor. Condé could ascribe his success to their indolence and want of common motive, as much as to his own energy.

After this splendid triumph Condé undertook to relieve Courtray, which, lying as it did in the midst of the enemy's forces, needed a convoy of victual and powder to enable it to hold out. He sent the material down the Lys to Wervick by water, where it was discharged in such shape as to be quickly loaded on horses and carts. Shortly after midnight on the day appointed, the column of cavalry destined for the expedition was ready; each horseman took a bag behind his saddle; the rest was laden on carts, and the column advanced between Menin and Ypres, in each of which places the enemy had forces. Before he had marched many leagues, the duke of Lorraine and Piccolomini came out to dispute his passage, but Condé held himself so compact and ready that, barring a rear-guard fight, which fell out to the advantage of the French, no serious attempt was made. The prince entered Courtray without the loss of a man.

The return trip might be none the less perilous; for Lorraine and Piccolomini chose the best positions to cut Condé off, along whatever road he might choose. The column returned by the same route; and Condé's countenance was so firm, he marched with so much good order, and held himself so ready for a combat, that the allied generals left him free exit.

Beyond this handsome feat, nothing was done this year in the Netherlands which deserves especial mention. Condé's operations kept him away from the German theatre and left Turenne freehanded.

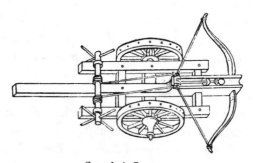

Crusader's Cannon.

XL.

TURENNE AND WRANGEL. 1646–1647.

In 1646 Turenne and Wrangel conducted a joint campaign. After some noxious delays due to political scheming of the rival courts, the French and Swedes joined in the Cologne district and advanced on the imperial army, which, under the archduke, lay on the Nidda. Arrived in presence, Turenne made a handsome movement around his opponent's left flank, and, cutting him off from his base, advanced to the Danube. Thus compromised, after an attempt to march north, the archduke followed. The allies crossed the Danube and besieged Augsburg, until the archduke returned and drove them off, taking post at Kirchheim. Here the allies again made a brilliant movement around the imperial left and marched on the interior, causing the Bavarian troops to separate from the imperial, and the elector was forced into a peace. In 1647 the emperor was quite alone; but the political necessity of not allowing the empire to be crushed resulted in withdrawing Turenne and Wrangel from the completion of their work of 1646. Turenne returned to the left bank of the Rhine, and, after suppressing a mutiny among his German troops, confined himself under Mazarin's orders to minor operations in the Netherlands. In 1648 he again joined Wrangel, who meanwhile, single, had been forced back to the Weser.

THE campaign of 1646 in Germany, save an early interruption by Mazarin, was conducted on Turenne's own plan, in connection with the Swedish general Wrangel. The latter was operating in Hesse and lower Saxony; Turenne proposed to join him, and to manœuvre in one body against the imperial army, half of which consisted of Bavarians, and which until now had usually stood and operated between them. This was a soundly conceived plan, looking to concentrated instead of scattering operations, and for a wonder Mazarin approved it. It was agreed with Torstenson and Wrangel that the Swedes should march by way of Hesse and the French by way of Nassau, to join hands. Turenne, who had wintered in the Rhine-Moselle region, concentrated in May, and was on the point of building a bridge of boats at Bacharach to cross the Rhine, when Mazarin suddenly forbade this movement, on the plea that the Bavarians had promised not to unite with the imperialists if the French would remain on the left bank of the Rhine; and much as he disapproved the orders, Turenne was bound to obey. He saw through the promise, which the Bavarians had only given as a ruse; for they did unite with the imperialists and move against the Swedes with scarcely a semblance of delay, taking post beyond the Main. This treachery again brought Mazarin's orders for action, but it altered the entire plan of campaign. The junction of French and Swedes must now be made by a circuit, for it was impossible to accomplish it by crossing at Bacharach. Turenne was compelled to throw a garrison of several regiments into Mainz, ford the Moselle some twenty miles above Coblentz, move through the electorate down to Cologne, and thence on Wesel and east to Lippstadt, keeping Wrangel apprised by couriers of his whereabouts. All this consumed more than a month of hard marching and much negotiation with neutral states, and Wrangel was meanwhile compelled to maintain himself by a system of manœuvres and intrenched camps, which, relying on the fact that field-works were rarely attacked at that day, he very cleverly did, and thus saved himself from being drawn into a general engagement.

When the enemy learned that Turenne was near at hand, they went into camp. Joining at Giessen, the allies had seven thousand infantry, ten thousand cavalry and sixty guns, with which they advanced to the vicinity of the enemy, but did not see their way clear to an attack. The imperial army was under the command of Archduke Leopold William, and lay behind the Nidda in a strong position near Ilbenstadt. The allies camped near Friedburg. After a short delay for reconnoitring and preparation, they developed the plan of moving around the enemy's left, leaving Frankfort on their own left, and through the hill country to Heilbronn, thus forcing the imperialists back, or perhaps cutting them off from the Main, the Neckar and the Danube. This, on due consideration, proved to be too much of a circuit, and the allies shortly adopted another route with the same object in view. About the middle of June they sent fifteen hundred cavalry to seize the passage of the Nidda at Bonames, and so soon as this was done they moved at daylight

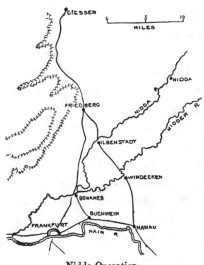

Nidda Operation.

one day by their right around the left of the archduke to the Bonames ford. The archduke, unaware of what they intended, put his men under arms, but did not attack them on the march: it took many generations to teach soldiers the advantage of falling on a marching column. The allies crossed the Nidda, drove back Werth's cavalry, and reached Buchheim the same day. From here they marched on the morrow to Windecken on the left bank of the Nidder, a confluent of the Nidda, and by taking and occupying it in force, cut the enemy off from access to the Main, except by a difficult circuit.

Thus separated from Franconia, Swabia and Bavaria, the archduke took a bold step and determined to move into the Hesse and Cologne district; if followed, to go as far as Westphalia, and thus draw Turenne and Wrangel away north and relieve the imperial lands from invasion. But this manœuvre was of no avail, for while the archduke started northerly on his errand, Turenne and Wrangel, guessing his intention, marched to Aschaffenburg, crossed the Main, — Turenne calling in his Mainz garrison, — and moved southward. There are few things which show the able soldier more than the power to retain his initiative, and to pay so much heed only to the enemy as will suffice for safety, and not so much as to weaken his own plans. This manœuvre had been beautifully planned as well as admirably executed. It was, says Napoleon, " plein d'audace et de sagesse."

The allies had now no more to fear from the imperial army. To cover the country more effectually, they marched in two columns a number of miles apart, the French by way of Schorndorf and Lauingen, and the Swedes by Nördlingen and Donauwörth, captured and garrisoned these towns, crossed the Danube, and found themselves in a rich and plentiful country, where they could victual their troops to great advantage, and had the enemy's land at their mercy.

From the Danube Turenne sent a detachment of five hundred men to Augsburg, and was himself about to move on the place, when Wrangel, who had crossed the Lech, and in the blockade of Rain had met with stubborn resistance, called for aid. Turenne moved on Rain, whose capture his presence assured, but he thereby forfeited his chance to take Augsburg, which the enemy meanwhile occupied with a force of fifteen hundred men from Memmingen. The archduke, moreover, gained time by this delay to return to the Danube and Lech from his attempted diversion north. It was an

error on Turenne's part not to capture Augsburg first, and
then to march to the assistance of Wrangel, who could just
as well have waited. Rain once captured, Turenne and
Wrangel determined to withdraw to the left bank of the
Lech, and to undertake the siege of Augsburg; but though
their siege operations were as rapidly and skillfully pushed as
without siege-guns they could be, and though they did indeed,
at a loss of five or six hundred men, advance to the main
ditch, the archduke got back through Franconia and the Upper Palatinate, and before they could reduce it, reached Augsburg by the right bank. Augsburg was then a short distance
from the Lech, and the space and works between the town
and river were made quite untenable by the enemy's heavy
artillery. Though the marshals sought to drive the enemy
away from his position, they were unable to do so, and the
archduke forced the allies, by his constant and well-directed
fire, from the siege and back to Lauingen, where they fortified a camp as well as strengthened the town defenses.

Having gained so much, the archduke moved across the
Lech and out on the road to Memmingen. Turenne and
Wrangel believed that he was aiming at Ulm, Tübingen and
Heilbronn, so as to pass around their right, manœuvre them
from their rich holding about Lauingen, and push them back
to Franconia. This would have forfeited the results of the
entire campaign, and have left them no satisfactory winter-
quarters, nor the chance of accumulating material so as to
afford promise of doing better in a new one. Moreover the
imperial army was much superior in numbers, and better provided for. The allied generals determined to move straight
at the enemy despite that they were not well equipped, and
to attack or manœuvre in his front as circumstances warranted; for the whole German campaign depended on what
they should now do. They moved from Lauingen Novem-

ber 5 towards Memmingen, and next day after reaching it, on the enemy's camp at Kirchheim, which they reconnoitred. The fact that this camp was so well protected by marshes and ravines in front that it could not be attacked with success led to a superb manœuvre. Leaving two thousand cavalry in their front to hold them there, the allies moved, November 7, unnoticed past the enemy's left to Landsberg, in the archduke's rear, captured the Lech bridge at that point and all the imperial magazines in the place, which had

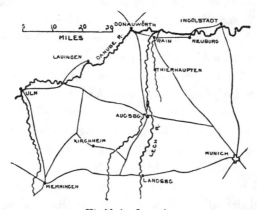

Kirchheim Operation.

but one hundred men as garrison, and projected a column of three thousand cavalry against Munich. They had completely cut the archduke off from Bavaria, which now lay open to their good pleasure. Thunderstruck, the archduke was compelled to follow.

This brilliant proceeding threw the elector of Bavaria into a ferment of uneasiness, created dissatisfaction with the management of the archduke and the Bavarian generals, and was the origin of the elector's making a separate peace with France. Cut off from his supplies, the archduke had difficulty in regaining his own base by crossing the Lech near

Thierhaupten. The imperial troops moved to Ratisbon, leaving the Bavarians to defend their own land,

"Les manœuvres pour déposter l'archiduc de son camp entre Memmingen et Landsberg," says Napoleon, "sont pleins d'audace, de sagesse et de génie; elles sont fécondes en grands résultats; les militaires les doivent étudier." This praise is well earned; the march on the Nidda and the march on Landsberg combine to make this campaign a marked one.

The allies remained three weeks on the right bank of the Lech, and then, November 23, moved to Memmingen and into extended winter-quarters; the French spread out as far as the Danube, and the Swedes towards the Lake of Constance. The French captured the castle of Tübingen, the Swedes took Bregenz and Meinau, but they failed to win Lindau. During the winter, however, Turenne and Wrangel, in a raid with six thousand cavalry, beat the enemy, who had rendezvoused at Rain, in a smart action, with heavy loss.

The Congress of Ulm now assembled. In the following spring, March, 1647, a treaty was made by which the elector of Bavaria cut loose from the emperor, and Lauingen, Gündelfingen, Hochstädt, Ulm, Donauwörth, Memmingen and Überlingen remained in the hands of the allies. This was to forestall a fresh alliance between the elector and the empire.

This campaign is remarkable in several ways. The junction of the Swedish and French armies in the presence of the imperial forces was admirably managed. The campaign was conducted by two armies, under two generals who remained in accord throughout, — a noteworthy circumstance, fit prototype of the coöperation of Marlborough and Eugene. The allies were weaker than the archduke, but they twice outmanœuvred him. The decisive nature of the campaign was shown by its results, — the separation of Bavaria from the

empire. The credit of the campaign is no doubt due to both
Wrangel and Turenne. Napoleon only praises Turenne, but
Wrangel must be given a share of the credit. Though in no
sense Turenne's equal, he was a soldier beyond the average.
No doubt Banér and Torstenson had done more brilliant
work; but they were not fortunate enough to be associated
with a man like Turenne, and their labors came to naught.

The emperor was now alone. He had no allies left. The
Swedes and French were decidedly superior. The latter
had in the field fourteen thousand infantry and twenty thousand cavalry; the emperor but five thousand foot and six
thousand horse, under the Archduke Leopold. This was a
small showing compared to what Wallenstein and Tilly had
made; but the whole of Germany was exhausted, both in
men and means.

Turenne and Wrangel were ready to reap the advantages
of their last year's operations. But the policy of the French
court prevented this. It would not do to permit the emperor,
who was the head of the Catholic rulers, to be quite subdued. Turenne was ordered from Germany, where he would
have done good work, to the Netherlands, to conduct with a
limited force a slow and profitless campaign of sieges. All
Turenne's protests were in vain, despite the best of reasoning. Condé had been ordered with a larger force to Catalonia,
where he was able to accomplish little.

On the way to his new field of operations, Turenne had
taken Höchst, Steinheim, Aschaffenburg and other places;
had crossed the Rhine at Philipsburg, and marched into the
country between Strasburg and Zabern. But the German
cavalry, late Weimar regiments, General Rosen commanding, declined to advance further until paid six months' arrears
then owing them. They had an idea that they could do
better by enlisting in the emperor's service. Turenne had no

funds. The mutineers in a body, under Rosen, recrossed the Rhine. Turenne followed them with part of his force, and for several days endeavored to pacify Rosen and them. But finding clemency of no avail, he carefully laid his plans, arrested Rosen at Ettlingen, and sent him under guard to Philipsburg. Thus left without a leader, part of the mutineers gave in; part marched towards the Tauber country. Turenne attacked these, killed two hundred and dispersed the rest. Some were reorganized; some went into the Swedish service.

In quelling this mutiny Turenne had lost much time. Mazarin's policy had negatived all the utility of the French army for the year, and had practically lost the German regiments. It was typical civilian management.

There is no pretense that the management of the affairs of nations would be safer in the hands of the army commanders than in those of the statesmen. Such a theory in America would tend towards the substitution of autocracy for republicanism. Those versed in statecraft ought to be able to hold the nation's helm to better advantage than men educated solely to arms; but it is the misfortune of generals that the real or alleged necessities of the state must so often interfere with military operations; and as we are looking only at the military side of history, we are compelled at times to lay the blame of the failure of campaigns upon those statesmen who use war, as they often must, not to succeed from a purely military standpoint, but as subsidiary to their own scheming, to win or to risk loss as may at the moment be most expedient.

It is often said that our operations during the civil war were interfered with by the Washington politicians. So they were, from a soldier's point of view; but the soldier looks at things from but one side; there were many other and weighty questions to be considered, which involved not only success in the field, but the integrity of the nation ; and it may be said that, on the whole, the political management was good ; certainly so according to the light the country's leaders then had, if not according to what shines on us now.

After this serious delay Turenne reorganized what was left of the Weimar regiments, and, sending part of his cavalry to Flanders, he moved into Luxemburg, where he was ordered to pursue a negative rôle, and to hold the enemy's attention by the capture of a few small places. This woeful policy of the prime minister placed his allies, the Swedes, in bad case. The Bavarians were again prevailed on to join the emperor ; took from the Swedes all their hard-won conquests, and forced them back to the Weser country, seizing all the terri- tory so laboriously gotten from them by Turenne and Wran- gel. Then, after all was gone, and there was danger that the balance might tip in the other direction to the disadvan- tage of France, Turenne received orders from the court again to join the Swedes. This well illustrates the idea of civilian management. So far as statesmanship goes, this may (or may not) have been good policy ; but from a military stand- point, how lamentable !

Turenne moved rapidly on the Main, raised the siege of Frankenthal, marched on Mainz, captured the castle of Fal- kenstein, crossed the Rhine at Oppenheim on a bridge of boats, and in January, 1648, went into winter-quarters in Hesse-Darmstadt. But as the Swedes were not ready in numbers or equipment for an immediate campaign, Turenne retired to Strasburg the same month.

Breech-loading Portable Gun.   (15th Century.)

XLI.

THE THIRTY YEARS' WAR ENDS. 1648.

TURENNE joined Wrangel in 1648 in Franconia, and after a slight disagreement as to plans, the two operated towards the Danube. Crossing at Lauingen, they followed the imperialists up to Zumarshausen, and in May drove them back to the Lech with heavy loss, despite their fine rear-guard fighting under Montecuculi. They then crossed the Lech and moved to the Isar, the enemy falling back behind the Inn. Following across the Isar, they occupied the whole country up to the Inn, which rapid river, having no pontoons, they were unable to pass. To punish the elector for last year's treachery, they devastated all Bavaria in their control. They were now on the edge of the emperor's hereditary lands; but a new imperial army arriving at Passau on the lower Inn, the allies retired to the lower Isar, whither the imperialists followed, and both sides intrenched camps. As autumn came to an end, the allies, whose bold operations had contributed effectually to the Peace of Westphalia, retired behind the Lech. During this campaign Turenne had fed his men on the country without interfering with his strategic manœuvres. In August of this year, after a fruitless campaign in Spain, Condé was transferred to the Netherlands, and defeated Archduke Leopold at Lens.

IN February, 1648, when Wrangel got ready to move and so notified Turenne, the latter, though not yet well equipped, crossed the Rhine at Mainz and joined the Swedish army in Franconia. The allies had nine thousand foot, twelve thousand horse and nearly fifty guns; not a large force, to be sure, but one whose strength lay in its commanders. Turenne frankly declared to the elector of Bavaria that he should treat him as for his late treachery he deserved to be treated; and the allies crossed the Main and followed the imperial army towards the Danube, as far as Ingolstadt, until the latter went into camp under the guns of the fortress. The two allied generals now for the first time disagreed as to plans. Wrangel wanted to move on the Upper Palatinate, Turenne to stay in Swabia, as being a better territory to victual troops, the former section having been eaten out. The disagreement in no wise interrupted good-will, though there was no inconsiderable friction among many of the minor generals, which it required all Turenne's patient persuasiveness to allay. The French army moved to the Bamberg country, Wrangel toward his goal, and after a short separation, the latter becoming aware that without Turenne he was helpless, the allies again joined at Rothemburg on the Tauber, and both armies moved to Würtemberg, and took up quarters at Reutlingen and Göppingen. This tribute to

Zumarshausen Operation.

Turenne by Wrangel shows where lay the greater strength and ability.

Hearing that the enemy was not far from Ulm, the allies marched toward the Danube, while the imperialists took position between that place and Augsburg, at Zumarshausen, ten miles from the river. Arrived at Lauingen, Turenne and Wrangel personally headed three thousand horse and advanced on a reconnoissance across the river, to within no great distance of the enemy. Hidden by a marsh through which they threaded, they ascertained that the imperialists were carelessly stationed ; were pasturing their horses, and had no outposts or patrols. They determined on attack, and sheltering the three thousand horse where they stood, sent back orders to the two armies to advance at night in light order, leaving the train behind. The orders were executed with exceptional speed ; the allied divisions reached the scene, were quickly rested, and again ployed into column ; and at 2 A. M. on May 17, they approached the enemy's lines, the French army in the lead with a van of cavalry. But, alive to their coming, the enemy had determined not to await attack, had thrown out thirty squadrons to cover their movements and protect the train, had burned their camp, and were already in full retreat. Count Holzapfel and Count Gronsfeld, who commanded the imperial and Bavarian forces respectively, after the experience of 1646, had feared to be cut off from Augsburg by another turning manœuvre, and had marched at night, the armies in the van followed by the train. The moral effect of the 1646 operations had already half won this campaign. The enemy's rear-guard was under command of Montecuculi, with but sixteen hundred horse, eight hundred musketeers and four guns. The route lay through a wooded and marshy territory, and the train could be got forward only with extreme difficulty. Following hard upon, the French van of cavalry at 7 A. M. fell sharply on the rear-guard, under Montecuculi, who, though reinforced by about one thousand men under Holzapfel, and though holding his own with great ability and fierce determination, was forced back in confusion. Count Holzapfel was killed, and Montecuculi barely escaped capture.

The French thus kept the rear busy while Wrangel sent his horse forward on either flank of the marching rear-guard column. The main army was prevented by the laboring train from coming back to the assistance of the rear-guard, and of this whole body of infantry, thirteen hundred were taken prisoners, while the rest dispersed ; eight guns and a number of standards and wagons were captured. The horse cut its way through to the main body. At night the imperial army, hard pressed by the allies, took position in much confusion behind the little river Schmutter. Turenne and Wrangel endeavored to force the passage, but they had no guns, and it was stoutly defended by Duke Ulrich of Würtemberg, who held his men together under extremely severe losses. As the troops and artillery had not yet got up, the attack was put off till daylight next day, May 18, the enemy meanwhile being cannonaded by what guns happened to be on hand. But during the night the enemy, now under Fermor and Gronsfeld, retired behind the Lech to the protection of the guns of Augsburg, having lost twenty-three hundred men in killed, wounded and prisoners, eight guns, six standards and three hundred and fifty-three wagons. The loss of the allies was also heavy. The enemy would scarcely have lost more men in a general engagement had they stood their ground; and the allies had accomplished much with small means.

The main Franco-Swedish column had not been able to follow, and the bulk of the fighting had been by the van. As a sample of stout pursuit it was excellent, and the defense by Montecuculi during the retreat, and that of Ulrich at the Schmutter, were of the best.

The allied marshals rested a day, — May 18, — to enable the main force to come up, and on the next Turenne and Wrangel moved on Rain. The Bavarians burned the bridge over the Lech, and took up the old position Tilly had held sixteen years before against Gustavus Adolphus; but after some cannonading they retired at night on Munich. The allies restored the bridge, crossed the Lech, leaving two thousand men to hold the bridge, and, sending one thousand horse to harass the enemy's retreat, moved on Neuburg, and then, June 12, on Freising on the Isar. The Bavarians fell back behind the Inn, sending strong infantry detachments to Munich and Ingolstadt and garrisoning Wasserburg, while the elector personally went to Salzburg and thence to the Tyrol. The allies now crossed the Isar, occupied Landshut, broke the bridge at Freising — preferring to use that at Landshut — and pushed towards Wasserburg, which, however, proved to be so strongly garrisoned that it could not be well taken. Marching downstream to Mühldorf to cross the Inn, they were again balked, having no pontoons, and the river being exceptionally wide, deep and rapid, with a rocky bed, in which piles could hardly be driven.

Turenne and Wrangel had now manœuvred and forced their way to the very boundary of Upper Austria, had taken possession of all Bavaria, and had rationed their troops on the country. As a lesson to the elector for his treachery in breaking his treaty, all the overrun portion of Bavaria was devastated. This was done with no light touch, and the Bavarians, who sixteen years before had prayed openly in their churches to be delivered from the "Swedish Devil," found in Turenne and Wrangel a foe as bitter and unrelenting as Gustavus Adolphus had been upright and placable.

If they should cross the Inn, the allies would find a great deal of support, for the population of Upper Austria, as for many years it had been, was still in the mood for revolt from the emperor. This advance they were prepared to make and no doubt would have done, but for a sudden turn in fortune, which, as usual all through the Thirty Years' War, seemed to protect the hereditary possessions of the emperor. Field-Marshal Piccolomini and General Enkevort early in July had assembled ten thousand foot and fifteen thousand horse with a lot of guns at Passau and Wilshofen, had crossed the Danube and moved to Eggenfelden, on the allies' left flank, which stood near Mühldorf. Thus threatened, Turenne and Wrangel found it essential to retire, which they did via Landshut to Dingolfing on the lower Isar, where they in-

trenched a camp and built a bridge. Piccolomini and Enkevort did the like near Landau, a dozen miles below.

The habit of intrenching was with Turenne, who preferred
the offensive in all cases, a mere relic of the system of the
day. We shall, in the next century, see it disappear in
favor of battles in the open; and yet even Marlborough and
Eugene did not quite cut loose from the habits of thought
they had inherited.

In this situation the rival armies remained till midsummer.
About this time the imperial forces endeavored to entrap a
Swedish outpost at a village near their camp, and made a threat
as if to approach the allies. But nothing came of either
attempt. There were one or two attacks on the other's position by either army, — particularly one on the enemy's camp
by Wrangel with his batteries; but they were fruitless.

Piccolomini was now compelled to send reinforcements to
Bohemia to save Prague, which had been raided by Königsmark from the Franco-Swedish army, and Turenne and
Wrangel by the end of August had exhausted the victual of
the vicinity of Dingolfing. They therefore moved via the
Landshut bridge to Moosburg back of the Isar; the enemy
followed and took up a new camp at Landshut. For more
than a month — till the end of September — inactivity
reigned. Then Turenne and Wrangel retired behind the
Lech, and on October 11 established themselves between
Augsburg and Landsberg at Schwäbisch-München. Hence
they marched to Donauwörth, crossed the Danube and moved
on Eichstädt. The imperial army followed from the Isar, as
far as the Lech.

Shortly after came the Peace of Westphalia, to which
Turenne's and Wrangel's operations had much contributed.
Turenne took up winter-quarters in Swabia, and Wrangel
near Nürnberg.

This last joint campaign of Turenne and Wrangel worthily crowned the Thirty Years' War. After those of Gustavus Adolphus, this and the campaign of 1646 are the most noteworthy and the most productive of results. The allied generals, says Napoleon, moved through the length and breadth of Germany with a rapidity and decision unknown to war at that time. Their success came from their ability and proper method, from the strong feeling for the offensive which characterized Turenne, and from the boldness and intelligence of their every step.

The armies were fed largely on the country. This was possible from their small number, and the usual friendliness of the population during the advance. But in retreat the allies still found the magazines they had prepared absolutely essential, and they mixed the system of requisitions with that of magazines in an effective manner. Since Gustavus' time, the magazine system had been the only one in use. Gustavus' victualing was done by magazines and regularly-paid-for contributions from the territories traversed. Turenne made war nourish war, — a method which is, however, incompatible with the humanity inculcated by Gustavus. From a military aspect, the one system contributes to speed, the other to security. Turenne had small armies to feed, and could easily live on requisitions from the surrounding towns. The true system is a proper combination of the two : magazines at proper places on the line of advance and at places of possible refuge, and requisitions — paid or enforced — on forward and flank movements and on retreats.

The last years of the Thirty Years' War were mixed up with the war of France against Spain in such a manner as materially to enlarge the theatre and scope of operations. The war was no longer one of Protestant Germany against the Catholic emperor to secure freedom of worship. It became a general European war, waged between France and the Hapsburgs for the supreme control of European politics.

France was shortsighted in many ways. She constantly divided her forces so as, for instance, in 1635 to have armies in Germany and the Netherlands, in northern Italy, in the Valteline, in Roussillon and in Spain, not to count immense resources spent upon the navy. The result naturally was that instead of accomplishing results so that a peace with Spain should accompany the general Peace of Westphalia in 1648, the Franco-Spanish war dragged along a dozen years more.

Almost the only noteworthy operations during this whole period occurred in 1635 to 1637 in the Valteline, where the Duke of Rohan defended that territory with a small force against Spanish troops advancing from northern Italy, and against an imperial army which sought to join the former by way of the valley of the Adda. As a sample of mountain warfare, these operations deserve study.

In 1647 Condé was sent to Catalonia, where he failed in the siege of Lerida, owing to lack of men and material. The operations have no especial interest, save to recall those of Cæsar on the same terrain. The great Roman won, as he always did, in the end ; the Frenchman lost; but it is perhaps no blot on a captain's record to fail in Spain, that graveyard of military reputations. It needed the genius that inspired a Hamilcar or a Hannibal to succeed in such a country.

In 1648 Condé was again in the Low Countries, and at the end of May took the town of Ypres after a siege of two weeks. His biographers make much of many of Condé's operations which wear, on the whole, an air of triviality ; and without underrating this great soldier, it is noticeable that much of Condé's best work was done when associated with

Turenne, and his worst when opposed to this commander. Later in the year Condé won a battle at Lens over Archduke Leopold. The civil turmoils of the Fronde had begun, and the Spaniards believed that a great battle won would give them a permanent footing in France, if not indeed access to the capital. The archduke had eighteen thousand men and thirty-eight guns, and the army was really commanded under him by Baron Beck. He had, after taking the town of Lens, marshaled his line facing northerly, with the right leaning on that place, and the forces posted on high and excellent defen-

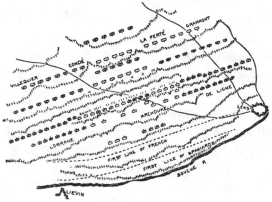

Battle of Lens.

sive ground. He hoped that Condé would attack, as he had at Allerheim, and in such case felt confident of success. But Condé, who was approaching from the Ypres and Dunkirk country, and who had but fourteen thousand men, of which six thousand were horse, and less artillery, was too circumspect to blindly attack; though he drew up in line, he declined an assault, and strove by every means to lure his opponent down into the plain. The armies lay in parallel order; the day of grand-tactics had not come. Finding that his efforts produced no result, Condé determined to fall back for forage and victual to La Bassée, north of Lens, and at day-break on August 20 he moved to the rear in six columns. Thus tempted, Beck sallied out with his light horse and attacked the French, badly defeating the cavalry rear-guard. Condé answered with his heavy cavalry; but this, too, after a preliminary success, was beaten back. Under cover of this engagement, and seeing that he could do no less, Condé faced about, and drew up on the heights half way between Lens and Neus, a village on the road to La Bassée, mean-while essaying a charge in person to extricate his heavy horse, which was hard pressed. Though ill delivered and driven back, the general result of the entire series of combats was to give Condé time to marshal his line; and what was really a lost opening had induced the Spaniards to leave their advan-tageous post in the expectation of improving a victory already half won. The cavalry which had been beaten Condé wisely put in second line, and then advanced to attack the archduke, who still lay on higher ground than the French, but not as favorably as before. The cavalry lines which opened the battle came into very close contact, — four paces, say the old records, — before a pistol shot was fired. Then the horse-men clashed, and while the foot in the centre of each army advanced, the squadrons swayed to and fro in the usual con-fusion of a parallel battle. Finally, on both wings, the French horse won the day, and was able to turn inward on the Spanish foot, with which the French *corps de bataille* was already fiercely engaged.

The battle was gained. The enemy lost four thousand killed, and six thousand prisoners. The rest of the army broke up, and nearly all the officers, — some eight hundred, — all the guns and one hundred and twenty standards were taken. Lens made a fourth spendid victory in Condé's neck-lace of gems, though it was by impulsive fighting and not manœuvring that it was won. It checkmated the Spanish efforts for the year. Beck died of his wounds.

The operations from the battle of Lützen to the Peace of Westphalia redound almost as much to the glory of Gustavus Adolphus as those which he himself conducted in Germany. The manœuvres of his successors were indeed brilliant, but they lacked the solidity and the results of those of the great Swede. What Gustavus did stayed done; and it was he who built the foundation of the structure of Protestant success in Germany. A century of operations such as those which preceded and succeeded his could not contribute as much to the cause as did his manœuvres in the few months he remained upon the theatre of war. It was exhaustion pure and simple which put an end to the Thirty Years' War; that the end was in favor of Protestantism was solely due to what Gustavus had done.

The Peace of Westphalia was the fruit of negotiations which dragged on from 1643 to 1648. Sweden received, as a fief of the empire, all western Pomerania, Stettin, Garz, Damm, Gollnow, Wollin and Usedom in eastern Pomerania, Wismar, the secularized bishoprics (not the city) of Bremen and of Werden, and an indemnity of five million rix dollars. She became a member of the Diet with three votes. France received outright (not as a fief of the empire) Metz, Toul, Verdun, Pignerol, Breisach, about all Alsace, and the right to garrison Philipsburg. Strasburg remained free, as did some other towns. Hesse-Cassel got Hersfeld, Schaumberg, the fiefs of the foundation of Minden and six hundred thousand rix dollars. Brandenburg was indemnified for her loss of Pomerania by the bishoprics of Halberstadt, Minden and Camin, and by Magdeburg after the death of August of Saxony. Mecklenburg and Brunswick received small territorial rights.

The secular and ecclesiastical affairs of the empire were rearranged so as to place Catholics and Protestants on a substantial equality; and the ownership of ecclesiastical estates was to remain forever as it existed January 1, 1624. The Austrian and Bohemian Protestants gained nothing; but elsewhere freedom of worship was fairly well established. The imperial courts in the several Circles were to be equally divided between Protestants and Catholics.

The peace was guaranteed by France and Sweden.

Three-barreled Carbine.   (16th Century.)

XLII.

CONDÉ AGAINST TURENNE. 1650–1656.

THE war between France and Spain went on, and the civil war of the Fronde grew to larger proportions. Condé was imprisoned, and Turenne, seeking aid from Spain, led an army into France from the Netherlands. After some insignificant operations the French laid siege to Rhétel, and Turenne attempted to relieve it; but he was met by Duplessis and seriously defeated. In 1651 Turenne returned to Paris under an amnesty. In 1652 the Fronde broke out again, and Condé took up arms against the court, while Turenne defended it. The court moved from place to place, under escort of the army, while the princes held Paris, and a campaign of manœuvres south of the capital resulted. The duke of Lorraine was called in by Mazarin as an ally, but he went over to Condé, and was got rid of only after he had collected much plunder in France. La Ferté and Turenne later transferred the war to near Paris, and in July a battle was fought in the Faubourg Saint-Antoine, in which Condé was only saved by being admitted through the gates into the capital. Later he was crowded to the frontier, and the court returned to Paris. In 1653 Condé was in the Spanish service and Turenne opposed him; Condé made several attempts to march on Paris, but Turenne cleverly kept between him and the capital, and checkmated all his efforts.

DESPITE the Peace of Westphalia, the war between France and Spain went on, and the unhappy French were consumed not only by a harassing conflict upon their borders, but by the still more disheartening civil war of the Fronde at home. Stripped of its complex character, the Fronde was an insurrection under some of the French princes against Mazarin's government for Anne of Austria, queen regent during the minority of Louis XIV. Political difficulties during this period obliged Turenne to flee to Holland until an amnesty was declared at its close. His political course at the opening

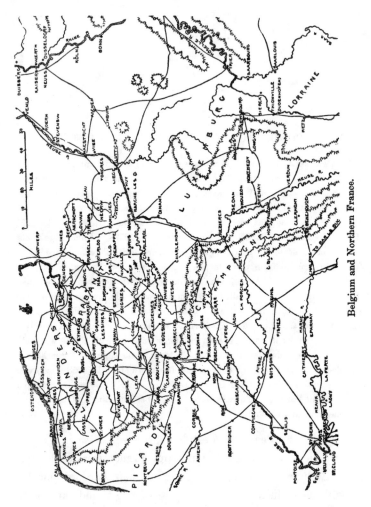

Belgium and Northern France.

of the struggle has been much criticised; but it was a time to try men's souls, as every civil war must do, and there were multitudes of honest men misled.

In 1650 the internal trouble grew apace; Condé and others of like sentiments were seized and imprisoned by Mazarin in the castle of Vincennes. Turenne sought to head the old troops of Condé at the castle of Stenay, on the Meuse, for the purpose of rescue, but, unable to gain over more than a few Frenchmen, he entered into negotiations with Archduke Leopold William, governor-general of the Spanish Netherlands, who gave him two hundred thousand thalers to raise troops, and fifty thousand thalers a month for rations, together with a personal subvention, and further agreed, in addition to what Turenne should enroll, to furnish and keep two thousand foot and three thousand horse under the latter's orders. Having reached a further understanding with the Spaniards, looking towards the forcing of a peace by Spain on Mazarin, and having made of the queen regent a respectful but fruitless demand for negotiations, Turenne led a Spanish army into France. Having, with the money furnished him, gathered together a few thousand men, and with these joined the Spanish army put on foot according to agreement, he crossed the border from the Netherlands. The Spanish idea was to invade Picardy while Turenne should invade Champagne; but Turenne insisted on marching in one body, to seize strong places in the interior, and to work in unison with the adherents of the Fronde, who had armed in Bordeaux and elsewhere. The small fortresses of Le Catelet and Guise were invested in June, but Guise could not be taken, owing to the presence of the royal French army, and to a very rainy season which made operations all but impossible. The allies drew back, a week later captured La Capelle, and thence moved to Vervins, where the archduke took command. The rival armies were of about equal strength, ten to twelve thousand foot and six to seven thousand horse. Turenne induced the Spanish army to move forward to the Aisne, taking and garrisoning Château Porcien and Rhétel, and the French army retired to Rheims. Turenne suggested the advisability of moving along the Aisne,

turning this army by the left, and marching straight on Paris
to free the imprisoned Fronde leaders, Condé among them; but
the Spanish commander had not the stomach to agree to such
a manœuvre, which was not perhaps as discreet as it was bold,
— though indeed in its very boldness lay safety, — and refused even to cross the Aisne. The princes were transferred
to another prison near Orleans. But Turenne undertook a
grand reconnoissance towards Fismes with three thousand
horse and five hundred musketeers, attacked ten regiments of
French cavalry which were stationed there and threw them
back on Soissons, capturing five hundred prisoners. The
Spaniards, sending a detachment to La Ferté-Milon, at
Turenne's suggestion, then marched on Fismes, to a position
between the French army at Rheims and the capital; but, for
what reasons cannot be said, took no advantage of their
favorable situation, further than to undertake a month's negotiations with the duke of Orleans, which eventuated in nothing. The Spaniards then retired to the east and besieged
Mouzon on the Meuse. After a seven weeks' siege Mouzon
surrendered, the Spanish troops retired to winter-quarters in
Flanders, and Turenne remained with his eight thousand
men near Montfaucon, in the hills between the Meuse and
Aisne. The French army sat down idly in Champagne, and
finally, in December, laid siege to Rhétel. Turenne hurried
to its relief, but as he arrived too late, the place having surrendered December 13, he started to return to Montfaucon,
marching by his left.

Intent on bringing Turenne to battle, the French commander, Marshal Duplessis, followed him south from Rhétel,
and reached his front December 15. Though Turenne preferred to retire, he nevertheless drew up on the heights to the
left of the valley route he was pursuing. Duplessis did the
like on the right of the valley, and both armies in parallel

order marched at half a cannon-shot distance by the flank
five or six miles along the valley. Inasmuch as he could not
well avoid battle, and observing that on the French right
flank there was but little cavalry, Turenne drew his own horse
together and marched down into the valley to turn the enemy
near the Champ Blanc. At first the operation looked like a
success, as the French cavalry of the right wing was somewhat dispersed; but the second line remained firm, and
Turenne's troops — mostly raw levies — grew unsteady. The

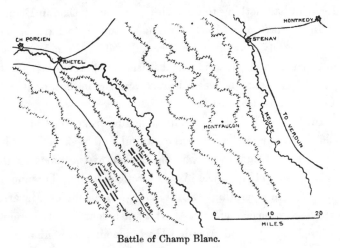

Battle of Champ Blanc.

same thing took place on Turenne's right, where an attack at
first promised success and then miscarried. So soon as he
perceived the weakening of Turenne's troops, Duplessis drew
some cavalry from his right, brought it over to his left, and
charged in with a vigor which completed Turenne's defeat.
The men behaved badly, and the great French soldier was
routed. He lost the bulk of his force in prisoners, several
general officers, and by good luck only saved himself by a
flight with five hundred cavalry south through Champagne to
Bar le Duc. Here he reassembled part of his troops and

moved back of the Meuse to Montmédy, where he went into winter-quarters. Napoleon's criticism on his engaging in battle does not seem to be sound. He was justified in fighting, even though the enemy outnumbered him; in fact, he could scarcely avoid accepting battle, for Duplessis forced it on him; but luck was against him, and his men were not his old soldiers, on whom he could rely.

During this campaign Turenne was dependent on the archduke, and could not operate on his own ideas, though Leopold had nothing to do with the defeat at Champ Blanc.

In the next year (1651) Turenne returned to Paris, a general amnesty having been granted. The French princes were freed, and Mazarin was banished. Turenne sought to patch up a peace between France and Spain, but, unable to do so, he returned to France.

In 1652 the Fronde troubles again broke out, and the court was obliged to leave the capital and seek refuge with the army. Condé, who was the leader of the party of the princes, sought to induce his old brother soldier, Turenne, to join him in operating against the government of Mazarin, who had returned after a short banishment. But Turenne refused, and he and Marshal Hocquincourt, with nine thousand men each, mostly horse, were sent to operate against Condé, who had taken command of the army of the Fronde that had been under the leadership of the duke of Beaufort, and, fourteen thousand strong, lay in position between Montargis and the Loire.

Condé held Montargis, and lay near by. Turenne was camped at Briare, with Hocquincourt at Bléneau, covering the peripatetic court which was sojourning at Gien. Their cavalry was dispersed for ease of foraging. Learning that Condé was approaching in person, the two royal generals were about to concentrate their forces further to the north.

If he would strike either singly, Condé had no time to lose ;
and having ascertained their situation by a spy, he made a
night attack on Hocquincourt, whom, leading a small body of
horse with his accustomed rapidity and success, he surprised
and drove in disorder from his post. He then turned towards
Briare, hoping to take Turenne unawares in the same manner. But the latter had
caught the alarm, and was
already in line between
Ozouer and Bléneau, where
he held a position he had
previously reconnoitred, and
which was the sole route by
which Condé could advance,
a defile between a wood and
a marsh. Condé was checked
at this point after a smart
combat ; Hocquincourt, finding that he was not pur-
sued, rejoined his colleague
by a circuit, and Turenne,
whose plan was to guard the
court rather than conduct
a brilliant offensive, retired

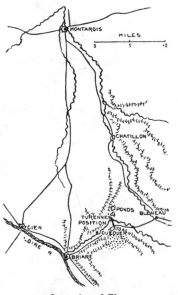

Operation of Gien.

to Gien. His total loss had been six hundred killed and six
hundred prisoners, but Hocquincourt had forfeited his guns ;
Condé's loss was but four hundred men. Had Condé won
in this first operation, the court would have been *in extremis ;*
but the prince retired to Chatillon with his army and personally went to Paris, where he arrived April 11, and, though
he had accomplished naught, assumed the rôle of conqueror
among his many adherents in the capital.

On learning Condé's absence, Turenne at once moved to

Auxerre. His (or Mazarin's) plan was to fix the theatre of war as near Paris as practicable. From Auxerre, by an able and rapid series of marches, Turenne kept on to Sens and Corbeil. Tavannes, in command of Condé's army, could

Paris-Orleans Country.

do nothing to arrest his movement, and when Turenne finally camped at Arpajon he had cut Tavannes from Paris and his chief. Tavannes advanced to Étampes. Thus isolated from his army, Condé, with but a few recruits, sought to place in a state of defense St. Cloud, Charenton, Neuilly and other suburbs of Paris. Negotiations — largely underhanded — were meanwhile afoot, in which Mazarin on one side and Condé on the other acted the principal rôles, each vainly seeking to outwit the other.

Turenne kept up his activity. He attacked Tavannes during a military fête at Étampes, and did him damage to the extent of two or three thousand men ; but Hocquincourt managed his part of the enterprise so ill that Mazarin concluded to send him to Flanders, and to rely solely on Turenne, who thus assembled under his own colors twelve thousand men. Tavannes had but eight thousand.

Meanwhile Condé took St. Denis. The court went to Melun, and Turenne laid siege to Étampes. Tavannes defended the place furiously. Once out of material, he was about to surrender, when Condé, from Paris, succeeded in throwing a convoy of munitions into the town. The king sought to exert the influence of his personal presence, but in vain ; Tavannes pleaded sickness and would not appear on the walls to parley with Louis, and the town was again on the point of surrender, when the duke of Lorraine came upon the scene. This treacherous ally had been called in by Mazarin, who imagined that he could control him ; but no sooner had Lorraine safely passed the army of La Ferté than he declared for Condé, and was warmly welcomed in Paris.

It seemed as if Condé, with the duke of Lorraine's army, could now move to Étampes and deal the last blow to Turenne. But though the duke was both a knave and a fool, he was not to be easily led ; plunder was more in his line than fighting ; and his army merely passed through the land, ravaging right and left, finally reaching Villeneuve St. Georges. Mazarin began again to negotiate with him ; Turenne advanced towards him ; and on the promise of the royal army giving up the siege of Étampes and permitting the duke to leave with the booty which he had gathered all along his route, the new-comer was got rid of. Turenne, who had lost nearly four thousand men in the siege of Étampes, and was on the eve of success, was thus by political necessity compelled to retire; but he moved to a position near the duke of Lorraine, prepared to force him to carry out his shameful contract. By a sharp march across the Seine, he reached the duke's camp, and at a risk of pushing him to

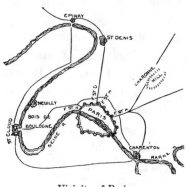

Vicinity of Paris.

battle, obliged him to sign a new agreement to leave for good, and actually to march away before Condé, who was on the road, could join him. The calling in of an outsider had merely resulted in ravaging a large section of France, and had done no good to either party. The duke of Lorraine alone had made a gain. He had moved away with an enormous amount of plunder, the result of Mazarin's interference in the military operations.

Condé, with his army of but five thousand men, was in camp at St. Cloud. He had possession of the sole near-by bridge over the Seine, and by crossing to one or the other side could thus hold head the better to Turenne's eleven thousand men; and the latter, though he advanced into the vicinity, for the moment attempted nothing against the prince. The queen, however, had disgarnished the frontiers and created a new army under La Ferté, equal to Turenne's, which was designed to operate in conjunction with him.

Turenne had moved to Lagny sur Marne to head off reinforcements for Condé, said to be approaching from the Netherlands; but finding them still far away, he preferred to
attack Condé in connection with his new coadjutor. He had
constructed a bridge at Epinay, and it was agreed that La
Ferté should cross and fall on the left flank of Condé's camp,
while Turenne should remain on the right bank to prevent
his repassing the river. Condé guessed the plan when he
saw the building of the bridge ; and was compelled ere
the two armies should be down upon him to seek refuge
beyond Paris, for the fickle capital was now as fiercely
opposed to him as it had been friendly, and would not allow
him inside the walls. He chose Charenton, at the confluence
of the Seine and Marne, as his retreat. From his camp at
St. Cloud he could move thither along the left bank, or he
could move through the suburbs of Paris on the right bank ;
and the latter being an equally short route and with better
roads, he chose it, — unwisely, as the event proved. Starting out early July 5, he had already traversed the Bois de
Boulogne, the Faubourgs St. Honoré, Montmartre, St. Denis
and St. Martin, and the van had got beyond St. Antoine,
when he perceived the head of the king's column approaching from the north. Turenne had ascertained his movement,
and determined to attack him on the march, a fact which prevented Condé's reaching Charenton without a battle. It was
manifest that, if he continued his march, his rear would be
fallen upon ; and there was no probability that so able a soldier as Turenne would permit him to cross the Marne. He
was trapped, but he did the only possible thing : he recalled
Tavannes, who led the column, and who managed to rejoin
his chief with some loss.

Condé was indeed in ill case. In his front the king's
army, thrice his size, in his rear the walls of Paris, manned

by the militia, determined to bar his entry to the town, now
his only refuge. His defeat seemed so certain that the walls
were crowded by Parisians, then as now eager sight-seers;
while on the heights of Charonne stood the king and court
to witness his inevitable destruction. Condé, as was always
his mood, determined to sell his life and his cause dear.
There were some intrenchments in his front which had been
erected to arrest the duke of Lorraine should he attempt to

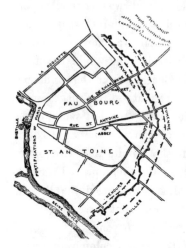

Battle of St. Antoine.

levy blackmail on Paris, and
these defenses he utilized.
His position was good in having concentric roads in his rear
which enabled him to sustain
his fighting lines; but he was
in a bag; Turenne well knew
it, and drew his line around
him from Charonne to the
river. He then organized
three attacks: himself in the
centre, Marquis St. Maigrin
on his right, and the duke of
Noailles on his left. Condé
opposed him with Nemours
and Tavannes on right and left, holding himself with a small
following ready to march to any point seriously endangered.
Each French general knew the other: it was surely to be a
death struggle.

Desirous of making a certainty of the fight, and, as was
his wont, seeking to save lives, Turenne began to skirmish,
while waiting for La Ferté, but Mazarin ordered him instantly
to close with the prince and destroy him. He could not tell
what might occur within the walls of Paris. Turenne obeyed.
Condé met the first assault on the centre by a sortie, and

repulsed it; and shortly a sanguinary struggle was engaged in all along the line. St. Maigrin carried the works in the Rue de Charonne, and despite the fire from the housetops and windows, kept on his way. Condé met his battalions at the market-place and drove them back headlong, with a heavy loss in officers. In the king's centre progress was made only at yet more severe loss, for Condé had posted troops in every house and garden, and the fire was deadly. It was a hand to hand fight at almost all points. Meanwhile Noailles carried the intrenchments in his front, and was fast closing in on Nemours, when Condé appeared upon the scene and thrust him back. But despite all Condé could do, Turenne, at the head of the royal army, still forged on; and though several times driven back, kept steadily gaining ground. He finally reached the abbey; and thence worked his way along the Rue St. Antoine until Condé in person stopped him west of its walls. At this point the conflict was desperate. The men fought like devils. Turenne sent in Noailles anew, and forced the fighting everywhere, while La Ferté arrived and prepared to get in Condé's rear. Condé was being netted; his annihilation appeared certain; when fortunately, by the intercession of Mlle. de Montpensier, daughter of the duke of Orleans, the gates of Paris were opened to him and he was allowed to pass in, as to a temple of refuge. He retired into the Quartier St. Jaques. He had lost two thousand men; Turenne probably more.

Condé did not long remain in Paris; he had but four thousand men left, and could not undertake to face both Turenne and La Ferté. He turned to Spain, which had had an easy task since the court had drawn the forces from the frontiers, and had recaptured many fortresses. Even Dunkirk, won at such risk and cost, had fallen to them. The archduke saw that Condé would be an exceptionally valuable ally, and dispatched Fuensaldegna to his aid; and the duke of Lorraine, who was again afoot, entered Champagne at the same time that Fuensaldegna entered Picardy. And though the Spaniard yielded no hearty assistance to Condé, on the other hand the duke of Lorraine remained with the prince some time.

Alarmed at this new alliance, the court was for retiring to Burgundy and Lyon, but Turenne persuaded them that flight was the one thing to ruin the cause, and induced them to stay near the army and to move to Pontoise, behind the river Oise, north of Paris, where he assured them that he could afford them due protection.

Learning of the approach of the duke of Lorraine, Turenne advanced to Compiègne, hoping to prevent his junction with the Spaniards. He failed in his efforts, but shortly the bulk of the Flanders contingent returned home, leaving but a small detachment of cavalry with the duke of Lorraine; whereupon Turenne retired to near Paris to prevent Condé and Lorraine from joining hands. But this project likewise failed, owing to the interference of Mazarin; Condé and Lorraine met at Ablon, and as they considerably outnumbered Turenne, the latter was driven to resort to the defensive. He placed his army behind the forest of Villeneuve St. Georges, in the angle of the Seine and Yères, from which place, by a *coup de main*, he ousted Lorraine. The allies were unwilling to attack him in this excellent position, but sought instead to cut off his convoys and to hold him to his camp. Condé posted his forces in four corps around the royal army and in close proximity to it, but was unable to cut Turenne from access to Corbeil, where lay his munitions, despite his numerous parties sent abroad to worry him and starve him out; and though for the moment Turenne was almost in a state of blockade, he was never out of victual. But Condé fell sick and left the army; and the duke of Lorraine had neither the ability nor the steadiness to carry out the plan Condé had inaugurated. Turenne managed safely to get all his convoys in, and on the fall of Montrond, which another royal army had been besieging, he received three thousand men as reinforcements.

The ill management of the campaign had disheartened the fickle Parisians as much as the eating out of the entire vicinity, and had predisposed them to any change. Turenne, who had exhausted his Corbeil magazines, now undertook a splendid manœuvre. By a night march on October 4–5, he made his way to Corbeil; thence he started, in two columns so disposed that he could at short notice wheel left into line, for Tournan, and in three days crossed the Marne at Meaux and reached Senlis; and thence to Pontoise, where lay the court. Condé, who had now been definitely abandoned by the Parisians, left the capital for Champagne, as the neighborhood of Paris could no longer sustain an army. While Condé and the duke of Lorraine retreated towards the Aisne, the king, via St. Germain and St. Cloud, reëntered Paris, — a triumph for which he might thank the constancy and skill of Turenne, whose courage and steadfastness under the pressure of grave difficulties had been altogether beyond praise.

In Champagne Condé took Château Porcien, Rhétel, Mouzon and Ste. Ménéhould, and made a definite treaty with the Spaniards, by which in consideration of his serving as generalissimo of their armies, all joint conquests on French territory should be his. He now had twenty-five thousand men under his orders; success appeared about to smile upon him; but the treaty was never carried out with any show of fairness. The means of securing any such conquests as had been contemplated were afforded him but for a short period, though he was able to take Bar le Duc, Void, Commerci and many small places. These gains were in a sense losses; they left him but a small relic of his own army, for his foot was all distributed in the captured places.

Turenne and La Ferté, after quieting the centre of the kingdom, moved forward to the Lorraine frontier, and laid siege to Bar le Duc. Condé came to its rescue, but his men became unmanageable at the capture of a small town through which they passed, and where was stored a good deal of wine, and he was driven off and returned to Clermont and thence to Stenay. The royal army took Bar le Duc, Barrois, Château Porcien and Vervins. Turenne would now have been glad to bring Condé to battle, but the latter retired into Luxemburg.

Only Condé and the duke of Orleans now held out; the Fronde was practically at an end, a work clearly due to the patient skill of Turenne.

At the opening of 1653 Condé held Rhétel, Ste. Ménéhould, Mouzon, Stenay and Clermont in Champagne; in Burgundy, Bellegarde; and he had seven to eight thousand men in Champagne, as many in Guienne, and numerous secret partisans all through France. The operations at the opening of the year were lax, for both the Spaniards and French were much weakened by the never-ending wars; and the era of big armies had not yet come. It needed a new generation to grow up to furnish men. The existing generation had been killed off.

The French opened the campaign in Champagne, Burgundy and Guienne; the Spaniards were late in coming into action, owing to impoverished resources. Turenne and La Ferté, who had ten thousand horse, seven thousand foot and a few guns, took Château Porcien, which had again fallen to the Spaniards, and Rhétel. Condé's possession of Mouzon, Stenay and Rhétel kept open an entrance into France, and the capture of the latter upset his plans. In July the archduke and he entered Picardy with nearly thirty thousand men, Spaniards, Germans, Italians, Lorrainers, Walloons and French refugees. Of this body eleven thousand were horse, and there were forty guns. They assembled at La Capelle, and pushed by a rapid march to Fonsomme ; whence Condé hoped by lively measures to reach Paris. But Fuensaldegna, jealous of Condé's success, was purposely slow; he wished to besiege Arras, because this town, if taken, would belong to Spain and not to Condé ; while Condé naturally desired to advance. The dispute consumed much time, and gave Turenne and La Ferté leisure to return from Rhétel, and to reach Ribemont via Vervins with twelve thousand men, accompanied by Mazarin and the king. Many opinions of what it was best to do were given, but Turenne had his way. " The danger is great," said he. " What we need is to concentrate all our forces, march to meet the enemy, choose the best places for defense, hold head to his superior forces without fighting him, and wait until Condé divides his forces, — as he must do if he would march on Paris, — to attack the parts in detail." Accepting this very sound advice, the court retired to Compiègne.

The French passed the Oise, and with care approached the Spaniards under Condé, who had also crossed and advanced with the Somme on their right and the Oise on their left. Along Condé's route all the undefended towns opened their gates, but he put in no garrisons, contenting himself with taking an oath of fealty, for fear of depleting his forces. This was his last chance, and he would take no risk. Rations and money he got in plenty ; and by way of Ham he advanced on Roie, and took it in two days. Here Fuensaldegna refused to go further. Turenne moved to Guiscard, a wooded country, good for defense, and sat down to watch Condé. The latter proposed to turn on La Fère, but Fuensaldegna was slow, and Turenne, guessing his intention, reached it first and garrisoned it. Failing at La Fère, Condé suggested Peronne or Corbie as a good objective, but Fuensaldegna would accept neither suggestion ; he kept his eye on Arras as the preferable scheme, and Turenne, moreover, forestalled Condé by throwing a garrison into both places. Hearing, at this time, that a

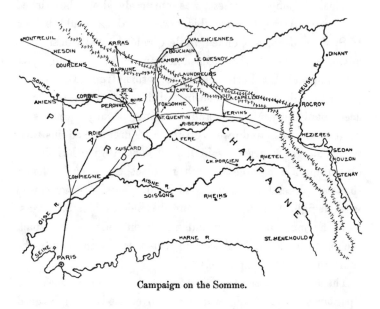

Campaign on the Somme.

large convoy was on the way from Cambray to the Spaniards, and crossing the Somme at Ham, Turenne marched by Peronne to Bapaume, and drove the convoy into Corbie for his own use. Thus met at all points Condé determined on fighting, as he had superior forces ; but how should he bring Turenne to battle ? He put all his skill to work. As says his biographer Desormeaux : " At one time he approached him threatening attack with his whole force, at another he moved away precipitately to entice him to decamp so that he might take him unawares on the march ; again he offered him the bait of a signal advantage which was but a trap in reality; and again he moved on the principal towns of Picardy, as if to undertake their capture. But in vain did he display all the resources of the art, — suspicion, circumspection and wisdom guided all the steps of Turenne. It was Fabius against Hannibal." And despite his superiority of force, Condé did not dare to advance on Paris with Turenne in his rear.

The French had gone into camp at Mont St. Quentin north of and covering Peronne; the Somme between the enemy and Turenne seemed to protect him, and neither marshal sought a cover behind intrenchments. Condé, by a circuit and a secret march, crossed the Somme and a brook which flowed in front of the royal camp, deceived La Ferté, and appeared suddenly on Turenne's right flank. At once catching alarm, the latter cleverly withdrew by his left; Condé followed with the cavalry ready for action. Turenne took up a new and very strong position a couple of miles to the east on a wooded plain near Buire, and began to intrench. Condé followed, occupied an adjoining position, and made preparations to attack; but the Spanish foot was late in coming up, and the favorable moment passed; Turenne's works grew too strong to make an assault advisable. The Spanish forces remained three days in front of Turenne, seeking by skirmishing and feints to draw him out; but Turenne's rôle was a defensive one, and Condé could accomplish nothing.

The prince then sought to invest Guise; but the Lorrainers would not coöperate. Turenne threw two thousand men into the place, and the Spaniards remained in camp at Vermand. Hither came Archduke Leopold, but his presence added little to the military scheme and internal troubles were increased. The treaty he had made with the Spaniards gave Condé the rank of generalissimo and was supposed to invest him with the

supreme command, but to this power the archduke and Fuensaldegna sought to put a limit; they effected their purposes
by inciting the several corps commanders against him; and
there being a number of separate bodies composing the Spanish army, only absolute obedience to one head could keep it
efficient. With the smallest opposition, no satisfactory military progress could be made; and there were never-ending
quarrels. Condé returned to near St. Quentin; Turenne
changed his position to Golancourt near Ham. He could
not be reached, and was yet a never-ceasing threat.

Having failed to accomplish aught in Picardy against
Turenne, Condé changed the theatre of war to Champagne,
and resolved to besiege Rocroy. The archduke finally
yielded him the command. To accomplish his end, Condé
must deceive Turenne. He dispatched several small bodies
to Bapaume, Dourlens, Hesdin and Montreuil, and while
Turenne was speeding detachments to head off these threatened attacks, Condé moved rapidly to Rocroy and invested it.
But he had more difficulty in taking it than he formerly
had had in beating the Spanish army under its walls. The
valorous defense of the garrison; continual rains; the jealousy of Fuensaldegna; the defection of the duke of Lorraine,
who left in the middle of the siege with all his troops, and
many other minor difficulties told against him. Turenne
made no effort to disturb the siege, for Condé had too
strongly held all the defiles which approach the plain in
which Rocroy is situated. He preferred instead to take
Mouzon. After a siege of twenty-five days Condé captured
Rocroy, and from here he made raids all through the country, and even to the vicinity of Paris.

A new royal army now besieged Ste. Ménéhould, and
Turenne and La Ferté covered the work. Condé endeavored
to raise the siege, but uselessly; he was tied hand and foot

by his allies. Thus the campaign ended with Turenne's complete success, though he had but half his opponent's forces. Condé's cause was falling into ruin.

This campaign has been much praised by military critics, but it is chiefly of interest to show the difference between Condé and Turenne. By many Condé has been called the greater man; but despite his exceptional boldness and skill in battle, his restless energy, his high military capacity and his many splendid successes, he did not have the power to work against fortune which Turenne so constantly exhibited. No doubt Condé was hampered by his allies; but so, in nearly all his campaigns, was Turenne by his superiors; and yet he rose above them and accomplished results on the whole greater than any of Condé.

Portable Gun. (15th Century.)

XLIII.

ARRAS AND VALENCIENNES. 1654–1656.

As 1654 opened, while the French besieged Stenay, the allies began the siege of Arras. The French covering army had been surprised by Condé, and the garrison was small. The allied works were strong, and stretched in a circle of fifteen miles. There were two lines, with ditch and wall and wolf-pits. Turenne came to the relief of Arras while Condé and Fuensaldegna were opening the trenches, and by clever positions cut the allies off from nearly all their supplies. Stenay was taken and its force sent to Turenne, who finally determined on assaulting the Spanish lines. This was done August 24, and despite heroic fighting by Condé, proved completely successful. The Spanish army was almost broken up, and Arras was relieved. In 1655 there was some handsome manœuvring, but to no great effect. In 1656 the French sat down before Valenciennes, a very strong city on the Scheldt, Turenne and La Ferté occupying the right and left banks respectively. Don John of Austria and Condé came to its relief, made works opposite Turenne, and inundated the country to distress the French. Building bridges over the Scheldt, Condé on July 16, at night, assaulted La Ferté's works and completely defeated him. Turenne was forced from the siege. Valenciennes was a good offset for Arras.

The 1654 campaign opened with the besieging of Stenay — sole relic of Condé's immense possessions — by the French army under Marshal La Ferté. Turenne with fifteen thousand men was in Champagne, covering the siege and watching the frontier. The allied army of Condé and the archduke, thirty thousand strong, moved from the Netherlands and sat down to besiege Arras. To cover this fortress General de Bar had been lying near by with a flying column; but he was negligent; Condé with ten thousand cavalry cleverly interposed between him and the town, and was so speedily followed by six thousand Lorrainers that he was able to invest it; while next day the archduke and Count Fuensaldegna arrived with fourteen thousand Spaniards, Italians and Walloons and completed the work.

Arras was one of the ramparts of France, but de Bar's failure to throw himself into the town on the appearance of Condé's column left the garrison under Montdejeu far too weak. Condé began lines of circumvallation in a circuit of eighteen miles. These consisted of a ditch twelve feet wide and a wall ten feet high, added to which, on the low land, was an outer ditch nine feet wide and ten deep; and along the whole of the line were erected redoubts every hundred paces, amply armed with guns. Between the double lines were twelve checker-wise rows of wolf-pits for defense against cavalry; and a line of contravallation was erected over much of the distance to hold head against sorties. In ten days, with the labor of the whole army and twelve thousand countrymen impressed into service, the work was completed. Though the garrison was small, the French were enterprising, and in three successive attempts they broke through the lines before they were complete, and threw six hundred horse into the town, losing, however, an equal number in the venture.

Fuensaldegna was still at odds with Condé. This feature is so constantly dwelt on by his biographers as an explanation of Condé's failure to accomplish what he set out to do, that it reads like a stereotyped excuse. That there was friction cannot be doubted, but Condé would have seemed greater had he been able to surmount this difficulty. It is success in the face of obstacles which peculiarly appeals to us; and surely Gustavus had more obstinacy among his allies to contend with than Condé ever dreamed of. Too much insistence on the interference of superiors or colleagues does not tend to raise the reputation of a general.

Condé knew Arras well, and advised two approaches, so as

to divide the enemy's efforts; Fuensaldegna chose an apparently easy but really difficult place for one approach, and insisted on so opening it; and as a result, at the end of a month he had made no progress worth mention.

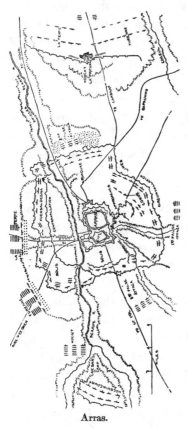

Arras.

The danger to Arras induced Mazarin in July to order Turenne and La Ferté from the Meuse to its relief. Condé, learning of their march, proposed to go out and give the enemy battle; but Fuensaldegna would not budge, and on July 19 Turenne put in an appearance on the east of the place and seized Mouchi-le-Preux, cutting the Spaniards off from Douay, Bouchain and Valenciennes; and by cleverly disposing his parties, — sending a suitable detachment to Bapaume, one to Lens and one to Peronne, — was able to intercept their convoys from Cambray, Lille, Aire and St. Omer. He set up his camp between the Scarpe and the Cogeul, on ground high and dry, and threw his works along his front from one river to the other. St. Pol alone was left to the allies: they were thus all but besieged in their own lines, and could get no victual except what was brought in by horsemen and packs. Shortly Stenay was captured, and under Hocquin-

court its besiegers moved to join Turenne, who with fifteen
squadrons went out to meet him at Bapaume, took St. Pol
and Mont St. Eloi on the way, and on his return placed him
on the opposite side of the town, on a hill known as Cæsar's
camp. This absence of Turenne was the proper occasion for
an attack on the French, which Condé was eager to make;
but Fuensaldegna was self-opinionated, and apparently possessed the power of enforcing his views.

The besiegers began to lack victual; they were at one time
all but starved out, and had it not been for a cleverly conducted convoy of provisions from Douay, they would have
been driven from the siege. For two weeks longer — the
Spaniards had been seven weeks on the spot — the two armies
lay in presence, exchanging only artillery fire. Turenne had
reconnoitred carefully on two separate occasions. Where
Condé had taken position, on the south of the town, he
found it impracticable to attack, but he thought the line
could be broken elsewhere. His lieutenants were not of his
opinion; in fact, he was the only one of the French who
saw any chance of success in the offensive. But Turenne
was determined to relieve Arras, for Montdejeu was getting
out of powder, as he managed to let Turenne know; and
it was finally agreed that each French marshal, at the head
of his own corps, should fall on the quarters of Don Ferdi-
nando de Solis on the northwest side, and on that part of
Fuensaldegna's quarters on the north nearest to Solis, these
being the furthest from the quarters of Condé and apparently
the weakest part of the line; and that to create a diversion
there should be made three false attacks, one on Condé, one on
the Lorrainers, and one opposite the archduke. The attack
was set for the night of August 24–25, the eve of St. Louis.

At sunset Turenne and La Ferté broke up, and so soon as
it was dark crossed the Scarpe on four bridges prepared

beforehand, leaving only the sick and non-combatants in camp. Arrived at the rendezvous given to Hocquincourt, they found him delayed by more than two hours, an unpardonable blunder, as he was close to the place of attack. The moon shortly became obscured, and the southeast wind blew towards the assaulting party. Under such favorable conditions Turenne deemed it wise not to wait for Hocquincourt. The columns of Turenne and La Ferté were each preceded by five battalions in line, to cover as wide a space as possible, and these were headed by pioneers with fascines, hurdles, ladders, picks and shovels. La Ferté was on Turenne's left; Hocquincourt was to have formed on his right. There were twenty-six thousand men in line; the enemy still had more by two thousand.

Turenne reached the foot of the enemy's works at 2 o'clock without discovery; so soon as his matches were seen by the enemy, he at once threw forward his men; and without much loss pushed his way across the first and second ditches. The enemy's fire was wild; the password, " Vive le Roi et Turenne ! " always fired the French heart, and the assault was given home. The Italian foot was driven in, and Montdejeu from within Arras made a sortie to aid the attack, of which he quickly got notice.

La Ferté was not equally successful opposite Count Fuensaldegna, but Turenne's success enabled him finally to push forward; and when Hocquincourt at length arrived and drove in the Lorrainers, the defeat of the Spaniards was complete; the French held half their works, and could communicate with the garrison of Arras. Not until five o'clock, it is alleged, did Condé learn of the disaster. The false attack which was to have been made on his lines was for some reason not delivered. Why the sound of the exceptional firing did not arrest his notice is not stated. It must have been a strong wind to blow it from him. Condé at once flew to arms, headed some of his cavalry, crossed the Scarpe by way of the archduke's quarters, and fell furiously on a part of La Ferté's troops that had dispersed for plunder, and on his line which had come down into the low land, and threw them into disorder; and had not Turenne gathered his own forces and La Ferté's artillery, taken post on the hill La Ferté had abandoned, and met Condé's stout assault in person, the result might even at this late hour have been changed; for Condé always charged like a whirlwind. Finding himself opposed by Turenne, and being moreover taken in rear by Montdejeu from Arras and by Hocquincourt on the flank, after a two hours' gallant fight Condé was forced to retire, which he did towards Cambray with the wreck of the army. The archduke fled to Douay, where Fuensaldegna joined him. It was Condé who saved what remained of the Spanish forces.

The Spaniards lost but three thousand men killed and wounded, but they left all their sixty-three guns on the spot; two thousand train wagons, nine thousand horses and great booty fell to the French.

This was a brilliant operation of Turenne's, full of able combinations, and added greatly to his repute. Louis XIV., who with the court was at Peronne, visited Arras and conferred on him command of all the French forces here. Turenne crossed the Scheldt, intending to march on Brussels. He actually did cross the border, but Condé gathered forty squadrons and the militia of the country, and though weak in numbers, with that restless activity which was so marked a characteristic when roused to action, manœuvred athwart his path; and Turenne, aware that there were many divisions to back Condé up in case the French advanced too far, retired to Maubeuge and then into winter-quarters in December. The operations at Arras deserve close study.

In 1655 both armies were equally strong, some twenty-five thousand men each. The French stood at Guise and Laon, the Spaniards not far from Landrecies, where Condé was in command, and at Mons, where the archduke lay. Turenne besieged and successively captured Landrecies and La Capelle. While he lay at Landrecies, Condé advised a diversion on La Fère, where the French court was at the moment resident, thinking to lure Turenne from his work; but Fuensaldegna would not undertake the operation, and Condé contented himself with heading sundry raids into Picardy. The siege of Landrecies lasted a month; Condé could not interrupt it, for Turenne had provisioned for a long siege, and to cut his convoys was of no avail.

Operation on the Scheldt.

Turenne, joined by the king, then advanced down the Sambre as far as Thuin; Condé and the Spaniards retired beyond the Scheldt and Sambre, and erected an intrenched defensive position behind the Haine in a country so inundated that an approach to it was impracticable. The lines, strongly garrisoned, extended from Condé to St. Ghislain. The king thought it would redound to the honor of the French arms to force them; but Turenne showed how he could turn this position by a flank manœuvre and by twice crossing the Scheldt, once above Valenciennes, and again below the fortress of Condé; and his plan was adopted. The French crossed the Sambre, and via Bavay marched towards Bouchain. Masking this fortress, Turenne crossed the Scheldt at Neuville, and the enemy, who had retired to Valenciennes, likewise crossed and established themselves with their left leaning on St. Amand. Arrived opposite them, Turenne sent Castelnau to fall on their right flank, while he attacked them in front. The enemy retired towards the fortress of Condé, and though Turenne ordered Castelnau to fall on their rear so as to hold them until he could come up, this was so weakly done that they escaped. Turenne's presence forced Condé and the Spaniards to retire toward Tournay, nullified any value their defensive line might have had, and enabled the French to lay siege to Condé.

Up to this moment Condé and Turenne, though on opposite sides, had been firm friends. But at this time Condé intercepted a dispatch of Turenne's in which the latter referred to his late retreat as a flight, in a manner which Condé could not forgive; and for a time the warring friends were foes in earnest.

In the last half of August Turenne captured the fortresses of Condé and St. Ghislain, and the enemy continued his retreat, though Condé undertook some smaller operations, and conducted them handsomely with his body of six thousand cavalry. The archduke, afraid of the French advance, strengthened the fortresses, by so much weakening his army, and did practically nothing. Late in the year, in November, both armies sought winter-quarters.

Next year, 1656, Don John of Austria replaced Archduke Leopold in command of the imperial forces; Condé was second to him, and could not operate on his own judgment. Don John, who brought the manners and ideas of the court to the conduct of the army, did nothing but move to and fro, and besiege small forts on the line between Tournay, Valenciennes, Quesnoy, Lens, Bethune and St. Quentin in southern Flanders, and on the northern boundary of Artois and Picardy. In resisting this ill-considered species of aggression,

Turenne exhibited remarkable powers of manœuvring. Both parties aimed for Tournay; but Condé threw a body of four thousand men under the works, and anticipating the French in a surprise of the place, held on until the Spanish army could come up and invest it. Though tied by the inertness of the Spanish generals, Condé, on this and other occasions this year, must be said to have operated with ability.

At the beginning of summer, on June 14 and 15, Turenne opened trenches in front of Valenciennes, building lines of circumvallation on both sides of the Scheldt, he occupying the right bank, La Ferté, who came up later, the left. Turenne had sixteen thousand men, half cavalry, La Ferté a less number. Valenciennes was a strong and rich city on the Scheldt, which with its affluents flowed through and around it, and made the country a network of marshes up and down river. From Valenciennes to the town of Condé is a vast plain; but on the west the town and river are dominated by a hill, Mont Azin. Turenne occupied the plain on the east of the town, the army of La Ferté the west, including Mont Azin, and over the Scheldt were a bridge above and another below, by which the two armies could intercommunicate. Turenne's plans were well laid; there were but two thousand men in the garrison, though some ten thousand citizens were drilled, and the capture of Valenciennes seemed but a question of time.

Don John had not yet got his forces in hand; but Condé had a flying corps, and his first scheme was to open the reservoir sluices of Bouchain to throw the waters of the river down upon the French. The inundation increased the width of the river to one thousand paces, and kept the French generals busy diverting the floods by canals and embankments. Finally they succeeded in throwing the inundation back from their camps and into the city, flooding one of its quarters.

Don John and Condé, with twenty thousand men, now moved from Douay towards Valenciennes, and, establishing their main camp on the south of the city opposite the left of Turenne's lines at half cannon-shot distance, with their own left on the Scheldt and the right on the Rouelle, they occupied both banks of the river, and threw several bridges across. The bulk of the force lay where it threatened Turenne, and this general believed that the attack would be made, if at all,

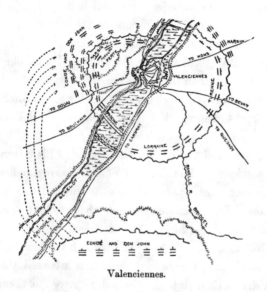

Valenciennes.

on him. Condé, for a week or more, made nightly attacks on Turenne or La Ferté, always at new points, and after so lively a fashion that the French troops were kept under arms until they were almost tired out. Then, for the night of July 9–10, he prepared an attack on La Ferté. Marshal Marsin from St. Amand was to hold Turenne in check by demonstrating with his six thousand men, while Condé and Don John should fall on his colleague. Notice was contrived to be got to the garrison to increase its fire and to open the sluices, so as, if possible, to make the French bridges unavailable for mutual succor. Condé remembered Turenne's brilliant operation at Arras and proposed to have his revenge.

The garrison had been much reduced, and had Turenne assaulted before this moment, the town must have fallen. It was time that the Spaniards should act, if at all. From the preparations of the allies Turenne divined that La Ferté would be attacked, and offered him half his army; but La Ferté, who was absurdly jealous of his colleague, rejected the offer. Before his arrival, Turenne had built strong defenses to his camp, but La Ferté had demolished half of them, as being quite unnecessary. Condé and Don John meanwhile assembled their men on the evening of the 16th of July, moved across the river, and reaching the ditch of La Ferté's works before they were discovered, delivered an assault so suddenly as to be completely successful. Though La Ferté gathered the cavalry and defended his ground manfully, Condé drove him in, and of the six regiments which Turenne sent over to La Ferté's assistance, two met the same fate. The inundation and short shrift prevented Turenne from aiding him with more men, though he made a stout effort to do so. While the Spanish foot made its way into Valenciennes, Condé and the horse attacked the flying French, drove them into the flooded river or cut them down, and of all La Ferté's forces only two thousand escaped the sword, drowning or capture, the Spanish loss being a bare hundred. The fight lasted an hour only. Marsin had meanwhile attacked Turenne, but was repulsed. Thus rudely interrupted, Turenne abandoned the siege and hastily retired to Quesnoy, where, with the sixteen thousand men and six guns left him, he took up a stand to meet Condé, who, he believed, would follow and urge battle. But Don John would not leave Valenciennes for immediate pursuit, and when he finally followed, Turenne was ready for an attack. He feared that to retire too far would alarm the court and unduly encourage the enemy ; and, against the advice of all his officers, prepared for battle. Nothing but his own courage kept his men in hand ; and, seeing his firm front, the Spanish army declined to attack, and retired to Condé.

The whole operation at Valenciennes was an able piece of work by Condé, and though it apparently succeeded because Turenne had not been as careful as he might in his outpost service, and did not soon enough receive notice of the enemy's manœuvre, it was none the less a fair match for Turenne's success at Arras. The fault mainly lay with La Ferté, who was unwilling to heed any suggestions of his colleague.

Turenne was by no means disheartened. He lost none of his activity, and constantly annoyed the enemy to sustain the morale of his troops. Turenne's elasticity under defeat is one of his highest qualities. Apparently unwilling to push Turenne further, the enemy now besieged the town of Condé, as if for lack of a better objective ; captured it, and moved successively on Cambray, Lens and Bethune. Constantly hovering around them, seeking an advantage, Turenne followed their movements, and held himself ready for battle at any auspicious moment. It is a subject of regret that so little space can be given to operations which are altogether admirable. Finally Condé and Don John retired to Maubeuge. Turenne went into winter-quarters behind the Somme.

When they are the only ones in the field, the operations of smaller bodies are as interesting and may be quite as skillful as those of the larger ones ; when they are mere detachments from the main army, contributing to and following its manœuvres, they do not command the same attention, however worthy of study. But though an enormous army compels a certain admiration which is inseparable from mere bulk (whether indeed in art, architecture, engineering or even literature), a general does not necessarily earn praise for ably commanding it beyond what we bestow on the leader of the smaller army. We admire Napoleon's 1796 campaign more than that of 1812; nor can it be said that Grant's Wilderness campaign was as able as that of Jackson in the Valley. While Turenne led smaller armies than Eugene or Marlborough, they were none the less the armies which enacted the principal rôles in the wars in which he was engaged, and deserve as ample recognition as if he had stood at the head of thrice the force. He later showed his capacity to handle large armies with equal ease.

Knight.
(15th Century.)

XLIV.

DUNKIRK. THE BATTLE OF THE DUNES, 1657. MAY AND JUNE, 1658.

Louis had agreed with Cromwell to capture Dunkirk, which had again fallen to the Spaniards, and turn it over to the English, against a contingent of six thousand men. In 1657 the campaign consisted solely of manœuvres between the coast and the Scheldt; but in 1658, after there had been a number of serious desertions from the French to Condé, and the affairs of the king seemed desperate, Turenne undertook to retrieve them by the capture of Dunkirk, under peculiarly harassing conditions, which almost promised failure. The time of year was bad, the difficulties greater than when Condé had taken it, and the threat of a relieving army certain. The English fleet, however, assisted Turenne, and later the English contingent. Finally, after the trenches were opened, Don John and Condé appeared at Furnes, and, leaving six thousand men at the siege, Turenne went out to meet them. On June 14 was fought the battle of the Dunes; the English ships assisted with their fire; the Spaniards had brought no artillery; the ground was ill-adapted to horse; and after a stout conflict Turenne won the day, and drove back the enemy, who retreated to his fortresses. Dunkirk shortly surrendered. After some minor operations the campaign ended, and next year came the Peace of the Pyrenees.

Louis XIV. had made a treaty offensive and defensive with Cromwell, by which England was to furnish six thousand men to France, and Louis agreed to capture Dunkirk and deliver it to the English. In consequence of this treaty, Charles II. and his brother, the duke of York, who so far had been depending on the countenance of the French court, left for the Netherlands, where the dukes of York and Gloucester thereafter commanded a small Irish contingent in the Spanish army. In May, 1657, Turenne concentrated at Amiens, intending to march to the seaboard in pursuance of the projected capture of Dunkirk. But the late arrival both of his new recruits and of the English contingent prevented his accomplishing any result. The Spaniards concentrated in Flanders, and Turenne conceived a new plan which the court approved. La Ferté with fifteen thousand men was sent to the border to hold Condé in Luxemburg, where he had been wont to winter, while Turenne himself, with twenty-five thousand men, proposed to march to the river Lys, as if bound for the coast, whence he would sharply turn on Cambray, whose garrison was reduced by detachments; and during this operation he would rely on the English, who were soon to land on the seaboard, and on the activity of La Ferté, to divert from his purpose the attention of the enemy. This plan Turenne inaugurated by a rapid march toward the Lys, which led Don John to fear for the coast fortresses and cease to watch Cambray; on perceiving which, Turenne broke up with all his horse, and by a rapid day and night march reached Cambray May 29, and blockaded it. The infantry followed close behind. Turenne crossed the Scheldt near the town, and stood across the road to Bouchain; threw bridges, and hurried forward his works so vigorously that in two days the blockade was complete.

The Spaniards had already begged Condé to leave Luxemburg to care for itself and come to the protection of the Netherlands, and La Ferté having failed to keep him busy, he had got to Mons, from whence, with three thousand horse, by rapid marching he reached Valenciennes May 29, the day on which Turenne blockaded Cambray. From Valenciennes Condé's guide happened to mislead him, and gave his column a wrong direction from which he emerged on the main road, while Turenne had made preparations to meet him on a road through a densely wooded country, which in fact Condé had intended to take. Thus by mere accident Condé went around

Turenne ; and having, from Valenciennes, succeeded in notify-
ing the commander of the Cambray garrison of his purpose,
while Turenne's lines were disgarnished by his absence, he
contrived, under cover of a smart night attack on the French
cavalry, and at a loss of thirty officers and three or four hundred men, to enter Cambray. This was a very handsome
operation, in which Condé's energy was deservedly aided by
his luck.

As the rest of Condé's army was near at hand, Turenne
retired from Cambray, marched up the right bank of the
Scheldt, and moved on Le Catelet and St. Quentin. With
the St. Quentin garrison of four thousand men he reinforced
La Ferté, who had been sent to besiege Montmédy, the key
of Luxemburg, in the hope that the vigorous prosecution of
the siege there would attract the attention of the enemy and
lead him to separate his forces, or to commit some error of
which he could take advantage. After a heroic resistance of
six weeks, Montmédy succumbed, and La Ferté turned over
his forces to Turenne. The latter was now joined by the six
thousand English who had landed on the coast, but this fact
drew the attention of the enemy to operations there ; and
with every means of assuming the offensive, Turenne, as he
says, felt constrained, while in the midst of so many strong
fortresses and in the presence of so strong an enemy, to act
on the defensive. If he undertook a siege of any of them,
he feared that the enemy would make a raid into the interior,
or snatch from him some one of his own ill-garrisoned cities.
The situation required a defensive attitude ; by waiting he
might gain an opportunity of taking the enemy at a disadvantage ; and he sat down in the region between the Scheldt
and Sambre.

No captain is always at his best. When we see him conduct a splendid campaign one year, we are naturally led to

expect equal originality, boldness and skill in the succeeding year. But history shows us no man who is uniformly on the same level ; and this was peculiarly the case in this era, when soldiers were under the restraint of a certain formality in the military art. In the game of war there constantly occur, moreover, situations which appear to paralyze the action of the rival leaders ; situations where, as at a game of chess, one moves in the dark, or tentatively, or in such a manner as to invite a move from the opponent. To sit down and wait for the next operation of your opponent is a very common occurrence in every campaign. Not to do so is the province of few men.

Don John had manœuvred meanwhile between the Meuse and Sambre, but finding no opportunity for action, he marched on Calais, which Condé had suggested a plan to seize out of hand by an attack at low tide from the sea front. As matters turned out, he found himself too late by a couple of hours ; and seeing that he could not seize the place, Don John returned to the Meuse, thinking to relieve Montmédy. Arriving after its fall, he continued to march to and fro without any apparent aim, fatiguing his army and gaining not the least result. Purposeless marching is not activity; this word presupposes a clear objective or a well-conceived plan. Finally, having gathered reinforcements at Luxemburg, it looked as if Don John was preparing to invade France; Condé indeed suggested a raid on Paris. To give the Spaniards something else to think of, Turenne, by a march of seventy-five miles in three days, reached the Lys and blockaded the fortress of St. Venant. Whatever Don John's intentions, he now advanced to the rescue, but sat down to besiege Ardres instead of relieving St. Venant. After much difficulty, and the loss of several of his convoys, Turenne took St. Venant, and then sent five thousand cavalry to the assistance of Ardres. Don John, who could easily have taken the place by assault, gave up the siege and, sharply pushed by the French, retired on Gravelines and Dunkirk. Turenne followed, took Mardyk under his nose, and put an English garrison into it. This ended the year's manœuvres, and the rival armies went into winter-quarters. Though the operations had been small, Turenne had fitted his work to his conditions and to his opponents as well. Condé had as usual been controlled by the Spanish generals, who well knew, by petty opposition and by subterfuge and half-hearted work, how to nullify his best efforts. His power, moreover, lay more in his *coup d'œil* and fervor on the battle-field than in manœuvring in the open field, or in stemming a disastrous tide which in any campaign might set against him.

Matters turned against Louis XIV. during the winter of 1657–58, and as a result Turenne got placed in a most difficult situation. Hocquincourt, with the garrison of Hesdin, went over to Condé; several fortresses surrendered; Marshal d'Aumont, in an attempt to surprise Ostende, was captured; Normandy rose in revolt; the long-continued weakness of the government brought about, in all classes of the people as well as in the army, a marked spirit of dissatisfaction; the number of troops was small; Cromwell was impatient to get Dunkirk, and threatened to withdraw his troops and fleet, unless this place was speedily captured. Everything conspired to give an ill turn to the situation.

But Dunkirk presented singular difficulties. The Spaniards had broken the dikes and flooded the whole vicinity to Bergen. The fortress itself lay in the midst of three others, Gravelines, Bergen and Furnes, all in the hands of the Spaniards. This made the victualing and the delivery of material to an army besieging Dunkirk a task almost beyond execution. France had no one to look to but Turenne, and he was at the head of a woefully small army. What could he do? He had no one but himself to rely on. But the man grew as the horizon blackened: he resolved to have Dunkirk; and by undertaking the almost impossible, he showed himself to be truly great.

He concentrated part of his army near Amiens in April, and marched with eight thousand men to St. Venant on the upper Lys, while three thousand men accompanied the nomadic court to Calais. On the way to Dunkirk, he sent out a detachment which took Cassel; repaired, as he advanced, the roads, which were almost bottomless, with boards, fascines and stones; turned Bergen by the right, and in early May, having learned that the garrison of the place was weak, and that the forts on the Bergen canal, which if in good condition might arrest his advance, had not been completed, he determined to push on Dunkirk, between this place and Furnes, over the flooded district. East of Dunkirk was a redoubt built on the only practicable road, but this had not been suitably garrisoned and was readily taken.

It was a desperate undertaking to advance over a country where the floods grew deeper every day, but Turenne happily found a dike available, which led up to the two forts between Dunkirk and Bergen. To utilize the dike the forts must be first captured, and Turenne, who had been fortunate enough to receive six thousand fresh men, moved against them. The enemy sent a detachment from Dunkirk to their aid; but Turenne drove this back, reduced the redoubts, which had not been kept up in proper shape for defense, and utilized them himself.

It was too early in the year to expect to succeed in crossing the flooded region with all his material of war; and yet Turenne looked not back. He debated whether he had not best first besiege Bergen, which would be easier to capture than

Dunkirk; but he saw that if for a moment he turned from his declared intention of besieging Dunkirk, he would lose the moral control of his army and of the situation. It was Dunkirk alone, not Bergen, which would satisfy Cromwell and conserve the English alliance. Only Turenne's wonderful personal enthusiasm and the devotion of his troops enabled him to get so far as to undertake the siege. Though up to their middle in water, ill-housed and ill-fed, the men worked with a will; bridges were built over the flooded low

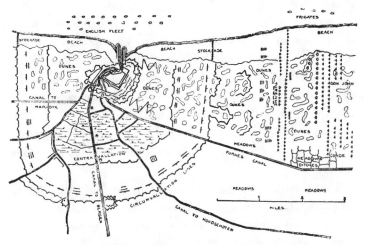

Dunkirk and the Battle of the Dunes.

lands, the canals from Hondschoten and Furnes were repaired, and in twenty-four hours after their completion the army stood upon the Dunes.

The garrison of Dunkirk, though not as large as it should have been, yet numbered nearly three thousand men. Part of these troops had been camped outside, but they were now drawn into the fortress. Don John and Condé, who with their armies were in Brussels, supposed that as a matter of course Turenne would first besiege Furnes, Bergen and

Gravelines, and thus consume much time. Indeed, Don
John reinforced the garrison of St. Omer, believing it to be
threatened rather than Dunkirk. They never gave a thought
to the French being able to reach Dunkirk; nor did they
believe Turenne could there victual his army. Had the
enemy been on hand near Furnes or Bergen, even in small
force, Turenne could hardly have prevented their marching
into Dunkirk and forestalling his operations; but, as is wont
to be the case, Turenne's boldness was an appeal to Fortune
which the fickle goddess could not disregard.

Having reached the place and invested it before the Spaniards knew of his intention to do so, Turenne was scarcely
better off. No materials were at hand to build a line of circumvallation; the wind overnight would blow down the
works which the men had piled up during the day, or the
tide would wash them away; all material had to come from
Calais as well as forage and rations. Turenne was repeating
Condé's experience of a few years before under vastly worse
conditions.

Thunderstruck at the news that Turenne had laid siege to
Dunkirk, Don John and Condé speedily started thither, but
Turenne had already blockaded the sea front by means of the
English troops under Generals Lockhart and Morgan, aided
by the fleet of twenty ships of the line and a number of
frigates, and had protected himself by a line of circumvallation on the land side. The labors of the men were a fit complement of the constancy of their leader. The marshal had
put himself and them in a place where there was but one
outlet, — victory. Had he failed and the French been compelled to retreat, the whole force would beyond a peradventure have been destroyed. There was no choice except to
win; Turenne determined to win, and fortune smiled upon
his efforts. Trenches were opened at the beginning of

summer, on the night of June 4–5, one set for the English, one for the French, and a number of sorties were repulsed. Seven days later, on July 12, Don John, Condé and the whole Spanish army came up, and at once sent forward a force to reconnoitre Turenne's position.

Turenne had already heard of their arrival at Furnes. They had marched so hurriedly that they had brought no artillery, and were ill supplied with infantry ammunition, believing that they could relieve Dunkirk by a *coup de main*, and that Turenne's lines could not be so stout but that they could break through. This was an assumption which might hold in the case of a fortress approachable on all sides, but not in the case of Dunkirk.

Don John called a council of war. Condé advised camping between the canals of Furnes and Hondschoten, to wait for the artillery, and meanwhile to harass the enemy and cut off his rations. Don John decided to advance on Turenne's lines in his actual condition and at once, though the ground was such that his cavalry had not space to manœuvre; nor were there any guns to oppose to those of the French.

The only means of arriving from Furnes, which is near the coast, to the dunes or sandhills on which Dunkirk lies, was by marching between the sea and the Furnes canal. This path was composed solely of beach and dunes, and narrowed as it approached Turenne's lines. It was, moreover, cut up by innumerable little canals and waterways, natural and artificial. However difficult it was to marshal troops on such terrain, the archduke was determined to raise the siege, and Condé had no means of opposing his will.

Turenne, who was not aware of the badly equipped condition of the enemy, saw that his lines were not strong enough to defend against a well-directed attack in force; and he was by nature more inclined to the offensive. He left six thousand men in the trenches to push the work on the siege, which had already reached the counterscarp, but which had not yet got a secure footing, concentrated the rest, nine thousand foot and six thousand horse, with ten guns, behind the works near the sea opposite where the enemy was approaching; personally headed a regiment of cavalry; and on June 13 attacked the Spanish van, consisting of a large force of horse, and drove it back. In the combat Hocquincourt, who had recently gone over to Condé, was killed.

The enemy's main force was still five miles distant. Turenne marched out of his lines and drew up to await the Spaniards, who on the same day advanced into closer contact, while the marshal did the like, seized some of the higher dune-hills, and threw up such works as the sandy soil and absence of material permitted. The rival lines were now within two thousand yards, and both bridged the Furnes canal in several places. A deserter — a page who had fled from his master — came in during the succeeding night and found Turenne wrapped in his mantle, cogitating the events of the morrow. The page brought the news that the enemy had no guns, a fact which gave Turenne fresh ardor. He determined on summary attack, and sent to ask his English allies if they sustained his reasons. " Whenever Marshal Turenne is ready, so are we," said they; " he can give us his reasons after we have whipped the enemy."

The Spaniards probably had no great confidence in Condé; they certainly did not listen to him; they were convinced that Turenne would not attack them, and their dispositions were far from sound. Turenne had sent his train to Mardyk and neighboring places, so as to be prepared for failure as well as success. He now drew up in two lines, with the right flank on the canal and the left on the sea, where the English fleet supported it, the foot in the centre, and the horse, sustained by a few battalions, on either flank, ten squadrons in reserve behind each wing. The English were in the left wing, the French composed the right and part of the left. A flying column of horse lay behind the army to head off sorties from the town, or to help any part of the line which might become depleted.

The Spanish army had fourteen thousand men, of which six thousand were horse, but their artillery, as reported, had not come up, and all their force was not put in; for part, it is alleged, had been sent out foraging. They approached quite near the French position, having set up the foot in the front line, the horse in the second, posted on the right in four lines, on the left in six or eight lines, on account of the narrow terrain — which was barely a league in width — between the Furnes canal and the sea. Don John commanded the Spanish right, Condé the left. In this position they spent the night. Next day, June 14, Turenne, with entire confidence that he should beat the enemy, marched forward, attacked them at daybreak with a heavy artillery fire, and then followed up the attack with his troops. The enemy's outposts were driven in, and Turenne was anxious to get at the main line; but in his memoirs he complains of the slowness of the march in line of battle. It was indeed slow at that day, and the guns, hard to work, could deliver but four or five shots during the advance.

When Don John observed the English fleet manœuvring off the shore, he feared to send his cavalry into action along the beach, lest it should be destroyed by the fire of the ships, and drew it up in rear of the infantry. Thus his right flank was not protected in the usual manner by horse, and the foot felt the less secure. The English regiments advanced with determination and fell on the enemy's right, where stood the best

Spanish foot, well posted on a dune-hill; and they were sustained by cross-fire from the fleet and by the action of the left-wing French horse, which joined in the attack on the Spanish right, and then outflanked it by moving along the beach. The English charge, despite stubborn courage, was not at first successful; they advanced thrice, and were thrice rolled back from the dune-hills by main push of Spanish pikes. But British blood was up; they would not be denied; the old Cromwellian heart was there. " The French fight like men; but those English fight like demons," said Don John, who with Caracena bravely sought to repair their errors by honest Spanish gallantry. The beach being disgarnished of Spanish troops, the French were able in addition to the cavalry to get some guns trained on the Spanish right flank on the dune-hills and to batter it heartily. The Spanish cavalry was well to the rear, and in such close masses that it could not disengage itself to charge.

Meanwhile the French infantry of the centre, struggling through the deep sand, smartly fell on the main line, and after some close work drove it in. The Spaniards of the right, thus taken in front and on both flanks, were finally defeated with great slaughter, fled in confusion, and were sharply pursued, though Condé sent some horse out to take in reverse the French squadrons, which had advanced too far.

On the Spanish left, where Condé stood, the ground was not so easily won. Condé had divined that defeat lay before the allies. " Have you ever been in a battle? " asked he of the duke of Gloucester before the action opened. " No." " Well, you 'll see a big one lost in half an hour," rejoined Condé. But he hoped to cut through and succor Dunkirk. Créqui commanded on the French right; Turenne was everywhere. At the outset the Spanish first line of troops was unsettled by the demoralization of two battalions, who fled

after one discharge. Turenne attacked with his cavalry and
drove back Condé four hundred paces; but Condé rallied,
charged with his massed column on the less numerous French
horse, threw it back six hundred paces, and all but broke
through Turenne's line, though the infantry behaved with
stanchness; and finally the mass of foot on the dunes
stopped his progress. Fearing disaster in case Condé made
another charge, Turenne headed some fresh horse in person
to forestall such an event, and after desperate fighting, — the
Spanish left being weakened by the disaster to the right, —
drove in his line and almost captured the prince himself,
whose cavalry had got dispersed. The victory was complete,
and Turenne, careful not to give Condé an opportunity to
rally, followed it smartly up.

During the battle the garrison under the marquis of Leyden made a hearty sortie, and reached and burned the tents
of the battalions in the besieging lines; but he was eventually driven back.

The French loss was small; the Spanish army lost one
thousand men, killed and wounded, and three thousand prisoners. It fled to Furnes, to which place Turenne followed,
and here, under the guns of the fortress, pursuit was checked.
On the advice of the duke of York, the Spanish army shut
itself up in the fortresses, Condé in Ostende, Fuensaldegna
in Nieuport, Don John in Bruges, and the prince of Ligny
in Ypres. Such was the battle of the Dunes.

Having pursued the beaten army as far as Furnes, Turenne
returned to the siege, which he prosecuted with vigor. The
English had been gallant and useful in the battle, but they
were less practiced in sieges and could not do much here. A
lodgment was made on the counterscarp by a sharp attack,
and the besiegers made their way to the foot of the last
work. Shortly, on June 25, Dunkirk surrendered, it being

the ninth day after the battle, and was, according to agreement, delivered to the English. The siege had cost many men on both sides ; one half the garrison had fallen. Leyden was killed.

Few sieges redound more to the credit of any captain than Dunkirk to that of Turenne. The courage with which he undertook an almost hopeless task, because it was the thing to be done, and the constancy with which he carried the work to completion, are admirable from every standpoint.

Two days after the surrender of Dunkirk, Bergen was surrounded ; trenches were opened ; next day the outworks were captured and a lodgment made in the counterscarp ; and on the 29th the place surrendered its garrison of nine hundred men as prisoners of war. Furnes, which had but eighty men, also capitulated. Turenne sent a body of troops to Rousbrügge to watch Ypres, and marched to Dixmuiden, which lay between the four fortresses above named, took it July 6, after no great effort, and thus cut the Spanish army in four parts. He was planning to move on Nieuport and Ostende, hoping to destroy the enemy in detail, when Mazarin, owing to the king's illness, unwisely commanded him to cease operations.

On the king's recovering, to give La Ferté a chance to distinguish himself he was sent to besiege Gravelines, while Turenne sent an observing detachment to Nieuport, held his own position at Dixmuiden, and thus protected him, in addition to reinforcing him with a thousand men. An army under Marsin coming from Luxemburg by the upper Lys and Ypres to relieve Gravelines, Turenne took post at Dunkirk, and put out a curtain of detachments to head Marsin off ; the latter retired again to Ypres and the upper Lys. La Ferté took Gravelines in twenty-six days, after much loss and rather inexpertly, and then went back to France.

Partly from La Ferté's troops, Turenne then placed a reserve of ten thousand foot and ten thousand horse at Hesdin to protect the frontier; assembled the rest at Dixmuiden, and marched on the Lys and the Scheldt, sending raiders as far as Brussels; won Oudenarde, surprised and beat the prince of Ligny at the Lys, captured Ypres, September 26, in a five days' siege, rested his troops a few days, covered for four weeks the new building of works at Menin and Oudenarde, and took Grammont and Ninove. He had thus overrun a large part of the Spanish Netherlands. As December came on, Turenne left five thousand men in the captured fortresses, and returned with the rest to France.

This remarkable campaign — the siege of Dunkirk, the battle of the Dunes and the overrunning of the Netherlands — greatly aided in making the terms of the treaty of the Pyrenees favorable to France. Turenne was created Maréchal général des armées; had he been willing to change his religion, he could have become constable of France.

Turenne exhibited military and personal gifts of the very highest order. If he had been independent so as to work on a larger scale, he might possibly have reached equality with the six great captains. But he was always hampered by the political difficulties of the king, and particularly by the enmity of the ministers. He possessed the intellect and character, but never had the requisite opportunity. On the other hand Condé, while full of the resources which make the battle-captain, and brilliant in some ways which Turenne was not, boasted qualities of endurance, patience and equanimity less marked than his opponent. One can imagine Condé beating Turenne in a great battle, but one would expect Turenne to win any campaign from Condé under equal conditions.

After the peace of the Pyrenees in 1659, Condé was reinstated in all his honors and property, returned home and

entered the service of France. France received some territorial enlargements, especially in the Spanish Netherlands;
the duke of Lorraine was partially reinstated; and Louis
XIV. married Maria Theresa, daughter of the king of Spain,
who, in consideration of a dowry, renounced her right of
inheritance.

French Dragoon.
(17th Century.)

XLV.

ARMY ORGANIZATION AND TACTICS. EARLY SEVEN-TEENTH TO EARLY EIGHTEENTH CENTURY.

STANDING armies became common in the seventeenth century. No great improvemepts were made, except in details; the method was cumbrous; Gustavus' system was imitated in letter and not in spirit. Bayonet and flint-lock were introduced; cavalry grew lighter; uniforms came into general use; and companies, squadrons and regiments were more regular in strength. Artillery was not up to Gustavus' scale of lightness, but ordnance and the theory of gunnery improved. In 1648 the foot still habitually stood in eight ranks; but Turenne reduced the depth, and later it got down to three. The horse also rode in three ranks; but the cavalryman rarely used cold steel. Marches were in several columns, and were slow, as roads often had to be made. Good positions rather than intrenched camps came into favor; but battle was less considered than manœuvring. Pursuit was rare; outpost service began; armies grew to be larger; pontoons were now common; and the baggage trains were enormous. Rationing was awkwardly done, but medical service grew in efficiency. Generals were usually much hampered by the governments. Engineering developed more than any other art; fortresses became numerous and strong. The era was one of sieges, manœuvres on the enemy's communications and small war. Battles lacked character and were usually accidental. The spade almost replaced the musket; armies moved from one strong place to another, or from siege to siege. War lost some of its horrors, but was still costly in men and material. Whatever success was won by any general came from his own ability.

By the middle of the seventeenth century nations had learned, in large part from the lessons of the Thirty Years' War, that there was not only more security, but more economy in keeping on foot at all times at least the skeleton organization of a considerable body of troops, than there was in discharging at the end of every campaign the men who had fought through it, and making new levies for the next one. Hence, following in the footsteps of Sweden, standing armies may be said to have become universal towards the end of this century, a fact which naturally fostered more careful discipline and a deeper study of the real problems of war. After Sweden, France was the first country, under the leadership of Louvois, the Great Monarch's great — if narrow — war minister, to found a permanent force; Brandenburg, under the Great Elector, followed; and other nations gradually dropped into line. After this period only a part of the forces under the colors were disbanded at the close of any given war.

The period following the Peace of Westphalia in 1648 gave no great impulse to the art of war proper, but though the foundation on which men worked was an unreal one, there were many and marked improvements in matters of detail. During the era of Gustavus Adolphus it was Sweden that led in shaping war towards its modern conditions; during the era of Louis XIV. (*le grand siècle*) it was France.

So far as the infantry went, the chief improvements were in the armament, — the introduction of bayonet and flintlock. The bayonet, said to have been first used in 1660 by General Martinet (father of rigidity in.drill and discipline), and to have originated in Bayonne, gave the death-blow to the pikemen, for the musketeer was now equipped for both distant and hand to hand fighting; and the flint-lock made the fire of a line of foot much more rapid and telling. The several armies of Europe, which had essentially varied in form from the Spanish masses to the Swedish three-rank line, grew to a much greater resemblance in organization and appearance; the light and heavy foot, as separate arms, disappeared, and the only light troops remaining were the *compagnies franches* of France, the *Jäger* or *Schützen* of Germany, and the *Pandours* of Austria. Grenadiers for hurling hand grenades made their appearance, first by companies, then by regiments.

Uniforms were introduced by Louis XIV. in his guards in 1665, and gradually came into general use. There had been uniforms before, but all the troops did not wear them; a company or a regiment was a harlequin affair compared to the troops of the eighteenth century.

The company was the tactical unit, but it consisted of varying numbers, from fifty or sixty men in France to two or three hundred in Austria. Battalions varied equally, from five companies in Brandenburg to seventeen in France.

The cavalry was made lighter in arms and equipment. The first idea of the knight, on the discovery of gunpowder, had been to encase himself and his steed in impenetrable steel; but as firearms had gained in penetration, horse armor finally disappeared, and only helmet and breastplate remained to the heavy trooper. Pistols, carbines and musketoons were the firearms of the cavalry; a sword or sabre the cold weapon. Dragoons carried the infantry musket with a bayonet, and came more and more into favor. They, with cuirassiers and irregular light horse, made up the bulk of the mounted troops; but mounted grenadiers were also introduced.

The squadron was the tactical unit of the cavalry, and consisted of a total of about one hundred and seventy men in three companies. The regiments varied from four hundred to eighteen hundred men in strength, according to the decade or the country.

Artillery ceased to be merely a guild of cannoneers, as it had long been, and became an inherent part of the army. More intelligence was devoted to, and more money spent on, this arm; it grew in strength and importance, and was markedly improved. But while artillery service ceased to be a trade, it did not put on the dignity of a special arm, nor was artillery of any great utility in the field until well along in the eighteenth century. Guns, however, in imitation of the Swedes, were lightened, particularly so in France; powder was gradually compounded on better recipes; gunmetal was improved; paper and linen cartridges were introduced; gun-carriages were provided with the aiming wedge; and many new styles of guns and mortars, and ammunition for them were invented. Science lent its aid to practical men, and not only exhausted chemical ingenuity in preparing powder and metal, but mathematical formulas were made for the artilleryman, and the value of ricochet firing was discovered. Louis XIV. founded several artillery schools, and the creation of arsenals was begun. Finally the artillery was organized on a battery and regimental basis, and careful rules were made for the tactics of the guns. These were served by dismounted men and generally hauled by contract horses.

But although sensibly improved, the artillery, in addition to being slow of fire, was still unskillfully managed; it stood in small bodies all along the line of battle; and being heavy and hard to haul, principally because the same guns were used for sieges and for field work, it was far from being, even relatively to the other arms, the weapon which it is to-day.

At the end of the Thirty Years' War the infantry habitually stood in eight ranks, the pikemen in the centre and the musketeers on the flanks. Gustavus had made a six-deep file, which deployed to fire into one three deep; but though this was not at once taken up by the other nations, even those who were his admirers and imitators, still the improvement in firearms necessarily led to a less deep formation. It was Turenne who first reduced the French file to six men; whence it was further diminished to four, three and even two men. The ranks stood four paces apart, but closed up to fire, and doubled up for a charge. The formation of squares was common, a relic of the Spanish "battles."

The horse rode in three ranks, of which the third was often trained to file out, ploy into closer order, and envelop the enemy's flanks. The squadrons stood at squadron distance from each other. The French at times rode in two ranks, to make a longer front. The drill manœuvres of the cavalry were simple, and commonly performed at a trot.

The improvement of firearms had one lamentable sequence, — the troops forgot that at times they must still rely on the cold steel; they deemed a stout fire the best attack that could be given; and a bold and skillful manœuvre or an assault, even though crowned with success, was looked upon as a dangerous departure from correct precedent, — a blunder. Even the cavalry (except the Swedish) so far forgot its rôle as to believe that its fire was its strongest point. In any event a few salvos were given before a charge, if one was made, and by such tactics cavalry soon lost its *élan.* Even in a charge they rode at a slow trot, and the dragoons mostly fought as and with the infantry. Few men were capable of doing what Condé did at Rocroy. He was an exception in the use of cavalry.

Marches were conducted in what seems to us a highly cumbrous fashion. As a general rule, an army moved in three, five or more columns, the middle one consisting of the artillery and trains, and the outer ones of cavalry. This demanded the preparation of roads, and cost much labor and loss of time, compensated for only by the enemy being tied down by the same method. To change a camp to a place ten miles distant, if in the presence of the enemy, roads would be constructed so as to enable the troops to move according to a given formula in a set number of columns. The roads all over Europe, from early winter to late spring, fully six months, were impassable, and necessitated going into winter-quarters, and during this season superior officers were apt to go off on leave of absence. It was only a man of exceptional energy who would conduct a winter campaign.

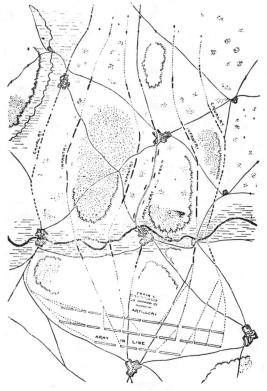

Army on the March.

Armies no longer so uniformly intrenched their camps; they took up advantageous positions; and tents replaced barracks. They camped in a sort of order of battle with company streets, the foot in the centre and the cavalry on the flanks. Able generals made their camps coincide with the topography; not so the average officer.

But the lack of mobility of organized forces was their chief characteristic. Manœuvres were slow and cumbrous. Even the French could not manœuvre as we understand it; and so soon as an army sought to go beyond the simplest tactics or to change its parallel order in battle, so soon did it run the risk of dissolution. What Gustavus had accomplished in this respect did not outlive him. He was away in advance of his era. His adaptation of the smaller details to the movement of an army was as skillful as his larger views of strategy were profound. Not even Swedish troops after his death manœuvred as rapidly and skillfully as his own Royal Army.

Battle was the last thing thought of except by such men as Condé, Turenne, Prince Eugene or Marlborough. When one occurred, it was rather apt to be a battle of accident; a deliberately planned engagement was rare. A decisive battle like Rocroy, Allerheim, Blenheim or Turin was yet more rare. Few generals, when they fought, did so in other than in parallel order. Flank attacks, not to speak of grand-tactics, as Frederick or Napoleon understood them, were almost unheard of. The English were perhaps as original as any other people in this matter, and sought to make the infantry and cavalry sustain each other in their attack.

Pursuit, as Alexander had pursued, was unknown. Even after a great victory, the victors remained on the field of battle. It was looked on as a sort of blunder to pursue, lest the enemy should turn and renew the battle. A bridge of gold was to be preferred.

Outpost service was begun in this era, and reached a considerable development. This was looked on as the best school for the soldier. Small war and manœuvring over extensive territory were the operations most highly considered. To manœuvre your enemy out of his chosen position was deemed

a greater feat, and more in accordance with the true princi-
ples of the art, than to destroy or disable his army in a great
battle.

Compared with earlier times, the armies of the last part
of this era were numerically large, — the armies of France
reaching often a total as high as two hundred thousand men.
The proper ratio of the three arms was by no means settled. Cavalry was proportionately numerous, at times quite
equaling the infantry, or even exceeding it, while in line it
occupied thrice the space. Artillery averaged one gun per
thousand men.

Pontoon trains grew to be more common, and an immense
amount of private baggage and numerous camp followers
cumbered the army trains, to such an extent that the tale of
non-combatants often rose to equal the for-duty roster.

It had become the fashion to imitate the methods of Gustavus Adolphus, but it was generally only the letter and not
the spirit which was imitated. This applied to the system of
victualing armies from established magazines. The principal
magazine of any given army was as a rule a fortress, where
large supplies were accumulated. In case of danger, the
meal or flour was baked into bread at the magazine ; otherwise
it was transported two or three days' march towards the
army, and there baked in field bakeries. Bread for from six
to nine days was sent forward to the troops. As the ration
was not composed of concentrated material, this required
immense trains, which were managed by contractors. Soldiers were expected to carry three days' rations in their hav-
ersacks, a supply which they eked out by depredations on the
country. Detachments baked in the neighboring towns :
small ones were boarded by the inhabitants.

All this practically prevented troops from moving to any
distance from their magazines. When an army had got five

days' march away from its principal magazine, it must sit down and wait for the establishment of a new one. While this made it reasonably certain that the troops would be fed, it prevented any but the slowest and most limited movements. Turenne broke through this magazine habit, and frequently rationed his army by forced requisitions on the country. At times his marches were rapid and extensive.

Medical service was more carefully attended to in this era than ever before. Especially the French had an excellent hospital staff attached to its armies; not excellent in the sense of our Sanitary Commission or the Red Cross service, but a marked gain on what existed in the previous generations. For in almost all wars prior to this period, to be severely wounded meant, if massacre was escaped, to be left to the tender mercies of the elements, or to the robbery and violence of the human wolves who prowled about the battlefields.

A marked factor in the slow and trammeled method of the armies of this era was the control exercised over generals in the field by the home government, either king or minister. A general had his plan of campaign marked out to him by men quite unfamiliar with war, and certain geographical limitations were set to his action, irrespective of any conditions which might arise. Marshal Turenne was a noteworthy example of this pernicious interference. And as, moreover, wars were wont to be conducted by allies, the general of each army being subject to separate control, as well as not infrequently at odds with his fellows, the lack of vigor and purpose was scarcely to be wondered at. We have only to recall Condé in the service of the Spanish government, to see how great this evil might be.

But in the armies themselves, the imitation of Gustavus, even if misguided, had brought about a much better state of

discipline than had theretofore existed.   Except that gold
and family influence were potent to secure military commis-
sions or unearned promotion, and that luxury was rampant
in many of the armies, — things never tolerated by Gustavus,
— this feature is a distinct tribute to the great Swede.

The end of the seventeenth and beginning of the eighteenth century formed a brilliant epoch in engineering.   Especially in France and the Netherlands, such distinguished men
as Vauban and Coehorn carried this branch of the military
art far beyond other countries.   Fortifications covered every
part of Europe.   Whole frontiers bristled with them, and
every important town became a fortress.   The skill with
which works were erected to resist the armament of the day
is beyond praise.

The art of besieging was equally advanced by the introduction of parallels and ricochet firing, and in the improvements of the methods of approach.

This era, then, is one of the growth of deployments for
firing, as against the massing of troops ; of the use of cold
steel ; of brilliant advance in engineering ; of wrong or mistaken theories and singular immobility of armies.   Yet it
was an era which continued the good work begun by Gustavus Adolphus, and helped to lay the foundation for the
new art of war to be soon expounded by the great masters,
Frederick and Napoleon.

Owing to the general introduction of firearms, and to
the vast increase of material of war, which it was deemed
essential to transport with the armies ; and owing to the
necessity of securely keeping this material and of safely
bringing it to the front, there grew to be a nervous dread on
the part of the commanding officers, of being severed from
their communications.   Gustavus had introduced method into
war ; his successors and imitators sought to reduce his

method to a set of theoretical rules, which should bind every one, under however varying factors. As in the case of other great captains, Gustavus' imitators failed to understand his method, and while copying his detail, quite lost sight of his general aim. Unmindful of changed conditions, forgetful that Gustavus could be bold and rapid as well as methodical and cautious, the theorists of this era sought, by blind adherence to his system of slow and cautious manœuvres, to develop a new art of war. So soon as they entered a territory, they intrenched themselves so as to be sure to hold it; they contented themselves with capturing or defending fortresses; they dared not move far from their magazines lest these should be cut off by the enemy, and they rarely went beyond the conduct of small war. The fact that the early wars of this era were largely in the Netherlands, a country dotted with fortified towns, and cut by numerous rivers, dikes and artificial streams, increased the timidity of the prevailing method, and reduced operations to cautious manœuvring to cut the enemy's or preserve one's own communications with important magazines.

It was deemed practically impossible to pass an enemy's fortress without leaving a large force to observe it. Sieges were long, and costly in men and material; a captured town was wont to be destroyed during or after the siege; and the vicinity was invariably reduced to a desert. Or, at a given period in the siege, the garrison capitulated, marched out to join its own forces, and large sums were spent to repair the damage done. The more fortresses an army of invasion captured the more garrisons it detailed, and the weaker it became; the enemy, meanwhile, gaining as it lost.

The objective of a campaign was, as a rule, the capture of some special fortress, and one half the army would besiege it while the other manœuvred to keep the enemy from approaching to raise the siege. If it was a campaign of manœuvres on the enemy's communications, the army was split up into detachments, each of which conducted an absurd small war, in the belief that the sum of the small successes would add up to as much as the result of one great victory. More than half the time, armies were consuming bread, and using up material, without doing any acts which, according to our estimate, fall under the head of conducting serious war.

As pursuit was never made, so battles lacked character and decisiveness. This grew to be so marked a feature of the system that military men finally came to condemn battles as costly in lives and unfruitful in results. To come to battle was deemed almost a blunder; such a campaign as 1646 or 1675 was deemed to show higher skill than those culminating in distinguished battles, even if decisive; and except Blenheim, Turin and Ramillies, all the general engagements of this era might in a sense be called useless, for no results followed on a victory. The march on and battle of Turin was a brilliantly conceived and ably conducted operation, taken as a whole, the best of this era; but even Blenheim and Ramillies were fruitful quite as much by accident as by design. The battles of Condé and Turenne were in no sense as clear in design and decisive in results as was Turin; or indeed as were Breitenfeld or Lützen.

With the disappearance of battles as a factor in the success of operations, there arose a false estimate of the value of movements or positions taken to sever the communications of the enemy, or to conserve one's own. A general who compelled his enemy to retreat by cutting him off from his magazines of food or war-material was held to do a more able act than one who in a great battle destroyed his enemy's army; and he was honored accordingly. Thus the usual campaign was narrowed down to operations against the enemy's communications, to feints to draw his attention from the real manœuvre, to attacks on isolated places by lesser detachments, and to small war of all kinds. Armies sought positions of security and intrenched, or else shut themselves up in fortified towns or camps. Nothing was done without the aid of strong lines. It was the era of the spade. The general who best understood how to suit his works to his position was the man who won. For to attack a fortified line was deemed a hazard not to be lightly undertaken.

War lost somewhat of its horrors, to be sure, but the loss of men, owing to the long drawn out character of the operations, was no less than of yore ; and the expenditure of wealth was greater. Wars were wont to be ended by the exhaustion of the exchequer of one or other opponent, not by any particular military success.

The result of all this misapplication of principle was that, with the exception of a few brilliant generals, war was conducted on an entirely fictitious basis. Nothing in war except the campaigns of these generals can be deemed other than trivial. Even they were often trammeled by the slow and ill-conceived method of the day. Whatever success was won by Turenne, Condé, Eugene, Marlborough, Montecuculi, Vendome and Villars was due to their own individuality and strength. But though it is their campaigns which developed whatever growth there was, none of them can be said to have earned the place in the rank of Great Captains which is clearly due to Gustavus Adolphus.

Pistol Sword. (16th Century.)

XLVI.

TURENNE IN HOLLAND. 1672.

WHILE the other European powers were busy, Louis XIV. saw a chance to conquer the Netherlands, and in 1667–68, with Turenne leading, he overran Flanders, and Vauban fortified it. Meanwhile Condé conquered Franche Comté. The Dutch formed a Triple Alliance with Sweden and England to restore the balance of power ; but in 1672 this was broken up, and Louis had such allies that he could invade Holland from the east. Under Turenne and Condé, Louis' army, one hundred thousand strong, entered Holland. The generals advised destroying all the fortresses they took so as not to parcel out the troops in garrisons, and to push on to Amsterdam ; but Louis and Louvois, his war-minister, could not see so far ; time was lost, and William of Orange flooded the country, and prevented an advance. In August Turenne, with seventeen thousand men, was sent to head off the two armies under the Great Elector and Montecuculi, forty-three thousand strong, which were marching to the relief of Holland ; and was ordered also to protect Alsatia. Though much hampered by his instructions, he was able, by skillful operations, to prevent the two allied armies from joining, and both returned homeward.

RICHELIEU had left France the most powerful nation of Western Europe, and Mazarin followed in his footsteps. The native abilities of Louis XIV., who succeeded to the government in 1661, were well seconded by the executive power of his ministers, Colbert and Louvois, of whom the first doubled the revenue without correspondingly oppressing the people, and the latter reorganized the army and made it an excellent fighting machine.

The other European powers had each its own serious troubles. Spain had been drained by the late wars ; England under the Stuarts had lost the importance it had possessed under Cromwell ; Holland was mainly devoted to fostering its trade, and increased its fleet to the detriment of its army; Germany was so completely exhausted by the Thirty Years' War as to be out of the race; Austria was equally weak, and could scarcely hold head to the Hungarian insurrection and the war with Turkey.

Louis XIV. saw an excellent opportunity of increasing his territory by conquering Brabant and Flanders, to whose possession he alleged a right on behalf of his wife, the daughter of Philip IV. of Spain, just dead. The right was no better nor worse than any other *casus belli* of the day; the ambition of Louis is a sufficient explanation. The alleged claim was that the Spanish possessions in the Belgian provinces were personal estates of the Spanish Hapsburgs, and that their descent should naturally follow local law, which would give these provinces to Maria Theresa. That she had renounced her right of inheritance was voided, Louis alleged, by the non-payment of her dowry.

In 1667–68, with Turenne at the head of his principal army, Louis overran Flanders, in a campaign which was more like a triumphal march than serious war; and Vauban was directed to put the conquered fortresses in a condition of perfect defense. In 1668 Condé conquered Franche Comté with equal ease, overrunning the province in two weeks.

John De Witt, Pensioner of Holland, alarmed at these unwarranted proceedings, and fearful for the independence of his fatherland, formed with England and Sweden a Triple Alliance to preserve the balance of power. This temporarily forestalled Louis' plans, and at the peace of Aix la Chapelle in 1668, France returned Franche Comté to Spain and received in exchange twelve fortresses, among them Lille, Tournay and Oudenarde, on the Spanish Netherlands frontier. This was but an interlude, for Louis harbored a solid hatred for Holland, where refugees from France were protected and allowed to issue their abusive pamphlets. In 1672 Louis, with that clever diplomatic intrigue in which he and his advisers were easily first, made a private treaty in which he purchased Charles II. of England, and another with Sweden. These treaties broke up the Triple Alliance; and by able manipulations Louis managed to enlist against Holland the sympathies of Emperor Leopold I., the Great Elector Frederick William of Brandenburg, the duke of Neuenburg, the pope, and the duke of Savoy; while other interested powers, including the king of Denmark and the electors of Trier and Mainz, remained neutral. Savoy promised three thousand men. Cologne and Münster were prevailed on to join France, and this important accession enabled Louis to create magazines near by her border and to invade Holland from the weakest spot, the east, where only partially fortified cities, such as Arnhem, Doesburg, Zütphen and Deventer, lay; whereas, on the south, opposite France, Holland was very strong, being protected by the Meuse and the Waal, and by a series of strong places, among them Bergen op Zoom, Breda, Herzogenbusch (Bosch), Grave and Nymwegen, in addition to the outlying fortress of Maestricht with a heavy garrison of thirteen thousand men; and on the lower Rhine, Wesel, Emmerich, Rheinberg and other fortified towns. That Louis was angry at Holland for setting bounds to his late attempt at conquest, and jealous of her blooming commerce, was an augury that the war would be more than mere play. The German alliances procured for Louis an accession of twenty thousand troops. He was overwhelmingly strong.

Turenne drew up the plans for the campaign, to which Condé contributed his approval. Depots of victual and material were to be established in the territory of Cologne and Münster, whence the invasion was to be made as a base; and instead of wasting time on besieging sundry fortresses, the armies were to disregard these, turn them or observe them, and march as a body on Amsterdam, the capital. If fortresses were taken, they were to be dismantled, to save the detailing of garrisons, and thus weakening the main body of troops. This excellent plan, which distinctly foreshadowed the new art of war, was carried out so far only as the march

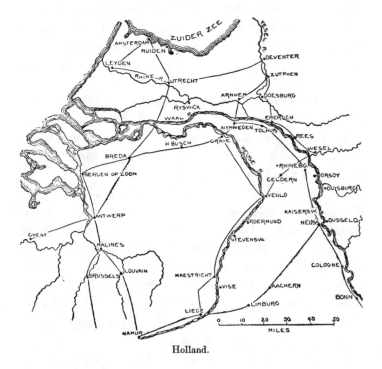

Holland.

into Holland from the east was concerned. Louis and Louvois were not abreast with such intelligent ideas. It was only such an intellect as Turenne possessed which could grasp the advantages and promise of such a scheme.

The French army was one hundred and two thousand strong, and was early assembled in cantonments: sixty thousand between the Sambre and Meuse, thirty thousand between the Meuse and Moselle, and twelve thousand in the Cologne district. This force was then concentrated in two main bodies, one of sixty thousand men under the king, with the duke of Orleans and Turenne as leaders, and one of twenty-five thousand men under Condé, while a number of smaller detachments were to be devoted to various outside purposes. At sea the Count d'Estrées, with forty-four ships of the line, was to join the duke of York with fifty. It should be noted that Condé and Turenne had become reconciled; the pique of the former had died with time, and they worked in unison and goodfellowship thenceforth.

The Dutch had but twenty-five thousand land troops, and these were mercenaries. But gallant De Ruyter commanded ninety-one ships of the line; the land, cut up by canals and dikes, was excellently calculated for defense, and John De Witt was a man of force and ability.

The French had established magazines in Bonn, Neuss and Kaiserswerth, a fact from which De Witt drew a correct inference as to their intentions; and he proposed that Holland should take the offensive and move into the electorates of Cologne and Münster, there to destroy these stores before the French army had rendezvoused in the vicinity. But jealousies and enmities prevented the recognition of his wisdom; the states-general decided against his plan on the silly plea that France had not yet declared war.

Early in 1672 the French invaded Holland without delaying to besiege Maestricht, which they masked. The main body, under the king, but really led by Condé and Turenne, crossed to the right bank of the Meuse at Visé, above Maestricht, marched on the lower Rhine, and occupied without difficulty the ill-defended fortresses of Orsoy and Rees, which were taken by Turenne, and Wesel and Emmerich, which surrendered to Condé, as well as some others, the garrisons of all of which were either frightened into surrender by the native populace, or their commanders — as a cheaper plan — bribed by the French generals. Condé and Turenne then, in the face of the enemy, and with a promptness which gave them a marked moral advantage over the Dutch — though the operation itself was easy — crossed the Rhine near Toll-huis, below Emmerich, at a place where, owing to the low water of this year, the most part of the stream could be forded by the cavalry, and there was scarce a hundred feet to swim. There was some small opposition made by a body of Dutch troops, but the French cavalry van soon drove it off; and a bridge having been thrown, the rest of the horse and all the foot speedily crossed. Condé was wounded, and being moreover prostrated by the gout, Turenne remained in sole control.

The prince of Orange had taken position at Arnhem beyond the Yssel with the Dutch army, but on Turenne's advance he retired from this position towards Utrecht, rather than have Arnhem turned, as Turenne manifestly proposed to do. Turenne passed the Yssel near its mouth and occupied Arnhem. He now urged the king to push immediately on with the entire force towards Amsterdam, to which the road was quite open, and to within a few miles of which city some advanced parties, four thousand strong, sent ahead under Rochefort, had already penetrated.

De Ruyter had some success against the allied fleets; but at this time — August 27 — the De Witts fell a sacrifice to an unreasoning popular tumult, and had Turenne's plan been carried out, nothing could have saved Holland. William of Orange, then twenty-two years old, was made stadtholder, and put at the head of affairs. Louis, at Louvois' instance, did just the reverse of what Turenne advised; he divided his army into detachments and set to work besieging the fortresses of Nymwegen, Doesburg, Grave, Herzogenbusch and others, and parceled out his forces in garrisoning the captured places. The Dutch were never lacking in self - sacrifice for their little land, and they now resorted to extreme measures. The opening of the sluices and the cutting of the dikes put the whole country under water, and saved Amsterdam and the province of Holland from the French invasion. This inundation could have been prevented by Rochefort's seizing Muiden, where is situated the inlet of the canals ; but this he foolishly omitted to do, though the place was within his grasp ; and, having covered the country with water, William placed his army of thirteen thousand men upon the principal dikes leading to Amsterdam, now the only high roads for advance or retreat. The operations were thus limited so that a small force was the equal of a big one, and William was able to conclude alliances with Austria, Spain, Brandenburg, most of Germany and Denmark, and later too with England. Thus came about a general European war.

To the peculiar terrain of Holland was in large measure due the course undertaken by Louis and Louvois. No country has ever been so profusely sown with fortresses, small and great; no country is easier to defend, harder to attack. The Dutch were good soldiers, and fought tenaciously for such fortresses as Maestricht, Lüttich and Namur, such towns as Brussels and Antwerp. Another reason prevailed for the peculiar irregularity of Dutch operations. During all the wars of this era in the Low Countries, the troops under arms belonged to many nations and races, and served under many commanders ; and it was no more due to the numerous fortresses than it was to the jealousies of the respective allied governments and of the rival generals, that the campaigns on Dutch soil were wont to be so singularly unsystematic.

Until the opening of winter the flooded country precluded manœuvres of any kind; and Turenne counseled a movement in force against Germany to forestall an attack by the new allies of Holland. But Louvois would not give up his plan of reducing the strong places, to which duty he assigned the duke of Luxemburg; and the latter, with sixteen thousand men, was ordered to take position near Utrecht, which had been recently captured, while Turenne was detached with a paltry force of twelve thousand men to operate to the east of the Meuse and Waal and watch for the crossing of the elector of Brandenburg. Thus by fruitless detachments and sieges, out of a force originally of one hundred thousand men, a bare eighth was allotted to the leading French general with which to do an all-important part of its legitimate work.

Louvois always acted in a jealous, almost a childish spirit towards Turenne, and was constantly doing uncalled-for and unwise things. On payment of a small ransom, for example, he discharged all the garrisons captured in the towns he took, — some thirty thousand men, — thus furnishing the Dutch with fresh troops; while the French were depleting their own numbers by garrisoning these same fortresses. Not that such action was unwarrantable from Louvois' standpoint; but if success was to be sought in worsting the enemy, this was no way to accomplish that end.

In August two new armies came upon the scene: one of twenty-four thousand men, under the Great Elector, moved from Halberstadt towards Hildesheim, and an imperial army of nineteen thousand men under Field-Marshal Montecuculi advanced from Bohemia towards Erfurt; and these two proposed, after making a junction, to cross the Rhine and operate in the rear of Luxemburg, to cut him off from France or compel him to retreat from Holland. The only force to oppose these armies and prevent their crossing the Rhine was

Turenne's army of twelve thousand men. This was in truth a lamentable ending of the brilliant array which crossed the Rhine at Tollhuis not many weeks before.

Turenne knew his opponents, and gauged their plans with skill. He had only boldness and energy to oppose to their numbers. He knew that they would not enter Alsatia, but push direct for Holland; and he believed that they would not operate with unity. Despite his being but one third of the enemy in strength, with a boldness quite at odds with the timorous habit of the day, he determined not to defend the left bank, but to cross the Rhine himself, and by an active offensive seek to checkmate their plan on the right bank. Indeed, Montecuculi had orders, though Turenne was unaware of it, not to conduct an offensive campaign, but to oppose such an one on the elector's part; for the emperor was kept in a state of anxiety by the Turks in Poland and by Hungarian revolts, and was afraid to launch out in a whole-souled manner. Turenne increased his force to seventeen thousand men by detachments from the garrisons of Wesel, Rees and Emmerich, and marched from Wesel up the Lippe to Westphalia. The allies, who were aiming at the same general point to compel the elector of Cologne and the bishop of Münster to restore to the Dutch the territory taken from them, and to give up their alliance with the French, on hearing of Turenne's movements changed their course southerly towards Fulda. Turenne pushed on up the right bank of the Rhine to Coblentz, and forced them to move still further south into the Main region, so that they could not approach the Rhine to effect a crossing until after passing to the south of the Main.

Fearing for Alsatia, though indeed there was no threat to that province, Louis ordered Turenne back to the left bank of the Rhine, and sent Condé with eight thousand men to support him. The prince of Orange made a feint towards the Rhine to aid his allies in crossing it; but the operation, owing to the many though dispersed French detachments in Holland, proved to be slow and weakly conducted. He only captured Fauquemme and made an attempt on Charleroi. The allies, after failing to cross on the usual bridges at Mainz and again at Strasburg, finally managed to put their army over at Mainz on a bridge of their own; but they were soon forced by Turenne and Condé to recross, and winter, sickness and hunger drove them, in January, 1673, back to Lippstadt in Westphalia. This was well; but from Lippstadt there was danger that the allies might march to the west and cross the Yssel into Holland; and Turenne determined to prevent this also.

He had been forbidden by Louvois to again cross the Rhine; but he went back of the minister and, on laying out his scheme, obtained permission from the king to do so. Moving down to Wesel, he put over and marched on Lippstadt with sixteen thousand men. Unable to act together, as Turenne had rightly estimated, the allies gave up the idea of wintering in Westphalia, and retired, the elector to Brandenburg, after Brunswick had refused him shelter and winter-quarters, and Montecuculi to Bohemia.

Thus by cleverly utilizing the want of unity of the allies, Turenne's manœuvres had driven them from the Rhine region back towards their respective bases, and had robbed Holland of two strong allied armies. The Great Elector, dissatisfied with the emperor's laxness, concluded peace with France. This peace was, however, of short duration; for in 1674 he renewed his alliance with Holland.

Pistol Sword. (16th Century.)

XLVII.

MONTECUCULI. 1673.

In 1673 the emperor sent Montecuculi with twenty-five thousand men to join the prince of Orange at Bonn. Turenne, with twenty-three thousand, was given the task to protect Alsatia and to prevent this junction, — two irreconcilable duties. He advised marching to the Böhmerwald, if this was to be done; but permission was refused. Montecuculi feinted towards Alsatia and then marched on the Main. The bishop of Würzburg, though a neutral, opened his bridges to the imperialists and closed them to the French, and Turenne was much delayed. Montecuculi manœuvred with exceeding ability; avoided battle, which Turenne sought to force on him; and made good his crossing of the Main. Turenne, taking out garrisons, had but eighteen thousand men, and could not operate as boldly as he would have liked, owing to his orders to protect Alsatia. Though he knew that Montecuculi would not attempt to enter Alsatia, he yet had to keep south of the Main, having only one bridge. Politics had aided Montecuculi's able manœuvres, and he made his junction with the Dutch at Bonn. This campaign redounds much to his credit.

ONE of the best generals of this era, and the more interesting on account of his Military Memoirs, was Count Raimondo Montecuculi. We have from time to time met him in minor commands previous to the last campaign. Born in Modena in 1608, of a military family, he ran away from home to embrace the career of arms, enlisted and rose from the ranks. He served with Tilly in 1629–30, where he won a name for exceptional bravery. He was in numerous engagements, at the battles of Breitenfeld and Nördlingen, repeatedly led storming parties, was often wounded and captured; and wherever he stood, he distinguished himself. By 1642 he had passed through all ranks to major-general, and two years later he became field-marshal. In the emperor's service he was never out of employment and always at the front. In 1657 he first commanded an independent army, which consisted of twenty thousand men and operated in Silesia, and later he served in Denmark and against the Turks. No general of this period has a better claim to rank with such men as Turenne, Eugene and Marlborough, than Raimondo Montecuculi.

In the spring of 1673 the emperor made a formal declaration of war against France, and planned to push a heavy column under Montecuculi from Bohemia towards the Rhine, where, near Bonn, it should cross and join the prince of Orange, who would pass the Meuse to meet him. Turenne wisely advised that an army be sent to the Böhmerwald — the rugged mountainous country which forms the western boundary of Bohemia — to forestall this movement. But Louvois opposed the plan, and insisted that Turenne should take up a position on the left bank of the Rhine in Alsatia and confine himself to its defense, and to interrupting the two allied armies in their projected junction. He was given twenty-three thousand men to carry out these two utterly inconsistent projects. Again appealing to the king, Turenne obtained leave from him to conduct a defensive campaign on the right bank of the Rhine, but though he desired to manœuvre well to the north of the Main, where he had a number of magazines left over from the last campaign, when he was opposing the junction of the elector of Brandenburg and Montecuculi, he was limited to operating in the Main country proper; and he was particularly warned to do nothing which might

Montecuculi.

offend the neutral states. In other words, his hands were absolutely tied. He furnished the brain and force, but his superiors would not afford him the opportunity. He was held to prevent the junction of the imperial and Dutch armies on his left and to protect Alsatia on his right, and was limited in his movements,— instructions which before he opened the campaign promised failure in both tasks. In his frank but clear manner, Turenne protested that the French troops in the Netherlands were the ones to prevent the junction of the Dutch and imperialists; that to protect Alsatia was quite inconsistent with this duty; but Louvois would no longer give way, and Turenne set about his thankless task.

To mislead Turenne as to his intentions, Montecuculi, after crossing the Böhmerwald, which he did in all security, directed his march, not on Bonn, but towards Nürnberg, as if to move well south of the Main and threaten Alsatia. Turenne, instead of being allowed to manœuvre as he deemed best, was at once ordered from the right to the left bank of the Main, with a strict injunction to pay first heed to Alsatia; but the German princes, who were more inclined to favor the emperor than the French, denied him the use of the neutral bridges at Aschaffenburg and Würzburg; and he was in consequence compelled to build one for himself near Seligenstadt. The spun-out negotiations in respect to these bridges materially delayed him, and when the bishop of Würzburg finally promised neutrality and Turenne was half unwillingly permitted to cross at Aschaffenburg, Montecuculi had already got from Nürnberg into the Main country. After occupying Aschaffenburg and sending his van to establish magazines in Miltenburg, Bishofsheim and various other places along the Tauber, which he deemed the best line to prevent the enemy's access to Alsatia, Turenne crossed the Main with the bulk of the army, and moved to Mergentheim early in September, to get nearer the enemy and ascertain his movements.

Montecuculi was evidently hugging the Main, and Turenne, so soon as he perceived his direction, crossed the Tauber and moved towards the Rothemburg country. The enemy, on September 10, took up a position at Windsheim; Turenne sat down in his front ready to move to right or left as his opponent should head to the Main or towards Alsatia. He was limited in his orders, and knew that he was facing an able general.

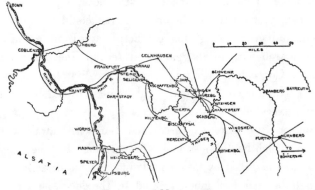

Turenne and Montecuculi.

The imperial general had fifteen thousand foot and ten thousand horse; Turenne, taking out garrisons, had fourteen thousand foot and four thousand horse. Montecuculi's intention was clearly to draw Turenne away from the Main, and then, himself speedily crossing, to oblige the French to take the longer road on the south bank, while he should push straight for Bonn. Although on general probabilities Turenne may have presumed as much, yet he could not divine the purpose of his antagonist, and to defend Alsatia had been made his paramount duty.

Turenne desired battle. If he beat the enemy, he would

have accomplished his end of holding Montecuculi back from both the Rhine and Alsatia; if beaten, he could still retire fighting to the Tauber or the Rhine, and he felt, as always, confident that he should prevail. The object of Montecuculi was to join the prince of Orange intact; to fight was not in his programme; but he did not want Turenne to think so. He had a solid respect for his great opponent, and cared to take no liberties with him. Both generals manœuvred as for battle not far from Rothemburg; and the imperialists drew up in battle-order; but Montecuculi kept out his first line, made no special advances towards accepting battle, and under its protection and before Turenne could marshal his forces and get into fighting contact, started on a skillful flank march with his baggage and second line towards the Main. Concealed by rising ground, the first line followed before Turenne could attack. The manœuvre had been brilliantly executed.

So soon as Turenne discovered the withdrawal of the enemy, which he did just as his preparations had been completed, he marched by his own left in the same direction, and though he had lost much ground by the delay, he overtook the enemy. The imperial army, for fear of having its tactical shifting of ground turned into a retreat by an attack on its rear, again stopped and drew up; and soon reaching a point opposite the new position of the enemy, Turenne reconnoitred and found that the imperial general had drawn up his line with a hill in his rear and a swamp on both flanks and in front, where he could not be assailed with any chance of success.

That the two armies thus marched on parallel lines in the immediate neighborhood of each other, and without any attack on the part of Turenne, is explainable only by the difficulty in those days of deploying the cumbrous battalions into battle-order. Even the flankers did not seriously exchange fire, and Turenne was able to pick up but a few stragglers and wagons. The ideas of old soldiers who have served in these days of rapid manœuvres must be modified before they can appreciate the operations of an army of the seventeenth century.

Both armies thus marched north to the angle of the Main, where, September 12, Montecuculi took up position at Markt-breit, and Turenne, restricted in his operations, placed himself in his front, on the hills not far back from the river, watching his chance to attack the imperialists when they should attempt to cross.

Montecuculi had worked hard, and had manifestly gained the advantage. He could now cross the Main. Had Turenne been able to prevent his so doing, it would have seriously limited the operations of the imperial general, and at the same time have protected Alsatia. But Montecuculi had out-manœuvred him, and was well posted on the river. Some critics make this march a long-pondered and deep-laid plan of the imperial marshal; but he himself does not claim it to be so, and it appears rather to have been an operation undertaken on the spur of the moment when he met the French at an unexpected place.

Montecuculi was now admirably placed; the result of his manœuvres was all that he could ask. Nearly all the bridges up the river were at his disposal, for, after some negotiation, the bishop of Würzburg broke his neutrality and allowed Montecuculi any privilege he asked; so that he could take the straight road by Würzburg and Lohr, threaten Aschaf-fenburg, where Turenne had his only bridge, and thus sever his communications with the lower Rhine country. Politics was fighting against Turenne as well as the able conduct of his adversary. Well aware of this fact, Turenne hurried a

few hundred dragoons to reinforce the garrison of Aschaffenburg, and remained with the balance to confront Montecuculi
on the Tauber; for if he committed the error of crossing the
Main before his opponent, the road to Alsatia would be left
open; and though convinced that Montecuculi had not the
slightest intention of invading Alsatia, Turenne might not
disregard his instructions.

Unwilling to remain in the camp he had taken up back
of Ochsenfurt, not only because he saw small chance of interfering with Montecuculi, but because the water supply was
difficult and had already led to some hostile exchanges,
Turenne sent the train ahead September 19, and next day
the army followed. Wertheim and places enough on the
Tauber were occupied to protect the magazines and to
overawe the population, which was anti-French to the core.
Glad to be rid of his opponent without battle, Montecuculi,
whose reinforcements had run his force up to forty thousand
men, left Marktbreit September 26, and pursuing the straight
road, crossed the Main at Kitzingen September 27, and
again at Würzburg next day, and camping at Zellingen,
began to construct two bridges at Lohr to again reach the
right bank. Once there, Montecuculi would have all Turenne's magazines north of the Main at his mercy, and indeed
did carry off one convoy.

While at Zellingen, Montecuculi's army was in the *cul-
de-sac* here formed by a northerly bend of the Main; but
Turenne declined to attack him, as the country was heavily
wooded and unfavorable, contained no suitable battle-ground,
and especially as since Montecuculi's reinforcements had
arrived, he had with him but an inferior force. Circumstances had compelled him to parcel out his army, because
limited to a defensive campaign; while Montecuculi kept the
imperialists in one body and well in hand, with a clean-cut

purpose. What here happened well illustrates the advantages of the initiative.

Anxious to ascertain Montecuculi's intention, whether to march on Coblentz or to attack Aschaffenburg, whose garrison he had now increased to one thousand men, Turenne sent a large cavalry party to Wertheim to observe the river up and down, and throw a bridge at Miltenburg, to which he built a bridge-head. Montecuculi, with his larger army, could readily hold Turenne on the left bank and commit havoc on the right by suitable detachments; and Turenne, under his limited instructions, had to be watchful to commit no error. He sent and led out several reconnoitring parties, but ascertained little, for the enemy kept a heavy curtain of parties out. On October 3 Montecuculi crossed at Lohr and broke the bridges. He was now nearer Aschaffenburg and Frankfort than the French, and he made a clever feint as if to threaten Turenne's bridge. With the idea, fostered by the parties which the imperial general sent out to observe the river, that Montecuculi might possibly recross the Main, if only as a diversion, the French marshal strengthened all the places from Rothemburg to Aschaffenburg so as to make the line of the Tauber and Main a network of troops. But when Turenne learned that Montecuculi had marched to Gelnhausen on the road to Frankfort, he made a strong demonstration on Steinheim, opposite Hanau, to lead his opponent to believe that he would cross there, — an operation which had some effect on the neutrality of Frankfort, but in no wise hindered the enemy. Montecuculi then pushed straight on to Coblentz, where he crossed the Rhine, and marching rapidly on Bonn, joined the prince of Orange, as projected. He had, assisted by the friendly neutrality of the bishop of Würzburg, fairly outmanœuvred Turenne, whom he had been able, by marching behind the Main, to keep in ignorance of his movements, and who was hampered by his absurd home orders, and by the necessity of handling the neutral territory with delicacy. His instructions compelled him to hold fast to the Tauber and Aschaffenburg, while Montecuculi had a clearer purpose, a larger force and an open road. For all this the manœuvre redounds to the latter's credit as one of the most interesting pieces of work of this war.

In 1673 Condé had been conducting a campaign in Holland, while Louis XIV., aided by the skill of Vauban, personally besieged and took Maestricht; but from a multiplicity of reasons, Condé accomplished nothing against William of Orange, who managed, as agreed, to advance to Bonn to meet Montecuculi. In order to victual, Turenne withdrew to Philipsburg, where he crossed the Rhine, but to find none of the rations which had been promised by Louvois. All these adverse circumstances so greatly delayed his operations that he could in no event have reached the Netherlands in season to be of service. He had been able to protect Alsatia, but this province had in reality not been threatened, and Louvois' nervous fear for it had prevented Turenne from heading off the imperial army from its actual objective.

Spain had joined the allies. The prince of Orange had thirty thousand Dutch-Spanish troops, and with Montecuculi he captured Bonn, and overran the whole region between the Meuse and Rhine, a proceeding which Condé with his twelve thousand men had been unable to prevent. By the operations, originating in the hostility of Spain, the duke of Luxemburg, still conducting a war of sieges in the Netherlands, was practically cut off from France, but under Louvois' orders he garrisoned such of the strong places as he could, and, despite all the allies' efforts, made good his junction with Condé. Maestricht was retaken from the French, a loss Louis could ill afford.

The elector of Cologne and the bishop of Münster now forsook .France for the allied cause; and England, for lack of supplies which the parliament would not vote, made peace with Holland. The whole aspect of the war changed.

In this campaign the allies had the advantage. The French had to vacate Holland, and the allies set themselves down firmly there. It was a campaign of manœuvres solely, marked by not a single battle. Turenne had done all that his impossible orders and his limited force permitted; but circumstances favored the enemy and not Turenne. His advice in 1672 to raze the captured Dutch fortresses was now well proven to be sound. By their retention nothing whatever had been gained, and by garrisoning them heavily the forces in the field under Luxemburg, Condé and Turenne had been kept at such low water mark that nothing could be expected of them.

Montecuculi deserves all credit for cleverly utilizing·his advantages. Opposed to Turenne, another might have let them slip.

Garde du Corps.
(1688.)

XLVIII.

SENEF, AUGUST 11, AND SINSHEIM, JUNE 16, 1674.

FRANCE now assumed a defensive rôle. In 1674 Condé fought a drawn battle with the prince of Orange at Senef to prevent him from invading France. There is little in this engagement except the large forces and the desperate fighting to make it noteworthy, and Condé attacked with but a portion of his army. The rest of the campaign was trivial. Turenne, with a much smaller force, had Alsatia to defend, and did this by crossing the Rhine to attack the enemy. He found them at Sinsheim, where they had taken up an almost unassailable position on a high plateau. Here, quite against the rules of the art of that day, Turenne attacked the enemy and defeated him badly. There was no more actual gallantry in his assault than in Condé's at Senef, but there was vastly more calculation, and the battle had better results. Still, the whole Sinsheim operation was not much more than a raid, — a blow at the enemy to forestall one by him.

By the extensive combination against her, France was now reduced to a defensive rôle; but this did not prevent her generals from attacking the enemy. In 1674 Condé again commanded in the Netherlands, and on the 11th of August, to check the Dutch advance, he fought the bloody but drawn battle of Senef with the prince of Orange, who had advanced well on into Brabant. No peculiar results followed what the French deemed a victory.

There is little about the battle of Senef except the furious fighting pushed by Condé, and the enormous loss stated to have been suffered by the allies, which commends it to our notice; and it is quite doubtful whether the statement that the priests and their helpers, after the battle, buried twenty-seven thousand bodies (or half the number) within a space of three leagues, is true. It was said in a letter of the Marquis of Louvois, written at the time, that the French loss was seven thousand men killed and wounded; and that it was suspected that in this number had been counted all those who, since the campaign opened, had died or deserted.

The Stadtholder had sixty-five thousand men; Condé forty-five thousand. The allies had advanced to Nivelle, where they threatened Courtray and Oudenarde, and were thought to be projecting the invasion of France by way of Mons and Cambray. Condé lay not far from Charleroi, on a species of island surrounded by a marshy stream, where the prince of Orange could not well attack him; and deciding therefore to advance on Quesnoy, the allies marched south to Senef, thus presenting the flank of their long column. On August 11, at the point of day, they broke camp in three columns, the imperialists, the Dutch and the Spaniards, with four thousand horse as rear-guard, heading along the Binche road for Fayx. Condé had likewise broken camp and moved towards the marching allies; and so soon as he perceived the order and direction of their columns, he resolved on attack. Though he had but his van with him, he sent a force to occupy Senef, and himself, at the head of his best cavalry, advanced on the rest of the allied rear-guard, which, so soon as the French were discovered, took up on their line of march a good position for defense. The preliminary attack succeeded in breaking up the rear-guard, and Condé, placing his battalions of foot, as they successively arrived, in the most advantageous

Condé (late in life).

positions, advanced on the rear column of the enemy, which
he had now got near. To hold head to Condé until the main
body could return, this column had drawn up on a height
approachable only through orchards and fields whose hedges
had been filled with musketeers, and was backed by a heavy
line of cavalry; but Condé's brilliant charge, well seconded
by his lieutenants, bore fruit here also; and this column was
driven back to the village of Fayx. The French leader had
opened with all the fire he had shown at Rocroy.

To hold head against Condé's violent onset, the prince of
Orange retraced his steps and drew up on the hills behind

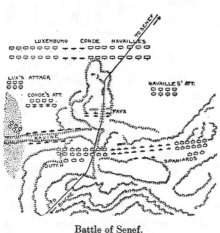

Battle of Senef.

Fayx, which stand
from a hundred to a
hundred and fifty feet
above the surround-
ing country, and
whose slopes were at
that time covered by
gardens, hop-fields,
quickset hedges and
ditches. Into a ra-
vine or hollow way on
his left leading to a
thick wood he threw
some troops; on the
right, say the accounts, were marshes and orchards, and the
ground was cut up so as to be capable of stubborn defense.
Fayx, in front of his left centre, was held by the foot and
artillery; the entire position was excessively strong.

Condé reconnoitred the new line, and despite its strength
determined on attack. Luxemburg commanded the French
right; Navailles the left; Condé and his son, the duke
d'Enghien, the centre. Unwilling to wait for all his forces

to come up, lest the prince of Orange should make his position still more impregnable than it already was, Condé delivered battle with but a part of his army, and especially lacked infantry. Opposite Luxemburg were the Dutch; opposite Navailles the Spaniards. Condé in the centre proposed to attack that side of the village where lay the ravine. If he could occupy and hold this ravine, he would take the enemy in reverse and cut off the *élite* of their foot, which had been posted in Fayx. As he advanced, a body of imperial cavalry debouched from the wood to take his column of attack itself in flank, and Condé sent Luxemburg to head it off, which was successfully done. Meanwhile Navailles was keeping the Spaniards busy, but making no progress.

Condé's onset was superb, and its vigor hustled back the first line of the enemy; but the cool-headed prince of Orange promptly replaced it by the second. A repeated charge drove the enemy beyond the ravine, and the French were on the eve of raising the cry of victory. But to save the day there came to the rescue the heavy cavalry of the Stadtholder, and, outnumbered four to one, Condé was forced to a precipitate retreat.

Condé was always at his best in the glow of battle; defeat never cast him down. He gathered a column of cavalry and dragoons from Luxemburg, and once more drove in the enemy and solidly occupied the ravine. But horse alone could not keep what the impetuous rush had won. It needed foot. To hold the ravine definitely, Condé ordered forward two battalions of Swiss infantry, the only ones which happened to be at hand; but these men, already decimated, could not be got to advance; they had lost stomach for the day; and before other troops could be got up, the *élan* of the manœuvre was lost; the ravine was retaken by William, and with it the battle was forfeited.

Condé was in ill case. If he retired, he might be followed
and beaten by superior numbers. He had no more foot
which he could put in; his vanguard columns had hurried
ahead of his *corps de bataille;* no artillery was at hand.
All he could do was to hold his own till night; and this
he did by repeated attacks, headed by Luxemburg and
Navailles, on the village. Had the prince advanced in force
on Condé he would have annihilated his army; but William,
though astonishingly indifferent to defeat, always lacked that
instinct of the captain which enables him to seize the auspicious moment, and was not enterprising in victory.

Night put an end to the battle; but desultory fighting was
kept up till near midnight. The loss had been tremendous.
Both armies were exhausted and terror-stricken, and both
retired from the field. Condé's belated artillery and foot
arrived during the night, too late to retrieve the disaster.
It is said that Condé proposed to renew the combat on the
morrow, with what was left of his cavalry and the foot and
guns which had come up. But this was not to be.

It has been alleged that the allies confessed to fifteen thousand killed and five thousand captured. The number of officers lost was appalling. Few generals but had been killed or
disabled. The retreat of the allies left the French a number
of trophies. Condé treated the prisoners with generosity.
Count Stahremberg, who was sent to Rheims, drank, at a
banquet there held, to the health of the prince of Orange,
who, he said, had promised him a glass of champagne in
Champagne, "and he has kept his word!"

The rest of the campaign lacked importance. Condé had,
to be sure, saved France from invasion, but at a very heavy
cost. It seems as if he had been over eager in attacking with
but a part of his force. He had won on other fields by the
charges of cavalry alone, but this is not good tactics. "*C'est*

magnifique, mais ce n'est pas la guerre!" He could not
expect that charges of horse, however ardent, would always
demoralize the enemy, or insure his holding what he might
win. Cavalry is limited by the terrain.

The elector of Brandenburg had again joined the allies;
some minor princes had also sided against Louis XIV.,
and the task assigned Marshal Turenne in 1674 was that
of defending Alsatia and the middle Rhine, for which duty
twelve thousand men were given him. His main magazines

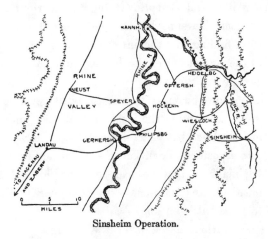

Sinsheim Operation.

were at Zabern (Saverne), and in its vicinity he took his
stand. Near Heidelberg, on the other side and down the
Rhine, lay an imperial and allied camp of ten thousand men
under the duke of Lorraine and Marshal Caprara, and reinforcements from Franconia were on the way to join them
under General Bournonville.

At the beginning of summer Caprara showed signs of opening operations, and the French commander decided to strike
the imperial officer before his reinforcements should arrive.
He had some fear that Alsatia might be attacked from the
Moselle region, but he provided against this by a detachment

of cavalry on the Saar; and with nine thousand five hundred
men he crossed the Rhine on June 14 at Philipsburg, where
he built a bridge; and having drawn in a few thousand foot
and horse, with six guns, from this fortress, as a vanguard, he
moved towards Heidelberg by the straight road, to seek the
enemy. At Hockenheim he ascertained that Caprara and the
duke of Lorraine, having heard of his crossing, had broken
up to march on Wimpfen, in the hope to forestall the French
advance into the interior and prevent its arresting the march
of Bournonville; and sharply turning to the right on June
15 to Wiesloch, Turenne headed the imperial generals off.
On the 16th, finding that the enemy was busy crossing from
the left to the right bank of the Elsenz, he advanced on him
and stopped him at Sinsheim.

Caprara, whose business it was to await reinforcements,
should have, according to the ideas of that time, and indeed
of any time, declined battle, as he could well have done by
moving into a position which Turenne could not attack. But
though he imagined that he had so done, his calculations
proved unsound, and Turenne with characteristic boldness
decided to force battle on him.

There are various accounts of the strength of the rival
armies, but on the field they were not far from equal.
Caprara and the duke had with them seven thousand horse,
but not exceeding two thousand foot; and they had taken up
their stand on a plateau back of Sinsheim, with a steep access
on all sides, and with the Elsenz like a double ditch in its
front. They had occupied Sinsheim, an old fortified abbey
near by, and the edges of the plateau, and deemed themselves
quite secure. It was indeed a dubious place to attack. South
of Sinsheim is a plain shut in by hills, and into this plain,
south of the river, Turenne had debouched and formed line.

Caprara ought to have held Sinsheim in greater force; but

he had placed only one thousand foot and four hundred dragoons in the gardens of the town, the town itself, the abbey and along the bank of the river, and had not sustained them by artillery. As Turenne had no excess of force, — five thousand foot and four thousand horse, — the task was a serious one to face. The imperialists had had a long rest and the troops were fresh, while the French had marched about ninety miles in four days and were tired and footsore. But Turenne wished to strike the enemy before he was reinforced, so as to open the campaign by a gain in moral force; and he decided on battle. There was, according to our ideas, an excellent chance of an attack on the enemy's right flank by a circuit around Sinsheim and up the Heidelberg road, but this was not within the ideas of the day. Parallel front attacks were universal. Despite their long march the spirit of the men was good, and with his usual confidence Turenne moved to the attack, meanwhile using his six guns to open his way.

In front of Sinsheim were gardens and hedges proper for defense, and though near the river were a number of low marshy places, it was fordable. Turenne detached a force of thirteen hundred foot and four squadrons of dragoons to attack the town. The troops went at their work cheerily, and in an hour had forced the river, driven the enemy out of the gardens and back into Sinsheim, and had reached the town ditch. Here was met a sharp fire, but the French waded the ditch, planted their ladders, and after another hour and a half forced an entrance, though the place was well defended, and had its streets barricaded with wine-barrels filled with earth and heavy beams from the houses. The abbey offered no defense whatever; its garrison fled, and reinforcements sent to it came too late. In Sinsheim Caprara forfeited a large part of his infantry force, — four hundred men being taken prisoners.

Having captured Sinsheim and driven the enemy away from the river, Turenne, not to allow him to recover from his surprise, turned quickly on his main force.

The plateau on which stood the imperialists was an immense triangle, at whose apex, near Sinsheim, was a ravine, up which Turenne must work his way in order to debouch in the open; and at the top there was but narrow space to

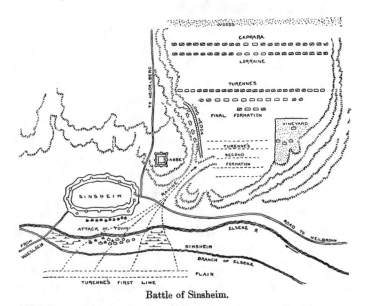

Battle of Sinsheim.

deploy his men. On each side of the defile lay steeps, covered on the right by orchards and vineyards, on the left by a long quickset hedge, and everywhere practicable for unmounted men only. Marshaling his foot in the two wings so as by occupying the hedge and a walled vineyard to be able to drive out the enemy's light troops, still on the edge of the plateau, and placing his cavalry in the centre, he advanced. This was an intelligent formation, though a decided innovation on the rules of the day for battle-order; but Turenne was, if anything, original. In this order the French vigorously advanced up the heights, and, as they debouched, the lines were formed with platoons of foot interspersed with the squadrons in the fashion of Gustavus. The guns were got up with the cavalry. Instead of disputing the possession of the ravine, the enemy had drawn up his cavalry well back on the plateau to keep away from Turenne's artillery fire, Caprara in the second line, the duke of Lorraine in the first; and this enabled the French the more easily to make their way up the slopes, and gave them more chance to deploy.

Turenne's bold advance on the enemy, rarely paralleled in those slow and unenterprising days, met with its well-deserved success. The foot, which had to climb up the rough, steep hillside, so as to leave the ravine for the cavalry, no sooner reached the level than it fell smartly on the imperial troops, which defended the edge of the plateau, and after a stout tussle, drove them in. Turenne had meanwhile been getting the cavalry forward into line, and, as it moved onward, its front was widened by additional squadrons on right and left. The French horse already in line vigorously charged home on the allied centre, but the right having gone ahead with too much ardor, Lorraine met it with a counter charge and drove it back. In following it up, however, he came on the French battalions, which met him with so hot a fire that he recoiled, and Turenne's horse again formed. When fully deployed, the first line was composed of cavalry with foot on either flank; and the second line of foot with horse on its flanks; while a mixed line of horse and foot stood in reserve. The field was covered with dust so thick as to quite hide the operations, but the lines fought stubbornly, and flags were taken and retaken again and again. Turenne, as always, was in the heat of the fray; with a few squadrons he was for an hour in the midst of the enemy's cuirassiers; after a struggle which reflected credit on both sides, French fervor prevailed, and with much pushing to and fro, but without loss of courage or ground, the French drove the enemy from the field. The battle had lasted seven hours, much time having been consumed in preliminaries. Caprara and Lorraine retired very much broken, but not so well pursued as they might have been, by a circuit through the woods to Heilbronn, whence they returned, back of the Neckar, to Heidelberg.

The victory was complete; the French loss was thirteen hundred killed; the imperial loss two thousand men killed and six hundred prisoners. But even Turenne did not know how to utilize the gain. He retired June 20 — possibly by orders from the Court — across the Rhine at Philipsburg and took post at Lachen near Neustadt, content with the punishment he had given the duke and Caprara. He shortly strengthened his force up to sixteen thousand men.

There was no more gallantry in Turenne's attack on Sinsheim than in Condé's at Senef; but the former battle, associated with its entire operation, strikes us more favorably than the latter. Though the numbers engaged were less, the work was done in a broader style.

In a certain sense, in this raid, for it was little more, the gain was hardly worth the loss. We are not given Turenne's ideas with reference to it; and the old military writers devote much time to the description of battles, while rarely giving reasons for a captain's larger operations. A battle is the cutting of the knot; though it appeals to our sympathies, it is important mainly in its results; whereas the reason for this or that strategic manœuvre is of vastly greater moment. But we are rarely permitted to know what most interests us, — the impelling causes to any given manœuvre or battle. It is left to the military critic to guess these if he can; they alone elucidate the grand operations.

The province of war is not to kill. Killing is but an incident, and an unfortunate one, of war. To inflict a loss on
the enemy unless such a loss accomplishes some end — as to
put the enemy out of capacity to do harm for a season, and
thus enable you to manœuvre to advantage — is no gain. To
have a clearly defined purpose for a battle, or to utilize a
victory properly, was, until the days of Frederick, almost an
unknown thing. Gustavus was an exception; so, frequently,
was Turenne, but not here, unless it can be claimed that the
defeat at Sinsheim forestalled the allies in an invasion of
Alsatia, of which there was no immediate probability. Turenne had struck the enemy before their junction with
Bournonville, and had to a certain extent neutralized them;
but this was all.

French Musketeer.
(End of 17th Century.)

XLIX.

ENTZHEIM, OCTOBER 4, 1674. TÜRKHEIM, JANUARY 5, 1675.

SHORTLY after Sinsheim, to forestall an invasion of Alsatia, Turenne again crossed the Rhine, advanced on the enemy, who lay back of the Neckar, and drove them towards the Main. Hereupon they crossed the Rhine and marched up towards Speyer, where, seeing no chance to operate advantageously, they recrossed, managed to reach Strasburg, and again entering Alsatia, took up a position at Entzheim. Here, October 4, Turenne attacked them. The enemy had over thirty-five thousand men; Turenne had but twenty-two thousand; but he put his men to good use, and fell with some effect on their left wing, so as to crowd them towards the Rhine. Though hotly contested, the battle was drawn and both armies retired; but the enemy vacated the field, while Turenne held it with a small force. The enemy was now joined by the elector of Brandenburg, which gave them fifty-seven thousand men, with which they went into winter-quarters. To crowd them out of Alsatia, Turenne made a winter march back of the Vosges Mountains, and debouching on their left flank, forced them towards the Rhine. Then, following them up, he attacked them near Colmar January 5. By turning their left flank at Türkheim, he managed to drive them from the field; and owing to disagreement among the commanders, the allies retired definitely across the Rhine. This campaign had been vastly to Turenne's credit.

SHORTLY after his return to the left bank of the Rhine after the battle of Sinsheim, Turenne learned that the allies, largely reinforced, had taken position between Mannheim and Ladensburg, north of the Neckar and near its mouth. Bournonville had joined, and the forces, to which the Worms garrison was added, had grown to five thousand foot and nine thousand horse. To check the enemy in any attempt they might be about to make on Alsatia, the French captain determined on dealing them a fresh blow.

Having strengthened Zabern so that he would have a secure *point d'appui* in Alsatia, Turenne gathered his forces near Neustadt, and giving out that he would shortly move on the Saar, he headed his van of five hundred cavalry on Kaiserslautern July 3, while the main army marched towards Philipsburg.

He again crossed the Rhine at that place, from which he took four battalions, six guns and twenty copper pontoons, and marched via Hockenheim to the Neckar at Wieblingen, where the enemy's officers came down to reconnoitre. The river was fordable, but Turenne, who was always careful of his men when without detriment he could be so, built a pontoon bridge, after driving away the enemy's cavalry with his guns, and sending over some squadrons to hold the further bank, he crossed. His purpose was to turn the enemy out of their position. Having passed the river, he demonstrated towards Ladensburg, while the enemy made small resistance and retired summarily on Frankfort, via Zwingenberg and Darmstadt, reaching Langen the same day. Turenne followed, but got no further than Zwingenberg. Here he saw that he could not prevent them from reaching Frankfort, gave over the pursuit, and deeming it essential to keep his eye on the Moselle region, from which there was danger, he retired and took up a position at Weinheim and Gross-Saxen. The enemy withdrew beyond the Main, having suffered the loss of a large number of prisoners and a yet greater moral depletion. They expected further reinforcements, and Turenne believed they would then seek to carry the war into Alsatia; to watch which purpose he determined to remain awhile on the right bank. In order to spare his own magazines at Philipsburg, Hagenau, Germersheim, Landau and Neustadt, and in accordance with orders to prevent the allies from again establishing themselves in the Lower Palatinate, or in the region between the Main and the Neckar, and thus be a threat to Alsatia, he devastated the entire region, destroying everything he could not carry off. Done under explicit instructions from the French government, barbarous as it was, this work was thoroughly done. Such vandalism was the order of the day; it cannot well be laid at Turenne's door. A generation later, Marlborough devastated Bavaria; and have we not the work of Sheridan in the Shenandoah Valley to regret?

The allies, as Turenne had feared, now threatened Alsatia from the Moselle region; and at the end of July the French army was transferred to the left bank and was established near Neustadt, and later in the Landau region, where Turenne remained a month, closely watching the enemy by means of parties scouting on both sides of the Rhine. By sundry rein-forcements Turenne managed to raise his army to twenty thousand men. The details of the minor operations at this period are extremely interesting to the student, but from lack of space cannot be given. Having received large accessions from Germany and Lorraine, with thirty-five thousand men the allies crossed the Rhine at Mainz, the last days of August, and marched slowly on Speyer, which they reached September 6. The commanding because senior officer, Bournonville, could not agree with his subordinates; and not liking the task of attacking Turenne's lines near Landau, for Philips-burg was on their flank, and being hard up for victual, the allies recrossed the Rhine above Speyer, September 21, on three bridges which they threw, and camped at Lusheim and later at Wiesenthal, north and south of Philipsburg. Antici-pating that the enemy was aiming to control Strasburg, Turenne sent a detachment out from Philipsburg to hold the road to that place at Graben, and to head off approaches by the enemy; and dispatched a considerable body under Gen-

eral Vaubrun to seize the bridge-head fort on the west bank of
the Rhine at Strasburg; but the latter officer negotiated in
lieu of acting, the former detachment came too late, and on
September 24 Caprara, who had meanwhile marched up river
and acted with commendable vigor, seized the Strasburg
bridge-head himself. This was unfortunate, for Strasburg,
which was considered to be neutral, opened the gate of upper
Alsatia.

That Alsatia was the allies' objective Turenne now clearly
saw; he had already headed up river, and by September 29
he placed his entire army in a position behind the small
stream Süffel, just north of Strasburg, with his right flank on
a morass, his left on the Ill, and Wantzenau in his rear. The
allies were slower, but their main army again crossed, the
end of September, and took up a position near Strasburg,
behind the Brüsch, in the villages of Entzheim, Geispoltz-
heim and Blesheim, where they could await reinforcements
while holding part of upper Alsatia. But they lay too far
back of the Brüsch to make this stream serve as a defense.
This period is full of interesting and skillful manœuvres; and
Turenne deserves credit for rarely failing to divine the enemy's purpose. If one were to write a manual which should
cover all the operations of war, minor and major, illustrations,
and apt ones, could be taken for every principle from the
life of Turenne alone.

Louvois was for holding Turenne to task for allowing the
allies to enter Alsatia, despite his fine work against great odds
in defense of the province; and wanted him to retire at once
to Lorraine, lest the enemy should march into the interior;
but Turenne obtained from the king permission to act as he
deemed best, and to remain in Alsatia, for here alone could
he prevent the enemy from invading France. His letter to
the king is reasonable, strong, — much like the man: —

"Les ennemis, quelque grand nombre de troupes qu'ils ayent, ne sauraient dans la saison où nous sommes penser à aucune autre enterprise qu'à celle de me faire sortir de la province où je suis, n'ayant ni vivres ni moyens pour passer en Lorraine que je ne sois chassé de l'Alsace: si je m'en allais de moi-même, comme V. M. me l'ordonne, je ferais ce qu'ils auront peut-être de la peine à me faire faire; quand on a un nombre raisonable de troupes, on ne quitte pas un pays, encore que l'ennemi en ai beaucoup d'avantage; je suis persuadé qu'il vaudrait beaucoup mieux pour le service de V. M. que je perdisse une bataille, que d'abandonner l'Alsace et repasser les montagnes; si je le fais, Philipsbourg et Brisac seront bientôt obligés de se rendre; les imperiaux s'empareront de tout le pays depuis Mayence jusqu'à Bâle, et transporteront peut-être la guerre d'abord en Franche Comté, de là en Lorraine, et viendront ravager la Champagne; je connois la force des troupes imperiales, les généraux qui les commandent, le pays où je suis. Je prend tout sur moi, et je me charge des événements."

To be able to hold himself, he strengthened his magazines, particularly Zabern, and closely watched the enemy. He was now placed where a battle won would drive the enemy out of Alsatia; while from a battle lost he believed he could retire under the guns of Zabern; lest the allies should become too strong when the elector should have joined them with his twenty thousand men, Turenne determined to strike them before that event; and with this end in view made preparations from his camp at Wantzenau to move on them at Entzheim. It required all the self-reliance and enterprise which Turenne possessed to face the difficulties of the situation. The enemy had twice his force; they backed on upper Alsatia, rich in victual, while lower Alsatia had been largely stripped by the late operations; they were placed where an invasion of France was easy, and they were awaiting twenty thousand fresh men while Turenne could hope for no reinforcements. But to attack was the safest defense, and Turenne did not hesitate.

At nightfall of October 2 Turenne sent dragoon parties

out to bridge all the streams he must cross to reach the Brüsch, — the Rhine-Ill region is a perfect network of marsh streams, — and at midnight the whole army followed to Achenheim, crossing the Süffel at Lampertheim, and advancing in three columns: the cavalry on the left, the foot in the centre, the artillery and baggage on the right. A steady rain made the roads extremely heavy, and the advance was slow. It was not the habit of the day to keep outposts at any great distance; the enemy had none out beyond a mile from Entzheim, and the movements of the French army were not discovered. Reaching Achenheim in the afternoon of the 3d, Turenne reconnoitred carefully, and pushed forward his van of dragoons to Holzheim; during the following night the entire army followed,

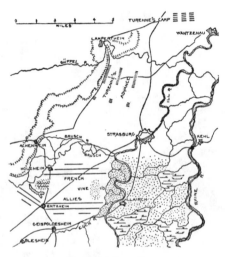

Entzheim Operation.

and after crossing took up a position beyond the Brüsch, with its right leaning on Holzheim. The army had worked hard to get at the enemy.

Before it stretched a triangular plain three or four miles long, in the middle of which the enemy had drawn up when they heard of Turenne's advance, with the centre behind Entzheim, held in force by foot and guns; while the left, thrown forward, reached out towards the Brüsch and the right towards the Erger, a small stream across which they had their bridges and line of retreat to Strasburg. Small ravines bordered by hedges cut up the plain; one of especially large size lay in front of the left like an intrenchment; and near Entzheim were patches of woods, hedges and gardens.

The morning of October 4 opened foggy, and shortly rain began to fall. The enemy, already aware of Turenne's advance, now discovered the immediate presence of the French. Turenne, cheerful and bright in word and deed, as

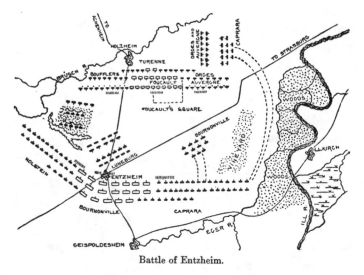

Battle of Entzheim.

he always was on the day of battle, himself led forward his lines. He had twenty battalions of about six hundred men each, and eighty-five squadrons of one hundred and twenty men, in all a force of about twenty-two thousand. His order of battle was the common one: ten battalions in the first line, eight in the second and two in reserve, with six squadrons in reserve and five between the lines. The cavalry and dragoons were on the flanks, and in the first line little bodies of fifteen musketeers stood between each two squadrons. Thirty guns were placed in front of the wings and centre.

The enemy had twenty-seven battalions, averaging six hundred and seventy men, and one hundred and twenty-three squadrons, numbering, including dragoons and cavalry, nineteen thousand men ; total, thirty-eight thousand. Some French records only allot them thirty-five thousand men ; but they had fifty guns. They stood in two lines and a reserve ; and, according to some accounts, were in six bodies, with more or less open intervals between them. The line had a reëntering angle at Entzheim ; and the left wing had in its front a wood which was about three quarters of a mile long by nearly half a mile wide, called in the various accounts of the battle the " little wood ; " while on the right extended a much larger one called the " big wood." In front of the right was an extensive patch of vineyards and hedges. It was a good position for the defensive battle on which the allies had determined. Caprara commanded the right ; the duke of Holstein the left ; Bournonville stood with the *corps de bataille* in the centre. The duke of Lorraine, the duke of Baden and some other German princes commanded their own forces. Bournonville had occupied the little wood with foot, and had thrown up two lines of works in it, on which some guns were mounted.

Turenne opened the attack by a cannonade all along the line, which was well sustained throughout the day. It seems as if he might have turned the little wood, and taken the force there in reverse ; he did not do so, but pushed a force of dragoons under Boufflers directly into the wood, hoping to take it and fall on the enemy's left. This attack was promptly met at the first line of works, and Boufflers recoiled. Turenne sent him some reinforcements, and despite additional troops put in by the enemy, Boufflers carried the first line and captured the guns. He was, however, stopped at the second line of works, and here for three hours the fight was

kept up, hot and bloody. Turenne again and again sent reinforcements to Boufflers, and the enemy did the like to their
divisions. Not until the French had been thrice forced out
was the wood definitely taken and the enemy driven to shelter behind the ravine in their rear. It was at this point that
the English contingent fought, in which the later great duke
of Marlborough commanded a regiment.

The attention of Turenne had been so constantly taken up
with the fierce fighting at the little wood that there had been
no set attempt to manœuvre the centre or left of the French
army; it was probably not intended that there should be
more than a partial attack here, for his plan manifestly was
to crush their left and throw them back towards the frontier; and there is some doubt whether the French or the
allies first advanced. But Bournonville initiated an onset
with a heavy column of cavalry *d'élite* on the centre of the
French line, advancing on the left of the vineyards, while
Caprara was sent out with another column on the right of the
vineyards to fall on the left flank of the French, and take
the infantry centre in reverse.

On the French left stood the cavalry of Counts d'Auvergne
and de l'Orges. These officers had advanced, or were preparing to advance, towards the big wood on the enemy's right,
and the movement was to be followed by General Foucault
and seven battalions of foot from the centre; but the French
had scarcely started when they became aware of the column
of eighteen squadrons which, under Caprara in person, was
about to fall on the French left, and of the advance of Bournonville. Foreseeing danger from front and rear, General
Foucault ployed his foot into a square — " fit face des deux
côtés " — and awaited attack, ordering the men to reserve
their fire; but when Bournonville perceived the firm front of
the French *corps de bataille*, he declined to deliver the blow,

and rode back whence he came. Caprara, on the other hand, boldly rode around the French flank, and by the violence of his onset came close to breaking it up, but d'Auvergne and de l'Orges returned to the line, faced to the left, took Caprara himself in reverse, and hustled him back.

The fighting at the little wood had ceased; not so the fighting on the French right. The enemy, unwilling to give up their point, now sent out a heavy force of foot under the duke of Lüneburg to retake it; but Turenne, determined to win success at this part of the line, called for reinforcements. He met Lüneburg's advance with the bulk of the first line of the right wing, the second moving up into its place; and after another period of heavy fighting, in which the enemy and the French were each driven back four times, and four times again came to the charge, Turenne pushed Lüneburg well back into Entzheim. The work here was so hot that the French left was now instructed to remain on the defensive; but it kept up a heavy cannonading meanwhile. The battle on the right flank had been hotly contested; but, though it had lasted all day, it had led to nothing definite.

Turenne's willingness to attack shows a keen knowledge of the weakness of the enemy's army, which, though numerous, was made up of so many different parts as to lack cohesion. It has been suggested that his proper tactics on this field was to attack the allied right, which was easier of access, and if once demolished would enable him to cut them off from Strasburg. Their fear for this flank would probably have given him a better chance of driving them off the field, if he could give them a sufficiently hearty blow at this point; and it was feasible, as their main infantry force was massed near Entzheim. But Turenne's plan seems to have been to break the enemy's left, lead to the capture of Entzheim, which would thus be taken in reverse, and throw the enemy back on his line of retreat and across the Rhine. This was indeed more in accordance with the ideas of the day, which did not look favorably upon a battle which would drive the enemy, especially a superior one, into a corner where they must absolutely fight. It was deemed too dangerous an experiment; and here the French were outnumbered two to one. In his effort to accomplish his design, Turenne ran the risk of so depleting his centre and left that, had the allies stoutly pushed home in these quarters, Turenne must, with his smaller force, have suffered a galling defeat. But the allies fought feebly, and only defended themselves from Turenne's attack; they had not the enterprise to push in with any vigor.

The French had been marching and working hard for the two preceding nights and days, in the rain without camping; all had been on a plain deep in mud, under heavy fire, and half the army had been fighting desperately all day. They were exhausted, and Turenne clearly saw that he could not carry out his plan against the heavy odds of the enemy. He determined to retire to his camp. Under a cannonade which lasted well on into the night, and leaving a brigade of cavalry to hold the field as an assertion of victory, Turenne moved his army back to Achenheim.

Neither side could fairly claim the victory, for the allies at the same time withdrew to their old camp at Illkirch, having lost three thousand killed, three thousand wounded, eight guns and twenty standards. The French loss was two thousand killed and fifteen hundred wounded, with several colors. Why the French loss should be the smaller does not appear from the course of the fighting; but these are the figures usually accepted as correct. Turenne had a horse shot under him, and the loss in officers was heavy. The allies remained near Strasburg, and Turenne placed himself at Marlenheim, in advance of Zabern, where he protected his magazines at this place and Hagenau, to recuperate and prepare for a fresh blow.

The battle had consisted solely of an isolated attack pushed home on the left of an enemy who fought on the defensive, and of a second attempted attack on his right, met half way. Much discussion, coupled with the usual critic's "if," has been had on this battle; but it was so far a gain to the French as it prevented the allies from making any effort to penetrate into France. For this accomplishment Turenne deserves high credit, as he clearly does for his splendid courage in attacking such superior forces. With reference to Turenne's withdrawal from the field, Napoleon says: "Il a poussé dans cette occasion la circonspection jusqu'à la timidité; il savait mieux que qui que ce soit l'influence de l'opinion à la guerre." At all events, Turenne had made a handsome bid to drive the allies out of Alsatia; and if he had not fully succeeded on this field, he shortly would on another.

The elector of Brandenburg finally joined the allies on the 14th of October at Strasburg, making a total force of thirty-three thousand foot and twenty-four thousand horse. To meet this serious threat, the *arrière-ban* of France was ordered out and a number of regiments brought back from Flanders. Despite their strength, the allies were slow and inactive, though they indulged in much manœuvring, ostensibly with a view of attacking Turenne's depots at Zabern and Hagenau; but eventually making no progress, for Turenne headed them off at every point, meeting them by concentrating and ably posting his forces behind the Zorn, at Detweiler, they returned to the vicinity of their old camps, and later went into winter-quarters, the elector establishing his court in Colmar. Turenne then put his men in quarters behind the

Moder, having strengthened Hagenau and Zabern, and cut all the bridges leading north from the Strasburg region.

The explanation of the allies' laxness lay in the jealousy of the several leaders and the entire want of unity in their proceedings. By utilizing his knowledge of this fact, Turenne, who lay near his magazines watching the enemy, and had been also reinforced by a few thousand men, conceived the idea that, after the beginning he had made, with some further skillful feints, he might push the allies back on Strasburg and perhaps crowd them out of the country. They manifestly desired to winter in Alsatia, not only because it saved their own supplies by consuming the enemy's, but because it gave them a starting-point for the invasion of France the succeeding spring. Both Franche Comté and Lorraine were ready to welcome them, and this serious threat to France Turenne determined to undermine. With a view to so doing, and against the rule of the day, which was to go into winter-quarters early, Turenne obtained permission from the king to conduct a winter campaign. The allies had so heavily intrenched their position that there was no chance for a front attack, and both armies extended from the Vosges to the Rhine, so that there was no means of reaching either flank.

In order to mislead the enemy as to his intentions, Turenne put his own forces into winter-quarters between his magazines at Zabern and Hagenau, both of which he had strongly fortified and garrisoned, and gave out that he had done with operations for the year. He needed patience as well as activity, for victual and forage were both hard to get. The allies were so thoroughly deceived as to spread their own troops over a wide territory backing on the Rhine between Belfort and Benfelden.

On November 29 Turenne started with fifteen thousand foot and thirteen thousand horse, and via Lützelstein and

Lixheim, which he left December 4, he led his men across the
Vosges mountain paths, and along their west slope through
Lorcheim, Blamont, Baccarat and Padoulx to Remiremont.
The march was admirably planned; each column was given
its daily route, and the rendezvous was at Belfort; but no one

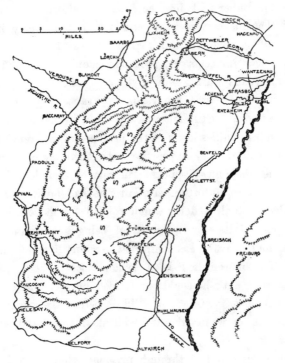

Türkheim Operation.

except Turenne knew its purpose. He may have hoped to
surprise the allies, but they were not inactive, and got wind
of the manœuvre while Turenne was waiting at Remiremont
for his infantry column, belated by snow and bad roads, to
come up, as well as to collect victual. To lead the allies to
believe that he might debouch on them through some of the
mountain gaps, as well as to prevent their using the gaps

themselves, Turenne sent several detachments due east across
the range to move to and fro on the eastern slope. These
indulged in a number of exchanges with the enemy, while
with his main force Turenne marched still further south.

His journey had been as fast as could be, and yet slow;
it was December 27 before he reached Belfort. As he had
hoped that his movements would act on the enemy in the
nature of a surprise, this march of less than five miles
a day seems unnecessarily protracted; only by remembering
Virginia roads during our civil war can we account for
it; in Turenne's time, the roads in France were not what
they are to-day. Still Turenne was right in his calculations;
for though the allies knew of the presence of a French force
at Remiremont, they appear to have been taken unawares
when the whole army appeared in rear of their left flank at
Belfort. Here, unfortunately, Turenne had again to remain
to collect victual, a delay which robbed his movement of a
great part of its effect: instead of being able summarily to
attack the enemy, he was compelled to resort to small manœuvres. The march had been exhausting; his column was
much strung out; he could barely feed his men ; and though
he had come so far to get in a blow before the enemy could
concentrate, he was unable to undertake a smart and immediate attack.

Having ascertained through prisoners that the allied left
wing was under orders in case of attack to rendezvous, part
at Altkirch and part at Colmar, Turenne sought to separate
these two detachments by pushing in between them, and
marched on Mühlhausen; but he was able to take with him
only three thousand cavalry, while a small body of foot was
ordered to follow as speedily as possible. The allies, astonished at his appearance, yet anticipated his manœuvre; they
set out at once, and their van reached Mühlhausen first.

Though with a force so small as to be merely a reconnoitring party, Turenne attacked the enemy near Mühlhausen,
but without advantage other than to gain a handsome victory
and some information. The loss of the allies was three hundred men. Turenne returned towards his main force; he
was yet again compelled to victual, get his troops together
and rest them. The intelligent conception of this operation
was quite ahead of the means of carrying it out. Everything
was cumbrous in those days; and in winter, especially in a
sparsely settled mountain country, it was impossible to march
fast and suitably ration a column. Neither had the country
supplies, nor could a train be carried along at any reasonable
pace.

On January 2 the army was advanced to Ensisheim, on
the 4th to Pfaffenheim, marching near the hills to avoid
Colmar, and because the valley roads were impassable.
Pushing on towards Colmar on January 5, Turenne found
the main force of the allies in line of battle, behind a branch
of the Fechte called the Logelbach, and covered by a number
of works. Their left leaned on Colmar; in front was a' low
plain, too much cut up for advantageous manœuvring; a
mile beyond their right lay, on the main stream of the
Fechte, the village of Türkheim, which the allies had but
slightly occupied. The branch in their front had been
strengthened with works, and the troops stood in two lines
with a reserve. The French army marched from Pfaffenheim in three columns, and at Eggisheim threw back eight
squadrons of the enemy which were out reconnoitring. Drawing up his army of thirty thousand men, of which half was
foot, in line but beyond artillery range, in order to impose
on the allies, Turenne with a small force reconnoitred, and at
once saw that Türkheim was the most promising point for
attack. He proposed to try the same tactics which had

half succeeded at Entzheim: turn the flank furthest from
their line of communications, and by pushing boldly in, facilitate their exit from French soil. In pursuance of this
design, while the army filed into line, the two first lines stood
ready to engage the enemy, and were instructed to feel him,
but not so strongly as to bring on an engagement, while the
third column marched over roads supposed to be impassable,

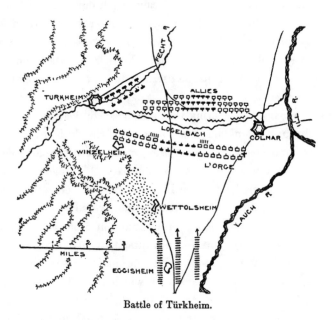

Battle of Türkheim.

behind vineyards, and then through a mountain gap to the
Türkheim valley, intending to seize the place and thus
threaten the allied right. Meanwhile, Count de l'Orges, in
command of the French right wing, demonstrated towards the
enemy in Colmar to prevent their sending reinforcements to
Türkheim. In this village were two battalions of the enemy,
which were withdrawn as the French approached. Turenne
occupied the place, threw a force into a mill which stood on

both sides of the stream, and drew up in line behind the Fechte, across the allied flank.

No sooner had the allies perceived Turenne's manœuvre than they undertook to retrieve their error, and sent twelve battalions, thirty squadrons and six guns from their second line to retake Türkheim. There was a sharp fight in and near this village, in which General Foucault was killed and Turenne had his horse shot under him, and each side lost some two hundred killed and wounded; but the French held their ground. Of the main army facing the allies, Turenne's left flank leaned on vineyards at Winzenheim, the right on a church — often a good rallying-point — half a mile from Colmar. While Turenne was thus making sure of Türkheim, the artillery of the French left wing moved somewhat to the left and front, so that the guns might half enfilade the enemy's line; and Turenne was preparing to follow up his attack by an advance in force on the enemy's right flank, when, toward nightfall, the allies concluded to retire, though they had suffered small loss; and during the next night, January 5–6, rather than further try the fortunes of battle, they left the field.

The French bivouacked where they fought; the next day, Colmar, with hospitals and magazines, fell to them, and thirty squadrons were sent in pursuit of the retiring enemy. The allies manifestly had no desire to engage in a winter campaign; they made their way to Schlettstadt and shortly to Strasburg; and from here, to get safely away from touch of the all too active French commander, they crossed the Rhine and went into winter-quarters on the right bank. Strasburg was glad to resume its neutrality.

That Turenne by manœuvres, without delivering a pitched battle, — though he had been quite ready for one, — had thus been able to thrust the enemy out of Alsatia was, according to the idea of his day, the highest honor. While he was on the march, there had been a great outcry in Paris about his retreat into Lorraine and his abandonment of Alsatia to the enemy; but on the completion of the operation, of which he had in October given the king an outline, he was applauded by all France, indeed even by his enemies.

Perhaps, judged by the standard of Frederick or Napoleon, this manœuvre might be criticised in some of its details: the slowness of the march, the inability to strike a hearty blow so soon as the army debouched from the mountains, the letting the enemy escape without a fatal blow. But this is hypercriticism. We must judge Turenne by his age and the steps he made in advance of it. It was quite outside of rules to make a winter campaign: Turenne braved one in a mountain district. He had no modern railway on which to transport his rations: he carried or collected his food by whatever means he could. The roads were called impassable for an army: Turenne nevertheless marched on them, and reached his goal in condition for battle. It was deemed hazardous to attack a superior enemy: Turenne disregarded numbers. And best of all, he succeeded in what he started out to do, — to thrust the allies out of Alsatia. Turenne was well ahead of his own day; we can hardly expect his method to equal that of later and greater captains ; and it remains true that the French had won a magnificent success, thanks solely to him.

It is generally acknowledged that this was Turenne's best campaign, though the following one comes close to disputing it that title. Sinsheim, Entzheim and Türkheim, three great victories in seven months, make a wonderful string of jewels.

French Carbine.   (16th Century.)

L.

TURENNE'S LAST CAMPAIGN. 1675.

In 1675 the imperial forces were under Montecuculi, who tried to seize Strasburg. Turenne's duty was to keep him from this city and Alsatia. The campaign was one strictly of manœuvres. Montecuculi crossed to the left bank, but could accomplish no result. Returning to the right bank, he began a series of able operations to seize on the approaches to Strasburg; but Turenne met him at every point. Failing in his victual, Montecuculi moved close to the Rhine, so as to get convoys down the river; but this source Turenne also cut off. The rival armies lay on the Rench, and finally on the same night each sought to surprise his opponent, with the result that Montecuculi was compelled to withdraw. Following him up, Turenne prepared to attack the imperialists at Nieder-Sasbach, when he was killed by a cannon-ball. The French were now forced across the Rhine, and the war was carried into Alsatia. Few soldiers have left as enviable a reputation as Turenne. After his death the French cause retrograded fast.

THE emperor had no cause to be satisfied with the campaign of 1674. He saw that enormous forces had accomplished nothing; that divided authority lay at the root of their failure, and in 1675 he gave sole command of an army of twelve thousand foot and fourteen thousand horse to Field-Marshal Montecuculi, who purposed to anticipate Turenne by crossing the Rhine at Strasburg, and by pushing sharply into lower Alsatia. On the last occasion, two years before, when he had matched himself against Turenne, this brilliant soldier had shown wonderful capacity to manœuvre, and it was with strong expectation of renewed success that the emperor now intrusted the opening campaign to him.

From the Ulm region Montecuculi marched toward the Rhine, and took position near Willstädt, where he rendez-

voused the troops from the Neckar and the upper Rhine.
The population favored the imperial forces; there were considerable magazines still holding over from the last year;
and Montecuculi's object was to conduct a campaign in Alsatia.   To Turenne's part fell the task of holding head against
Montecuculi's projected inroad.   His forces concentrated at

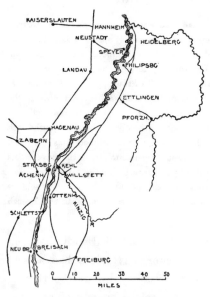

Theatre of 1675 Campaign.

Schlettstadt, on the left
bank above Strasburg,
and he joined them
from Paris on May 29.
Strasburg was the
main objective of both
generals, but Turenne
had the harder task.
His army was smaller,
twelve thousand foot
and ten thousand horse,
and Strasburg inclined
to the emperor ; yet, as
we shall see, Turenne
succeeded in his object
of keeping the enemy
away from the city by
skillful manœuvres, in

a campaign which worthily crowned a typical soldier's life,
and one which had at that day few equals; which, judged
by the state of the art, the condition of the country, the
quality of the troops and their equipment, and the cumbrous
artillery, has had few superiors at any day.

Though he was aiming at Strasburg, as well as the enemy,
it was Turenne's purpose to cross to the German side of the
Rhine ; and his original plan was to do so at Philipsburg.
On the right bank he would be freer to operate, and less

hampered in the defense of Alsatia than by manœuvres on
the left bank; he could better impose on Strasburg and the
other German neutrals, and he could feed his army on the

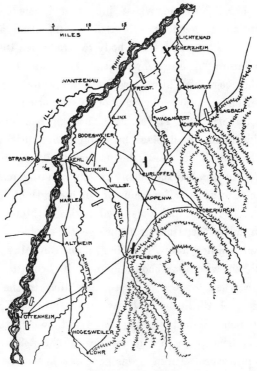

Campaign of 1675.
(The blocks show the successive positions.)

enemy's country. He appears this year not to have been
interfered with by the court.

It was May when Montecuculi reached Willstädt. Turenne
moved from Schlettstadt on Strasburg and threatened it with
bombardment, in case neutrality was violated or the imperial
army harbored. To entice him thence, Montecuculi moved
towards Philipsburg and took measures to besiege it, leaving

behind at Willstädt a force of six thousand men with orders to occupy Strasburg so soon as Turenne's back should be turned. Though Montecuculi carried out this scheme with consummate skill, and spread rumors that he would lay siege to Philipsburg, Turenne, whose judgment in such matters was exceptionally keen, saw through his intention and did not follow; but he sent a small body to strengthen the garrison. To enforce his apparent purpose, Montecuculi not only opened the siege of Philipsburg, but put a force over the Rhine at Speyer, and made signs of an intention to besiege Landau, Zabern and Hagenau. Turenne had moved to Achenheim, from which place he could dominate Strasburg or quickly march to these depots, or to Philipsburg, as required. He watched the enemy closely, sending many parties out to seek news. Conscious of the strength of his magazine-towns, Turenne took no special notice of Montecuculi's threat, but made preparations to bridge the Rhine at Ottenheim, twenty miles above Strasburg; and on May 30 put over Vaubrun, with four thousand men, in boats, to protect the bridge when thrown. He thought that if the enemy really besieged Philipsburg, he would march on Freiburg, where Montecuculi had his magazines, and by this threat to his commissariat frighten him away. On May 31 another body was put over. Turenne was now astride the river, with good communications, and ready to act on either side.

Montecuculi himself crossed with the main army to the left bank at Angelhausen above Speyer June 1, as a further attempt to draw Turenne away from Strasburg, took up a position south of Mannheim, backing on his bridge, and gave out that he would attack the French army. But Turenne was not troubled, sent out detachments to Neustadt, Kaiserslautern and Landau, and notified Metz and Nancy not to fear raids if they should occur, as they would be mere demonstrations made for effect. Seeing that none of his operations could intimidate or draw Turenne away from Strasburg, Montecuculi after but a few days retired to the right bank, and camped not far from Philipsburg. Having failed to transfer the war to the left bank, he now had his choice between forcing battle on Turenne, starving him out, or capturing his bridges, and to the business of determining which was best he now addressed himself.

Once rid of his adversary on the left bank, Turenne himself crossed the Rhine at Ottenheim, June 7 and 8, took Willstädt, transformed it into a French depot, captured a lot of forage which had been shipped down the Kinzig to the enemy, and there took up a position between the Kinzig and Schutter, covering Strasburg, which he thus neutralized. As Strasburg was approachable only by way of Kehl, which lay behind the Kinzig, Turenne's presence at Willstädt sufficed; but he later broke the Kinzig bridge at Kehl, which made access to the city harder. Turenne's position was one which threatened Montecuculi's magazines at Offenburg, and the latter, on hearing that the French had crossed, at once broke up and marched south, hoping to forestall Turenne at Willstädt; but finding himself too late, he stopped at Lichtenau. He now had thirty thousand men. Turenne had won the first round of this manœuvring match by permanently moving the theatre of operations to the right bank of the Rhine; by freeing Alsatia from the hardship of war; and by barring the way to Strasburg.

The next move of the French marshal was to make an attempt on Offenburg and on Oberkirch, both magazines of the enemy. The latter place was taken, but the former held out, and when Montecuculi marched from Lichtenau to the relief of Offenburg, which he reached June 15, Turenne to meet him changed his front at Willstädt, and sat down

closely to watch his opponent, who, as he was now cut off
from Strasburg, where he had much breadstuff, made a
demonstration against Kehl, but accomplished nothing.
Turenne protected his communications with the left bank by
heavy detachments at Altheim, six miles below Ottenheim,
and at the bridge at Ottenheim ; but he kept his headquarters in Willstädt.

Still Turenne's position was not secure. His front was
twenty miles long. To the enemy at Offenburg his bridge at
Ottenheim was nearer than he was himself, a situation, indeed,
of which Montecuculi took advantage. Had the imperial
general moved sharply on Ottenheim, he might have caught
Turenne in an awkward dilemma; but fortunately for
Turenne he was too slow. As on June 21 he approached the
Schutter, the fact that his men were taxed by the heavy
roads induced him to stop for the night; seeing which
Turenne changed his position by leaving part of his army at
Willstädt to protect Strasburg, and by moving his bridge and
protecting force to Altheim, where all preparations for such
an operation had been made ; and thither he also transferred
his headquarters. Montecuculi made preparations for action,
extending his left as far as Lohr, but preferring not to attack
the new position, which was strong, he withdrew and again
camped at Offenburg.

Now that this threat to his bridge had failed and his line
was less long, Turenne, who suspected some design on Strasburg, moved to Neumühl to hold the road to Kehl. Montecuculi was now nearer the Altheim bridge than Turenne, but
not caring to duplicate his late operation, he took no advantage of the fact, and moreover Turenne had made it too strong
to be lightly assailed. From Offenburg, on June 28, for lack
of victual and forage, the imperial marshal moved to Urlof-
fen, leaving three thousand men in Offenburg. To meet this

manœuvre, Turenne changed his position in prolongation of his left and again stood athwart Montecuculi's road to Strasburg, taking post in front of Botesweyer.

Montecuculi saw that he had failed in his undertaking to get hold of Strasburg with its munitions and food; and as he lay in a poor country, and was forced to move to seek rations, he made a rapid flank movement back of the Rench at the end of June, reached the Rhine, and took up his stand at Scherzheim, with his right leaning on the Rhine, hoping to get victual and pontoons by water from Strasburg. Turenne, though the country was woody and hard to operate in, followed him on the opposite side of the Rench, placed himself at Freistädt, and erecting batteries on the Rhine islands and anchoring boats with troops in the current, prevented the use of the waterway. He also ordered the Hagenau people to post a detachment at Wantzenau on the Rhine, and to stop all boats which might try to move down the river.

The land along the Rench being low and swampy, the armies, with only the stream between them, remained quietly *en face* for three weeks, rather than manœuvre; want of food, it was thought by each, would soon compel the other to withdraw. In fact, the unhealthful situation, the lack of forage in the French and lack of rations in the imperial camp finally drove each army to activity. Turenne determined to stretch his line up the Rench and turn Montecuculi's left flank, meanwhile watching Caprara in Offenburg. While meditating an attack on Montecuculi, Turenne had been improving and fortifying a small foot-road, which had been found across the river near Wagshorst, by which he proposed in due time to move his army. On getting knowledge of Turenne's first movements, Montecuculi, not anticipating an attack, concluded that Turenne had spread himself out too much and offered a fair chance for a blow; and he prepared to attack

the position on the Rench in the rear by a portion of the
Offenburg garrison, while personally with another part of his
army he should move upon its front. The dispositions were
these : Caprara with two thousand men was to make an attack
from Offenburg on the rear at Wagshorst; the duke of Lorraine was to attack the centre with five thousand men ; a force
of four thousand was detailed against the front of the intrenched
ford ; and Montecuculi in person was to move on Freistädt.
The attack thus planned was actually made at night on July
23–24, but it quite lacked *ensemble* and remained without
result, though delivered on Turenne's depleted lines. The
ground was difficult in the day-time; at night it proved
impracticable.

When this imperial operation had failed, Turenne, leaving
a half of his force well intrenched at Freistädt, advanced
July 25 with the other half of his force over the Rench to
turn Montecuculi's left and cut him off from Offenburg. He
had fortified his ford over the Rench on both banks, and had
established posts to hold communication with the Freistädt
force. His manœuvre was a bold one, which exposed each
half of his army to be overwhelmed by the entire force of the
enemy ; but Turenne had a way of relying on his knowledge
of his opponent's character, and moreover he had diligently
prepared his ground. He would not move his entire force,
lest he should open the way to Strasburg to the enemy, and
he believed that a threat on his magazine would compel Montecuculi to retire. Nor was he disappointed. The several
attacks prepared by Montecuculi, as above said, quite failed
to work together, and Turenne had got no further than Gams-
horst, when Montecuculi, hearing of his presence there in
force, concluded that he was to be cut off from Caprara at
Offenburg, and hurriedly withdrew in the night of July
25–26 to Nieder Sasbach. Here he stood on the road which

preserved his communications and ordered Caprara up to the same place. Turenne at once drew in the Freistädt half of his force and followed to Achern. In this position at Nieder Sasbach Montecuculi skillfully drew up his forces, and Turenne, proposing to push his opponents to battle, did the like. He is said to have felt confident of a victorious issue; but while he was marshaling his forces, and just before moving to the attack, he was struck to death by a cannon-ball.

Operations were suspended. The French generals — de l'Orges and Vaubrun — could not agree as to who should take command, and summarily withdrew over the Rhine at Altheim. Montecuculi followed, defeated them and carried the war into Alsatia. However interesting the details of this remarkable campaign, space forbids us to give more than its salient features.

In 1676 Condé conducted a campaign against Montecuculi in Germany, on the whole successfully. It had no remarkable details.

Turenne stood decidedly at the head of the generals of his time. He was singular in his ability to correctly gauge his opponents and the conditions under which he was called on to act. He himself was self-contained, shrewd and enterprising, and far above the foolish military prejudices of his day. He was willing to conduct operations at any season, and decidedly opposed to the devotion of unnecessary time to sieges and the parceling out of troops in minor operations. Ready to fight whenever he had morally or physically the advantage of the enemy, he often engaged against marked odds. His tactics was original; he was the first who in his day began flank attacks, and who thoughtfully prepared his turning manœuvres. Unlike Condé, whose most stirring work was done in his youth, Turenne grew every year of his life, and his last campaigns were by far his best.

Sometimes over careful of his men, Turenne inspired them with confidence in the greatest danger, and with energy to undertake the most difficult operations. He won their devotion by his kindness, reasonableness, unflurried temper and never-ceasing acts of generosity. Always among his men, his keen eye singled out the worthy soldier, and his good nature never wearied in rewarding him. On one occasion he noticed a lieutenant of dragoons, whose assiduity in his duties had quite worn out his horse. Turenne accosted him and, after some conversation about his outpost, fell to admiring the subaltern's poor steed, and presently suggested a trade with his own, — a noble creature, such as he always rode. Alleging a liking for the color and the shape of the other's head, the marshal of France insisted on the trade, and rode off on the lieutenant's horse, leaving his charger behind. Anecdotes such as these abound in the accounts of this great man.

Turenne was a soldier pure and simple. From early youth until his death he was that and only that. Few captains lead a life so uniformly devoted to arms. Nearly every one of his active years was passed in the field. To judge Turenne's real value as a captain we must study the conditions under which he worked. He was always hampered by the home government, by the paucity of his troops and by the jealousy of his superiors. His work was narrowed far below his capacity. In view of what he accomplished under generally unfavorable conditions, and especially against such opponents as the Great Condé and Montecuculi, he must be said to have earned the highest rank of all the generals of his day.

Louis XIV. had so far conducted his war of conquest with credit and advantage; but what occurred in the following years undid much of what had been gained.

In 1678 and 1679 there was negotiated with each of the enemies of France — Holland, Spain, the Empire, Sweden,

Denmark — the peace of Nymwegen. The various cessions of territory were complicated, but in general terms Holland got back her entire territory. Spain ceded to France Franche Comté, Valenciennes, Cambray, Ypres, Bouchain and other towns, in exchange for Charleroi, Oudenarde, Courtray, Ghent and other places. The emperor ceded Freiburg, and France her right to garrison Philipsburg. The duke of Lorraine refused to receive back his duchy on the terms offered. The Great Elector was forced to return what he had conquered from Sweden.

This peace, won by his able generals, Turenne and Condé at their head, placed Le Grand Monarque at the summit of his power. Nothing now sufficed to his boundless ambition, and owing to the weakness of the empire he continued his territorial thefts under whatever pretext he could invent. Saarbrück, Luxemburg, Zweibrücken and even Strasburg were seized and annexed to France. Trier and Lorraine followed ; the emperor protested, but allowed the occupation to continue.

Finally, the revocation of the Edict of Nantes, Louis' attempted seizure of the Palatinate and his interference in the election of the archbishop of Cologne roused the enemies of France, and in 1686 the League of Augsburg was entered into by William of Orange, the emperor, the kings of Sweden and Spain and the electors of Saxony, Bavaria and the Palatinate ; and this, owing to the French invasion and barbarous devastation of the Palatinate in 1688, culminated, in the succeeding year, in the Grand Alliance. The prince of Orange had become king of England, and it was he who organized this new alliance against France, which was joined by the members of the Augsburg League, by Holland, Denmark, Savoy, by some of the smaller German princes and the pope. France had grown too powerful to make peace a probability. Louis responded by espousing the cause of the exiled James II. The war concerning the succession of the Palatinate ensued. All western Europe was arrayed against Louis. For nine years war was waged in the Netherlands, along the Rhine, in Italy, on the border of Spain, in Ireland and at sea. Either the triumph or the destruction of France should have followed this widespread warfare. Neither occurred, owing to the peculiar laxness of the conduct of war at that day. In Ireland and at sea the French lost; elsewhere there was a balance of success. But neither side knew how to improve its gains.

In this war, which raged from 1689 to 1697, there were a number of splendid French victories to which we shall return, meanwhile turning aside to a brilliant feat of arms, upon which that radiance is shed which always illumines the saving of a Christian state from the dominion of the pagan.

Mounted Arquebusier. (16th Century.)

LI.

THE SIEGE OF VIENNA. 1683.

THE emperor had always been at war with the Turks, and harassed by insurrections in Hungary. In 1682 both again occurred, and in 1683 the Turks marched on Vienna and laid siege to it. The emperor fled. Count Stahremberg defended the city, while Charles of Lorraine with a small force kept open the routes by which an army of relief might come. The Germans sent several divisions, and John Sobieski, king of Poland, marched to Vienna with twenty-six thousand men. The grand vizier, Kara Mustapha, had been slow in his siege, and the defense of Stahremberg had been stubborn to the last degree. Finally, after over two months' siege, when the garrison and citizens were at the end of their powers and almost starved, the army of relief came up; Sobieski and Lorraine attacked the enemy and defeated them in a hard-fought battle at the very gates of the capital. The Turks summarily retired, and were, during the following months, quite pushed out of the land.

EXCEPT that the heroic defense of Vienna by Stahremberg and its relief by John Sobieski and Charles of Lorraine was one of the notable feats of arms of the seventeenth century, it should scarce find a place in these pages, for there is no special lesson to be learned from it, nor was any one of the actors in the splendid drama a captain of the greatest note. It was, however, in this siege that Prince Eugene, who has done so much for the art of war, played one of his earliest, though a modest rôle, at the age of twenty.

In 1661 a war broke out between the emperor and the Turks, to which an end was put in the splendid victory of St. Gothard by Montecuculi. In 1682 a second war broke out, fostered openly by the Hungarians and secretly by the French. In 1683 the Turks invaded Hungary and laid siege

to Vienna. Their army, two hundred thousand strong, was
under command of Kara Mustapha, grand vizier, to whom
was intrusted the old green eagle-standard of the Prophet as
a badge of success; and on May 12 this force left Belgrade on
its march to Vienna. Aware of its destination, the emperor,
Leopold I., called on the princes of the empire for assistance, and made a treaty with John Sobieski, king of Poland,

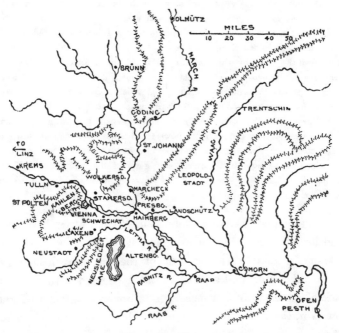

Vienna-Ofen Country.

to come to his aid with forty thousand men, the emperor
promising sixty thousand men to join him. The imperial
army was mustered in May at Presburg under Charles of
Lorraine, a soldier tried in the school of adversity, robbed of
his inheritance by the French, and a connection and devoted
servant of the emperor. It numbered thirty-three thousand

men, and with this handful Charles was holden to defend the
land, and to garrison Presburg, Raab and Comorn.

The Turks were already near Ofen, and on June 25
Charles intrenched himself in a camp between the Raab and
the Rabnitz, while Esterhazy held the line of the Waag, and
a Polish force lay at Trentschin.

The grand vizier had been counseled by Count Tököly, the
Hungarian insurgent, and some of his own
wise lieutenants not to march on Vienna,
but Kara Mustapha heeded not, and pushed
his van of horse out past the Neusiedler
Lake and to the line of the Leitha, leaving Raab, Comorn and Leopoldstadt on
his flank. Charles sent his foot back to
Vienna, and with his horse retired to Haim-
burg. The Turkish van attacked him July
7, and gave his cavalry a hard blow. Vienna was in a panic, and the emperor left it
next day for Linz. Count Stahremberg
was given command of the abandoned city,

Turkish Soldier.

from which a stampede of all the population able to leave
soon followed, to the number of sixty thousand souls.

The defenses of Vienna were wretched; the counterscarp
was only partly palisaded; gabions were wanting, barely ten
guns were mounted in the bastions, and the ditch was dry in
many places. The entire garrison consisted of the common
city guard and scarce one thousand troops of the line. On
July 9, however, Charles came up with his eleven thousand
horse, followed by some twelve thousand foot, — what was left
after taking out garrisons. Stahremberg was a man of experience and worth, stern and unflinching, who had won his way
by merit. He was just the man for the work; but he had
only six days to complete his preparations, for on July 13 the

whole country round the capital smoked from the burning villages fired by the Tartar horse. In these six days Stahremberg did wonders; every man in Vienna was got to work; the priest and the nobleman vied with the merchant, the laborer, to help on the cause. Victual was collected up and down the river, north and south; munitions were got from every point, and by July 13 over three hundred guns had been mounted. The spahis of the enemy's van now swarmed all round the town, from the mountains to the river; and a column of foot appeared in the suburbs, which Stahremberg received with a cannonade, and drove out by destroying everything outside the walls. As good luck would have it, the line troops sent to garrison the city marched in on this same day from across the river fourteen thousand strong; and with citizens, guilds, students and others, Stahremberg found under his command some twenty-two thousand men. On the 14th Kara Mustapha and his entire army stood before Vienna.

Turkish Soldier.

The Turks lost no time. On the night of the 13th–14th the van had opened trenches on the west of the town, at three points, and these stood under the grand vizier's own command, and that of Kara Mohammed and Ahmed Pasha. Charles, who had been lying with his cavalry in the Unter-Werd, retired across the Danube to the Bisamberg, pursued by the enemy's horse, which pressed him hard. The Turks then camped in a huge half-moon, along the hills from the river at Schwechat to the river at Nussdorf; and during the rest of July they built batteries of heavy siege-guns to back up their trenches.

Stahremberg was the life and soul of everything. Thrice a day he visited the works, and though repeatedly wounded, desisted not from his constant efforts. He was relentless against the cowardly or treacherous or lazy ; equally generous for courage or intelligence in the service. The grand vizier was no less active. On the tenth day of the siege the first mines were exploded, and sorties and assaults were of daily occurrence. Not to recount all these operations, suffice it to say that during the siege the Turks delivered eight assaults and sprung forty mines ; the besieged made twenty-four sorties, and fired ten counter-mines. Only seven times did the besieged hear from the outside news of the eagerly hoped-for army of relief.

Until the arrival of relief armies from Silesia, Moravia, Bohemia, Poland and the principalities of the empire, Charles of Lorraine was to keep open the fords of the Danube and hold the river from Presburg to Tulln. Tököly, on the other hand, led a raiding party to head off the Poles, and easily captured the town of Presburg ; the citadel held out. Hereupon Charles descended from his Bisam eyrie, sharply followed up the Hungarian, beat him at Landschütz, drove him beyond the Waag, and recaptured Presburg. The garrisons of Comorn, Raab and Altenburg proved useless, allowing Turkish convoys to pass under their walls unmolested. Tököly rapidly recovered from his defeat, forced his way August 6 across the March at St. Johann, purposing to join a Turkish force which should cross the Danube at the Tabor island, and then drive Charles from the Bisam hills, aided by a demonstration of Tartar horse on St. Polten to engage his attention. But Charles was equal to the situation. Sending a force against the Turks at Tabor, he prevented their crossing, and himself moved against Tököly and threw him back across the March. Shortly after, he retired

to Tulln to protect the building of bridges for the approaching armies of relief, a movement which Tököly improved by
again crossing the March at Göding with his own forces and
ten thousand Tartar cavalry, and devastating to Wölkersdorf.
In connection with this raid, a Turkish force crossed at Mar-
check, joined a body from Vienna, and advanced twelve thousand strong up the Danube ; but Charles, on August 24, fell
on this body and beat it so badly at Stamersdorf, that a mere
fraction was left to escape by swimming across the river.
This handsome operation speedily recalled Tököly from his
foray.

Meanwhile Sobieski's van had reached Olmütz August 25,
and on September 4 the Tulln bridge. Tököly had been
able but slightly to annoy his advance. Two days later the
entire Polish army of twenty-six thousand men reported.
The Bavarians and Saxons, the Swabians and Franconians,
had come down the Danube, and reached Krems September
7. During the succeeding days the passage of the Danube
was effected. The total forces thus reunited came to thirty-
nine thousand foot and forty-six thousand horse. In the
absence of the emperor, the command fell to Sobieski, who,
though a king, was a plain soldier and an able man, self-reli-
ant and bold, who had fought against the Great Elector, the
Swedes, the Cossacks and the Turks, and always with honor.
Charles and he had been rival candidates for the Polish
crown ; but they were none the less good friends. " Prince,
take that great soldier as a model ! " said Sobieski to his son.

Rather than consume time by marching round by the valley roads, Sobieski and Charles agreed to speed their advance
over the Kahlenberg to the city, which was already in the
extremity of danger. Sobieski took command of the right
wing, Charles of the left.

For two months the grand vizier had lain opposite Vienna,

and had not detached a man from his enormous forces to forestall this army of relief, or to interfere with its passage of the Danube. " Such a man," said Sobieski, " is already beaten ! " From day to day Kara Mustapha had expected to force an entrance within the walls. He had been so blinded

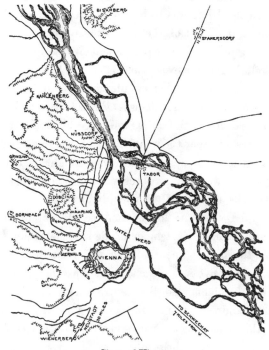

Siege of Vienna.

by the work in his front that he knew nothing of the operations on his flank, and expected the army of relief by way of the plain and the Wienerberg. Leaving part of his forces in the trenches on the 9th, he moved the rest of his troops to a camp at Laxenburg and Neustadt, sending detachments only to the Kahlenberg and to Grünzing. He did not believe that the army of relief was a well-organized one ; he did not

know that it was led by Sobieski; he had no great opinion
of Charles.

The king's battle orders were brief : the imperial troops
were to hug the river so as to throw relief into Vienna; in the
advance, the infantry and artillery were to precede the cavalry; once in line the latter was to fill the intervals of the
former ; a third line was to be held in reserve ; the first and
generally sharp onset of the Turkish cavalry was to be met
by throwing out the light Spanish squadrons.

The relief came none too soon.   Vienna had been pounded
into ruins; but Stahremberg would not give up ; every breach
was repaired, every assault was thrown back; every man,
under his stern eye and active presence, did his duty.   The
question was, whether the weakened garrison and works could
resist a general assault, — and when might it not come ?
Happy indeed was the sore beset Kaiserstadt, when rockets
from the hills announced the friendly advance !

The grand vizier no longer doubted the intention of the
Christians when, on September 12, he saw the columns emerging from the hills.   The challenge was answered.   He drew
up his army in five heavy lines, from Nussdorf to Dornbach,
and himself commanded the centre, the pashas the wings.
Sobieski's address to the troops was fervent : " We have
beaten this same enemy, you and I.   To-day you fight not
for Poland but for Christianity; not for your king, but for
your God !   I have but one order for you : wherever you see
your king, follow and fear not ! "

The line was formed, and the artillery at 7 A. M. opened
from Kahlenberg village against Nussdorf.   The Poles on
the right had a long and difficult route through the mountain roads to pass over before they could reach the Turkish
left ; and the German troops fought seven long hours against
heavy odds and desperate resistance through the glens and

defiles of the foothills, making with splendid gallantry a marked advance. Five times did the Turkish serried masses charge in on the German lines; but these wavered not, though a heavy Turkish battery on the Döbling hill finally put a term to their gain. It was 2 o'clock and neither centre nor right had come into close quarters with the enemy. Finally Sobieski emerged from the Dornbach hills and fell sharply on the Turkish array. Their onset was gallant; their king was present at the point of grav-est danger; but the deep masses of the Turkish for-mation resisted their bravest charges. Finally a regiment of lancers broke, and in its retreat threatened to force back the line in disorder. But Charles was near by; he ordered an advance on the Turkish centre; it was given with a will; under it the Poles rallied; one more charge and the Turkish left

Polish Cavalryman.

was rolled up on its centre. Charles captured the great Döbling battery, drove back the enemy, and forced his way, fighting for every step, to Währing, while Sobieski pursued the now broken enemy to Hernals. Louis of Baden headed a few squadrons, and fought his way to the west gate of Vienna, where he and Stahremberg at once made a sortie on the janis-saries, who still kept up a fire from their trenches. Soon a panic seized the Turks, and once the flight began there was no more organization left. In a *sauve qui peut* rabble the entire army fled — barring a slight stand at St. Ulrich's — back through the Wienerberg defiles to Raab.

The loss of the Turks is given as from ten thousand to twenty-five thousand men. That of the allies is not known. In the siege there had fallen in Vienna five thousand men from wounds, twenty thousand from disease. The booty was enormous. There was no marked pursuit.

On September 14 the emperor, whose capital had been saved as by a miracle, reëntered the city. Next day, invited by Sobieski, he went out to view the Turkish camp. A curious scene ensued. The pride-beridden successor of the Cæsars, for fear of losing some of his imperial dignity, treated the king of Poland, his saviour, *de haut en bas*, to the infinite disgust of the Polish army, and the annoyance, mixed with a keen sense of ridicule, of Sobieski. The Pole had too much good sense not to wash his hands of the absurd business; but to Leopold, the personal attitude of the German emperor towards an elective king was a matter of moment. It had been a question of discussion in the cabinet, and on Charles of Lorraine being asked how the emperor should receive such a monarch, he replied: " When he has saved the empire, with open arms !" But Leopold's ideas of rank could not permit him so far to condescend.

In the grand vizier's tent was found clear proof that the war had been fostered by France; and Sobieski could not deny himself the pleasure of sending a report of the battle in his own hand to the Most Christian King Louis XIV.

The grand vizier was able enough to cast the blame on his subordinates, many of whom he executed, and to justify his conduct to the sultan, by whom he was at first liberally rewarded. The retreat of the Turkish army was hastened by Charles and Sobieski, who followed it up as far as Ofen. Other engagements ensued, but they have no part in the relief of Vienna.

LII.

LUXEMBURG AND CATINAT. 1690–1693.

LUXEMBURG was naturally a good soldier; but he was stunted by the narrow method of Louvois, which was a mere war of sieges that parceled out the army in small detachments. In 1690 Luxemburg had one hundred thousand men in the Netherlands, to oppose less than sixty thousand allies. He met Waldeck at Fleurus in July, and coupled with a cavalry flank attack, his assault was stout enough to win a handsome victory. The road to Brussels was open, but Luxemburg did not know enough to improve the occasion. In 1692 William III. fell on Luxemburg at Steenkirke, but owing to difficulties of the ground, was beaten with very heavy loss. In 1693 Luxemburg again met William at Neerwinden, where the allies were heavily intrenched, and again won a hard-fought victory. But despite all these triumphs the French gained no headway, and the allies kept the field. In this same year Catinat defeated the duke of Savoy at Marsaglia. The result of these splendid victories was comparatively little.

BEFORE proceeding to the brilliant campaigns which characterized the War of the Spanish Succession, short mention should be made of three of the battles of the French under the duke of Luxemburg. This officer, who certainly possessed many of the qualities which go to make up a solid general, and who covered with renown the arms of France in the Netherlands, is nevertheless an excellent example of how depressing an effect the unenterprising method of that day could exert on even an able man, and brings out in stronger relief the immense personality of such a soldier as Turenne, who was able to cut loose from the hard and fast rules of the then art, and despite the inert tendencies of Louvois, put his own individuality into what he did; and of such men as Eugene and Marlborough, who cast to the winds the ancient ways, refusing to be tied by an obsolete system, and thus paved the way for a Frederick and a Napoleon. Guided either by the narrow rules of the art as he understood them, or by the narrower instructions of Louvois, who, though a great war minister, did not understand war, Luxemburg was

Luxemburg.

able to accomplish less than his opportunities and his opponents should have yielded him. With such resources, what might not a Turenne have won for France! What we might call Louvois' one maxim of war was : Take all the enemy's strong places which you can lay your hands on so soon as you reach his territory ; and though he had seen the most splendid victories and the greatest successes of France won by men who disregarded the rule and moved on the enemy, he could not get beyond this point in his comprehension of war. That this system called for the parceling out of troops in petty detachments in the various sieges, to much useless small war, and to the loss of many men in efforts to accomplish what was scarcely worth the while, he did not consider. His system made him naturally timid ; the advent on the theatre of operations of a force so small that he could afford to despise it sent him into a tremor of caution, and resulted as a rule in his giving his generals orders to act on the defensive. He spent much time and more money in spying out what the enemy was doing, when he might have kept the initiative. One of his pet schemes was to rob the enemy of means of subsistence by devastating wide districts, or by devising extensive operations to cut off the enemy's supplies. All this was done with immense outlay and with vast intelli-

gence ; but it lacked that divine spark to which, if to anything, the genius for war is due.

At the opening of 1690 there stood one hundred thousand
French under the duke of Luxemburg on the borders of the
Netherlands. Opposite them were eighteen thousand Spaniards under Castanaga ; while thirty thousand allies under
Prince Waldeck lay between the Meuse and Dender. A body
of eleven thousand Brandenburgers was approaching, and
their coming so strongly impressed Louvois that he ordered
Luxemburg to stand on the defensive. The huge French
force was in three corps : Marshal Boufflers leaning on the
Meuse; the duke in the centre ; and Marshal Humières
between the Scheldt and Lys. The latter body took no part
in the operations, but remained in its fortified lines. Luxemburg began by devastating the
region occupied by his left;
but learning that Waldeck
had marched towards Dinant
on the Meuse, he drew in
Boufflers and advanced on the
prince with forty thousand
men. At Fleurus, northeast
of Charleroi, he met Waldeck
at the head of twenty-five thousand allies on July 1. The
prince was drawn up with
Ligny and St. Amand in front
of his left, and Fleurus some

Battle of Fleurus

distance in front of his right. A small stream ran in his
front, and the land rose towards his right, and then suddenly
dipped so as to conceal the movement of troops beyond the
edge of the hill to any one on the level. Beyond the brook
was land of about equal height, on which lay the French.

Drawing up in two lines of infantry, with the horse in two lines on the flanks, Luxemburg sent Gournay, an excellent cavalry officer, with the entire left wing, under cover of the hill of Fleurus, around to fall on the right flank of the allies.

Waldeck neglected to scout the vicinity of his position, and knew nothing of the manœuvre. While Gournay was on the way, the French infantry made a stout front attack by crossing the stream and marching up the slope of the plateau, which assault Waldeck met in good style, and drove back. But Luxemburg rallied his battalions and again led them to the attack; and this being nicely timed, so that Gournay could simultaneously fall on the flank of the allies, their array was broken up with extremely heavy losses, — said to have been six thousand killed. The victory was decisive. The road to Brussels was open; but neither would Luxemburg of his own initiative advance farther, nor could he do so without orders from Louvois. He celebrated his triumph by camping six days on the battle-field, and then retired across the Sambre, and permitted Waldeck at his leisure to join the elector of Brandenburg in Brussels.

Catinat.

In this same year Marshal Catinat won a victory over the duke of Savoy at Staffarda. There were but eighteen thousand French in Italy, but they were assisted by the incompetence of the duke. Crossing the Po from Turin, he marched against Catinat and met him at the monastery of Staffarda. He intended to attack, but assuming a defensive position full of faults, Catinat took advantage of one of these, turned his left flank and utterly worsted him. The French then captured

Susa and overran Savoy. There are no reliable accounts of this engagement.

For the next year (1691) France put one hundred and twenty thousand men into the field. As it was his occasional pleasure to do, Louis XIV. took the field in person and besieged Mons; having taken which he returned to Paris. Luxemburg was left in command, with instructions not to indulge in battle unless victory was secure, and to rely mainly on his cavalry. Neither party had any apparent liking for the offensive this year; Liège was burned by Luxemburg from political spite; and William III. moved on Dinant, expecting to attack Marshal Boufflers singly; but Luxemburg came up to his aid. Far outnumbering the enemy, he would have liked to fight; but his rigid instructions held him back. This was the sort of campaign which Louvois deemed a handsome one.

William III. was as if created to oppose such an unscrupulous conqueror as Louis XIV. He was not of the mould which is instinct with great projects; he had no craving for extension of territory; but he was determined to keep what he rightfully owned, and to do this, as he said, " he could die in the last dike." Few men have lost so many battles and still kept the field; fewer yet would have broken the dikes and let the ocean in to destroy the work of generations in order to preserve the autonomy of his country and the faith and liberty it enjoyed. He was of the stuff which would have given Holland as a whole back to the waves, and have begun afresh a republic in the New World.

Without being in any sense a great soldier, William accomplished results where men who had many of the captain's traits would have wrecked their cause. Beginning with but a tithe of the gigantic forces of the French, he slowly worked up to an equality with them; meanwhile, with a per-

sistency rarely matched, wresting from them and holding
more and more ground. He was so fond of war that he
fought at St. Denis after he knew that peace had been concluded. He was not a brilliant soldier, but he was a safe one
in the rôle which he enacted.

Next year, 1692, Louis in person besieged Namur. Louvois had died. On the capture of the place, Luxemburg was
again left in command with defensive orders, and he chose to
retire to the Brussels country, where was more forage for his
large force of cavalry, artillery and train horses. William

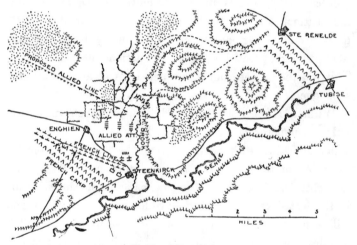

Battle of Steenkirke.

spread a report that he would undertake to recapture Namur,
and having made some feints in that direction, Luxemburg
weakened himself to send a detachment to the aid of Namur,
and gave William the opportunity to fall on him at Steenkirke.

Luxemburg was camped with the right leaning on Steenkirke and his left near Enghien; William lay between Tubise
and St. Renelde; the ground between the two armies was

well accentuated by hills of one or two hundred feet above
the bed of the Senne, and so much cut up by woods, marshes
and hedges that it was a network of defiles, through which it
was almost impossible to manœuvre to advantage. Neither
army could approach the other except by passing through
such defiles. There happened to be a spy at the allied headquarters who sold news to the French. This man William discovered and compelled to write to Luxemburg that the allies
were about to seize the defiles along the Steenkirke brook in
order to protect their foragers, but without the intention of
making any special movement; and under this *ruse de guerre*
managed to mass his men and to debouch suddenly on Luxemburg July 24, to the utter surprise of the latter, who had
explained away the news which his scouts brought in by the
information received from his old spy. William had done
well, but the event was not as fortunate as the beginning.

The French right, composed of horse, lay in advance of
Steenkirke, and to protect this a brigade of foot had camped
in its front. Upon this force the blow of the allies first fell;
its guns were taken and turned against the French, and the
right seemed threatened with destruction. But the allies
could not debouch rapidly enough from behind the brook.
Luxemburg was active, speedily sent succor to the right,
where the damage was repaired, and got his forces into line
with what was, under the circumstances, most praiseworthy
speed. Luckily for the French, their front was covered by
fields inclosed by hedges, which prevented the allies from
summarily attacking their line *en masse*. William's front
attack was feeble, and was driven back by the French first
line, which then advanced and enabled the second line to
form in its rear and get out beyond the camp. Once in line,
the French fought well, and William, whose own right had
been led astray by a night march and had not come up, had

really accomplished nothing but a surprise of the French
right. The fighting was tenacious to the last degree on both
sides. The ground was unsuited to the operations of cavalry, and the whole affair was a mêlée, quite lacking anything like grand-tactics. The battle was in an irregular parallel order, and the allies were not so well marshaled as to
deliver a sudden and effective blow. Much fault was found
on the allied side for the failure of Count Solmes to sustain
the English column. The result of the battle was the defeat
of the allies, with, it is claimed, ten thousand dead and as
many wounded. The French loss must have been as great.
The allies abandoned most of their guns. Had William
delayed his attack until he was sure that his right had come
up, the victory would probably have been his, for his stratagem worked well; he was hidden by the ground and by the
deceit practiced on Luxemburg, and the French were quite
taken by surprise.

Despite this splendid victory, Luxemburg did nothing. On
the other hand, William, who was curiously hard to discour-
age, managed to join fifteen thousand English troops, which
had landed in Ostende, and then captured Furnes and Dixmuiden. On his leaving the Netherlands these places were
recaptured by the French.

For the campaign of 1693 Louis put no less than one hundred and thirty thousand men in the field, and personally
undertook the siege of Liège, a work which, for lack of a
better objective, William determined to interrupt. About
this time Heidelberg fell, which gave the French a chance to
win success in Germany, and forty thousand men were sent
thither from the Netherlands, while Louis left Luxemburg
to continue the operations against William, instructing him
to keep the allies from manœuvring towards the sea-coast.
To carry out these orders, Luxemburg threatened Louvain

and then Liège, and lost much time in useless operations; but learning in July that William had depleted his force by a number of detachments, and lay at Neerwinden on the Geete, he marched to attack him, though he had but half his force under the colors.

Neerwinden is close to the Little Geete, and the village of Romsdorf lies east of it on the brook of Landen or Molen-

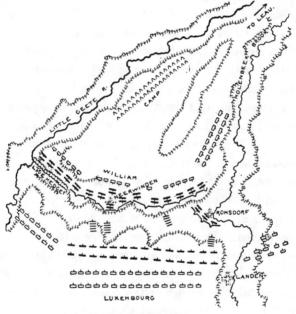

Battle of Neerwinden.

beck, both of which streams unite to the north and form a triangular plateau five miles long. Here William had camped, between Neerwinden and Romsdorf, and, hearing of Luxemburg's approach, had fortified his lines, and believed the position impregnable. The line was convex. Neerwinden and a small ravine with a quickset hedge from the village to the Geete protected the allied right; the centre was covered by somewhat lower land in its front to Romsdorf; the left was thrown back *en potence*, and proved useless in the battle. The weakness of the position was that it was a crowded one. The right was made especially strong, Neerwinden was filled with foot, and Romsdorf was intrenched. One hundred guns stood in battery along the line. The horse was in reserve or on the left. The land to the south is slightly higher than the Neerwinden plateau, but gently descends towards it. The beds of the brooks are sixty to eighty feet lower than the rolling hills.

On the afternoon of July 28 Luxemburg arrived in William's front with his van of cavalry and reconnoitred. His first duty was to expel the enemy from Landen, which he did, so as to lean his right on it in the battle he proposed to deliver next day, and here he put forty battalions of foot. At daylight of July 29 the guns opened, and under a severe fire, the French formed for the attack. They were substantially in two lines of foot with two lines of horse in their rear, and cavalry on both flanks in three lines.

The main attack was opened at 6 A. M. by the French left on Neerwinden. The French pushed vigorously in, took the village, but were fiercely met and driven out. On the French right the fighting was less marked. A second time Luxemburg assaulted Neerwinden and successfully gained an entrance, but only to be a second time ejected, partly because the assault on Romsdorf was not pushed home, so as to give the enemy more to do.

Luxemburg deserves great credit for not losing courage at these two failures. He prepared for a new assault on Neerwinden, and as he saw that in anticipation of it the allies were disgarnishing their left centre to protect Neerwinden with more troops, he directed Marquis Feuquière to assault the intrenchments on the west of Romsdorf in force. This

was done in good form, and Feuquière made a lodgment on
the highest part of the ground held by the allied line, and
thus took the foot defending Neerwinden in reverse, and in a
determined assault at the same time the duke took Neerwinden and held it. This was the moment for the allied cavalry
of the left to put in its work. There had been and was nothing
in its front; and had it been well commanded, it could have
changed front and hustled the French under Feuquière back
by a charge on their flank. But this body of cavalry, without firing a salvo or drawing a sabre, saw fit to retire to Léau,
and between the duke and Feuquière the bulk of the allied
foot on the right was driven into the Geete, with a loss of
eighteen thousand men killed, wounded and prisoners, one
hundred and four guns and numberless trophies. The French
loss was heavy. There was no attempt at pursuit; Luxemburg was held by his orders to obtain further instructions
from the king; and finally he sat down to besiege Charleroi.
The result of this splendid victory was naught, owing to the
mischievous system ingrained in all the French generals by
Louvois. The taking of Charleroi ended this campaign. It
is a remarkable fact, and much to his credit, that despite all
these defeats William kept the field. It would have been
otherwise had Turenne stood in the place of Luxemburg.

Luxemburg died in 1695. Villeroi succeeded him, but
accomplished nothing. The year which saw the victory of
Neerwinden in the Low Countries added one more victory to
the French arms in Italy. In 1691 Prince Eugene came to
assist the duke of Savoy, and the French accomplished little.
In 1692 the duke raised his forces to fifty thousand men
and made a raid into the Dauphiné, but without much result.
In 1693, as he was besieging Pinerolo, Catinat, who had
been pushed well back into the mountains, escaped from his
trap, turned the duke's flank and obliged him to retire, and

then forced battle on him October 4 at Marsaglia, southwest of Turin.

When the duke became aware of the approach of the French, he crossed the little river Cisola and drew up his army, leaning his left on this stream, and extending his right across to a small patch of woods which lay near another small stream, unnamed. On his left was the height of Piosaca, on which he might have leaned this flank to effect; but neglecting to do so, he left it for the enemy to occupy, and thus threaten his line in reverse. Both streams were almost dry at this season, and the wood on the duke's right was so open that even cavalry could ride through it. Catinat at once seized on the salient errors of the duke, and occupied the Piosaca heights. He then pushed a stout attack all along the

Battle of Marsaglia.

Savoyard line, and followed it up by enveloping its left. Success began here. The duke's army was rolled up on the centre and right, and so badly defeated that some time after he concluded peace.

During this period the operations on the Rhine were insignificant. The war on the border of Spain was enlivened only by the conquest of Barcelona (1697). In Ireland the cause of James was lost in the battle of the Boyne; and at Cape La Hogue the English fleet destroyed the French fleet in 1692.

There is no denying to the French a number of brilliant

victories on land; they were in a sense almost as splendid as the later victories of the allies under Marlborough and Eugene. But the latter knew how to utilize them and generally did; not so the Louvois-taught French. And the result of all their victories did not offset the general downhill tendency of the fortune of France.

France had lost so much that it would seem as if the allies could have imposed harsh terms on her. But in the Peace of Ryswick (1697) she was no further mulcted than to make her yield up, except Alsatia and Strasburg, all her conquests in the Netherlands, on the Rhine and in Spain. In this peace William III. was acknowledged king of England and Anne as his successor. The main fortresses in the Spanish Netherlands were to be garrisoned by the Dutch. Freiburg, Breisach and Philipsburg went to the empire; Zweibrücken to Sweden; Lorraine was restored to Duke Leopold; the Rhine was made free.

Except the work of Luxemburg and Catinat, nothing in the operations since the death of Turenne is worthy of extended notice.

French Musketeer. (17th Century.)

LIII.

PRINCE EUGENE AGAINST CATINAT. 1701.

THE death, childless, of Charles II. of Spain left France, Austria and Bavaria to claim the throne; and the War of the Spanish Succession resulted. Prince Eugene of Savoy was French by birth, but, unable to get military preferment at home, he sought his fortune at the court of the emperor, whom thereafter he served throughout life. By his exceptional skill, courage and services he early rose to be field-marshal, and in 1697 won the splendid victory of Zenta against the Turks. In 1701 Prince Eugene with thirty thousand men was sent to Italy against Catinat. He cut a new road down the Adige, crossed below Verona, and gradually forced the French back. Catinat was restricted by his orders, and had not been able to manœuvre as he otherwise might. By skilful operations, Eugene regained all northern Italy as far as the Oglio.

THE intermarriages of the reigning families of Europe have generally resulted in rival claims of territory or in jealousy of a preponderating political influence. In the opening year of the eighteenth century a serious European question arose from the death of Charles II. of Spain. A genealogical table best explains the facts.

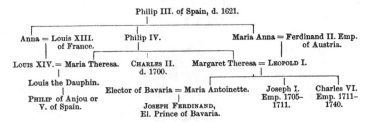

Inasmuch as Charles II. was childless, and the Spanish Hapsburgs threatened to become extinct after the general settlement of the Peace of Ryswick, the question as to who should succeed to the Spanish throne became the leading one among all the nations of Europe. In 1698 the powers made a treaty of partition, by which Spain, the Indies and the Netherlands should go to the electoral prince of Bavaria; Naples and Sicily and some other minor places to the Dauphin; Milan to the Archduke Charles. This treaty, concluded without the consent of Charles II., provoked this monarch into making the prince elector of Bavaria his sole heir; and to this the naval powers agreed; but the death of the prince in 1699 reopened the entire question. In 1700 another treaty of partition was made, by which Spain and the Indies should go to the Archduke Charles; Naples, Sicily and Lorraine to the Dauphin, and Milan to the duke of Lorraine as a compensation for his own land. But again changing his mind, Charles II. made a will leaving his entire possessions to Philip of Anjou, and in 1700 died. Louis XIV. then chose to disregard the treaty of partition and to act under the will; and the duke of Anjou was proclaimed as Philip V., and started for Spain amid the cries of "Il n'y a plus de Pyrenées!"

The complex nature of this question, which was what led to the War of the Spanish Succession, thus had a legal and a political aspect. On the one side there were three claimants to the throne of Spain: Louis XIV., son of the elder daughter of Philip III. and husband of the elder daughter of Philip IV., both of which princesses had renounced their inheritance; Leopold I. of Austria, son of the younger daughter of Philip III. and husband of the younger daughter of Philip IV., both of which princesses had reserved their inheritance; Joseph Ferdinand, electoral prince of Bavaria, great-grandson of Philip IV. Louis XIV. claimed the throne for his second grandson, and Leopold for his second son. On the other side, the balance of power forbade that either France or Austria should succeed to the enormous Spanish territory, and England and Holland joined hands to enforce this view. The naval powers and estates of the empire, with Prussia (and later Portugal), joined the emperor in a Grand Alliance to prevent France from securing Spain. As allies France had Savoy and Mantua, Bavaria and Cologne, but in 1703 Savoy deserted France. The three great men of the Grand Alliance were Eugene, the emperor's general, Marlborough, the commander of the Anglo-Dutch, and A. Heinsius, pensionary of Holland. After the death of William III. in 1702, Spain played no great part in the war, and being safe on her weakest point, the Pyrenees, France could devote her energies to Italy, the Rhine and the Netherlands. France had interior lines and a single purpose; the allies had exterior lines and very divergent purposes. In population the two contestants were about equal; but Austria was kept busy by her Hungarian troubles and the Turkish wars. England was wholly in earnest; Holland needed to defend herself against France, from whose ambition she had in the late wars suffered so much. The other members of the Grand Alliance were not easy to persuade into giving active succor. It was in the War of the Spanish Succession that we find the best work of Eugene, Marlborough, Vendome and Villars.

Prince Eugene of Savoy was fifth son of Prince Maurice of Savoy-Carignan, count of Soissons, commander of the Swiss in the French service, and governor of Champagne. His mother was niece of Cardinal Mazarin. He was born in Paris, October 18, 1663, and early destined for the church. His father died when he was ten, and his mother fell into disfavor. Eugene sought admittance to the army, but could not obtain it, as his diminutive stature and slight physique spoke against him. But from childhood up he had pored over Plutarch's Lives; his firm desire was to be a soldier; his studies

all tended in this direction, and he made himself proficient in
every technical branch of the military art.

Unable to get military preferment in France, Eugene went
— as many other young noblemen did — to Vienna, where
the Emperor Leopold was seeking well-trained volunteers to
resist the incursions of the Turks. Here, in 1683, he especially
distinguished himself in the re-
lief of Vienna by Sobieski, rose
speedily to be colonel, did a
great deal of staff duty, and
earned universal commendation from his superiors. In the
wars against the Turks, Prince
Eugene showed himself to have
not only a true military eye,
but a quite uncommon courage,
moral and physical. His acts
of gallantry were exceptional,

Prince Eugene.

and he proved that he could shoulder responsibility. In 1686
he rose to be major-general, and two years later field-marshal
lieutenant, being then but twenty-five years of age. He had
already been several times wounded.

The Netherlands War had again broken out in 1689. The
emperor, with Bavaria, Sweden and Spain, took the part of
the prince of Orange against France, and Leopold sent Prince
Eugene to Turin to negotiate a treaty with Duke Victor Ama-
deus. The prince would have preferred to remain in service against the Turks, but he accomplished his mission well.
(1689–1690.)

Learning of this treaty, Louis XIV. sent Catinat with
twelve thousand men into Piedmont.' Prince Eugene was
dispatched with eighteen thousand men to reinforce the duke;
and, in connection with him, or at times alone, Eugene fought

handsomely in the Italian campaigns of 1690 to 1696, when
by mutual agreement Italy became neutral.

Louis XIV. now tried to win Eugene back, by offering him
the grade of marshal of France, the governorship of Champagne and two hundred thousand livres salary; but Eugene
clave to the emperor, who had steadily befriended him, and
for this act of loyalty was placed in larger commands.

His first independent campaign was in 1697 with fifty
thousand men against the Turks under the Sultan Kara Mus-

Zenta Campaign.

tapha, who had advanced on the empire a hundred thousand
strong. He moved down between the Save and the Drave
rivers to the Danube-Theiss region, where, after some manœuvring between these two rivers, he checked the Turks in
the siege of Peterwardein and of Szegedin. Among the most
interesting campaigns of this great soldier during his long and
laborious life are those against the Turks, but they do not come
within the scope of this work. The battle which practically
ended this campaign is, however, characteristic of the man.

The sultan planned to cross to the left bank of the Theiss, intending to pillage and devastate upper Hungary and Sieben-bürgen (Transylvania) ; and Prince Eugene determined to attack his army at the passage of the bridge which it held, before it had completed the operation. At the moment of attack the prince received dispatches, but he is said, rather doubtfully, to have refused to open them, rightly guessing that they were orders not to be led into battle.

The Turkish army was drawn up in a great bow in front of the bridge near Zenta, protected by earthworks, by the baggage wagons lashed together Zisca-fashion, and with an inner bridge-head. About one hundred guns were in position. Zenta was near the right. The river was covered with transports, and a part of the Turkish army under the sultan had already crossed to the other side ; and for this reason Eugene was anxious to attack. It was September 11.

Having left his infantry resting under arms, the prince rode forward to reconnoitre ; and ascertaining that the Turks were hastening to get across, — a fact which was apt to breed confusion, — he at once brought his army into position, with the right on the Theiss, and swung it by a right wheel so that it enveloped the enemy's lines. There were. but three or four hours of daylight. His concentric fire of artillery was highly effective and that of the Turks the reverse, for their guns were big and cumbrous and their ammunition ill-assorted. The attack was begun by the grand vizier sending out a cavalry detachment, which was, however, quickly driven back ; General Rabutin on the Austrian left opened the assault ; the centre under Prince Eugene and right under Count Stahremberg followed. The Turks resisted stoutly, but the Austrians, though outnumbered two to one, stormed the earthworks and an hour later the bridge-head. Here the fighting was desperate and the Turkish loss fearful, for the

Austrians gave no quarter. The victory was complete. From ten thousand to twenty thousand Turks are said to have fallen, among them many pashas and the grand vizier. The camp on the other bank and an enormous booty fell into the Austrian hands; guns and flags were captured wholesale; and the Turks retired east to Temesvar. The Austrian loss was but two thousand killed and wounded.

This first victory of Prince Eugene's does him great credit, especially in view of the responsibility he took. After a three days' rest he followed the Turks, but they had retired south to Belgrade, leaving a strong garrison in Temesvar. The siege of this place promised to occupy so much time that it would practically consume the rest of the campaign; and Eugene preferred to quarter his troops and undertake an expedition with twenty-five hundred foot, four thousand horse and twelve guns into Bosnia, to capture the capital, Bosna-Seraj. The Turks were far from expecting an incursion, and in less than three weeks the prince overcame the whole province and returned. The capital was captured and accidentally burned; the citadel held out. On the home march the Austrians destroyed the defenses of all captured towns, and the army then went into winter-quarters.

On returning to Vienna Prince Eugene found that his enemies, under the lead of Field-Marshal Caprara, had managed to rouse the anger of the emperor against him for disobedience of orders in fighting the battle of Zenta, and he was placed in arrest. The people, rejoiced at the splendid victory, were, however, with him; the disfavor of the emperor lasted but a short while, and resulted in the justification of the prince, who next year was again placed in sole command in Hungary, and made independent of the Austrian council general of war. His short humiliation, which is also doubtful, in no wise harmed his eventual reputation.

In 1698 the Austrian army continued under command of Prince Eugene, who manœuvred over much the same territory; but we cannot detail the operations, and the war eventually languished into a truce and peace.

Prince Eugene was next employed in the War of the Spanish Succession.

At the opening of 1701 the emperor had under his control not exceeding eighty-five thousand men. Of these thirty thousand, one third horse, were sent under Eugene into Italy, and assembled at Roveredo; twenty-one thousand were on the Rhine, and the rest were in Austria and Hungary. Louis XIV. and his allies had over two hundred thousand men, of whom seventy-five thousand were in Flanders, not including the garrisons of the strong places, fifteen thousand on the Moselle, forty-one thousand on the Rhine, three thousand in Alsatian garrisons, and in Italy thirty-three thousand in the field and eleven thousand in garrison, not to count some twenty thousand Savoyards and Wolfenbüttel troops. Louis' large preponderance of force and his alliance with Bavaria opened a promising chance for a summary march on Vienna with his main army, which should cross the Rhine and join the Bavarians and Wolfenbüttel troops, the whole to be sustained on the right by the advance of the Italian contingent. Such an operation might have settled the war in his favor in one campaign. The emperor would probably have succumbed, and the allies been dispersed. But Louis chose to act on the defensive, for he no longer had a Turenne to advise him; the emperor joined hands with the other enemies of France, and during the long war which followed, the empire, England and Holland were held together by the splendid abilities of Eugene, Marlborough and Heinsius.

In the early part of 1701 there were then in Italy some thirty-three thousand French in the field; five thousand in

Mantua, and six thousand in the strong places of Mirandola, Cremona, Pizzighetone, Lodi, Lecco and other towns. They were of good quality, but scarcely as able as the imperial troops, who had seen war in Hungary and were service-hard-

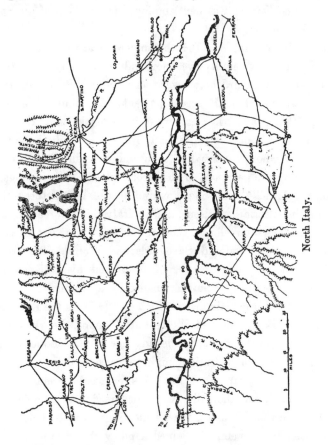

North Italy.

ened. Marshal Catinat, who was in command, with orders to remain on the defensive and not to cross to the left bank of the Adige, — in other words not to invade Venetian territory, — took up his stand at Rivoli between the lake of Garda and the Adige, where he lay athwart the imperial advance from the Tyrol into northern Italy. Prince Eugene, whose task it was to drive the French from Italy, and who joined the army at Roveredo May 20, at once perceived that he had no resource but to violate the neutrality of Venice by crossing her territory, and determined to move down on the left bank of the Adige, and cross the river below. This was a thing he would scarcely have dared to do unless he had known by means of a secret understanding with the duke of Savoy, the happy relic of their recent joint campaigns against Catinat, that the French marshal had orders not to cross the Adige; for without this certainty Eugene laid himself open to being absolutely cut off from his base. The only good road, at that day, lay over the foothills of Monte Baldo along the right bank, and was in possession of the enemy. The route Eugene proposed to take was then a mere footpath, and a proper road over thirty miles long had to be built at vast exertion. A force of six thousand pioneers was set to work, and within a week several roads down the valleys of the Adige affluents were made practicable; but they remained so poor that the cavalry was compelled to lead the horses in single file, and the wagons and guns had to be dismounted at some places, and at others to be lowered or raised by windlasses up or down perpendicular rocks.

On this road, despite the difficulties, which were surmounted by wonderful persistence and ability, Prince Eugene moved south, and on May 28 reached Verona undiscovered by Catinat, whose orders not only tied his hands, but who must have relaxed his usual vigilance; for while Eugene worked and marched behind the mountains, a proper system of spies or scouting would have revealed his project. Eugene quite outwitted his opponent. So soon as the French general discovered the imperial manœuvre, he left part of his army at Rivoli and marched down the right bank of the Adige with the rest; but Eugene had disposed his troops from Verona down in such a way as to make Catinat string out his own forces over a long line. He utilized the southwesterly bend of the Adige below Cologna so as to compel Catinat to occupy the bow on bad terrain, while he himself held only the chord on good, and by skillful feints managed to convince his opponent that he would pass the river above Verona, though his troops already reached down as far as Legnano. Catinat did not fathom Eugene's scheme, and tired his troops by restless marching up and down; and the prince, meanwhile keeping Catinat busy at Rivoli by a small detachment, bridged the swollen Adige and the several canals to the west, put his forces over at Castelbaldo on July 9, and taking Carpi, in front of which he beat a large French cavalry party with loss of one thousand men, he crossed the Tartaro and threatened Catinat's right flank. In this engagement Eugene himself was wounded. Like Gustavus, he was always in the thick of the fray, and his wounds were frequent, but happily not often severe.

In this combat at Carpi, it is noteworthy that Eugene employed his dragoons in exactly the same manner as we were wont to use our cavalry in the civil war: he dismounted them on ground unsuitable for cavalry, and on good terrain sent them in at a charge against the enemy. We could ask no better precedent for our American method.

When Catinat found Eugene in force below Verona, he imagined that he was about to push towards the Po, cross it and enter the Modena territory, and he still further divided his forces, leading a strong party down to Ostiglia. He had started on a wrong theory, and could not cast it off. Had Eugene pushed home at this moment, he might have turned his flank and rolled up the entire French army like a scroll; but bad roads, which made concentration difficult, and the delay in the crossing of his heavy artillery and trains held him back, and Catinat managed to save himself by summary retreat on Villafranca, where he concentrated his scattered forces. Eugene made preparations to attack him the next day, but Catinat had now gauged the enemy's purpose, gathered his dispersed forces, withdrew in the night across the Mincio and escaped. His main force he posted between Goito and Vallegio. The prince's whole operation had been admirably planned and executed, and deserves study in detail. In fact, one can scarcely appreciate the niceties of Eugene's strategy otherwise than by following every one of his movements day by day.

Shortly after, Prince Eugene made a flank movement up river past and near by the French army; and purposing to cross the Mincio and aim for Castiglione, he assembled his bridge-material at Salionze, where on July 28 he put over the army. He expected a French attack, but Catinat declined it, and retired behind the Chiese. While in this region, Eugene tried one of his fertile schemes to get hold of Mantua by treachery, but it quite failed; the enemy kept the place.

Louis XIV., dissatisfied with Catinat's apparent neglect, and unmindful of how he had been hampered by his orders, replaced him by Villeroi, until the arrival of whom the duke of Savoy as senior assumed supreme command. The latter brought a reinforcement of seventeen thousand troops, which increased the French-Savoyard army to fifty thousand men.

By advancing a wing to Peschiera and Lonato, Prince Eugene securely regained his direct communications with the Tyrol, but the French made no signs of attacking him. He then pushed forward to Castiglione and Montechiaro, and thence to Brescia, a manœuvre which turned the left flank of the French and threatened their communications with France through the Milan district, but which in turn laid him open to the same danger from the larger French army, that could always base on Mantua. The duke, however, thought not of any such bold scheme as a grand turning operation, but retired behind the Oglio, drawing in the troops from its upper waters down to Caneto, so as to present a new front to the imperial army.

Eugene had been victualing out of the Mantua region, but now transferred his commissariat. He had learned from the duke of Savoy that Villeroi had fighting orders, and though always active, had kept to small war only, for the enemy, now reinforced, quite outnumbered him. But in order to hold himself better, he advanced to the Oglio, took up a strong position at Chiari, and sat down to await some ten thousand reinforcements of his own which were to arrive from the Tyrol along the road west of Lake Garda, and via Salo down to Brescia, which city his position protected. He lay in the open country, but he could lean his flanks on small streams too deep to ford, of which the basin of the Po is full; and, in his front, he threw up some works. To all appearance fronting oddly in a strategic light, he was tactically well placed. Though Chiari belonged to Venice and was occupied by a Venetian garrison, Eugene put his own troops in it by force; he had already violated the Venetian territory by marching on the left bank of the Adige, and this seizure of Chiari made matters no worse. The enemy lay opposite him on the other side of the Oglio.

Catinat had in many campaigns shown himself to be a good officer, and deserved better of his king. Villeroi was a favorite at court, and got his command on that score, for he had no merit. Eugene is quoted as saying before the campaign opened, " If Villeroi is my opponent, I shall beat him ; if Vendome, I shall fight with him ; if Catinat, he may beat me." At that time he knew Catinat better than Vendome.

LIV.

EUGENE AGAINST VILLEROI AND VENDOME. 1701–1702.

Villeroi's first act was to attack Eugene at Palazzolo. He had forty-five thousand men to Eugene's thirty thousand; but his attack was weak and without result; and in November he went into winter-quarters. The year's campaign had been a brilliant one on Eugene's part. Early in February he made a sudden attack on Cremona, broke in and captured Villeroi, but could not hold the city. Vendome was sent to take command of the French army, now numbering fifty thousand men. Eugene had been blockading Mantua, but Vendome, by a skillful manœuvre, cut him off from his communications and revictualed the place; then moving around Eugene's flank, he forced him back across the Po. A battle ensued at Luzzara, which was drawn, and in November both armies went into winter-quarters. Vendome held the honors of the campaign. One of the greatest generals of this era, John Churchill, now appeared on the theatre of war. Born in 1650, he early approved himself a good soldier, and served with distinction in the English corps under Condé and Turenne. Under James II. and William III. he rose in his chosen profession by skill and courage; was made duke of Marlborough, and finally, in 1701, became general-in-chief of the allies in the Netherlands. His campaigns of 1701 to 1703 were not remarkable.

Villeroi shortly came upon the scene, and as he was ordered, determined to attack the prince before he was reinforced. Catinat, his junior, remained with the army. With some forty-five thousand men, Villeroi crossed the Oglio at Rudiano on August 28 and 29, and so certain was he of easy victory that he neglected to fetch most of his artillery with him. Much in accordance with his character, this proved to be a foolish error. On the afternoon of September 1 he moved on the imperial army, after the barest semblance of a reconnoissance. With his thirty thousand men, Eugene had made good dispositions, and his outposts gave him early

notice of the coming of the French.   He had three lines, the
cavalry in the third, and in Chiari, on his left flank, and in a
number of houses near by, he placed foot and artillery.   His
line faced nearly east, and his right leaned on two brooks.
His position was strong.   Villeroi advanced in good heart,
never doubting victory ; but his attack on the prince's position, though heartily enough delivered and followed up, was

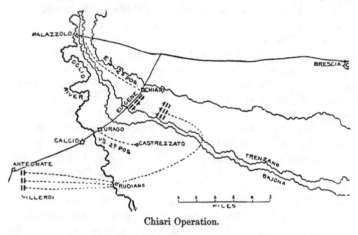

Chiari Operation.

beaten off by the imperial forces, with the loss of over twenty-
five hundred men and many officers, while Eugene lost little.
The prince declined to pursue the advantage against the odds
existing ; Villeroi retired in good order to Urago, near by,
and intrenched between that place and Castrezato ; and
Eugene slightly changed his position to one leaning his
right on Palazzolo, and his left on Chiari.   Autumn was at
hand, and the rest of the year was eaten up by small war,
conducted by the imperialists with great vigor and constant
success.

Each day some expedition against the enemy's foragers,
outposts or convoys was undertaken, but Eugene, who considered that he had won enough for this campaign, did not care

to risk what he had already gained by uncertain operations on a larger scale against so superior a force. Catinat suggested some bolder manœuvres to utilize the French excess of forces, but Villeroi was not abreast of them.

At the end of these small operations, Villeroi, on November 13, retired across the Oglio below Urago so carefully that Eugene had small chance of attacking him, and the French went into winter-quarters in the country along the Oglio and down to Cremona. The Venetians refused Eugene the right to winter on their territory, but as he could not well retire to the Tyrol and have all his work to do over again next spring, in order to drive the enemy out of the Mantua region he undertook operations which secured him a number of places, including Marcaria, Rodondesco, Torre d' Oglio, Ostiglia, Borgoforte and Ponte Molino, in fact all the towns of importance save Mantua and Goito; he captured Mirandola, where was much material, in the middle of December, and Guastalla shortly after; strengthened the crossings of the Oglio, nearly all of which he controlled, cut the French off from Mantua, and himself went into cantonments in three lines along the Oglio and Mincio, with his left resting on the Po. Headquarters were at San Benedetto, and a big outpost lay in the Parma territory, while Parma itself was occupied, though against the consent of the duke. The imperial general had a good country to victual from and could quickly concentrate. The Savoyard army marched back to Piedmont.

According to the ideas of the day, Prince Eugene's campaign had been exceedingly brilliant; he had kept the initiative at all times; but it is true that he was aided by the limitations of the generals opposed to him. Catinat could not cross the Adige, a fact which allowed Eugene all the liberty of action he desired on the east bank; the secret understanding with the duke of Savoy, which gave the prince access to all the news he desired, was a vital point in his favor; and finally the breaking up of the French army into small detachments, together with the poor management of Villeroi, made in his favor. But he had shown exceptional activity and enterprise; his work in all respects had been able and soldierly, and the campaign redounds much to his honor. He had taken advantage of all the openings the enemy had given him, and if we should gauge all generals by the opposition they encountered, there would be few great reputations. It is rare that great captains have been matched by equal talent.

In 1702 Prince Eugene was again in command of the imperial forces with which he had in the previous campaign pushed the French back to the Milanese, and which he had withdrawn towards winter to the neighborhood of Mantua. He had kept up an activity all winter to which the inertness of Villeroi formed a great contrast; he had blockaded Mantua, which at the beginning of January he proceeded with some twelve thousand men to shut in more thoroughly; and in order to hold his lines securely, he watched the Po above his position with much care, and collected supplies in the towns of Brescello, Guastalla, Luzzara, Mirandola and Borgoforte. The enemy considerably outnumbered him; and his task in this campaign was to hold himself in Italy rather than to push the enemy out of it. General Vaudemont was stationed in the Parma country.

On the 1st of February Prince Eugene carried out a scheme which he had for some time had in view, against the fortress of Cremona, where the bulk of the French were stationed, and where Villeroi had his headquarters. In his pay was an admirable corps of spies, from whom he got much information. By corrupting a priest, whose house was near the north city wall, a few imperial soldiers got admitted through a drain into the city, and at the preconcerted hour of 3 A. M., opened one of the adjacent gates to a force headed by Prince Eugene. Within a few minutes the latter was inside, with two thousand infantry and somewhat more cavalry, and before the garrison was aware of any danger the place was taken, and Villeroi, whose quarters were close at hand, was made a prisoner.

But the event was not as fortunate as the beginning. General Vaudemont (the son, for the father was serving under Villeroi) had been instructed to aid the stratagem from Parma by attacking and taking the Cremona bridge-head from the south, and thus opening communication with Eugene and an outlet for retreat; but he failed to do this, and when the scheme was on the very eve of success, the garrison got under arms, and during the whole day energetically fought to expel the enemy. Finally the French gained their point, and Eugene, with a loss of twelve hundred men, was obliged to retire. The marquis of Créqui was on the march to help the garrison, and had he come up, Eugene might have been captured himself; but on hearing a report that Cremona had been taken, Créqui pusillanimously turned back without attempting to verify the rumor, and Eugene got away by the Margaret gate on the east, crossed the Oglio, and retired to camp with his prisoner.

When, on March 1, Vendome, the successor of Villeroi, arrived in Cremona and took command of the French army lying on the Adda, he first sat down to wait for some twenty-five thousand reinforcements to arrive, and then planned to march to the Mincio, place himself on the communications of Eugene with the Tyrol, and either force him to battle, or compel him to throw up the blockade of Mantua. While waiting his accessions and the proper moment to act, he made an attempt to help Mantua by moving on Eugene's position on the Po ; but Eugene outmanœuvred him, met him at every point, and not only held fast the blockade, but kept up a series of annoying raids into the Milanese and Cremona districts.

Louis Joseph, Duke of Vendome, was born in 1654, had early served in the Gardes du Corps in the Netherlands,  under Turenne on the Rhine, and under Condé in Flanders. He became familiar with Italy by serving as a junior in the campaigns conducted by Catinat. In 1695 he commanded the French army in Spain, freed Palamos, and captured Barcelona. A splendid soldier, in private life he was shiftless, indecorous and showed little ambition ; it required the stimulus of arms to rouse his naturally indolent nature ; and sometimes even this failed to do so. In the field he often showed determination unsurpassed, as well as a marked gallantry and intelligence ; but he was not always careful to guard the secret of his operations.

Vendome.

Having had his forces raised to over fifty thousand men, Vendome left Cremona well garrisoned and the line of the Adda and Po sufficiently posted, and with twenty thousand men marched, May 12, over the Oglio at Pontevico, crossed the Mella, May 15, at Manerbio, turned to the right over the Chiese at Medole, and reached Goito May. 23. This handsome march, made before Eugene could do aught to interrupt or neutralize it, was a clear check to the imperial commander, for it not only cut him off from his main line of communications, — the direct road to the Tyrol, — but at the same time raised the blockade of Mantua on the north. The prince at once recognized his situation. He might readily have been drawn into fatal manœuvres or a still more fatal battle; but he quietly withdrew to his lower Mantua lines with troops which had been reinforced up to thirty-nine thousand men, took up a strong position, May 17, near Montanara and Curtatone, intrenched it, and here still held Mantua in a species of blockade. But Vendome's presence in superior force between Goito and Mantua could not fail to become dangerous to the imperial army, and Eugene concluded to draw in his forces from the towns surrounding Mantua, and to watch for further developments while victualing his forces over the bridge at Borgoforte from the magazines which he had so judiciously established in the Modena country on the other side of the Po. From Brescello to Ostiglia his possession of the Po was made secure.

Upon this withdrawal of Eugene, Vendome was enabled to revictual Mantua, and then took up his post opposite Eugene near Rivalto, where both armies remained *in situ* for a month, indulging only in small war and cannonading. An attempt to duplicate the capture of Villeroi by seizing Vendome in his quarters at Rivalto came so close to success as to make the French general careful where he established himself.

Eugene's position was peculiar. He stood between the Po and the Mincio, the enemy, who outnumbered him, in his front, and Mantua on his right, against whose sorties he now had to intrench himself. The neutral Venetians held the line of the Adige with twenty-six thousand men for their own protection, and Eugene could have a line of retreat on its left bank by marching over their territory; but his original line of retreat was gone. Now again heavily reinforced from Spain, Vendome was anxious to oust Eugene from his position; but, as he did not like to make a front attack, he left Vaudemont with twenty-three thousand men in his Rivalto lines astride the imperial communications, and boldly started, July 7, with the van of other twenty-three thousand, towards Cremona and Casal Maggiore, proposing to cross the Po and by a flank attack seek to cut off his opponent from his Modena holdings and capture his magazines. Thus, he thought, he would force him into a situation which would compel him to leave Italy. His object in marching so far up the Po as Cremona was perhaps to meet Philip V. of Spain, who was coming on a visit to the allied armies.

Eugene guessed his opponent's intention, and increased his detachments at Borgoforte and Brescello, where he had bridges over the Po, and at Guastalla.

Crossing the river, July 14, in two columns, at Cremona and Casal Maggiore, Vendome met at Santa Vittoria some imperial horse which Eugene sent out to watch the operation, beat it with a loss of six hundred men, captured Reggio, Modena and Carpi, and having got together thirty-six thousand troops, marched to Luzzara, August 15, hoping to seize on Eugene's bridges over the Po. He was doing brilliant work.

Matters looked threatening for Eugene. It seemed as if battle with a superior enemy was his only outlet, and on this he determined. By skillfully deceiving Vaudemont, he withdrew most of his forces from his front, crossed the Po at Borgoforte August 1, reinforced his army from garrisons up to twenty-six thousand men and fifty-seven guns, also marched straight on Luzzara, and on August 3 reached Sailetto, just south of the crossing. Strong garrisons were left in his magazine towns.

Vendome had called on the commander of the place to surrender, and on refusal had taken the town but not the citadel; and then, heedless of Eugene, prepared to camp near by. The old accounts of this battle are a good deal confused,

and the old charts do not show the topography of to-day.
Along the Po near Luzzara there was said to be a canal or
an embankment to arrest the frequent inundations of the
river, and high enough to conceal a considerable army. The
old charts call it the Zero Canal. At all events, it is certain
that the country was much cut up by embankments, dikes,
ditches, hedges, patches of woods, so much so that only careful scouting would discover an enemy. On this terrain
Eugene, who with his entire force of infantry and cavalry
had advanced in two columns along the Po, and now lay in a
sort of ambush, hoped to fall suddenly on the French when
they should go into camp, as he was advised by his scouts

that they were
about to do. Ven-
dome's people were
exceedingly care-
less in outpost
duty, and the
French army had
marched up and
was preparing to
camp without dis-
covering the pres-
ence of the ene-
my. Just before
Eugene was ready

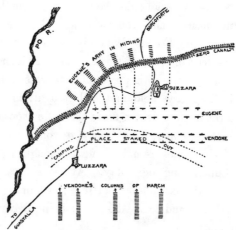

Battle of Luzzara.

to debouch from hiding and fall upon the French, Vendome,
by the curiosity of an outpost commander, was fortunate
enough to discover the ambush, and by the time Eugene had
got his men through the difficult country and into line, so
had Vendome. It was 5 P. M. The imperialists of the right
wing worked their way through the many obstacles and fell
on the French left with great fury ; but they were met by

equal gallantry, and for hours a bloody struggle was maintained. Eugene reported that in several regiments every officer fell, and that the fighting was kept up under command
of the sergeants. In the centre Vendome opposed Eugene,
but the latter gained some ground. On the left the imperial
gain was more marked, as the ground was more open and the
cavalry could better operate. In every respect it was a
fiercely contested battle, but without any special show of
grand-tactics. Up to past midnight the struggle went on
along the line in places, breaking out at intervals on either
side; and it had been hot enough to cost each army some two
thousand killed, and on the French side four thousand and
on the imperial side two thousand wounded. Eugene had by
no means made the gain he had anticipated, which was to
drive the French from his vicinity; nor indeed had he lost
the battle, for both sides claimed a victory.

Eugene, who is unusually accurate in his reports, says that
he kept the field and collected all his wounded, while the
French were driven more than one thousand paces back from
it, a statement which seems to vouch for an imperial success.
Both armies remained near enough together to indulge in
cannonading next day. At all events, Eugene had accomplished his end by putting a summary stop to Vendome's
advance and to the danger of being driven out of the Modena
country.

Vendome ordered Vaudemont to blockade Borgoforte; but
Eugene kept free enough to send his light horse out on
raids, even so far as into the Milanese. One enterprising
raid is worth mentioning. A party of six hundred hussars
under General Davia started from camp, rode up the Po,
crossed the Enza, Parma, Taro, Rura and Trebbia, seized the
bridge at Arena, crossed, forced a heavy contribution on
Pavia, and marched on and into Milan. Thence easterly

they crossed the Adda at Cassano, the Oglio at Calcio, the Mincio at Valleggio, and arrived safe and laden with enormous booty at Ostiglia. This was the sort of work Eugene's tremendous vitality was apt to inspire in his subordinates. For fifty-five days the armies stood *en face* near Luzzara, and Vendome only captured Guastalla. Eugene was too weak to do more than hold his own; but Vendome was able successively to seize several of Eugene's Modena magazines, though not Mirandola. He made an attempt on this place by moving on Bondanello on the Secchia; but while on the march to this latter place, Eugene quietly drew in most of the Borgoforte garrison, rapidly moved across the Secchia, and on November 8 drew up to defend the river; and though Vendome had much the larger force, he declined to attack. But he shortly got Borgoforte, whose garrison was thus depleted.

Prince Eugene attempted later to gain possession of the Guastalla bridge, as well as made an attack on Mantua; but failing in both efforts, he gave up all his holdings on the left bank of the Po and went into winter-quarters in the vicinity of Mirandola. The French, in November, also put their fifty-six thousand men (not counting garrisons) into winter-quarters, with headquarters in Guastalla.

The campaign had been decidedly in favor of Vendome, who with his superior forces had conducted it with much ability, and may be said to have gained substantial repute by his boldness and intelligence. Prince Eugene, though to be sure his army was but half that of his opponent, had been forced back to the right bank of the Po and been cooped up in the Mirandola country; but he had not been driven out of Italy; and all his operations were active and able. Though Vendome had accomplished more, yet Eugene had shown the greater ability. An exceptional circumstance in the cam-

paigns of 1701–1702 is that Prince Eugene called on Austria
for scarcely any support. He built his road from the Tyrol
down, and subsisted his men on the enemy's territory. He
so disposed his magazines that being cut off from his direct
communications with the Tyrol by no means fatally compromised him. All this was an unusual thing in those days.
The operations had cost Austria little in men or material.
Eugene had, considering his force and the fact that his opponent was one of the best soldiers of the day, conducted a
very handsome campaign. Perhaps the most noteworthy fact
of the 1702 campaign is that Eugene grasped and acted on
the theory that the weaker of two generals must never await
attack, but himself assume the offensive. This was Frederick's great power; and Eugene distinctly exhibited it. At
Luzzara he advanced on the enemy ; during the whole campaign his activity in small war never relaxed ; and he always
managed to keep a central position with interior lines. He
was recalled to Vienna, received with enthusiasm, and made
president of the imperial council of war. During the succeeding year he was not in the field.

There had come upon the theatre of the War of the Spanish Succession a soldier as remarkable as Eugene, and one
with whom his name was to be imperishably coupled. John
Churchill was born in Devonshire July 5, 1650, thirteen
years before his colleague, his father being a royalist, his
mother a daughter of Sir Francis Drake. Educated at St.
Paul's school, he entered the army at sixteen years old, under
the patronage of the duke of York, and first saw service in
the war against Tangiers, where he was distinguished as a
volunteer in all hazardous exploits. In 1672, at the beginning of the second Netherlands War, he was captain in the
English corps, and at Nymwegen Turenne highly and justly
complimented him. A certain position under a French officer

had been lost by a Dutch attack. Turenne is said to have bet a champagne supper that "*son bel Anglais*," with half the troops which had just been driven back, would take it; and Churchill gallantly won him his bet. Next year he earned the public thanks of Louis XIV. for services at the

siege of Maestricht, was soon made colonel, and, as such, in 1674, served under Turenne on the Rhine.

Four years after, he participated in the campaign in Flanders, and for three years succeeding was with the banished duke of York in the Netherlands and Belgium. His fidelity earned him his baronetcy and promotion; and

Marlborough.

when the duke became James II. he was made peer and French ambassador. Engaged at Sedgmoor against the insurgents, he afterwards went over to William III., and was made lieutenant-general and duke of Marlborough in 1686.

At the battle of Walcourt (1689) against the French, in the Netherlands, he showed marked skill, and the king desired him to go to Ireland in 1690, to serve against James II. But Marlborough declined to go thither until after James had left that country, when he drove back the insurgents in Cork, Kinsale and Ulster. Notwithstanding his treasonable correspondence with James, the king kept him in favor, and took him to the Netherlands in 1691; and though in the next year he fell from favor and was imprisoned in the Tower, he was again called to court, showered with honors and dignities, made captain-general, and sent to the Netherlands as plenipotentiary, in 1701. Queen Anne, on her accession, commissioned him general-in-chief of the English forces, and, in 1702, conferred the Garter on him.

Although, under the common belief that the divine right of ruling confers like military skill, there were many claimants to the command of the allied armies, — the king of Prussia, the Archduke Charles, the elector of Hanover, the duke of Zell, and especially Prince George of Denmark, husband of Queen Anne, — the Dutch estates insisted upon their own choice, and the duke of Marlborough, in 1702, was made commander-in-chief of the allies in the Netherlands. For this action there were two good reasons : the confidence of the Dutch in his ability, and their desire to have a commander whom their field deputies could control. Owing to political complications, Marlborough did not reach his army till midsummer, the earl of Athlone having meanwhile been engaged in the siege of Kaiserswörth, which fell June 15, and in checking Marshal Boufflers' raid on Nymwegen. Three weeks later Marlborough crossed the Maas at Grave with his sixty thousand men, made up of English, German and Dutch troops. He was anxious for battle with Marshal Boufflers, who had some forty thousand men, but the Dutch field deputies held him back, and he was reduced to a campaign of sieges. Capturing Venlo, Roermond, Stevensweert and Lüttich (Liège), he forced the French behind the Mehaigne. This was already a marked gain ; it put the situation in the Netherlands on a new footing ; the French were cut off from what they had deemed their highway, the Rhine, and a secure waterway was open from the Dutch ports to the army of the allies at the front, — no mean success. The allied position moreover threatened Brussels and Cologne, and Marlborough began to be looked on as the saviour of the Netherlands. Had he been given his own way, he might have spared much future waste of lives and treasure ; for

Marlborough belongs to those generals who only now and then were given an opportunity of doing their very best; of whom it cannot be said how great they might have become had they possessed unlimited power.

Next year (1703) was a repetition of the same story. Holland at that day bristled with fortifications, built under the eye of the most distinguished engineers, the Frenchman Vauban and the Dutchman Coehorn at their head, and the presence of these interfered with free manœuvring. A single fortress in its rear may not be dangerous to an army; but when they are so numerous that detachments from their garrisons can make up a body able to threaten the communications of an army advancing beyond their lines, greater caution is required; and unless a commander had sufficient troops to detail large observation parties for each strong place, it could scarcely be deemed wise to leave them behind him. This view, then universal, was warmly espoused by the Dutch deputies. They constantly restrained Marlborough, who had designs on Antwerp and Ostende, and who in any event was inclined to fight as the best military policy; and he was now fain to be content with besieging Bonn. Villeroi, who had returned from Italy, sought meanwhile to interfere with Marlborough's siege by an advance on Maestricht; but Bonn fell May 15, — in season to allow Marlborough, who with his lieutenant Overkirk had fifty-five thousand men, to head him off. Villeroi and Boufflers, however, quite negatived his attempt in June on Antwerp, in which operation Boufflers beat a large force of the Dutch who formed the right of the concentrically operating forces, and Marlborough had no success. Later he fell back behind the Maas, and in August and September took Huy and Limburg, and the Prussians, under Count Lottum, Geldern.

This campaign is neither of especial interest, nor does it

reflect any great credit on its management; but from giving it its trivial character Marlborough must be absolved; for the Dutch deputies were constantly at his elbow, and their view of the military necessities of the case savored of astigmatism. Tired of his slow-moving masters, — for he saw other generals winning victories, and felt conscious of his own power to do the like, — Marlborough determined to march into Germany in 1704, and there conduct his campaign. It was evident to all that Bavaria was the key of the theatre of war.

French Cannon. (16th Century.)

LV.

VILLARS. 1703.

IN 1703 Vendome opposed Stahremberg in Italy, but the latter outmanœuvred him, and finally, Savoy having joined the allies, made a splendid march
around his position to Piedmont. On the Rhine Villars opened the campaign
by a brilliant foray. Crossing at Hüningen, he marched down the river to the
Stollhofen lines, capturing everything on the way. Later, he again crossed,
advanced to the Danube country, joined the elector of Bavaria, and proposed
to march on Vienna; but the elector declined the operation as too hazardous.
Some interesting manœuvres occurred between him and the prince of Baden
when Villars was succeeded by Marsin. He had operated with boldness and
skill. In this campaign occurred the first bayonet charge on record. Bavaria
was looked on as the battle-ground for 1704, and both France and the allies
made preparations to concentrate their efforts there.

IN the Italian campaign of 1703 Vendome did not do himself the same credit as in the previous one. His opponent
was Count Stahremberg, whose position on the right bank of
the Po, where Eugene had left the army, was one of much
difficulty, as his communications with the Tyrol and Austria
ran across the Po at Ostiglia, the Adige at Castelbaldo, and
up to Triente, a treacherous route, full of obstacles, through
Venetian territory, and easy to interrupt. Vendome had
sixty-two thousand men to Stahremberg's twenty odd thousand, and a decided advance in force on his opponent at
any suitable point must have resulted in crushing him. But
his natural love of ease appearing this year to get the better
of him, Vendome preferred slower operations, and divided
his forces. With twenty-seven thousand men, he himself
marched to Ostiglia and sent his brother, who was his second
in command, with twenty thousand on the south of the Po

to the Secchia, behind which lay Stahremberg. The latter,
well aware of the movements through his scouts, carefully
held Ostiglia, covered the Po bridge with a suitable force,
and waited. As Vendome approached on the north of him,
and the younger Vendome had actually crossed the Secchia,
which operation Stahremberg did not attempt to prevent, and
as General Alberghatti with four thousand men had penetrated to Finale on the south of him, Stahremberg opened
the sluices of the Po at Ostiglia, laid the entire country
under water so as to prevent Vendome's advance, and turning sharply on Alberghatti, gave him a severe beating, and
again took up his post in the Mirandola region. Quite
unsettled by this unexpected and original proceeding, the
French retired up the Po along both banks, and Vendome
remained inactive for six weeks.

The duke of Savoy, with whom Prince Eugene had been
sedulously laboring, now declared for the allies. This proved
a great gain : it secured the passes in the Alps against falling
into the hands of the French, and made more difficult their
reinforcing their Danube army from Italy. Vendome, after
a fruitless because indolent march to join the elector of
Bavaria in the Tyrol for an advance on Vienna, — the emas-
culated outcome of an excellent scheme of Villars, — returned
to Italy. He had large forces, and his position between Stahremberg and the duke of Savoy would have enabled him to
operate successfully against each in turn ; but he did nothing,
despite his superiority, and finally went into winter-quarters
at Asti, leaving his brother to face Stahremberg.

The Austrian now saw his chance, and executed the one
manœuvre which makes this campaign worth a notice. It
was a fine one. He concluded that the war in Italy could be
conducted to better advantage if he should join hands with
the duke of Savoy than by operating in two bodies, each of

which was too weak. A part of Vendome's force was in his front; but, throwing up his communications with the Tyrol, as well as his Mirandola magazine, he moved around the French left, deceived the enemy as to his intentions, pushed rapidly up the left bank of the Po, and joined the duke in Nizza della Paglia in Piedmont. The French hovered on his flank and rear, not infrequently placing him in grievous danger, but Stahremberg turned and twisted with rapidity and skill, and forestalled all their efforts. This operation was entirely sound, but it was quite outside of the usual system and deserves all praise. Stahremberg was the hero of the Italian campaign of 1703.

At the opening of the War of Succession, as above observed, Louis XIV., with his overwhelming forces and allies, missed his best opportunity in not taking the offensive. In 1703 he determined to repair his error. The theatre of the German campaign was again curiously divided, for Prince Louis of Baden was the ally of the emperor, while the elector of Bavaria was allied to France, thus placing both Baden and Bavaria between two fires. Resolved to conduct no longer a war of sieges, Louis XIV. conceived the brilliant strategic plan of a march on Vienna down the Danube, utilizing his connection with the elector of Bavaria to afford him a secondary base. Simple as the problem appears to us, the scheme really showed strong penetration on the part of Louis and his counselors.

Louis was to begin by uniting an army of thirty thousand men under Villars with that of the elector of Bavaria, who also had thirty thousand men in the field, and twenty odd thousand in garrison in his various cities: Ingolstadt, Neumarkt, Munich, Augsburg and smaller towns. Villars was on the upper Rhine at Hüningen and Neuenburg, while Tallard with twelve thousand men was on the Moselle, holding the border fortresses.   The plan of the emperor, on the other hand, was to attack the elector and sunder him from the French alliance before Villars came up; and for this purpose he collected on the left bank of the Danube nine thousand men under Marshal Styrum, and twenty thousand on the right bank under Marshal Schlick.   Prince Louis, with thirty thousand imperialists, occupied the right bank of the Rhine, from the Lake of Constance to the Stollhofen fortified line, strung along the whole distance in small detachments; held Breisach and Freiburg, and posted his main

body on the Kinzig near Kehl, where he dominated the crossing.   A body of nine thousand men was ordered from Holland to the Moselle to hold head against the French at that point, and to draw them from operations on the Rhine.

Louis Hector de Villars came of a noble family, but poor and out of favor.   He was born in 1653, and at twenty distinguished himself at the siege of Maestricht by such ex-

Villars.

ceptional bravery that he attracted the king's eye.   After the bloody battle of Senef, he was promoted on the field to the command of a cavalry regiment.   He was ambassador to Vienna in 1678, and again later, and in the Netherlands war in 1689, he rose to be field-marshal.   He served under Villeroi and Catinat, and in October, 1702, won a handsome victory at Friedlingen over the prince of Baden.   He now for the first time received command of an important army.

Villars opened the campaign in February by a brilliant *coup*.   He crossed the Rhine at Hüningen and Neuenburg, marched rapidly down the right bank, passed under the very walls of Breisach and Freiburg, beat a body of nine thousand men on the Elz, and drove the imperial forces, which were yet in cantonments, to take refuge in the Stollhofen lines. He then took Offenburg, with the abundant supplies of material and victual of the prince of Baden there lying, left a force to observe Kehl, which capitulated March 10, moved back up the Kinzig valley, and made another big capture in Haslach.

The emperor, quite aghast at this sudden irruption into his ally's territory, hurried some troops from the Danube to Swabia. Villars, one third of whose troops were without muskets, and who it was purposed should march to Bavaria, deferred this advance, occupied Kehl, and retired across the Rhine. His brilliant raid, for such it was, formed a curious contrast to the slow and tedious operations of the other generals of this year.

This foray of Villars was really what enabled the elector of Bavaria to turn against the imperial marshals, Styrum and Schlick; and to beat their depleted forces in detail in the Inn-Danube region, an operation which he conducted with marked vigor, winning in two important engagements and pushing the enemy well back. Had he operated with his entire fifty thousand men, instead of leaving nearly half of them dormant in his fortresses, his success would have been of more value. As it was, the enemy's forces were not definitely crippled, for the imperial generals had as many men as he had put afield.

Not long after, Villars, who had got his army into better shape, to counteract the renewed efforts of the imperial forces on the Danube, added Tallard's Moselle force to his own, and crossed the Rhine at Strasburg with fifty thousand men, purposing to capture the Stollhofen lines. But Prince Louis met him with such good countenance that he gave up this

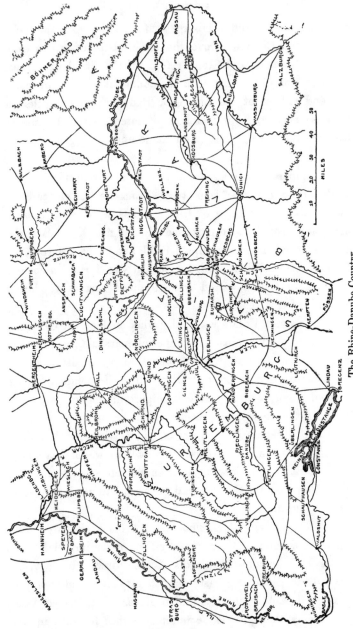

The Rhine-Danube Country.

plan and, leaving Tallard to observe the lines, he moved with thirty thousand up the Kinzig and down the Esch to Tutlingen, through the Danube valley, and May 10 joined the elector of Bavaria at Riedlingen on that river. The two armies numbered sixty thousand men. Unable to forestall it, the prince of Baden cleverly matched this manœuvre by leaving fifteen thousand of his forces at Stollhofen, and by moving with sixteen thousand men to Stuttgart, where he joined Styrum, who had advanced to meet him, and thus made up an army of thirty-six thousand men.

Villars now proposed to the elector to carry out the masterly plan already mentioned, by a march with their sixty thousand men down the valley of the Danube, straight on Vienna, leaving Tallard to hold head to the prince of Baden. But the elector, fearing that Tallard might fail in this duty and that his own territory might be devastated meanwhile, was unwilling to enter into so extended a plan. Villars then suggested a march through the Tyrol, whither Vendome could send twenty thousand reinforcements from Italy. The first suggested march was a bold one to make; it might have put an end to the war; but speed alone could lend it success. The second necessitated waiting for the Italian contingent, and this forfeited the most essential element.

Uncertain of himself, the elector was intractable with Villars, and this enterprising general was fain to lie still and see the precious opportunity slip away. Neither plan was carried out. Villars placed himself on the left bank of the Danube between Lauingen and Dillingen, to protect Bavaria, while in June the elector marched to the Tyrol to meet the French forces which should come from Italy under Vendome; but these, as we have seen, never reached him, and he got no farther. Meanwhile the duke of Burgundy, with a fresh army of nearly forty thousand men, operated against the

Stollhofen lines. There was no lack of men; a leader was wanting in the French army.

Unwilling to attack Villars in his strong position at Lauingen, and having had a division, which he sent to manœuvre against the French, beaten at one of the near-by Danube crossings, the prince of Baden conceived a bold plan for turning Villars out of his holding, and for compromising the elector as well. Leaving Styrum and twenty thousand men to watch Villars at Lauingen, he marched with twenty-seven thousand up the river to above Ulm, crossed, moved rapidly on Augsburg and took it; and then assumed a strong position between the Lech and the Wertach, where he cut asunder the two armies of the enemy.

Although this movement compelled the elector to withdraw from his advance on the Tyrol, it was a mistake, in that the prince of Baden himself divided his forces; and if the elector had speeded his return, Villars and he between them could have crushed the prince with his smaller force beyond a doubt. But the elector was too slow to cut off Prince Louis, who on his approach retired north from Augsburg; and having joined Villars, the bulk of both allied armies retired to Donauwörth, where their efforts were now devoted to keeping the imperial armies apart.

Shortly after, in September, Marshal Styrum moved to Hochstädt on the left bank of the Danube, expecting to join the prince of Baden somewhere west of the mouth of the Lech. Villars and the elector determined to destroy him before he could complete the junction. Sending from Dillingen, by a circuit, a force under General Jusson to attack Styrum's rear, the Franco-Bavarian army, on September 19, prepared to fall upon his front. But Jusson advanced on Styrum too early and was thrust back, and when Villars and the elector reached his lines and drove Styrum in, Jusson made no second attack, but allowed the imperialist to slip from between the two armies and retire to Nördlingen. Villars' dispositions, though smartly carried out, thus failed to accomplish the destruction of the imperial force; Styrum still aimed to join the prince; but as he could not well do so in Bavaria, he sought to move up river.

Leaving a body on the Lech to cover Bavaria and to insure against a junction of the enemy there, Villars marched with twenty-five thousand men to Wieblingen, on the Iller near Ulm, to head off the prince in his efforts to reach Styrum further up the Danube. The prince marched to Kempten, a cross-roads on the east of the upper Iller, if perchance, by a long circuit, he might accomplish his purpose; and Villars, reinforced up to fifty-four thousand men, marched to Memmingen, resolved to force battle on him as a preventive measure; but the prince kept well ahead of him, and fearing battle at a disadvantage, passed on a line well to the south of Villars, and made good his retreat to Leutkirch on the other side of the Iller.

Villars still followed, with a view of forcing him to battle before Styrum could come up; but his relations with the elector had become so strained that while he was preparing a fresh manœuvre he was relieved of his command. His successor, Marshal Marsin, put the troops into winter-quarters on the Lech, an example which was followed by all the armies. The prince of Baden finally joined Styrum, who marched west from Nördlingen, and went into winter-quarters covering a wide territory, between Lake Constance and the Neckar.

France lost much in removing Villars. It was such exceptional boldness and energy as his which promised to accomplish the results which would tell in her favor. Had Villars been unhampered, we must conclude from what he did under unfavorable circumstances that he would have worsted the average generals opposed to him, and have placed France much nearer to success. His 1703 campaign was a remarkable one; it showed great ability, singular push, and a decided preference for fighting over manœuvres. Moreover he was opposed by an active and intelligent soldier, the prince of Baden.

The operations on the Rhine, this year, were not important, nor characterized by anything out of the ordinary, except the first bayonet charge on record, not preceded by fire. The prince of Hesse was advancing on Speyer, at the head of twenty-four thousand men, purposing to relieve Landau, when Field-Marshal Tallard, who had just blockaded the place, went out to meet him with nineteen thousand. As the prince was crossing the Speyerbach, Tallard's column reached the stream. Seizing the instant, and without waiting to form line of battle, Tallard ployed his marching columns into column of attack, and just as they were, charged in on the enemy with the bayonet. The result was a brilliant victory. It is odd to note that military critics looked on this charge as a gross error, an inexcusable variation from the rules of the art, and universally condemned it; though had Tallard commanded pikemen merely, the charge would have been his only resource, and would have been considered bold and skillful. In any event, Tallard had won, and concluded his work by the capture of Landau, to the confusion — in our eyes — of the critics.

In the campaign of 1703 the emperor had been sadly hampered by the rebellion in Hungary, which monopolized many troops and more attention. The year had made the French masters of the middle Rhine crossings. Landau and Neu-Breisach enabled them to debouch into the enemy's country, and Bavaria was a salient thrust forward into it by which to reach and manœuvre on the Danube. In the Netherlands

France had lost nothing. The allies in 1704 needed the most brilliant of success to retrieve their cause; and thanks to Marlborough and Eugene, they won it.

The alliance of Bavaria was particularly important to both contestants, and at the opening of the campaign the generals on both sides looked upon that electorate as the objective and probable theatre of operations. Elsewhere the campaign was less marked. For France, Bavarian amity was useful because it would keep the war off French territory, and made a secondary base for the French operations against the emperor. To the emperor, Bavaria was necessary because by occupying it he robbed France of a strong ally, and from Bavaria, with Baden in his favor, he could carry the war into France, instead of seeing it waged near or within his own frontiers. Bavaria was ill placed, being the battle-ground of both contestants.

It was planned for 1704 to send Tallard and Marsin with fifty thousand men into Bavaria, where, added to the elector's troops, there would be ninety-five thousand men, and it was hoped that such a force might make a decided impression on the war. But Tallard was anxious to operate alone, and the king was prevailed on to order Marsin, who had wintered in the Augsburg country, to march towards the sources of the Danube, take ten thousand men over from Tallard, and with this reduced force to operate with the elector against the emperor. Tallard, thus left to himself, proposed to manœuvre against the Stollhofen lines, and actually opened operations.

If the imperial generals had concentrated their forces on the middle Rhine against either Tallard or Marsin, they could have beaten the French marshals separately. The prince of Baden did assemble thirty-five thousand men at Rothweil, and strove to cut Marsin off from Bavaria; but he

was slow and undecided, and instead of moving on Tuttlingen, so as to reach Marsin's flank and rear, he marched to
Villingen, and thus opened to Marsin the main road to
Bavaria; after which he could only follow him up and take
post at Munderkingen on the Danube, while Marsin took
position at Ulm.   Meanwhile Marlborough was ordered from
the Netherlands to Germany.

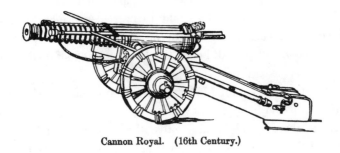

Cannon Royal.   (16th Century.)

LVI.

MARLBOROUGH AND EUGENE. 1704.

THE Dutch deputies had tied Marlborough's hands in the Netherlands ; but in 1704 he got their consent to move to Bavaria, marched unopposed up the Rhine, crossed, joined Louis of Baden, and reached the Danube with sixty thousand men. Eugene remained at Stollhofen to contain the French, while Marlborough and Baden opposed the elector of Bavaria and Marsin. Moving down to Donauwörth, Marlborough captured the Schellenberg with excessive loss, crossed to the south bank, and moved on Augsburg. Tallard now left the Rhine and marched to the relief of Marsin and the elector; Eugene at once followed, leaving part of his force in Stollhofen, for without him the allies might be overwhelmed. The French withdrew from Augsburg to the left bank of the Danube; Baden besieged Ingolstadt, and Marlborough and Eugene joined near Donauwörth. They had fifty-six thousand men; the French and Bavarians perhaps sixty thousand. Near Hochstädt (or Blenheim) the two armies came into accidental collision, and both were willing to fight.

MARLBOROUGH had determined to shake the Dutch shackles from his wrists, and his skillful diplomacy proved equal to the task. The Dutch estates first gave their consent to his advancing up and across the Rhine, and later, if he could neutralize Villeroi, to his continuing on to Bavaria. The emperor, with the Hungarian rebellion and the French successes of 1703, was in ill case; Vienna seemed to be threatened; and this danger to one of the principal allies was peril to all. With reinforcements Marlborough had got thirty thousand English troops in the Low Countries, fifty thousand in all under his immediate command; with sixteen thousand men, on the opening of operations early in May, he crossed the Meuse at Maestricht, proceeded to Bonn and up the left bank of the Rhine, passed at Coblentz May 26, after taking in enough garrisons to nearly double his force; and on June 3 had marched to Ladenburg on the Neckar near its mouth, where he crossed a few days later. His progress, according to modern ideas, had been quite slow, but good for the times. Becoming aware of his advance, the French seemed to lose their heads; they grew fearful for their Alsatian fortresses, particularly Landau, and quickly concentrated here from the Netherlands, the Moselle and the middle Rhine all the troops of Villeroi, Coigny and Tallard, nearly sixty thousand in the aggregate, to check Marlborough, whose intention they could not divine. Luckily for him, however, they made no attempt to interfere with his progress as they readily might have done, but allowed him to cross the Rhine and move up to Ladenburg unmolested. From here Marlborough, as if aiming for Ulm, marched via Heilbronn (June 8) through the rugged country which ends in the Geislingen defile, debouched into the Danube flats, and in good order, June 22, joined Prince Louis' thirty-two thousand men from the upper Danube, making an army over sixty thousand strong, with forty-eight guns. The road was new to him, but an old one to the French and German generals.

This march is spoken of by English authors as an entirely exceptional performance. Though as a strategic operation it was in truth a stroke of the happiest, it was no more than had been frequently made before. Not to speak of the greater, many of the lesser lights had often done as much. Duke Bernard had gone from the Rhine way beyond the Isar; Banér had marched from the Baltic to the Danube; Torstenson had marched from the Baltic to Vienna; Turenne and Wrangel had repeatedly started from the upper or the lower Rhine and had pushed far into the empire, — once to the banks of the Inn; Montecuculi had forced his way from Vienna to the Netherlands, with Turenne to oppose him; Eugene had pushed across the Alps into Italy and well up the Po, fighting for every step; in this very campaign he marched from his base to the Rhine, quite as far as the Anglo-Dutch. It is quite inaccurate to call Marlborough's unopposed march an unheard-of enterprise. However successfully the knot of the difficulty may have been cut by Eugene and him at Blenheim, the bald fact is that Marlborough marched to the Danube because, as all the military world knew, he was needed there; but he does not even appear to have had any immediate strategic objective. He was only, like the true soldier he was, marching toward the sound of the guns. In common with the others he saw that the allied cause could be best helped on the Danube, because the French were most seriously threatening this section; and, getting leave from the Dutch, he marched his army into the enemy's country, a thing in which he had a host of predecessors. The idea may indeed not have been originally his. There is on record a letter of Eugene's to him suggesting this very performance, and if the scheme was of Marlborough's own devising, he was not the only one to see its value. In fact, until he had reached the Neckar, Eugene was the duke's only confidant; and it is certain that the campaign was concerted between them long before it opened. It by no means helps Marlborough's splendid reputation to overstate his case. It is because we English-speaking peoples slur over the deeds of all but our own heroes that we are wont to make Marlborough the only general of his day; that one often meets folk who place Wellington as a soldier on a plane above Napoleon; or that many of us ascribe the victory of Waterloo solely to the Iron Duke, forgetful of "Marschal Vorwärts" and his Prussians. All nations suffer from want of perspec-

tive in gauging their own military history; and in writing
the biography of a single general it is perhaps impossible not
to err; but we Anglo-Saxons are almost the worst offenders.
It is not to belittle Marlborough, — his reputation as a soldier
is beyond any one's ability to disturb, — it is to be just to his
colleagues and contemporaries that so much must be said.

Marlborough, Eugene and Louis personally met in Hep-
pach in June — it was the first meeting of the two former —
and, after discussion of the situation, it was determined that
Marlborough and Louis should operate against the elector of
Bavaria and Marsin, while Eugene, to whom Marlborough
and Prince Louis sent ten thousand men, with the thirty-
seven thousand he would then have, should remain in the
Stollhofen lines to contain Tallard, Villeroi and Coigny.
There was no difficulty in Eugene and Marlborough agreeing
upon plans. They would, in this instance, have liked to operate together and leave Prince Louis on the Rhine; but the
latter would not agree to this, and claimed all the rights of a
senior in command. He had been a pupil of Montecuculi;
he had won battles; he had served at Vienna with Sobieski;
and he was high-strung, jealous and hard to please.

The joint forces of Marsin and the elector of Bavaria, who
on May 4 joined at Wieblingen, were sixty-three thousand
men and one hundred and thirty guns and mortars; and to
prevent Marlborough and the prince of Baden from crossing
the Danube and marching into Bavaria, they had taken post
in June between Lauingen and Dillingen with their back to
the river. The forces were about equally matched: the allies
had sixty thousand men and forty-eight guns. During Marlborough's march there had been some manœuvring in the
Black Forest country, but it resulted in nothing which affected
the year's campaign.

Marlborough and Prince Louis, who, though the latter was

acknowledged to be senior, had resorted to the questionable, but at that day common, device of commanding the whole army on alternate days, proposed indeed to force their way into Bavaria, but they did not try to cross at Ulm, as the enemy expected them to do. They moved up to Giengen on the Brenz, and thence, at the end of June, by a flank march in the presence of the enemy's army, to Donauwörth. The enemy held to his lines, and did not attack them on the march, but allowed them to pass unmolested within a few miles, over bad roads and under marked difficulties. The march of the duke and prince was bold ; but had there been at Lauingen such a man as Turenne, it would have scarcely escaped leading to a battle. To march to Donauwörth was an excellent manœuvre ; to march so near the enemy by the flank was a risk pardonable in those days, but hardly permissible in front of an active enemy. The allies were taking liberties with unenterprising opponents. Not only was the enemy indolent, but the position of the elector and Marsin was thoroughly false. Lauingen was not the place to defend Bavaria with the allies headed for Donauwörth, and even when they awoke to this fact they contented themselves with sending ten thousand men to Count d'Arco, who commanded at Donauwörth, and was expected to head off a force of sixty thousand men well equipped and led, with a fifth the number. Such adversaries promised to be an easy prey.

Donauwörth was not over well fortified, but the Schellenberg, near by, was intrenched, and was joined to the town by lines not quite completed. Within these works lay d'Arco's camp.

No general ever possessed the instinct of fighting to a keener degree than Marlborough ; this instinct at times overrode his judgment, and as he was determined to cross the river at Donauwörth, he had no sooner reached the vicinity

than he undertook an assault on the Schellenberg, to seize
the bridge over the Danube, by which alone he could make
his way. He was led to do so by the belief that if he delayed
d'Arco would strengthen his works so as to make them inexpugnable ; that the French and Bavarians were concentrating
opposite to bar his passage ; and by the fact that this was his

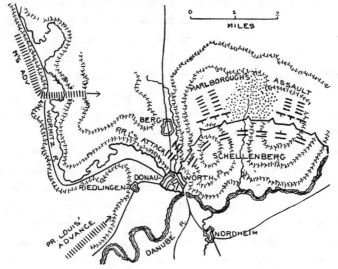

Assault on the Schellenberg.

day of command, and that Prince Louis was not of a mind
to make the assault.

It was July 2. Marlborough headed a vanguard of ten
thousand men, followed closely by the rest of the army. He
reached the Wörmitz, a small affluent of the Danube, which
flowed past the Schellenberg lines, at three o'clock, crossed
the stream above the place, and gave his men, who had been
marching since early dawn, two or three hours' rest. Aware
from what he could learn of the terrain that the place was
very strong, he detailed a picked force from each battalion,
which, with thirty squadrons and three regiments of Prince

Louis, made up a column of ten thousand five hundred men. Count d'Arco had some two thousand more.

The Schellenberg lines were old fortifications erected by Gustavus Adolphus, and d'Arco was at work with a large body of countrymen in repairing them. The hill itself is about three hundred feet above the river. Donauwörth was a fortress, but not well kept up nor sufficiently garrisoned; and the force d'Arco sent to hold it was badly stationed and worse led. From the town, which lay in the confluence of the Wörmitz and Danube, the lines which d'Arco was seeking to intrench and hold ran over the hill and back to the Danube. Opposite the centre of the hill lay a thick wood, through which a column could not well advance. After reconnoitring, Marlborough determined to attack on either side of the wood; the assault between the wood and Donauwörth to be made in force. It looks as if he had not sufficiently studied the situation, for he chose the strongest part of the line for the assault, whereas he could more easily have broken through nearer the town, where the half-finished works were barely waist high. Nor was there any greater gain to be had by getting a foothold on the Schellenberg; the town was nearer the bridge Marlborough wanted. But the assaults were delivered by his *corps d'élite* in gallant style. The first one was met with equal courage, was repulsed, and the Bavarians made a sortie with the bayonet, which in its turn was met and broken by an English regiment, which took the enemy in flank. A second assault had no better result. A third failed, and the Bavarians again issued in a bayonet charge from their works, and were only checked by the cavalry. Failure was imminent, and the loss had been fearful. Marlborough had undertaken a desperate task.

But help was at hand. Prince Louis' column now arrived, crossed the Wörmitz near Berg, and fell on the defenses of d'Arco at the town. With scarcely any opposition he broke through the weak intrenchments, and thus took d'Arco in reverse. Marlborough had for hours been hammering at a spot which he could not break, when close at hand was a weak one he had not heeded. At once recognizing that the position was lost, d'Arco put himself at the head of two French regiments of dragoons, ployed his foot into close columns, cut a path through the Baden troops, and made his way to the bridge at Donauwörth, where he crossed to the south bank of the Danube. Though Marlborough had done all the fighting, Prince Louis arrogated to himself the credit of the victory, as having been first inside the works.

The loss of the allies was six to seven thousand men (fifteen hundred killed and four thousand wounded, say the English authorities); that of the Bavarians only sixteen hundred; but the bold assault, though it seems, as says Lossau, to have been delivered rather prematurely, and was very costly, made such an impression on the elector, who with Marsin still stood at Lauingen, and had acted with unwarrantable lethargy, that he crossed the river, threw the bulk of his Bavarian forces into his fortresses, where they were useless, retired to Augsburg with all Marsin's and five thousand of his own men, and sat down in an intrenched camp.

It may be asserted that this assault was as justifiable as that of Gustavus at the Lech or at the Alte Veste; but in the latter case, the Swede had exhausted every other means to bring his opponent to battle, as an outlet to a situation growing daily more intolerable, while in the former the king, once set on crossing in the face of the enemy, carefully selected his point of attack and actually got the best one. It seems to be agreed by the best Continental critics, and these are all warm admirers of the duke, — as who indeed is not? — that the assault here was a mistake.

Marlborough and Prince Louis crossed the Danube July 5, took Rain, and appeared, July 23, at Augsburg, camping at Friedberg, on the road from Augsburg to Munich. Augsburg was too strong to attack, and no terms could be made with the elector ; but the allies began to devastate Bavaria as a means of detaching him from his alliance with France. This devastation was thorough, and conducted, says Alison, with savage ferocity. Three hundred towns or villages were consumed, a species of vengeance for the devastation of the Palatinate by Turenne. Despite this terrifying havoc the elector stood to his alliance.

Meanwhile Tallard and Villeroi had been idly watching these operations with their fifty-eight thousand men, which Eugene was holding by his presence at Stollhofen ; but Tallard, who had received orders to hurry to Bavaria with some chosen troops to the aid of Marsin and the elector, crossed the Rhine at Strasburg, July 1, with twenty-six thousand men, and marching through the valley of the Danube, reached Augsburg August 5. Villeroi and Coigny, with thirty-two thousand men, remained to confront the Stollhofen lines and protect Tallard's rear. So soon as Prince Eugene became aware of Tallard's march, he grasped the danger to which his allies would be exposed by these reinforcements to an army already outnumbering their own, left twenty-one thousand men under the count of Nassau in Stollhofen, and July 18 marched with sixteen thousand on a parallel line but through more rugged country on the north, to prevent Tallard from doing his colleagues a mischief. He reached Dillingen August 4 ; his speed had been good, but Tallard had started and kept ahead of him ; and as the French commander had much the larger force, Eugene would not have deemed it wise to attack, had he overtaken him. Now that he was so far, however, he determined not to return, but to reinforce the allies, and marched to Münster, near Donau-wörth. Tallard effected his end, and with the elector of Bavaria and Marsin, the army numbered some fifty-seven thousand men, with all the fortresses heavily garrisoned. It was now the manifest duty of the French and Bavarians to attack either Marlborough or Eugene singly ; but they hesitated so long as to lose their opportunity. Marlborough and the prince of Baden were not on good terms, and the English general finally induced Louis to undertake the apparently useful but not essential siege of Ingolstadt with fifteen thousand men, while he himself first covered it and then joined Prince Eugene. For the former purpose he marched by Aichach to Schrobbenhausen August 5, and thus took post between Ingolstadt and Augsburg.

To draw the allies from Bavaria, the French and the elector adopted the singular plan of themselves moving to the left bank of the Danube, whereas by remaining where they were, they would have kept the allies inactive, or have obliged them to resort to besieging the strong places of the Danube country. They thought, moreover, to threaten Eugene, and to draw Prince Louis from the siege of Ingolstadt. Crossing at Lauingen, August 9, they moved down towards Hochstädt, on hearing of which, and on consultation with Marlborough, Eugene, who had returned to Dillingen, marched to the Schellenberg, while Marlborough moved to Donauwörth. This still secured the siege of Ingolstadt, which was now fully invested. The enemy had been operating on exterior lines, leaving the interior lines to the allies.

Marlborough sent twenty-two battalions and twenty-seven squadrons ahead to Eugene, and next day, August 10, followed in two columns, one crossing the Danube at Nieder-Schönfeld and the other at Rain over the Lech, and then over the Danube at Donauwörth. Eugene on August 11 joined

Marlborough's army. The two had fifty-six thousand men; the enemy perhaps five thousand more. They were now to act as colleagues in daily operations for the first time.

No difficulty ever existed between Marlborough and Eugene as to command. They were men of altogether too big calibre to be jealous of each other's precedence, or to waste time discussing trifles. Whenever they acted together, they commanded each his own army, and the joint forces on alternate days, and never failed to agree as to the advisability of any special operation. It was not a question of either, whose day it was, giving orders to the other; a suggestion sufficed, for the mind of each could grasp the situation and argue correctly with reference to it.

Following is Prince Eugene's estimate of forces, given in a letter dated August 25, 1704, viz.: —

ALLIES.					FRENCH.				
		Battalions.	*Squadrons.*				*Battalions.*	*Squadrons.*	
Eugene r. w.	Prussians	11	15		Marsin l. w.	French	29	50	18,000
	Danes	7	0			Bavarians	13	37	12,000
	Austrians	0	24	20,000			—	—	—
	Empire	0	35				42	87	30,000
		—	—						
		18	74						
Marlborough c. and l.	English	14	14						
	Dutch	14	22						
	Hessians	7	7		Tallard r. and c.	French	42	60	30,000
	Hanoverians	13	25	36,000			—	—	—
	Danes	0	22			Total	84	147	60,000
		—	—						
		48	90		Guns 90				
	Total	66	164	56,000					
Guns 66									

In the above estimate of the allied forces, presumably as correct as any we can find, though there are many others, all varying somewhat from each other, the very small percentage of British troops is striking. We are brought up to believe Blenheim (or Hochstädt) to be an English victory; and it cannot be denied that half the glory of the battle belongs to the English general. But only a fifth of the allied foot was English; less than a sixth of the cavalry. England in this war, as in most other land-wars she has done, fought with her money-bags and not her men. At sea the case was different. There the British tars always bared their breasts, and fought as Anglo-Saxons have always fought, on land or sea, like heroes. But if, in the battles of Marlborough for instance, we gauge the credit of the English according to the troops they furnished, Blenheim and Malplaquet, Oudenarde and Ramillies, cease to be English victories, — a distinct loss to Greater Britain.

It was here, near Hochstädt, that the rival armies fell into almost accidental battle. Though ready for it, neither army had anticipated a general engagement at any particular time. The French and the elector desired a battle in order to drive the allies out of Bavaria, and it was better that it should occur on the left bank of the Danube than on the right; Marlborough and Eugene were eager to measure arms because they believed that they could beat the enemy and thus release the empire from its difficulties. It was evident that the situation must breed a battle before many days; for the commanders on both sides had determined on fighting.

The two allied generals had early on the 12th ridden out on a reconnoissance, during which they caught sight of the enemy in full march. They withdrew to Tapfheim, and having from the church tower observed the French and Bavarians go into camp, at once returned to headquarters.

Marsin and Tallard had assumed that the allies were on the way to Nördlingen, to which view some movements of the allied cavalry, according to their reports, contributed. So confirmed was Tallard in this view, indeed, that he mistook the "assembly" blown in the allied camp on the morning of the battle, for the order to march. The Franco-Bavarians had not expected an immediate encounter, nor indeed taken up any distinct order of battle; they had rather camped in order of march, and as each French general as well as the elector

commanded his own forces, they had advanced in three separate bodies. Tallard was on the right; Marsin on his left,
and the elector beyond him. The cavalry had been as usual
disposed on the flanks of each army, and thus the bulk of the
French mounted men, when emerging from camp to form,
would occupy the centre of the whole line, separating the
infantry wings. This queer order neither suited the ground
nor was adapted for battle. In fact, owing to the leaning of
the flanks on Lützingen and Blenheim, which were held
mainly by foot, the amount of cavalry in the centre during
the battle was increased.

Knowing the enemy to be near by in force, the French
general had made suitable dispositions. Where the cavalry
stood, near the village of Oberklau, the line made a slight
salient, so as to include the village in its scheme. In their
front, but too far off to be of much good as a defense, though
doubtless it would detain the assailants, ran the Nebelbach
in a low, deep, marshy bed. Above Oberklau the brook was
divided into, or rather fed by, four small streams, making the
ground opposite Marsin and the elector much harder to cross
than below the village. Tallard's right leaned on the Danube
at Blenheim, which village he now occupied with twenty-
seven battalions and twelve squadrons of dragoons, — about
fifteen thousand men, a detachment which dangerously reduced his force of infantry elsewhere. Marsin had taken
possession of Oberklau and Lützingen, and there placed a
number of battalions of foot mixed in with the horse.
Though the French lay at the top of a gentle, long slope
which ran downward to the Nebelbach, yet the position was
bad, for the troops did not correspond to the terrain ; the
several arms were not placed where they could do effective
service or sustain each other. Yet one may imagine the
French marshals arguing that the ground in the centre was

excellent for cavalry to act upon, as on right and left it
was not; but in that case they needed heavy infantry supports for the horse thus massed.   To neglect this point was to
invite defeat.

The bulk of the foot was thus in two bodies on the extreme
flanks.   These were strongly posted, the right in Blenheim
and the left at the foot of rugged hills which cavalry and
artillery could not cross.   But though the left centre was sustained by Oberklau, yet the centre was far too extended, and
between Oberklau and Blenheim there stood eighty squadrons
of horse and only ten battalions of foot in reserve.   The guns
were fairly distributed all along the line.   To the villages
some attention had been paid; they had not only intrenchments, but the streets were barricaded with carts and the
furniture from the houses.   Their strength did not, however,
help the weakness of the centre against a suitable attack.
Nothing but the marshy Nebelbach, no insuperable obstacle,
protected it.

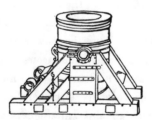

French Mortar.   (16th Century.)

LVII.

BLENHEIM. AUGUST 13, 1704.

MARSIN and the elector held the left; Tallard the right. They had formed in line as they marched, so as to throw the bulk of their cavalry in the centre. In the allied army, Eugene stood on the right, Marlborough on the left, each leading his own army. There was absolute good-will and helpfulness between them; though alternating daily in command, they acted together as one man. In their front ran the Nebelbach, which must be crossed, and Tallard had occupied Blenheim in force. The allies attacked. On the left, Marlborough devoted much time to capturing Blenheim, but fruitlessly; on the right, opposed to heavier forces, Eugene struggled hard for victory, but was thrice thrust back. Finally he drove in the elector and Marsin, while Marlborough, giving up his direct assaults on Blenheim, attacked and broke through the French centre of horse and took the village in reverse. Eugene followed up the retiring French; Marlborough captured Tallard in Blenheim. The victory was complete, and decisive in its results. The French fled to France; the Bavarians gave up their alliance with them, and surrendered their fortresses. One victory had done more than several campaigns.

ON returning to camp from their reconnoissance, a council of war was held by the allied commanders, and, though a number of officers voted nay, Marlborough and Eugene both decided on battle. They feared delay, lest the enemy, anticipating their action, should make their field-works stronger; they were themselves suffering for lack of forage; their victual from Nördlingen was not always secure; and Villeroi was rumored to be advancing to reinforce Tallard and Marsin. Moreover, Marlborough had been roundly abused in England for advancing so far from the Netherlands, and he desired to justify his action. The armies lay but three miles apart, the allies encamped on the heights behind Tapfheim, back of the plain which stretched between them and the French. Attack being decided on, they broke up, August 13, at daylight, and advanced on the enemy in a number of columns. Their movements had been observed by the French, but the advance was deemed a manœuvre to protect a flank march to Nördlingen. That the French generals did not expect a battle that day is shown by the fact that much of their cavalry was out foraging; but this was called in and the order given to prepare for action; the outposts were ordered back from the villages north of the Nebelbach, and these were set on fire to prevent their being used for defense.

Marlborough and Eugene are said to have again reconnoitred, and to have recognized the errors in the enemy's dispositions. By some authorities it is said that the morning was hazy, in which case they can scarcely have learned much beyond satisfying themselves that the enemy had not substantially changed the formation of the day before. But a note by Tallard, penned at the time, states that he could see the allies on the hills, so that the day was probably only overcast. It was at all events first determined between the commanders that Eugene, who held the allied right wing, should make an attack on Marsin to hold his attention as well as that of the elector of Bavaria, while Marlborough should assail Blenheim.

It is generally stated in the accounts of this battle that Marlborough, or Eugene, or both of them, on recognizing the weakness of the enemy's centre, then and there determined to break through at this point and cut the enemy in two. Whatever plan was adopted was a joint one between the allied commanders; and it does not appear from the initial attacks that they had so soon perceived that the centre was the proper place on which to deliver the vital blow. If it is true that they did so, then Marlborough's early expenditure of force on Blenheim was an error, and not in accordance with the plan adopted. To carry out the idea of breaking the centre, only partial attacks on Blenheim and opposite Lützingen should have been made, stout enough to hold the enemy from reinforcing the centre from these places, but no

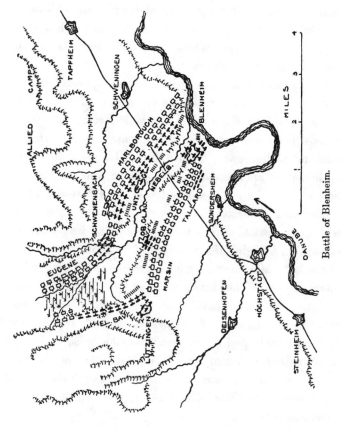

Battle of Blenheim.

more. The action taken by Marlborough does not warrant the belief that the generals founded their initial plan for the battle on the enemy's weak centre.

The bulk of Tallard's foot was thus engaged in defending Blenheim, which he, as well as Marlborough, at first deemed the key of the battle-field. From Blenheim to Oberklau there was nothing but horse. Oberklau had nearly thirty battalions in and about it; then came some Bavarian and French cavalry, and then eighteen battalions of foot thrown forward of Lützingen in a crotchet along the foot of the hills. Tallard had but ten battalions to sustain his cavalry. Marsin and the elector had a second line in which foot stood behind foot and horse behind horse. Batteries lay all along the line, judiciously disposed.

In Eugene's front the ground was exceptionally difficult, and it was high noon before he was able to make it practicable by filling up the worst places with fascines and logs, or boards from the houses in Schwenenbach; but being covered by undergrowth, he had been able to push his skirmishers over unobserved; whereupon he sent word to Marlborough that he was ready to cross. The batteries of both armies had been steadily at work ever since eight o'clock, with quite marked effect; the engineers had been meanwhile engaged in bridging the Nebelbach in several places in front of the left; Marlborough gave his orders to his wing, and the attack began. The duke's wing was in four lines, two of infantry, and two of cavalry between them; it was intended that the footmen of the first lines should push over the brook and take such position as to enable the horse under their cover to get across and form, — the two rear lines to remain in reserve. On the extreme left was a heavy column of the three arms under Lord Cutts, ready to be launched against Blenheim.

This column was first across the Nebelbach; it is stated to have been sent to the attack by eleven; Coxe says one. Eugene was not fairly across until half-past twelve, owing to the bad ground and the opposition of the enemy's light troops, but the crossing was finally accomplished under cover of the guns. The French batteries had been so well served that a loss of at least two thousand men is said to have been inflicted on the allies before they came to close quarters. Though the ground he had to cross was not only marshy but cut up by bushes so as to break up the alignment of his men in their advance, Eugene made his attack in good heart, and on his first assault took a battery of six guns; but when he had broken Marsin's first line, the second charged. in on his own, broke it, and drove it back across the first brook. He suffered seriously from lack of sufficient infantry, and the guns from Oberklau could enfilade his line. A second charge by the horse was driven back by the elector; and a third one was rather weakly delivered by the tired troops, though headed by Eugene in person. It became evident to the prince that he had too heavy a force against him. He was, in fact, with a third of the allied numbers, and nearly all cavalry at that, facing half the enemy, and on the worst possible ground. Nor indeed, save the Prussians, did his cavalry behave as it should. The prince was called on to shoot down numerous runaways; the material was far less good than that of Marlborough. That Eugene kept them at their work, however, the fearful list of casualties abundantly testifies. Nothing daunted, notwithstanding backsets and poor response to his exertions, he so ably utilized his squadrons, both afoot and in the saddle, that neither Marsin nor the elector sent any reinforcements to the centre.

While the prince was preparing and pushing his attack, Marlborough had got over the troops on his extreme left, and these had fallen on the village of Blenheim in six heavy lines. Lord Cutts assaulted in gallant form, but he was violently thrown back; successive bodies of troops were sent on to aid in the attacks, but no impression whatsoever was made. General Clérambault, with the infantry in Blenheim, held his own with ease; and the French horse, breaking out on the

allied columns with much effect, drove them back across the
brook, and it was with difficulty, though the assaults were
renewed again and again with brilliant courage, that the
allies held their ground at all in front of the place. No
lodgment was made in Blenheim. Meanwhile the forces of
the allied centre had been preparing to push their way across
the Nebelbach.

It was a sad mistake that Tallard, during this time, did
not make a counter attack. Had he done so, Marlborough
might have been unable to get his men into line. But the
French contented themselves with cannonading from the
front, and enfilading the allied centre with the batteries of
Blenheim and Oberklau.

Finally, Marlborough became convinced that he could not
take Blenheim, and having debouched from Unterklau and
pushed his first two lines of the centre under Churchill across
the Nebelbach, though much hampered by a serious flank
attack from Oberklau, he finally drew up his cavalry in
front, and his foot behind, with intervals through which the
cavalry, if thrown back, could retire, and delivered an impetuous assault. It was already five o'clock. From four to six
hours had been wasted on Blenheim; no gain had been made,
and Eugene had been struggling against heavy odds ever
since half-past twelve. But once started, the left wing cavalry rode at the French line in close ranks with good effect;
and though in its turn several times repulsed, on each occasion the pursuing French squadrons came upon the infantry line in the rear, and were severely handled by the salvos
of musketry. They had not enough foot in the centre to
follow up and hold what gain they might make. Finally,
the French horse and the ten supporting battalions of foot
gave way; Marlborough seized on the propitious moment
with the keen eye of the battle-captain; one more charge, and

the enemy broke and retired in great confusion. "Le gros de la cavallerie a fait *mal, je dis très mal*," wrote Tallard in his official report. Still they had held their own gallantly; they were simply ill-placed. Part were cut down, part captured, part pursued to Hochstädt; Marlborough now turned on the fifteen thousand men in Blenheim, and after hard fighting, surrounded and captured the entire body, including Marshal Tallard, who from the centre was seeking to join the Blenheim force.

While Marlborough was thus earning a difficult success on the left, and before he had actually broken the centre, Prince Eugene, though thrice repulsed, had, after collecting and resting his men, a fourth time led an attack on Marsin's and the elector's front and left flank; and this time successfully, driving the enemy well back beyond Lützingen. His task had been the harder one. It was at the time Marlborough ruptured Tallard's centre and captured that marshal, of which fact the news spread rapidly, that Eugene broke down Marsin's resistance, and when Marlborough had definitely thrust back the French cavalry, the elector and Marsin were in full retreat.

Tallard had committed a grave mistake in cooping up so much of his infantry in Blenheim, and leaving nothing but cavalry to oppose to Marlborough's centre. The latter made a lesser mistake in giving so much of his attention to the capture of Blenheim. He may have been somewhat delayed by bridging the Nebelbach; but not much beyond noon. It was only at five o'clock, when he threw up his attempts there and devoted himself to breaking through the cavalry-centre of the enemy, that he contributed his best efforts to the victory. Had Marsin and the elector had opposite to them a less strong opponent than Eugene, they would have certainly detached some of their forty-two battalions to aid the centre, with what result it is hard to say. And in the later phases of the fight, had Marlborough left a smaller force to engage the Blenheim body, and turned with his bulk against Marsin's naked right flank, the latter would have been annihilated, and Blenheim would have fallen later. As it was, Marsin made good his escape. But when Marlborough had made up his mind to break the centre of the French army, he put his whole soul into the work, and won.

The French, out of sixty thousand, lost thirty thousand men, of whom fifteen thousand were prisoners, two hundred flags, fifty guns and all their baggage. The allies lost over eleven thousand men, — forty-four hundred killed, seventy-three hundred wounded. Eugene pursued Marsin some distance; Marlborough, busy with Blenheim, attempted no tactical pursuit. The allies, according to the questionable custom of that time, remained five days on the battle-field. Strategic pursuit, unusual then in any event, was delayed by the allies because bread and forage had partially failed them.

The French, with the thirty thousand men they had left, crossed the Danube at Lauingen, left fifteen battalions in Ulm, gathered in the garrisons of Augsburg and other places, and leaving Bavaria to her fate, fled along the Danube valley to the Rhine, crossed that river, August 31 to September 2, at Strasburg, joined the twenty thousand men of Villeroi and the ten thousand of Coigny, and thus made up again an array of sixty thousand men for the defense of France.

The troops besieging Ingolstadt were withdrawn and part of them put at the siege of Ulm, which surrendered September 11 with two hundred and fifty guns and twelve hundred barrels of powder.

The victory of Blenheim, won in consequence of the errors of the French, had immense results. After taking Ulm, the allies marched to Philipsburg, crossed with sixty-five thousand men, captured Trarbach on the Moselle, and besieged Landau. Marlborough and Eugene were anxious for another battle; but Prince Louis would not agree to it, and insisted on a war of sieges. The French had recovered equality in force, but had lost all morale; the allies were allowed to take Landau and Trier; and only winter put an end to their successes. The Bavarians made a treaty in November, by which their fortresses were surrendered, and the Bavarian garrisons discharged.

This campaign, thanks to these two great leaders, showed again the superiority of concentration and battle over detailed operations and sieges. Forces had been concentrated in an important territory, and the result of a victory had been decisive. Even before the battle, the assault on the position at the Schellenberg, though delivered with too little deliberation, had won marked moral results, and all his fortresses did not save the elector of Bavaria: after one real victory, even without pursuit, they succumbed. On the other hand, the Stollhofen lines were of no use whatever to the allies. Despite them, or because of them, Tallard first sent part of his troops to Marsin and then marched to Bavaria.

We must allow Eugene a full half of the credit for this memorable victory. From his earliest day he was unquestionably as much a fighter as the duke, he conducted more campaigns and won more victories. There prevails among us Anglo-Saxons an impression that Marlborough was the one who urged on to battle, as he is often assumed if not asserted to have been the chief in command. All this is quite unwarranted. As the responsibility was equal, so must be the credit for the victory. Not that English historians fail to praise Eugene; some, as Coxe, are honest eulogists of the prince; but by implication he is treated as if he had been

Marlborough's lieutenant and not his equal in command; every strategic march is ascribed to the Briton, every tactical manœuvre posted to his credit; and the inference drawn by the average reader is necessarily wrong. To some historians there was only one directing influence in this war, and that Marlborough's; the existence, in success, of any other force is ignored. In failure, of course, the Dutch deputies are omnipotent.

No criticism can belittle Marlborough's splendid conduct on this field; nor, on the other hand, must we rob Eugene of one of his laurels. On the allied right, with twenty thousand men, of which only a small part was foot, the gallant prince had defeated Marsin and the elector with thirty thousand men, on ground worse adapted for attack than that opposite Marlborough, and especially bad for cavalry. Had Eugene not contained nearly half the enemy, Marlborough would scarcely have been able to break the centre, for this would assuredly have been reinforced from the heavy masses of foot under Marsin and the elector. As it was, when Tallard appealed to Marsin for aid, the latter replied that he was himself too hard beset. That Eugene's fighting was of the hottest is shown by the fact that out of his twenty thousand men he lost six thousand, — nearly a third, while out of thirty-six thousand men Marlborough lost but five thousand, — only a seventh. And as Eugene's force was mostly cavalry, which cannot as a rule be put over such bad ground or into such close contact, and rarely loses as heavily as foot, this is all the more a tribute to the prince's exceptional vigor and determination.

As children we have been taught from our schooldays up to look to Marlborough rather than to Eugene for the success of Blenheim, and it is hard to eradicate the feeling. But when we weigh the part of each, from the moment that saw

Eugene without waiting for authority from any source march out of the Stollhofen lines to follow Tallard, — a brilliant inspiration that lay at the very root of success, — to his last moment of pursuit of the flying French; the part which Eugene bore against greater difficulties on the allied right, so as to enable Marlborough to succeed on the left and centre; when we remember Zenta, Turin and Belgrade, and the whole military life of the wonderful imperial marshal, we must cheerfully allow him full half the credit for this great and decisive victory.

Let us lay our tribute equally at the feet of both. Following in the footsteps of Gustavus, they inaugurated the era of great battles and of battle-tactics. Blenheim, though the tactical combinations were by no means perfect, was a worthy successor of Breitenfeld and Lützen; was one of those object-lessons in war which teach even the obstinate; and which here showed the world that intrenched lines, fortresses heavily garrisoned, and other defensive devices are as nothing compared to offensive energy and skill on the battle-field. As the modern art of war is distinctly dependent on manœuvres leading up to battle, so we owe to Marlborough and Eugene, as successors of Gustavus and predecessors of Frederick, a debt for their grand conception of the value of fighting over mere manœuvring.

Nor is this said in forgetfulness of the battles delivered and won by Turenne and by Condé. It was such men as all these who first saw the error of carrying the theory of fortified lines too far, and who prepared the way for Frederick and Napoleon to make perfect; and it may well be said that the two last captains would scarcely have risen to the height they reached but for these same predecessors in the art of war.

With Marlborough's splendid diplomatic services during

the War of the Succession this history has nothing to do; it is only as a captain that he is gauged. But even in diplomacy, the accomplishment of Eugene may well be placed beside his colleague's.

We are often told about the untutored soldier, whose keen military instinct, power to divine the intentions of the enemy, and courage of his convictions make him superior to the book-worm who is full of military saws and warlike instances; and Marlborough has been held up as a sample of the uneducated general. Such, to begin with, is not the fact; Marlborough had received the best practical education of the day under its greatest leaders; and history moreover shows us that the great captains of the world have been men to whom a generous providence gave the one quality, and whose own industry and intelligence have made good use of the other. No one doubts the superiority of the gifted unread man over the highly educated weakling; but Alexander, Hannibal, Gustavus, Frederick and Napoleon were all born soldiers, deep-read and trained to arms as well. Cæsar is perhaps the exception that proves the rule; and yet he got a fair military education in the Spanish peninsula, and the best one in the world in Gaul; and who knows how much he had studied the military works and generals preceding his day? It is probable that he had Arrian and Xenophon and Polybius by heart. Had he not indeed taken all learning to be his province? It might be claimed because Frederick hated war, that he was an unread soldier; but who except he unearthed and profited by Epaminondas' matchless oblique order, which had lain buried for two thousand years? The same thing applies to all captains of the second rank: Miltiades, Epaminondas, Hasdrubal, Pyrrhus, the consul Nero, Scipio, Sertorius, Turenne, Eugene, Marlborough, Wellington, Lee, Moltke, — all were men who were educated to war, and who had read military history. A man need not become a book-worm to assimilate the lessons of history; and the keen per-ceptions of a Marlborough in the field would soon make the lessons of a Turenne his own, and better on them, if it were possible, in his own campaigns. It is true that to reduce war to a science of diagrams and nothing more does not make a soldier; but given equal intellect, character and opportunity, it is certain that, of any two men, the one who has faithfully studied what his predecessors in the art of war have done will be by far the better. All great captains have profited by reading and study; most of them have been keen students of the deeds of the great men before them; and if there has been one who has become truly great without such study and training, I have failed to find him in history. I do not refer to mere conquerors; I speak of great captains whose work has instructed mankind in the art of war.

It is possible that the present estimate of Marlborough, the placing him on a lower level than Gustavus, on the same level with Turenne and Eugene, may evoke a protest in Greater Britain. But it remains no less the true estimate. *Cuidem in sua arte crede experto;* and no doubt those who have best made war are the safest critics of war. No one will be found to deny that, naval war apart, the Continental nations have, in the past two generations, outstripped the English in capacity for the military art; their critics will be found the safest ones to follow; and an examination of the best critical work of all the Continental nations will sustain the views herein expressed.

To quote Kausler with reference to this campaign, than whom there is no more honest panegyrist of Marlborough: " If we subject the conduct of the several commanding gen-erals to a critical examination, it appears that only Eugene stands forth fault free."

As has always been and is to-day usual with the English, — as is in fact proper, — the most extravagant rewards and honors were heaped upon Marlborough. Prince Eugene, who had borne his full share in the campaign and in the battle, and whose master the emperor had gained more than Queen Anne, for his country was saved from the brink of ruin, won nothing but the additional fame which posterity awards him.

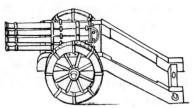

Four-Barreled Gun.   (16th Century.)

LVIII.

EUGENE AND VENDOME. 1705.

In 1705 Vendome and Eugene manœuvred in Italy. Stahremberg and the duke of Savoy had been pushed up into a corner of Piedmont. The campaign here was one of the old-fashioned kind, in which Vendome on the defensive rather outmanœuvred the prince, and held head to him in a battle at Cassano. The operations were between the Oglio and Adda, and both armies early retired into winter-quarters. In the Netherlands the campaign was equally fruitless, and consisted merely of secondary operations. Marlborough was hampered by lack of men and money; and the year was frittered away on work which is scarcely worth the recital except to show what the old method was, out of which able generals were gradually but only slowly working. Marlborough sought to open the campaign on the Moselle; but the French seized the initiative in the Netherlands, and obliged the duke to return to protect Holland. The plan that had been made for an invasion of France ended in only protecting Holland from invasion.

AFTER the serious defeat of 1704, Louis XIV. determined to operate defensively next year. To Villeroi was given the duty of defending Brabant; to Marsin was intrusted the Rhine, to Villars the Saar and Moselle; while Vendome was instructed finally to reduce the duke of Savoy, who in the last campaign had lost Susa, Pignerol, Aosta, Bardo, Vercelli and Ivrea, and now stood on the brink of ruin.

In 1705, in Italy, Vendome and Eugene were consequently once more opposed to each other. Field-Marshal Stahremberg and the duke of Savoy were in a bad situation; Vendome had already reduced the northwestern part of Piedmont and Savoy, and soon after captured the fortress of Verona, which enabled him to control the line of the Adige. Some seventy-seven thousand French troops were in Italy, of which Ven-

dome commanded twenty-two thousand in Piedmont, where
he had just captured Verona; his brother, with fifteen thousand in the Brescia country, faced the imperialists, who with
eight thousand had retired to the west shore of Lake Garda;
La Feuillade held the Nizza country with eleven thousand;
Laparace with five thousand was besieging Mirandola, and
twenty-four thousand men were in fortresses. To oppose this
extensive but in the highest degree ill-disposed array, Stahremberg and Savoy had only sixteen thousand men. Prince
Eugene was given twenty-eight thousand men and ordered to
Piedmont to their relief. The odds were decidedly against
him; and he had indeed found much difficulty in procuring
this many troops from the short-sighted Vienna ministers.

When Eugene arrived, via Triente, at Roveredo, he moved
down the Adige and attempted to cross the upper Mincio,
intending to relieve Mirandola; but checked at this river by
the French, and hearing that Vendome was approaching the
scene, he put part of his army across the lake in boats to
the west bank, sent the others around the north shore, and at
the end of May took up a strong position between Salo and
Gavardo. Hoping to neutralize the prince, Vendome fortified a position in his front, hemmed him in between the mountains and the lake, where he was cut off from foraging in the
open country, left the younger Vendome to hold him there,
and returned to Piedmont, where, by drawing in some of his
scattered forces, he soon captured the last outstanding fortresses of Nizza, Villafranca and Chivasso, and drove the
duke of Savoy back to Turin in sore distress.

Eugene remained a month in his position, waiting for
essential reinforcements from Austria. This was not brilliant
conduct, but in front of such numbers it was safe. The desperate situation of the duke finally constraining him to
attempt a march to his relief, he threw up his communica-

tions with the Tyrol, turned Vendome's position by the left, marched in the night of June 22 through the mountains via Nave to Brescia, where he anticipated young Vendome by a number of hours, and pushing on, crossed the Oglio at Calcio June 27 in the face of opposition. The French general did not attack him on the march, but moved on a parallel line to the south of him, via Montechiaro and Manerbio, himself crossed the Oglio at Pontevico, and took up a position against him between Crema and Lodi. Eugene took Soncino, but only moved as far as Romanengo. Alarmed at this sudden progress, the duke of Vendome left Piedmont for the moment, came up to join his brother, at once recrossed the Serio, and drew up opposite Eugene near Casal Moraro. Both generals began to manœuvre, Eugene to reach Piedmont, Vendome to prevent his so doing. The former tried several operations, but none proved successful; he could better perhaps have accomplished his object by a battle. He had on the spot an army fully as large as those under the duke and the younger Vendome; but the enemy lay across his path, and, fearing the depletion of even victory, he preferred manœuvre to battle, and sought to steal a passage of the Adda, either up or down the river, to join the duke of Savoy with forces intact.

He first moved by a cautious night march on August 10 to Paradiso on the upper Adda, thinking, if Vendome did not follow him, to find a passage to Piedmont that way. But Vendome knew Eugene's shrewd ways, and discovering his absence next day, made speed to follow. Leaving his brother with thirteen thousand men on the left bank at Cassano, where there was a bridge protected by a strong bridge-head and the Ritorto canal, he crossed to the right bank of the Adda, on the Lodi bridge, with nine thousand, and marched up river, where he attempted by fortifying the banks to fore-

stall a passage by the imperialists.   An accident to his pontoon train delayed Eugene, and before he could cross, Vendome had put in an appearance.   Eugene then, on August 17,
stole another march back to Cassano, hoping to catch young
Vendome at that place and beat him; but with the idea that
Eugene would march to Cremona, the latter had been ordered
by the duke farther down the left bank to Rivolta, his rear-
guard only being left in the Cassano bridge-head.   Prince

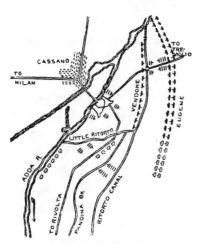

Eugene was about to attack,
when Vendome, fearing just
this contingency, returned
from the upper Adda, and
resumed his position in
those defenses.

Eugene had now tried
schemes for stealing a passage of the Adda above and
below the French; he had
failed in his every device,
and was confronted with
the question whether he
should force a passage or
not.   His activity had kept

Battle of Cassano.

the French commander in his front, and had relieved the duke
of Savoy to this extent, for Vendome's lieutenants at Turin
were not able.   But the prince was constantly urged by the
emperor to reach and release the duke from his predicament;
Vendome had a scant ten thousand men in his front, though
in an exceptionally strong position behind the Ritorto canal,
while he himself had some twenty-four thousand; young Vendome was in Rivolta, and with his hyper-indolent character,
was scarcely apt to come up in season to aid his brother;
if Eugene attacked and could not force Cassano, he would

not be compromised; and if he won, he would gain much. He decided on attack.

Cassano lay behind the Adda, over which the bridge had a strong bridge-head. In its front was the Ritorto canal, with a branch running back to the river. Vendome was in a species of fortress, with a wet ditch twenty odd feet wide and four or five feet deep. A stone bridge crossed the canal on the Treviglio road, and was stoutly held by the French. Eugene first sent a column against this bridge under Count Leiningen, who with a gallant rush seized it, crossed, and was forming line on the other side, when heavy reinforcements came up and he was hustled back. Returning boldly to his work, after a short rest, Leiningen again took the bridge, aided by parties who waded the canal up to their necks in water; but at the critical moment he was killed, and the assault again came to naught. Meanwhile all along the line, at close range, the rival battalions were pouring a deadly fire into each other's ranks. Eugene now determined to have the bridge at any cost. Heading a column of troops gathered from the right, he led them against it in person, carried it, and drove the French well back into the bridge-head. In and near by this the French made a stand. A sort of wagon-burg had been erected in its front, and the fighting was tenacious to the last degree, for if Eugene won, he would drive the French into the Adda. After a long and desperate contest numbers prevailed, and the wagon-burg was taken. Vendome came in person to the rescue, but Eugene, still in the thick of the fray, drove the French back into the bridge-head. One more effort and the battle would be won. Inspired by the tremendous fire of their gallant chieftain, the imperialists followed him over the breastworks, and the garrison began to fall back, hundreds throwing themselves into the river. But again Vendome came up and stemmed the tide, as Eugene reached the inner works of the bridge-head, and again Eugene rallied his men and pressed on. The two commanders were almost face to face. The French left wing was cut off; Vendome was on the point of retiring, when, in quick succession, Eugene received a ball in the neck and another in the knee, which obliged him to go back to the surgeons. General Bibra took his place; but the effort had exhausted itself, and, in the absence of Eugene, the French crowded the imperialists back to the stone bridge. This, however, Bibra held.

Meanwhile Eugene's Prussian troops had made a gallant but ineffectual attack on the French right; but in wading the canal their ammunition was wetted, and they had only their bayonets to rely on. With the wounding of Eugene all chance of success against Vendome had gone. The imperialists, after a four hours' battle, retired to camp. Vendome kept the battle-field.

The casualties were heavy. Eugene lost two thousand killed and two thousand one hundred wounded. The French, who had been subjected to the close-range fire of superior numbers, are said to have lost many more, — estimates went as high as six thousand killed and four thousand wounded, a sum equal to Vendome's entire force. Perhaps two thousand five hundred killed and three thousand wounded would be a fair guess. The loss in officers of rank was terrible; few escaped being disabled.

Both sides claimed the victory, and *Te Deums* were sung in Paris, Vienna and Turin. But Vendome had countered his adversary's blow.

Eugene retired to Treviglio August 17 and intrenched a camp. Vendome joined his brother at Rivolta. The latter had had a chance to distinguish himself on this occasion by falling on the Austrian flank and rear from Rivolta; but as he did not do so, — though the messenger dispatched to him with orders to this effect was captured, — Vendome deprived him of command.

For two months both armies, now about equal in numbers, faced each other between the Adda and the Serio. Eugene was still waiting for reinforcements from the Tyrol, and Vendome closely watched him. Both indulged in an active small war. Finally, October 10, Eugene undertook a secret flank march by the lower Serio via Crema around Vendome's right, to try thus to break through to Piedmont, or, if not this, to cut the French off from, and himself secure better winter-quarters near, Cremona. But the rains delayed his bridge-throwing at Montadine so many hours that Vendome forestalled him by marching rapidly via Lodi and Pizzighe-tone, where were bridges and good roads, took post opposite the prince, and beat back his attempted passage of the river with considerable loss. Both armies then marched upstream on either bank of the Serio, and the prince, the river having fallen, finally succeeded in stealing a passage over a ford near by, and took up a position at Fontenella. Vendome sat down opposite him, and captured Soncino with its imperial garrison. Finally Eugene, seeing that he could not succeed in joining the duke of Savoy, gave up the idea of doing more this year, and at the beginning of November retired by a rapid secret march across the Oglio to Chiari, and a few days later started for Castiglione, intending to seek winter-quarters near Mantua. But Vendome again anticipated him by a parallel march to his right, and by occupying the heights south of Lonato, thus cutting him off from the Mantua country, and forcing him to seek winter-quarters on the west shore of Lake Garda. Vendome himself went into cantonments in the Mantua country; Eugene, between Salo and Monte Chiaro. Leaving Count Reventlau in command, the prince returned to Vienna in January.

Vendome had acted with consummate ability, quickness and decision. This campaign redounds much to his credit. He largely outnumbered Prince Eugene, his total in Italy being seventy-seven thousand men to his opponent's thirty-two thousand; but he checkmated the imperial general in all attempts to reach Piedmont, and fought him with smaller forces. At the same time Eugene had done well for the duke of Savoy. He had kept Vendome so busy that he could not besiege Turin; and while he had not been able to join his ally, he had accomplished the spirit of his task if not the letter.

This campaign — except at Cassano — was conducted according to the old fashion, by manœuvring instead of fighting, and, on the French side, by holding and besieging fortresses. Vendome could have placed sixty thousand men in the field, with this force have annihilated Eugene's army, or have crippled it for the campaign, and then, turning on the duke in Turin, he would scarcely have needed to besiege the place. Or, indeed, he might have captured Turin before Eugene reached the field. But the old idea still held men fast, and out of seventy-seven thousand men, Vendome opposed the prince in the field with but twenty-two thousand, the rest being planted all over Italy in fortresses. Not only that, but he again divided his force into two parts, one on either side of the Adda. Eugene was not fortunate in his efforts to take advantage of this opening, but his forces were always well concentrated, and he kept them actively employed. Vendome's were not so well in hand, but he displayed exceptional rapidity and energy. Had he concentrated his forces for a single hearty blow, he might have saved Italy to the French arms.

It has been said that, as the opening move, Eugene chose a roundabout and difficult road into Italy, via Triente and the

Adige, in lieu of the road up the Inn and down the Adda, which was the nearer route to join the duke; that after he had taken Soncino, he remained at Romanengo instead of crossing the Adda ; that he kept quiet, a month at Gavardo and two at Treviglio, while the duke of Savoy was in utmost need. That Eugene weighed the advantages of both routes across the Alps can scarcely be doubted, though we are not told why he did not march by the Inn-Adda ; and the delays mentioned are not only explained by the attendant circumstances, but during these weeks Eugene never ceased from an active small war. Of all the generals of this era, Eugene was the one who least often, from whatever cause, sat down to inactivity. His constant push, in great and little operations, was unequaled. The thing this year which is most noteworthy in Eugene's manœuvres is that he did not blindly cling to his communications with Germany, but gave them up and relied on the country, when it became desirable. And it is particularly to be noted that it was he who constantly retained the initiative and dictated the manœuvres. Vendome was following his lead at all times.

As is usual after a brilliant success, the English made no great effort for 1705, either in men or money. Only forty thousand men were authorized, not so much as England's share of men to be furnished. At the opening of the year was the time to follow up the fruits of Blenheim ; but neither London, La Hague nor Vienna seemed to see the wisdom of making a strenuous effort to improve the occasion ; whereas Louis did all that in him lay to retrieve himself.

Marlborough and Eugene jointly drew up a plan for 1705, and proposed to the allies early to concentrate on the Moselle their main force, which should reach ninety thousand men, capture Diedenhofen, Saarlouis and Metz, and invade France through the Duchy of Lorraine, Trier and Trarbach having already been taken and garrisoned. Marlborough's column should march up the Moselle, the prince of Baden up the Saar; Alsace would thus be taken in reverse, and the French would be thrown into a defensive attitude. In half-pursuance to this advice, but with a slowness which argued ill for the campaign, the allies began to assemble sixty thousand men on the Moselle, and to place thirty thousand each on the Meuse and the Scheldt. Louis XIV. on his side determined to act defensively in the Netherlands, to put thirty-two thousand men under Villeroi at Maestricht, to which number the army of the elector of Bavaria would be added later; to send Villars with forty-six thousand men to the Moselle; to intrust Alsatia to Marsin with twenty-six thousand; and to garrison all the Flanders towns. Despite these enormous forces, which presaged a conflict of the giants, the campaign was one of manœuvring only, and without any worthy result. Marlborough purposed to hold the French from activity in the Netherlands by his operations on the Moselle; but they were speedier than he was and took the initiative from him.

The allies concentrated so slowly that Villars was able to cover Diedenhofen and Metz by taking up an admirable position above Sierck on the right bank of the Moselle, sustained by Saarlouis, Metz and Luxemburg in a circle in the rear. Marlborough reached the vicinity of Sierck at midsummer, long before the prince of Baden was ready to join him; but as men and material were both lacking, he was able to accomplish nothing; the invasion scheme quite failed; and Marlborough was suddenly forced to return to the Netherlands, where Villeroi and the elector had captured Huy by assault, and had occupied the town and besieged the citadel of Lüttich. So far from being able to carry the war into France, he was himself threatened with an invasion of the country he was held to defend. Under these annoying conditions, Marlborough could well understand why other generals sometimes failed in their efforts. He was certainly not to blame for the lack of support given him; but it was on this same rock that so many of the allied generals had been wrecked.

Marlborough broke up and headed for Maestricht, crossing the Meuse at Visé. Upon his approach the French retired from Lüttich, and Marlborough joined Overkirk, who had

been in Villeroi's front and had recaptured Huy. But in his absence from the Moselle things went quite amiss. Villars sent Villeroi twenty-three thousand men from his own command, left

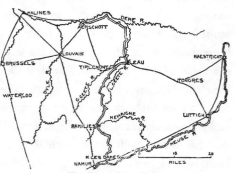

The Line of the Dyle.

nine thousand men on the Moselle to oppose the prince of Baden, who later arrived there with nineteen thousand, headed twenty-seven thousand men and captured Trier from the forces left there by Marlborough, and marched to the middle Rhine to join Marsin. All the advantage hoped from the proposed plan had vanished into thin air, and the Anglo-Dutch were put on the defensive.

When Villeroi knew that Marlborough was coming, he withdrew to the sources of the Méhaigne into fortified lines, which was, according to the ideas of the day, a profitable thing to do. These lines were, however, altogether too long to be safe. The right rested on the Meuse at Marché les Dames, ran north to the upper Méhaigne, thence along the Geete to Léau, and on to Aerschott back of the Demer.

Villeroi had force enough to conduct extensive operations, but not enough to keep intact so long a line, however skillfully he might hold it.

Marlborough had sixty thousand men, but it was only after great difficulty that he persuaded the Dutch to agree to any active measures. Villeroi had fortified every obstacle, and, curiously, intrenched lines were supposed to be hard to break through; but Marlborough went intelligently at it. In order to weaken Villeroi's centre, he demonstrated in force towards the right of his line, which leaned on the Méhaigne, and persuaded the French general to draw from the other points a large body to reinforce it; having accomplished which, on the night of July 17 Marlborough made a forced march with his choice troops to the vicinity of Léau, and here, at early dawn, broke through the depleted French lines by a massed attack pushed home, with slight opposition or loss. Seeing that his intrenched line was no longer tenable, Villeroi fell back behind the Dyle with his left on Louvain. This was a fresh proof of the uselessness of such positions; but they remained a favorite defensive scheme for many decades more.

After much opposition by the Dutch deputies, Marlborough made another attempt to force the Dyle; but the Dutch troops refused to do their part, and the project, though happily initiated, proved a complete failure. Later in mid-August, Marlborough turned the Dyle position by its headwaters and forced the French back towards Brussels, thus cutting them off from the direct road to France. On August 18 there was a skirmish at Waterloo; Marlborough made preparations to attack the French; they facing as Wellington did in 1815, and he facing north, in exactly reversed positions. But again, when everything was ready for attack, the Dutch deputies interposed their veto, and by the next day the French had made their position too strong to be assaulted by even the hero of the Schellenberg. Forced to retire, Marlborough took Léau and Santvliet, and leveled the lines of the Geete. This campaign must be pronounced a failure. Though it is true that the duke was not to blame for his lack of support and had many things to contend against, yet these are the same conditions which neutralized the best efforts of many another general of his era. And though, as is so often asserted, it is true that Marlborough never lost a battle or failed to take a place he laid siege to, it is also true that, from one or other cause, he conducted as many barren campaigns as any of the other generals whom we place in the same rank with himself. But this year bore one good fruit : the ill-success of the Flanders campaign had the effect of stimulating the allies to proper exertions, and in 1706 Marlborough could take the field with a suitable equipment of men and money.

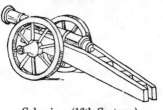

Culverin.   (16th Century.)

LIX.

RAMILLIES. MAY 23, 1706.

In 1706 Villeroi with sixty-two thousand men lay at Tirlemont. Marlborough concentrated his sixty thousand allies near Maestricht, and marched on Namur. Villeroi moved by his right and met him at Ramillies, May 23, drawn up on high ground. Marlborough, always ready for battle, made an able feint on the French left, to meet which Villeroi transferred much of his force to that flank; upon which Marlborough attacked the French right with great determination, and though forced back more than once, by bringing all his available forces to bear, broke in the enemy's defense and drove him from the field. The effect of this magnificent victory was immense. Nearly all the Austrian Netherlands fell to the allies. Ramillies saved Holland. Villeroi was replaced by Vendome.

In 1706 Louis XIV. put three hundred thousand men into the field, and proposed to act offensively. Turin and Barcelona were to be vigorously besieged, and the French generals in Flanders and Italy were given fighting orders. Villeroi, with the elector of Bavaria, was to command in the Netherlands; Villars on the Rhine; Marsin on the Moselle; Vendome was to push back the imperialists to the Tyrol while La Feuillade captured Turin.

It would, this spring, have well suited the inclinations of Marlborough to go in person to Italy, as he had formerly marched to Germany, and there work with Eugene, instead of being tied to the narrow ideas of the Dutch deputies; but the states-general would, under no circumstances whatsoever, permit any of their troops to go to the south of the Alps. The successes of Villars had so far modified the courage of the deputies, however, that, somewhat to his surprise, the duke was given freer play than usual in the Netherlands.

The French, some sixty-two thousand strong, and with one hundred and thirty guns, under Villeroi, lay near Tirlemont, east of the Dyle, in fortified lines covering Namur, against which they believed the allies had conceived an intention to operate. About May 20, in the Maestricht country, near Tongres, Marlborough concentrated his English and Dutch troops, a force of about sixty thousand men and one hundred and twenty guns. His objective was in fact Namur. To cover this fortress, Villeroi moved forward by his right and took post on Mount St. André on the Great Geete near Ramillies. Marching towards Namur on the old Roman road which here runs along the Méhaigne from east to west, Marlborough's van soon gained sight of the French camp, and perceiving the approach of the enemy, Villeroi drew up in line. The French lay on high ground — a sort of plateau — where rise the Great and Little Geete rivers and several other minor brooks. Marlborough, well aware of the commanding nature of the position, would have been glad himself to seize it; but Villeroi had anticipated him and now stood on its summit in battle array, long before the bulk of the allied columns reached the ground. His army lay in a species of concave order on the slope of the hill back of which runs the Louvain-Namur turnpike, with the marshy ground along the Little Geete in his front, the left leaning on the village of Autre Église, the right stretching out towards Tavières on the Méhaigne, and the centre strengthened by the villages of Ramillies and Offuz. The position, not very expertly taken up, was good only for defense, and Villeroi was constitutionally inclined towards a defensive battle. The cavalry of the left was behind the Little Geete, where it could not manœuvre if needed; Ramillies in Villeroi's front-centre was well held by foot, but could readily be turned and captured; the cavalry of the right stretched out towards Tavières, but had nothing to lean on, nor were any foot supports near by it. Tavières and an outlying hamlet beyond it were strengthened by some bodies of foot but lacked numbers; the other villages had more, Ramillies being held by twenty battalions; and the rest of the infantry was marshaled in two

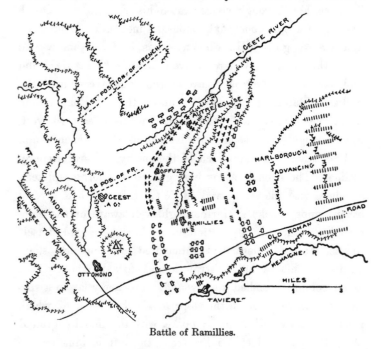

Battle of Ramillies.

lines, with the one hundred and thirty guns suitably posted in batteries in its front. The array was formidable. It was because the enemy was looked for along the old Roman road that Villeroi had massed most of his cavalry on his right, in two lines, covering this approach; and because the cavalry comprised the Maison du Roi, he deemed it invulnerable. He forgot the lesson of Blenheim. Despite errors, the line was strong; and few armies are drawn up for battle, in whose setting up one may not discover flaws.

Knowing himself to be in the presence of the enemy, Marlborough had advanced in ten columns, six of foot in the centre, two of cavalry on each of the flanks. Riding ahead to reconnoitre, he at once perceived that the highest point of the French line, the right, where stood the tomb of Ottomond, a German hero of olden times, was the key of the position, and he determined to make it the object of his main attack. But in order to mislead the enemy so as to deliver his assault under the best conditions, he organized at the same time a diversion in some force against the other wing at Autre Église. The concave position of the French aided him in the execution of this task, as he himself held the chord of the arc along which lay their line. With a good deal of show he massed a heavy column and marched it to a point opposite this village; on perceiving which, Villeroi drew most of the reserves from his centre and dispatched them over to sustain his left, which he deemed to be thus threatened. An abler general would have divined that this was no real attack; and would have acted less hastily, for the left was abundantly able to protect itself, for a while at least. This allied column was drawn up in two lines and a reserve, and having sufficiently paraded it to produce the desired impression, Marlborough ordered all but the first line, under cover of some rolling ground which prevented its being seen, over to his left, and at the same time instructed the bulk of his cavalry so to manœuvre as to sustain this flank.

Shortly after noon the attack was opened by the guns, the French devoting their best efforts to the column supposed to be opposite their left, whose first line crossed the Little Geete, advanced to the foot of the crest opposite Autre Église, and opened fire; while under the smoke of the fusillade, the second line and reserve was enabled, as stated, to move off to the left to sustain the main assault.

To give Villeroi no time to repair his mistake, the attack was at once precipitated. A body of Dutch troops moved on Tavières, while a heavy column of twelve battalions was launched against Ramillies; these attacks were driven home, and though Villeroi soon perceived that he had been misled by a sham attack, it was already too late. He had no reserves of foot to meet the onslaught on his right and was compelled to put in some horse, which he dismounted for the purpose, to sustain Tavières. But even this proved unavailing; the Dutch carried the place, while a column of allied cavalry fell on the dismounted horsemen and cut them to pieces. The French horse, of which the right was mainly composed, was now put in; but Overkirk threw back their first line by a handsome charge. The French second line, the Maison du Roi, — the flower of the French heavy cavalry, — was not, however, so easily disposed of. Riding down on Overkirk when this officer was somewhat disordered by success, these superb horsemen clave their way through the astonished allied squadrons, and drove them back so far beyond the line of Ramillies that they would shortly have been enabled to take in reverse the foot battalions assailing that village. It was a critical moment, the instant which makes or mars a battle. Perceiving the imminence of the danger, Marlborough in person headed a body of seventeen reserve squadrons which he found ready to hand, sent an urgent order recalling all the horse from the right, where lay twenty squadrons likewise in reserve, and himself led in the column against the cuirassiers, under a telling fire from the French batteries. In the fray he was all but captured, but his opportune charge for a moment checked the enemy; and the aid of the twenty squadrons from the right, which came up at a gallop but in fine close order, reëstablished the battle at this point. At the same moment a body of Danish horse debouched from the

Méhaigne lowlands and fell smartly on the right of the Maison du Roi, and another body of Dutch fell on their left. Thus surrounded, the French cuirassiers, finally losing heart, turned from the field ; and Marlborough, seizing the moment of their backward movement as opportune, and giving his men the impetus which success makes so telling after hours of combat, pressed on with all his troops to the top of the plateau. As is usual in offensive battles, Marlborough had outnumbered his opponent at the point of fighting contact, and the battle was won. But Villeroi was not so readily driven from the field ; he strove desperately to establish a new line by throwing back his right to Geest a Gerompant, and by holding fast to Offuz and Autre Église, so as to form a convex order instead of the concave one with which he first received the allied attack. Ramillies was not yet taken, and that would make an outwork which might perhaps arrest the victors while he patched up the new line. But Marlborough gave him no time ; he knew too well how much the minutes count at the instant of victory. Though the plateau around Ottomond was crowded with men of all arms, guns and caissons, much disordered and mixed up from the late desperate battle, he pushed on in whatever order he could. No one better understood the meaning of " Action, action, action ! " and while this advance was making, despite the hottest defense, Ramillies fell to the allies, and the ground was such that Villeroi could marshal no new line in any practicable order. Many a general would have now paused to re-form. Not so Marlborough ; there was no let up to his blows. A general advance all along the allied line was sounded, and the whole mass pushed on. Offuz and Autre Église were taken, sweeping the entire field clear of the French. In utterly disorganized masses, bearing no semblance to an army, Villeroi sought refuge at Louvain. The British horse pursued the enemy almost to the gates of that city, on which Marlborough advanced next day.

The French lost seven thousand killed and wounded, six thousand prisoners, fifty-two guns, eight standards and all their baggage. The allies lost one thousand and sixty-six men killed and three thousand six hundred and thirty-three wounded. Following the noble example of Gustavus as well as his own generous instincts, Marlborough showed great consideration for the enemy's wounded, who had equal care with his own.

Ramillies won nearly all Austrian Flanders; Brussels, Louvain, Mechlin and most other towns of Brabant opened their gates without delay. Only the coast towns, Antwerp, Ostende, Nieuport and Dunkirk, held out. The battle of Blenheim had saved Germany. Turin was to save Italy. Ramillies saved Holland; and the Dutch put no bounds to their joy or gratitude. Marlborough was the national hero; he was no longer hampered by the deputies.

The discipline enforced by Marlborough had an equally happy effect, and went far to win the good-will of the country. On June 6 Antwerp surrendered, and Oudenarde followed suit. Siege was laid to Dunkirk, and that great fortress succumbed on July 6. Menin followed August 22, Dendermonde September 5, Ath October 4. An aggregate of twenty thousand prisoners fell to Marlborough's arms this year.

After this crushing defeat, Vendome was called back from Italy and took the place of Villeroi; and twenty thousand reinforcements came to hand. But the moral depression caused by the defeat of Ramillies was so great that the French only pretended to defend the northern border of France.

LX.

TURIN. SEPTEMBER 7, 1706.

IF Marlborough won a great triumph at Ramillies, Eugene won an equally splendid victory at Turin. When he was on the Adige the French had begun to press Turin hard. Luckily Vendome was called from Italy to supplant Villeroi, and the duke of Orleans, with Marsin as second, took command. Eugene determined to march to the relief of Savoy, and leaving the prince of Hesse on the Adige, crossed the Po and advanced rapidly along its south bank westward. The duke followed him, but Eugene got to the pass of Stradella first, which enabled him to pursue his march. Reaching Turin, he joined the duke, which gave him thirty-six thousand men to the sixty thousand of the French. The lines about Turin were very strong, but Eugene, after a careful reconnoissance, attacked them from the west, and so effectually did he follow up his assault that he drove the enemy out of their works, broke up their army and forced them into headlong retreat. As Ramillies saved Holland, so the battle of Turin saved Italy, and, moreover, it resulted in driving the French permanently from the land. This triumph against a heavily intrenched enemy of nearly twice his strength was indeed a glorious one. Perhaps this campaign, including both the march and battle, is the best of the war. It has few superiors in any war.

IF in the Netherlands Marlborough was helping to teach the world the advantage of battle over manœuvring and intrenched lines, so, in this year, Prince Eugene in Italy gave us a brilliant lesson of the same nature.

From the new emperor, Joseph I., Eugene received the same consideration and support which the crown had always vouchsafed him. Early in 1706 several columns of reinforcements were directed towards Italy, to the army which lay on the west bank of the Lake of Garda. Eugene reached Roveredo in mid-April, and Gavardo April 20, but only to find the army in bad case. Its situation had not been over and above

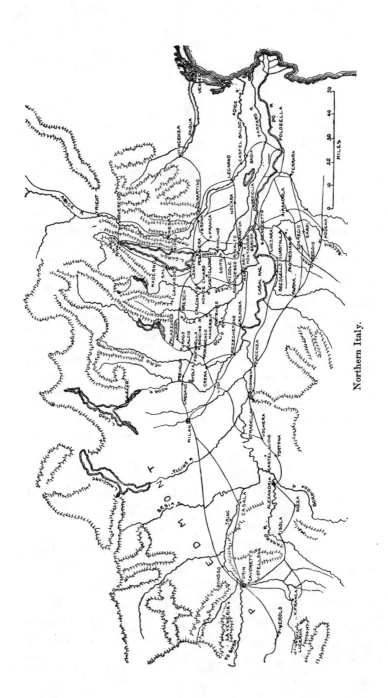

Northern Italy.

secure, nor had the lines been sufficiently watched to have timely notice of the enemy's approach.

On the 19th of April Vendome, who had forty-four thousand men and fighting orders, made a sudden attack on the imperial winter - quarters, which were under command of Count Reventlau during the absence of Prince Eugene, hoping to overwhelm his army and to push it quite out of Italy. Reventlau had been in an intrenched camp, but a threatened turning movement by way of San Marco induced him to come out into the open. The assault fell first on Montechiaro, which Vendome took, and then on Calcinato, with equal success. The troops retired over the bridge of San Marco in much disorder, with a loss of three thousand men. On his arrival Eugene collected some troops, and sought to hold a position he had previously occupied between Gavardo and Salo, but the French on April 22 pushed Salo hard. Vendome sought to cut him off by a flank march near the lake, and making up his mind to take the Adige route, Eugene retired by way of Riva to the Triente country. In a rearguard fight in Maderno, the enemy was worsted, and Eugene quietly marched around the lake and concentrated on the east shore, hoping to push unopposed down the Adige on the right bank. But as the French had taken possession of both sides of the lower part of the lake, he was forced to fight his way through to the other side of the river. Luckily the French had omitted to hold the passage at Chiuso, else they would have quite barred the imperial passage down the valley of the Adige. Prince Eugene marched through the Polesella valley, and, May 17, took post along the left bank at San Martino. He here awaited his reinforcements and pontoons, which on arrival would give him all told some thirty-eight thousand men and full equipment, not counting ten thousand Hessians still on the way. Vendome left thirty thousand men to watch the west shore of Garda, and, committing the same error as Catinat, assumed a position in detachments from Salo down, a large part lying opposite the prince, on the right bank of the Adige. He had nearly forty thousand men thus employed. Here the armies remained two or three weeks inactive. Eugene could go no further until his reinforcements came up to replace him when he left.

Meanwhile La Feuillade had besieged Turin in May with forty-two thousand men and two hundred and thirty-seven guns and mortars; and leaving twenty thousand men to defend the capital, the duke of Savoy took refuge with eight thousand men in the Cottian Alps at Luserna, and loudly called to Prince Eugene for aid. Determined to retrieve his last year's failure by moving to Piedmont along the right bank of the Po, Eugene left eight thousand men at Verona to hold the line of the Adige, which force was later joined by the prince of Hesse with his ten thousand, started with the rest in two detachments, July 4 and 5, down the left bank, and crossed at Boara and at Badia, below Castelbaldo, between the 9th and the 14th. So well concealed had been his operations that he met with but slight opposition, though there were twenty-seven thousand French on the right bank from Verona to Badia.

Luckily for the Italian situation, the king now called Vendome from Italy to the Netherlands, where Villeroi had been defeated at Ramillies, and the duke of Orleans, with Marsin as second, was given the command. Vendome had been a worthy antagonist, and his removal was the death-blow to the French successes in Italy. Eugene was as fortunate in his new opponents as Marlborough had been in Villeroi. The change of command upset all calculations, and the new commander found himself face to face with an awkward duty; but he took some healthy measures, called in thirteen thousand men from La Feuillade, and placed ten thousand under Mendavi opposite the prince of Hesse.

Prince Eugene had crossed the numerous canals and waterways south of the Adige, and the Po at Polozella, by July 24. He was detained near Finale until, on July 27, he heard of the actual arrival of the prince of Hesse, when he moved upstream and over the Secchia past Carpi, and August 1 over the Ledo canal; thence up to the line of the Parmegiano, with a column nearly twenty-five thousand strong.

The duke of Orleans, meanwhile, fell back behind the Mincio, and thinking to arrest Eugene's further march, he left thirty thousand men on that line, crossed at San Benedetto with twenty-six thousand to the south bank of the Po, and took up a position on the Parmegiano. Finding his opponent on hand, Prince Eugene reconnoitred, and ascertained that the duke lay behind a marsh made by the stream, where he could not be readily attacked, and concluded to turn him out of this position by the south.

At this time the prince of Hesse began operations, and advanced to the Mincio, and the duke, lest the situation on the north bank should be changed to his disadvantage, left the Parmegiano, and retired across the Po, thus opening the road to Piedmont along its right bank; and to cap the French troubles, when he reached the Mincio he found that the prince of Hesse had already secured the passage of that river at Goito. Thus, despite his rapid movements, he had failed to stop either of his opponents in their westward march. His activity had been weak and misplaced; mere manœuvring between two enemies will not suffice; it requires battle.

Prince Eugene utilized the enemy's absence by capturing Carpi August 5, Correggio August 8, Finale and Reggio August 9 and 14, and advanced on and took Parma August 15, where the troops were given on the 16th a day of rest on account of great heat; and thence marched to Piacenza. The season was dry, and the numerous streams did not greatly delay the march.

The duke of Orleans recognized his mistake; he now had one more chance to stop Eugene, and that was at the pass of Stradella, where the possession of the defile between the Apennines and the Po would have shut Eugene out from reaching Piedmont on the right bank of the river. It was the key to northwestern Italy, and could be held by a small body against a large army. We remember that it played its due part in Hannibal's campaign along the Po, as it always has in all operations in northern Italy. To his credit the duke of Orleans saw this chance, hurried seven thousand men ahead to this pass, and followed with the bulk of his army. The march was along the left bank, and the foot was carried in wagons to make speed. But Prince Eugene was fortunate, while the duke was not. So soon as he heard that the French were heading for Stradella, he himself speeded a detachment of seven thousand men towards the defile, followed after a few hours by a second one, and the prince later joined the column with all his cavalry. He reached San Giovanni July 21, and learned to his gratification that the commander of the leading detachment had seized the defile, and that the second one had gone on to Voghera. On the 23d the rest of the foot came up; next day they marched to Voghera, and on the 25th went into camp at Castelnuovo, while the van pushed on. On the 26th the van crossed the Bormida, and on the 27th it stood at the Tanaro. The army followed, marched between the fortresses of Alexandria and Tortona without blockading or besieging either, — an unusual proceeding in those days, as they were held by French garrisons, — and marching to Nizza, crossed the Tanaro, August 28, at Isola, with van at Villafranca. From the Tanaro Eugene,

on the last day of August, joined the duke of Savoy on
the upper Po, at Villastellona, whither the duke had come to
meet him. Between them they had some thirty-six thousand
men. The sick and baggage were sent to Alba.

The duke of Orleans, having failed to anticipate Eugene
at Stradella, and thus to prevent his junction with the duke
of Savoy, still managed to get to Turin first, marching, as he
did, by the shorter road up the left bank of the Po. With

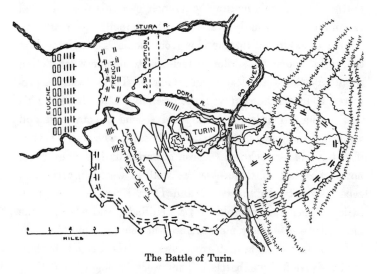

The Battle of Turin.

La Feuillade he had ninety battalions and one hundred and
thirty-eight squadrons, some sixty thousand men.

Turin lies on the flat left bank of the Po, and at that day
had a strong bridge-head and line of works on the hilly right
bank. In his prolonged siege of the place, La Feuillade had
directed his main attack against the citadel, and though the
siege had lasted four months, and the town had been much
bombarded, the whole operation had been so lamentably conducted that its works were still strong. A breach, to be sure,
had been made in the citadel, but several assaults had been

driven back. On the left bank was a line of contravallation, and the troops used in the siege were protected by a line of circumvallation a dozen or more miles long, whose left flank leaned on the Po and the right on the Stura, which falls into the Po not far below the city. The lines were cut by the Dora, which falls into the Po at Turin.

The one policy of the French, who were two to one of the allies, was clearly to move on the imperial army and give it battle; but in this matter the French generals were divided in opinion; and finally Marsin, at the council of war of September 5, exhibited instructions from Louis XIV. giving him the right above the duke of Orleans to decide what action should be taken in case of an attack on Turin; and he preferred to await the enemy in the circumvallation lines. This was a singular order to a supposed second in command and a marked indignity to the duke of Orleans, who was a better, if not an older, soldier. These circumvallation lines were, however, weak of themselves as well as weakly garrisoned, especially between the Stura and Dora rivers, where no attack had been anticipated by La Feuillade, and where at the moment were scarcely more than eight thousand men.

It was in the highest degree unwise in the French to fight a strictly defensive battle. They were stronger than their adversaries, but their strength was wasted in the extent of their lines; and the men, knowing that they were in superior force, lost much of their spirit behind intrenchments. The French generals believed that the allies were too weak to attack with any chance of success; that they could not cross the Dora without exposing themselves to a dangerous sortie, and that therefore they would not try; and it was for this reason that to the intrenchments near the Dora proper attention had not been paid. This was a curious but not uncommon lapse of judgment.

Meanwhile Eugene and the duke of Savoy crossed the upper Po and camped at Pianezza, six miles from Turin; they then passed around the lines of the besiegers by the south and west, leaving some bodies to make demonstrations from the east, and took up a position between the Stura and Dora, with headquarters at the castle of La Veneria. A large convoy coming from France was cleverly seized by the duke, and came in good stead.

The commandant of Turin, General Daun, was notified that next day, September 7, an attack would be made, of which a certain signal would be given.

On the other side of the Po, across the bridge, on the Capuchin hill, lay General Alberghatti with a force of twenty thousand French, to shut in the city from the right bank. General Daun sent a force of six thousand militia across to the bridge-head to prevent Alberghatti from detailing any of his forces to aid the rest of the besiegers, or, in case he did so, to make a junction with a big convoy and six thousand Piedmontese troops which were waiting a chance to enter the city.

After a careful reconnoissance Eugene saw that north of the Dora the French line was the weakest; and it was here, on September 7, that the imperial army attacked the circumvallation lines of the French. Eugene's orders for the attack are a model of minuteness, care and intelligence. He had thirty thousand men in line, of which six thousand were horse, and these he ployed into eight columns, and started from camp at daylight. His right leaned on the Dora, his left on the Stura, and he deployed just beyond artillery range. His foot stood in two lines, his cavalry in a third and fourth line; there were three to four hundred paces between lines, and he delivered his assault about an hour before noon, with all the *élan* of which he was capable.

There were but from eight to ten thousand foot here and about four thousand horse; and General Daun at once sent six thousand men from within walls to assail them in rear. The allied left was the first to reach the enemy's lines and to make an impression, as the right had less good ground to pass over. There was the usual swaying to and fro of an assaulting line, and the allied cavalry was once thrust back and threatened with demoralization; but it was not long, under the always gallant personal conduct of Eugene, who here ran his risk with the junior officers, before the line of circumvallation was broken through and the French defenders driven back. The French reinforcements all came up too late, and were successively beaten in detail. The duke of Orleans had called for twelve thousand men from General Alberghatti on the right bank of the Po; but this officer deemed himself neutralized by the six thousand Piedmontese who were trying to throw relief into Turin and by the bridge-head garrison, and did not respond.

The garrison of Turin now made a sharper sally on the French rear. The duke of Orleans and Field-Marshal Marsin were both wounded, the latter mortally; and the French, ill-led and dispersed, were quite broken up and many driven into the Po and drowned. They lost two thousand killed, twelve hundred wounded and six thousand prisoners, over one hundred guns and all their baggage and material; and, lacking leadership, fell back, not by way of Casal or the Milan region, where were Mendavi and a number of strong garrisons, but towards the Alps at Pinerolo, which direction Alberghatti also took, crossing the Po at Cavoretto. Their direct route to France via Susa was already cut off by the allied position. The allied loss was nine hundred and fifty killed and twenty-three hundred wounded.

Meanwhile, the prince of Hesse, besieging Castiglione, had

been attacked by Mendavi, who had defeated and thrown him back behind the Mincio with a loss of six thousand men. Had the beaten Turin army actually retired on Milan, the campaign might not have been entirely lost. But the allies now began gradually to capture the strong places in Piedmont and the duchy of Milan, twenty-three of which fell to them in the succeeding three months; and seeing that he could no longer hold himself in Italy, Louis XIV. recalled the troops and gave up his fortresses against free exit for the garrisons. The victory at Turin had the same immense results which those at Blenheim and Ramillies had had. The allies gained all Italy, and were able to carry the war to the borders of France. Indeed, the results were greater, for Italy was permanently freed by this noted victory, as Germany and Holland were not.

So splendid a success against an enemy double his strength rarely falls to the lot of any captain. This one was fairly earned, coming as it did from Eugene's decisive march to Piedmont, where he lay upon the communications of the French with France; the forcing of battle at Turin after the selection of the best part of the line to attack; and the good fortune which attended him. The prince's march to Piedmont is one of his best operations. It was bold and well conceived. He threw up his communications with Germany, and thus all hope of reinforcements, for the duke of Savoy had but few troops left, as well as of victual, for the enemy held the entire country. The right bank of the Po was a difficult route, cut up by many streams; and the defile of Stradella must be reached before the French could take it. The question of rationing his men was at that day an almost insuperable obstacle. But fortune this year smiled upon the prince, and lent herself to his bold and clever manœuvres.

The French made mistakes. Vendome began with the

same error which Catinat had made, of trying to watch the entire line of the Adige; but circumstances prevented the error from bearing fruit, and the calling away of this general was a great misfortune. Vendome had the only true theory: beat the enemy and Turin will fall. But the duke of Orleans worked on the converse plan. At all times the French were strong enough to overwhelm the allies, but Vendome had no chance to show what he might have done, and after his recall the French operated badly. They opened the road to Piedmont to Prince Eugene, did not dispute the defile at Stradella, and while of twice his strength at Turin, instead of moving out to fight him, remained in the Turin lines to be beaten.

Had Vendome been kept in command, or had the French army retired on Milan, Prince Eugene's triumph might not have been so brilliant. Without underrating the splendor of this campaign, it must be granted that the errors of the French, and good fortune, helped him as much as Villeroi's weak methods helped Marlborough. But even a Cæsar had sometimes to thank mere fortune that he was not overwhelmed; and as Napoleon's brilliant successes were often due to the fatuity of his opponents, so with Eugene and Marlborough. It was Hannibal alone who constantly worked against fortune, and fought able opponents.

Here again battle had done more than manœuvring. On the whole, this campaign is the most brilliant one conducted by any general during the War of the Spanish Succession.

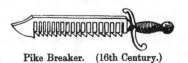

Pike Breaker.   (16th Century.)

LXI.

OUDENARDE AND LILLE. JULY 11 AND OCTOBER 22, 1708.

In 1707 little was done. In 1708 the French had one hundred thousand men near Mons, under the duke of Burgundy and Vendome; Marlborough was at Brussels with sixty-five thousand men. Eugene's army was kept on the Rhine until other troops replaced it, when he was to join the Netherlands army. After some manœuvring Marlborough, who feared that the French would take Oudenarde, determined on battle. Eugene was personally with him, though his army was still on the march from the Rhine. Vendome desired to fight the allies before Eugene's army could come up; but Burgundy was slow and undecided. Finally Marlborough forced operations, and attacked the French while both armies were crossing the Scheldt below Oudenarde. Eugene joined in the battle and commanded part of Marlborough's army. After a long and bloody struggle — somewhat irregular in character — the allies turned the right flank of the French, enveloped them, and drove the wreck of their army back to Ghent. When Eugene's army arrived, he and Marlborough had one hundred and twenty thousand men, with which they undertook the siege of Lille. The French had ninety-six thousand men, but they did nothing effective to interrupt it, and finally, despite a handsome defense by Marshal Boufflers, Lille fell, and the French retired from Flanders.

THE spring after the battle of Ramillies (1707) Vendome, with his eighty thousand men, was ordered to operate defensively against the allied army of but thirty-six thousand. Marlborough was inactive; but it was the Dutch officials who held him back from active work, quite as much as it was limited numbers, and the entire campaign was composed of unimportant manœuvres and petty operations. The theatre of war had become more complicated. It was decided among the allies to protect Savoy against a probable French attack, as well as to prevent French reinforcements from being dispatched to Spain, by undertaking an invasion of southern

France; but this campaign had no better result. Prince Eugene and the duke of Savoy undertook the expedition into France by way of the Maritime Alps, in connection with a British-Dutch fleet, and operated against Toulon. After a long and difficult march, the army reached that port at the end of July, and found the garrison so depleted that energetic measures would have resulted in its capture. But the duke insisted on a regular siege; this lasted a month, and during the delay the place was relieved by the French. Eugene conducted a handsome retreat, capturing Susa at its close. The whole affair was a failure, apparently owing to jealousy and consequent want of energy of the duke of Savoy. That the blundering was not Eugene's there is clear evidence; and the operation does not bear his thumb-marks. It had no special effect on Spain, for on April 25, at the battle of Almanza, Marshal Berwick, in command of the French forces, totally defeated the allies, and placed Spain in the possession of the Bourbons. On the other hand, with an army of thirteen thousand men, General Daun conquered Naples and ejected the Bourbons; but to offset this success, Villars beat an imperial army on the Rhine, destroyed the Stollhofen lines, invaded Swabia and levied contributions on the land.

In 1708 the French Netherlands army was raised to a force, not including garrisons, of one hundred thousand men, and concentrated near Mons, from which quarter it was to operate under the duke of Burgundy, grandson of Louis XIV., with Vendome as his second and mentor, on a plan which should be offensive, but without running any serious risk. Villars had a small force on the borders of Switzerland. An army of fifty thousand men, under the elector of Bavaria and Field-Marshal Berwick (who, after his victory at Almanza, had been ordered north), stood at Strasburg, and was to be faced by the elector of Hanover; but until the forces of the latter were all concentrated, Prince Eugene, with his army of thirty-five thousand Saxons, Hessians, Palatinate troops and imperialists, was ordered to remain near Coblentz, and when relieved to march to the Netherlands to join the Anglo-Dutch army under Marlborough. The excellent result of the generous coöperation of these two captains was recognized. It was manifest that the heavy work was to be done this year in the Low Countries, and Eugene and Marlborough met in the Hague in April to confer as to the plan of action; but the imperial exchequer was so empty that many serious additional duties were laid upon the prince. Well it was that the sea powers had abundant resources and were willing to use them. Eugene had actually been sent to campaign in a friendly land, where he might not take supplies, and without money wherewith to buy them.

There were also annoying difficulties with all the German princes, — the electors of Hanover, Saxony, Mainz and the Palatinate, and the landgrave of Hesse, all of whom disliked the secondary rôle they had to play, and made impossible demands. But the diplomatic good-nature of Marlborough and Eugene finally smoothed over these troubles before the campaign opened.

Marlborough had been lying near Brussels with sixty-five thousand men (English, Dutch, Danes, Hanoverians and Prussians) and one hundred and thirteen guns. There had been some anticipation of treachery on the part of the garrison of Antwerp, and fearing that Vendome, who had been moving into Flanders, would go thither to take advantage of the fact, Marlborough marched, May 24, to Hal, to bar the way to that important harbor. The French, May 26, marched to Soignies, and on June 1 moved further on and camped between Genappe and Braine l'Alleud, about three leagues from Marlborough, on the allies' left flank. Marlborough did not understand Vendome's purpose, but from his position conceived fears for Louvain or even Brussels; and as he needed to keep the road open for Eugene, who was by and by to come on from Coblentz, he moved by a quick night march, June 2–3, to a position near Louvain. He urgently needed Eugene's assistance, but the latter could not yet leave the Rhine, for Berwick was on hand in force, and the Hanoverian contingent had not yet come up. Both armies here remained a month. Marlborough would have liked to attack Vendome and cut the knot by a battle; but he did not feel strong enough to do so. He had not — no one ever had — the utter disregard of numbers displayed by Frederick. Few ever led such battalions as the last of the kings.

Vendome was energetic meanwhile; he had a very clear purpose. His diversion towards Louvain was a simple ruse to keep Marlborough's eyes away from the Scheldt. The provinces acquired by the allies as a result of Ramillies were full of malcontents. They were Catholic; the people cordially hated the Dutch; and the latter were not wise in their treatment of the case, but levied taxes remorselessly. Ghent was a most important place. In the hands of the allies it was a sort of advanced work which defended Flanders, and a base from which Lille, the great French fortress, could be threatened. Vendome proposed to have it, and for some time had been working with the authorities within walls to induce them to play into his hands. In this he succeeded, and by able dispositions, energy and a sharp march by his left on the night of July 4 to the Senne, the French got well ahead of Marlborough, advanced across the Dender, and on July 5 one of their parties seized Ghent by a *coup de main*. Another party laid hold of Bruges on the same day, and Plassendael, one of the defenses of Ostende, was captured by storm July 10. This was a blow straight in the face of the Anglo-Dutch.

On learning of Vendome's operations Marlborough, on July 5, had advanced with the hope of arresting his progress ; but the French marshal was too speedy, placed himself back of Alost to protect Ghent, and Marlborough took position at Asche, west of Brussels. He was ready to attack the enemy on the Dender July 7, but the harm had been already done, and battle would correct nothing. He now feared the enemy would capture Oudenarde, as was indeed Vendome's next projected step ; and he threw into it a force taken from the garrisons of neighboring places, sufficient to hold it, just before the French came to invest it.

These successes of the French had the effect of depressing the Dutch to so alarming an extent that the English commander determined to force a battle even before the arrival of Eugene's corps, if he could do so, lest the Dutch should become so far demoralized as to conclude a separate peace. Indeed, Marlborough, whose health was far from good, was himself much down-hearted, and it was well that Eugene arrived at this time to cheer him up. An occasion was not long in presenting itself, and Marlborough, with the countenance of Eugene, who, escorted by a small cavalry force, had hurried ahead of his corps, was not slow to embrace it. Having failed to seize Oudenarde out of hand as he had Ghent, Vendome determined to besiege the place, and detached a force to make preparation for so doing. The fortress was central, commanded a passage of the Scheldt, whose high banks make it an easily defended river, and gave its possessor singular facilities for manœuvring in both Brabant and Flanders. To cover the projected siege as well as Ghent and Bruges, the French position between Oordegen and Alost was as good as any. Marlborough, still fearing for this important fortress, to him a link in his home communications, as well as apprehensive that the enemy would occupy and eat out all northern Flanders, thus consuming victual he needed himself, determined to forestall both accidents. His plan to secure battle was to move on Vendome's communications with France, instead of directly on his main body; and this had manifest advantages, as the event showed. He hurried a detachment of three regiments each of foot and horse, and six guns, under General Cadogan, July 9, to the Dender at Lessines, with orders to bridge it; the army moved forward by its left to the same place on the 11th, and Cadogan was again sent with sixteen battalions and thirty squadrons to bridge the Scheldt below Oudenarde. The main force speedily followed, and next day reached and stood ready to pass that river. In forty-eight hours the troops had marched some forty miles, had crossed one river and made ready to cross a second. This was fast work at that day, good for any day.

Hoping to prevent the allies' passage of the Dender, of the march on which he was informed, Vendome had, July 9, advanced to Ninove, where, finding that he was too late to accomplish the end in view, and ascertaining that the allies were bridging the Scheldt, he conceived fears for Ghent, and in order to cover that fortress, turned back to the river, which he prepared to cross on his bridge at Gavre, a short distance below Marlborough's bridges. The Oudenarde detachment was ordered in.

It was apparent to Vendome that the thing to do was to fight Marlborough before Eugene's corps came up, and he advised his chief, the duke of Burgundy, to cross the Scheldt as soon as he could possibly put the troops over, and be ready to fall upon the enemy. In pursuance of this idea, in fact, Vendome sent to the other side the van under General Biron,

with orders to hold the allies till the French army should
have got over, so that the whole force could then fall upon
them while in the confusion of crossing. Biron occupied
Eyne. The operation could very well have been carried out,
as the allies at this moment were still busy completing their
bridges and the French had their own all ready; and when
the first allied detachment, under Cadogan, pushed out
towards the high ground, they ran across these very forces of
Vendome's. No better plan could have been devised, for the
French were several hours in advance of Marlborough; but
it was not promptly carried out, and its very essence was
speed. The duke of Burgundy had been, so far, a passive
tool in the hands of his able second; but as dangers thick-
ened, and the pulse of Vendome, soldier-like, began to throb
in quicker beats, the duke grew nervous and undecided, and
instead of pushing the troops over the river, as advised by
his lieutenant, consumed the precious time in coming to a
conclusion as to what he had best do. He appeared to be
afraid to go into a general engagement, and finally thought
wise to return to Ghent. But it was already too late to avoid
the one or accomplish the other. It was not long after noon
that Cadogan had crossed the Scheldt and pushed his horse
and twelve battalions of foot out to the higher land towards
Eyne and to its left. He soon struck the French van from
Gavre, which stopped him in a smart encounter and seized
Eyne. Notwithstanding the laxness of Burgundy, Vendome
still hoped to be able to catch the English astride the river,
and as troops got over, he formed line of battle on the high
ground behind the Norken. Some eighty thousand men were
thus set up. Meanwhile Marlborough and Eugene pushed
forward the crossing, and by two o'clock had got over a substantial part of their equal numbers. It had been a race of
speed and purpose: Marlborough and Eugene were instinct

with a single idea, while Vendome was hampered in all he
did by his inexpert and hesitating chief. Had he been sole
ih command, the battle of Oudenarde might not have proven
an allied victory. Some critics underrate Vendome's ability

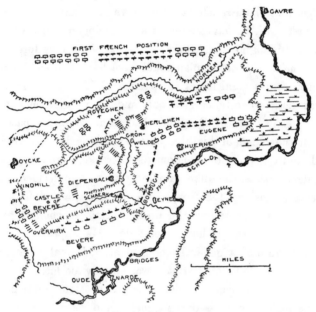

Battle of Oudenarde.

in this campaign. At times he exhibited his best qualities ;
at others he lapsed into his indolent mood.

Vendome's idea of the best way to fight the battle was to
drive an attack firmly in on the allied right, and by breaking
it, cut it from the river and the bridges ; and he dispatched
a force under General Pfiffer from the left to open up the
manœuvre ; but Burgundy, technically in command, would
not permit the operation, alleging unsuitability of ground
near the river. Advancing along the Ghent road, Pfiffer
did, however, get as far as Huerne and Eyne. These contin-

ued delays and irresolute orders were fatal to the French. Burgundy now desired to retreat, but Vendome showed him that it was no longer feasible; the enemy was already upon him. The brilliant opportunity for overwhelming the allies while astride the river had faded as the sun grew lower.

As the allied troops were got upon the field, they were marshaled on the first high ground to the west from Eyne, and so soon as enough men were on hand, Cadogan was again pushed in on that village, which after a sharp half hour's fighting he took, by attacking it in front with his foot and riding around its left with his squadrons. Pfiffer withdrew to the vicinity of the Norken. Added to Burgundy's fatuity, it was Cadogan's activity which had prevented the French from disturbing the crossing, now completed under the cover he had afforded.

The position behind the Norken was a serious one to attack ; and when he found that he had been prevented by Burgundy from seasonably initiating an offensive battle, Vendome bethought him to invite attack here. But nothing would suit his chief, who now ordered some cavalry forward from the right to see if he could occupy the Huerne plateau. This force he shortly followed up by some foot, and presently a large part of the French right was marching out to the attack.

It was well after four when the French attack became serious, and by this time the allies were ready for it. The cavalry force pushed out from the right, having met some of the Prussian horse, fell back to Royeghem. There was no system in the manœuvres of the French, who, now that their opportunity had passed, advanced their right in earnest. Divining that they would make their main effort with this wing, Marlborough had deployed his troops accordingly, pushed forward the forces from Eyne towards Huerne and

Herlehem, and threw out small parties to seize and defend
the woods and hedges beyond the line, so as to hold the
advanced ground for the troops to occupy as they arrived.
The Prussian horse was sent out to the left of this body
beyond Huerne, while Shaecken was held by twenty battalions. As yet little artillery had been got up; time had not
sufficed.

No sooner had Marlborough reached this advanced position
than the French right was upon him. Thirty battalions of
French and Swiss guards debouched from the covered country
on Groemvelde, fell on a small allied force posted there, cut
it up, and pushed on down the little brook, taking Marlborough's advanced force absolutely in reverse. Not slow to
perceive or utilize their advantage, the French all too soon
caught the inspiration of success, and already the cry of victory began to resound along their lines. But Marlborough
was happily equal to the occasion. Eugene, the ever ready,
was at hand; to him Marlborough confided the work upon
the right, giving him his English troops, while, seizing the
Dutch and Hanoverians, he set himself to stem the threatening tide of defeat on the left of Schaecken. Foreseeing that
the French would soon attack in force on their immediate
front, he sent twenty more battalions under Count Lottum to
Eugene, intending that by and by the decisive blow should
be given by the right; so that the prince now had about one
third of all the allied foot — sixty battalions — under his
command, — more than twice what Marlborough retained on
the left. Well that it was so, for the French columns between
Groemvelde and Schaecken were making desperate efforts to
follow up their supposed gain, and Eugene had all he could
do to hold them in check. Moreover, at this moment the
infantry of the French left-centre advanced across the Norken, and the cavalry of their left followed to sustain them.

Cadogan was hustled out of Herlehem by the sudden onslaught; but the reinforcement enabled Eugene to reëstablish the fight, and having first driven the French back across the Eyne, he turned to the plateau and broke the French first line, while the Prussian horse followed up this gain and charged clean through the French second line, being only stopped by the reserve of cuirassiers in the rear, which drove it back.

There being few guns of either army on the field to make a pronounced effect, the battle was one of musketry only, and it took the form of desperate contests by small bodies at every little patch of woods, every hedge, ditch or hamlet.

Opposite Marlborough west of Schaecken, where he was striving to turn the tide of French success with the Dutch and Hanoverians, the fighting was similar and equally severe. Every obstacle was utilized, and a series of partial and desperate encounters resulted all along the S-shaped line. Cavalry was of small use in the country covered with hedges and copses, unless dismounted. But the foot fought tenaciously, and finally, under Marlborough's strong will, the allied line compelled the retreat from their advanced position of the French, who too soon had deemed the victory secure. But it was only by desperate hand to hand fighting that they were forced back to Diepenbeck; and here ensued a pause. Neither party could gain a step.

Marlborough's eye was keen. Spying the windmill of Oycke on his left, he detached Overkirk with the reserve cavalry and twenty Dutch battalions to occupy it, move beyond and turn the French right. With marked speed, despite the heavy ground cut up by all manner of obstacles, the veteran general made his way thither, and defeating a French force which held the castle of Bevere, threw it off toward the west. He soon got himself into a position on the

French right flank, which was in the air, and, extending his left under the prince of Orange as far as he could reach, he enveloped their forces from Bevere to Royeghem. This manœuvre was in reality what won the battle, for the French troops along the Eyne, startled by a fire in their rear, quickly fell back, and in much confusion, and this was carried throughout the army, and grew into a panic as darkness settled on the field. From a species of convex order, the allies now swung forward into a huge concave semicircle, and drove the French before them at every point, crowding them in more and more. Thus huddled together on the plain, there was little chance to fight to good effect, and even the stoutest resistance of the French gendarmes, who did their duty nobly, could effect nothing.

Vendome sought to stem the tide by a heroic assault on the right-centre and right of the allies with all the forces he could muster on his left; but cheered with the marked success of the allied left, Eugene held his own against the heavy onslaught. The ground was so much cut up that the French could not advance in order, and the Bavarian horse held bravely to its line on the edge of the plain. Eugene now advanced his wing to cut off the enemy from the river, and so fully did the concave order of the enveloping force complete the circle, that the two outer flanks met on the heights in the French rear, and indeed exchanged volleys at each other in the dark.

It was through this gradually narrowing gap that the French left and centre made their escape. Their right was nearly all taken, a few only making their way through openings in the allied line to Bevere and thence towards France; and Eugene captured prisoners from their left wholesale. It occurred to him to have the French "appel" (assembly) beaten by his drums, which brought in a vast number of

men to swell his prisoners. Had daylight lasted, the French
army would have been forced into surrender.

The French lost three thousand killed, four thousand
wounded, nine thousand prisoners, three thousand deserters,
one thousand officers and one hundred standards. The allied
loss was two thousand killed and three thousand wounded;
or, as otherwise stated, only eight hundred and twenty-five
killed and two thousand two hundred wounded.

In this battle of Oudenarde the French army was almost
broken up. Vendome was the one who most contributed to
repair the disaster. He gathered a handful of troops less
demoralized than the others, formed a rear-guard, arrested
the flying army and reëstablished a new line three or four
miles in front of Ghent. When next day (July 12) Marlborough sent twelve battalions and forty squadrons on Ghent,
expecting to complete his yesterday's work, the force was
received and checked by Vendome at this place. Shortly
after, the French army fell back through Ghent and took up
a position with its back to the sea, behind fortified lines and
the Bruges and Ghent canal. With a heavy force at this
point, from which Brussels could be threatened, Vendome
believed that Marlborough would not advance into France.
Ypres, with its fortified lines, which the French had built to
hold the Lys-Scheldt region, soon fell to an expeditionary
force sent out under the Prussian marshal Lottum; but
nothing further was immediately undertaken; Marlborough
moved up to Helchin on the Scheldt, and later, to a position
on the Lys above Menin.

About the 15th of July Eugene's corps arrived at Brussels, thirty-five thousand strong; and to strengthen the
French, the duke of Berwick who, when he became aware
that troops were moving from the Rhine country towards the
Netherlands, had left part of his army *in situ,* and had

headed with the rest to the assistance of Vendome, also came up from the middle Rhine, with twenty-four thousand men, and took post near Valenciennes and Douay. It now appeared how valuable had been Marlborough's action in moving on the communications of the French army before engaging it. He had thrust the most important force of the enemy back into a corner of Flanders, and there was no army left except that of Marshal Berwick between his own divisions and the French capital. How should he utilize the favorable position?

At Brussels, Ath and on the Lys, with one hundred and twenty thousand men, the allies lay between the two French armies, Vendome's large numerically but demoralized by defeat, and Berwick's not strong enough to stand long against their heavy onset flushed with victory. It has been suggested by some critics that the joint commanders should have now marched on one or other of these divided forces. But it is never easy at any one era to frame your military work to the pattern of future critics of another era; and as Vendome was for the moment neutralized by defeat, and Berwick by lack of numbers, there were many other schemes for reducing the land equally advantageous for the allied commanders to consider. Both of the French armies were perhaps in their judgment too strongly placed to warrant attack, when equal results could be otherwise obtained. Whatever their reasons, nothing of the kind was attempted. The month of July was consumed in raids for material and forage, or in other small war by both armies.

In discussing plans, Marlborough is said to have advised an invasion of France and a march on Paris. In view of the fact that Eugene could have been left behind to prevent Vendome from mischievous diversions in Flanders while the invading army should be absent, of the comparative prox-

imity of the French capital, and of the lack of strong forces
in his front, this was much the same operation as the march
to Vienna urged on Gustavus after the battle of Breitenfeld,
and which so many critics still maintain he should have undertaken. But Eugene could not have been given a force large
enough to contain both Vendome and Berwick, who would
at once have united forces, without reducing Marlborough's

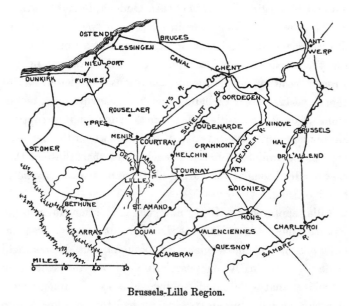

Brussels-Lille Region.

army below the number requisite for such an invasion; and
the two French armies, the heavy garrisons of the intervening
fortresses and the militia of the provinces were too great
an array in his rear to make the operation safe for the English general. In any event, the Dutch deputies would not
hear of Marlborough's absenting himself from the Low
Countries while Vendome remained there; and the suggestion
was incontinently shelved. Eugene was inclined at first to
agree with Marlborough; but he now thought that prior to

such an operation, some great fortress on the frontier should
be taken as a *point d'appui* and magazine. Obstinate as
Marlborough was in the prosecution of a manœuvre to which
he had put his hand, he was equally diplomatic and reasonable in the cabinet, and he was moreover unable to insist on
his own view. The allies decided to undertake the siege of
Lille, which Eugene was to run while Marlborough should
cover it by posting himself between Oudenarde and Tournay.

The presence of Vendome in his lines between Ghent and
Bruges made the undertaking far from an easy one. Lacking the navigation of the Scheldt, now interrupted by the
French position, the ordnance, munitions and victual had to
come overland from Holland; and huge convoys must be got
from Brussels to Lille safe from Vendome's interruption.
Nothing exhibits the severity of the blow which the battle of
Oudenarde inflicted on the French more than the fact that
they confined themselves during all these preparations strictly
to minor schemes.

Lille, captured in 1667, now chief frontier fortress of
France and commanding the Lys-Scheldt country, was not
only one of the masterpieces of Vauban, but it was held
by an exceptionally big garrison — fifteen thousand men
— under that celebrated soldier, Marshal Boufflers, who,
shrewdly anticipating an investment, had thrown himself into
the place at the end of July. The troops were mostly raw,
but their spirit was excellent. The means of defense was
ample; the scheme had been drawn up by Vauban himself,
and was under control of his nephew, General Vauban, who
was serving in the town; and no stone was left unturned to
make the defense a success. Many celebrated French officers and noblemen were within walls, and many well-known
foreigners joined the army of the besiegers, — among them
perhaps the most noteworthy, a slender lad of twelve, later the

great Marshal Saxe. The siege, whichever way it turned, was destined to be a remarkable one, — for a large and amply equipped army was to conduct it; this was protected by a larger one; and a third of over one hundred thousand men lay ready to interrupt it.

The first great step was to get the initial convoy safely to the place, without an attack by Vendome. Luckily the latter never dreamed of a siege of Lille; he imagined Mons to be the objective of the convoy of which he had heard, and he made no other motion to disturb it than to send a column of eighteen thousand men part way to the Dender. Indeed he jeered at the idea of so able a man as Eugene undertaking so impossible a thing. The convoy was well conducted. It consisted of five

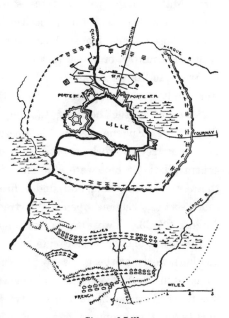

Siege of Lille.

thousand wagons containing one hundred and twenty heavy guns, sixty mortars and twenty howitzers, was fifteen miles long, and left Brussels August 6, — via Soignies and Ath, whence it turned off by way of Helchin towards Lille. The Brussels garrison protected it as far as Ath; thence the imperialists undertook its safety to Helchin, where Marlborough received and escorted it. The details of its management furnish a fruitful study in the art of protecting convoys. Marshal Berwick, who had pushed forward to St. Amand, had suggested to Vendome the advisability of interrupting the allies' plan by moving in force to some point between Brussels and Lille; but Vendome, who had his lazy as well as energetic moods, would not listen to him.

While Eugene undertook the siege with forty thousand men, Marlborough, with a force stated between sixty and seventy thousand, took up his position at Helchin. This was a well-chosen place, from which Marlborough could readily scout the country, or move to any threatened point; and in order to facilitate the speedy delivery of supplies, six bridges were built at various places on the Scheldt.

So soon as the head of the big convoy reached Lille, August 14, Eugene began his operations. Ten thousand men were set at work on the lines of circumvallation and contravallation, which were nine miles in extent. Long before these were completed, and under fire of the besieged and some sorties, Eugene opened his trenches on the night of August 22–23. Two attacks were chosen, both on the north of the town, one on either side of the Deule, and opposite the horn-works at the gates of St. André and of the Madeleine. On August 24 fire was opened; the second parallel was finished on the 25th, and a heavy fire was at once begun. Sorties were frequent, in one of which the works erected at the chapel of the Madeleine were destroyed.

On August 30 a junction was made between the armies of Vendome and Berwick. It had required a great deal of persuasion to induce Vendome to throw up his Ghent-Bruges lines; but he finally left La Motte in Ghent with twenty thousand men, and moved via Oordegen and Ninove on Grammont, while Berwick advanced from Mons towards the same place. After the junction the army — under supreme orders of the duke of Burgundy — marched to Tournay, crossed the Scheldt and camped on the west of that fortress. As Burgundy was a mere figurehead, and Vendome and Berwick, both able men, were at swords' points, there was small unity in the French army. Marlborough had made a movement to interrupt the operation by which the French thus concentrated, but could not do so. The French generals now had a force of over one hundred thousand men, and though their counsels remained divided, there was manifestly but one thing to do, and that was to relieve Lille; with which intent, on September 2 they started towards the beleaguered place, and soon took up a position along the Marque on its east bank, hoping to find a chance to raise the siege. Marlborough was early instructed of their advance, which he had been expecting, at once guessed their object, and, anticipating the manœuvre, slipped in between them and Lille, and himself on September 5 assumed a position behind the Marque. He was none too soon. Within two hours after he had established himself the French van came up. The enemy had with them some two hundred guns.

Either Vendome or Berwick of his own motion would have fought; but as orders from the court of Versailles had impressed caution, and the two generals were so jealous of each other and agreed so ill that Burgundy could not control them, no plan of action could be agreed upon. Finally, on referring the case to Versailles, the king sent the war minister on to decide the action to be taken. Chamillart knew nothing of war, but he concluded that a battle might be delivered to advantage, and Vendome and Berwick moved closer to Marlborough, taking up a position between the Marque and the Deule; to meet which Marlborough had already constructed a strong line to face them. But after all this preparation, except a two days' cannonade, no attack was made. Eugene detached enough of his besieging force to run Marlborough's strength up to eighty-five thousand men, and battle was anxiously awaited, but in vain.   The colleagues indeed were eager to attack the French, but the Dutch deputies, content with the situation, vetoed the project, and Marlborough then fortified his position.   Finally, September 15 Vendome and Berwick returned to Tournay and stretched out towards Oudenarde, and Marlborough, following, camped near the Scheldt. Though still between Lille and the French, they yet had managed so cleverly as to sever the allies' communications with Brussels, and only the road to Menin remained open. Shortly the French captured the bridges over the Scheldt, and what they had not accomplished by a battle, they now had a prospect of accomplishing by famine.

In the siege-lines, sorties and assaults were of daily occurrence, and the fire from both sides was constant; but despite hearty pushing, the progress of the siege was slow; Boufflers was as able as Lille was strong.   Not until September 7, when an assault in force at a loss of three thousand men gave the allies a footing on the works, was there any special gain; and with Ghent, Bruges, Douay, Tournay, all in French hands, the case was beginning to look desperate.   On September 20 another assault in force, headed by a column of five thousand picked English troops, was delivered; though given with the utmost gallantry, it was thrice repulsed, when Eugene in person headed the fourth assault, and after two hours' fighting a good lodgment was effected, at a loss in the English column of two thousand killed and wounded. Eugene was himself among the wounded, a fact which for a few days seriously increased Marlborough's duties.   On September 23 still another assault was delivered in two columns of five thousand men; and another lodgment was effected at a loss of one thousand killed and wounded.

Both besiegers and besieged were getting out of powder; but the French cunningly introduced a supply into the town by some eighteen hundred horsemen, who, each carrying a sixty-pound sack, managed to break through the investing lines; while at the same time, near the end of September, Marlborough managed to replace his exhausted store from England via Ostende, by a convoy ably led, but with a loss of at least one thousand men. The siege still dragged along. On September 30 yet another stout assault was delivered; the fire from the works never ceased, and gradually the capacity of the town to resist was destroyed. Finally, on October 22, just before a final assault was to be made, Marshal Boufflers surrendered the town and retired into the citadel, where he held himself six weeks longer, nor capitulated until December 11, notwithstanding a number of assaults, in which, as was his habit, Eugene frequently led the column.

No commander of a great army can be praised for thus risking his life. Marlborough was less wont to be tempted out of the general conduct of operations into such moods of daring. But while condemning the act, one cannot but admire the dash of the imperialist, in whose diminutive body throbbed the heart of a lion, as in his brain there worked a military intellect not surpassed by any man of his generation.

Out of a force of fifteen thousand men, increased by eighteen hundred horsemen, the garrison lost all but four thousand five hundred. The allied loss was three thousand six hundred and thirty-two killed and eight thousand three hundred and twenty-two wounded; but many more died of sickness. It was the victory of Oudenarde which so demoralized the French that they did not interfere to better effect with this memorable siege.

Vendome had rejoined the force at Ghent. Burgundy and Berwick remained on the Scheldt, where, from Tournay to

Oudenarde, they fortified all the crossings with carefully
constructed works, often in double and triple lines, purposing
to cut the allies permanently from Brussels. From Ghent
Vendome moved out and captured a number of small places
in front of Bruges and Ostende, opened the sluices at Plassendael near Ostende and at Nieuport, and overflowed the
country so as to cut off Marlborough's line of supply from
England. The latter moved across the Lys to attack Vendome, but the Frenchman retired to Bruges. The flood and
the capture of Lessinghe by Vendome obliged Marlborough
to send foraging parties all over the country and well into
Picardy, to victual the army, as well as to build high-wheeled
carts to haul powder through the inundated districts. At the
beginning of November the French generals were ordered by
Louis XIV. to extend their line along the Scheldt, and to
take up positions all around Lille in a great semicircle of
fifty leagues. The cordon thus formed lay at Bethune, Arras,
Douay, St. Amand, Saulces near Tournay, the right bank of
the Scheldt to Ghent, and behind the canal to Bruges.
Small bodies only were placed along the cordon, except at
Tournay, Melchin, Ghent and behind the canal. The object
of this plan was to cut the allies off from both the coast and
Brussels, and meanwhile to protect France. The weakness
of so long a line did not occur to the king; but it is certain that Vendome can have had nothing to do with the
scheme. His ability in this campaign had been overlooked,
and his wonderful services of the past forgotten, — a fact to
which his own difficult disposition contributed not a little.
Both armies thus remained a month, when Berwick was
again sent to the Rhine.

At the end of November the French dispatched a body of
fifteen thousand men under the elector of Bavaria, who
moved from Mons by Braine l'Alleud and Hal, behind the

Scheldt curtain, to take Brussels; and trenches were opened against that city on the 24th. Brussels had only an old and weak wall, but the garrison held bravely out, and Marlborough and Eugene, with sixty-five thousand men, joined hands at Marlborough's camp at Rouselaer, crossed the Lys, by clever dispositions misled the enemy, and forced the Scheldt near Oudenarde. The French line was broken, despite its careful construction, and the army cut in two, of which one part retired to Tournay and Grammont, and another to Ghent. Having thus broken the Scheldt lines, Eugene returned to the siege of Lille citadel, and Marlborough went to the relief of Brussels, from which the elector, on hearing of his approach, speedily decamped; whereupon Marlborough marched back to Oudenarde.

The allies were not content to go into winter-quarters while Vendome lay in his Ghent-Bruges line. Ghent, which Vendome had left to La Motte while he operated in the Ostende region, was accordingly attacked and taken by a summary siege in December, capitulating January 2, and Bruges followed suit soon after. The French thereupon retired within their own border, Vendome going into winter-quarters between Ypres and Furnes.

During this year the main struggle between France and the allies took place in the Netherlands, and the campaign here had been one exhibiting consummate ability in strategy, tactics and logistics. Elsewhere the operations were confined to manœuvring, but they are more interesting as samples of the unenterprising system of the day than as military studies. At the end of the campaign both parties appear to have shown more signs of exhaustion than they had since the beginning of the war.

LXII.

MALPLAQUET. SEPTEMBER 11, 1709.

EFFORTS at peace were fruitless, and Villars opened the 1709 campaign with over one hundred thousand men in intrenched lines near Bethune. The allies had one hundred and ten thousand men ; but Villars' position being too strong for attack, they laid siege to Tournay and took it in July. They then sat down to besiege Mons, from a position which rendered the French lines useless. Villars marched to its relief, took up a defensive position at Malplaquet, and the allies advanced on him. The armies were about equal, each short of one hundred thousand men, Villars being very stoutly intrenched. The bulk of the fighting, though not the most bloody, was in the forest of Taisnières, on the right, in front of Eugene. The Dutch on the left assaulted with equal heart ; but the battle was not won until the French centre was disgarnished to save the left, and Marlborough made the final assault which ruptured the French line. Boufflers, who had taken wounded Villars' place, withdrew in good order, with a loss of fourteen thousand men ; the allies had lost twenty thousand. The result of the victory was naught. The allies turned to the siege of Mons, which they took September 26. With Malplaquet, Marlborough's brilliant military career ends. Together, he and Eugene had won Blenheim, Oudenarde and Malplaquet ; separate, he had won Ramillies and Eugene Turin. Honors in this war were equal.

THE efforts to conclude peace during the winter of 1708–1709 were unavailing. The allies made their demands so harsh that Louis felt that he could not honorably accept them ; and his appeals to the French people were so effectual that, despite unusual distress throughout France, the power with which the new campaign was opened exceeded that of any other in which France had ever engaged. To Harcourt was intrusted the defense of the Rhine and Alsatia ; to Berwick the task of holding head to the duke of Savoy, who threatened to debouch from the Alps ; but Flanders was again to be the main theatre of operations. The *ban* and *arrière-ban* were called out; forces were drawn from the Rhine, and Villars, who had replaced Vendome, entered the field with one hundred and twelve thousand men, instinct with enthusiasm and courage. A preliminary position was taken up from Douay to the Lys, strongly fortified with all manner of works, marshes and inundations, and with detachments out at Lannoy, Touflers and Templeuve, in a strong but extended line, holding Bethune and covering Lens. The left was made the stronger flank because Villars believed that the allies, not to lose touch with the coast, would be apt to approach this way; and the object of the whole line seemed to be to protect Arras and Douay, fortresses which were essential to the safety of France. The line was later prolonged far to the east, and ran, more or less well held, by way of Marchiennes and Denain, Condé and Mons, and backward to Maubeuge.

By great exertions, Marlborough managed to get sufficient supplies voted; and ten thousand men were added to the English forces in Flanders. All told, the allies under Eugene and Marlborough opened the campaign with one hundred and ten thousand men, — a motley array of many nationalities, but held together by good discipline and success, and by ardent belief in their distinguished leaders. They were in a mood to attack the enemy; but owing to the late season, it was June before their forces could assemble, and at the end of June they moved forward up the Lys, and on either side of the Deule, towards where Villars sat behind his inexpugnable defenses in the plain, and where he would have been only too glad to accept a battle. He at first imagined from their direction that the allies proposed to take Aire and St. Venant on his left, and then move into Picardy, or perhaps on Paris; when they had, however, reached a point well south of Lille, he concluded that they were about to attack him, and prepared for the event by manning his lines.

Eugene and Marlborough carefully reconnoitred Villars' position, which they found to be altogether too strong to attack. The right leaned on the Lille-Douay canal; the centre had the marsh of Cambrin as a shield; and the left, which had received especial attention, was protected by streams and hills near Bethune. Intrenchments lay along the front; inundations alternated with regularly built lines; palisades and earthworks were erected everywhere, and the entire front had a ditch fifteen feet wide and six feet deep, with corresponding rampart. The army was encamped behind this defense, in two foot-lines, with cavalry cantonned in the rear. It was found essential by the allied generals to adopt some other means of opening the campaign than a foolhardy assault. By taking Tournay they might go far to turn Villars out of the strongest part of his intrenched line by the right, and after due deliberation they set themselves this task.

But first it was wise to deceive Villars, and the allied commanders made a demonstration in force towards his lines, as if seriously to attack them. On July 23 Eugene with the right crossed the Deule below Lille; Marlborough with the left, consisting of the Anglo-Dutch, crossed the Marque; and the whole force concentrated on the upper Deule. Villars believed that their attack was certain, withdrew all his detachments, strengthened himself with parts of the garrisons of Tournay and other fortresses, and lay waiting his opponents. On the night of June 27 the allies made a march in the direction of the enemy in such fashion that he should observe it; and then, by a sudden file to the left, behind a curtain of troops, marched straight on Tournay. So admirably was this done that by seven next morning they had reached and completely invested that fortress.

When Villars perceived that the allies had sat down before Tournay, he did not deem it essential to interfere with the siege, but holding fast to his position, made two or three isolated attacks on the protecting force of Eugene at Mortagne and St. Amand, as if to feel him. He understood that his rôle was to protect the French frontier rather than to do battle with the enemy.

Lying on the Scheldt, the town of Tournay was well fortified and full of military stores, but the garrison was not large, nor was victual abundant. The outworks had been drawn by Vauban, and the citadel was of the best. The colleagues reversed the rôles of Lille : Marlborough undertook the siege; Eugene covered the operation by a position in a semicircle southwest of Tournay from St. Amand through Orchies to Pont à Tessin. Approaches were opened July 6; but not until the 10th were the heavy guns got up by the river from Ghent. After repeated assaults and sorties repulsed, on the 21st a lodgment was effected in the covered way; on the 27th a strong horn-work fell, and July 29 the town surrendered, and the garrison, still four thousand strong, retired into the citadel. The latter offered exceptional difficulty, and owing to lack of ability in the corps of engineers, a siege of mines and counter mines went on for weeks, with great loss of life. It was not until September 3 that the citadel surrendered.

Villars had done nothing to interrupt the siege, but to answer the demonstration on his right had been extending his lines from Douay along the Scarpe to Condé, and beyond the Scheldt. Finally, but too late to prevent the fall of Tournay, he made another demonstration on St. Amand. Eugene's position was too strong : it failed.

The allies were still too much hampered with the network of fortresses in their front — Douay, Bouchain, Valenciennes, Condé — to think of advancing into France without further siege operations. They had tried August 18 to seize Marchiennes so as to threaten Douay, but the French had been too watchful. Deciding to complete the turning of the enemy's position then compelled them to resort to the siege of Mons, which lay well beyond Villars' right. This fortress, with Valenciennes, Douay and some minor ones, which could be observed in case of an advance, alone remained to protect the French frontier at this point. But a passage of the Haine, the line of which was essential to secure the siege of Mons, must be had, and Orkney was dispatched August 31 to St. Ghislain to get hold of the crossing. This likewise failed, but another expedition was sent out under the prince of Hesse-Cassel, who on September 3, with four thousand foot and sixty squadrons of horse, after a march of forty-nine miles in fifty-six hours, seized the passage at Obourg and Havré east of Mons. Marlborough at once ordered this gain to be followed up, occupied the heights of Jemappes west of the fortress, thus turned Villars' long lines, which he had been so laboriously constructing for months, and was enabled safely to invest Mons from the French side. The Tournay forces then passed the Scheldt, marched rapidly up the right bank of the Haine, crossed at Obourg and Havré, and made the investment of Mons secure. Villars did nothing more ; and about this time gallant Boufflers, though his senior, came to the army to serve under his orders, anxious solely to add his efforts to the success of the French arms.

So soon as Villars perceived that the allies had laid siege to Mons, it was evident to him that his stronghold was of no further value. He had received from Versailles orders to prevent the siege of Mons even at the risk of a general engagement; had drawn in a large body of troops at Valenciennes, had crossed the Scheldt there, and on September 4 had reached the Honneau; and September 8 he moved by his right still further towards the east, purposing to attack the allies under the walls of the fortress. In order to reach Mons, he chose to pass through the intervening forests by the gap of Aulnois, and on September 9 moved in this direction.

Every one was surprised at the ease with which the lines that had cost such time and labor were rendered useless, — no person more so than Villars. He had expected an attack, but was ignorant as to where it might fall; and the seizure by Hesse-Cassel of the crossing of the Haine first instructed him. The outposts of the allies had been thrown out to the Trouille; and as Villars moved onward, his van of cavalry struck these outposts September 4. Fearing lest he had the entire allied army before him, he did not take measures to attack, though the moment was opportune. With a little more speed, indeed, Villars would have caught the allies separated, but when he found the enemy's van in his immediate front, he arrested his advance. At this moment the allies, taking out the forces at Mons and Tournay, would scarcely have equaled Villars; but he credited them with much over one hundred thousand men and one hundred guns, and declining to attack he took up a defensive position. This was unlike Villars.

When two armies are *en face* manœuvring towards battle, the one who first attacks will in two cases out of three strike the enemy before he is quite ready, and had Villars known all the facts, he might have made a marked gain by assuming a sharp offensive. But he preferred to utilize his time in strengthening his position. Though usually the attacking party, at this time the French had adopted the fashion of defensive battles, — a thing less suited to the Gallic character than the impetuosity of assault. They had been made cautious by the vigor of the allied generals.

On September 7, having learned that Villars had sat down near Malplaquet and that he had fighting orders, the allies moved forward, leaving a small force to observe Mons. In a number of columns, headed by Eugene and Marlborough and so disposed as to cut off from the French the avenues of approach to Mons through the forest-gaps, the allies debouched into the plain of Quarégnon. Unless Villars retired, a battle must supervene.

Villars had a good army, on which he had spent much time and effort, homogeneous, well-rested, in good spirits, and able in every sense. Among the officers serving under him no less than twelve became marshals of France. He had no idea of declining battle. He may have outnumbered the allies by five thousand men; the forces are variously stated, both in organizations and numbers. Kausler gives them in one place as: Allies, one hundred and thirty-nine battalions, two hundred and fifty-two squadrons, one hundred and five guns; total ninety-three thousand men. French and Bavarians, one hundred and thirty battalions, two hundred and sixty squadrons, eighty guns; total ninety-five thousand men. In another place he quotes the allies at ninety thousand men; the French at eighty-one thousand.

The theatre of the immediate operations is a square inclosed by Mons, Quiévrain, Bavay, Givry, and bounded by the Haine on the north, and the Trouille and Honneau on the east and west. On the south were a number of brooks.

The terrain of Malplaquet is a plateau some two hundred feet above the low grazing-land of the Trouille. At that day so many woods covered the ground that it could not be bettered for defense. The village of Malplaquet lies in open ground at the summit of this plateau, and from here the brooks flow either towards the Trouille or towards the Hon. The brooks cut well into the surface of the country; in places, as at Aulnois and Blaregnies, running through deep ravines. The ridges between the brooks are marked. To the right of Malplaquet as one looks towards Mons stretches the great wood of Lanière; to the left, the forest of Taisnières, often called the wood of Blangies. In the many accounts of the battle, the woods are variously named, often breeding much confusion. Between and beyond these woods lies open ground, which, separated by another small wooded stretch, makes two avenues of approach, the left one being the "wolf-gap," the right one the gap of Aulnois.

In the allied army there were two separate corps; but each was instinct with the same spirit of generous rivalry which inspired the two commanders. Eugene was on the right of the allies with about two fifths of the joint forces; Marlborough was on the left with the larger half.

From the windmill of Sart, on an eminence some three miles from Malplaquet, whither, with a big escort, they had ridden to reconnoitre, the allied commanders on September 9 perceived the French army at Malplaquet, where it had occupied the woods and the plain between. Marlborough at once ordered his wing, the left, forward, and took position athwart the gaps, penetrating so close to the French line as to bring about a smart exchange. Both generals were for immediate attack; Eugene the more so, for Marlborough was held back by the Dutch deputies, who insisted on waiting until a belated column of nineteen battalions and ten squadrons under Count Lottum could arrive from Tournay, and also until St. Ghislain was taken, so that the allies might have a secure crossing over the Haine in their rear. All this was the more readily accomplished because Villars, on perceiving the enemy in force in his front, withdrew his outlying detachments. On September 10 St. Ghislain was taken by escalade ; the Tournay troops came up ; and so soon as the French retired from the Haine, Eugene advanced his, the right, wing and took place in prolongation of Marlborough's line.

What had been gained by the delay was more than twice offset by the time afforded Villars to intrench. His men had recently been trained to just this work, and they lost no time in making their position impregnable. The edge of the wood of Taisnières became a fortress, and the artillery in front of the two gaps lay in such defenses that it could scarcely be taken, while, trained as it was, down a gentle slope towards the allied position, it admirably covered everything in its front. Abatis was laid before every intrenchment; redoubts arose as by magic, topped by palisades ; and the troops were protected by stockades placed wherever the ground allowed and with much skill. In the intrenchments which lay across the gaps there were left intervals, through which the cavalry might debouch. To the works on the edge of the wood of Taisnières the brooks acted as a ditch, and the left was protected by a swampy stream-head. Batteries which should give a cross-fire on the two approaches were set up ; a single one of twenty guns stood in the centre. The place was as desperate a spot to assault as the Bloody Angle. It was called, and in truth was, a " trouée d'enfer." Its one fault was being cramped.

The ground was such as to make the French position a peculiar one. The approach to Malplaquet itself was admirably defended, and the edge of the Forest of Taisnières was held so as to throw the French left almost a mile beyond the centre, like a species of outwork. On the right, through the wood of Lanière, ran the Bavay-Binche turnpike; and though the edge of the wood near Malplaquet was fortified, and the works leaned on the sources of the Honneau, which

were rather low and swampy, it does not appear that the
road was held in force, a fact which would have permitted
the French right to be easily turned. But no advantage

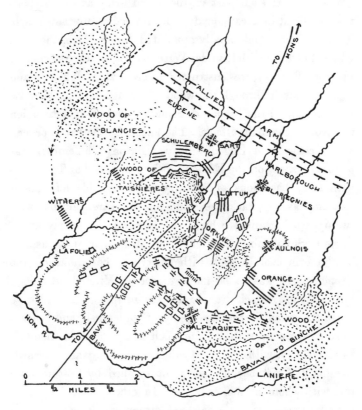

Battle of Malplaquet.

was taken of this fact; front attacks and hard fighting were
the order of the day. Throughout the battle the assault
was practically one in front, mainly by the right, with a feint
which became a real attack on the French right, but in effect
all along the line.

Villars had generously given the post of honor, on the

right, to Marshal Boufflers, and himself took the left. D'Artagnan commanded the front line of the right; Legal that of the left. Alberghatti had general charge of the left.

On the 10th such part of the allied army as was in position indulged in a cannonade, duly replied to by the French. To aid in the attack finally appointed for the 11th, the force which Lottum had left under Withers, and which was coming up from Tournay, was instructed to cross at St. Ghislain and then to march through the wood of Blangies, so as near La Folie to fall on the French extreme left and make a diversion in favor of the main attack. The latter, by the battle orders, was to come from Eugene's corps : Baron Schulemberg was to force his way on the French left into the wood of Taisnières with forty battalions of infantry, while on his left Count Lottum was to attack the same line of intrenchments with twenty-two battalions, which would crowd the enemy at an angle to Schulemberg's onset. Half an hour later, an assault by the prince of Orange with thirty-one battalions on the French right was to be made to occupy Villars' attention ; but Eugene's attack was to be the main one, intended to crush the salient left of the enemy. Schulemberg and Lottum were to draw up with a front such as the ground dictated. Lord Orkney, with fifteen battalions, was to advance towards the gap, but not beyond the point reached by Lottum, on a line with whom he was to keep. In other words, he was to remain in reserve until he could attack with success. It is said that these orders were later somewhat changed, but the course of the battle ran in accordance with them. The day was the anniversary of Eugene's great victory at Zenta.

On the French side all was enthusiasm. If behind such works as these they could not defeat the allies, what had become of French valor? There could be no doubt as to the result. The enemy would here meet their match.

St. Simon relates that by a clever *ruse de guerre* the allies, under a pretense of parley, got within the Taisnières intrenchments and were able to gauge their strength; but the fact, if such, had small influence on the battle.

At 3 A. M. religious services were held throughout the allied army.

At half-past seven on the eventful day the morning fog cleared away, and the guns opened fire. After an interval, not exceeding an hour, the assaulting columns were started on their perilous errand. The orders to the Dutch, under the prince of Orange, were to wait thirty minutes before assaulting in earnest, and the prince began with only an artillery duel; but Schulemberg forged straight ahead with his forty battalions, while Lottum, with his twenty - two, swinging somewhat round to the right, advanced against the right of the French outworks on the edge of the forest of Taisnières, thus working in towards the left of Schulemberg. Lord Orkney at the same time advanced his fifteen battalions to a point on a line with Lottum and out of range. The cavalry, owing to the awkward terrain, lay in groups in the rear, but had orders to press in after the foot as occasion warranted.

The first assault of Schulemberg, who, in five lines, headed the advance of Eugene's wing, though stoutly delivered, was repulsed, after a struggle of some duration; but headed by Eugene in person, who was ever reckless of his life, and aided by the smart diversion made by General Gauvain with a detached party of three regiments on the extreme French left, a second assault succeeded better, and in not much over an hour the enemy under Alberghatti were driven out of their intrenchments and well back into the wood.

Marlborough meanwhile was sustaining Lottum with a number of squadrons. Some time later than Eugene had penetrated the works, Lottum carried those in his own front,

but after the lapse of a brief holding was expulsed by a
charge led by Villars in person; whereupon Marlborough,
at the head of his cavalry, rode in on the over-eager enemy
and recaptured the works, aided by a renewed threat of
Lottum. By this time Withers at La Folie began to make
some headway, and as Eugene had actually captured the
works in his front, it looked as if he would push Villars
entirely from the wood of Taisnières.

On the left, meanwhile, where Field-Marshal Tilly was
in nominal command, after his half hour's pause the prince
of Orange delivered his assault with unequaled ardor. His
troops were made up of auxiliaries in the Dutch service,
including a Scotch brigade. On the first rush and without a
stop the French intrenchments were carried, and had there
been a reserve, the French right might have been then and
there permanently broken. But the prince had but forty
battalions; Boufflers met him in the rear of his works with
seventy, turned his guns inward and enfiladed his line, and
after an obstinate and bloody struggle the Dutch were thrown
out, but in no disorder. The French second line now closed
up, and the prince of Orange could make no further headway. He drew off with, it is said, three thousand killed and
six thousand wounded, casualties which prove the bitterest
kind of fighting. No sooner had they expelled the enemy
than the French sallied out of their works and made a gallant advance with heavy columns of foot and horse. There
was danger that the allied left would be broken, but Marlborough opportunely came up from the wood of Taisnières,
and put in a few Hanoverian battalions to check the French,
while Eugene brought some reserves over from the right.
The matter was reëstablished, and Boufflers withdrew within
his works.

Villars believed that, by giving up the advanced position

of his left, he would jeopardize his centre, and now resumed the offensive in the wood of Taisnières; and in order to do this with sufficient vigor, he reinforced his left with a number of battalions of foot withdrawn from his centre, — among them the two Irish brigades. Eugene, aided by Withers' diversion, had pressed him so hard that his entire left wing was in peril, and he now pushed his counter attack with the utmost vigor. Lottum called for help, and Marlborough flew to his aid.

Villars had miscalculated the conditions of the battle; his weakening of the centre proved his ruin; the allied commanders soon became aware of it, and were able to take a telling advantage of the lapse. Eugene, who had visited the left to aid the prince of Orange, rejoined his wing and forced the fighting on the right. It was already noon, and Eugene had pushed the French left well through the wood and had joined hands with Withers; and Marlborough now sent the column under Orkney forward to make its way in at the disgarnished French centre, which so far had not been attacked in force. The fighting became hotter than ever. Eugene had had the bulk of the French foot to contend with; though again wounded, he persisted in leading on his men in person, and he made marked progress, which Villars, likewise wounded, was unable to resist. Withers, too, pressed on; and the French left was practically broken. The weakened centre was now open to a stanch assault notwithstanding its intrenchments; it gave way before Orkney's gallant onset and the works were entered. The cavalry followed hard upon the foot, and after getting through the lines, charged in with a will. The French guns were seized and turned on the enemy, who were now crowded into too small a space to be able to act effectively, and were fast losing ground. But Boufflers would not give up the fight. He headed the Maison du Roi, and charging in on the allied horse, completely broke it up; but he was himself in turn broken when he reached the line of Orkney's infantry, which now held the French ramparts, and decimated by point-blank musketry and by the cross-fire of some batteries judiciously if hastily placed, he retired. Once more he collected a column of foot as support to his squadrons and returned to the fray. Time and again was either line forced back, and not until Eugene came up with his reserve cavalry, and Marlborough with his English horse, could Boufflers' noble effort be checked. On the allied left, simultaneously with the centre, Orange and Hesse-Cassel again advanced, took the works on the French right and held them. Ousted from his intrench-ments and with his left crushed beyond usefulness, Boufflers saw that his chances were gone. The bloodiest battle of the war was over.

But the gallant French marshal made a masterly retreat to Bavay, in what was, under the circumstances, astonishingly good order. No pursuit could be undertaken by the allies, exhausted by their fearful losses. Though the breaking of the centre threw the French wings off in eccentric directions, they reunited a dozen miles in the rear of Malplaquet. Bouf-flers carried off all but his dismounted guns; there were losses of flags and guns on both sides.

The wounded were returned by the allies a few days later. The French loss was not over fourteen thousand men. It has been given at eight thousand killed and four thousand five hundred wounded. In such a mêlée there was small chance for a wounded man.

The allied loss was fully twenty thousand men. It is stated in the Memoirs of Count Schulemberg as follows: Eugene's loss, officers, eighty-nine killed, two hundred and sixty-eight wounded; men, two thousand and ninety-nine killed, three thousand four hundred and nine wounded; Marlborough's loss, officers (including the Dutch), two hundred and seventy-four killed, seven hundred and twelve wounded; men, three thousand eight hundred and twenty-one killed, nine thousand eight hundred and forty-eight wounded. Total, twenty thousand five hundred and twenty killed and wounded. The official account gives for the infantry alone five thousand five hundred and forty-four killed, and twelve thousand seven hundred and six wounded and missing; add the losses in the cavalry, and the same result is got.

The credit of the victory was equally shared between the prince and the duke. It was Eugene's hearty work on the allied right which induced Villars to disgarnish his centre, and thus enabled Marlborough with a gallant onset to break through where he would have vainly essayed before. What British there were in the battle behaved, as always, with true Anglo-Saxon grit. But the Dutch regiments lost the most heavily, showing determination quite equal to the British battalions.

The battle had been one of prolonged and bloody fighting, in which mere endurance and the persistent courage of Eugene and Marlborough contrived to win.

The French had fought superbly, and the allies had bought the victory dear. Some French accounts of the battle ascribe the defeat to the faulty position. It was rather the stubborn push of the two allied captains. Almost any generals would have retired before they had lost so heavily.

In this battle the allies formed their troops for attack in columns of deployed battalions. The French centre, both horse and foot, used the same formation. The innovation had not been so generally employed before, though by no means new.

It is curious to state that the result of this costly victory

was naught. The allies merely besieged Mons without interference. The trenches were opened September 25; on
October 9 a lodgment was made in the covered way; on
October 17 the outworks were stormed; and on the 26th the
town surrendered. Brabant was entirely occupied.

With Malplaquet, the brilliant part of Marlborough's
career came to an end. In this Succession War, he and
Prince Eugene had won five splendid victories: three in joint
command, Blenheim, Oudenarde and Malplaquet, though
at Oudenarde Eugene was without his own troops, but present
in person and commanding a part of Marlborough's; and
one singly each, Eugene at Turin, Marlborough at Ramillies.
Though Eugene had fought and won a number of battles
aside from these, as battle-commanders glory may be evenly
awarded to each. In their separate victories Marlborough
had been opposed by Villeroi at Ramillies, and Eugene by
Marsin and the duke of Orleans at Turin. Neither singly
had defeated a really able opponent.

Marlborough is incontestably one of the most splendid military figures of this era of giants. From the battle of Lützen
to the battle of Mollwitz, only Turenne and Eugene stand
out to share with him equal honors. He had the true battle
fervor, and the *coup d'œil* which is allotted to so few generals. He handled large armies with the same ease as he
commanded small ones; and no occurrence on the theatre
of war or on the battle-field ever threw him off his balance.
His strategic plans were often pared down to suit the puny
taste of the Dutch deputies; had he been left to his own
devices, he might have undertaken larger operations, and we
may believe would have conducted them with the same ability which characterized his lesser ones. Opportunity was
denied him.

If Marlborough cannot claim to stand among the six great

captains, he may certainly be placed on the first step of the military dais. But his eulogists do his solid reputation no good by such panegyrics as that of Alison, who, after claiming every other success in this war as the work of his hero, goes so far in his homage as to say that " by the succors " — some ten thousand men — " he sent to Eugene, he conquered Italy at Turin."

Marlborough is a splendid enough leader of men, just as he stands, not to make it essential to rob others to clothe him. It is quite as natural that some of the foreign military critics should err in making Eugene the greater soldier of the two ; though it is rare that ample justice is not done Marlborough in the annals of the continental writers. He is one of the greatest men of the second rank ; but he may not even be said to be *primus inter pares.*

The operations of the French this year were hampered by want of victual, in consequence of a poor harvest, and after Malplaquet, by the wounding of Villars. The operations of the allies after the battle were not remarkable.

Bombard.   (15th Century.)

LXIII.

SPAIN. 1704–1710.

THE operations of the War of the Spanish Succession were generally outside of Spain, but in 1704 and 1705 the allies invaded Spain under the Archduke Charles, while the duke of Berwick commanded the army of Philip. In 1706 Lord Galway, for Charles, took Madrid, but Berwick soon drove him back to the coast. In 1707 Galway and Berwick met at Almanza, and the former was defeated; and French reinforcements coming into Spain, the allies were crowded back to Catalonia. Their forces had been too much dispersed. In 1708 and 1709 comparatively little was done; but in 1710 Marshal Stahremberg beat Philip's army on the Ebro and marched to Madrid. Vendome now came into Spain, and he and Stahremberg conducted an admirable campaign, in which the French were fully successful, and the allies were again pushed back to the coast.

ALTHOUGH the great war which had desolated Europe from 1701 to 1714 was caused by the question of who should succeed childless Charles II. on the throne of Spain, yet that peninsula itself saw but a small portion of its horrors. Barring one or two campaigns, there was not much to interest the military student in comparison with the work of the giants in the Netherlands, in Germany and in Italy.

There were no operations there until 1704. Towards the end of 1703 the claimant of Spain under the treaty of partition, the Archduke Charles, with some nine thousand Anglo-Dutch troops, reached Lisbon. Adding to his force the Portuguese militia, he undertook in 1704 to defend the frontier of Portugal against the army of France and Spain under the duke of Berwick, a natural son of James II. In this he succeeded, but an attempt to advance to Madrid miscarried.

During this same year Gibraltar fell to the fleet of England and Holland. In 1705 the archduke landed in Catalonia, where he gained a foothold, roused the Spaniards to insurrection against Philip V., and aided by the gallant exploit of Lord Peterborough, captured Barcelona; but this city was soon again laid under siege by the Franco-Spanish army.

Spain.

In 1706, after the arrival of a British fleet, the archduke drove the French with loss from the siege of Barcelona and made it his base, while the enemy retired to Madrid. Lord Galway, with the Anglo-Portuguese army, captured many strong places, and in June took Madrid and reduced all middle Spain for Charles, who was proclaimed as king. But this success did not last long. The jealousies usual in Spain put an end to Galway's activity; and Berwick, aided by

Philip's adherents in Andalusia and the Castiles, managed to regain Madrid and push the English general out of nearly all his conquests and towards Portugal ; while Charles returned to the eastern coast. Berwick had thus manœuvred himself into a position between his opponents' two armies. Still, despite these losses, the archduke, at the opening of 1707, held Catalonia, Arragon and Valencia, that is, the north-east corner of Spain, with a force of forty-five thousand men under Galway, who had also returned to the eastern coast. Berwick had nearly forty thousand men, and fourteen thousand more were on the way from France. In April, 1707, Galway concentrated some thirty-three thousand men in the province of Valencia ; he was active and enterprising, but he accomplished nothing of importance. He harbored the idea of moving on Madrid, but Berwick, with an equal number of men, moved on Almanza, a position from which he might threaten Galway's communications with Barcelona. Galway saw that he must do battle for his holding, certainly so if he would advance on the capital ; he likewise marched to Almanza, where he drew up in two lines, with squadrons in between his battalions of the first line. Berwick had also two lines, but his foot was in the centre, his horse on the flanks. Galway opened the attack ; but his hermaphrodite first line did not work well, probably from inexperience in this formation. The cavalry attacked twice, but, after some work, was twice broken by the French horse, and found refuge under the fire of the foot. Finally Berwick strengthened his cavalry wings with foot from the second line, advanced for the third time, and succeeded in breaking Galway's left wing. In pushing back the French foot, Galway's centre had got itself forward in a salient from the main line, and somewhat separated from the right, which enabled Berwick to take the infantry in flank where the gap occurred, and by advancing his right smartly he secured the victory. None of the accounts of the battle is very clear; but the English, as always, fought stanchly, and their allies left them in the lurch. Galway was cut up, with a loss of five thousand killed and wounded and ten thousand prisoners; he lost all his artillery and train, and retired through the province of Valencia towards Barcelona, with but sixteen thousand men. Berwick placed some garrisons in Valencia, and followed Galway with twenty-three thousand men, forcing him back across the Ebro through Tortosa to Lerida. Philip V. was now king in earnest.

About the same time the duke of Orleans came by way of Navarre to Spain, and with nineteen thousand men advanced to Saragossa, where Berwick, crossing the Ebro, joined him. This made thirty-two thousand men, and they shortly drove the English out of Lerida and back into Catalonia, after which both armies went into winter-quarters.

The error of the archduke had been to disperse his none too large force of forty-five thousand men in various garrisons, so as to be unable to meet the enemy in sufficient strength. Had he kept his army in full force and taken his stand between Berwick and the duke of Orleans, — say in the Tudela country, — he might have beaten either in succession. In like manner, had Berwick got the duke of Orleans to move down towards the lower Ebro, and he himself at once followed up Galway, between them they might have captured the entire body.

Berwick was now ordered to the Netherlands; and the duke of Orleans was unable to profit by the gains of 1707. Though he had some forty thousand men in Catalonia, and was faced by Stahremberg with not much over half the number, he did nothing during 1708 and 1709 but besiege a few fortresses; so that Stahremberg even threatened to penetrate

into the interior. At the opening of 1710 Stahremberg's
forces rose to twenty-six thousand men, and a Portuguese
army of thirty thousand foot and two thousand horse assembled at the fortress Elvas ; while the forces of Philip V. were
sensibly diminished by drafts for the defense of the French
frontiers. He had not much exceeding thirty-five thousand
men all told ; and after detaching a suitable force against the
Portuguese to Estremadura, another to Andalusia, and making sundry smaller details, he had less than twenty thousand
with which to operate in Catalonia. The early manœuvres
were more for the purpose of collecting victual and of devastating the land to prevent the enemy's so doing, than for any
other apparent object ; but Stahremberg finally determined
to march on Madrid, join the Portuguese, and definitely place
the crown on Charles' head.

Advancing in pursuance of his design, he won a handsome
advantage on the Segre, and drove the Spaniards back to
Lerida, in so much disorder that had he followed them up
he might have destroyed them. But waiting for victual
and material, he remained inactive for two weeks, when he
advanced on Saragossa. This gave Philip time to repair his
losses and to move up the right bank of the Ebro to oppose
his passage ; but Stahremberg threw a pontoon bridge over
the river, crossed, attacked the Spanish army, which numbered but nineteen thousand men to his own twenty - four
thousand, and beat it badly with loss of half its force. The
wreck, nine thousand strong, retired to Tudela, and thence
via Aranda and Valladolid to Salamanca, which had been
made the rendezvous for a new Spanish army that Vendome
had just come to organize. With the new army the French
marshal hoped to march to Almaraz on the Tagus, and prevent the junction of the Portuguese and Stahremberg ; or at
least give them battle.

The archduke should have devoted his energies to preventing the formation of this new army; but he was eager to do great things, and deserve as well as get the crown; and Stahremberg could not restrain him. He chose to march on Madrid, which he took, as well as Toledo, and parceled out his forces uselessly. The Portuguese attempted to advance towards Madrid, but the appearance of a Spanish force of twelve thousand men in Estremadura headed them off, and they returned to Elvas.

Vendome, on the other hand, went sensibly to work. He began by sending out small raiding parties of horse to cut the archduke's communications with Saragossa, and capture his convoys. This, indeed, he accomplished so frequently that provision grew scarce in Madrid. By this time Vendome's army (Philip was formally in command) had grown to twenty-seven thousand men, and with these he made a clever march on the bridge of Almaraz over the Tagus, and pushed a large force of cavalry to Talavera. This, as Vendome had calculated it would be, was the end of any coöperation of the half-hearted Portuguese, who summarily left; Stahremberg could no longer hope to hold himself, and began his retreat to Catalonia with sixteen thousand men. He moved in three columns, each a day's march apart. Vendome followed him sharply, and at Brihuega, on the river Henares, cut off Stanhope and five thousand men who formed the rearguard of his army, and who had kept no outposts to notify him of danger. Stahremberg quickly turned in his tracks, but was two days too late at Brihuega to rescue his lieutenant; and Vendome, not permitting him to retire from the vicinity without fighting, attacked him at Villa Viciosa, near by. The battle here was drawn; but Stahremberg hastened his retreat, with less than ten thousand men he now had left, to Saragossa and thence to Catalonia. He was really in grave danger, for Marshal Noailles was advancing across the Pyrenees on the east with twenty-seven thousand men, and might fall on his rear and completely destroy him. But Noailles contented himself with besieging Gerona in lieu of advancing to the Ebro. Vendome followed up Stahremberg, and, crossing the Segre, went into winter-quarters.

These operations are interesting. Vendome's work was especially handsome. He had not only raised an army, but, by skillful manœuvres, had separated the allies, had ousted Stahremberg from Madrid, and had driven his enemy back to the sea with a loss of two thirds his force.

Heavy Cavalryman.
(16th Century.)

LXIV.

VILLARS AGAINST MARLBOROUGH AND EUGENE.
1710-1712.

IN 1710 the allies conducted a war of sieges. Douay was first invested, after breaking through the French fortified lines. Villars came to its relief, but did not push the allies to battle, preferring to protect Arras from attack. Having taken Douay, the allies in fact turned on Arras, but Villars headed them off. They then invested Bethune, proposing to capture all the strong places up to the coast, with a view to a new base. Villars took up a position in the Hesdin line, and after Bethune fell, the allies moved on and captured St. Venant and Aire. But they were no nearer Paris. In 1711 Bouchain was captured. In 1712 the English, with peace in sight, acted on the defensive; Eugene captured Quesnoy, but failed before Landrecies, owing to a handsome attack by Villars on his communications. In 1713 Eugene defended the Rhine against Villars with twice his force. Peace supervened.

IN 1710 the allies raised their forces to one hundred and forty thousand men, of whom eighty thousand took the field. In April Eugene and Marlborough met at Tournay, where their several columns rendezvoused out of winter-quarters, and opened the campaign by the recapture of Mortagne, which had just been seized by the French, and was essential as a step to attacking Douay. The French still held the strong line created by Villars the year before; and this had to be forced before Douay could be thought of. Speed being of the essence, the army advanced in two columns, the right under Marlborough, the left under Eugene. Marlborough crossed the Deule at Pont à Vendin, unopposed; Eugene, finding that he would have to fight for his passage at Pont d'Auby, filed to the right and crossed at Courière. The two columns reunited at Lens on April 21, and the French under

Montesquieu retired so hurriedly behind the Scarpe at Vitry as to forfeit much of their baggage. Marlborough crossed the Scarpe and closed in on Douay on the right bank, while Eugene remained on the left bank and invested it from the north.   The French then retired to Cambray.

Douay had been captured by the French in 1667.   It was a large and powerful fortress, the work of Vauban, astride the Scarpe, whose inundations made approach to it difficult.

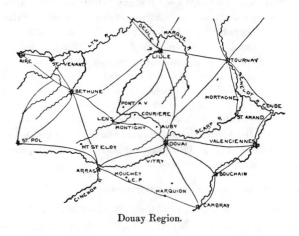

Douay Region.

It was not of the newest construction, but still a strong place of the first class, and the ditch was wide and full, and the covered way excellent.   It had eight thousand men in garrison, under Alberghatti.   The trenches were opened May 4–5. On the 9th a big siege-train arrived from Tournay; on the 11th the batteries were pushed up to the covered way.   The danger to the fortress caused Villars to be sent to its relief with ninety thousand men.   Berwick was with the army under special orders to report to the king.   Assembling at Cambray, Villars, under protection of a feint on the allies by way of Bouchain, moved by his left via Arras across the Scarpe and into the Lens plain, facing towards Douay, with reserves

at Mt. St. Eloy, intending battle. In anticipation of what
might occur, the allies had fortified two lines, one facing east
and one west, for the protection of Douay; and so soon as
Villars' manœuvres became clear, Marlborough and Eugene
depleted their Douay lines, advanced to meet him with sixty
thousand men, and on May 30 took up the position on the
west of Douay, which extended from Vitry north to Mon-
tigny, backing on the fortress. A strong outpost at Pont à
Vendin protected the right. Here they drew up for battle,
which seemed inevitable, as Villars never lacked pugnacity.
On June 1 he advanced to the front of the position of the
allies, whose rôle was, as covering the siege of Douay, necessarily a defensive one. On reconnoitring, both Berwick and
Villars deemed the line too strong to be forced. The French
retired June 4, hoping that the allied generals would follow;
and finally took up a position backing on Arras; and the
siege went on, in the presence of a relieving army of five-
score thousand men! By mid-June the fortress was *in extremis*, and Villars made another feint as if to relieve it by the
right bank of the Scarpe. Marlborough barred his advance
and Villars again retired, and in order to prevent the allies,
after capturing Douay, from further penetrating into France,
took up a position with his right on Cambray and his left out
towards Arras. On June 19 the prince of Orange failed
in an assault, but on the 24th made a lodgment. The sap
had reached the counterscarp, and on the 26th Alberghatti
surrendered. He had lost three thousand five hundred men;
the allies eight thousand.

Early in July, after a short rest, Eugene and Marlborough
advanced on Arras, the last of the triple line of French fortresses at that point. But Villars had ably placed himself to
prevent their advance. His left was on the Crinchon; his
centre from Marquion to Mouchy le Preux; his right between

Valenciennes and Bouchain. He had nearly one hundred thousand men and one hundred and thirty guns; and so soon as he saw that the allies were aiming for Arras, he moved by his left so as to prevent them from reaching the place to invest it. They then decided to lay siege to Bethune, a fortress whose capture would lead probably to the fall of Aire and St. Venant, and thus open up communication with the coast; and they invested the place July 15. Villars became nervous for the safety of Montreuil, Hesdin and Dourlens, towns in Picardy, the second of which places the allies indeed desired to seize; and again moved by his left to a position with his right on Arras and with his left stretching out towards St. Pol; and here he threw up a new line of defense. He did not care to risk a battle, which, if lost, might now be fatal for France. For the same reason it has been suggested that the allies might have sought battle to marked advantage; but they did not. Perhaps the losses of Malplaquet were deterrent. Bethune, though well garrisoned and well provisioned, fell at the end of August. The details need not be given.

As Villars lay so strongly posted that the allies did not wish to attack him in his lines, they now resorted to the siege of St. Venant and Aire. These towns lay on the Lys, which river their possession would open, and they might form the base for a movement on Calais and Boulogne, which had been in contemplation. On September 2 the allies moved forward as if to reconnoitre Villars' lines; and then suddenly filing to the right, marched on St. Venant and Aire along such a route as to prevent Villars from interfering with the operations. Both places were quickly invested. St. Venant was very strong and had eight thousand garrison, but despite the loss of an important convoy coming to the allies from Ghent, which Villars cleverly captured or destroyed, it fell the end of September. Aire held out till November 12. The capture of these towns, however, brought the allies no nearer Paris; and before Douay, Bethune, Aire and St. Venant, the allies had lost twelve thousand killed, thirteen thousand wounded, and seven thousand prisoners or missing, — a loss which could ill be afforded. They had captured four of the strong places of the French, with nearly thirty thousand men; but they had made no essential progress in this campaign. Louis' intrigues were bringing peace nearer, and the military success had not been brilliant. It was one of the old-model campaigns, the knot of which a victory would have cut. But political matters had been going against Marlborough at home; his hands were even more tied than usual; Eugene suffered from the same cause; and the campaign lacked vigor accordingly.

The campaign of 1711 in the Netherlands was conducted under difficulties. The change of ministry in England had brought Marlborough into disfavor, and we have Eugene's testimony to show that this reacted upon his military ardor. The new ministry was set for peace, but allowed war to go on. Eugene was ordered to the Rhine to protect the election of a new emperor in Frankfort, and took twenty-three thousand men from the army.

France now had but her third line of fortresses left, of which Arras and Cambray were of the first order. Villars had created another long line of defense, extending from the Canche all the way to Namur, along the Scarpe, Sensée, Scheldt and Sambre. Marlborough had cut out for the year's work the capture of Bouchain, Arras and Le Quesnoy, hoping to winter near the French frontier and invade France in 1712. Bouchain was his first objective, to reach which he must break through Villars' lines. These were too strong to assault, and Marlborough tried ruse. Moving by his right from the position to which he had advanced south of the Scarpe, he crossed at Vitry and marched towards Bethune. Villars moved by his left on a parallel route to a position west of Arras. Here Marlborough made a feint to attack him, and having convinced him that he was about to do so, under cover of a cavalry demonstration on Villars' left he marched rapidly back, crossed the Scarpe at Vitry, and easily breaking through the French lines, passed the Scheldt at Etrum and invested Bouchain. Part of his column had marched thirty-six miles in sixteen hours. Villars sought to entice him into battle near Cambray, but to no purpose, though it has been thought that Marlborough would have done well to fight. Invested August 17, Bouchain fell September 11. Beyond this nothing was done in 1711. In the way of manœuvring, part of the campaign had been brilliant; but it was not otherwise so ; nor had its activity been comparable to some of Eugene's.

In 1712 peace-negotiations were begun at Utrecht, and the English army received orders to act on the defensive; Prince Eugene, who succeeded Marlborough as commander-in-chief of the Dutch forces, being meanwhile under orders to continue the offensive, the two allies for the first time could not act in unison. They had possession of Antwerp, Oudenarde, Tournay, Ath, Mons, Dendermonde, Menin, Lille, Bethune, Aire, St. Venant, Douay and Bouchain. They could well have pushed into Artois and Picardy, and have taken Boulogne and Calais, as proposed two years before. But Eugene was seriously hampered by his dealings with the Dutch as well as those with the English allies, and was unable to carry out his own ideas. It would have been much more in his style, and indeed he frequently urged the Dutch deputies, to seek to try conclusions with Villars in a great battle rather than to sit down to a series of sieges, especially as a battle lost would now all but destroy France. The plan of 1710 was abandoned, and Eugene chose as a starting-point for his march into France the other flank, because the country was more fruitful and easier, and because Quesnoy and Landrecies were far less serious obstacles than Arras and Cambray.

Eugene assembled the troops early in April in the Douay-Marchiennes country. Lord Ormond was in command of the English contingent. The total force was some one hundred and twenty thousand men and one hundred and thirty-six guns. Villars had perhaps twenty thousand less, and lay from the headwaters of the Scheldt at Le Catelet along the left bank of the river to Cambray, and thence stretching out towards Arras. These two strong places he was bound to preserve from investment if possible. But his position left Condé, Valenciennes, Quesnoy and Landrecies outside his scheme of defense.

Towards the end of May Eugene crossed the Scheldt above Bouchain. Ormond advanced with him; but he had secret orders, the fruit of the recent negotiations, to take part in neither a battle nor a siege, and of this fact knowledge had been afforded Villars, — bad faith little creditable to the British ministry. The French were in poor military case; but this treachery saved them harmless.

Prince Eugene opened the siege of Quesnoy June 8, and undertaking, as a further menace, to devastate the French borders, so as to intimidate the population and to keep his army at their cost, he sent twelve hundred horse into Champagne and Lorraine, while from the Rhine, at the same time, another raiding party was sent into the Metz region.

Eugene had for some time suspected the bad faith of the English, but was scarcely prepared for so bald a breach of common military honor as was contained in the secret instruc-

tions to Ormond.   Had he not been wise, he might have got
into a situation where Villars could have destroyed him.
About midsummer the matter came to a head, and the English left the army ; the other allies kept faith ; and having,
July 4, captured Quesnoy, Eugene moved forward to the
siege of Landrecies.   He marched over the Escaillon to the
Selle, and sent the prince of Dessau ahead with thirty battalions and forty squadrons to shut in Landrecies.   His main

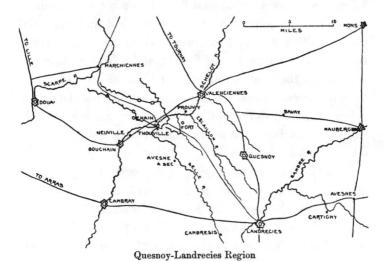

Quesnoy-Landrecies Region

force to cover the siege was placed between the Sambre and
the Scheldt, and his chief magazines were in Marchiennes,
behind the Scheldt and the Scarpe.   To hold communications
with these places, there had, at Denain and at Prouvy over
the Scheldt, been built bridges and on the right bank bridge-
heads ; and between Denain and Marchiennes a double line
of works running nearly the entire distance of ten miles,
behind which the trains could safely move.   These were part
of Villars' old lines, and the men called them " The Road to
Paris."   Denain had works all around it, and a garrison of

thirteen thousand men under Albemarle ; Marchiennes had
four thousand. Prince Eugene's communications with his
magazines were thus apparently protected ; but they were not
actually so. The position was strategically faulty, in that the
depot of all supplies lay beyond the right flank in prolongation of the front of the position. It was quite against
Eugene's advice that he was thus posted ; Marchiennes had
been selected by the Dutch because of its water approaches
by the Lys and Scheldt. After the capture of Quesnoy,
Eugene would have been glad to move the depots thither,
but the Dutch looked at the matter from the economic standpoint solely, and not from the military ; they declined the
expense of moving the depots, alleging that Douay and Bouchain sufficiently protected the line, which ran behind the
Selle.

Villars received orders from Versailles to compel Prince
Eugene to raise the siege of Landrecies. He had long been
ready to so act on his own judgment ; for Prince Eugene
was now much weaker than when he had the English contingent with him ; actually weaker than Villars. Moreover,
the French army was concentrated and in good order, while
Eugene's was in several detachments and much spread.
Villars had reconnoitred the Landrecies position and Eugene's position behind the Selle, and found both too strong
to assault. But he saw that he could easily make an attack
on Denain or Marchiennes, and this he began to consider.
Although the niceties of strategic manoeuvring had not yet
been studied as they were after Jomini began his work of
showing why Napoleon did what he did, yet a problem so
simple as this of necessity forced itself on a man of such
military intelligence as Villars, and he soon formed his
plan.

In order to be sure of success, Villars must first draw

Eugene's attention away from his right flank. He crossed the Scheldt, began to prepare military roads towards the Sambre, advanced towards the headwaters of the Selle, and July 22 camped at Cambresis and south of it. This operation convinced Eugene that his siege of Landrecies was threatened. Villars further made a number of demonstrations against the allied left on the circumvallation lines at Landrecies, and instituted such preparations as looked like a serious attack in that quarter; he sent a cavalry party to Cartigny to make a lively demonstration; he issued orders for a march against Landrecies, of which Eugene got notice by his spies. In the belief that the manœuvre was a real one, Eugene concentrated a large part of his infantry force on his left, and gave undivided attention to the siege works. Villars left a small force to engage him, detailed strong cavalry parties to observe Bouchain and hold the fords of the Selle, so as to prevent Albemarle from discovering his march; filled the country full of his hussars; and on the evening of July 23, sending his pontoons suitably guarded to Neuville, three miles from Bouchain, he marched unnoticed with the main force in close columns in their rear. A demonstration was made at the same time on the Landrecies lines to arrest the attention of Prince Eugene. Villars crossed the Scheldt at Neuville early July 24. Albemarle must have been singularly careless in his outpost service, for up to 7 A. M., when he discovered the marching French column at Avesne le Sec, he had no information of their movements. Even Bouchain had sent him no word of the passage at Neuville, or else the messengers had been picked up.

Going ahead, the French cavalry had at once fallen on and taken the southerly line of the Road to Paris; while the commandant of Valenciennes headed part of the garrison to take the northerly line. When Villars came up with his infantry, he found the lines in his possession and Denain open to assault. Upon this town he at once directed his march.

So soon as notified, Eugene had speedily reached the ground, had ordered Albemarle to hold the post at all hazards, and he would within a few hours sustain him with a heavy force; and had galloped back towards Landrecies to collect troops. But he counted too much on Albemarle, or on any delay on the part of Villars. So soon as he reached the ground, Villars drew up his column of attack. According to some authorities, he organized eight columns two hundred paces apart; according to others, he drew up in one column of forty deployed battalions — the Denain column — and firing not a shot, but standing three volleys from the allies, he charged in with the bayonet and swept over the intrenchments like a flood. The resistance was as naught. The allied force was overthrown and largely driven into the river, with a loss of eight thousand men. The French lost a bare five hundred.

For the second time in modern warfare, an attack solely with cold steel had been successful, — the first time at the battle of Speyerbach in 1703. Villars deserves great credit for his speedy and bold attack; he knew he had not a minute to lose, and as a fact Eugene came up too late: Albemarle had been overmatched; the damage was already done. Having taken Denain, and the bridge and redoubt at Prouvy, Villars turned back and captured Marchiennes on the 30th, with all its garrison, material, food and two hundred pieces of ordnance. Eugene was compelled to raise the siege of Landrecies, and retired by Mons on Tournay. Villars incorporated in his army the garrisons of Ypres, Dunkirk and other sea fortresses, which, now that the English were out of the game, were of no more use; and was by twenty thousand men stronger than Eugene; and having the advantage of moral gain of victory, he ended the campaign by besieging and recapturing Douay, Quesnoy and Bouchain.

Villars earned unstinted praise for this handsome piece of work, which cost little in men, made great gains, and quite upset the calculations of the enemy. It was at a moment, too, when Louis XIV. was hard pushed, and it had a marked influence on the negotiations for peace.

The emperor would none of the Peace of Utrecht, which England and Holland had made with France. Prince Eugene, in 1713, was ordered to operate along the Rhine from Switzerland to the boundary of Holland, the Ettlingen lines to be the central point of his scheme. Villars lay on the other side with one hundred and thirty thousand men, and after some manœuvring began the siege of Landau. Prince Eugene had sixty thousand men at Ettlingen, and might, perhaps, have crossed the Rhine to hamper the operation. But he lacked numbers; Villars anticipated him, put over a division near Fort Louis June 4, sent some horse to Rastadt, and concentrated his force on the right bank opposite as a demonstration; while he himself returned to the left bank, captured Speyer, blockaded the Philipsburg bridge-head, where he made a fortified camp, and took that at Mannheim, cut Landau off from all communications with the Rhine, sent eighty squadrons to Worms, captured Kaiserslautern, and thus, by every means, forestalled a crossing by Eugene. Two months later (August 20) Landau surrendered. Villars' army still increased, while Prince Eugene received no reinforcements, and was forced to keep to a quiet defensive. He feared a crossing at Freiburg, and sent General Vobonne thither with eighteen thousand men to reoccupy the old fortified lines. Villars dispatched forty battalions to Freiburg and drove Vobonne out of his defenses; the latter left twelve battalions in Freiburg and retired to Rothweil.

Villars began the siege of Freiburg, which lasted many weeks, but finally, on November 13, the town fell, and the garrison received free exit. Both parties now went into winter-quarters, and Eugene and Villars began to negotiate. The result was that the Peace of Rastadt was concluded in the spring.

Prince Eugene in this campaign had but half of Villars' troops, and was unable to effectuate anything. He remained in the Ettlingen lines, strictly on the defensive, but was constantly watchful and active in small war. He did well to confine Villars to the capture of Landau and Freiburg, and to prevent his penetrating beyond the Rhine country, as with his huge army he well might do.

A new war breaking out with Turkey in 1716, Prince Eugene was put in chief command of one hundred and twenty-five thousand men in Hungary, and a flotilla on the Danube. After some preliminary manœuvring with sixty thousand men, near Peterwardein, Eugene attacked the Turks, who had nearly one hundred and fifty thousand. On August 5, after a hotly contested battle, in which Eugene's left was successful, his right defeated, but saved by cavalry charges on the Turkish flank, the imperial army won a very splendid victory. The Turks fled to Belgrade with six thousand killed, the loss of one hundred and sixty-four guns, one hundred and fifty flags and other trophies. Prince Eugene lost three thousand killed and two thousand wounded.

Next year Eugene captured Belgrade after a handsome campaign, in which he attacked and defeated under its walls a force sixfold his own, and received his thirteenth and last wound on the field of battle.

Much of the brilliant work of Eugene was against the Turks, a subject of marked interest, but beyond the scope of our subject. From 1718 to 1737 he was not in active service.

The last two campaigns of Prince Eugene in the war of the Polish Succession were conducted against very superior numbers, but were weak. The brave and able soldier was feeling the weight of his seventy-one years. He had done enough to send his name down to posterity as one of the brightest in the annals of generalship.

In this war, young Frederick, Crown Prince of Prussia, was for a few weeks present at the headquarters of the splendid old warrior, an occurrence which pleasantly links the era which Marlborough and Eugene so highly distinguished with the magnificent era of the Last of the Kings.

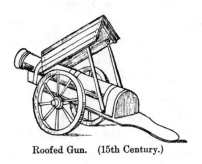

Roofed Gun.   (15th Century.)

LXV.

CHARLES XII. 1700–1709.

DURING the War of the Spanish Succession two remarkable men were in conflict in northeastern Europe: Peter the Great, who made Russia, and Charles XII., who undid Sweden. Charles inherited much of the Vasa ability, but lacked its common sense. On his accession Sweden was threatened by Denmark, Poland and Russia. Charles was a mere lad, but he showed wonderful ability. He attacked and brought Denmark to terms, and then, turning on Russia, defeated Peter at Narva in a most brilliant engagement. Hence he turned against Poland, fought his way across the Dwina, and beat the Poles at Klissow. In the course of a couple of years, despite the aid of Saxony, Charles completely reduced Poland, and in 1706 invaded Saxony, dictated terms to both countries, and threatened to take a hand in the Succession War. But foregoing this, he turned again on Russia. Peter had well used his respite in creating an army; Charles ventured too far into the bleak plains of Russia, was sadly used by the winter of 1708, and in 1709 was wholly defeated at Pultowa, and became a refugee among the Turks. He later returned to Sweden; but his country, meanwhile, had been despoiled of her glory. Charles XII. would have been a great soldier had he possessed a balance-wheel; as it is, he was a mediocre one.

WHILE central Europe was being convulsed with the gigantic contest of the Spanish Succession, a war in the north went on which has some interest for us, though fruitful rather in negative than in positive lessons. Two remarkable men enacted the chief rôles, — Peter the Great, who began the work which has made Russia what she is to-day, and Charles XII., who undid all that his great predecessor, Gustavus Adolphus, had won for Sweden. Both these men were strong and able; but Peter's practical intelligence lacked brilliancy, while Charles' brilliant intellect ran off into the unbalanced trait which ever and anon cropped up in the Vasa family.   Peter was a magnificent passionate animal, who civ- ilized his subjects with the knout, but who in government and politics had a thorough, patient, reasonable habit of mind, which viewed things as they actually were and marshaled them in methodical array.   Charles was strict in his morality,

Campaigns of Charles XII.

had none of the passions of his great opponent, and possessed all the virtues of private life; he was a king who indulged in neither wine, women nor song; but in political matters he was headstrong, foolish and senseless.   He had much of the Vasa intellect; he had much of the equipment which made Gustavus so great; but he quite lacked that astonish- ing mental poise which kept Gustavus from falling into a network of errors.

Peter had found the Baltic a Swedish lake, and he determined to make it an open sea, and to own harbors in it of some value to Russia, — a thing which must of necessity lead to war. Another breeder of trouble for the Swedes was the attempt of Augustus, king of Poland and elector of Saxony, to reconquer Livonia, which Gustavus had taken from Sigismund. Still another was that Frederick of Denmark had a quarrel with the duke of Holstein-Gottorp, the brother-in-law of Charles XII. ; and the latter, a mere boy of fifteen when, in 1697, he ascended the throne, embraced the duke's cause. These three monarchs, Peter, Augustus and Frederick, who deemed Sweden an easy prey, concluded a union against her. The Danes invaded Schleswig; the Saxons laid siege to Riga, and the Russians invested Narva. The eighteen-year-old king had as much on his hands at the opening of his reign as Gustavus Adolphus.

Instinct with the true Vasa courage, Charles rose superbly to the occasion. Not waiting for Denmark to attack him, he sent eight thousand men to Pomerania, and started from Stockholm in May, 1700. The English and Dutch fleets were on his side, — that of free commerce and an open Sound, which Denmark threatened to close. On forty-three ships he embarked his Swedes, crossed over to Zealand, and, threatening Copenhagen, compelled an immediate contribution of money and victual. Not anticipating so speedy an attack, Frederick was at a distance; but though he hurried to the spot, he found himself summarily driven into the peace of Travendal, in August, by which he indemnified Holstein and agreed to future neutrality towards Sweden. This was a handsome gain. Charles had bettered on Gustavus' Danish war. But he was aided by what his great predecessor had not, a now powerful country and a splendid army. Though Denmark was shelved, the two other enemies were yet

threatening.   Peter had assembled one hundred thousand
men to invade Livonia, and Riga was being stoutly pressed
by the Poles, and ably defended by the veteran Alberg.   In
the event, Riga being a free town of great commercial value,
the Poles retired from it, lest they should embroil themselves
with England and Holland.

Passing through and ravaging Ingria, Peter, with eighty
thousand men, appeared
before Narva in Octo-
ber, 1700.   They were
not soldiers in the sense
of the Swedes, who still
retained what Gustavus
had willed them, and
though Peter was grad-
ually seeking to teach
them discipline, they
were an ill-fed, ill-armed
and half-organized rab-
ble, of whom the larger
part had only arrows
and clubs, and in lieu of
soldierly instinct had
but the dogged, persist-
ent obedience for which

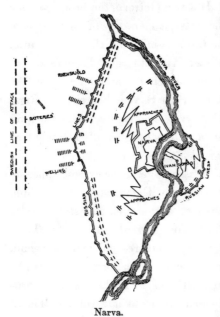

Narva.

the Russian has always been famous.   And although Peter
had purchased a great number of guns, there was scarcely any
knowledge of artillery practice in his army.   Not arrogating
to himself the divine right, Peter's forces were commanded
by a German, and the leaven of the troops was German.
Nothing shows the low condition of the Russian army more
than that their poor knowledge of sieges had enabled them
in ten weeks to make scarcely any progress.   Charles

crossed the Baltic in two hundred vessels, and landing at Pernau, in the gulf of Riga, advanced with twenty thousand men, of which four thousand were horse, to the relief of Narva. Hurrying forward to Revel, he started from here with the horse and four thousand foot, and leaving his baggage at Wesenburg, half way to Narva, marched through a country which the enemy had ruthlessly devastated, struck the Russian outposts in a defile which a handful could have defended, and drove them in. No resistance was made worthy the name, and in order to utilize the moral effect of his first gain, without waiting for the rest of the army, Charles pushed on, and November 29 stood in front of Narva.

Lying on the west of the river of the same name, Narva was fairly strong. On the east bank was a small town, also fortified. The Russians had mounted many batteries, had made approaches to both places, and had built a line of circumvallation from the river above to the river below, nearly three miles long. It was of earthworks, with a deep ditch, some outworks well flanked, and covered by abatis and *trous de loup*. Peter had gone towards Moscow to bring up an army of reinforcements; and General Croy (Kreuz) was in command.

Tired as the troops were, indefatigable Charles set them at making gabions and fascines while he reconnoitred the lines. Though he had but one man in ten of the Russians (five thousand foot and three thousand horse), he would not wait for the bulk of his army to come up, but ordered an assault. He knew his troops, — ever since the day of Gustavus the Swedes had outranked every army in Europe, — and took counsel of his own superabundant gallantry. Charles had the *élan* of the true cavalry leader; but he lacked the reserve of the great captain. He possessed Gustavus' fiery boldness, perhaps the great Swede's worst trait as king and army leader; and lacked his methodical caution, unquestionably his greatest virtue.

Two columns were organized, the right under Welling, the left under Rhenskjöld, and such batteries as had come on with the king were planted so as to aid the assault. The cavalry was held in reserve, with orders to ride in so soon as the foot should have made a passage for them, and to drive home with the cold steel. At 2 P. M. of November 30, on the signal given, two "fusees," the columns rushed forward with the watchword "With God's help!" Luckily a storm of sleet was blowing in the faces of the enemy; and so hot was the assault that in a quarter-hour the lines were taken and a breach practicable for cavalry was made. Believing in themselves, believing in their king, the Swedes, in spite of numbers, broke through the Muscovite array, and cut the enemy down by thousands. It was like the old battles of Alexander against the Oriental hordes. The enemy turned and fled, part towards the river on the north, where their mass broke down the bridge, part to some barracks on the bank, where they offered a desperate resistance. The Russian generals of the right wing were all captured; and by nightfall that part of the line was secured. The Russian left was still unbroken, and promised another battle on the morrow, for which Charles duly prepared; but during the night, in imitation of the left, they concluded to surrender also.

The Swedes, out of eight thousand men, lost six hundred killed and one thousand four hundred wounded. Of the Russians over eighteen thousand are said to have been cut down. Innumerable trophies were taken, and one hundred and forty-five new bronze guns. The victory was complete, the triumph of a disciplined handful against an unorganized multitude. But it would not always be thus. To Peter, who came up too late with his forty thousand reinforcements, the battle of Narva was a lesson by which he failed not to profit, to arm and discipline his forces while he was civilizing his people. Charles would have been wise to bring him to a peace or to cripple him before turning on Augustus. But Charles XII. lacked wisdom and was a slave of blind prejudice. His chief desire was to humble Poland; he could not see that Peter was a vastly more dangerous opponent than Augustus; and in his pursuit of the latter, he lost sight of the growing power of the Czar.

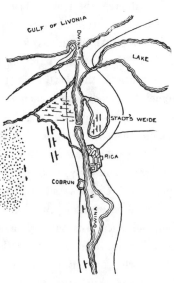

The Dwina.

That Russia and Poland must not be allowed to work into each other's hands Charles saw clearly enough; but the easiest way to prevent this was to push Peter to the wall, as Charles now could do, but by and by might not. He chose to leave his work half done, and so soon as the season opened, advanced to the Dwina to relieve Riga. He reached the river the middle of July, and camped in the Stadts Weide north of the town. By sending a column with a train of artillery *en évidence* up river, Charles persuaded the enemy that he would seek to cross above, and led them to disperse their forces in detachments along the banks, having done which he bridged the river and ferried over his troops under cover of a heavy smoke of dampened straw, which the north wind blew towards the enemy. The latter had assembled to oppose the crossing, and the left bank was covered by numerous defenses; but they remained in place and awaited attack instead of interfering with the passage. After an initial check at landing, Charles defeated the enemy, with small loss to himself, and drove them back into Courland, whither he speedily followed, taking the same cities, and covering much the same ground, as Gustavus did nearly a hundred years before. Thence during the rest of 1701 he advanced into Lithuania, taking place after place, unswerving in his determination to dethrone Augustus as king of Poland. In this he was aided by the Sapieha party, between which and its rivals, the Oginskys, the land was torn. His route lay up the Memel to Grodno, and thence down the Bobs and Narew to Warsaw, which opened its gates to him May 15, 1702.

Augustus saw that he had to fight for Poland, and the two kings met near Klissow, a small place between Warsaw and Cracow, in July, 1702. Augustus had twenty-four thousand men; Charles but half as many. The Swedes were marshaled as usual in two lines, with cavalry on the wings. Their advance was through a wood, and some manœuvring had to be resorted to to get the army on suitable ground. But Charles pushed his offensive vigorously, and the Poles, who formed Augustus' right wing, fled early in the battle and left the latter to fight with the Saxons alone. Despite the good conduct of these, Charles won handsomely, at a loss to the Swedes of three hundred killed and eight hundred wounded, to two thousand killed and wounded of the enemy. There were forty-eight guns and one thousand seven hundred prisoners taken. The Polish king fled to Cracow, whither Charles followed, and took the place. To overrun the country and defeat Augustus did not mean that the land was under the control of the conqueror. Charles had not Gustavus' solid method. The months were consumed in taking and garrisoning the towns, and in dispersing the roving bands of soldiers of fortune to whom peace could be no gain ; and a considerable force was kept out on the borders of Poland to head off the raids of the Russians.

Next year, in May, 1703, Charles defeated the Saxons with ridiculous ease at Pultusk, northwest of Warsaw, where Augustus had assembled, each army having some ten thousand men. The name of Swede was enough to rout any opponent ; a bare six hundred men were lost by the enemy, so rapidly did they flee. Augustus retired to Thorn on the Vistula ; Charles laid siege to it, and Danzig and Elbing were mulcted for interference with his transports. Having finally got control of the land, Augustus was legally deposed and the Protestant Stanislaus Lesczinski was elected king of Poland.

During these three years devoted to the control of Poland, Charles had lost sight of Peter and his doings ; but this most dangerous opponent had not only been creating an army, but had founded St. Petersburg in 1703 and captured Narva in 1704. He promised to give a better account of himself when he next met the Swedes.

Augustus made one more effort for Poland. Charles was still engaged in reducing the land, of which hundreds of towns sent him the keys so soon as he approached. While he took Leopold in September, 1704, Augustus advanced on Warsaw, from which the new king fled, and captured it. Charles and Stanislaus advanced against his army, of which Schulenburg was in command. This was an able general, but he needed all his skill to control the troops, discouraged by long ill-success. They were made up of Poles, half-hearted in his cause and ready to fight for either king, raw Saxon recruits, who had seen no war, and vagabond Cossacks. To fight such men was, as Charles said, hunting, not war. And be it observed, Charles so far had met no one worthy of

his steel. The effort of Schulenburg, his first able opponent, was rather to keep the army intact for his master than
to aim at an impossible victory. His was a policy really
Fabian.

In the Posen country, on the Warta, Schulenburg learned
that Charles and Stanislaus, whom he thought far off, had
reached his vicinity by a march of fifty leagues in nine days.
Charles pushed his troops faster than any man of his day.
Schulenburg had eight thousand foot and one thousand
horse. In the belief that he could make his foot stand up to
cavalry (Gustavus had done so in these same countries), he
drew up in extra close order on ground where he could not
be surrounded, but had his retreat open; his first rank of
pikemen and musketeers mixed, kneeled; the second, slightly
stooping, fired over the first; the third over the two others.
To the surprise of Charles and Stanislaus, their cavalry
could not be driven in upon this array of pikes vomiting
lead. Schulenburg, five times wounded, held himself all day,
and at night retired in a hollow square to Guhran, east of
Glogau, not far from the Oder.

The kings followed him up sharply. Beyond Guhran as
far as the Oder the country was heavily wooded ; and through
this wood the Saxon general led his army, now reduced by
half. The Swedes followed through almost impassable paths.
Near Rutzen, at the outlet of the woods, Schulenburg crossed
the little river Bartsch just in time to escape Charles; but
this indefatigable monarch found fords, led over his cavalry,
and penned Schulenburg up in the confluence of the Bartsch
and Oder. Schulenburg seemed lost, but by sacrificing a
rear-guard, he got across the Oder the succeeding night.

Schulenburg had saved Augustus his army, but the Saxon
king made no use of it. He again abandoned Poland, personally retired to Saxony, and fortified Dresden. While

Charles and Stanislaus were busy driving back sundry Muscovite raids on the eastern border of Poland, Schulenburg again assembled an army and recrossed the Oder. But he was met by Rhenskjöld (the " Parmenio of the Northern Alexander ") at Frauenstadt, February 12, 1706, and though he had twenty thousand men to Rhenskjöld's ten thousand, was utterly defeated, — the Saxon recruits decamping as at Breitenfeld. The unequaled discipline which Gustavus Adolphus had introduced among the Swedes had lasted one hundred years. The Russians in Schulenburg's army were cut down to a man to save taking prisoners.

In September, 1706, Charles invaded Saxony. Augustus, who had shut himself up in Cracow, dared not return to his Saxon capital. At Leipsic Charles camped on the field of Lützen. His army, be it said to his credit, was governed by the same splendid discipline he had inherited. Peace was dictated at Altranstädt, near Leipsic, by which Augustus renounced the Polish crown and recognized Stanislaus ; abjured his treaty with Russia and provisioned and paid the Swedish army for the winter.

There was some question as to what part this brilliant soldier would take in the Succession War ; but Marlborough visited him this year, and with his persuasive tongue and some English gold, well laid out, won him to the cause of the allies. Charles, however, took no part in the war.

Comparisons have sometimes been drawn between Charles and Gustavus. The structure erected by the one, who saved Protestantism to Germany, and the wreck left by the other, who found Sweden the great kingdom Gustavus had made it, and left it stripped of all save honor, speak for themselves. Merely to compare the work done by Charles from 1700 to 1707 — his period of success — with that done by Gustavus from 1630 to 1632 suffices to gauge the two men.

Gustavus, opposed by the best generals of the day, in twenty-eight months reduced to control all Germany; had he outlived Lützen, he would have at once dictated peace in Vienna. Charles, against opposition barely worth the name, in seven years reduced Poland and invaded Saxony; but his holding was insecure; what he took he did not keep, and what he had received from his ancestors he lost. At the same time Charles was a brilliant soldier within his limits. As a lieutenant, guided by the discretion of some great captain, he would have been incomparable. He was a good disciplinarian, an untiring worker, gallantry personified in battle, and with the true soldier's ambition and skill. He lacked but one thing, — the breadth which puts aside prejudice, which gauges things as they really are, and which truthfully forecasts the future.

While Charles was permitting his hatred of Augustus to lead him to the Elbe, he lost sight of the fact that his worst enemy, Peter, had been given years in which to build up an army, and had utilized the time well. The Russian army now numbered many German officers of experience. The czar invaded Poland with sixty thousand men, to which force Charles' lieutenant, Levenhaupt, with his regiments scattered along the border in Livonia, Lithuania and Poland, could not hold head, and sat down at Leopold and later at Lublin to gain control of Poland. Between conquering Swedes, and pillaging Russians and Poles, the poor land groaned under fearful oppression. Charles might even now have made a peace with Peter at the price of allowing him a port at his new capital; but he would have all or none, and the Baltic belonged to Sweden.

Stanislaus returned to Poland with Rhenskjöld in August, 1707; Peter prudently retired into Lithuania. Having spent a year in Saxony, Charles left for Russia in September, 1707, at the head of forty-three thousand men; Levenhaupt had twenty thousand in Poland; there were fifteen thousand in Finland, and recruits were coming from Sweden. This was no longer an army of Swedish veterans. So many of the old soldiers and officers had been sent home that the solidity of the force had been impaired. But it was still a Swedish army, and with it there was no doubt in the mind of Charles that he would dethrone Peter as he had done Augustus. At this point began his miscalculations.

Peter was at Grodno on the Memel, and here Charles sought him out in January, 1708, at the head of his cavalry; and though, riding on with his wonted recklessness, he reached the place at the head of but six hundred horse, Peter, who was almost taken prisoner, precipitately retired. With prudent foresight the czar had made up his mind not to fight Charles, but to starve him out. What he lacked in brilliant conduct he more than made up in good judgment. Three routes were open to Charles: on newly founded St. Petersburg via Pleskow and Novgorod, safe and apt to yield good results; on Moscow via Smolensk, a marsh part way, a desert the rest; a southern route, the least good of all. On the first he was always near his base; on the second there was peril enough; to select the third was a leap in the dark.

The whole Russian army had rendezvoused in the province of Minsk. Despite the perilous route and the sparsely peopled country, quite unequal to subsist an army, Charles pushed on, and by June 25, 1708, he had reached the Beresina at Borissov, where the czar had assembled to defend his land. Charles, by a march up river, turned him out of his intrenchments, and he retired, devastating everything on the way to retard the Swedes. Charles followed, defeating by a bold attack a body of twenty thousand Rus-

sians intrenched behind a marsh at Hollosin, and crossed the
Dnieper (Borysthenes) at Moghilev, then the most easterly
of the Polish cities. Peter retired by way of Smolensk along
the great highway to Moscow. He was gaining in strength
as Charles lost. On September 22 Charles came near meeting his death in one of the numerous vanguard fights which
daily occurred, and in which he exposed himself as Gustavus
used to do.

His position was becoming a perilous one, but he could not
see it. To fight an enemy who will stand, to pursue a flying
enemy into a populous country, is one thing ; to follow an
ever-retreating foe into a desert is safe to no captain. It is
scarcely doubtful that Charles would have been lost, as was
later the great Corsican, had he pushed on to Moscow ; but,
worse still, he was persuaded to turn aside from the straight
road to a southerly one into the Ukraine, by the Cossack
hetman Mazeppa, who proposed to revolt from the czar, and
who promised to join him with thirty thousand men on the
Desna, and with abundant provisions and gold. Allies and
food were what Charles now most needed. On the Desna
Charles purposed to winter and prepare for a march on Moscow in the spring. But anticipating the plan, the Russians
destroyed Mazeppa's preparations, and when Charles reached
the rendezvous, it was to find only a fugitive demanding help,
not a prince with reinforcements. Charles' only hope was
now based on Levenhaupt, who was following with fifteen
thousand men and a convoy of eight thousand wagons. But
the Swedish general had already fallen a prey to Peter's
army of forty thousand men, who day after day forced battle
on him, and with his now much better troops, though at fearful cost, cut Levenhaupt's numbers down to five thousand
men, and seized the convoy. Levenhaupt joined Charles with
a wreck of brave men and without victual or munitions. The

Swedish monarch was cut off from Poland and Sweden, was reduced to twenty-four thousand half-starved men, was obliged to abandon his guns from lack of horses to haul them, and had no prospects for the future unless Stanislaus could reach him with a new army. It was boldness unmixed with caution which had led him to this; inability to gauge facts as they were, to foresee contingencies. The winter was passed amid constant attacks by the roving bodies of Russians. In April, 1709, Charles had but twenty thousand Swedes left, — but, with a courage worthy of a better fate, he still aimed at Moscow. Towards the end of May he undertook the siege of Pultowa, with the aid of native tribes which about doubled his numbers; the place was of no importance, but contained an abundance of victual. Charles had taught the Russians how to make war, and he found Pultowa well garrisoned and hard to take. The czar came to its relief with eighty thousand men of regular troops, plus forty thousand Calmucks and Cossacks. Charles went out to meet the enemy, and on the 7th of July beat one of its detachments; but he was unfortunately wounded. Peter came up, and Charles had to confide the attack of the 8th to Rhenskjöld, he himself being carried on a litter.

The Swedes had been besieging Pultowa from one side only. The Russians approached from the other and, after crossing the Vorskla, built an intrenched camp, which shortly they gave up for a second one nearer the town. As a wing to this, opposite the Swedish camp, a number of redoubts were constructed between two patches of woods, a body of troops was sent to attempt a crossing of the Vorskla at a point nearer the town held by the Swedes, and Peter sat down to await events, as he could well afford to do. As usual, Charles determined on summary attack, despite disparity in numbers, and on the morning of July 8, 1709, the Swedish foot in four columns advanced to assault the redoubts, followed by the horsemen in six columns. Between the redoubts had been set up a large body of Russian horse; this was summarily attacked and driven in confusion well back beyond the large camp. The two woods were too near together to afford a chance to form line, and the king's intention was to pass between the redoubts without attempting to

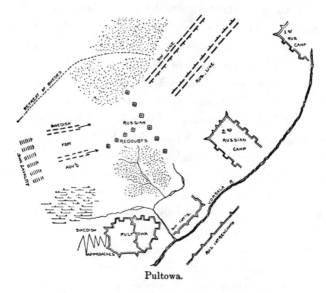

Pultowa.

capture them, form opposite and assault the intrenched camp. The bulk of the army carried out this programme, but the left wing took to assaulting the redoubts in its front, and finally, after great loss, got cut off from the rest of the army.

Backing on one of the woods, the king formed line, under the fire of one hundred and twenty Russian guns, and advanced to the assault of the camp. Parts of his line reached it, penetrated it; parts did not. But all along the line the gallant Swedes encountered opposition such as Russians had never yet shown. Peter's seven years had borne

fruit, and he now had a stanch army. Gradually falling
back, the Swedes were followed up, and a heavy battle ensued
at the edge of the plain. Charles, on his litter, could do but
little ; General Rhenskjöld was captured, and after sacrificing
a large number of his men, the king saw that the battle
was lost. He retired by the way he had come, and moved
in fairly good order to the confluence of the Dnieper and
Vorskla. There he counted, all told, invalided and for duty,
sixteen thousand men. The loss in the battle had been fully
four thousand.

The battle of Pultowa ended the career of Charles XII., so
far as any but trivial operations were concerned. The position of Sweden was rudely disturbed; Peter
established that of Russia. Having taken
refuge with the Turks, Charles remained
with them until 1714, obstinately seeking
through their means to conduct further
campaigns against Russia. In 1711 he
did succeed in placing Peter in a questionable situation on the Pruth, but the
czar cleverly managed to buy a peace from
the Turks, in which it was provided that
Charles might return unmolested to Sweden. But, angry at the peace, the king
would not leave Bender, a camp in Bessara-
bia where he played the rôle of a species of

Russian Soldier.

royal captive, and which, indeed, in 1713, he undertook to defend against an army that sought to compel him to withdraw.

Nothing militates so greatly against the reputation of
Charles XII. as a soldier, as this refusal to return home. In
this era of danger, Sweden needed her king. Charles had
ability enough, Sweden had elasticity enough, between them
to bring matters back to some kind of satisfactory basis.

His strategic errors in his Russian campaign are easily forgiven : another and greater soldier committed such.   But no
strategy is sound which has not patriotism as a basis.   The

greatest soldiers have sought primarily the
good of the fatherland: Alexander made Macedon govern the earth ; Hannibal had Rome at
his feet, but stupid Carthage would not accept
the gift ; Cæsar and Napoleon, on the theory
of L'Etat c'est moi, were patriotic strategists ;
Gustavus and Frederick were truly such.   On
this test the military reputation of Charles
XII. is shattered.   From mere childish prejudice — spite is the better word — he would not
return to his country when his country needed
him, because a free return was given him, not
conquered.   He remained in Bender yet three
years, wearing out his welcome, but treated

Turkish Soldier.

with great magnificence.

Many volumes have been written about this singular monarch ; nothing is easier than to fill others.   He was a man of
genius, without a balance-wheel, and in war the latter is the
greater part of genius.   Brilliant as few men have ever been,
a soldier to his finger-tips, he remains on the page of history
as holding no greater rank than a magnificent corps-com-
mander.   He returned to Sweden in 1714, and was shot, by
an assassin probably, in front of Friedrichshall, in 1718.
Sweden was despoiled of all her provinces, and became a
minor power.   What she owed to Gustavus she lost through
Charles XII., — a monarch possessing abundant courage,
abundant skill, abundant means, but lacking the one trait
which he needed to make him truly great, — discretion.

APPENDIX A.

SOME MODERN MARCHES.

MARCHES, in the seventeenth and eighteenth centuries, were apt to be slow, owing to bad roads, long trains, numerous non-combatants, and the habit of ploying an army into several columns, for some of which roads had to be prepared. Following are a few samples, most of which, tried by our standard, are ordinary; a few, good for any era.

1. In October and November, 1632, Gustavus, with about 20,000 men of all arms, marched over bad roads, from Donauwörth to Naumburg, some 270 miles by the route he took, in 18 days, or 15 miles a day.

2. In August, 1644, Condé, with about 10,000 men of all arms, marched from the Moselle to Freiburg, 210 miles in 13 days, or 16 miles a day.

3. In 1657, Turenne, with over 30,000 men of all arms, marched from the Scheldt-Sambre region to the Lys, 75 miles in 3 days, or 25 miles a day.

4. In June, 1674, Turenne, with 9,000 men of all arms, marched from the Rhine to Sinsheim, 90 miles in 4 days, or $17\frac{1}{2}$ miles a day.

5. In October, 1704, Charles XII., with 20,000 men of all arms, marched from the Vistula to the Oder, over bad roads, 180 miles in 10 days, or 18 miles a day.

6. In August, 1706, Eugene, with 25,000 men of all arms, marched from Reggio to Villa Stellona, 240 miles in 16 days, or 15 miles a day. Counting out a rest-day, owing to intense heat, the rate was 16 miles a day.

7. In July, 1708, Marlborough, with 65,000 men of all·arms, marched from near Brussels on Oudenarde, 40 miles in 48 hours, or 20 miles a day.

8. In September, 1709, the duke of Hesse-Cassel, with 10,000 men of all arms, marched from Douay to Obourg and Havré, 49 miles in 56 hours, or 21 miles a day.

APPENDIX B.

CASUALTIES IN SOME MODERN BATTLES.

Battle of	Date	Number Engaged	Nationality	Number Killed	Per-centage	Usual Per-centage[1]	Killed and Wounded	Per-centage	Usual Per-centage[1]	Loss of Enemy[1]	Remarks
Breitenfeld...	Sept. 7, 1631	26,800	Swedes	-	-	-	2,100	8	13	13,000	{ a Variously stated at 2,000 to 4,000.
Alte Veste....	Aug. 24, 1632	20,000	Swedes	-	-	-	3,000 a	15	13	2,000	a As generally given. Uncertain.
Lützen	Nov. 16, 1632	20,000	Swedes	-	-	-	10,000 b	50	13	-	b "
" "	" "	20,000	Mixed	-	-	-	10,000 b	50	13	-	c Attack ending in rout.
Nördlingen .	Sept. 15, 1634	26,000	Swedes	-	-	-	12,000 c	46	13	1,200	"
Rocroy.....	May 18, 1643	23,000	French	-	-	4	2,000	8¾	13	9,000	
Marston Moor	July 2, 1644	50,000 g	English	4,000	2	-	-	-	-	-	g On both sides.
Freiburg.....	Aug. 3–5, 1644	20,000	French	-	-	-	6,000	30	-	-	Three days' fighting.
Allerheim ...	Aug., 1645	15,000	Bavarians	-	-	-	9,000	60	13	-	" "
" "	" "	16,000	Hessians, French	-	-	-	4,000	22¾	13	-	
Lens	Aug., 1647	18,000	Bavarians	4,000	22¾	-	4,000	25	13	-	
St. Antoine .	July 5, 1652	5,000	Spanish and Dutch	-	-	5	2,000	40	20	-	
" "	" "	11,000	French	-	-	-	2,500	23	20	-	
Arras.......	Aug., 1654	30,000	French	-	-	-	3,000	10	13	-	
The Dunes ..	June, 1658	14,000	French	-	-	-	500	3¾	13	-	
" "	" "	14,000	Spanish and Dutch	-	-	-	1,000	7	13	-	
Sinzheim ...	June, 1674	9,000	French	1,200	13¾	-	-	-	-	-	
" "	" "	9,000	Imp'l-Lorraine	2,000	22	-	-	-	-	-	
Senef.......	Aug., 1674	45,000	French	-	-	-	7,000	15¾	13	30,000 d	{ d Loss said to have been half the army.
Entzheim....	Oct., 1674	65,000	Spanish and Dutch	15,000	23	4	30,000 e	16	-	-	Doubtful.
" "	" "	22,000	French	2,000	9	5	3,500	16	13	-	
Narva.......	Nov. 9, 1700	38,000	Germans	3,000	8	4	3,000	8	13	-	
" "	" "	8,000	Swedes	600	7½	4	2,000	25	13	18,000 h	h Massacre.
Luzzara.....	Aug. 15, 1701	36,000	Austrians	2,000	5½	4	5,000	14	13	-	
" "	" "	36,000	French	2,000	5½	4	5,000	14	13	-	
Klissow......	July, 1702	12,000	Swedes	300	2½	4	1,100	9	13	-	
" "	" "	24,000	Poles and Saxons	-	-	-	2,000	8	13	-	
Schellenberg..	July 2, 1704	10,500	English	1,500	14¾	5	5,500	52½	20	-	

	Date		Nationality							Remarks
Blenheim	Aug., 1704	58,000	{ English, Dutch, Germans	—	—	—	11,000	19	13	Heavy losses in the defeat.
"	"	63,000	French	—	—	—	15,000	24	13	
Ramillies	May, 1706	60,000	Anglo-Dutch	1,066	1¾	4	3,633	6	13	
"	"	62,000	French	—	—	—	7,000	11⅜	13	
Turin	Sept., 1706	36,000	Austrians	1,000	3	4	3,350	9	13	
"	"	60,000	French	2,000	3½	4	3,000	5	13	
Oudenarde	July, 1708	80,000	Anglo-Dutch	2,000	2½	4	5,000	6¼	13	
"	"		French	4,000	5	4	2,000	2½	13	
Maiplaquet	Sept., 1708	93,000	{ Anglo-Dutch and Austrians	6,000 ƒ	6½	4	18,250	20	13	{ 5,544 in infantry; estimated in cavalry and artillery.
"	"	95,000	French	—	—	—	14,000	15	13	
Pultowa	July 8, 1709	20,000	Swedes	—	—	—	4,000	20	13	

¹ For armies of this size in a very stubbornly contested battle.

INDEX.

LIST OF DATES.

LIST OF DATES.

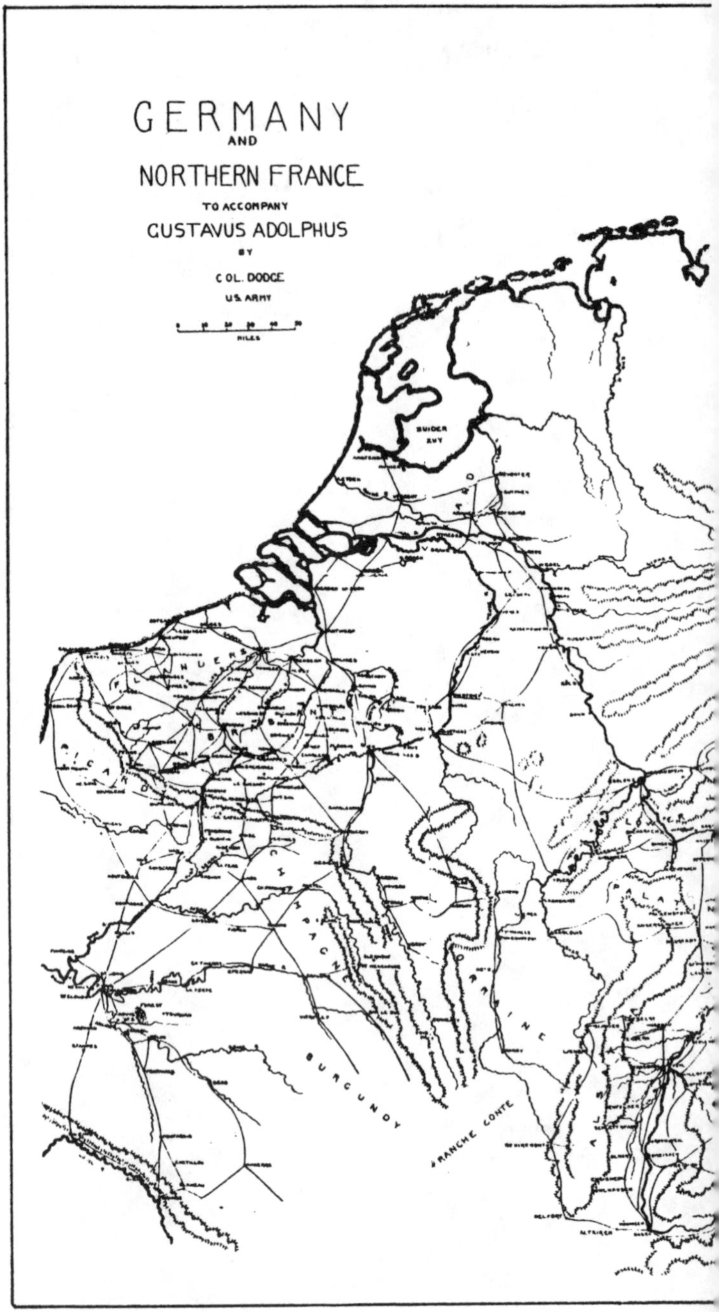

GERMANY
AND
NORTHERN FRANCE
TO ACCOMPANY
GUSTAVUS ADOLPHUS
BY
COL. DODGE
U.S. ARMY
MILES
ZUIDER ZUY
FLANDERS
BURGUNDY
FRANCHE CONTE

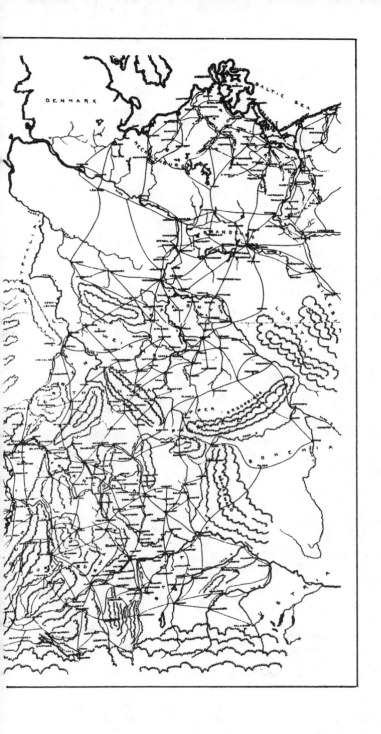

Other titles of interest

**WORLD EXPLORERS
AND DISCOVERERS**
Edited by Richard E. Bohlander
544 pp., 170 illus., 50 maps
80824-2 $25.95

**A BIRD'S-EYE VIEW
OF OUR CIVIL WAR**
Theodore Ayrault Dodge
376 pp., 47 maps and charts
80845-5 $15.95

**THE REVOLUTIONARY
WAR MEMOIRS OF
GENERAL HENRY LEE**
Edited by Robert E. Lee
New introduction by
Charles Royster
647 pp., 6 illus., 5 maps
80841-2 $18.95

**THE DISCOVERY AND
CONQUEST OF MEXICO**
Bernal Díaz del Castillo
Translated by A. P. Maudslay
New introd. by Hugh Thomas
512 pp., 33 illus., 2 maps
80697-5 $16.95

GEORGE WASHINGTON
A Biography
Washington Irving
Edited and abridged with an
introduction by Charles Neider
790 pp., 3 illus, 5 maps
80593-6 $18.95

**GEORGE WASHINGTON'S
GENERALS AND OPPONENTS**
Their Exploits and Leadership
Edited by George Athan Billias
766 pp., 23 photos, 9 maps
80560-X $19.95

MONTCALM AND WOLFE
The French and Indian War
Francis Parkman
Foreword by C. Vann Woodward
674 pp., 116 illus., 9 maps
80621-5 $18.95

GERONIMO
Alexander B. Adams
381 pp., 18 illus.
80394-1 $14.95

**MEMOIRS OF GENERAL
WILLIAM T. SHERMAN**
New introduction by
William S. McFeely
820 pp.
80213-9 $17.95

**PERSONAL MEMOIRS OF
U. S. GRANT**
New introduction by
William S. McFeely
Critical Notes by E. B. Long
648 pp.
80172-8 $16.95

**THE WARTIME PAPERS OF
ROBERT E. LEE**
Edited by Clifford Dowdey and
Louis H. Manarin
1,012 pp.
80282-1 $19.95

MEMOIRS
Ten Years and Twenty Days
Grand Admiral Karl Doenitz
Introduction and Afterword
by Jürgen Rohwer
New foreword by John Toland
554 pp., 18 photos, 5 maps
80764-5 $16.95

PANZER LEADER
General Heinz Guderian
Foreword by B. H. Liddell Hart
New introd. by Kenneth Macksey
554 pp., 22 photos, 37 maps
80689-4 $17.95

**THE PATTON PAPERS,
1885–1940**
Martin Blumenson
1,048 pp., 32 photos, 5 maps
80862-5 $24.50

**THE PATTON PAPERS,
1940–1945**
Martin Blumenson
944 pp., 31 photos, 5 maps
80717-3 $19.95

THE ROMMEL PAPERS
Edited by B. H. Liddell Hart
544 pp., 17 photos
80157-4 $16.95